Marriage and the Family

Marriage and the Family

Development and Change

Stephen R. Jorgensen

TEXAS TECH UNIVERSITY

Macmillan Publishing Company

NEW YORK

To Julie and the boys

Photos on pages 115 and 116
by Marc P. Anderson.

Copyright © 1986, Stephen R. Jorgensen

Printed in the United States of America

Macmillan Publishing Company
866 Third Avenue, New York, New York 10022

Collier Macmillan Canada, Inc.

Library of Congress Cataloging in Publication Data

Jorgensen, Stephen R.
  Marriage and the family.

  Bibliography: p.
  Includes index.
  1. Family life education — United States.   I. Title.
HQ10.J669   1985   306.8   84-11291
ISBN   0-02-361420-X

Printing: 1 2 3 4 5 6 7 8   Year: 6 7 8 9 0 1 2 3 4 5

ISBN   0-02-361420-X

Preface

After teaching college courses in marriage and family life education for more than nine years on two large university campuses, the University of Arizona and Texas Tech University, I have learned a number of things that motivated me to write this book. The more than thirteen hundred students who have enrolled in these classes are typically some of the most energetic, enthusiastic, and intellectually curious students one can find in the college classroom, and I owe thanks to them for stimulating my interest in writing what may appear to be, on the surface, "just another text" in the field of marriage and family relationships. My goal is to have this book viewed in a different light, as a text that is not like "all of the others," but which still provides the essential information for useful application.

The first thing my students taught me is that young adults in the 1980s continue to have romanticized and idealized views of marriage and family life. Many simply have not given the subject much thought, even if they are involved in a serious dating relationship, or plan to be married after the school year is out. They enroll in marriage and family education courses in order to confirm their visions and dreams of marriage as a blissful and "happy ever after" existence. Fortunately, both as an experienced social scientist in the marriage and family studies field, and as someone who himself has experienced fifteen years of marriage, I am able to convince them otherwise. The course I teach actually evolves into a type of "reality therapy" by the middle of the semester, akin to taking the students "by the shoulders and shaking them" until they understand that marriage may be one of the most difficult and painful undertakings that they may ever experience. On the very first day of class I ask them,

> "How many of you are planning to be married at some time in your lives?"

Almost everyone's hand goes up, enthusiastically. However, there are two or three holdouts in every group, who are brave enough to admit that marriage is not for them. They are in the class to find out if they are crazy or weird and I assure them that they are *not!* Then I ask those who raised their hands,

> "How many of you who are planning to get married are also planning to get divorced at least one time during your lives?"

No one now raises a hand because, obviously, no one would ever dream that *they* would be one of *those* (divorced people). Then I say,

> "Look around you, look at the people sitting next to you, in front of you, and behind you. If you are at all a fair representation of the young adult population in the United States today, at the current rate, one of two of you will be divorced at least once, and close to one of five of you will be divorced twice or more."

I give them a chance to squirm in their seats a bit, and mumble some sort of reaction. Then I ask,

> "You know, when you make a commitment to marry someone, you are telling that person that you are going to live, eat, sleep, and wake up with that person virtually every day, of every month, of every year, for somewhere between 50 to 75 years. How many of you would commit yourself to *anything* for that long a time, especially with as little training and formal preparation as you are likely to have prior to marriage?"

The typical response, usually unsolicited, is, "Gee, I never thought of it that way!"

And so the reality therapy begins. My goal is to get the student to think about it "that way," to question their unquestioned intentions to get married and have children, and to realize what marriage and parenthood can do *to,* as well as *for,* you. For sixteen weeks, we explore the various aspects of the development of marriage and the family over time. We examine the nature of love, sexuality, economic survival, and gender roles, from premarital relationship development, to the early years without children, the years with children, the postparental or "empty nest" stage, and the aging years. We examine the problems, stresses, and strains that married couples in our society must confront as they seek personal growth and fulfillment in a relationship which, one hopes, will endure. We pay close attention to research studies in order to get an accurate and, as much as possible, unbiased picture of reality in marriage and family life. Of course, we examine the factors that contribute to those marriages which are considered by both marriage partners and researchers to be truly successful, and, in doing so, realize that there is more to building a successful marriage than simply enduring without divorce. By semester's end, most of the students have discarded their idealistic views of marriage and parenthood, and in their place have substituted more realistic views.

Both the students and I have found this approach to teaching about development in marriage and the family to be effective, in terms of increasing their understanding about such complex relationships. It is in this spirit, then, that this text is written: realistically, honestly, and to the point. The perspective is a scientific one, borrowing heavily on current and past research on marriage and family relationships to provide an empirical basis for understanding what they are all about. The perspective is *not* prescriptive—telling students that they should or should not get married, that they should or should not have children, or that both partners in marriage should or should not work outside the home. The approach is to identify the various options relating to marriage and family life, determine what the research literature has to say about what consequences flow from choosing one option over the other, discuss the implications of making various choices, and let the *student* decide which path, or paths, to follow. In this way, this book is different from several others that make judgments about what successful marriage and family life is, and what recipe to follow in order to realize success. The book focuses on what *is* rather than what *should be* happening to marriage and the family as institutions in our society.

A second lesson I have learned from my students is that they tend to view marriage as a uniform and undiffer-

entiated relationship—"one gets married, settles down, has children, and that's it." They lack a coherent and meaningful *conceptual framework,* and therefore do not understand the interpersonal dynamics of premarital and marital relationships, and how they influence, and are influenced by, ties with social networks such as friends and relatives; involvement in extramarital systems such as the occupational, legal, and religious; and changes in the broader society taken as a whole. The lack of a conceptual framework prevents them from seeing that the shape and content of a marital relationship go through significant changes and transformations as the relationship develops over time. We are fortunate, in the field of marriage and family studies, to have at our disposal a variety of conceptual frameworks to provide a coherent, cohesive, and more or less integrated picture of marriage and family relationships. I have chosen the *Family Development* framework to guide the organization of this book. The Family Development approach is a hybrid of the most useful concepts from the fields of psychology, sociology, education, and biology. Marriage is viewed as a *career,* with discernible *stages of development,* separated by one or more *critical transition points* (e.g., marriage, parenthood, retirement, death, and divorce). Other concepts useful in this approach are *developmental tasks, normative scripts, roles, role sequences, interdependence, selective boundary maintenance,* and *role reciprocity.* Application of these concepts helps to provide a clear picture of the continuity, discontinuity, and cumulativity of development in the marital relationship as it moves from one stage of the marital career to the next. Moreover, the Family Development framework provides a useful bridge between scientific theory and research, on the one hand, and practical application on the other. In sum, it is a good teaching tool. Hence, I have chosen to cast the discussion of marriage and the family in this book in a developmental perspective, utilizing appropriate concepts of the Family Development framework and providing a definite *time* perspective to development in marriage.

The chapters of the book are organized accordingly. In Chapter 1, an overview of current trends in marriage and the family is presented, with particular emphasis on the challenges that married couples and families of the 1980s are facing, and the dramatic changes that the marital and family institutions in our society have undergone over the past two decades. Chapter 2 covers the rationale underlying the scientific study of marriage and family relationships, and provides the basis for understanding development in marriage and the family by using the growing body of knowledge provided by scientific researchers in this area. The limitations and proper caveats associated with this research will also be noted here. The major assumptions and concepts of the developmental perspective are also defined in Chapter 2. Chapters 3 through 8 provide detailed coverage of the fundamental bases upon which marriages and families are built. The bases determine, to a large extent, how marriages and families (1) are able to satisfy the needs of all members; (2) provide an environment for growth and development; and (3) come to be viewed as successful or unsuccessful, fulfilling or empty, congenial or conflict-ridden, by each member. In Chapters 9 through 14 we explore each of these fundamental bases of marriage and family life, stage by stage across the marital career, pointing out the continuities and discontinuities associated with development in marriage and the family over time. Because the typical years for divorce are the second and third, the most logical place for a chapter on divorce and remarriage might be somewhere between Chapters 10 and 11 (the early years and the childbearing years). However, a nontrivial number of couples are now dissolving their marriages after 20 or 25 years together, often after the children are in various stages of being launched from the home. The chapter on divorce (Chapter 15), therefore, follows the other stages in order to provide a comprehensive picture of divorce as it occurs across all stages of the marital career. The book closes with a chapter on the future of marriage and family relationships in contemporary society, Chapter 16.

Although the future is uncertain in many respects, it is sure to hold a number of fascinating challenges and opportunities for us as we continue to seek intimacy and satisfaction in marriage and family relationships. It is in this spirit of openness to the possibilities and challenges of the future that this book is written.

Acknowledgments

One cannot truly appreciate the challenge and utter difficulty of writing a textbook without first putting pen to paper and doing it. The task is a monumental one, but ultimately it is extremely gratifying. However, the task is not done by the author alone. I have learned that a textbook results from a team effort, and I would like to thank each and every one of the team members who contributed in various ways to the successful completion of this book. Each of them deserves credit for a job well done.

First, the comments and helpful suggestions that the following individuals made during various stages of writing are gratefully acknowledged: Joan Aldous, University of Notre Dame; Kathleen Auerbach, University of Nebraska-Omaha; William J. Brindle, Monroe Community College (New York); Kathleen M. Campbell, Bowling Green State University; LeRoy Gruner, Northern Kentucky University; Reuben Hill, University of Minnesota; David M. Klein, University of Notre Dame; Brent C. Miller, Utah State University; Marie W. Osmond, Florida State University; Jill S. Quadagno, University of Kansas; Ellen Rosengarten, Sinclair Community College (Ohio); Robert A. Rotz, Millersville University of Pennsylvania; Jean P. Scott, Texas Tech University; Peter J. Stein, William Patterson College; Janice G. Stroud, University of North Carolina-Charlotte; Thomas P. Thompson, Berry College (Georgia). A special thanks goes to two others who read in great detail and commented on several chapters of the book: Sharon J. Alexander, American Association for Counseling and Development, Alexandria, Virginia, and James Hine, Division of Child Development and Family Relations, University of Arizona. Their comments and suggestions were among the most useful.

I must also acknowledge, and express my sincere appreciation, to the professionals at Macmillan who stuck with me throughout the many trials and tribulations of the book's writing and production. Ken Scott, formerly Senior Editor in the College and Professional Division, and now with the University of South Carolina Press, was instrumental in his support of the initial proposal for the book. He also was an expert reviewer and consultant for several of the chapters in their first draft stages of development. Jim Anker, Senior Editor, picked up where Ken Scott left off and provided timely and much needed encouragement to keep the ball rolling to the end. George Carr, Production Supervisor, was simply a delightful person to work with during the entire production process. His attention to detail and easy-going friendly demeanor made this part of the effort a pleasure rather than the chore about which most authors complain.

One can never adequately acknowledge and express appreciation for the scholarly heritage imparted by academic mentors. I am pleased to have the opportunity to thank those individuals who guided my graduate education at the University of Minnesota and equipped me with the skills necessary to conduct social science research, and with the knowledge and ability to write about it in a book such as this. They are as much a part of this book as I am. To Reuben Hill, my dissertation advisor, friend, counselor, and godfather; to Ira Reiss, who taught me how to think critically and to know that "the examined life is more worth living;" to Joan Aldous, who taught me the value of the developmental approach to family study, which shines through in this volume; and to David Klein, who shared with me the many and varied experiences of conducting original doctoral dissertation research on marriage and the family. My intellectual debt to these scholars can never be fully repaid, and I thank them for being such excellent teachers.

Last, and in no way least, I wish to express my appreciation of, and unrequited love for, my own family. From Julie, my loving wife who has experienced with me over the past 15 years many of the vicissitudes of married life described in this book, my faith in the concept of "successful marriage" is continually renewed. From Jesse, Erik, and Brett, "my three sons," I am continually reminded of the challenges and gratifications of parenthood that many may write about but never feel. This book would never have been without all of you by my side.

Stephen R. Jorgensen
Lubbock, Texas

Brief Contents

III. Careers in Marriage and the Family   247

IV. Contemporary Issues in Marriage   439
and Family Life: Marital Dissolution
and the Future of Careers
in Marriage and the Family

Detailed Contents

7. Communication and Conflict Management   187

*IV.*Contemporary Issues in Marriage and Family Life: Marital Dissolution and the Future of Careers in Marriage and the Family   *439*

15. Divorce: Social, Emotional, and Legal Issues   441

Marriage and the Family

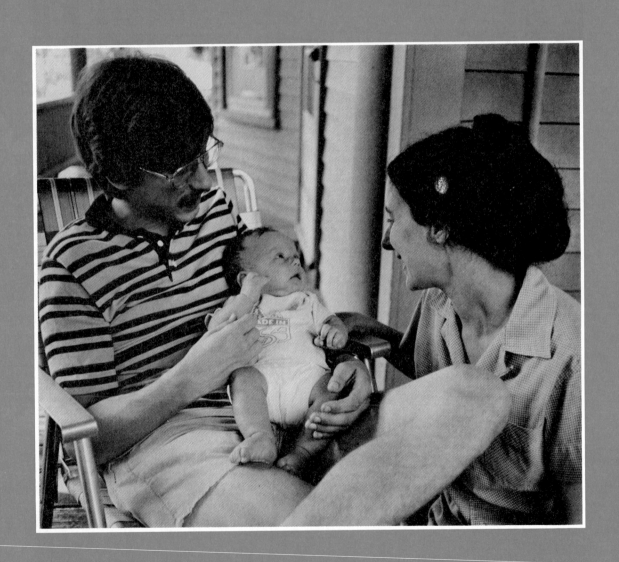

PART I

The Study of Marriage and the Family from a Developmental Perspective

In order to acquire an understanding of the possibilities and options relating to marriage and family relationships of today, along with the problems and stresses most married couples are likely to face at some point in their lifetimes, it is important to first examine the changing environment and social context impinging on marriages and families. Chapter 1 will take us on a brief excursion through our recent history, to explore the changing forms and functions of marriage and the family in the traditional preindustrial and modern postindustrial societies of the Western world. Although many observers have for years predicted that traditional forms of marriage and family living would become obsolete as we charge ahead into a future of technological wonders and space-age possibilities, such has not been the case. As we shall see in chapter 1, marriage continues to be a dominant means by which adults seek emotional and physical intimacy with each other, and the family continues to be the single most important source of the physical and psychological nurturance necessary for healthy child growth and development that society has to offer. In chapter 2, we will review the importance, and limitations, of social science research as a means of acquiring knowledge about marriage and family relationships in contemporary society. There, we will also introduce important concepts that will help to organize and integrate material to be introduced in subsequent chapters, when we explore the major bases of marriage and the family and the possible changes that occur in marriage and family relationships over time.

CHAPTER 1

The Shape of Marriage and the Family in Contemporary Society

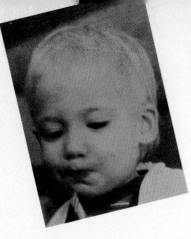

Perhaps the most prominent feature of human existence in the twentieth century has been the monumental growth of industrial and scientific technology. In the past eighty years, we have seen the development of such modern means of transportation as the automobile, airplane, and space shuttle; such high-speed means of mass communication as television, worldwide telephone systems, and communications satellites; and the construction of awe-inspiring cities characterized by their hundreds upon hundreds of mammoth skyscrapers. Indeed, the accelerative growth of technology and modern industrialism in the twentieth century has no precedent in human history, in terms of the rapidity with which such environmental changes have occurred.

As we approach the year 2000 and the beginning of the twenty-first century, it is becoming painfully clear to many people that these rapid changes in our technological environment are not all to our benefit. Air and water pollution, resulting from industrial waste and mass use of the automobile, continue to exist despite the efforts of environmentalists, government, and several industries to prevent it. We are seeing the rapid depletion of world mineral and energy resources, such as coal, natural gas, and oil, which must be relied upon to feed our modern means of production and technology. Although we have developed and implemented the use of nuclear power in response to this situation of dwindling energy resources, we have managed to turn it into sophisticated modern weaponry that is capable of virtually destroying civilization with the push of a single button. Unfortunately, political conflicts between nations of the world, often over the limited energy resources, have been volatile and frequent enough in the past several years to make total nuclear destruction of the world a distinct possibility.

In spite of our technological developments, moreover, the world's "population bomb" continues to tick away, and does so despite the warnings of experts that food and energy resources of the twenty-first century will be insufficient to meet the demand of the increased numbers of people (Brown, 1954; Meadows, et al., 1972). We entered the twentieth century with fewer than two billion people in the world. In 1982, there were 4.67 billion people on our earth, and the number is expected to top 5 billion by 1987 and 6 billion by the year 2000 (Arizona Family Planning Council Newsletter, 1983b). Related to this is the continued hunger and starvation in many societies of the world. Pictures of starving adults and children in many areas of Africa, Latin America, and India are commonplace, serving as a continuing reminder that starvation claims thousands of lives every year. Although our modern technological accomplishments in contraception have provided the means for effective population control, and modern agricultural technology is capable of providing food for the world's hungry without significantly affecting the life-styles of others, people continue to starve. Countries such as India, Mexico, and other Latin American nations continue to have birth rates that would double their populations in 25 to 35 years, if left unchecked — populations which already are crowded into massive and impoverished urban centers. Foodstuffs, and the natural resources necessary to produce them, are unequally distributed, and political bickering often prevents food exports from reaching those for whom they are intended. Indeed, many nations of the world spend more money on defense weapons than they do on the social and economic welfare of their people.

Marriage in a World of Challenge

An understanding of the rapid technological progress, industrial growth, and environmental changes that have occurred in this century is critical for developing an accurate understanding of marriage relationships in a modern, complex society. Not only have rapid technological development and modernization of society created a complex and overwhelming set of problems related to our survival as a civilization, but it has also had multiple and profound effects on patterns of marriage and family relationships. Let us take a brief look at how patterns of human relationships, both inside and outside of marriage and family contexts, have changed in response to the development of modern scientific technology and a mass society.

GEMEINSCHAFT AND GESELLSCHAFT

Philosophers and social theorists of the late nineteenth and early twentieth centuries detected a fundamental change in the way people related to each other in progressing from simple rural societies, which relied upon agriculture as the primary means of production, to more organizationally complex and differentiated societies, which relied primarily upon industrial technology for production of goods. Ferdinand Töennies (1855–1936) was a German social theorist, who, in 1887, wrote a most influential treatise on the changing nature of social relationships caused by technological changes (industrialization) and urbanization that were beginning to accelerate at that time. He labeled this dichotomy *Gemeinschaft and Gesellschaft,* which was translated into English as *Community and Society* (Martindale, 1960). Töennies viewed *social relationships* as the most basic, and most important, aspect of society. All social relationships, and the total collective of social relationships (i.e., society), could be placed in one of two categories: (1) *Gemeinschaft,* which are social relationships based on the belief that the bond between members of a relationship is a sacred and natural gift that is supernaturally endowed; and (2) *Gesellschaft,* in which members of the relationship base their interaction on purely rational grounds, as determined by the social class and authority differences between those members. As societies became increasingly urbanized, industrialized,

and differentiated in terms of the types of occupations available to people, Töennies saw the nature of relationships between people moving from basically warm, friendly, and integrative bonds to those that were basically cold, indifferent, and based purely on rational motives. From 1750 through the entire 1800s, laws were formed to regulate social life, including life in marriages and families, in a manner consistent with the demands of an industrialized system. New machinery and factories demanded a pool of labor to operate them and to produce the goods of a changing economic system. Families were the primary source of that labor, as men, women, and even children were drawn into factories and commercial centers. At the same time, social life was becoming increasingly impersonal and contractual in nature; life was no longer based on the philosophy of "I like you for who you are," but rather, "I will relate to you only as long as you can do something for me." Figure 1.1 summarizes some of the basic distinctions Töennies made between the two types of societies he saw emerging out of an industrializing modern world.

Another social theorist writing about that time was the American, Charles Horton Cooley (1864–1929), who shared Töennies's concern for the direction in which interpersonal relationships appeared to be moving. In 1909, Cooley presented the concept of the *primary group,* which complemented Töennies's notion of moving from *Gemeinschaft* to *Gesellschaft* as a basis for human relationships. According to Cooley, the degree to which a person is able to develop as a human being depends upon the ability to nurture a favorable self-concept. Moreover, we come to form concepts and evaluations of our selves by means of perceiving how *others* are judging our appearance, habits, motives, personality, family, and friends, and then reacting with some type of feeling, be it pride, disgust, frustration, or shame. This is the concept of *looking-glass-self.* We come to develop a sense of who we are and what we are worth on the basis of how significant other people who are important or close to us are reacting to us, and how they appear to be evaluating us. That is, we see ourselves as we are "reflected" in the eyes of others, as if peering into a "social mirror." For example, if your best friend comments on your new $200 suit by saying how sharp and sexy it makes you look, you are likely to feel quite good about your appearance and proud of yourself. On the other hand, if your friend says that the suit makes you look "slouchy and dumpy," you are likely to look for the first hole to crawl into. Your feeling of self-worth, then, is

FIGURE 1.1.   Töennies' Typology of *Gemeinschaft* and *Gesellschaft*.

Social Characteristic	Societal Type:	
	Gemeinschaft	*Gesellschaft*
Dominant Social Relation-ship	Fellowship Kinship Neighborliness	Exchange Rational calculation
Central Institutions	Family law Extended kin group	State Capitalistic economy
The Individual in the Social Order	Self	Person
Characteristic Form of Wealth	Land	Money
Type of Law	Family Law	Law of contracts
Ordering of Institutions	Family life Rural village life Town life	City life Rational life Cosmopolitan life
Type of Social Control	Concord Folkways and mores Religion	Convention Legislation Public opinion

(SOURCE: Martindale: *The Nature and Types of Sociological Theory,* Second Edition. Copyright © 1981 by Houghton Mifflin Company. Used with permission.)

highly susceptible to the reactions of certain significant others with whom you interact on a regular basis.

Given the importance of a person's self-concept and the reflective process by which it develops in interaction with significant others, Cooley stated that the primary sources of self-concept formation and the healthy integration of people into society are one's *primary groups.* These are groups composed of the significant others in one's life, and are characterized by intimacy, cooperation, and face-to-face interaction. Members of primary groups nurture the healthy development of each others' self-concepts by having a common purpose and allegiance to the group, and by sharing a high level of mutual trust, exchange of affection and love, and caring for each other's psychological and emotional needs. As Coser (1971) pointed out, one's primary groups are composed mainly of friends, family, and, as children, one's playmates. They are based upon one's intrinsic valuing of and appreciation of others in the group. It is the primary group that supplies the caring, concern, and understanding that are so critical for

the development of one's self-concept and sense of self-worth; that is, the "looking-glass self." Rather than seeking individual gain at the expense of others, relationships to people in one's primary groups are

> built upon the diffuse solidarity of its members rather than upon an exchange of specific services or benefits. It (the primary group) is, moreover, a nursery for the development of human warmth and sympathy, which is contrasted to the formal coldness, the impersonality, the emotional distance of other types of relations. (Coser, 1971:308)

Clear parallels exist between Cooley's concept of the primary group and Töennies's *Gemeinschaft-Gesellschaft* typology. The *Gemeinschaft* society of preindustrial, small town, rural days was characterized by the general immersion of the individual in primary-group associations. Relationships with others with whom one would come into contact on any given day would, to a considerable degree, be based upon mutual recognition, friendship, concern and, in some cases, intimacy, affection, and understanding. Of course, the most important primary group consisted of relationships between parents, children, spouses, and other family members. But other social contacts were primary in nature as well, including those one might make with the town banker, grocer, sheriff, mayor, doctor, or blacksmith. People knew one another in terms of family histories, personalities, habits, and problems, and this mutual knowledge functioned to bind and integrate these communities by means of a group identity and a sense of *we-ness* which set them apart from other communities or larger cities.

However, as our society continued its phenomenal growth in technology and industry, the economic system demanded that relationships between people become more fleeting, impersonal, and fragmented. The transition from *Gemeinschaft* to *Gesellschaft,* caused by the rapid urbanization and population growth accompanying industrialization, created a new social order—one built upon *secondary* relationships. Now, people with whom one would come into contact on a given day were suddenly impersonal, distant, and generally not known to one another more than before. Relationships with others became fragmented in that our contacts with them were limited to brief encounters for a specific reason, like applying for a loan or buying a ticket at a movie counter, and then not seeing that person again for a long time, if ever. The person to whom one related in a bank, grocery store, or government office no longer mattered because all that was necessary was that whoever occupied that position perform their duties efficiently, with as little personal contact with the client as possible. It was no longer considered appropriate to reveal aspects of one's self, or know the other person in any intimate or personal way in conducting day-to-day business. In urban areas of today, for example, a person would be considered a bit eccentric if, in approaching the ticket window of a movie theater, said to the ticket seller, "How is the spouse? How are your kids doing in school this year? How about coming over to our house after the show for beer and peanuts?"

The direction in which social relationships were moving as a result of urbanization and industrial growth, and the transition from *Gemeinschaft* to *Gesellschaft,* was one of increasing impersonality, individualism, and alienation of individual from individual. There existed a decreasing sense of community identity, belonging, and meaningful integration in society as a whole. Töennies and

The shift toward a *Gesellschaft* society has included increasing impersonality, individualism, and alienation in relationships among people. *(Photo by Ron Jenkins.)*

Cooley both looked back at the *Gemeinschaft*-primary-group style of relating with fondness and nostalgic pride, and regarded the future of *Gesellschaft*-secondary-group society with dismay and, indeed, some disgust. As we shall see, however, both types of societies have their positive and negative aspects, particularly in regard to the relationships of men and women in and out of marriage.

MARRIAGE IN A *GESELLSCHAFT* SOCIETY

Actually, it is somewhat of an oversimplification to look at social relationships in a dichotomous fashion; that is, as *either* primary *or* secondary, *Gemeinschaft* or *Gesellschaft*. It is a matter of degree, as Figure 1.2 illustrates. There are probably few, if any, communities or societies that are pure *Gemeinschaft* or *Gesellschaft* types, or which are based exclusively on primary- or secondary-group relations. Moreover, within any given society there are undoubtedly elements of both types. For example, our society today is moving closer and closer to a *Gesellschaft* type, in that an increasing number of our social contacts are secondary in nature: the mailman, bus driver, taxi cab driver, stock broker, cashier at the grocery counter, clerk at the department store, waiter at the restaurant, and ticket seller at the theater are all typical daily contacts we make in a fleeting, transitory, and impersonal way. However, we have maintained our emphasis on satisfying humanistic needs for intimacy, nurturance, and self-affirmation by means of close friendships, marriage, and family relationships. We continue to seek emotional warmth, to satisfy our need for belonging to something meaningful, to know that we are loved and able to love, in our relationships with close friends, marriage partners, and other family members.

Some observers would say that relationships with marriage partners and other family members are the last remaining vestiges of *Gemeinschaft* society that we have today. This has created a dilemma for the person of the 1980s, whose work on the job is typically highly specialized, with the majority of daily contacts secondary in nature. For many, the *only* remaining means of fulfilling the human needs for intimacy, caring, affiliation, self-affirmation, and belonging reside in marriage and family relationships. Some who do not belong to a marriage or family relationship are able to compensate by forming close friendship ties, but others are left without such alterna-

tives. They may have limited opportunities for meeting other people, or they may be unaware of places to go to make social contacts that might result in close friendships. Without these ties, then, individuals are faced with increased chances of loneliness, alienation, and depersonalization. Perhaps this explains the fact that in contemporary American society more than 90 percent of all adults will marry at least one time, and of those who marry, 90 percent will bear or adopt at least one child (Glick 1979; 1984a). Marriage and family relationships, then, are today both "unusually valuable and highly demanding" in that they function to fulfill our needs "for meaning and emotional satisfaction" in a "culture that is chiefly impersonal and in which most relations are interchangeable" (Saxton, 1977:18–19).

Thus, the significance of our twentieth century growth in technology and urban expansion into a mass society is, for the marital institution, twofold. First, we live in a climate of uncertainty, unpredictability, and upheaval in our civilization as a whole. The stresses and challenges of individual survival have never been greater. The impact that this economic and social climate has had on marriage has been that of *highlighting its importance* as a haven from the uncertainties and the stresses imposed upon us by the world of challenge in the 1980s. Marriage and family relationships are shelters that function to provide fulfillment of our intrinsic human needs for security, nurturance, intimacy, and comfort in a world currently beset by hostility, turmoil, and threat. A list of such basic human needs, for which fulfillment is currently being sought in marriage and family relationships by the majority of our population of all ages, is contained in Table 1.1.

Second, the movement from *Gemeinschaft* to *Gesellschaft* society, and the accompanying shift from predominantly primary to secondary interpersonal relationships, has given even more impetus to the seeking of personal-need fulfillment and self-affirmation by means of intimate relationships, such as marriage. In a society predominated by transitory and impersonal contacts with

FIGURE 1.2.   *Geminschaft-Gesellschaft* as a Continuum.

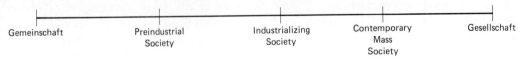

Gemeinschaft   Preindustrial   Industrializing   Contemporary   Gesellschaft
                     Society   Society   Mass
                                                                Society

TABLE 1.1. *Basic Human Physical, Psychological, and Socioemotional Needs Satisfied by Marriage and Family Relationships in a* Gesellschaft *Society*[1]

Intimacy	Belonging
Nurturance	Independence
Warmth	Affection
Food, clothing, and shelter	Love
Acceptance	Comfort
Affiliation	Social integration
Self-affirmation	Security
Stimulation	Sex
Encouragement	Recognition

[1] Undoubtedly, many of these overlap (such as affection and love), or might be considered synonymous (such as affiliation and belonging). This is simply a compilation of the vast number of labels experts attach to human needs which must be fulfilled if development and healthy psychological growth are to take place in childhood and adulthood.

SOURCE: A variety of introductory functional marriage textbooks.

others, it seems that people are, *more than ever before,* in need of some kind of psychological and emotional oasis to which they can retreat in order to satisfy basic human needs. Marriage and family have remained the primary means for meeting those needs, and will continue to assume increasing importance to people as we move closer to the *Gesellschaft* end of the relationship continuum.

Marriage and Family: Dying Institutions?

Given the continuing importance of marriage and family relationships in contemporary society, it is difficult to imagine that anyone would predict the demise of the marital and family institutions within the next several years. Yet, these predictions were made in the early 1970s, shortly after a noticeable increase in the divorce rate, downward trends in birth and marriage rates, and the growth of apparently viable alternatives to traditional patterns of marriage and family living for meeting our psy-

chological and social needs (see, for example, Gordon, 1972; Roy and Roy, 1972; Cooper, 1970). In Cooper's (1970) sardonic assessment of the manner in which families can smother, intimidate, and injure their members (which, indeed, they can), he predicted an end to the family as we know it.

The family form of social existence that characterizes all our institutions essentially destroys autonomous initiative by its defining nonrecognition of what I have called the proper dialectic of solitude and being with other people . . . Nothing is to be left to the Family. Mothers, fathers, brothers, sisters, sons and daughters, husbands and wives have all predeceased us. They are not there as people to be left with anything of oneself or left anywhere in oneself. The blood of consanguinity has already flowed through the gutters of suburban family streets. The age of relatives is over because the relative invades the absolute center of ourselves. (Cooper, 1970:140–141)

Others followed suit in their descriptions of marriage and family as "sick or dying institutions." It became fashionable to criticize the institutions of marriage and family in the late 1960s and throughout the 1970s. Often heard were cries that "the family is dead," "marriage is old-fashioned," "parenting is out," and so on. After all, given that we were living in a world with heretofore unknown challenges and uncertainties, and that our society was becoming increasingly depersonalized, fragmented, and characterized by secondary relationships, why did people *have to continue* satisfying their intrinsic human needs for intimacy and nurturance in the context of marriage and family relationships? What about a system of short-term commitments outside of marriage, such as cohabitation, short-term sexual affairs, or simply two people living together and fulfilling each other's intimacy needs indefinitely? What about permanent singlehood, in which people would satisfy their psychological and emotional needs in intimate relationships as they developed spontaneously? Why couldn't we satisfy our human needs by means of close friendships, which do not require a commitment such as marriage? What was to stop us from seeking need-fulfillment in communal or group-marriage situations, where we would have several partners to provide for us? For a number of reasons, to be detailed at appropriate points in subsequent chapters, these alternatives have never become popular choices in our society, and probably will not for some time to come.

A LOOK AT CURRENT TRENDS IN MARRIAGE, DIVORCE, AND BIRTH RATES

The belief that marriage and the family are dying is shared by a relatively small number of observers. However, it has since become magnified and overly dramatized by the mass media. Many, if not most, of these observers have demonstrated considerable naïveté in regard to current demographic and other scientific data relating to the popularity of traditional marriage and family patterns today. Many relied heavily on personal philosophies and the predictions of social commentators, whose preferences for alternatives led them to predict their ultimate large-scale acceptance. The predictions simply were not rooted in carefully designed and evaluated scientific research, research that could empirically demonstrate what *is* rather than what *should be*. The fact is that marriage and parenting in one form or another are thriving as highly desirable goals for the adult population of contemporary society in the 1980s, although both are *changing* in order to adapt to the rapidly changing economic and technological conditions that we have been experiencing over the past several years. None of these changes are signaling the demise or disintegration of the marital and family institutions. To the contrary, there is a substantial body of evidence showing that entering a marriage relationship or becoming a parent are still popular choices today.

Marriage.   From an historical perspective, Americans have been, and will probably continue to be, one of the most marrying societies in the world during the twentieth century. This is true in terms of the percentage of the population that will become married at least once, and in terms of our comparatively young age at marriage (see *Marriage and Divorce Today,* 1980). Throughout the 1970s and into the 1980s, the proportion of our adult population marrying at least once varied only slightly, between 94 percent and 96 percent (Glick, 1979; 1984a). The average age at first marriage has hovered around 23 for females and 25 for males. This can be compared with marriage rates of anywhere from 60 percent to 80 percent for other societies, including Ireland and Sweden, where the average age at first marriage often approaches or exceeds 30 for both males and females (Reiss, 1980).

The decline in marriage rates witnessed in our society in the early to mid-1970s (number of marriages per 1,000 population) led to predictions of the demise of the marriage institution. However, the drop in marriage rates was really because people *delayed* marriage in order to complete a college education, or to establish an adequate financial base (in an uncertain economy) prior to marriage, rather than because they decided never to marry (see Figure 1.3). This tendency to delay marriage is also occurring in Canada (*Marriage and Divorce Today,* 1980). A demographic phenomenon, known as the *marriage squeeze,* has contributed to both the delay of entering marriage for the first time, and to the apparent increase in permanent singlehood. The marriage squeeze is a result of two factors: first, men tend to marry women who are somewhat younger; second, the post-World War II baby boom created a large cohort of people who became of marriageable age in the 1970s. According to demographer Paul Glick, formerly of the United States Bureau of the Census, in commenting on the marriage-squeeze situation:

During recent years the number of women in the United States who were in the age range when most of their first marriages occur (18 to 24 years) has been up to 11 percent higher than the number of men in the age range when most of their marriages occur (20 to 26 years). This imbalance, or squeeze, is a consequence of past fluctuations in the birth rate. For example, many women born in 1957 at the peak of the baby boom were ready to marry at the age of 21, but the pool of men 3 years older—the men most likely to include a prospective husband for them—were born in 1954 when the birth rate was somewhat lower. (Glick, 1979:2–3)

Other factors also influenced young people to delay marriage, such as increases in the education and employment of young women, the concurrent difficulty of the large number of baby boom adults to find employment in the labor market, and the increase in the frequency of cohabitation ("living together") outside of marriage. Glick (1984a) estimated that around 90 percent of all young adults between the ages of 25 and 29 in 1980 would eventually marry, at least one time. In fact, the marriage rate actually reversed the downward trend of the early 1970s by remaining level in 1977; increasing 2 percent in 1978, 3 percent in 1979, 2 percent in 1980, 0 percent in 1981 (the year in which a new national record for the number of marriages was established), and increasing another 2 percent in 1982, before declining by 3 percent in

FIGURE 1.3.   Marriage Rates in the United States: 1925–1984. (Number per 1,000 population.)

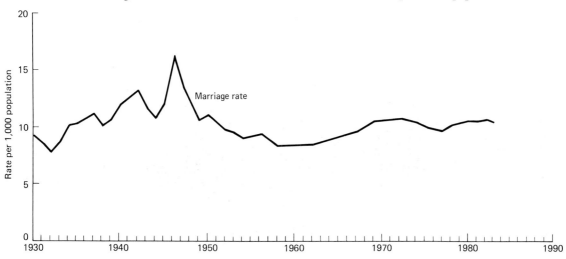

SOURCES:

(a) 1925–1977 data drawn from National Center for Health Statistics, DHEW (PHS) No. 79-1120, Vol. 28, No. 4 Supplement: p. 1, *Final Marriage Statistics, 1977.*

(b) 1978 data drawn from National Center for Health Statistics, DHEW (PHS) No. 79-1120, Vol. 27, No. 13, August 13, 1979, p. 11, *Annual Summary of Births, Deaths, Marriages, and Divorces, 1978.*

(c) 1979 data drawn from National Center for Health Statistics, DHEW (PHS) No. 80–1120, Vol. 29, No. 1, April 9, 1980: p. 2, *Births, Marriages, Divorces, and Deaths for January, 1980.*

(e) 1981 data drawn from National Center for Health Statistics, HHS (PHS) No. 82-1120, Vol. 30, No. 12, March 18, 1982: pp. 2–3, *Births, Marriages, Divorces, and Deaths for 1981.*

(f) 1982 data drawn from National Center for Health Statistics, HHS (PHS) No. 83-1120, October 5, 1983: p. 7, *Annual Summary of Births, Deaths, Marriages, and Divorces: United States, 1982.*

(g) 1983 data drawn from National Center for Health Statistics, HHS (PHS) No. 84-1120, March 26, 1984: p. 2, *Births, Marriages, Divorces, and Deaths for 1983.*

(h) 1984 data drawn from National Center for Health Statistics, HHS (PHS) No. 85-1120, March 26, 1985: p. 2, *Births, Marriages, Divorces, and Deaths for 1984.*

1983 (see Figure 1.3). If marriage is becoming unpopular, or if the marriage institution is dying, our statistics do not show it, at this point.

Divorce and Remarriage.
Another indicator of the potential decline of the marriage institution noted by several observers was the dramatic upswing in the American divorce rate, which began in the mid-1960s. The divorce rate per 1,000 married couples nearly doubled between the years 1965 and 1975, moving from 10.6 per 1,000 to 20.3 per 1,000 (Glick, 1979). Every year between 1973 and 1981 broke the all-time American record for the number of divorces set during the previous year (see Figure 1.4). In 1981, there were an estimated 1,219,000 divorces granted in the United States, more than ever before. This trend was a clear indication to many that the frequency of marriage breakups was reaching a dangerously high level which, if continued, would certainly spell disaster for the institution of marriage in our society. At the very least, it indicated a souring of people's attitudes toward marriage, and a growing propensity to turn away from it permanently.

As with the scientific evidence regarding the marriage-rate decline, however, the predictions of the demise of the marriage institution, based on trends in divorce, were premature. What must be understood is that our divorce rate, historically, has been low and surprisingly constant, with the exception of the years immediately

FIGURE 1.4.   Divorce Rate in the United States: 1920–1984.

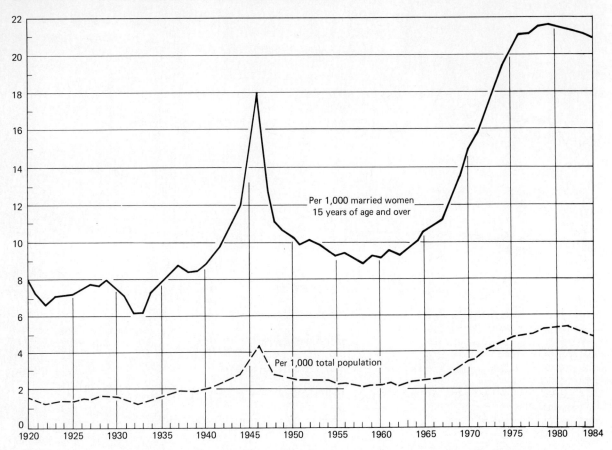

SOURCES:

(a) National Center for Health Statistics, DHEW, No. (PHS) 79-1120, Vol. 28, No. 2, May 16, 1979: p. 1. *Final Divorce Statistics, 1977.*

(b) National Center for Health Statistics, DHEW No. (PHS) 79-1120, Vol. 27, No. 13, August 13, 1979: p. 11, *Annual Summary of Births, Deaths, Marriages, and Divorces, 1978.*

(c) National Center for Health Statistics, DHEW No. 80-1120, Vol. 29, No. 1, April 9, 1980, p. 2, *Births, Marriages, Divorces, and Deaths for January, 1980.*

(d) 1980 data drawn from National Center for Health Statistics, HHS (PHS) No. 81-1120, Vol. 29, No. 13, September 17, 1981: p. 1, *Annual Summary of Births, Deaths, Marriages, and Divorces: United States, 1980.*

(e) 1981 data drawn from National Center for Health Statistics, HHS (PHS) No. 82-1120, Vol. 30, No. 12, March 18, 1982: pp. 2–3, *Births, Marriages, Divorces, and Deaths for 1981.*

(f) 1982 data drawn from National Center for Health Statistics, HHS (PHS) No. 83-1120, October 5, 1983: p. 9, *Annual Summary of Births, Deaths, Marriages, and Divorces: United States, 1982.*

(g) 1983 data drawn from National Center for Health Statistics, HHS (PHS) No. 84-1120, March 26, 1984: p. 3, *Births, Marriages, Divorces, and Deaths for 1983.*

(h) 1984 data drawn from National Center for Health Statistics, HHS (PHS) No. 85-1120, March 26, 1985: p. 2, *Births, Marriages, Divorces, and Deaths for 1984.*

FIGURE 1.5. Interval Between Divorce and Remarriage for Persons Born Between 1900 and 1949, By Sex: 1975.

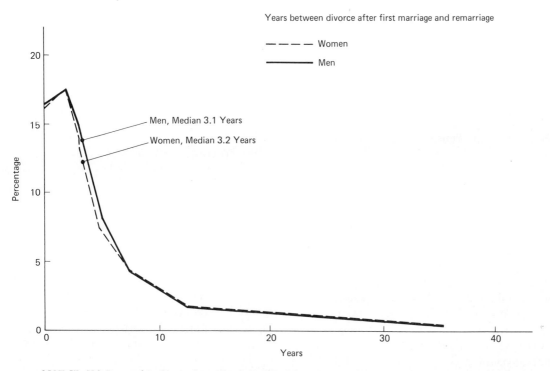

Years between divorce after first marriage and remarriage

– – – – Women
———— Men

Men, Median 3.1 Years
Women, Median 3.2 Years

Percentage

Years

SOURCE: U.S. Bureau of the Census, *Current Population Reports,* Series P-20, No. 297, p. 15: "Number, Timing and Duration of Marriages and Divorces in the United States: June, 1975."

following World War II. Hence, although a rapid move upward in the rate occurred in a period of only 10 to 12 years, the proportion of all marriages terminated by divorce, even at the end of this time period, was not great. In 1978 — the highest divorce rate on record up to that time — the 22 per 1,000 married couples divorcing translates into only one out of every 45 marriages, or 2.2 percent of the total. Moreover, the majority of marriages continue to survive without divorce and will not be terminated until one partner dies. Glick (1984a), who made projections of marriage survival rates based on current divorce statistics, estimated that among married people between 25 and 34 years of age in 1980, 51 percent of the first-time marriages will survive without divorce. Among those between 45 and 54 years of age in 1980, about 70 percent of the first marriages will survive, and for those in 65 to 74 year-old range in 1980, only 15 percent will end their first marriages by divorce (an 85 percent survival

rate). Certainly, our marital institution must show more distress than this if we are to believe that it is on the verge of collapse.[1]

A second indication that the climbing divorce rate is an insufficient basis for predicting the demise of the marital institution is provided by an examination of *remarriage* rates after divorce. One would think that there would be some merit to this prediction if divorced people stayed away from marriage by remaining single. To the contrary, the great majority of divorced people in our society eventually remarry, and most do so in a rather short period of time. As Figure 1.5 shows, more than half of all divorced people who remarry do so within three and one-half years, and 80 percent of all divorced persons remarry eventually (77 percent of divorced women and 84 percent of divorced men) [Glick, 1984a]. Hence, even among those who are sufficiently dissatisfied with their first marriages to terminate them by divorce, relatively few decide to avoid further contact with the marital institution. Moreover, despite the fact that divorced men and women who remarry are likely to wed another who has been divorced (as opposed to a never-married or widowed person), the majority of remarriages among those older than 35 years of age can be expected to survive. For example, among all 50- to 60-year-old Americans in their second marriages in 1980, around 2 in 3 (67 percent) are expected to survive without divorce. This is further evidence that marriage remains a popular method of satisfying basic human needs for intimacy, nurturance, and self-fulfillment in our modern *Gesellschaft*-type of society.

Finally, in evaluating the predicted disintegration of the marital institution by means of recent trends in the divorce rate, note must be taken of the fact that the divorce rate has leveled off considerably in the past few years. Indeed, in 1977 the divorce rate remained level for the first time since 1965, when the record-setting climb in the rate began. Since then, only miniscule fluctuations in the divorce rate occurred, and in 1982 and 1983, the American divorce rate, and the number of divorces, actually declined (National Center for Health Statistics, 1983c; 1984b) [see Figure 1.4]. In 1983, for example, the number of divorces declined to 1,179,000, and the divorce rate of 5.0 per 1,000 population was the lowest since 1977 (National Center for Health Statistics, 1984b). According to data from the United States Bureau of the Census:

During the next decade or two, barring unforeseen developments, the odds seem to favor some continuation of the current slow rise in the divorce rate, with the trend broken periodically by a year or more of stability or decline, (Glick, 1979:3)

Births.   In terms of parenting, the vast majority of married couples in American society will become parents at least once. According to one study (Blake, 1979), in the next several years, only 5 to 10 percent of married couples are likely to choose permanent childlessness, and another 5 percent will remain childless involuntarily because of sterility or subfecundity (difficulty in conceiving because of biological factors). However, many of these couples will become parents by adopting at least one child.

Although it is true that the average number of children per married couple is declining, and that more couples are deciding to limit the total number of children that they will ever bear to one or two (Glick, 1979; Hawke and

Knox, 1977), current evidence strongly indicates that parenthood will continue to be a popular choice well into the next two decades. An examination of the crude birth rate (number of births per 1,000 population) shows a dramatic decline during the 1960s and into the 1970s (see Figure 1.6). However, this trend has all but stopped in recent years; the birth rate increased by 3 percent from 1976 to 1977, remained about the same from 1977 to 1978, and increased again by about 3 percent in 1979, 3 percent in 1980, 1 percent in 1981, and 1 percent in 1982, before declining by 3 percent in 1983. Scientists believe that the previous decline in the birth rate had "gone about as far as it can go" (Glick, 1979:2). The reasons underlying the changes in the birth rate in our society will be discussed in greater detail in chapter 11.

ATTITUDES TOWARD MARRIAGE AND PARENTHOOD

The reader should not draw the conclusion from this evidence that marriage and parenthood are the only legitimate options open to young people today. Indeed, they are not. The point is that marriage and parenthood continue to be popular choices of adults in our society in the 1980s.

However, these statistics on marriage, divorce, and birth rates are indicators of the behavior of people in our society. They may not reflect changes in *attitudes* toward marriage and parenthood. Because attitude changes often precede actual changes in behavior among a large number of people in a society, it is possible that we are becoming increasingly negative in our attitudes toward marriage and parenting but have not yet changed our behavior to conform to those attitudinal changes. The available evidence suggests otherwise, however. National surveys have shown that marriage and a happy family life remain high on the list of personal goals for most young adults (Eckland and Bailey, 1976), even among career-oriented and college-educated young men and women, and that marriage will not become obsolete in future years (Hoge, 1976). A more recent study of nearly 1,000 18-year-olds in 1980 found that attitudes toward marriage remain positive, and do not appear to point toward dramatic behavioral changes in the form of permanent singlehood or childlessness in the years to come (Thornton and Freedman, 1982). For example, this study found that over 90

FIGURE 1.6. Birth Rates and Numbers in the United States: 1920–1984. (Births per 1,000 women aged 15–44.)

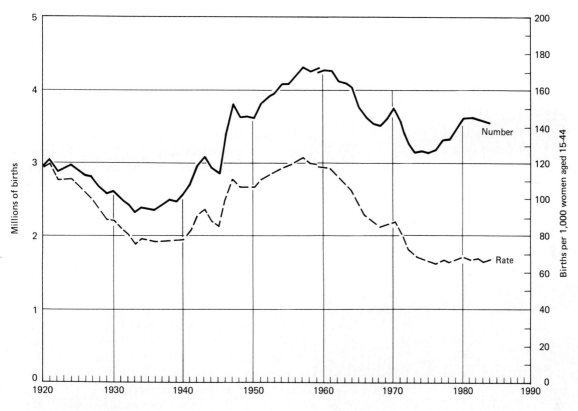

Note: Beginning 1959 trend lines are based on registered live births; trend lines for 1920-1959 are based on live births adjusted for underregistration.

SOURCES:

(a) 1920–1981 data drawn from National Center for Health Statistics, HHS (PHS) No. 83-1120, December 29, 1983, Vol. 32, No. 9, Supplement: p. 1, *Advance Report of Final Natality Statistics, 1981.*

(b) 1982 data drawn from National Center for Health Statistics, HHS (PHS), No. 83-1120, October 5, 1983, Vol. 31, No. 13: p. 1, *Annual Summary of Births, Deaths, Marriages, and Divorces: United States, 1982.*

(c) 1983 and 1984 data drawn from National Center for Health Statistics, HHS (PHS), No. 85-1120, March 26, 1985: p. 1, *Births, Marriages, Divorces, and Deaths for 1984.*

percent of these young single adults expected to marry some day, as one in three (33 percent) were currently dating someone they expected to marry. However, in comparing the responses of these 18-year-olds in 1980 with those of over 4,500 adults surveyed in 1957 and 1976, it was found that people today hold more positive attitudes toward those who choose not to marry. Being single is no longer viewed in such a negative light as it once was, and most young adults today view it as a legitimate life-style for those who choose it. Nonetheless, despite the more accepting attitude toward the singlehood of *others*, only 3 percent of those in the 1980 study stated that they themselves expected to remain single (Thornton and Freedman, 1982:299).

Attitudes toward marriage and parenthood remain highly positive in our society, despite changes in our views toward what constitutes legitimate life styles. *(Photo © Elizabeth Crews.)*

MARRIAGE: IS IT GOOD FOR YOU?

The research evidence discussed in the preceding sections shows that seeking intimacy and self-fulfillment

in marriage continues to be the most popular choice for young people in our modern *Gesellschaft*-type of society. In searching for reasons for the continued popularity of marriage, it seems logical to speculate that being married not only satisfies basic psychological and emotional needs of individuals in a relatively impersonal mass society, but also provides some protection from the daily stresses and pressures of our fast-paced and highly competitive system. Research indicates that for many this may indeed be the case.

One consequence of our highly industrialized and urbanized society, characterized as it is by a predominance of secondary relationships and an emphasis on achievement and success, has been to place people under considerable pressure. In a sense, we are a society "run by the clock." We undergo tremendous pressure in meeting deadlines, being on time to this meeting or that one, traveling great distances on business several times a year, or simply working long hours every day in order to please the boss and move up the ladder of success in one's field of work. This pressure creates a considerable degree of personal *stress,* a phenomenon well known by our recent concerns and controversies over high blood pressure (hypertension), heart disease, ulcers, and psychiatric and other mental health problems. It seems that stress is now a part of our everyday lives, taking its toll on the physical and mental health of many in our society.

Research has shown that marriage is capable of absorbing some of this stress, and functions as a buffer for many who might otherwise be more severely affected by the pressures of modern society. In analyzing data from a questionnaire survey of over 5,000 adults in California, Renne (1971) found that married people were less likely than divorced people to report physical disabilities, chronic illnesses, neurosis, depression, and isolation. In addition, Renne found that formerly divorced persons who had remarried and who were happier in their more recent marriages were *less* likely to report health problems than those in unhappy first marriages. It was also found that unhappily married people reported more health problems than either divorced or happily married people of the same age, sex, and race. This evidence suggests that marriage, if satisfying, can function as a protection against the stress and pressure of today's society.

A study by Pearlin and Johnson (1977) provides further evidence that marriage can function as a protective environment in a context of daily stress and strain so

FEATURE 1.1 First Loyalty

Although the increasing value on occupational pursuits among American women has not detracted from the high value they place on marriage, this does not appear to be the case for the Japanese. As the following news story indicates, among the Japanese, careers often take precedence over marriage — among men!

To whom does the average American owe his first loyalty — to himself, his wife, his family or his country?

Suppose the average American male were driving along a highway, and an earthquake occurred. Whom would he phone first?

In Japan, only 9% of the men would first phone their wives. Incredibly, 37% would first phone their employers — proving conclusively that a large segment of the Japanese value their jobs more than their wives. Which is one basic competitive advantage Japanese companies enjoy over their American rivals in the battle for world business, productivity increases and quality control.

Japanese women are aware of their husbands' slavish devotion to the corporation (they call it "Aisha Seishin") and regard it as a primary cause of marital disagreement, unhappiness and divorce. Many of the best-educated women believe job loyalty is an integral factor of Japanese culture that will not be altered for decades.

Last year when the prime minister's office took one of its periodic surveys on the state of Japanese life, 25% of the single women polled said they did not want to get married because for them this was not the road to fulfillment. Of the 62% who opted for marriage, only 12% said that they expected any happiness out of it. The majority realized that in the Japanese scheme of things, wives rank lower in the pecking order than they should.

SOURCE: Lloyd Shearer, *Parade Magazine,* June 15, 1980.

---

pervasive in our modern mass society. These researchers surveyed 2,300 adults, who comprised a representative sample of the Chicago metropolitan area, and found that married individuals experienced lower levels of depression than the never-married, widowed, divorced, or separated. Even more revealing were their findings that unmarried people were much more likely than married people to experience such life strains as social isolation, economic hardship, and parental-role overloads. These life strains *did not* account for the differences in levels of psychological depression between the married and unmarried, however; married individuals experienced *significantly less depression than did unmarried individuals at equal levels of life strain* (see Table 1.2). These researchers provide the following interpretation of their results, which supports the previous discussion of the important functions of marriage in a *Gesellschaft* society:

Clearly, it is where one is confronted both by social and economic strains *and* is single that one is most prone to depression. The combination most productive of psychological distress is to be simultaneously single, isolated, exposed to burdensome parental obligations and — most serious of all — poor. What we have learned is that marriage can function as a protective barrier against the destructive consequences of external threats. Marriage does not prevent economic and social problems from invading life, but it apparently can help people fend off the psychological assaults that such problems otherwise create. *Even in an era when marriage is a fragile arrangement between spouses, its capacity to protect people from the full impact of external strains makes it a surprisingly stable social institution, at least in the absence of alternative relations providing similar functions.* (Pearlin and Johnson, 1977: 714; *emphasis added*)

Still others have found that (1) married people have lower *mortality* (death) rates than the unmarried (Gove, 1973; Kobrin and Hendershot, 1977); (2) married people report being *happier* than those in any other status, such as the never-married, divorced, and widowed (Bradburn, 1969; Glenn, 1975b; Gurin, Veroff, and Feld, 1960); (3) married people have fewer *disabilities* and *chronic* and *acute illnesses* than do the never-married and formerly married (Verbrugge, 1979); and (4) married

17

TABLE 1.2. *Percentage Distributions from Pearlin and Johnson (1977): Marital Status and Depression by Level of (a) Economic Strains, (b) Social Isolation, and (c) Number of Children at Home*

(a) Level of Economic Strain

	Severe Strain		Moderate Strain		No Strain	
Depression	Married	Unmarried	Married	Unmarried	Married	Unmarried
High 1	26	50	19	29	9	15
2	17	15	22	21	12	18
3	8	12	16	27	19	17
4	26	16	27	13	30	26
Low 5	23	7	16	10	30	24
N=	(73)	(92)	(335)	(220)	(1175)	(383)

(b) Level of Social Isolation

	Considerably Isolated		Fairly Isolated		Not Isolated	
Depression	Married	Unmarried	Married	Unmarried	Married	Unmarried
High 1	13	28	11	24	11	21
2	15	19	13	15	14	16
3	18	19	18	20	19	22
4	28	21	30	21	29	20
Low 5	26	13	28	20	27	21
N=	(270)	(200)	(315)	(135)	(957)	(343)

(c) Number of Children at Home

	Three or More		One or Two		None	
Depression	Married	Unmarried	Married	Unmarried	Married	Unmarried
High 1	12	34	12	26	11	20
2	12	18	14	20	17	19
3	16	17	19	24	20	19
4	31	16	28	18	27	23
Low 5	29	15	27	12	25	19
N=	(458)	(89)	(715)	(179)	(416)	(435)

people have lower rates of *mental disorder* than do the unmarried (Blumenthal, 1967; Gove, 1972).

According to Verbrugge (1979), the comparatively better psychological and physical health status of married people is the result of two things. First, healthy people are good candidates for marriage, whereas severely ill or disabled people may experience greater difficulty in finding a suitable marriage partner, and are more likely to remain single as a result of their disabilities. Those who develop a serious health problem while married may also be more prone to divorce or separation, because of economic or emotional stress. Second, in line with Pearlin and Johnson's (1977) conclusions, married persons can take advantage of the security and social support that marriage has to offer; therefore marriage has a *protective* function. Those who are divorced or separated may experience negative health consequences if they choose to relieve their stress by "drinking, smoking, and other behaviors with high health risks (Verbrugge, 1979:268)." In addition, the single never-married person may be more likely to engage in "risky" life-styles, which include drinking, smoking, drug use, and frequent careless driving.

Although marriage appears to protect individuals from the stresses and pressures of our modern life, it does not appear to do so equally for all married people. Clearly, the *quality* of the marital relationship plays an important role in the degree to which it functions to maintain the psychological and physical well-being of the spouses. For example, one recent study found that husbands and wives who rated their marriages more favorably than others also reported having more positive self-concepts (Schaefer and Keith, 1984). In addition, marriage appears to affect men and women differently, although the research on sex differences varies in its conclusions. For example, some studies indicate that marriage plays more of a protective role for women than for men (Glenn, 1975b; Verbrugge, 1979), but others have reported that marriage is better for the physical and mental health of men than for women (Bernard, 1972; Gove, 1972, 1973; Kobrin and Hendershot, 1977; Radloff, 1975).

In support of the idea that marriage is more protective of the physical and emotional health of women, Glenn (1975b) studied the personal happiness of people in three large national surveys. He found the happiness differential between the married and unmarried to be greater for *women*. That is, marriage was more likely to be associated with overall psychological well-being for women than for men. Verbrugge (1979) seemed to confirm the results of Glenn's study in her examination of several national Health Interview Surveys, a national Health Examination Survey, and U.S. Census statistics from both 1960 and 1970. She found that

Surprisingly, women appear more sensitive to marital status than men. *Separated women* are strongly disadvantaged, compared to married ones, for acute incidence (of illness), all short-term disability measures, major activity limitation, and partial work disability . . . *Divorced women* are also strongly disfavored for several of the same indicators . . . *Widowed women* show higher ratios than widowed men for major activity limitation and partial work disability. In summary, the data suggest that marital dissolution has more negative impact on the health of women than men. (Verbrugge, 1979:283)

However, when looking at those who had never been married, the *single men and women,* Verbrugge found that *single men* experienced more chronic illnesses and disabilities than *married men,* although *single women* fared just as well as *married women.* In sum, whereas having been married at one time and having it dissolved by separation, divorce, or widowhood was more damaging to the physical and psychological health of women, having *never been married* was more damaging to men.

When examining additional evidence from national surveys, Gove (1972; 1973) and Bernard (1972) discovered that the "mental health gap" between single and married men was far greater than the gap between single and married women. Also, married women did not fare as well as married men in terms of being protected from various types of *mental* illness. They interpreted these differences as evidence that married women, particularly traditional housewives, are less protected than married men from psychological stress because they "find their roles constricted and frustrating," thereby reaping fewer of the benefits that marriage has to offer. Married men, who are more likely to undergo pressure and stress in the outside world as a result of their greater involvement in the occupational system, stand more to gain from marriage because it provides a therapeutic "oasis" at the end of every day. According to Bernard (1972), marriage is a "trap" for the wife who is confined to house and children for the seven days of every week, a phenomenon known as the "housewife syndrome."

This interpretation of the differential protective function of marriage for husbands and wives is elaborated by research on mortality and family ties (Kobrin and Hendershot, 1976) and depression (Radloff, 1975). Studying 20,000 cases from the 1970 National Mortality Survey, Kobrin and Hendershot (1976) found that death rates were substantially higher for the unmarried than the married at all age levels from 35 to 74, although the mortality differences were found to be greater between married and unmarried men than those between married and unmarried women. Radloff's (1975) study found that "married women are consistently *more* depressed than married men; both housewives and working wives are *more* depressed than working husbands of comparable age, education, income, happiness with job and marriage, and reported amount of housework"; and that "housewives are *not* more depressed than working wives" (Radloff, 1975:264). Hence, rather than concluding that "housewife syndrome" leads to psychological depression among married women, as Bernard (1972) had suggested, Radloff suggests that *women in general* experience *learned helplessness* throughout their lives. This syndrome involves women perceiving a lack of control over their lives, and an inability to improve an unsatisfying life situation.

The available research evidence generally supports the idea that married people, for whatever reasons, enjoy higher levels of psychological well-being and experience fewer physical health problems than do unmarried individuals. However, the effect of marital status on the psychological and physical health of males versus females appears to depend on the individual life circumstances of the persons involved. For example, some groups of married women report being "happier" than single women (Glenn, 1975b), but others report being "more depressed" than either their husbands or single women (Radloff, 1975).

Whatever the case, marriage seems to be a highly popular choice among young people today. Marriage has the potential to provide beneficial functions for people who undergo the stresses and strains of a fast-paced, competitive, and somewhat impersonal world. Marriage can offer a warm and supportive environment based upon values of caring, concern, cooperation, and respect, in contrast to an impersonal and indifferent occupational system based upon values of achievement, success, and competition. Marriage will continue to thrive as an institution so long as it continues to provide such a stark contrast to other relationships in our modern *Gesellschaft* society, and so long as it functions to satisfy the basic human needs for nurturance, intimacy, and self-affirmation that continue to be so critical to our survival as individuals in contemporary mass society.

Current Trends in Marriage and the Family: Where Have We Been, Where Are We Now, Where Are We Going?

Clearly, the institution of marriage is not dying or disintegrating. What has happened in the last two or three decades is that our institutions of marriage and family have undergone tremendous *changes* in response to tumultuous changes in our society as a whole. Nonetheless, the basic structure of formalizing intimate relationships by means of long-term commitments in marriage and parenthood has remained intact. In other words, the container is the same, but the contents have changed significantly. Let us look briefly at how some of the changes have taken place, and take a look forward to the probable shape of marriage in years to come.

WHERE HAVE WE BEEN?

To see the tremendous changes that our marital and family institutions have undergone, we must look back only three decades. The events that were taking place during the 1950s provide a useful benchmark to see just how much our patterns of marriage and family life have changed over the years in response to other events and changes occurring in our society at large.

The "Happy Days" of the 1950s. If we examine the trends in marriage, birth, and divorce rates (see Figures 1.3 through 1.6), it is evident that the decade of the 1950s was a family-oriented period (Glick, 1975). Following World War II, the United States entered a period of economic prosperity and high employment. Immediately after the war, all three indicators of marital and family patterns rose dramatically, as birth, marriage, and divorce rates shot skyward. By the relatively prosperous 1950s following the war years, all three indexes stabilized at a relatively high plateau, indicating that our new-found affluence was having an impact on marital and family patterns. The post-World War II baby boom continued well into the 1950s, peaking in 1957. *The Total Fertility Rate,* which is an estimate of how many children the average woman in the childbearing ages of 15–44 would eventually have, at current rates, was nearly four children per woman (Glick, 1975). The divorce rate stabilized for the entire decade, and continued to be rather stable until 1965. The marriage rate, which in Figure 1.3 appears to be dropping considerably during that time, was simply a reflection that *remarriages* were fewer because of the rather stable divorce rate and because most young adults were already married. According to Glick (1975:16):

After World War II, the marriage and divorce rates shot up briefly, fell again sharply, and then subsided gradually. By the mid-1950s, a relatively familistic period had arrived. Couples were entering marriage at the youngest ages on record, and all but four percent of those at the height of the childbearing period eventually married.

Clearly, the 1950s represented a period of involvement in families — marriage and birth rates remained strong and the rate of divorce leveled off.

Those of us who lived through the 1950s can surely remember the nature of society at that time, and will recall the pro-family sentimentality presented through such mass media channels as television programs, movies, magazines, and songs. The virtues of love, eventual marriage, and parenthood were important cultural themes, providing clear images of what marriage and family living are, or should be, all about. Melville (1980) provides a graphic account of how television portrayed the American family of the 1950s, reflecting our cultural values on marriage,

parenting, and living harmoniously without unnecessary or severe conflicts in "one big happy family."

In the decade of the 1950s, there appeared to be little reason for public concern about marriage and family. America at that time was a marriage-oriented society in which the state of matrimony was celebrated in songs and mass-circulation magazines . . . Through the new mass medium of television, millions of people were exposed to a new vision of the modern family in its suburban setting. The images of family life portrayed in such popular television programs as "Ozzie and Harriet" and "Father Knows Best" somehow reflected the mood of the times. To be sure, while the Nelsons had "happy problems" that were resolved by the end of each half-hour segment, the problems of real families of that era were not so easily resolved . . . The message of much of the writing about marriage and family life was that, with a

Marriage and family relationships continue to be an important source of emotional and physical intimacy in our modern, fast-paced world. *(Photo © 1980, Ellis Herwig.)*

little bit of personal effort, every family might attain the domestic contentment of the "Ozzie and Harriet" or the "Father Knows Best" model. (Melville, 1980:4)

The television programs mentioned by Melville are only two examples of the kind of programs that enjoyed overwhelming popularity at the time. Indeed, a more contemporary television program, set in that time period, was called "Happy Days." The important point to remember is that the mass media at that time portrayed a *cultural model* which in all likelihood did not fit well with the actual experiences, conflicts, frustrations, and problems of American marriages and parent-child relationships in that decade. Although it is true that Americans were marrying at quite young ages, were almost all marrying at least once, were having between three and four children per family, and the divorce rate was quite stable, the cultural model portrayed through mass media channels was an overly idealized and sentimental picture of the actual experiences of people as marriage partners and as parents — what some people *thought* was happening within American families at the time, without really *knowing* how accurate the picture was.

In the 1950s, then, our society was prospering economically, and floods of people were migrating from the urban centers to *suburban* areas. All major cities in our country, along with several others, were soon encircled by sprawling suburban areas characterized by a preponderance of split-level and ranch-style houses, neatly trimmed hedges and lawns, large single-dwelling lots, and two cars in every garage. This new and refreshing environment was particularly attractive to the group of families referred to as the *new middle class,* those who prospered economically along with the rest of the society.

A definite system of values emerged in conjunction with the development of the suburban middle class. Americans came to highly value occupational achievement and success (through husband's efforts *only,* of course), a respectable income, and the material possessions and modern conveniences that would not only make life comfortable and cushy but which would also demonstrate to others that they had *made it* in life. Advertising agencies assisted by convincing people that they *needed* the most recent devices and gimmicks that modern industry and technology had to offer. A subtle competitive game emerged, known as "Keeping up with the Joneses," which kept families more or less even in the race for symbols of

success. During that decade a society of *consumers* was created. This keeping up, via status symbols, was often very *conspicuous,* so that there would be no mistake in anyone's eyes, especially the neighbors', that we measured up to the American standard of competence and achievement.

Marriage, too, was maintained as a high-priority value in life, and married couples of the new middle class could now afford to have a full complement of children (approximately four, on the average), and were psychologically motivated to do so. Everything *seemed* so idyllic, perfect, and unquestionably fulfilling. It was this *image* of middle-class suburban life, provided by our prospering social and economic systems and our never-more-popular marriage and family patterns, that was developed into the cultural model of "the American Family" and presented to millions of television viewers around the country as something for them to value and, if possible, emulate. A happy marriage, four children, a house in suburbia, and an abundance of material possessions are what we all could, and indeed should, rank high on our list of priorities. *Then,* however, the children of the 1950s grew up to become the adolescents and young adults of the mid-to late-1960s and the early 1970s, and the fantastic American family dream dissipated as rapidly and as thoroughly as it had developed.

WINDS OF CHANGE

The cultural model of the suburban American family just described was superimposed on two aspects of American society which led to its eventual downfall: (1) a wide diversity of ethnic, racial, and economic patterns in regard to marriage and family living that continued to exist during the emergence of the suburban family model, yet were unacknowledged by that model; and (2) a continued emphasis on the basic American values of free speech; the rights of the individual; equal opportunity; equal participation of all citizens in the decision-making processes of the local community, state, and nation; and justice for all without regard to ethnic, racial, or religious background.

Although many young people in the 1960s and early 1970s actually grew up in a typical suburban middle-class family, many did not. Almost all, however, grew up with the *model* of that kind of family as presented and perpetuated on the "magic" screen of television and through other channels of mass communication. Youth in both categories became disillusioned rather quickly with the very essence of the suburban family model, viewing it as a manifestation of basic American values and practices that were either extremely unjust to many in the society or, if just, inadequately or inappropriately applied. The failure of "adult society" to recognize and acknowledge the existence of other patterns of marriage and family living, patterns that were direct outgrowths of continuing poverty, underemployment, and unemployment of many (especially Blacks and other minorities), developed into a pressure cooker of disillusionment, disappointment, frustration, and anger among young people from all segments of society—from the urban ghettos to the suburban communities.

There is a familiar America. It is celebrated in speeches and advertised on television and in the magazines. It has the highest mass standard of living the world has ever known . . . The nation's problems are no longer a matter of basic needs, of food, shelter, and clothing. Now they are seen as qualitative, a question of learning to live decently amid luxury. While this discussion was carried on, there existed another America. In it dwelt somewhere between 40,000,000 and 50,000,000 citizens of this land. They were poor. They still are . . . Tens of millions of Americans are, at this very moment, maimed in body and spirit, existing at levels beneath those necessary for human decency. If these people are not starving, they are hungry, and sometimes fat with hunger, for that is what cheap foods do. They are without adequate housing and medical care . . . The other America, the America of poverty, is hidden today in a way that it never was before. (Harrington, 1962:9–10)

So began Michael Harrington in *The Other America,* a book that signaled to many that the "affluent society" of the 1950s did not include everyone. It became painfully evident that the marriage and family arrangements of millions of Americans did not, and never would, conform to the cultural ideal: the "happily married, four-child, material wealth" family pattern of modern suburbia. Indeed, young people became aware that the very American values upon which the suburban middle-class family rested were being violated: there was *not* equal participation in the decision-making processes of the national community, and there was definitely *not* justice for all without regard to ethnic or racial background. Youth came to see our society as composed primarily of two groups: the

Haves and the *Have-Nots*. The Haves were able to realize the American model of the suburban middle-class family. The Have-Nots experienced high rates of marital separation, divorce, and desertion; high illegitimacy rates; multiple-family living in crowded and run-down urban dwellings; unemployment and underemployment of both husband-fathers and wife-mothers; and, for Black and other racial minorities, prejudice and discrimination.

Rightly or wrongly, the suburban middle-class family model came to be viewed by many as the embodiment of the social injustices and inequality which persisted well into the 1960s. This was all a part of the *Establishment* toward which youthful protest was directed. The reaction of youth against the Establishment was swift, and fanned out in different directions along many different fronts. According to some (Thornburg, 1975; Kenniston, 1967), youth were caught in a serious dilemma of rejecting the values and goals of adult society in regard to material possessions and conspicuous consumption, and, concurrently, they were searching for values and an identity in order to fill the void. According to Thornburg (1975:383–384), youth of the late 1960s and early 1970s sought identity in:

1. student activism, which represents a social and political alternative;
2. drugs, which often strengthen peer-group identity and provide a means of escape from the established culture;
3. greater sexual freedom, because it allows emotional commitment at an intimate level not found in the impersonal society or in conversation with parents;
4. alienation—the passive behavioral counterpart to activism—which, like activism, denies established social and political goals;
5. counterculture institutions—hippie life-styles, Eastern religions, trial marriages—because they provide new types of social structures and identities in place of traditional institutions that have been rejected—traditional religion, marriage, families, schools, and so on.

Clearly, some youth preferred tearing down the entire set of established social and cultural practices, such as the prototypical middle-class family. Others accepted the basic values of adult society, such as equality, justice, and freedom, but sought better ways of realizing them. Kenniston (1967) labeled these two types of youth the "alienated" and the "activist," respectively.

With the escalation of the war in Vietnam, added impetus was given to the disillusionment process among youth, and the roots of alienation from, and disenchantment with, the established order grew deeper and deeper. The societal upheaval of the 1960s, which began in the buses and businesses of the deep South as Blacks boycotted and staged "sit-ins" as a form of nonviolent protest against the white Establishment, was soon picked up by youth across the country and spread to the streets of every major city, where the protests were often much more violent. During the early 1970s, student protesters at such places as Kent State University and Jackson State University were killed by the guns of National Guardsmen or police officers, and several others, including law-enforcement personnel, were severely injured in other confrontations. It appeared to many that this youthful rebellion would eventually lead to a major overhaul of the American value system, including a complete rejection of traditional forms of marriage and family patterns. In ten short years, then, the children of the "idyllic" and "harmonious" middle-class family of the 1950s — the *cultural model* that was held as the epitomy of virtue and accomplishment in our affluent society of that time — appeared to be shaking the very foundations of that model and threatening its future existence, because these youth were to become the adults of tomorrow. Tomorrow has arrived, allowing us to take a look at what happened.

THE PENDULUM SWINGS BACK — THE 1980s

Predictions of the downfall of the marital and family institutions in our society, which were critically examined previously in this chapter, followed on the crest of this wave of youth alienation and rebellion. The search for viable alternatives to the Establishment's values on traditional marriage and family patterns was underway. Considerable attention in the media, and among sociologists, psychologists, and other observers of the marital and family institutions, was directed at new ways of structuring intimate relationships and meeting the basic human needs of emotional nurturance, security, and self-fulfillment. *Communes* appeared to offer a kind of group support in providing for the economic and socioemotional needs of their members. Permanent voluntary childlessness, singlehood, and sexually open relationships (both in and out of marriage) were appearing to replace the traditional marriage and family patterns of the 1950s.

Communal alternatives to traditional *nuclear family* arrangements (that is, husband, wife, and biological or adopted offspring) never flourished, and many dissolved as quickly as they were formed.[2] The same can be said for other alternatives, such as *group marriage,* in which three or more people enter a marital relationship, and *swinging (mate-swapping),* in which spouses are exchanged for sexual purposes while remaining emotionally committed to the married partner. We have already seen that permanent singlehood, and permanent childlessness among those who did marry, never emerged as popular choices, either. Those alienated and disgruntled youth of the early 1970s, who vowed never to commit the "sins" of their parents in forming long-term monogomous (two-person) commitments in such a mundane Establishment practice as marriage, and who swore they would never bring children into a world of hypocrisy and contradiction, actually wound up only *delaying* their eventual entry into marriage and parenthood. Even the seemingly popular practice of *cohabitation,* or "living together" outside of marriage, has not been practiced by more than 25 to 30 percent of the college-age population (Bower and Christopherson, 1977; Clayton and Voss, 1977), and comprised no more than 2 percent of all households in 1983 (Glick, 1984b). Moreover, those who enter a cohabitation-type relationship usually do not view it as a permanent alternative to marriage — virtually all will marry eventually, because cohabitation is viewed as "simply another form of courtship" before marriage (Reiss, 1980:105).

Despite the fact that such alternatives to traditional nuclear-family arrangements have not emerged as popular choices among young adults of the late 1960s and 1970s, the changing pattern of values emerging out of the youth versus Establishment conflicts of the 1970s has paralleled some rather radical *changes* in the form and function of interpersonal relationships within the confines of traditional marriage and family patterns. The two most important changes were (1) an increased emphasis on self-fulfillment and immediate self-gratification of the individual; and (2) changes in male-female gender-role perceptions.

The "Me" Generation. The cultural model of the 1950s clearly emphasized the importance of cohesiveness, cooperation, and togetherness among individuals in a traditional nuclear-family setting. With the dramatic course of events taking place in the late 1960s and early

1970s, however, such values tended to give way as young people began their search for alternative ways of seeking fulfillment and satisfaction of psychological and emotional needs. The uncertainty, unpredictability, and society-wide conflicts at that time seemed to result in a movement away from concern about others and selfless (altruistic) giving in such primary groups as the family, and movement toward a heightened self-consciousness—what "makes *me* feel good." This shift in emphasis is perhaps best illustrated by the tremendous increase in the popularity of such drugs as marijuana, heroin, cocaine, and LSD among the young. The increased use of psychoactive drugs among youth was associated with inward reflection, a search for the meaning of life, and to just "feel good," as an end in itself.

The search for the ultimate in quick and easy self-gratification has since shifted from a focus primarily on psychoactive drugs to what Melville (1980) refers to as "psychic self-improvement." Such activities as jogging, eating health food and organically grown food, seeking advice on being "in touch with ones feelings," dieting, "doing your own thing," exercising, and having one's own psychiatric analyst became the activities of people who emphasized their individuality and their immediate concern for the satisfaction of the needs of the self rather than striving to satisfy someone else's needs.

The rising divorce rate that began in the mid-1960s, and which appeared to some to be skyrocketing, was the result, in part, of the shifting emphasis from mutuality and commitment in long-term relationships to concern for immediate gratification of the needs of the individual. The declining marriage and birth rates provide further evidence that, indeed, this shift in concern was occurring. By the late 1970s, however, the pendulum seemed to be swinging back again as the divorce rate leveled off and the marriage and birth rates indicated *delays* rather than permanent singlehood or childlessness. As we move further into the 1980s, young adults seem to be striving to balance their concern with self-improvement and self-fulfillment with concern for assuming the responsibilities and commitment to such enduring social ties as those involved in a marriage or parenting relationship. As individuals, we continue to seek satisfaction of our basic psychological and emotional needs, as well as the enhancement and growth of ourselves as individual people, but the evidence clearly suggests that we will do so in a context of mutuality and commitment, in monogamous (two-person) relationships

such as marriage. An outgrowth of the *individualism movement* of the 1970s, however, has been to *raise our expectations* of our marriage partners in meeting personal needs and providing satisfaction. In a sense, we have made it more difficult for our spouses to adequately perform the marital roles that would provide satisfaction to us—such roles as sex partner, companion, decision-maker, and affection-giver. In commenting on the state of the marital institution in the 1980s, Reiss (1980:461–462) states:

> There is today an emphasis on the satisfactions available from dyadic relationships that rivals anything we've had in our history as a nation. I would submit that our expectations are quite high and our tolerance of dissatisfaction quite low. We want to obtain a great deal of satisfaction from marriage and if that is not clearly forthcoming, we often do not stay around . . . [I]t is no wonder that our divorce rate has risen.

The movement toward individualism of the 1970s has clearly had an impact on the shape of marriage by increasing our demands for satisfaction from it. The rising divorce rate and delay in entering first marriages are clear barometers of that trend. However, in view of our modern *Gesellschaft*-type of society, and the preponderance of secondary relationships, impersonality, and indifference that it entails, it is logical to predict that people in our society will continue to seek the security, nurturance, intimacy, self-affirmation, and commitment in relationships that endure while, at the same time, striving to enhance and develop themselves as individuals. This is a delicate balancing act that will provide a formidable challenge to marriage partners in the years to come.

Change in Gender Roles. The second major change that has altered the shape of marriage in today's society is the revolutionary shift in the gender-role perceptions of women, and to a lesser extent men, over the past 15 years. Research conducted in the 1950s revealed two characteristic features of marital relationships at that time.

First, marital roles were *scripted*. That is, what was considered appropriate role behavior for men and women in marriage was unambiguously defined, and left little doubt about what each person's rights and responsibilities were in the marital relationship. Husbands were expected to be the primary breadwinners, decision makers, problem solvers, and overall providers of the instrumental resources for the marriage and family. These expectations were firmly grounded in the belief that men were naturally more aggressive, assertive, courageous, and intellectually competent. Wives, on the other hand, were expected to care for the house and children, including of course, washing the dishes. They were expected to clean and cook; do the weekly shopping; mediate conflicts; nurse the children and husband back to health when ill; provide psychological and emotional therapy for the husband when he returned from a hard day on the job; and generally provide the expressive and socioemotional resources necessary to keep relationships within the family cohesive and stable. These expectations were grounded in the belief that women were submissive, passive, nurturant, warm, and cuddly creatures who were necessary to maintain equilibrium in the family unit and provide for everyone else's socioemotional needs.

The second characteristic feature of marital-role relationships was that in the face of disagreements, conflict, habits, or day-to-day living patterns, it was the *wife* who adjusted to the husband's point of view and who accommodated his habits in order to maintain a satisfactory level of harmony in the marital relationship (Bernard, 1964; 1972). Hence, the unambiguous definition of marital roles, in the 1950s, helped to keep levels of conflict and disharmony in marital relationships at a minimum; each partner had definite job descriptions which allowed for little overlap or uncertainty as to "who was to expect what from," and "do what for," whom. Moreover, included in the wife's cluster of roles was that of being able to figure out ways to give in gracefully in the event that conflicts should erupt, and go along with any habits or quirks that the husband might bring into the relationship. Is it any wonder that the divorce rate during this decade was comparatively low and stable?

This style of relating in marriage was not to survive for much longer. By the mid to late 1960s, a new wave of consciousness was sweeping the nation, with such labels as "Feminism," "Women's Liberation," "Sisterhood," and the "Sex-Role Revolution." The ideology of feminism emphasizes that women who immerse themselves in wifehood and motherhood to the exclusion of all else, particularly occupational careers, are severely restricting their own personal development for the sake of their husbands' and childrens' development (Duberman, 1975). Actually, this ideology was not new in the 1960s; feminist movements between 1840 and 1920 fought for legal and political equality between men and women, gradually gained

power, and won voting rights for women by 1919. As Duberman (1975:13–17) points out, though, the 1920–1963 period saw a lull in feminist activity. By 1965, however, the lull was broken and once again women organized across the country to gain social and economic equality with men, both inside and outside of marriage. By 1966, a group of women headed by Betty Friedan founded the National Organization for Women (NOW), and influential books on feminism and the underlying philosophy and goals of the Women's Liberation Movement began to appear. Friedan's *The Feminine Mystique,* although published in 1963, gained popularity and led the charge of the renewed consciousness of women. It was followed by Kate Millett's *Sexual Politics,* Germaine Greer's *The Female Eunuch,* and Robin Morgan's *Sisterhood Is Powerful.* Gloria Steinem became a charismatic leader by campaigning for women's rights and self-development, and by starting *MS.* magazine.

Before long, it became evident that many women in marriages characterized by the traditional male-female gender-role assignments were no longer willing to accept the scripted distinction between what was considered appropriate male and female behavior. The feminist point of view was invalidating the underlying perception of males as dominant, inexpressive, and intellectually competent and of females as submissive, nurturant, and always in service to the male partner. Researchers were finding, and feminist literature reported, that gender roles are more culturally than biologically determined, and that women are fully capable of functioning in realms formerly reserved for men. Neither were women willing to continue being the ones who did all the adjusting and accommodating to their mates. Moreover, changes in women's perceptions of gender roles occurred more dramatically and more suddenly than did those of men (Duberman, 1975; Walum, 1977). There was a significant lag between male and female acceptance of the "modern" gender role equalitarianism between the sexes, causing husbands and wives to enter a process of bargaining and renegotiation of role relationships as women strove to move from "junior partner" to "equal partner" status and men fought to maintain the *status quo* of male dominance (Scanzoni, 1972). That this lag has caused conflict in marital relationships is suggested by the fact that the divorce rate in our society began its historic climb at the same time that these cultural changes in gender role perceptions began, indicating that the bargaining and renegotiation processes were unsuccessful in many cases (see Figure 1.4). Although by no means the only cause of this growth in divorce rates, there is little doubt that the changing gender-role perceptions among wives, and the failure of their husbands to change accordingly, contributed significantly to the divorce rate phenomenon of the late 1960s and 1970s.

Changes in gender-role perceptions associated with the women's liberation ideology have effected a major restructuring of role relationships within many marriages in our society. The traditional male-female role scripts are no longer taken for granted, as they once were. Now more than ever, bargaining and negotiating skills between partners in marriage assume paramount importance. Moreover, this effort will become more sharply focused as women continue to pursue careers and work outside of the home while, at the same time, they marry and have children with male spouses who also will continue to work outside of the home.

We have only scratched the surface of the topic of gender roles and their relationship to marriage. We will devote more detailed attention to the development, change, and influence of gender roles in chapter 4. Of importance, at this point, is to understand the nature and magnitude of gender-role changes in our society, and to realize the swiftness of these changes and their impact on the internal dynamics of marriage.

Marriage and Successful Marriage: Working Definitions

Up to this point, we have not given a precise definition of the concept of marriage, nor have we given much consideration to what constitutes a successful marriage relationship. Surely, there are a number of possible definitions that could be provided for each concept, depending upon who was asked to provide it, and none would be intrinsically more valid than another.

Gender role changes have fostered a restructuring of male-female relationships in marriage and the family, including a new emphasis on the concept of fatherhood. *(Photo by Mary Arntzen.)*

The U.S. Census Bureau defines marriage as two people who have entered into a legal contract of marriage. Reiss (1980) developed a sociological definition of marriage by identifying the structure and function of marriages that exist universally in all known cultures, past and present.

Marriage is a socially accepted union of individuals in husband and wife roles with the key function of legitimation of parenthood. (Reiss, 1980:50)

This definition introduces the idea that the state is concerned with the care and nurturance of children, and that the institution of marriage will assure, as much as possible, that the married pair will provide a stable environment and be responsible for the proper socialization and protection of children born to it. This is true for cultures where *monogamy* (one husband married to one wife) is practiced, as is the case in our society, or in cultures where *polygyny* (one husband with two or more wives) or *polyandry* (one wife with two or more husbands) is practiced.

Although Reiss's definition may be technically correct in that it is universally applicable, it is not of sufficient scope to encompass the key features of marriage in contemporary American society. For one thing, not all marriages involve parenthood. Knox (1979) provides a more useful definition of marriage, for the purposes of this book:

Marriage in America is a relationship in which two adults of the opposite sex make an emotional and legal commitment to live together. Most marriages involve a public announcement and are undertaken with the hope of permanence. Subsequent children of the union are socially and legally recognized as legitimate. (Knox, 1979:5)

In addition to Reiss's concept of "legitimation of parenthood," Knox adds *emotional commitment, legal commitment* (akin to Reiss's notion of a "socially accepted union"), *public announcement,* and *hope of permanence* to his definition. Given that this is what marriage *is,* however, is there a way to define what constitutes *success* in marriage?

DEFINING SUCCESSFUL MARRIAGE

As a society, Americans continue to value success in anything that might be undertaken as a task, challenge, or commitment. Ours is a success-oriented society, granting

prestige and status to those who have "made it" in the occupational, political, educational, and social arenas (Williams, 1970). We like to be known as *winners,* not *losers,* as indicated by the differential reward structure established for each category—the winning team gets more money, the winning candidate gets the political office, the winning student gets the A's and scholarship offers, and so on. The same can be said for individuals entering marriage relationships. By whatever criteria those individuals have in mind when they marry, most people are hoping, and probably expecting, that their marriage will be a good one that will last "till death do us part." Rightly or wrongly, many people view divorce as a failure of one partner or the other. But undoubtedly there are other criteria for success in marriage beyond its simply lasting a long period of time, such as 50 to 75 years.

If you were to ask different people to provide a definition of what constitutes a successful marriage, you would get many distinct definitions. Finding a satisfactory definition of successful marriage is particularly difficult because of the tremendous range of values, life-styles, social classes, and ethnic backgrounds represented in our society. For example, some define successful marriage by its longevity, or stability over time without divorce. Others have called successful those marriages that have little or no conflict between spouses, or that comply with prescribed gender roles for husbands and wives (that is, the husband is a good provider and the wife is a good housekeeper, cook, and mother) [Olson, 1972]. However, these definitions fail to take into account the subjective feelings and perceptions of the spouses toward the relationship, and do not consider the diversity of roles and values now open to spouses of both sexes. Would *you* call a marriage successful that has lasted forty years without divorce when the partners have become indifferent toward one another, or where each wished they had never married the other? Probably not. Today, people in general are moving toward viewing successful marriage as one in which "growth and development of both partners is facilitated to a greater extent than it could be for either of these individuals outside the relationship" (Olson, 1972:390).

In short, a definition that is valid and meaningful for one individual or group of individuals may be highly objectionable to another. The nature of successful marriage depends upon the criteria adopted for assessing the quality of the relationship; the nature of the goals and expectations brought to the marriage by the individuals involved; and the particular person (husband or wife) being asked to assess the degree to which the marriage is successful. These factors, combined with the tremendous diversity in individual values, goals, and normative expectations characteristic of our society in general, make a definition of the concept of successful marriage susceptible to bias and value-laden prescriptions.

A useful and meaningful definition of successful marriage must therefore be phrased in such a way that is unbiased. Such a definition has been proposed by Burr (1976), and a somewhat modified version of it will be adopted here.

A successful marriage is one that in actuality fulfills the needs and achieves or approximates the goals, expectations, and values of both marriage partners over time.

Success in marriage, therefore, is accomplished to the extent that three criteria are met: (1) important goals, expectations, values, and needs for marriage are being realized, either in full or within an acceptable range; (2) *both* partners' goals, expectations, and needs are being met; and (3) criteria one and two are being met consistently over time. In addition, it is important to realize that successful marriage is not an either-or kind of situation in which a couple is labeled either successful or not successful. Successful marriage is a continuum that ranges from high to low, with many degrees in between. Where a particular couple ranks along this continuum at any one time depends upon the combined effects of these three criteria, because goal- and need-fulfillment may be accomplished in some areas but not in others; goals and needs vary in terms of their relative importance to the married pair; the two partners within a marriage may vary in their perceptions of goal- and need-fulfillment; and the perceptions of each will vary over the months and years of marriage.

Burr (1976) reviews several different marital styles and arrangements which, given the goals and expectations of the participants, could be considered "successful" according to our definition. Let us briefly review some of these types here.

1. *Traditional Marriage.* In traditional marriage arrangements, spouses tend to believe that the way in which their relationship has been structured is the most common and acceptable way, and is, as a result, somehow better than other arrangements. Role relationships in traditional marriage are defined according to gender

of the spouse, with clear rights and responsibilities associated with being either the "husband" or "wife."

The husband and wife roles will be fairly different in that the husband will be the primary source of income. The wife will assume the primary responsibility for running the household even though the husband will be expected to help out somewhat. If the wife works it probably will not be to have a career. She will work because they need the money or because she needs to get out of the house . . . The euphoria of the first few months will disappear as practical concerns such as house payments, vaccination, frayed cuffs, pay raises, strikes, insurance, dripping taps, promotions, PTA, Little League, buying shoes, and getting dishes done take its place . . . As the years pass the couple will spend less time going out. They will do some things together, and both will have important relationships outside of marriage . . . Married life will have its share of surprises, excitements, joys, and satisfactions, but most of the time it will be quite ordinary and routine. (Burr, 1976:18–19)

2. *The Intrinsic Marriage.* Based upon a study of 400 upper-middle and upper-class marriages in the United States, Cuber and Haroff (1965) identified a type of marriage relationship considered to be successful by the participants; the intrinsic marriage is one in which

couples have intense feelings about each other, and each considers the other person, as a person, to be of central importance . . . merging of two people that is so intimate and encompassing that it is the pervasive concern and source of pleasure in their lives . . . other aspects of life (e.g., careers, kin, friends, individuality) tend to be subordinate to the husband-wife relationship. (Burr, 1976:3–4)

3. *The Utilitarian Marriage.* A second type of marriage, found in Cuber and Haroff's study of "significant Americans," is known as *utilitarian marriage,* and consists of a relatively limited amount of mutual intimacy, companionship, and togetherness. It is one in which

only selected parts of the individuals' lives are shared. Other parts (career, friends, relatives), and frequently these are the most important aspects of the individual's lives, are viewed as separate concerns that are shared with others and not the spouse. (Burr, 1976:6)

4. *Open Marriage.* Drawing from the work of O'Neill and O'Neill (1972), Burr describes this marriage type as one that

> involves a unique balance of intimacy, interpersonal commitment, and flexibility. One of the most important aspects . . . is a recognition that individuals change throughout their lives, and the marital relationship is viewed as sufficiently flexible to permit both members of the couple to change and grow, yet maintain a meaningful relationship with each other . . . Other ingredients are living for now, realistic expectations, privacy, role flexibility, open companionship, equality, identity, and trust . . . Open companionship implies that both spouses are free to develop deep, involved, and important interpersonal relationships with other individuals. These relationships can be with persons of either sex, temporary or permanent, and limited to very narrow aspects or very broad and inclusive. (Burr, 1976:8–9)

5. *Two-Step Marriage.* The late anthropologist Margaret Mead has popularized a type of marital arrangement known as *"two-step marriage,"* although others have promoted a similar idea under a variety of different labels (e.g., Packard, 1968; Satir, 1967). Under this system, the couple enters a trial period, or quasi-permanent stage, lasting anywhere from two to five years. In this stage

> . . . the individuals usually live together, cohabit sexually, and form one economic unit, but they do not have children. (Burr, 1976:11)

At the end of this stage, the couple has the option of continuing in the relationship and making a more permanent, legally sanctioned commitment that involves the bearing and rearing of children, if desired, or terminating the relationship if after this trial and error stage the spouses perceive the relationship to be unsatisfactory.

6. *Group Marriage.* This type of marriage arrangement involves at least three individuals, and sometimes as many as six or seven, who consider themselves to be married to the others in the group. However, there is no legal basis for this sort of arrangement in our society at the present time. Hence, group marriage is based upon a *social* definition of the situation by the participants involved. According to Burr (1976:15):

> Group marriages include such combinations as a couple and a single person, two couples, two couples and a single person, three couples, and so on . . . Usually, but not always, intimate sexual activity, such as sexual intercourse, occurs in all of the cross-sex relationships and occasionally homosexual relationships develop in the same-sex relationships . . . Also, group marriage demands considerably more commitment, time, energy, and effort than do the simpler forms of marriage, and the larger the group the more demanding the interpersonal relationships . . . Given the tendency of humans to have such reactions as jealousy, feeling left out, resentments, and a need for esteem, group arrangements can become extremely complex.

7. *Swinging Marriage.* This style of marriage is one in which marriage partners are exchanged among a given number of couples for the purpose of sexual activity. Only a very small number of couples actually participate in sexual swinging activities; for those who do, the marital relationship in all other aspects appears to fall within the normal range for traditional marriages. According to Burr (1976:10):

> Usually the couples who engage in swinging have high commitment to permanence in their marital relationship, and most of the time they are fairly conventional in the other roles they occupy . . . Since sex is only one aspect of the total marital relationship it is possible to combine the swinging style of marriage with one or several of the other alternatives (e.g., Utilitarian or Open marriage).

Clearly, there is a wide range of options available to individuals considering a career in marriage. Although some options are more popular than others, any of those patterns can be found in society today. Which of the marital arrangements just described provides the best fit with *your* personal goals, expectations, and values regarding what marriage *ought to be?* Which one is the best for you? There are other possibilities for marriage relationships which have not been described here, so perhaps none of these fit into your life design. Moreover, you may wish to combine certain elements of two or more of these styles of marriage arrangements in your attempt to define what is right for you. The point here is that every individual who enters a marriage comes equipped with some idea of what a successful marriage *is,* what one can expect to put *into* it, and what one can expect to get *out* of it. In determining what a successful marriage is, therefore, we must give foremost consideration to these individual marital goals, expectations, and values in order to avoid imposing on other individuals our own values and conception of what is right.

A basic assumption of this book is that, although successful marriage as defined here is attainable, it is a difficult, and oftentimes elusive, state of existence to attain. This is because of the complexities involved in establishing and maintaining a fulfilling interpersonal relationship that is to span a long period of time; and the tremendous number and variety of choices and decisions that individuals in marital careers must make at many critical junctures along the way. There are also numerous societal constraints that impose limitations on the ability of people to realize their goals in marriage, such as differences in education, income, and other "life chances." Regardless of the numerous choices and constraints involved, however, it is important to realize that individuals in marriage often have more power to direct and control their own futures than they might realize. The power to structure and control the future comes primarily from within each marriage partner. Compared to other species, human beings are relatively autonomous and self-directed entities who have a strong ability to anticipate, structure, and prepare for the future. We sometimes become victims of circumstances, situations, and other sources of external influence because we *allow* ourselves to be so influenced. In working to construct a successful marriage, it must be realized, and accepted, that the *partners* share some of the responsibility for the shape that their future in marriage will take. To make marriage successful, partners must take the initiative to engage in the kind of preparation and work which is necessary to reach their goals, and be willing to make the choices and decisions necessary in order to meet the challenges that their future in marriage undoubtedly will pose. It is hoped that the material contained in this text will make this task a little more understandable and, consequently, a little easier.

Summary

The rapid technological changes that have taken place in our modern postindustrial society over the past century have created tremendous changes in our social and economic environment. We have been moving ever closer to a *Gesellschaft*-type of society, which entails a decreasing number of *primary relationships* that are personal, familiar, and close, and an increasing number of *secondary relationships* that are relatively impersonal, indifferent, and distant. The world we live in is also challenged by grave problems which threaten its survival, and which place all of us in a climate of uncertainty and unpredictability. In spite of these conditions of contemporary society, the institutions of marriage and family have continued to function as the primary means by which people satisfy basic psychological and emotional needs for intimacy, nurturance, self-affirmation, and security. However, the conditions and stresses of our modern society have created several noteworthy *changes* in the *range of options* people have available for structuring their relationships both inside and outside of marriage, changes perpetuated by the increased emphasis on individualism and the changes in gender roles over the past fifteen to twenty years.

The stresses of modern society are also clearly represented by changes in the three major barometers of the state of the marriage and family institutions: marriage, divorce, and birth rates. These indicators currently show that marriage and parenting will remain popular choices of individuals in our society for some time to come. This highlights the fact that marriage and family relationships are major societal stress absorbers, in the form of primary-group relationships carried over from the *Gemeinschaft*-type of society which existed prior to the development of modern technology and the industrial revolution. Although this movement toward a *Gesellschaft*-type of society has enhanced the significance of marriage, it has also placed considerable stress upon the marital institution and has affected the ability of marriage partners to fulfill each others needs. Particularly stressful is the modern occupational system, characterized as it is by daily pressures.

Because a dominant value of American culture is *to succeed* at anything one might undertake, most people entering marriage strive for success in that particular undertaking. Success in marriage was defined as the degree to which a marriage achieves or approximates the goals, values, expectations, and needs of both partners over time. The recently increased emphasis on individualism, rising expectations for the satisfaction of psychological and emotional needs in marriage, and changing gender-role expectations and behavior have rendered the attainment of success in marriage particularly difficult in the 1980s. This world in which we live is certainly not the "best of all possible worlds," nor is it the worst. Success in marriage, as difficult as it may seem given the present reality of our life circumstances, can be shaped and directed by those who enter it. The odds may be difficult, but partners in marriage will persist in confronting them by seeking fulfillment in marriage in the challenging world of the 1980s.

Questions for Discussion and Review

1. Examine the differences between *Gemeinschaft* and *Gesellschaft* society presented in Figure 1.1. What evidence of any of these differences do you see in contemporary society? Are people from rural areas or small towns more likely to see signs of *Gemeinschaft* than of *Gesellschaft?* Is *Gesellschaft* more apparent in larger urban areas?

2. Discuss the implications that you believe the transition from *Gemeinschaft* to *Gesellschaft* society has had for the status of women and men. How has this transition influenced the *relationship between* the sexes? Are these changes for the best?

3. Discuss the benefits, as well as the drawbacks, of life in *Gemeinschaft* society. What are the benefits and drawbacks of life in *Gesellschaft* society? In which type of society would you rather live? Why?

4. What are your most important primary groups? What role do they play in your life? Identify four major functions that primary groups have for you.

5. What are your attitudes toward marriage and parenthood? Just how important are these as life goals for you? Are they more, or less, important to you than a career in the world of work?

6. Try to think of ways in which marriage is good for the physical and psychological well-being of people. Under what conditions might marriage be better for men than it is for women? Under what conditions would marriage be better for women than for men? Under what conditions would remaining single be better than being married, for both men and women?

7. What is your definition of a successful marriage? How would you rate the marriages of people you know closely, such as friends, relatives, parents, or siblings? How would you rate each of the seven types of marriage described on pp. 29–30.

Notes

1. We will not be discussing the various *causes* of the rising divorce rate, nor its consequences, in this chapter. This issue will be detailed in full in chapter 15. We are simply concerned at this point with the extent of recent changes in the rate as they bear on the prediction that the marital institution is crumbling.

2. The structure, functions, problems, and popularity of communes and other alternatives to traditional nuclear-family arrangements (group marriage, cohabitation, singlehood, and so on) will be discussed at appropriate points throughout the book. They are mentioned in this chapter only to document emerging and declining trends in the way people have structured their marital and family relationships in the context of recent social changes.

CHAPTER 2

Development in Marriage and the Family:

Principles and Concepts

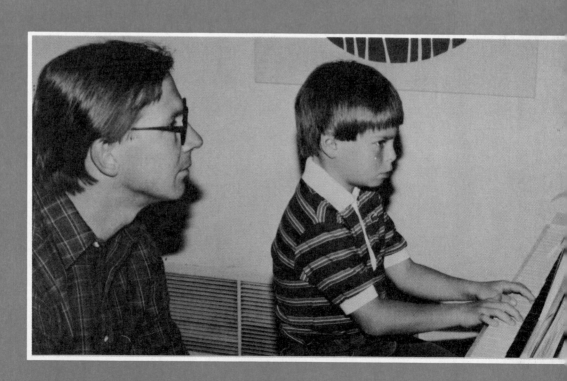

Scientific knowledge bearing upon marriage and family life in our society is in a continual state of flux. Not only is the shape of these institutions heavily influenced by changing cultural values and norms, as is the case in all kinds of social relationships, but the volume and quality of scientific research in this area continues to expand at an accelerating pace. This large volume of research on marriage and family relationships may prove to be a mixed blessing: it is becoming so expansive and diverse that it is difficult to gain a comprehensive picture of all, or even most, of what is known.

What should prove useful to the reader of this book is a *framework of concepts* within which to cast the knowledge acquired from various research studies. Conceptual frameworks provide a coherent and integrated picture of marriage. Although no single framework can claim to encompass all that is known about marriage and family life on the basis of existing scientific research, some sort of framework is necessary to pull together a large number of research studies, which must then be organized to provide a more meaningful picture of marriage and family than could be provided by a random and unfocused search of the research literature. In this book, the conceptual framework that will guide the examination of marriage and family life is known as the *Family Development framework*.

Conceptual Frameworks and Research on Marriage and the Family

Conceptual frameworks in the study of marriage and the family are simply clusters of clearly defined concepts that refer to specific aspects of marriage and family life

which anyone can observe. These concepts provide a language for the study of marriage and family relationships so that we can communicate more effectively and efficiently about them. Conceptual frameworks, then, function to sensitize us to particular aspects of marriage and family relationships, as well as to enhance our ability to effectively communicate with one another about the subtleties and complexities of development in these important areas of our lives.

Throughout this volume, specific concepts relating to marriage and the family will be employed. They will help us to make sense out of scientific research studies designed to provide knowledge in this important area. Research studies, often referred to as *empirical investigations,* are the scientist's means for establishing facts based on observations. In this way, our knowledge about a given topic is less likely to be biased; based on myth, conjecture, or someone's guesswork; or subject to a particular value system or point of view that distorts reality. Marriage and family life are complex aspects of our existence, and discussions of these topics often evoke our deepest values and emotions, such as in the areas of abortion and birth control; child or spouse abuse; how to be a good parent; and proper roles of men and women. Carefully conducted scientific research therefore assumes a critical role in our study of marriage and family relationships.

The Buyer Beware: Limitations of Social Science Research

In this book, we will rely upon social scientific research to organize our study of marriage and family relationships. Other methods may be preferred by many people, such as the astrological or the psychoanalytic; or one that is closely tied to a particular religious ideology, such as the Roman Catholic, Mormon, Judaic, or Protestant. Nonetheless, a widely accepted and utilized approach to the study of marriage and the family is the social science approach, one that uses specific concepts, employs logically developed theories, and follows certain rules of observation which most people can accept as legitimate.

The main advantage of the social scientific approach to the study of marriage and the family is that it strives for *objectivity*. It does not endorse one point of view or set of values relating to marriage and family life as inherently better than another. Just as our definition of successful marriage (see chapter 1) was made in a spirit of acceptance of a diversity of values, goals, and life-styles, so too the spirit of science is one that strives to provide an unbiased understanding of what *is* rather than what *should be*. Thus, a person is in the position of being able to make a choice in regard to how he or she wishes to behave or live. In other words, social scientists can and do *study* values, beliefs, and behavior of people, and the consequences that each might have, but social science cannot determine which system of values or beliefs is better than another, or *right* in a moralistic sense. It must be understood, however, that the quality and, consequently, the credibility, of research studies vary considerably. Therefore, as consumers of social science research, we must beware of false or overextended claims, and exercise caution in applying research findings to our personal lives. Just because someone's research found something to be true in regard to marriage does not mean that we should accept it uncritically. In evaluating the usefulness of any given study, and in deciding whether or not to accept it as a true picture of reality, the following points must be given consideration.

1. Scientific Research and the Knowledge It Generates Are Based on the Laws of Probability.

There is a saying, "To every rule, there is an exception." The findings of social science research never imply that they are true for *all* people at *all* times. Rather, the focus is on what is true "on the average," or what the tendency is "for most people." If 75 percent of all marriages of young people under the age of eighteen were found to be terminated by divorce within ten years, this research finding would be a valid and useful one, even though 25 percent of the marriages did not fit the pattern.

We would conclude that early age at marriage is *probably* related to marital instability. Of course, researchers can increase our understanding of this phenomenon by taking a closer look at the group of cases that did not fit the overall pattern, to see what, if anything, distinguishes them from the others. A familiar example of the use of the laws of probability has to do with cigarette smoking and the probability of contracting lung cancer and heart disease. Numerous studies have found that cigarette smokers experience significantly higher rates of lung cancer and cardiovascular disease, and that among those who smoke more cigarettes per day the morbidity rates are higher. Despite this causal relationship, which has been found to exist, we all know of smokers who have not contracted heart or lung disease. Some people smoke over two packs a day for fifty years or more and never become ill. These individuals have managed to "beat the odds" of contracting lung or heart disease, yet the fact remains that people who smoke are *more likely* than others to contract this disease.

The research evidence, which has provided the foundation for the chapters that follow, will alert you to the probabilities attached to various aspects of marriage and the family. For example, the current probability of your marrying at least one time is extremely high (well over 90 percent), the probability of your divorcing at least once is considerably lower (45 to 50 percent), and the probability of your experiencing some sort of physical violence with your spouse is lower yet (10 percent). Hence, you get married expecting that you probably will not divorce, and you feel secure in knowing that you are very unlikely to ever be involved in a physically violent situation with your spouse. If the probabilities of divorce and physical violence in marriage were considerably higher, say 60 or 70 percent, and if you were made aware of these probabilities, then you would probably give strong consideration to staying single. Indeed, in time we would probably see a tremendous drop in the marriage rate!

2. Exercise Caution in Generalizing Research Findings.

Related to the foregoing point one is a warning: avoid overgeneralization of research findings that are based on aggregates of people. You should be aware that social science research is not concerned with explaining anything about particular individuals, or marriages of specific couples; but it is concerned with understanding how and why people behave as they do, in the *aggregate*. There are therefore, two things to bear in mind.

First, it is true that all generalizations made on the basis of social science research have exceptions to the general case, and some have more exceptions than others. Therefore, do not automatically assume that the findings of research apply to your individual case, because you may be one of the exceptions. Remember that it is useful to be *aware* of the probabilities attached to various aspects of marriage and family life, so that you can weigh and consider them in making more informed choices and decisions in your life. Imperfect as they are, knowing the probabilities is better than having absolutely no information at all upon which to make a decision that is important to you. However, probabilities provided by research should only be viewed as rough guides, and should not be followed blindly and uncritically.

Second, you should exercise caution when generalizing from your own individual case to what is true in general, or true "on the average." A few years ago, a student in a marriage education class was describing the experiences that she and her husband had had in a communal living arrangement involving two other couples. She said that the other couples were quite messy, had different norms of cleanliness and tidiness, and the resulting conflict between the couples eventually led to the dissolution of the communal arrangement. The student commented, "Communes just don't work. It is too difficult to manage everyone's different habits, personalities, and life-styles." Just because a communal living arrangement did not work out for this student and her husband, she promptly generalized her experience to include other communal arrangements. Whether or not communes, in general, work for those in them is an *empirical question*. It can be answered only by conducting systematic observations across a number of such living arrangements, not by the outcome of one person's or one couple's experience. Again, what is true for you *may* be an accurate reflection of what is true in general, but only carefully designed and systematically conducted research will allow us to state, with any degree of confidence, whether or not it is true.

3. The Quality of Research Varies from One Study to the Next.

Social science can never prove anything absolutely, because of the imprecision and error that is present, to some degree, in our research methods. The generalizability of any research in the social sciences, including that on marriage and the family, depends upon several factors, including:

(a) *The size and nature of the sample drawn.* Large samples that are randomly drawn, and which represent a clearly defined population, are generally better than small or unrepresentative samples. Large samples, however, are not always superior to smaller ones. A large sample that is biased in some respect is inferior to a smaller sample that is more representative of a particular group or population. For example, a large national magazine recently published a questionnaire on the sexual interests and activities of its female readership. The fact that 50,000 people completed the questionnaire and returned it through the mail was a signal to some that this study provided a true reflection of the sexuality of the adult female in America. However, the fact that this magazine is more popular among a particular segment of the American female population, notably middle- to upper-middle-class females with reasonably high levels of education, suggests that the results are at best generalizable to that segment of the population only —and probably just to the readership of that magazine. A randomly selected sample of 1,000 drawn from all levels of society would provide a more representative and unbiased picture of sexuality among adult American females than this sample of 50,000. However, perfectly random and representative samples are hard to come by, as the following point illustrates.

(b) *Problems with respondents in social science research.* Because social scientists normally depend upon people to supply the data for research, usually by means of people who participate in a survey or experiment, the problem of *voluntarism* emerges. Social scientists depend upon people who are willing to participate in order to conduct their research. This is especially problematic in research on marriage and families because of the sensitive nature of the questions asked and the norms of privacy people usually have about such intimate relationships. It is not uncommon for marriage research to be conducted on 50 to 75 percent of those who were asked to participate. One often wonders what the 25 to 50 percent who refused to participate are like, and how the results of the research would have been altered had they volunteered to participate. For example, in a study of *satisfaction with marriage,* where only 50 percent of those who were asked to participate did so, it would be reasonable to speculate that those who refused perceived their marriages to be unsatisfying and wanted to hide that fact from some snoopy researcher. The researcher would certainly be getting a biased picture of marriage, if this was the case. Because the vast majority of research on marriage and family depends upon people volunteering to participate, and invariably a certain percentage will not be willing to do so, we must be aware of what those percentages are when evaluating the usefulness of a particular study.

Other problems in conducting research with human subjects, especially on marriages, also occur. Even among those who volunteer to participate in research, the problem of *social desirability,* or *conventionalization,* is a perpetual nemesis (Edmonds, 1967). People in general, and marriage partners in particular, often have a desire to place themselves in a favorable light, or to respond to a question in a way they think the researcher expects them to respond. Also, respondents in a study on marriage may *refuse to answer* particular questions that they find offensive, or that involve aspects of their lives they may wish to keep private. If too many refuse to answer certain questions, or simply don't understand a question that may be somewhat complex, the researcher is left with an incomplete set of data which are of questionable utility. There are ways of minimizing all of these problems associated with conducting social science research on marriage and the family, and the more carefully conducted research studies provide evidence that this has been done.

4. Statistics Do Not Always Tell the Whole Story.
Some people firmly believe that "numbers do not lie." In a sense, this is true. It is also true that social science research rests squarely on the use of statistics to help us understand the nature and magnitude of cause-and-effect relationships that are predicted by our theories. However, statistics can be quite misleading when researchers only present those that support their own point of view, and ignore those that might not be compatible with the outcome they had hoped for. In almost any report of research in the social sciences, it is the researcher who provides the *interpretation* of the numbers, in order to tell us what they *mean.* In many cases, the same numbers can yield quite different interpretations, depending upon who is doing the interpreting. For example, recall the mention, in chapter 1, of research on the physical and emotional health status of single versus married persons, and husbands versus wives. The findings of Glenn's (1975b) national surveys were that the gap in psychological well-being (overall happiness with life) between married and single women was greater than that between married and single men, and that wives showed a stronger relationship of marital happiness to overall happiness than did men. His interpretation of these findings was that, for wives,

> the psychological benefits of marriage are strong enough to outweigh, in the balance of positive and negative affect, the stressful consequences. . . . The data presented here . . . strongly suggest that contemporary American marriage, in spite of its many limitations, is typically beneficial to both husbands and wives. (Glenn, 1975b:599)

Bernard (1975), upon examining the data presented by Glenn, did not interpret the result in quite the same way. In referring to the concept of "affect balance" mentioned by Glenn, Bernard (1975:600) stated that

> perhaps the positive aspects of marriage for women outweighed the negative in view of the grim alternatives available to them in so many cases. In that sense they might well say that they were happy. But . . . the costs are far too high in terms of mental health. And the research literature on the mental health, even the mental illness, of married women is so overwhelming that their self-reported happiness seems almost like one of the symptoms.

Surely, whoever is right or wrong is not the point here. We may never know for sure. The point is that the statistics, in and of themselves, do not come fully equipped with meaning and significance. Researchers are the ones who provide that, and there is always the possibility that the statistical results of research will be cast in a light that is favorable to the researcher's own bias or point of view.

5. Research Findings Age Right Along with the Rest of Us.
Compared with other disciplines, the study of marriage and family life is more heavily influenced by the continually changing norms and values in our culture. In such disciplines as chemistry and physics, forming a particular combination of elements or forces today will result in the identical compound or outcome that would have resulted last year, five years ago, or even hundreds of years ago. There are laws of physical *nature* that are invariant — do not change. This is not so in the study of marriage, where the laws of *social nature* change according to the values and norms in a culture at any given time. Various combinations of male and female partners in marriage in the 1980s, (which, for our purpose, might be considered analogous to creating a compound in the chemistry laboratory) will surely result in

quite different outcomes than if those same individuals had been "combined" in the familistic era of the 1950s, when the recently evolved cultural values of individualism and gender-role equality were less prevalent. This means that much research conducted on marriage and the family is bound to the particular era in which it was conducted; what was considered "scientific knowledge" in the past may be quite different today. For example, we know that the attitudes and behavior relating to sex before marriage (premarital sex) were quite different in the 1950s than they are today (see chapter 9). Not only were young people more conservative in their attitudes, and therefore less likely to engage in premarital sexual intercourse in the 1950s, but the causes and consequences of such behavior were also quite different.

By the same token, the current state of scientific knowledge on marriage and family life today may be quite different several years from now. The body of knowledge in these areas is therefore relative to a cultural era. Clearly, as social and cultural changes bearing on our marriage and family institutions occur, research data collected at one time may become stale—no longer applicable to current conditions. But this is *not necessarily* the case with *all* research conducted in past years. We merely stress the importance of continuing research on marriage and the family, in order to keep us current in our knowledge about these institutions which are so critical to so many members of our society.

couples in the context of such major societal systems as the family, the occupational system, and the religious system. Some approaches to studying marriage and the family might assume that certain kinds of marriage relationships are better than others, such as those characterized by a high degree of consensus and companionship, and a low degree of conflict and change. One of the more fruitful approaches has been to *combine* several points of view to provide a more comprehensive picture of marriage and the family. Whatever approach is taken, however, it is impossible to include every research study (thousands have been done), or to cover all that is known about marriage and family relationships. The question then becomes, "What determines which research study, or other literature on marriage and family relationships, will be included or excluded? What are the criteria for the inclusion or exclusion of particular research findings?"

Three criteria will guide our coverage of research: (1) *recency,* (2) *scientific quality,* and (3) *practical applicability.* Also, because social science research and statistics on marriage and the family do not "speak for themselves," it is critically important to specify the principles and major concepts of the framework being used, so that the reader can place the information in the proper perspective. In the sections to follow, we will review briefly the underlying principles of the developmental perspective, and provide definitions of several concepts which will help to organize and integrate research data on marriage and the family in a meaningful way. These concepts will focus our attention on principles that should be useful for the reader.

Major Principles and Concepts of the Developmental Perspective

In seeking to understand the nature of marriage and family life, the role that marriage can play in satisfying the physical and emotional needs of marriage partners, and how to establish plans for building a fulfilling relationship that will endure over time, there are many approaches that could be taken. For example, we might focus on the psychological characteristics of each individual in marriage, their individual needs, goals, and expectations. Or we might adopt a sociological approach, which would focus on dating couples, engaged couples, and married

PRINCIPLES OF THE DEVELOPMENTAL FRAMEWORK

The perspective provided by the developmental framework is best described as being *eclectic* (Hill and Hansen, 1960). That is, it is a blending of the more useful principles and concepts from other frameworks in the marriage and family field of study. These principles and concepts have their roots in several disciplines, including psychology, education, sociology, biology, and anthropology. The following principles are stated in terms of the marriage relationship, although they also apply to other family members (such as children) and relationships within the family (such as parent-child and sibling relationships).

Principle 1. The behavior of marriage partners is the sum of their past experiences as incorporated in the present, as well as in their goals and expectations for the future.

Principle 2. Marriage relationships develop and change over time in similar and consistent ways.

Principle 3. Humans initiate actions as they mature and interact with others, and also react to pressures from their physical and social environments.

Principle 4. Married partners must perform certain time-specific tasks set by themselves and by persons in the broader society.

Principle 5. In viewing marriage within a social setting, the individual is the basic autonomous unit.

Principles 1 and 2 make clear the importance of the concepts of *time* and *change* in the developmental perspective. Marriage and family relationships are not static, unchanging entities that remain the same from one year to the next. For example, marriage for many has a dynamic quality in which partners initiate and experience, to varying degrees and in various ways, a multitude of changes in several dimensions of the relationship. In chapters 9 through 14, we will examine in detail the significant changes that occur over time in the following areas of marriage and other family relationships:

1. The definition of the concept of *love,* and the importance of this concept for families and partners in a marriage relationship (chapter 3).

2. The definition of appropriate male and female behavior, as determined by *gender roles* (chapter 4).

3. The nature and importance of the *sexual relationship* in marriage (chapters 5 and 6).

4. The processes and outcomes of *communication patterns* of various types, and the issues, strategies, and outcomes of *conflicts* between spouses and other family members (chapter 7).

5. The problems and prospects of family *economic functioning* in our modern affluent society (chapter 8).

Clearly, if we were to ignore the importance of *change over time,* we would be missing one of the most critical dimensions of marriage and family relationships, and, consequently, would acquire a rather stunted, short-sighted picture of what marriage and family life holds in store in the long run. In addition, the fact that marriage and family relationships are more or less patterned, regularized, and predictable has allowed social scientists to build a cumulative body of knowledge about the typical and not-so-typical problems, stresses, and strains experienced in marriages and families over time.

Principles three through five emphasize the *active role* each partner in a marriage relationship takes in influencing its development. The point here is that humans are not simply passive reactors to stimuli in their environment. Rather, each marriage partner is fully capable of initiating actions that in some way will influence the development of the relationship, either by promoting change in the patterns of interactions and their outcomes or in maintaining stability and continuity by preserving the status quo.

Moreover, these principles, particularly number 4, are related to a theme that runs throughout this book: Survival in marriage requires a certain amount of *work* on the part of each marriage partner. The criteria of marital success that most people hold, in terms of goal-attainment and need-fulfillment, do not come naturally. Contrary to what we might like to believe, we are not born as competent marriage partners, readymade expert lovers, problem solvers, sex partners, and conflict managers. These are skills acquired, to varying degrees, in our own families of orientation (families into which we are born) and in other educational settings, such as in school or among friends. In addition, these skills must remain relatively sharp, by using them at appropriate times throughout the years of a marriage relationship. The process of development in marriage and other family relationships clearly requires a continual and conscious *effort* on the part of each member in order to satisfy the criteria for success that each might have. Indeed, one of the first orders of business during the months prior to entering a marriage is to find out what each partner's criteria for success are; whether they involve expectations and goals or simply a particular kind of feeling in the relationship. Of course, some partners have more stringent expectations and loftier goals than others, thereby requiring more intensive and concerted work in the marital relationship if success in meeting expectations and reaching goals is to be realized. The point to remember is that *working* on a marriage or other family relationship is a continuing task that is critical for realizing success, for the vast majority of individuals.

CONCEPTS OF THE DEVELOPMENTAL PERSPECTIVE

The principles of the developmental perspective highlight the importance of time, change, and individual initiative in our thinking about marriage and family relationships. As illustrated in Figure 2.1, development in marriage is an ongoing and dynamic *process,* one that emerges as a result of past experiences of the married couple as well as their goals and expectations for the present and the future. In addition to the reciprocal influences of marriage partners on each other over time, there is a continual impact of children, friends, relatives, and the occupational and economic systems of society on the marriage relationship. Development in marriage and the family should therefore be viewed in a social context, both exerting influence upon, and being influenced by, experiences with the social environment over time. In Figure 2.1, the broken line around the marriage relationship represents the permeability of its boundaries, which provides for change and development in the relationship as it be-

comes increasingly involved in transactions with other social agents in the present and in the future.

The developmental perspective on marriage and the family, therefore, involves a set of concepts that are able to capture the ebb and flow of change in marriage and family relationships over time. It should also help us to understand the processes, problems, stresses, and strengths of marriage and family relationships at any particular time. Such concepts are useful if they point to meaningful similarities among events and experiences in our environment.

The following concepts and definitions were drawn from the family development conceptual framework in order to provide the reader with a set of tools for understanding the dynamics and outcomes of marriage and family relationships when viewed as developmental processes occurring over time. These concepts are also intended to organize the ever-increasing storehouse of knowledge provided by scientific research on marriage and family life in our society. The definitions presented here are based largely on the work of the author, Aldous (1978), and Duvall (1977). Here, we will focus on definitions rather than on application. The application of the concepts and examples appear at appropriate points throughout the remainder of this book.

Norms, Roles, and Positions.   *Norms* are the culturally defined *shoulds* and *ought to's* of individuals in a society. They represent our guides for acceptable behavior. For example, "children *should* obey their par-

FIGURE 2.1.   Marriage as a Dynamic Process in a Social Context.

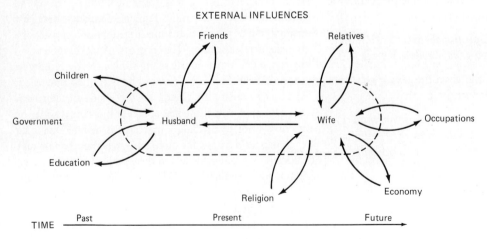

ents," "husbands and wives *should* share in the house-keeping duties," "marriage partners *should* have an equal voice in making important decisions," "wives *should* be primarily responsible for child care," "husbands *should* assume and maintain an occupation that will provide an adequate standard of living" are all norms to which many people subscribe. People learn particular norms for marriage and other family relationships in their families of orientation, from their friends and other adult contacts, and from the mass media of television, film, and literature (Hill and Aldous, 1969). Norms are often referred to as *normative expectations,* and are of critical importance in marriage, because each partner enters a marriage equipped with a "script" of such expectations for themselves and for their partners to follow. In addition to serving as guides for behavior, norms reflect the *perceived rights and duties* that each partner has in a relationship such as marriage. Problems are likely to arise when partners' normative expectations are in conflict; for example, when a husband has learned that housework should be a woman's task, and a wife subscribes to the norm that housework is drudgery and should be shared equally by both partners. Problems may also arise if the normative scripts of two people entering a marriage are undeveloped, and one or both simply do not *know* what to expect from each other, or have not thought about the appropriate allocation of rights and obligations between them. Many norms may be so subtle that people are not conscious of them until they find themselves in a situation that brings them to the surface. An example is the husband who did not know that he objected to his wife's working outside of the home until she started her new job. In addition to normative *conflict,* then, normative *ambiguity* can pose problems for partners in an intimate relationship, including marriage.

No less important than the concept of norm is that of *role*. A *role* is an organized clustering of specific norms that define a given activity for an individual. In marriage, for example both husbands and wives assume a variety of roles that are defined by distinct norms; that is, the behavioral expectations and perceived rights and duties held by each partner for the self and for the other person. The actual enactment of these expectations, rights, and duties are known as *role behaviors*. In addition, marriage and family life can be characterized as involving two basic types of roles: (1) *instrumental roles:* roles that require competence in dealing with objects in the environment as well as in performing particular tasks related to survival,

physical maintenance (food, clothing, and shelter), and decisions that affect the marriage partners and other members of the family; and (2) *expressive roles:* roles that require establishing and maintaining interpersonal relationships characterized by caring, intimacy, and trust (Parsons and Bales, 1955; Zelditch, 1955). Table 2.1 contains only a partial listing of the major instrumental and expressive roles that married persons play. Clearly, marriage calls for skilled behavior in a variety of areas. Marriage is unique in the relatively greater blending and balancing of expressive and instrumental roles than is true for other kinds of adult involvements, such as those with friends (which are mainly expressive) and those in one's place of work (which are primarily instrumental).

A particularly important dimension of role behavior in marriage and the family is that of *gender roles,* sometimes referred to as sex roles. These are roles related to conceptions of masculinity and femininity; that is, what are appropriate behaviors, rights, and duties for males and females? (see chapter 4 for a more complete discussion of gender roles). Some people subscribe to *traditional* gender roles as defined by the following norms, among others:

1. Males only should be the primary breadwinners earning income for the family.

2. Females only should assume responsibility for care of the home and children.

3. Males should be dominant and aggressive.

4. Females should be passive and submissive.

5. Males should be strong and emotionally self-sufficient.

6. Females should be weak and emotionally nurturant in relationships with others.

7. Males should manage the economic resources of a marriage and family.

8. Females should manage the conflicts and smooth over the tensions between family members (this means yielding to the husband, if necessary).

9. Male children should play with trucks, footballs, and engage in a rough-and tumble activities; females should engage in quiet and non-aggressive play activities.

Marriage and family life demand the peformance of a complex combination of instrumental and expressive roles.   *(Photo by Carl Hill.)*

Many people are likely to be more modern, or egalitarian, in their gender-role expectations, distinguishing less between males and females simply because they are of one sex category or the other. In the case of traditional gender roles, people are expected to behave in certain ways and accept certain rights and duties simply because they are male or female. These are *ascribed* roles, assigned on the basis of some characteristics that the individual possesses and over which they have little or no control, such as race, sex, or age. *Achieved* roles, on the other hand, are those that are attained on the basis of the individual's own efforts. In the case of modern gender roles, it is just as appropriate for females to be dominant, aggressive, the primary breadwinner for the family, or in control of eco-

nomic resources of the marriage or family unit. Likewise, males might legitimately choose to make efforts in assuming the primary child-care and home-care responsibilities, and in functioning as the major source of nurturance and intimacy in the marriage and family.

Related to the concepts of gender roles, ascribed roles, and achieved roles is the concept of *conjugal-role organization* (Bott, 1957). The concept refers to the manner in which marriage partners perform various marital roles having to do with household tasks, such as cooking, cleaning, repairs, and childrearing and child discipline. *Joint* conjugal-role organization refers to marriages in which the husband and wife share most or all of the household duties, or where the tasks are viewed as being

TABLE 2.1. *Roles That Marriage Partners Play*

Instrumental Roles	Expressive Roles
Provider	Confidant
Decision-maker	Affection-giver
Teacher	Affection-receiver
Leader	Sex partner
Budget analyst	Lover
Repair person	Face-saver
Cook	Ego-builder
Housecleaner	Companion
Mechanic	Conflict manager
Buyer	

Roles Involving Both
Instrumental and Expressive
Activities

Problem solver
Nurse

interchangeable. *Segregated-role organization* refers to marriages in which tasks are divided between the husband and wife, with little overlapping; roles are generally allocated on the basis of traditional gender-role prescriptions. In this case, husbands would handle the household repairs and heavier work, whereas wives would handle the cooking, cleaning, and child care.

Whether one assumes roles that are based on some characteristic over which the individual has no control (ascribed roles), or assumes roles based on individual efforts (achieved roles), all roles are based on a cluster of norms that define the appropriate behaviors, rights, and obligations for that individual in a given relationship at a particular time. Collectively, the cluster of roles that are assumed by an individual at any particular time constitute that person's *position* in the social system. In regard to marriage in our society, there are obviously two basic positions: the *husband position* and the *wife position*. When children are born, the labels for these positions are modified and become the *husband-father* and *wife-mother* positions, respectively. Children occupy the positions of *son-brother* or *daughter-sister* in a family.

The interrelationship of the concepts of norm, role, and position is illustrated in Figure 2.2, with a simplified

example of a hypothetical married couple. One *expressive* and one *instrumental* role are presented in this illustration, with the normative *scripts* of each role presented as they are viewed by each individual in the two positions. That is, the norms defining the sex-partner role for the husband position are those held by Tom; the norms defining the sex-partner role for the wife position are those held by Sue, and so on. It should be noted at this point that no judgments are being made in regard to what type of role configuration in marriage is better than, or preferred over, another. There exist a large number of possible role scripts in male-female relationships both before and during marriage. The reader should note the potential for role conflict in the case of Tom and Sue, pictured in Figure 2.2. In subsequent chapters, we will examine some of the more common problems and conflicts in role relationships of males and females, both within and outside the boundaries of marriage and family relationships.

Role Sequence. Recalling the importance of change over time in the developmental perspective, a concept is needed to denote the fact that the norms comprising various roles in marriage and the family actually change over the years. We will refer to the changes in the role behaviors and expectations in any family position over time as a *role sequence*. An example of a role sequence in the sex-partner role of a married couple should illustrate this concept.

John and Helen have been married for eight years. At the time they married, they found each other to be quite sexually attractive, and enjoyed a close and intimate sexual relationship during their first year of marriage. They engaged in sexual intercourse on the average of four or five times every week, and each found this frequency to be satisfactory in fulfilling their sexual needs. Soon the novelty of the sexual relationship wore off for both partners, however, and they reduced the frequency with which they sought sexual contact with each other. Each modified their expectations so that neither anticipated as much sexual contact as they had previously enjoyed, and the one or two sexual encounters per week they now had reflected a change in their role behavior. Their normative expectations and actual behavior were now compatible. Later, when Helen became pregnant for the first time, she experienced considerable nausea, backache, and some dizziness. These symptoms persisted for some time, and the fre-

FIGURE 2.2.   Hypothetical Examples of Norms, Roles, and Positions.

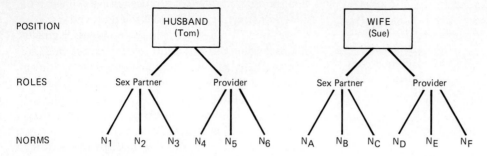

Key to Norms: Sex Partner Roles

N_1 = Sex is a man's privilege and a wife's duty
N_2 = The man should take the lead in initiating sexual relations
N_3 = Sex play outside of marriage is acceptable for males, but not for females
N_A = Sexual pleasure should be shared equally by husband and wife
N_B = Initiative taking is the female's responsibility
N_C = Sex play outside of marriage is inappropriate for both males and females

            Provider Roles

N_4 = The husband should be the primary provider of income
N_5 = The primary provider has the right to decide how money will be spent
N_6 = The husband should decide what job he will take
N_D = Women should make as much income as they can in order to contribute to the
        economic well-being of the marriage
N_E = The right to decide how to spend money should be based on the individual
        competencies of the spouses
N_F = Each partner should contribute to decisions on occupational involvements of
        the husband or wife

quency of sexual contact decreased even further. Neither partner felt that they should engage in sexual relations while Helen was feeling so miserable. However, after the baby was born, each partner soon found their sexual interest in each other rekindled, probably because of the extended period of sexual abstinence during the pregnancy, and the reduced frequency of intercourse even before that. The novelty of the sexual relationship had waned after the first year of marriage, but it had now reappeared after a period of relatively little sexual contact. Each partner expected more sexual contact, and the four or five sexual encounters that they were currently enjoying reflected the change in their role behaviors. Contributing further to the role sequence in their roles as sexual partners was the fact that they had been reading some new books on human sexuality. These were intended to increase the couple's enjoyment of the sexual relationship by providing ideas about different positions, methods of stimulation, and so on. Hence, not only did the frequency of sexual contact return to its original level, but the changes in their methods and patterns of sexual interaction, inspired by their reading of human sexuality books, reflected changes in the expectations and behaviors associated with their roles as sex partners — a *role sequence*.

Role Cluster and Role Complex.   The hypothetical couple illustrated in Figure 2.2 is clearly an oversimplification of the full complement of normatively scripted roles that one is likely to find in marriage and family relationships. We therefore need concepts that denote the full range and complexity of role relationships in marriage and the family. Picture, if you can, the complexity of Tom's and Sue's interpersonal relationship by taking all the roles listed in Table 2.1 (for a total of 21), making the appropriate specification of norms for each, and then assigning them to each position (husband and wife). If we take three as the number of norms defining each role (this is surely a conservative estimate for most roles), and each person has assumed 21 roles in their position as either husband or wife, we find that each partner is operating with a normative script which includes 63 normative expectations regarding appropriate behavior, rights, and obligations. The full complement of normatively scripted roles assumed by either the husband or wife is the *role cluster* for that position. Added to the complexity is the fact that Sue not only holds normative expectations for her own performance in a given role, say in the role of sex partner, but she also has expectations about *Tom's* performance in that role. Tom also has expectations for himself, as well as for Sue, across the range of roles in this relationship. The full complement of normatively scripted roles for both husband and wife combined, or for the relationship as a whole, is that couple's *role complex*.

As we shall see in a subsequent chapter, one of the important tasks confronting many couples contemplating marriage is that of establishing a certain degree of *role compatibility* prior to entering marriage, then working to maintain that compatibility as the marriage relationship develops over time. This means that a certain level of agreement on the various normative expectations for each partner must be reached in the couple's role complex. However, the magnitude of this task is often not fully understood by couples contemplating marriage, or even by those couples who have been married for several years. In the example of Tom and Sue, presented in Figure 2.2, there is potential for conflict over the normative expectations that comprise their role complex. For example, Tom believes that the husband should decide how their money should be spent, whereas Sue believes that the decision as to when and where to spend money should be made by the spouse who has the greatest ability to make money-spending decisions. If this situation causes a disagreement between Tom and Sue (when he wants to buy a stereo and she wants to save the money for a vacation), *role conflict* emerges.

As we have seen in the concept of role sequence, the normative expectations that partners bring to marriage change over the course of time. Hence, compatibility be-

tween roles that may have existed at one time may later become role *conflict* if the norms of one partner or the other should change. The potential for change, then, further magnifies the *complexity* of a married couple's role complex, and makes the task of maintaining role compatibility even more difficult over time as each partner strives to adjust to changes in the other.

When we add the role sequences of *parents* and *children* in the family, the picture becomes even more complicated. For example, the techniques that a parent uses to discipline a child's misbehavior at age two or three change markedly by the time the child reaches adolescence. Parents of young children may attempt to use physical restraint and more direct control, whereas parents of an adolescent may find that verbal reasoning and explanation are more appropriate, and effective, discipline methods. Likewise, expectations for a child's behavior change over time. Expecting a three year old to do heavy chores around the house, such as removing the trash or cleaning windows, is likely to be viewed by most people as less appropriate than to expect this type of role behavior from an adolescent. When one considers the many roles that parents and children assume—including those relating to discipline, communication, decision making power, affection exchange, and "teacher-student"—in addition to the multiple roles that marriage partners in a family play, the true complexity of marriage and family life becomes evident.

Role Reciprocity. Let us take the concepts of norm, role, and position one step further by introducing a concept that specifies how marriage partners and other family members are motivated to perform roles, and thereby maintain stability and harmony in the relationship. Based upon a perspective known as *social exchange theory,* people form and maintain relationships on the basis of perceived rewards and costs that those relationships might have for each person (Scanzoni, 1972; Nye, 1978). People usually get married because they are rewarded by the companionship, love, and affection received from the partner, and often because there are economic benefits to be gained by marrying. Moreover, at the time of marriage, the perceived rewards of the relationship usually outweigh the perceived costs. Costs may be in the form of an occasional argument or quarrel; having to move to a different city; or having to adjust to a less-than-friendly set of

The addition of children magnifies the role complexity of the family unit.   *(Photo by Stephen R. Jorgensen.)*

in-laws. However, when the costs involved in a marriage exceed the perceived rewards, as is often the case when marriage partners move toward dissolving the relationship by means of divorce, the partners become increasingly likely to seek rewards in other ways, such as in other intimate relationships, if such alternatives become available.

Role reciprocity directly links the process of seeking rewards in marriage to the norms and roles of marriage partners. This process is illustrated in Figure 2.3 (see also Scanzoni, 1972). Again, we have greatly simplified matters by limiting the number of roles involved. Actually, the complexity of the role-reciprocity process is much greater because of the large number of roles and norms involved in the role complex of a married couple. Each partner, for instance, has duties attached to the role of affection-giver in his or her respective role clusters. Let us assume that each holds the following norms for themselves and for the other partner:

Duties

1. Married people should take the time to show affection whenever one partner or the other desires it.

2. Married people are obligated to engage in sexual intercourse as often as necessary to fulfill each other's sexual needs.

FIGURE 2.3.   Role Reciprocity in the Affection Giving Role in Marriage.

SOURCE: Adopted from Scanzoni (1972).

Rights

1. Married people have the right to receive affection from their partners.

2. Married people have the right to be sexually satisfied.

So long as the husband fulfills his *duties* in the affection-giving role, to the satisfaction of the wife, he rewards the wife by fulfilling her perceived *rights* in this area. The wife will reciprocate by fulfilling her duties in terms of affection-giving, thereby fulfilling the husband's perceived rights and rewarding him in kind. He will thereby continue to discharge his duties, and so on, in a reciprocal fashion.

People are motivated to reciprocate by performing certain roles, for two reasons. First, we tend to feel a *moral obligation* to reciprocate when someone does something for us, whether it is paying us a compliment, giving a gift, or satisfying a need that we have for love and affection (Gouldner, 1960). Second, the rewards we receive from another tend to make us feel good about our relationship with that person, and we reciprocate because we wish to avoid threatening the future of the relationship. We all have norms of *fairness* and *equity* which, if violated, cause us to cry "foul," and we seek to restore the relationship to one that is viewed as fair and just by both partners. Indeed, the concept of role reciprocity implies that one partner can bring *sanctions* to bear on the other if the other fails to reciprocate by meeting his or her role obligations or by behaving in conformity with role expectations. For example, a husband who tires of showing affection when his wife expects it (in the morning, for example) may find his wife being cold and distant to him, as punishment. If the problem persists in spite of the sanctions invoked by the wife, she may eventually threaten, as a last resort, to end the relationship. Such sanctions are invoked to bring the wayward partner back into line with norms that had existed in the relationship prior to the time the partner stopped meeting his role obligations.

Let us look at another example to show how role reciprocity works, this time in terms of Tom's and Sue's *companionship roles*. For the two years they have been married, Tom and Sue have had few disagreements with each other, and even fewer arguments and quarrels. They have, in other words, managed to establish a high degree of role compatibility in their relationship. Central to this role compatibility has been their high degree of compan-

ionship and togetherness. They have come to look forward to arriving home from work each night so they can share each other's company. They share the cooking duties for dinner, and often have an evening activity planned, such as attending a concert or a movie. These exchanges have formed a behavior pattern that they have come to expect of one another, and each is highly satisfied with their ability to exchange, or reciprocate, in their companionship roles. These role exchanges have helped to create satisfaction in other areas of the marriage as well, such as sharing household chores and making decisions.

Recently, however, Sue's work associates at the real estate office have developed a routine of stopping at a local restaurant after work to enjoy the Happy Hour, and have asked Sue to join them. This seems like an excellent way to relieve some of the pressures and strains that build up over the course of a hard day, and she agrees. For two weeks, Sue arrives home late from work, and Tom is forced to prepare dinner for both of them. Moreover, the money that Sue is spending for Happy Hour drinks is money that otherwise would have covered their expenses for concerts and movies. Consequently, the shared activities they once enjoyed are declining in frequency. This situation bothers Tom, and he becomes resentful of Sue's after-work activities. Tom's resentment and displeasure signal that a relationship that once had a high level of role reciprocity is now in a state of role conflict and disharmony. Tom's resentment is bound to continue until the former pattern of role reciprocity is re-established, or until he is able to change *his* expectations about what constitutes fair and equitable exchanges in the marriage (his rights and Sue's duties).

The reader must be aware that the example provided here is an oversimplification of a complex and complicated process. There are numerous roles and even more numerous norms in a marriage, and their linkages and mutual effects are often difficult to comprehend or understand. Role reciprocity also operates in relationships between parents and children, as well as between siblings, which complicates matters even further. The point to remember is that marriage and other family relationships are, to varying degrees, based on a system of exchanges in terms of behavior, behavior which discharges one's obligations and fulfills the rights and needs as perceived by another person. When role reciprocity begins to break down, either partner can impose sanctions on the other to re-establish a state of equilibrium. Role sequences complicate matters, in that the normative expectations and perceived rights and duties of marriage partners, parents and children, and siblings often change over time. The role-reciprocity process is thereby in a constant, though gradual, state of flux that demands continual negotiation and bargaining by family members. Further examples and more details on the concept of role reciprocity are provided at several points in subsequent chapters.

Interaction Structures: Power, Communication, and Affection.

So far, we have focused on concepts relating to role relationships within marriage and the family, and the processes by which patterns of role behavior are maintained over time. The nature of role relationships within marriage also include the concepts of *power, communication, and affection.*

The concept of *power* is as old as the study of society itself. Philosophers such as Plato and Aristotle, as well as religious scribes from the Biblical era, have been intrigued by the idea of one person's or one group's power over another. Yet the concept of social power has been one of the most difficult concepts to define clearly and concisely so that a general consensus can be reached on its meaning (Cromwell and Olson, 1975). Following is the definition of *marital power* to be employed here:

> *Marital power is the actual ability that each spouse has to influence the present status and future direction of events in the marriage.*

There are many types of power arrangements in marriage, and several arenas in which power may be exercised. Power in marriage refers to (1) the decisions that are important to the functioning and survival of the marriage and family unit; (2) the power to get one's way in the course of a disagreement or conflict; and (3) the power, in a physical confrontation, to overcome the other by means of physical violence. In terms of power *relationships* in marriage, Blood and Wolfe (1960) found the following types, in terms of decision-making. More recent research confirms the existence of these patterns (Hallenbeck, 1966; Jorgensen, 1976).

1. *Syncratic power* — major decisions are shared more or less equally by the husband and wife.

2. *Autonomic power* — each spouse has control over his or her own areas, with relatively little overlap (separate but equal).

3. *Husband-dominant* — the husband controls most or all of the important decisions in the marriage.

4. *Wife-dominant* — the wife controls most or all of the important decisions in the marriage.

Varying types of power structures can also be seen in relationships between parents and their children, as well as between siblings. Parents may exercise considerable power over their children by virtue of the *authority* that our culture grants to parents. Parents have the legitimate right to exercise power over children, which is sanctioned by formal laws and social custom. Similarly, a sibling may have power over a brother or sister by virtue of being older or stronger. As we will see in chapter 13, families differ in terms of the degree to which power is shared, or equal, among members. Families also differ in terms of the major bases by which power is allocated. In some families, the powerful members are those who are older, stronger, or of one sex or the other; in other families, power is based more on the expertise of a person to get things done or to make certain types of decisions.

The second of the interaction structures in marriage and the family is that of *communication*. The topic of communication and the means by which individuals communicate with each other form the basis of virtually all aspects of marriage and family relationships, including power and affection exchanges. "Failure to communicate" is the most frequently identified reason given by married couples seeking a divorce for why their marriages have broken down (Brown, 1979). As is true for the concept of power, that of communication can be categorized in various ways. Based on the work of Raush, Goodrich, and Campbell (1963), Aldous (1978:67) identified three major functions of communication in marriage:

1. To provide the other with information about one's knowledge and intentions.

2. To underscore the solidarity of the couple, demonstrating their closeness and separating them from others outside of the relationship.

3. To share feelings, satisfactions, dissatisfactions, and other emotions, such as love, anger, pride, disgust, and sorrow.

Marital communication occurs in two broad areas: communicating about the marriage relationship and the way the partners communicate with each other, which is known as *metacommunication;* and communicating about anything else (Watzlawick, Beavin, and Jackson, 1967). We will examine marital communication in much greater detail in chapter 7. In chapters 12 through 14, communication in other family relationships will be explored.

The third of the interaction structures characterizing marriage and family relationships is the *affection structure.* Role behaviors in the affection structure involve the sharing of words of endearment; the exchange of verbal and physical signs of one's love and affection for the other, such as kissing, hugging, touching, holding hands, or simply saying "I love you"; and the *comforting* of one another in troubled times. Of course, the sexual relationship of husband and wife is central to the affection structure of marriage. Actually, the exchange of affection between married partners, parents, children, and siblings may be viewed as a special kind of communication within the family's communication structure, although the importance of affection-exchange in maintaining the morale and solidarity of family relationships renders it worthy of consideration in its own right.

Married people vary considerably in both the frequency and style of exchanging affection. This depends largely on the normative expectations each person brings to a relationship. Also, such norms may change, or emerge, over the course of time as the relationship develops. Research has shown, for example, that males in our society are socialized to be less expressive of their feelings than females. Males are, therefore, less likely to view the giving of physical and verbal signs of affection to their marriage partners as a duty in their role of "affection-giver" (Balswick, 1979). Indeed, often there is an imbalance in the affection structure of marriage when inexpressive males expect their female partners to be physically and verbally expressive of affection to them. This role imbalance may emerge as an important conflict if the wife expects her mate to be as expressive of feelings and affection as she is.

Selective Boundary Maintenance.   The illustration in Figure 2.1 shows that marriages and families are not isolated "islands," which are self-sufficient and closed to outside influences. The importance of economic survival in contemporary society means that one or both marriage partners are involved in some way in the occupational system. Friends, relatives, and religious involve-ments also affect the functioning and quality of marriage and family relationships. Acknowledging that both marriage relationships and families as a whole interact with outside influences, let us simplify matters by examining how married couples in particular establish boundaries and determine who can cross them.

Despite these multiple outside influences, a husband and wife develop ways to set themselves, *as a couple,* apart from other relationships and influences that each might encounter outside of the marriage situation. The concept of *selective boundary maintenance* refers to two processes: (1) marriage partners establish social and physical boundaries which set them apart from others; (2) they allow the influences of others to penetrate those boundaries in a more or less selective manner. Selective boundary maintenance, then, involves the processes invoked by a married couple to establish and maintain their *identity as a couple.* Included here are the formation of a separate residence; pet names; special phrases; and rituals, such as celebrating birthdays, anniversaries, and frequenting particular restaurants or social spots. Ideally, the influences of outsiders are permitted to penetrate the couple's boundaries when they are invited to do so, on a *selective* basis. Having unwelcome in-laws, or friends who are notorious for sponging, show up on one's doorstep unexpectedly for a two-week visit is an example of an uninvited intrusion of a married couple's boundaries. To most spouses, the involvement of their partner in an extramarital sexual affair would be one of the most flagrant encroachments of the couple's boundaries. Sexual affairs often pose a serious threat to the "couple identity" of the marriage.

Other outside influences are certainly more welcome, such as good friends who come over to visit or to play a friendly game of cards. Often the friends of one partner can create problems, however, as in the case of the husband whose four-times-a-week bowling league and after-the-game card party pose a threat to the solidarity of the couple; or in the case of the wife's best friend who drops in to chat five times a week—always at dinner time! Of course, the very act of getting married is a way of establishing a clear relationship boundary, signaling to others —including past or potential boyfriends and girlfriends —that these two individuals are now a *couple* and should be treated as such.

Developmental Tasks.   A major principle of the developmental perspective is that marriage partners and families must accomplish certain tasks if they are to realize success. According to Havighurst (1953), a *developmental task* is one that *emerges at or about a certain time in the life of a person, or in relationships among people, successful accomplishment of which will enhance the chances of success with other tasks later on, but failure may lead to difficulty with subsequent tasks.*

There are a number of key points relating to this concept of developmental task. In regard to marriage, for example, some of these tasks involve the efforts of one person, but others require the joint participation of both partners. We will refer to these as *individual* and *couple* developmental tasks, respectively. Second, for any given relationship, developmental tasks depend upon the criteria for success in that relationship. This means that the nature of developmental tasks varies from one person and couple to the next. For example, open and honest communication about feelings and emotions between a husband and wife may be an important criterion for success among some couples. Hence, an important developmental task for them would be to discuss communication in these areas, and resolve any problems *before* they become major obstacles in the relationship.

For couples who do not view such communication as a goal in the relationship, and who may view the accumulation of material wealth as a primary criterion for success, the pressing developmental task would be to discuss methods by which each partner can contribute most to their bank account and to the effective management of their financial resources. For these couples, then, communicating about their feelings and emotions would be less important (unless, of course, their inability to communicate was interfering with their ability to accumulate assets and effectively manage their resources because they were continually getting angry with each other!).

Third, the developmental-task concept has two qualities that make it useful: *timing* and *cumulativity*. Developmental tasks arise at or about a certain time, meaning that premature or late attempts to accomplish them may be more difficult, or may yield fewer payoffs than on-schedule task accomplishment. Also, just as youngsters must learn to crawl before they learn to walk, and learn to walk before they learn to run and jump, there is a sequential and cumulative ordering of tasks in the development of so intimate a relationship as marriage. For example, as we will see in chapter 10, an important developmental task for many couples is the establishment of

role compatibility prior to marriage. That is, the establishment of a "fit" between each partner's role expectations, values, and goals is critical during the period of time prior to marriage. The pressures and strains of adjustment to life after marriage, such as those involved in securing a good job, developing good communication habits, or experiencing a pregnancy, can complicate a relationship that begins with serious role conflicts. If role compatibility is established before marriage *(timing),* then a young couple can devote more energy and time to the typical adjustment problems and to unexpected situations (such as a pregnancy or a crisis) as they arise in the delicate months immediately following marriage *(cumulativity).* To establish role compatibility *after* marriage would be a difficult task, if they are struggling with other tasks and stresses at the same time. The importance of developmental-task accomplishment, and its related qualities of timing and cumulativity, will be documented further in subsequent chapters.

The Marital Career and Critical Role-Transition Points.   Researchers who have studied marriages and families as they develop over time have sought to create an accurate method of dividing time into meaningful *stages of development.* The concept of *family life cycle* was developed in order to describe the major events and time periods characterizing families as they exist from their beginning to their dissolution. The stages of the family life cycle denote time periods in the existence of a family that are distinctive enough from those preceding and following them to constitute separate periods (Aldous, 1978:80). These stages have clear points of entry and departure so that there exist a number of similarities among those families who find themselves in one particular stage or another.

We will modify the concept of the family life cycle and its associated stages of development to guide our study of development in marriage. The concept we will use is that of the *marital career.* A marital career is *the existence of a married couple from their initial dating and courtship activities to their dissolution either by divorce or death of one of the partners, as demarcated by a sequence of stages of development.* We will use the same criteria for demarcating stages of development in the marital career as those employed for the family life cycle: (1) changes in the number of family members; (2) developmental stages of the oldest child; and (3) retirement status of the income provider or

Married couples and families establish an identity by means of boundaries that set them apart from others, including customs, rituals, and companionship activities.   *(Photo © 1983, Nancy J. Pierce.)*

TABLE 2.2. *Stages of the Marital Career*

Stage 1.   The premarital stage (dating, courtship, and engagement).

Stage 2.   The early years before children (between marriage and arrival of the first child).

Stage 3.   The childbearing stage (between arrival of first child and school entry).

Stage 4.   Marriage with young children and adolescents (oldest child still in school).

Stage 5.   The postparenthood stage (youngest child has left home).

Stage 6.   The aging stage (retirement to death of one partner).

providers. As applied to the marital career, we will examine the stages of development identified in Table 2.2 (Aldous, 1978; Duvall, 1977).

The *Premarital Stage* is a time in the development of the male-female relationship which is of critical importance for subsequent developmental patterns and outcomes in the relationship. For most couples, the Premarital Stage sets the tone and tempo for (1) the development of marital-role expectations; (2) role reciprocity; (3) the ability to establish boundaries and maintain them selectively; and (4) the development of interaction patterns in terms of power, communication, and the exchange of affection.

Because we will be considering marriage to be a developmental process that proceeds according to discrete stages, we will be viewing marriages within each stage as having similar problems and vulnerabilities, costs and rewards, and developmental tasks. It also means that there exist significant differences in these areas *between* stages, so that knowing what stage of development a married couple is in will allow us to understand the problems and tasks they are likely to be confronting, as well as the rewards and relationship strengths they are likely to be experiencing.

We will refer to the points of entry into each stage as *critical role-transition points,* which are actually periods of time in the career of a married couple signalling significant changes in role expectations, role clusters, and the interaction structures of power, affection-exchange, and communication. These are periods of time when old patterns of role expectations and behavior are insufficient to meet the demands of new situations, a time when new patterns

must be developed. For example, the transition from an unmarried to a married couple involves a variety of changes in behavior and interaction patterns, even among those who cohabited (lived together) before marriage. The transition to the childbearing years is a critical role-transition point, in that the arrival of a baby competes for the time, energy, and economic resources formerly reserved exclusively for the married couple alone. As we will see in chapter 12, the transition to parenthood is associated with multiple adjustments which cause marked changes in the very shape and quality of the marriage relationship.

Each stage of development in the marital career, and the critical role-transition points signalling entry into each one, are important enough to deserve a separate chapter for each (chapters 9 through 14). In those chapters, we will trace the changes in role expectations and role behavior, role clusters and role sequences, selective boundary maintenance, and the interaction structures of power, communication, and affection exchange. The idea of *cumulativity* in developmental tasks will also become evident as we examine stage-specific tasks for marriage partners, parents, and children which, if successfully accomplished, will facilitate the accomplishment of tasks in subsequent stages of the marital career. Finally, we will examine trends in the definition and importance of love, the nature of companionship activities, economic functioning, and satisfaction with various aspects of marriage and other family relationships across stages of the marital career.

It must be clearly understood that the way the marital career has been divided into stages here is not the only way. Certainly, not all people marry, have children, and grow old together in the sequence suggested by the marital-career concept. Many couples will terminate their first marriages by divorce, and will never pass through all the stages together. However, the marital-career concept is the *least common denominator* among the various marriage-related life styles of today. Most people in our society (over 90 percent) will marry at least one time, and most married couples (around 90 percent) will have at least one child. Among marriages in existence today, most (around 70 percent) will be dissolved by the death of one partner, and *not* by divorce. Even among those who choose to remain permanently single or permanently childless, or who follow some other sequence of developmental stages in their intimate relationships as adults, the marital-career concept should provide insights into these alternative life-styles by comparing and contrasting the sequence of events in marriage. Thus the marital-career concept is a benchmark for making comparisons among all kinds of development in marriage or in other forms of intimate relationships.

It must also be understood that although we have divided the marital career into discrete (nonoverlapping) stages, in reality, married couples and families often do experience some overlap in the stages. Examples of this are couples who have a baby when their older children are teenagers, or those who find themselves combining early retirement with the transition to the postparental stage (after the last child has left home).

MARITAL AND OCCUPATIONAL CAREERS: A COMPARISON

It makes sense to view marriage as one kind of career that people undertake. Marriage is similar to a career in the world of work and occupations in at least three respects. First, both a marital career and an occupational career demand a certain level of *competency* in performing tasks demanded by that particular activity. Physicians must be skilled in the areas of diagnosing and treating a wide variety of ailments and illnesses, and, if surgery is involved, must have a sure and steady hand. Lawyers must be competent orators and knowledgeable about a tremendous quantity of legal proceedings and laws relevant to their specializations if they are to be successful in their careers. People in business careers must know the difference between legitimate and nonlegitimate business practices; know sound principles of economics in terms of supply, demand, and prices; know how to approach and handle laws of business taxation and profit-making; and must know how to establish healthy relationships with the clients and customers, who eventually will determine the public image and reputation of the business in the community. All of these careers require extensive preparation in terms of education, practice, and some sort of preparatory experience in the chosen field of work.

Marriage is also a career that demands of a person a certain level of competency and skill in order to be successful. As Table 2.1 indicates, there are many highly specialized roles and associated tasks that confront a person entering a marital relationship. The combination of instrumental and expressive role performances in marriage calls for a well-rounded individual who is skilled in a

variety of task-oriented and interpersonal relationship areas. Add to this list of marital roles those that must be adopted when marriage partners become parents for the first time, and we have a ''job description'' that is equal to or greater than the demands for competency attached to professional careers in the world of work.

A second way in which marriage can be viewed as a career is this: marriage proceeds according to various stages of development, each with its characteristic problems, challenges, and rewards. Successful careers depend upon the smoothness with which people can make the transition from one stage to the next, and whether or not the conditions are right for making the transition. Most occupational careers follow an established timetable in terms of promotion to a higher-paying position, taking on more varied and more important responsibilities, and obtaining a comfortable level of security within the company or profession. The marital career also has its characteristic timetable for making the transition from one stage of development to the next. The responsibilities, rewards, problems, and level of security presented by marriage undergo remarkable transformations as married couples move from one stage of the marital career to the next. The marital-career concept, and the idea of semidiscrete stages of development, render many of the problems, vulnerabilities, and rewards of marriage quite predictable.

A third way in which marriage can be viewed as a career is its *longevity*. Marriage is a long-term commitment, a commitment that most people make for life. Even though the divorce rate in our society has been climbing in recent years, the majority of all marriages are still broken by the death of one of the partners (Glick, 1979:1984a). Marriage should be viewed, then, as a commitment for a 50- to 75-year period of time. How many people would make a commitment to *anything* for such an extended period of time without a tremendous amount of forethought and consideration? Unfortunately, when it comes to marriage, many people do.

Summary

The rapidly increasing volume of research on marriage and the family in our society has increased our ability to gain a comprehensive, integrated, and meaningful picture of these important social relationships. The principles and concepts of the developmental perspective, which is based on the family development conceptual framework, provide a set of useful tools for viewing the typical and atypical patterns of development in contemporary marriage and family relationships. These concepts include norm, role, and position; role sequence; role cluster and role complex; role reciprocity; the interaction structures of power, communication, and affection-exchange; selective boundary maintenance; developmental tasks; and marital career. We will use these tools to help us understand the fundamental bases of marriage and the family, in chapters 3 through 8. The concepts will also be useful in studying the continuities, problems, and changes in the marital career, as we explore them in chapters 9 through 14.

Questions for Discussion and Review

1. Think of ways that scientific research influences your life. Have you ever changed your behavior or thinking on the basis of newspaper or television reports of scientific research? How much do you think that people in general are influenced by the results of scientific research?

2. Think of an occasion when someone you know *generalized* to most or all people, based upon his or her own experiences. Describe the situation and explain how you handled it.

3. Are people in marriages and families "masters of their own destinies," or are they "victims of circumstances" that are beyond their control? What are some of the constraints and barriers that prevent people in marriages and families from accomplishing their goals?

4. What are the most important roles that you play in your life? Identify several norms that define these roles you play. Where did you learn these norms?

5. Think of a time when you were involved in a serious role conflict with someone close to you (such as a parent, good friend, dating partner, or sibling). What were the specific norms that were in conflict? How was the role conflict eventually resolved?

6. Is it important that both a male and a female in an intimate relationship derive equal benefits and rewards from that relationship? Under what circumstances is it acceptable to "give more than you receive" in a relationship? Under what conditions is it acceptable to "receive more than you give" in a relationship?

7. Think of your parents' marriage. How would you describe their power structure? What sort of communication and affection-giving patterns did you observe them sharing?

8. What kinds of boundaries are maintained in your relationships with other people? What special things do you do that set these relationships apart from others? How do the boundaries you established in your family, while growing up, differ from those boundaries you share with a boyfriend or girlfriend, roommate, or sibling?

9. Compare and contrast the most important developmental tasks a person has in childhood with those that are critical during adolescence, in college, and in adulthood. Explain how timing and cumulativity are important for each of the tasks you have identified.

The Fundamental Bases for Development in Marriage and the Family

Development in marriage and the family is based upon a number of distinct, yet related, foundations. In this section, we will explore each of these in considerable detail. Love (chapter 3), gender roles (chapter 4), sexuality (chapter 5), family planning (chapter 6), communication and conflict management (chapter 7), and economic functioning (chapter 8) are essential ingredients in shaping an understanding of how marriage and family relationships develop, or fail to develop, as they do. In one way or another, each of these bases also influences the degree to which marriage partners are able to successfully reach their goals and objectives in their relationship over the years of the marital career.

Love:

The Tie That Binds

No three words in the English language have had a greater impact on the lives of men and women than the words, "I love you." Our culture is one where the romantic feeling known as *love* provides the basis for marriage, influencing male-female pairs to commit themselves to each other for a lifetime. "Love makes the world go 'round." "Love conquers all." Love is the "cement" that is supposed to hold a relationship together, "through thick or thin," "for better or for worse." Love is important to us because it is the primary means by which men and women, parents and children, fulfill each others psychological and emotional needs for human warmth, contact, and closeness; nurturance; security and caring; and acceptance and self-validation. Love also functions to fulfill social needs for companionship, togetherness, and integration in a relationship that is meaningful. In brief, love is the basis for intimacy in human relationships.

Most people view love as the primary, and often the only, prerequisite for marriage. If we love someone, then we have sufficient grounds for marrying that person. On the other hand, falling *out* of love is often viewed as sufficient grounds for dissolving a marriage through divorce. Love can entail pain, suffering, and disappointment for intimate relationships, in addition to personal fulfillment and happiness. For most people, though, the concepts of love and marriage go hand in hand.

In this chapter, we will explore the various dimensions of the concept of love. We will see that love is complex and often difficult to define. We will also provide an understanding of why love, as the primary means for satisfying the basic human needs for intimacy and emotional nurturance, is so difficult to realize in a long-term relationship such as marriage. Let us begin by examining the importance of love as a basis for marriage and family relationships.

Love and Attachment

There is no doubt that human beings need emotional and physical nurturance if they are to develop and grow as psychologically healthy individuals from childhood through adulthood. From the moment of birth, humans embark on a lifelong journey in search of closeness, contact, and warmth with other people. We seek others who will care for us, support us, and provide validation of us as worthwhile individuals. These needs for intimacy and nurturance are as basic as the needs for food and shelter.

The classic studies conducted by Harry and Margaret Harlow, on attachment behavior among infant monkeys, help to illustrate the importance of satisfying intimacy and nurturance needs (Harlow and Harlow, 1969, 1977). In their experiments, the Harlows placed infant monkeys in two different wire cages: one contained a wire "mother" equipped with a machine that would dispense milk; the other contained a terry cloth "mother" without a feeding capacity. The results were clear: the infant monkeys preferred the contact with the terry cloth "mother," and spent considerably more time clinging to her despite the fact that they received no nourishment. In essence, the young monkeys became attached to the warm and soft cloth mother. They showed considerably more signs of love toward it, such as clinging and stroking, than was true for the wire food-dispensing "mother." Moreover, when the researchers placed them in a strange environment, or inserted a fearful object into the cage, the infant monkeys would run and cling to the cloth mother time and again, in order to reduce their fear and anxiety. Clearly, the warmth of the cloth mother was superior to the wire mother, indicating the importance of warmth and comfort in physical contact relative to that of nourishment.

Other experiments by the Harlow team expanded upon their studies of infant monkey attachment, giving further support to the idea that contact, closeness, and warmth are critical needs that must be met if satisfactory emotional and social growth are to occur. When monkeys were separated from their mothers for extended time periods, or were raised in isolation, these researchers found that

Fear is the overwhelming response in all monkeys raised in isolation. Although the animals are physically healthy, they crouch and appear terror-stricken by their new environment . . . They cringe when approached . . . When the other animals become aggressive, the isolates accept their abuse without making any effort to defend themselves . . . Their behavior is a pitiful combination of apathy and terror as they crouch at the sides of the room. (Harlow and Harlow, 1977:156–158)

After years of being raised in isolation, these monkeys suddenly began to viciously attack the others, becoming totally unloving, distressed, and disturbed creatures. High levels of sexual inadequacy were also discovered when these monkeys became adults.

It could be argued that such experiments conducted on monkeys are unrelated to what might be true for humans. Surely, no researcher today would dare attempt to replicate the Harlows' experiments with human infants to see if they would react in a similar fashion. However, observations of human infants in both natural and experimental settings have shown conclusively that bonds of attachment between a warm, nurturant, caring parent and the infant grow in a reciprocal and mutually reinforcing manner (Stayton, Hogan, and Ainsworth, 1971; Bowlby, 1969). Moreover, the fulfillment of these basic needs for human intimacy and nurturance facilitates the social and emotional growth of the child (Clarke-Stewart, 1973). In Clarke-Stewart's study of 9- to 18-month-old infants and their mothers, for example, infants with the more responsive mothers (that is, those who demonstrated more positive emotion toward the infant) demonstrated greater levels of social development and language competence.

Mothers who were sensitive to the child's needs by providing visual, sound, and physical stimulation had infants who themselves were more responsive and socially mature than others. Other studies have observed children who were separated from a care-giving parent, or who were raised in relatively isolated and emotionally cold environments, where care was impersonal and distant (such as orphanages, or, perhaps, their own families). These studies show that such children experience difficulty in relating closely to other people, are emotionally and socially underdeveloped, and have some signs of language and motor-skill retardation (Bowlby, 1973; Yarrow, 1964). Our knowledge of *human* needs for care, intimacy, and stimulation therefore parallels that provided by the Harlows and the monkey experiments: these are basic human needs which, if unsatisfied, retard the person's emotional and social growth through childhood, and, in all probability, into adulthood (Otto, 1972a:9; Colston, 1972:175–178).

LOVE AND HUMAN NEED-FULFILLMENT

At the root of this seeking of need-fulfillment by means of attachment to others is the concept of *love*. Love is the process by which humans satisfy a variety of social and emotional needs: intimacy, nurturance, affection, caring, security, stimulation, acceptance, and self-validation. In adulthood, we find need-fulfillment in, and seek to marry, those with whom we are "in love." The majority of people in our culture get married because they "fall in love" with those who satisfy their needs for intimacy and emotional nurturance, expressing a commitment to spend the rest of their lives together. As Casler (1969:18) stated:

[T]he more needs that one person satisfies, the more likely are we to love that person.

The importance of love for the individual's psychological and social development is emphasized in the writings of psychologist Abraham Maslow (1954, 1968). Maslow defined a "hierarchy of needs," which suggests that people attempt to satisfy certain needs over the course of their lifetimes with varying degrees of difficulty and success (see Figure 3.1). Maslow's basic premise is that these needs are satisfied in a sequential pattern, so that such physical needs as those for food, shelter, and clothing

must be met before needs for safety, such as security, routine, and consistency in one's daily life. Also, one must feel relatively safe and secure if he or she is to be motivated to seek satisfaction of the need for love and belonging, and so on. People will not be motivated to seek love if they are feeling threatened or insecure in their surroundings (e.g., the Harlows' monkeys), or if chronic hunger forces the person to concentrate on basic physical survival.

LOVE AND SELF-ACTUALIZATION

Maslow's hierarchy of needs is based on the premise that humans are in a continual *process of becoming*. That is, individual development is marked by being able to successfully meet each level of needs in a progressive fashion so that the individual can mature and grow toward his or her full potential — toward all that they can be. The ultimate stage in this process is *self-actualization* — fully becoming the person that one is capable of being, or reaching one's potential on the human development spectrum.

Mouly (1968:125 – 126) defined the self-actualizing person as one who

1. has a more adequate perception of, and a more comfortable relationship with, reality than do others;

2. is willing to be a part of the process of change;

3. has a positive view toward the self and trusts his or her ability to develop adequate values and engage in appropriate behavior;

4. has a high degree of personal integration and is open to new experiences;

5. has a strong sense of identification with others.

It is important to note the pivotal role that love plays in the self-actualization process. For many individuals who grow up in a hostile, insecure, or physically deprived environment, the resulting tension and frustration may inhibit the ability to form and maintain loving relationships with other people. Surely, the ability to love will be made more difficult for those who have learned that people or other

Love is a primary means for fulfilling personal needs for warmth, intimacy, and self-affirmation.
(Photo by Sybil Shelton.)

FIGURE 3.1. Maslow's Hierarchy of Human Needs.

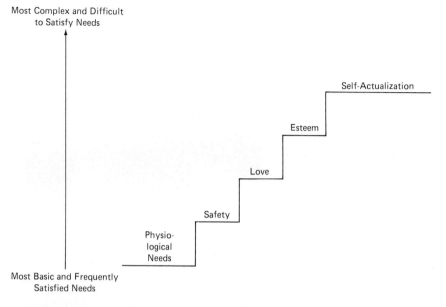

SOURCE: Maslow (1954).

objects in the environment are by nature hostile or threatening. To get too close to someone by opening up your thoughts and feelings to them risks getting hurt, being taken advantage of—"getting burned." The resulting tendency is likely to be a general avoidance of getting close to another, avoiding intimacy and interpersonal sharing, because others are not to be trusted (see discussion of self-disclosure, in chapter 7). Hodge (1967) referred to this as a "fear of love." However, the inability to fulfill the basic need for love, the need to be close to another person and engage in a mutual exchange of warmth and nurturance, is associated with disappointment, anxiety, frustration, self-doubt, and guilt (Rubin, 1976). As Adams (1972:29–30) pointed out:

Without love, physically expressed, infants will quite literally shrivel up and die. The need for love persists throughout life, and love deprivation always leads to some kind of weakness, strong though the individual may be in some respect . . . Without love, communication becomes not a form of intimacy, or even relatedness, but a means of manipulation. Thus deception, intrigue, and withholding of information, all of which create ignorance and delusion, will be prevalent. Deception, intrigue, and withholding of information will also create fear and alienation.

Love is essential for the self-actualization process because having one's needs for care and affection, acceptance and self-validation, nurturance and support fulfilled by other human beings promotes the development of a favorable self-concept. Our lives take on a new meaning and significance when another person confirms that we are valuable, worth something, and that we matter and belong. We come to feel good about ourselves, comfortable and satisfied in our relationships with others, and motivated to accept the challenges and assume the responsibilities that life poses for us. The way has been paved for self-actualization.

The self-actualization process is in a continual state of negotiation and reworking as the individual moves through childhood, youth, and the adult years. If a person is unable to satisfy basic needs for emotional nurturance, warmth, and support in intimate relationships, *at any time and for any reason,* the path to reaching a satisfactory level of self-esteem and of achieving one's potential as a self-actualizing person will be difficult. In brief, satisfying these needs is a *developmental task* which must be accomplished if the self-actualization process is to take place. In addition, most experts agree that the abilities to build and maintain loving relationships with others, to acquire a favorable self-concept, and to attain traits of the self-actualizing person are mutually reinforcing. That is, not only are those who are able to fulfill their needs for intimacy and emotional nurturance more likely than others to develop positive self-concepts and proceed in the self-actualization process; their positive self-concept will also enhance their ability to love and be loved.

LOVE AND MARRIAGE

Fulfilling needs for emotional nurturance and intimate contact with other people is increasingly centered in the marriage and family institutions, as our society becomes more automated, technologically complex, and *Gesellschaft* in regard to the nature of interpersonal relationships in our daily lives (see chapter 1). Over 90 percent of our adult population marries at least once, and over 80 percent of those who divorce their first spouses eventually remarry. This means that for the vast majority of adults in our society, marriage is viewed as a major vehicle of attachment by which the basic and continuing human needs for emotional nurturance and intimacy are fulfilled.

But what about marriages in which the partners are not in love with each other? Or those in which the marriage was entered on the basis of something other than love? Surely, there are many examples of each sort of couple: a man and woman marry because they love each other and somehow "grow out of love" over time; or when circumstances other than love prompt the marriage (such as financial gain, parental pressures, or pregnancy). Some spouses choose to fulfill their needs for emotional nurturance and intimacy outside of marriage by seeking love in extramarital relationships, sexual or otherwise. Although the culturally ingrained *ideal* is to fall in love with and eventually marry the person identified as being capable of fulfilling our needs, the relationship between love and marriage can, and often does, break down.

In the remainder of this chapter, we will examine the ways in which love can function to satisfy the basic human needs for emotional nurturance and intimacy, which are so critical for social and psychological development during the human lifespan. The concept of love also poses many intriguing questions, not the least of which is, "What is the definition of love?" "What does and does not constitute love?"

Falling in love and seeking intimacy in stable relationships, such as marriage, are viewed as primary means for avoiding loneliness and isolation in today's society. *(Photo by Mark Rogers.)*

The Meaning of Love

Our contemporary culture is love-oriented. By some appearances, we have a fixation about love. Try listening to a popular music station for one hour, for example, and count the number of references to love that are made in the songs that are played. You will probably be surprised by the number of times you count the word "love" being sung over the airwaves. The value of love is also extolled in contemporary television programs and movies. Love is seen as a virtue. It is something we all wish to experience, and, indeed, something our culture says we *should* experience. This normative aspect of love causes us to feel inadequate, or to believe that something is wrong with us, if we do not experience love with at least one other person. As Casler (1969:20) noted:

> For most of us, the internal and external pressures (to fall in love) are so great that we can no longer choose to love or not love. Loving becomes inevitable, like dying or getting married. We are so thoroughly brainwashed that we come to pity or scorn the person who is not in love.

As highly prized as the concept of love is, however, most people are momentarily stumped when asked to give a clear and concise definition of love. Stop for a moment and jot down *your* definition of love before reading on. What are the essential ingredients of all love? Are there different kinds of love? Do our definitions of love change over time? Does all love involve intense and passionate romantic feelings?

To illustrate the wide variety of elements that contemporary young adults consider as essential to all love, consider the list in Table 3.1 This list was generated from a questionnaire administered to over 1,300 undergraduate students in marriage education courses taught by the author between 1976 and 1982. The items are ranked according to the frequency with which respondents identified them as being part of their personal definitions of love. Of significance is the fact that no single item was mentioned by at least one-half (50 percent) of those responding. In fact, the most frequently cited component of love, *caring and concern for another,* was mentioned by just over

TABLE 3.1. *Essential Ingredients of Love As a Basis for Marriage*

Ingredient	Percent Responding*
Caring and concern for the other	39%
Respect for another	32
Acceptance of another	31
Understanding that is mutual	29
A shared relationship; togetherness, mutual give-and-take	27
Deep, strong feelings for another	27
Affection for another	24
Sacrifice and self-denial; putting the other first	22
Unconditional giving to another	20
Trust and confidence in another	18
Honesty	14
Compatibility with another in regard to life's goals	11
Friendship with another	9
Compassion for another	7
Support for another	5
Ability to communicate with another	4
Security	2
Dependency of one on another	2
Sexual attraction to another	2
Feeling of not being able to be without another	1
Having sex with another	1

* Percentages total more than 100 percent because respondents could list more than one ingredient. Based on the responses of more than 1,300 university undergraduates enrolled in marriage education courses, 1976–1982.

40 percent of the respondents. Another survey of 300 people, aged 18 to 38, yielded 383 different items, after duplications were eliminated (Swenson, 1961)!

The large number of "essential elements" of love in these surveys, none of which were identified by the majority of people, indicates that the definition of love varies considerably from one person to the next. In other words, there is relatively little agreement among people in regard to *what love is!* When you say "I love you" to another to whom you are close, then, your intended meaning may or may not coincide with their understanding of what was meant. Similarly, when someone says "I love you" to you, your interpretation may differ rather significantly from the meaning attached to those words by the other person. Do the words "I love you" imply that one is ready to be committed to marriage? Are they an invitation to the other to engage in sexual intercourse? Do they mean that each partner should be completely honest and open about all aspects of their personal lives? Or are they just a reflection of the positive feelings that one has toward the other at the present time? Surely, if people who tell each other that they are in love hold different definitions of what love is, then they may continue in the relationship and eventually marry each other without really knowing or attempting to find out how each is defining love. Consider the potential for misunderstanding, deception, and hurt that exists when partners attach different meanings to the concept of love. Owing in part to the pervasiveness of this concept in the mass media of television, movies, and popular music, people are lulled into assuming that there is a common definition of love which is shared by all. The statistics in Table 3.1 indicate that nothing could be further from the truth.

Not only may two people have definitions of love that vary, but research by Swenson (1972) has shown that marriage partners often disagree about how frequently expressions of love are exchanged. In describing these disagreements about the frequency with which affection is expressed, he notes:

> Both husband and wife agree that the husband has told his wife "I love you," but the husband is inclined to believe that he says it more frequently than his wife thinks he does. Apparently, husbands and wives have different standards by which they judge the frequency of verbal statements of love. (Swensen, 1972:95)

These differing perceptions of the meaning and communication about love can lead to considerable misunderstanding and conflict between marriage partners.

CHANGING DEFINITIONS OF LOVE

If people in general have such diverse ideas of what love is, we might ask if there is any more agreement among the experts on this topic. It seems, however, that there are about as many definitions of love as there are experts to define it.

Greek, Roman, and Early-European Definitions of Love. The seeds for the modern concept of love were planted as long ago as the fifth century B.C., when the Greek philosopher Plato detailed his view of love in *The Symposium of Plato*. Plato viewed love as one of the greatest of human virtues, one which inspires us to attain that which is most noble in life.

> So, there is agreement on many sides that love is the oldest (virtue) of them all. And as he is the oldest he is the source of the greatest blessing to us. I can't describe any greater blessing to a person in his earliest youth, than a good lover, and to a lover, his young friend. What men must follow for their entire lives if they intend to live beautifully and well, neither family nor public honors, nor wealth, nor anything else, can implant so well as love . . . So, you see I assert that of the Gods love is the most ancient, the most honorable and the most benevolent in bestowing virtue and happiness on men, alive and dead. (Plato, 1970:178c; 180b)

Even for Plato, love was not an easy concept to define, and he concluded his discourse by identifying two distinct types of love: one homosexual and the other heterosexual. Plato referred to these two types of love as *celestial* and *common,* respectively. According to Plato, the preferred type of love was the homosexual, or *celestial* type, that evolved between a man and a young boy. The *common* type of love, with its emphasis on physical gratification and lust between the male and female sexes, was viewed as less virtuous because it was not intellectually based, rational, or spiritual in nature (Reiss, 1980).

This Greek dichotomy between heterosexual and homosexual love, which placed higher value on the latter type, was rejected by Roman philosophers centuries later. The leading writer of the Roman philosophy of love was

Ovid, whose *Art of Love* became the book setting the stage for the evolution of the modern concept of *romantic love.* Contrary to Plato, Ovid defined love as heterosexual, giving emphasis to the lustful, sensuous, and physical nature of male-female relationships. What Plato viewed as *common love,* the least virtuous type of love, was now seen as the only real type of love. Moreover, for Ovid, love found its place primarily in extramarital sexual involvements, because marriages at that time were arranged by parents and were not based on any particular feelings of romantic attraction. The prototype of love, according to Ovid, was between a man and a married woman, and in the *Art of Love,* Ovid provides plenty of advice to both men and women on how to become involved in such love relationships. For example, he tells men how to pretend they are drunk when approaching a married woman, so if he is rejected he can blame the wine for his behavior.

Sing, if you have a voice; if your arms are lithe, dance; please by whatever gifts you can as real drunkenness does harm, so will feigned bring profits: make your crafty tongue stumble in stammering talk, so that whatever you do or say more freely than you should, may be put down to too much wine. And "Here's luck," say "to the lady," and "Luck to him who sleeps with her!": but in your silent soul let the prayer be "Deuce take the husband." But when the tables are removed and the company depart, and the crowd gives you chance of access, join the crowd, and gently drawing nigh to her as she goes, pull her sleeve with your fingers, and let your foot touch hers. Now is the time for talk with her; away with you, rustic shame! Chance and Venus help the brave . . . Each woman thinks herself lovable; hideous though she be, there is none her own looks do not please. (Ovid, 1929:55)

As this passage illustrates, Ovid viewed love as a game of deception and false pretense, move and countermove, between the sexes. At the core of this game was the drive for sexual union and the thrill of seeking "forbidden fruits" across the boundaries of marriage.

A fusion of the major elements of Plato's and Ovid's conceptions of love evolved in the twelfth century A.D., in Europe, combining the spiritual and virtuous features of Platonic love with the passionate and romantic aspects of Ovidian love. It also included the customs of courtesy and deference to women, which have been handed down through the ages into contemporary culture: the man opening the door for a woman, walking on the street side, and seating her at a table. However, marriages were still arranged by the parents, so true love often occurred across the boundaries of marriage (Reiss, 1980). Troubadours and knights sought love "which, while essentially adulterous, inspires the man with nobility of character and offers him, through the beloved, a transcendent experience" (Locke, 1957:vi). The major book on love during this period was Andreas Capellanus's *The Art of Courtly Love,* written sometime between the years 1174 and 1186. Capellanus was a French chaplain in the court of Marie, the Countess of Champagne. His book clearly shows elements of both Plato's and Ovid's concepts of love, and he pointed to the future of love as it is in its present-day form.

Capellanus defined love as follows:

Love is a certain inborn suffering derived from the sight of and excessive meditation upon the beauty of the opposite sex, which causes each one to wish above all things the embraces of the other and by common desire to carry out all of love's precepts in the other's embrace. (Capellanus, 1957:2)

Although Ovid's ideas of heterosexual passion shine through in this definition, Capellanus continued by invoking the Platonic notion of restraint.

An excess of passion is a bar to love, because there are men who are slaves to such passionate desire that they cannot be held in the bonds of love . . . Men of this kind lust after every woman they see; their love is like that of a shameless dog . . . Furthermore a love ought to appear to his lover wise in every respect and restrained in his conduct and do nothing disagreeable that might annoy her. (Capellanus, 1957:5, 25)

Capellanus also specified particular rules to guide people who are either seeking love or are in the process of falling in love (see Table 3.2). However, these rules and other advice given by Capellanus were clearly an effort to warn men of the dangers of passionate love. In his view, and undoubtedly in the view of others at the time, women are wicked creatures. Women are liars, slanderous, miserly, deceitful, vain, self-indulgent with food and wine, and fickle (Capellanus, 1957:48–51). This ambivalence about the value of love, and the different roles and responsibilities of the sexes in the course of love, revealed the bias in favor of males which existed at that time. This bias has faded away, for the most part, as the definition of love has evolved in the twentieth century.

CONTEMPORARY DEFINITIONS OF LOVE

After this rather brief historical overview of the concept of love, let us turn to more contemporary writers who have struggled with its definition. These modern definitions clearly reflect their historical antecedents: some emphasize the spiritual and soulful dimension of love, some the passionate and sexually sensuous side of love, and others have developed various syntheses of the two. In addition, some contemporary writers view love as a worthwhile and useful activity, contributing to the ability

TABLE 3.2. *The Rules of Courtly Love*

1. Marriage is no real excuse for not loving (someone other than your spouse).
2. He who is not jealous cannot love.
3. No one can be bound by a double love.
4. It is well known that love is always increasing or decreasing.
5. That which a lover takes against his will of his beloved has no relish.
6. Boys do not love until they arrive at the age of maturity.
7. When one lover dies, a widowhood of two years is required of the survivor.
8. No one should be deprived of love without the very best of reasons.
9. No one can love unless he is impelled by the persuasion of love.
10. Love is always a stranger in the home of avarice.
11. It is not proper to love any woman whom one should be ashamed to seek to marry.
12. A true lover does not desire to embrace in love anyone except his beloved.
13. When made public, love rarely endures.
14. The easy attainment of love makes it of little value; difficulty of attainment makes it prized.
15. Every lover regularly turns pale in the presence of his beloved.
16. When a lover suddenly catches sight of his beloved his heart palpitates.
17. A new love puts to flight an old one.
18. Good character alone makes any man worthy of love.
19. If love diminishes, it quickly fails and rarely revives.
20. A man in love is always apprehensive.
21. Real jealousy always increases the feeling of love.
22. Jealousy, and therefore love, are increased when one suspects his beloved.
23. He whom the thought of love vexes, eats and sleeps very little.
24. Every act of a lover ends in the thought of his beloved.
25. A true lover considers nothing good except what he thinks will please his beloved.
26. Love can deny nothing to love.
27. A lover can never have enough of the solaces of his beloved.
28. A slight presumption causes a lover to suspect his beloved.
29. A man who is vexed by too much passion usually does not love.
30. A true lover is constantly and without intermission possessed by the thought of his beloved.
31. Nothing forbids one woman being loved by two men or one man by two women.

SOURCE: Cappellanus (1957:42–43).

of the person to grow emotionally and socially. Others view love as a problematic aspect of human relationships, blinding us to the realities of life and causing deception, insecurity, and suffering. What has changed in the modern definitions is an increased emphasis on equality between men and women in love relationships; that is, women are no longer treated as the scapegoats for love gone awry. There is also a tendency to place love in the context of marriage, as opposed to love in the extramarital context of adultery. In addition, virtually all experts agree that love is a concept with many faces or dimensions.

To illustrate the many sides of love, and the synthesis of Greek, Roman, and early-European elements of love in contemporary culture, examine the following definitions of love:

Fromm (1956):

Love is an active process by which human beings attempt to overcome separateness by experiencing union with others. . . . love is union under the condition of preserving one's integrity, one's individuality. Love is an active power in man; a power which breaks through the walls which separate man from his fellowmen, which unites him with others; love makes him overcome the sense of isolation and separateness, yet it permits him to be himself, to retain his integrity. In love the paradox occurs that two beings become one and yet remain two (17).

Adams (1972):
[Love is a] . . . sentiment, i.e., a feeling for another person which is accompanied by desires and impulses to be intimate in some way (physically, emotionally, intellectually) with the loved person and to bring about pleasure, joy, relief from pain or fear, and includes the ability to experience pleasure and joy when such impulses and desires are consummated (29).

Lowen (1972):
Love is the promise of continued pleasure on the part of the person who gives his love and the expectation of pleasure on the part of the person who shares the love . . . Love is a feeling and, as such, is not subject to one's volition . . . (I)t is a feeling of total commitment that embraces the future as well as the present. It is unconditional in time or degree (19).

Jourard (1972):
I love her. What does this mean? I want her to exist for me, and to exist for herself. I want her alive. I want her to be, and moreover, to be in the way she chooses to be. I want her free. As she discloses her feelings to me, or before my gaze, my existence is enriched. I am more alive. I experience myself in dimensions that she evokes, such that my life is more meaningful and livable (44).

Casler (1969):
Love is the fear of losing an important source of need gratification (20).

Miller and Siegel (1972):
Love is a response to a generalized hope signal, a broad pleasurable expectancy. The love object, be it a "thing" or a person is a generalized secondary positive reinforcer. The loved object serves to attract and to hold. And it works across a broad spectrum of situations, circumstances, moods and motivational states both learned and unlearned (14–15).

These are only a few of the many and varied definitions that have been developed in modern times. These particular definitions were cited because elements of Plato, Ovid, and Capellanus cut across them. Moreover, it illustrates that the experts agree about what love is no more than do the students whose responses to the question, "What is love?" are listed in Table 3.1.

Regardless of how one defines love, agreement is likely with some of these experts, but not with others. Now, go back to the defintion of love *you* jotted down before beginning to read this section. Whose definition is closest to yours? Whose is least like yours? Let us look further at the various dimensions of love in order to crystalize our ideas about this concept.

Objects of Love. There are a variety of objects in the environment that one can love:

"I love my parents."   "I love that song."

"I love my dog."   "I love to work."

"I love ice cream."   "I love my girlfriend."

"I love James Bond   "I love money."
movies."

Although these may all be legitimate objects of one's affection and liking, that which will concern us for now is the *heterosexual love* that emerges in the relationships of males and females before, within, and outside of marriage.

Types of Love. Three concepts of love developed by the Greeks and passed on through the ages continue to influence contemporary ideas about love: *eros, agape,* and *philos.* Eros is the concept of love popularized by Ovid. It involves the sexual, sensuous, lustful, and erotic side of love, in which man and woman desire and seek total physical union. According to May (1969:72–73), however, Eros encompasses not only the sexual aspect of love but includes self-expansion, creativity, and intense self-fulfillment:

Eros in our day is taken as a synonym for "eroticism" or sexual titillation . . . Eros created life on earth, the early Greek mythology tells us. When the world was barren and lifeless, it was Eros who "seized his life-giving arrows and pierced the cold bosom of the Earth, . . . and immediately the brown surface was covered with luxuriant verdure

. . ." Ever since, Eros has been distinguished by the function of giving the spirit of life, in contrast to the function of sex as the release of tension . . . Sex can be defined fairly adequately in physiological terms as consisting of the building up of bodily tensions and their release. Eros, in contrast, is the experiencing of the personal intentions and meaning of the act. Whereas sex is a rhythm of stimulus and response, Eros is a state of being . . . The end toward which sex points is gratification and relaxation, whereas Eros is a desiring, longing, a forever reaching out.

Eros, then, is physical and sensuous love. It is love that involves sexual attraction and desire. Fromm (1956) refers to it as "erotic love," one that involves "physiological arousal." According to recent research investigations, the physical arousal experienced in passionate love with another can be heightened by certain factors. A number of studies have shown that such unpleasant emotional states as fear and perceived threat, and the embarrassment or anger at being rejected by another, can intensify a person's arousal and lead to feelings of romantic passion for a person of the opposite sex (Walster, 1971; Walster and Walster, 1978). In addition, passionate love seems to be great when the other person is "hard to get" rather than an "easy catch." Perhaps the greatest facilitator of passionate love, though, is sexual attraction for, and sexual gratification by, another person (Walster, 1971). As Casler (1969:19) noted:

Society emphasizes the necessity for love to precede sex. Although many disregard this restriction, others remain frightened or disturbed by the idea of a purely sexual relationship. The only way for many sexually aroused individuals to avoid frustration or anxiety is to fall in love — as quickly as possible. More declarations of love have probably been uttered in parked cars than in any other location.

For many people, it is difficult to tell which comes first — the feeling of passionate love, or the attempt to seek sexual gratification. In any event, many people associate love and sex in one way or another.

There is more to love than simple sexual arousal or sexual intercourse (Frankel, 1965; May, 1969). If two people engage in sexual intercourse purely for the purpose of relieving sexual tension and satisfying their physiological urges, then sexual relations are reduced to a purely mechanical act. Although people may say that they are "in love" at the time, these writers warn that those who engage in sexual behavior simply for reducing their sexual

drive are not experiencing love. According to Fromm (1956:45–46):

Because sexual desire is in the minds of most people coupled with the idea of love, they are easily misled to conclude that they love each other when they want each other physically . . . If the desire for physical union is not stimulated by love . . . it never leads to union in more than an orgiastic, transitory sense. Sexual attraction creates, for the moment, the illusion of union, yet without love this "union" leaves strangers as far apart as they were before.

Comedian Woody Allen put the issue of love and sex in a more contemporary perspective, however, when he stated, "Sex without love is a meaningless experience, but as meaningless experiences go, it's one of the best."

What is often missing in the sexual kind of love, or Eros, is the sort of love the Greeks referred to as *agape*. Agape involves genuine respect, caring, and concern for another human being; the exchange of tender signs of affection; and the "inner glow" that we feel just being near another person and knowing that we are loved by them. According to May (1969), our culture has become so sex-oriented, so obsessed with the mechanics of sexual techniques, sexual performance ability, and achieving orgasm, that we have lost sight of the caring, emotional commitment, and genuine sharing of each other's thoughts and feelings that being in love should involve; that is, *agape*.

The third type of love defined by the Greeks is *philos,* that which is equivalent to love for one's fellow human beings. It is this kind of love that sparked the intense protests in America against the Vietnam War during the 1960s and early 1970s. Philos is what is referred to in the Biblical commandment, "Love they neighbor as thyself." Philos is the sort of love manifested by Mother Teresa, whose selfless giving to the poor and hungry was recognized by the award of the Nobel Peace Prize in 1980. As Fromm (1956:39) stated it:

In brotherly love (philos) there is the experience of union with all men, of human solidarity, of human-at-onement. Brotherly love is based on the experience that we are all one.

LOVE AS LEARNED ROLE BEHAVIOR

Every individual develops his or her own definition of what love is on the basis of learning experiences in relationships with parents, siblings, and friends, and from religious teachings, books, and exposure to such mass media influences as television and Hollywood movies. And the ability *to act* upon our definitions of love, that is, to become involved in a love relationship according to our definition of love, and to maintain it over time, is also learned. In other words, the concept of love and the ability to love are acquired as we are socialized in our families and in the broader society. The ability to love is not innate, instinctive; we are not born with it. But we begin to form our concepts of love from the moment of birth, as we are comforted and soothed, or rejected and neglected, by our parents and others in the immediate environment.

The concept of love is molded further as we grow through childhood and adolescence, and begin interacting with others of the same sex and of the opposite sex. According to some, we learn to love those with whom we associate pleasure and reward, and with whom we dissociate pain and punishment (Miller and Siegel, 1972; Rubin, 1973). Miller and Siegel (p. 24) view honesty and openness in relationships as rewards which reinforce the partners' emotional commitment to each other, making it easier to predict and to avoid painful or unpleasurable experiences. If we are socialized by others who are dishonest, and who hide their feelings from us in deceptive ways, or who have a tendency to behave in negative ways toward others (complaining, criticizing, nagging, or belittling), then we will learn these patterns of relating to others; and we apply them later on when we become involved in intimate relationships of our own. If, on the other hand, these aversive patterns of relating have *not* been part of our socialization experiences, we will avoid people who behave in those ways because that behavior will be viewed as "painful or punishing."

[T]he best way to make someone love you is to make it very rewarding to be with you, and the best way to drive someone away is to fill that person's life with embarrassment, suffering, and pain . . . We also come to like people who are merely *associated* with good times and to dislike those who are merely *associated* with bad times. (Walster and Walster, 1978:10)

The concept of love, and the behavior that demonstrates our love, clearly become part of the *cluster of roles* that we bring to our heterosexual relationships in adulthood, including marriage. We develop norms for ourselves and others that guide our own love behavior and

Our concepts of love are learned in our experiences with others while we are growing up.   *(Photo by Paula Deering.)*

determine our expectations for those we love. For example, depending on how one defines love, a person may subscribe to any one of, or a combination of, the following norms for self and others in his or her *role as lover* in an intimate heterosexual relationship. A lover *should*

1. not share love with anyone else of the opposite sex.

2. devote his or her entire being to the other person.

3. freely show signs of affection by means of physical gestures, such as hugging, kissing, or sexual contact.

4. avoid showing signs of affection in public.

5. seek sexual contact only when the other person desires it.

6. not be jealous of the partner's contacts with others of the opposite sex.

7. reject or ignore the partner's attempts to show love in order to punish the other for some misdeed.

8. share all of his or her most personal and private thoughts, feelings, and fantasies with the partner.

9. maintain the "inner glow" and excitement in being around the other person, for the entire course of the relationship.

10. not disclose too much of his or her fears, feelings, and ideas in order to avoid the risk of being hurt, betrayed, or "burned."

Stop for a moment and consider *your* role expectations as a person who loves. Which of the foregoing norms, or any others, define your *role as lover?* How did you come to acquire these norms (from parents, friends, books)? How do your norms vary according to the person under consideration (parent, sibling, boyfriend, girlfriend, spouse)? How have your norms *changed* over time? That is, can you describe the *role sequence* you have undergone as

a person who loves? (See chapter 2 on the concept of role sequence.)

Role Reciprocity and Intimacy-Need Fulfillment. Orlinsky (1972) adopted the concept of role reciprocity to explain how two people can grow to be increasingly intimate and, as a result, satisfy their intimacy needs (see Figure 3.2). Each person in an intimate relationship has *growth needs*. These are certain conditions which are required if the person is to experience personal fulfillment and satisfaction, and which generally lead to personal well-being. For example, the needs to be understood, cared about, respected, trusted, and sexually satisfied are growth needs of many people. Orlinsky hypothesized (beginning with *a* in Figure 3.2) that we develop a sense of attraction toward those who appear to be able to satisfy our growth needs. We then respond to the other in a way that we hope satisfies his or her particular growth need. If this happens, the other person is likely to experience a pleasurable sense of fulfillment when the growth need is satisfied. A feeling of tenderness, or a caring and concern for the other, based on gratitude, will ensue. The other will respond in kind, according to his or her idea of what an appropriate response should be, and so on, in a mutually fulfilling spiral of need-fulfillment and interpersonal attraction.

Of course, it does not always work so neatly. Few individuals, if any, are able to satisfy *all* of their partner's growth needs. Partners may disagree about the nature of

Role Reciprocity and the Fulfillment of Growth Needs.

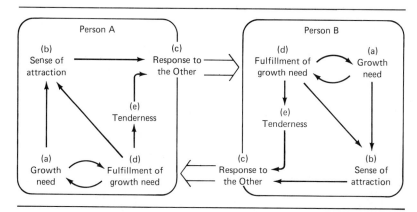

SOURCE: Orlinsky (1972:147).

their growth needs, or one partner's growth needs may change over time without the other realizing that the change has taken place. Nonetheless, this view of love as role reciprocity correctly points to the fact that love is a shared relationship, one which involves the mutual give and take of both partners.

Why Is Loving So Difficult? The Art of Love.

The fact that love is learned means not only that individual definitions of love will vary, but that individual *abilities* to become involved in love relationships and to realize the fulfillment of one's goals in love, either inside or outside of marriage, will also vary. According to Fromm (1956), for example, the ability to love is an *art*, and any one can become an *artist* by learning the necessary skills and applying them in life. According to Fromm, love involves four essential components: *care, responsibility, respect, and knowledge.* To *care* means to be actively concerned for the life and growth of that which is loved, as that of a parent toward a child. *Responsibility* implies the ability to respond to the needs of another as well as to one's own needs. *Respect* is the ability to see others as they are, to be aware of and accept their unique individual qualities, and to avoid exploiting others for one's own gains. *Knowledge* means that in order to love another we must be motivated to understand his or her thoughts, feelings, and perceptions; that is, to acquire knowledge of the depths of the other's personality—motivations, needs, concerns, and fears (Fromm, 1956:22–25).

These qualities of care, responsibility, respect, and knowledge are *learned* abilities. They do not come to us naturally. To learn them requires conscious effort and practice, according to Fromm. Such learning involves self-discipline, concentration, patience, and a genuine will to learn the art of love (Fromm, 1956:91–93). If they are not learned throughout childhood, by one's associations with such primary groups as family and close friends, then the task of learning will be difficult in adulthood.

Learning to love can be viewed as a *developmental task.* If we learn the skills as children, by having available those who can model these skills for us (such as parents or siblings), we will more easily enter love relationships as young adults, and we will be more able to maintain them throughout the years of adulthood. However, if learning to love does not occur early in life, we are more likely to find that the ability to love others may be a problem for us

as adults. It is not impossible to learn these abilities later in life, but it is true that our general orientation to those around us becomes *habituated* over the years. Such habits are hard to break, especially in the absence of some one who is able to facilitate our learning by modeling the skills for us.

According to Hodge (1967), patterns of loving and relating to others become quite difficult to change in adulthood. And some patterns of relating to others, learned during childhood, actually interfere with a person's ability to love in intimate relationships later on. (You will recognize the similarity of Hodge's theory and Maslow's concept of self-actualization.) Hodge noted that many people develop a basic *fear of love,* which is evident in the difficulty they have in becoming emotionally close to another person.

> It is one of the more puzzling facets of human existence that we often avoid those experiences that we most desire. We long to give and receive expressions of love, but at the critical moment we frequently back away. (Hodge, 1967:4)

There are two reasons for this fear of getting close to another person. The first is that to become emotionally close and intimate with another involves a certain degree of *risk.* To allow another to know us, our problems, fantasies, dreams, and fears makes us vulnerable because we leave ourselves open to getting hurt. Indeed, there is a certain degree of emotional pain and suffering in virtually all love relationships, as Hodge (1967:7–9) noted:

> The probabilities are that we *will* experience some of the hurt that we fear when we risk love . . . [W]e will sometimes be disappointed by those we love. If we share confidences, we will sometimes be betrayed. If we count on people, they will sometimes let us down. If we express warmth, others will sometimes seem indifferent or cold . . . The closer we are emotionally to another human being and the more openly we express our caring, the more open we are to the possibility of being hurt by that person and the more intensely the hurt will be felt. And it is this possibility that frightens us and keeps us wary about establishing close relationships . . . [W]e most often express our fear of love by maintaining our emotional distance from others.

A second cause of the fear of love is the *cycle of rejection.* This is truly a vicious cycle, and has its roots in childhood relationships with parents (see Figure 3.3). Children whose parents are overprotective, hostile, or ne-

FIGURE 3.3. Cycles of Rejection and Acceptance as They Relate to the Development of Self-Esteem.

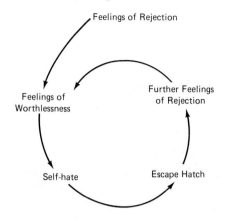

SOURCE: Hodge, *Your Fear of Love.* Copyright © 1967 by Marshall Bryant Hodge. Reprinted by permission of Doubleday & Company, Inc.

glectful are likely to develop a feeling of rejection. Even if parents do not consciously intend to create these insecurities, children may view their parents' behavior as rejecting. Over time, such children may grow to feel worthless and develop low self-esteem. The logic of this development is as follows:

"The most significant people in my life — that is, my parents — do not consider me to be of personal worth. Therefore, I must be worthless."

"All of my life I have never felt I really mattered to anyone and I have always felt there must be something wrong with me."

"I seem to be worthless. I appear inferior to my parents and other people around me. I cannot respect myself, since they don't seem to respect me. Since I am worthless, I hate myself." (Hodge, 1967:24–25)

Self-hatred is a bitter pill for anyone to swallow. Hodge identified several possible psychological *defense mechanisms,* or "escape hatches," people use in order to cope with "this terrible feeling that we are worthless and the object of our own hatred." These escape hatches might include bullying others or becoming a braggart; psychosomatic illness or psychosis; alcoholism and drug abuse; deflecting our self-hatred by hating others; or seeking escape in fantasy via television or work (for example, by becoming a "workaholic"). Each of these ultimately leads to further rejection by others, and the vicious cycle continues. The end result is that of increasing the emotional distance between oneself and others by the "psychological walls" that have been constructed. In the attempt to avoid further rejection, and to salvage some degree of self-esteem, these individuals avoid the risks attached to becoming emotionally close to or intimate with others — *without realizing that the very things they do to protect themselves from those risks contribute further to their rejection by others.* However, as the lower half of Figure 3.3 shows, the opposite cycle — acceptance by significant others, self-worth and self-acceptance, and seeking closeness with others — reduces the fear of involvement by increasing one's overall self-esteem and sense of security.

Love Today: Is it Good for You?

Centuries ago, philosophers debated the virtues of love, the relative advantages of various kinds of love, and the importance of romantic love in male-female relationships. So, too, contemporary experts disagree about the value of love in promoting the development of the individual and enhancing the quality of intimate relationships. Clearly, love has its advocates as well as its critics. We have already examined the evidence supporting the idea that love is good for the development of the person, and for relationships between people. Let us now take a look at some arguments that view love as having negative consequences for the individual person and for intimate relationships between two people.

LOVE IS NOT GOOD FOR YOU; A CRITIC'S VIEW

From a critical point of view, romantic love between a man and woman can interfere with the optimal choice of a marriage partner. First, the intensity of the physical and emotional arousal that is experienced when one "falls in love" can cause one to distort the image of the other person by seeing only his or her positive qualities. Love thereby blinds us from reality by causing us to ignore or gloss over the more negative traits of another. When we are in love, we often go out of our way to see the other person only as fitting an idealized picture that we have formed as a result of our romantic attachment. We do this in order to avoid risking the future of a relationship that is currently viewed as highly rewarding. Under these conditions, lovers may perceive themselves to be compatible, when, in reality, they are not. The idealized picture dissolves when we are forced to see the full range of the other's qualities, when many experience a phenomenon known as *reality shock*. Particularly after marriage, it becomes difficult to avoid discovering the most private and personal aspects of the partner's life.

Intimacy, infringement on privacy, confusion of identity, enforced interaction, as well as cold cream and curlers, unshaved stubble, body odors, halitosis, and dishabille may be involved as a concomitant of living together . . . How do people who are forced to live together (in marriage) reconcile themselves to the messy toothpaste tube, the singing in the shower, slovenly disorder, or compulsive neatness? (Bernard, 1964:685–686)

Because we know that the most divorce-prone years of marriage are the first two years, this ought to be a signal that romantic idealization before marriage, and reality shock after marriage, are problems for many. Therefore, romantic love — the intense physical and emotional experience that often involves somewhat irrational behavior and judgments about the other person — may be viewed as incompatible with the rational and careful choice of a marriage partner.

Second, some critics doubt that love, for many people, is a necessity. Casler (1969:19–20) notes that people fall in love for any of four basic reasons:

1. To satisfy needs for security, acceptance, and confirmation in a highly competitive and rather impersonal society.

Acceptance by others important to us fosters self-esteem, self-acceptance, and a willingness to seek closeness with others. *(Photo by Carl Hill.)*

2. To justify having sexual intercourse.

3. To conform to society's norms which say that people should fall in love if they are to consider themselves and be considered by others as psychologically healthy and normal, and which dictate that love should accompany marriage.

4. Out of fear of losing one's source of need gratification, fear based on the "possibility that the loved one will find someone else more gratifying."

Given these reasons for falling in love, Casler proceeds to argue that love is important only for those who are insecure, need to conform, and who need to be dependent on others. Love, then, can become an obsession or addiction, for many.

The person who seeks love in order to obtain security will become, like the alcoholic, increasingly dependent on this source of illusory well-being. The secure person who seeks love would probably not trap himself in this way . . . [I]f the need for a love relationship is based largely on insecurity, conformity to social pressures, and sexual frustration, then the person who is secure, independent, and has a satisfying sex life will not need to love. (Casler, 1969:75)

Peele and Brodsky (1975) actually defined love as one kind of "addiction," arguing that people lose themselves and sacrifice their very identities by falling in love and becoming increasingly dependent upon another person in order to satisfy needs for security, acceptance, and confirmation.

Finally, love can also be criticized because it incites the emotional response known as *jealousy.* For many people, love implies *ownership,* meaning that one's partner is exclusive property which simply cannot be shared with anyone else. The emotion of jealousy is so intense and so powerful in intimate relationships that innumerable divorces, conflicts, and, indeed, murders have resulted from the jealousy of one partner of the other's love for a third person. This is an example of *selective boundary maintenance.* We often allow only those who will not threaten the continuation of a love relationship to cross the boundaries that have been established to identify the couple as a unit. These boundaries set the two people in love apart from others, and function to keep potential competitors out. Jealousy, then, amounts to the anger, pain, and disappointment that accompany the perception that one is about to lose, or has lost, the person who is loved and, thereby, owned; that is, the person upon whom one has become *dependent.* Jealousy is associated with the idea that we cannot become intimate and love more than one person at a time. "You love either me or him — you cannot have both of us." However, as long ago as 1949, psychologist Albert Ellis found, in a survey of 500 college women, that 25 percent reported having been in love with two males simultaneously on at least one occasion (Ellis, 1949:66). More recently, Whitehurst (1977) found that 58 percent of the respondents (in a survey of 300 college freshmen) agreed that it is possible to love (including sexual love) more than one other person at a time. But *is* this possible

without jealousy? Can a person really love two others of the opposite sex at one time, without one or both of the loved ones being jealous?

The answer depends exclusively on one's personal definition of love and the mutual understanding of what is meant when the words "I love you" are exchanged in a relationship. If we accept the ideas that love involves caring, responsibility, respect, and knowledge; that the ability to love is a specific personality trait which influences the way that a person relates to others in general; and that love is much different from having sex with someone (Fromm, 1956; May, 1969; Hodge, 1967), then we might be able to accept the idea that we can actually love two or more people at the same time. According to Hodge (1967:174–175), jealousy of a partner's caring and concern for others is a sign of immaturity and insecurity:

The experience of love is not limited to those who are sexual partners or potential sexual partners . . . [O]ur ability to love grows out of the context of experiencing love and acceptance in the family or in other relationships. When we have this understanding of love it becomes a contradiction in terms to imagine that we could love one individual to the exclusion of all others . . . [I]t becomes evident that possessiveness in relationships is not a mark of love. It is a mark of insecurity and fear . . . If a husband, for example, resents other relationships that his wife may tend to develop, and if he demands that she severely limit her scope of activities and "devote herself" completely to the home and to him, he is almost certain to encounter resentment on her part . . . But even if he does not, how can he trust the "love" that she shows toward him even if it *is* genuine?

It is apparent that the *kinds* of love these writers are referring to are either *philos* or *agape,* and not *eros.* For most people, especially those who are married, love and sex are inextricably bound together. It is more likely that people in our culture would tolerate philos or agape types of love relationships between their partners and others of the opposite sex but would not tolerate eros, or sexual kinds of relationships. Jealousy tends to occur, then, when one's partner becomes, or is *perceived* to become, involved in relationships that fall outside the normative tolerance limits set by one's personal definition of love. Whether the human emotion of jealousy is intrinsically *good* or *bad* is impossible to determine in any absolute moral sense. Jealousy happens, and it does so when the norms of exclusivity determining the boundaries of a love relationship are believed to be violated by one's mate.

Love and Personal Development Over Time

In our culture, love is generally considered to be a prerequisite for getting married and having children. For many, love is necessary if the marriage is to be considered successful in the eyes of the partners. However, we have seen that definitions of love vary from one person to the next. Whether or not any given couple is sufficiently "in love" to marry is impossible to say without carefully examining what each person's concept of love involves, and what each person's definition of love implies to the other.

SELF-KNOWLEDGE AND SELF-LOVE

In order to love another person, we must first examine *ourselves* and determine just what we mean when we say "I love you" to another. This task should be undertaken with the full understanding that no single definition of love is inherently better than another. Whether you are aware of it or not, your concept of love has been shaped throughout your life in relationships with family members and friends; and there have been many other influences. Your definition of love *is as it is,* for whatever reason, and is not better or worse than anyone else's. Many people, however, never think of taking the time to look inward to discover what their concept of love is, and then attempt to develop an understanding of it. Because love, in our culture, plays such a critical role in the development of intimate relationships, including marriage, it becomes important to know what the use of this concept implies; that is, what we intend to communicate to our partner when we say "I love you."

Most experts agree that in order to love another we must first love ourselves (Adams, 1972; Hodge, 1967). Self-love does not mean that one is conceited or selfish. In Fromm's (1956) terms, self-love involves *caring* for what happens to you; assuming *responsibility* for your thoughts, words, and actions; *respecting* those qualities that are special or unique to you, and accepting yourself as you are; and seeking *knowledge* of yourself by discovering what motivates you to act the way you do. The lack of self-acceptance and self-respect inhibits a person's ability to love, as illustrated in the following example of a discussion a man might have with himself.

Mary says she loves me. But I'm inconsiderate and insensitive, and I really don't have much of a future. I'm not much to look at, either. Therefore, Mary is either lying to me in order to make me feel better, or she is a fool who doesn't know any better. In either case, I can't really trust her. I think I will keep my distance.

A good example of this attitude toward oneself is summed up in Groucho Marx's comment: "I would never join a club that would have someone like me as a member."

INFATUATION VERSUS MATURE LOVE

When we weigh the foregoing arguments, which either favor or oppose the idea of love as being important for the development of individuals in intimate relationships, it is useful to make a distinction between *infatuation* and *mature love*. The sort of love that leads to negative outcomes for relationship development is usually characterized by romantic illusions, idealization of the partner, and jealousy of the partner's other relationships, and can reasonably be called *infatuation*. The love that enhances the growth potential of both partners in the relationship can be called *mature love*.

According to Miller and Siegel (1972), infatuation with another is that "head over-heels, falling in love" feeling that strikes suddenly and without warning. It is the intense physiological arousal we feel when we meet someone who "sweeps us off of our feet." The most distinct feature of infatuation, however, is that while we are infatuated, we often fail to see the other person as he or she actually is.

Infatuation, then, is not as much a response to the actual attributes of a person as it is a response to characteristics that are similar to features found in an unrealistic idealized picture. Since infatuation, by definition, occurs rapidly, the characteristics that are perceived as similar to the fantasy must be readily apparent and may, therefore, quite often be superficial. (Miller and Siegel, 1972:70)

We become infatuated, then, with someone we meet who appears to fit our image of sexual or social desirability. People of all ages too often find physical attractiveness to be of the utmost importance in deciding whether or not to seek contact with another (e.g., asking someone to dance, asking for a date, and so on), or whether or not to continue in a newly established relationship. Hence, in our culture, the chances of becoming infatuated are rather high (Murstein, 1970). Becoming infatuated with another, then, is akin to what Walster and Walster (1979:2) labeled *passionate love*—"a wildly emotional state, a confusion of feelings: tenderness and sexuality, elation and pain, anxiety and relief, altruism and jealousy."

Because infatuation is by definition unstable and short-lived, it should not be the basis of a long-term relationship such as marriage (Miller and Siegel, 1972: 70). It is best to avoid committing oneself to marriage solely on the basis of infatuation. Hine (1980) identifies five types of love feeling that can properly be labeled *infatuation*.

1. *Eye Appeal.* This is love based upon the physical attractiveness of the other person. Many people's ideals of female and male physical beauty are molded by such influences as Hollywood film stars, Miss America, Mr. Universe, and the *Playboy* and *Playgirl* centerfolds. Youth, well-proportioned bodies, and vivaciousness are the foundation of our cultural models of beauty. When we meet someone who fits that image, or who approximates it, the tendency is to say, "This is the one for me!" We are swept off our feet by the other, causing us to overemphasize their physical characteristics and to underemphasize those features more important in long-term relationships: role and value compatibility, social and emotional maturity, and ability to communicate. The old maxim, "You can't tell a book by its cover," holds true, as we can be misled by a visual image and kept from knowing who another person really is.

2. *Surface Enchantment.* Often we focus on the superficial qualities of another person, rather than on physical attractiveness, and fall in love on that basis. Athletic ability, a sense of humor, a good party person (one who seems to keep people laughing by always knowing just the right things to say), financial wealth, and being in the in-group are all surface characteristics with which one can become enamored. Just as is true for eye appeal, however, such enchantment with surface qualities can prevent us from probing for knowledge of the other person's true personality.

3. *Fantasy Projection.* Many people enter intimate relationships with a previously established picture of the ideal marriage partner, perhaps based on a favorable "father image" or "mother image." This image, then,

is often projected onto the first convenient man or woman who happens to come along, causing us to actually *love the image* that we have imposed on the other person. We distort our picture of reality by placing others on a pedestal; we make them *fit* our predetermined mold, whether or not they do in reality; we adore them in a fantasy world. When marriage follows upon such a state of infatuation, the bubble bursts, and reality shock sets in: "He's not the one I (thought I) married!" Obviously, the potential for rapid deterioration of a marriage is high when fantasy projection is the basis of it.

4. *Narcissistic Love.* In Greek mythology, Narcissus was a character who fell in love with his own reflection while gazing into a pool of water. He became so enthralled with his reflection that he tumbled into the water, and was forever banished to the underworld. This myth is relevant to some contemporary love relationships: many people believe that they are in love with another when, in fact, *they are loving themselves as reflected in the other.* The person who "loves" another in order to impress friends, or to inspire envy among potential competitors, is engaging in narcissistic love. This person may actually believe that love exists when, in fact, he or she really wishes to enhance his or her own self-image. This kind of love is merely exploitative, egocentric, and self-gratifying—"I love you not for who you are, but for what you can do for me."

5. *Love As Dependency.* This sort of infatuation involves using another person as a temporary solution to a personal problem. We let go of all other activities and interests in order to devote our full time and energy to the other person. In extreme instances, people cut themselves off from life, moving ever closer to what Peele and Brodsky (1975) call "love as addiction." Essentially, love as dependency involves sacrificing one's identity by incorporating it into the other's existence. Love as dependency often occurs after an intimate relationship is dissolved and we latch onto the first convenient person who comes along, in order to fill the void left by the former partner. This is "love on the rebound," and can seriously affect the development of future relationships among those who have recently broken an engagement or been divorced. The tendency is to jump too quickly at the first opportunity, before we have taken the time to develop a realistic understanding

of the other's goals, values, role expectations, and general personality characteristics.

Mature Love.   In contrast to infatuation, mature love involves the genuine caring, responsibility, respect, and knowledge of the other which provide the space for each partner to mature and develop. It is the active process of exchanging affection and warmth, without one partner exploiting the other, and where mutual enrichment of the partners can and does take place. Mature love provides a more solid foundation upon which to build a relationship which involves a lifetime of commitment, such as marriage.

It would be an error, however, to assume that infatuation has no useful function. On the contrary, mature love relationships often do grow out of ones that began as infatuation. Infatuation begins to shade into the more mature aspects of love as the relationship is put to the test of time. Time will allow for the interaction between partners to become more varied, and to take place under a variety of circumstances and in many different situations. With time will come increased knowledge of the other person, because fantasizing will lessen after numerous experiences together (Miller and Siegel, 1972). The point here should be obvious: *Never marry a stranger!* A relationship needs time to develop from infatuation to mature love, if it is to provide a firm basis for a lifetime together in marriage.

LOVE AND THE MARITAL CAREER

In previous sections of this chapter, we noted that love is a multifaceted concept; there are many types, and many ways of defining love. It is also important to view love on the *continuum of time.* The nature of our interpersonal needs for intimacy and security change as we grow older and more mature. Consequently, as we grow through childhood, young adulthood, and into the later years of life, our definitions of love change as well. The concept of *role sequence* applies here, because our role as "lover" changes over time, in response to our changing needs and definitions of love.

The changing nature of love is significant for marriage because the partners' definitions may or may not change in a parallel fashion. Both Swenson (1972:88) and Jourard (1972:48) note that partners often find that the passionate love, which characterizes the period of court-

ship and the first few months or years of marriage, wanes over time: the novelty wears off, the pleasant little surprises end, the relationship becomes predictable, and continues largely on the basis of habit. The *agape* side of love, the concern, caring, and respectful nature of love, begins to overtake the more physiological, erotic *(Eros)* aspect of love. In the words of Walster and Walster (1978:124), we move from *passionate* love to more of a *companionate* love, based on lower-key emotion, friendly affection, and deep attachment to someone "with whom our lives are deeply intertwined." Some people find this role sequence to be disappointing, but others are rewarded by it.

The changing nature of love is illustrated by the following division of the human life span into stages, according to the types of love that characterize them (Shostrom, 1972:187–188):

1. *Affection* (ages 1–6):   the nurturing form of love, as characterized by the unconditional giving of a parent to a child.

2. *Friendship* (ages 6–12):   love based on common interests and respect for each person's equality; often seen in same-sex peer relationships;

3. *Eros* (ages 13–21):   the romantic form of love which includes inquisitiveness, jealousy, and exclusivity as well as sexual desire and an experience of strong elation;

4. *Empathy* (ages 21 +):   a charitable, altruistic form of love expressed by a deep feeling for another person as a unique human being, and which involves compassion, appreciation, tolerance, empathy, and the psychosocial maturity that increases with age.

This ability to learn and apply each kind of love is a *developmental task* that exists across the years of the marital career. That is, learning affection and friendship during the childhood years contributes to one's ability to engage in more mature forms of love relationships in later years. The ability to love, then, is a developmental process that is cumulative across stages of the individual's life and the marital career.

LOVE AND COMMUNICATION

Effective communication between partners in intimate relationships is critical if the future is to be one that is viewed by each partner as satisfying and fulfilling. Given the tremendous diversity in the way people define love, and the potential for change in the definition of love which either partner in the relationship may experience over time, the need for partners to talk to each other about their definitions of love seems obvious. Yet it is doubtful that many people actually communicate about their concepts of love prior to marriage. What is meant when one partner says to the other, "I love you?" How does this definition of love change after five, ten, or twenty years of marriage, when compared with the time when the partners were "head over heels" in passionate love, and those words were first uttered to each other during a particularly tender moment before marriage? Failure to communicate about the meaning of love can lead to confusion, misunderstanding, or, worse yet, a marriage that neither partner really wanted or actually needed (Otto, 1972b).

Making Your Own Decisions About Love

There is little that can be said about love that would be of practical use to all people. Nonetheless, there is sufficient research evidence to justify giving consideration to the following points, each of which is based upon information presented in this chapter. Although it is important to exercise caution when applying general principles to your individual case, these points should give pause for thought:

1. Love has many faces; that is, there are many types of love and many possible ways to define each. It is important to develop an understanding of the ways in which love can be categorized and defined in order to clarify and gain a proper perspective on your own definition of love.

2. Regardless of how you define love, it is important to develop a realistic understanding of what you intend to communicate when you say, "I love you" to another person (does it imply sex, marriage, commitment, exclusivity?).

3. Although most people believe that romantic love and marriage go hand-in-hand, too many believe that love, in and of itself, is a sufficient basis for marriage. Love alone is not enough. As we shall see in chapters 4 through 8, gender roles, value and role compatibility, sexual attitudes and sexuality, communication, problem-solving, conflict-management skills, and economic considerations all must be weighed in the decision to marry.

4. If love is the basis for a male-female relationship that is to extend into the future, whether or not marriage ensues, then it is important that partners communicate about their definitions of love and state what it is that their concept of love implies for the future of the relationship. Communicating about the concept of love is a *developmental task* that should be accomplished prior to marriage, for those who plan to spend their lifetimes together in a marriage relationship.

5. Individual definitions of love and role behavior as lovers change over the course of the person's life, as well as over the course of the marital career. The task of understanding one's partner is a continual one across all stages of the marital career.

6. The types of love categorized as infatuation generally do not provide a firm foundation for a long-term relationship such as marriage. At least some elements of mature love should be present if the relationship is to be expected to have a future.

7. In determining whether one is sufficiently in love with another to marry that person, there are no clear guidelines to follow. It is impossible to know for sure whether or not someone else will come along in the next week, months, or year who we might love even more than the current partner. The decision to marry based on feelings of love for another ultimately involves what existential philosophers refer to as a "leap of faith." You estimate the probabilities that this person is "the right one" for you, and if they are high enough, you make the leap. According to another old maxim, it is best to "look before you leap."

Summary

The romantic feeling known as love is an important basis for marriage in our society. Other types of love feelings form the basis of other family relationships, such as those between parents and children. Love is the means by which basic human needs for intimacy, warmth, security, self-affirmation, and acceptance are satisfied. Love is a crucial point in the process of self-development because the ability to enter and maintain loving relationships depends upon satisfaction of the basic needs for survival and security; success in loving enhances self-esteem and the ability of the person to grow toward his or her potential as a person.

As important as love is for marriage, not all people enter marriage on the basis of love for the other. Nor do those who marry out of love for each other necessarily define love in the same way. Among the different types of love defined were *Eros, agape, philos,* and *infatuation.* Also, definitions of love are in a gradual, but continual, process of change over the life of a person and across the stages of the marital career. Because definitions of love vary from one person to the next, and may change over time, there is great potential for misunderstanding and conflict between partners who define themselves as being "in love."

In order to avoid or overcome some of the potential difficulties with the concept of love that partners might encounter, several recommendations were made that can be considered developmental tasks to be undertaken by each person or by the couple as a unit. These include developing self-knowledge and self-acceptance; being able to distinguish infatuation from mature love; communicating openly and honestly with each other about definitions of love and what the words "I love you" imply for each partner; and realizing that, by itself, love is not a sufficient basis for marriage.

Some experts view being in love as a difficult task; others see the following negative aspects of love: making a poor choice of marriage partners as a result of being "blinded" by the physical arousal and/or romantic idealization of the partner; becoming overly dependent upon, or "addicted to," the loved one; and becoming jealous because one views one's partner as exclusive, "owned" property.

The debate about what love is and what role it plays in the development of individuals and marriages will probably never end. Love is a mysterious and slippery concept which, at times, seems to defy definition. In this chapter, we have raised many more questions than we have answers for. Yet, when it comes to a concept as personal and individual as love, each person must supply his or her own answers to the question of what love is, and what the words, "I love you," mean.

Questions for Discussion and Review

1. What is your personal definition of love? In what respects is it like any of the definitions stated in this chapter? In what respects is it unlike certain definitions that were stated?

2. Can one love two people of the opposite sex at the same time?

3. If you really love a person, are you likely to be jealous of that person's relationships with others? Is jealousy ever justified? Under what conditions is jealousy a legitimate response in an intimate relationship?

4. Is love a sufficient basis for marriage? Why or why not?

5. How do contemporary musicians define love when they sing about it in popular songs?

6. Where did you learn to define love as you do? Who, primarily, helped to shape your definition of the concept of love?

7. Have you ever told a person in an intimate relationship that you loved them? Under what circumstances did you do so? Have you ever regretted telling someone that you loved them? If so, why?

8. What is your view of the relationship between love and sex? Why do you feel the way you do about this relationship?

9. What are your major "growth needs?" How can these needs best be met for you?

10. Have you ever been afraid to get *too close* to someone because of a fear of love and the risks of getting involved? If so, what were the circumstances? How did you and the other person respond? What was the outcome of this relationship?

CHAPTER 4

Gender Roles and Sex:

Biological and Cultural Determinants

An important aspect of male-female relationships both within and outside of marriage and the family concerns each person's perceptions of *maleness* and *femaleness,* or masculinity and femininity. In our culture, we often attribute certain characteristics to others, come to expect particular kinds of behavior, and associate with others certain privileges and obligations, on the basis of whether they are male or female.

In chapter 1, we discussed some potential consequences of male and female roles both in and out of marriage. Some experts view the traditional masculine roles adopted by men as creating health problems. The strain and anxiety associated with pressures to succeed occupationally and financially are believed to result in greater frequencies of heart disease, high blood pressure, and earlier death among men. Other experts argue that the traditional feminine roles adopted by women are constricting and inhibitive of the developmental potential of individual women. The "housewife syndrome" affects women whose adult lives are limited to housecleaning, cooking, continual accommodation to the needs and preferences of husbands, and childbearing and child care.

In this chapter, the physiological and behavioral differences between males and females will be examined. The relative contributions of genetic heredity and the social-cultural environment in shaping those differences will be explored. We will also discuss the implications of these differences for the development of the individual. The concept of *role* will help us to understand the dynamics and consequences of psychological and behavioral differences between men and women. Clearly, biological and cultural differences between males and females have a considerable impact upon the experiences, degree of fulfillment, and

long-term stability of interpersonal relationships between the sexes, including those in marriage and the family.

Sex and Gender

To fully understand the nature of male-female differences and the impact these differences have on the development of interpersonal relationships, it is important to distinguish the two major sources of these differences: the *biological-physical* and the *cultural*. The concept of *sex* refers to the biological and physiological differences between males and females, as determined by one's *genetic structure (genotype)*. Anatomically, males and females generally differ in the shapes and sizes of their bodies, the amount of hair covering the face and body, genitalia and reproductive apparatus, and physical strength. These differences are established before birth as a result of the genetic makeup inherited from one's parents. An individual's *sexual identity,* on the other hand, is the "person's private and personal assessment of his or her sex," as reflected by "saying inwardly, 'I am a male' or 'I am a female'" (Diamond, 1979:41). However, one's genetic sex does not always correspond with one's sexual identity. Some people are born and raised as genotypic males or females, yet consider themselves to be of the opposite sex. "I am really a man born in a woman's body," or "I am really a woman born in a man's body," are typical comments of such individuals, known as *transsexuals* (see Feature 4.1). Transsexuals are caught in a vicious bind, in that their physical qualities cause society to expect them to behave in ways that are appropriate for their sex; but

—They were married three years ago, uncertain of the attraction between them but aware that something had drawn them together.

It was Harry and Jean Reynolds then. They had a child; they stayed together. But though they never spoke of it, they knew something was wrong.

Six months ago, with the never-mentioned tension driving them apart, Harry admitted out loud, for the first time, what he had known about himself for at least nine years.

Harry was a transsexual, psychologically and emotionally a woman but trapped in the body of a man.

Jean understood. The fear that had kept them from discussing the matter before proved to be unfounded. Because, Jean said, she, too, was a transsexual, a man existing in a woman's body.

In March, Harry changed his name to Sheila Marie Reynolds. Sheila wears women's clothes, has started electrolysis treatments and is taking hormones in preparation for a sex-change operation. After all those years of suppressing her instincts, she says, she can finally act as she feels.

"You can't bury your true self; it's impossible," Sheila said. "Believe me, I tried."

After Sheila has her operation, Jean plans to have one, too. They say that their marriage, with sexes reversed, will continue.

Sheila is afraid to leave the house anymore. She is 6-foot-8, 168 pounds, and is heckled when she goes out in public. Jean is afraid to leave her home alone, so neither has a job.

They support their two daughters, 2-year-old Kathy and 7-year-old Barbie (Sheila's from a previous marriage), on Sheila's $900-a-month veteran's disability check for severe asthma and emphysema.

"I don't work because I don't think anybody would hire a secretary with an Adam's apple that has to shave off a 5 p.m. shadow," Sheila said.

"I can't go anywhere. I wonder when somebody comes to the door what are they there for. I feel totally insecure. I would just like to be allowed to live like any other woman."

Jean says they have had problems getting credit and problems with the phone company since Sheila started living as a woman. They have to be out of their rented house this week, and say they can't find anyone in town willing to rent to them.

Sheila says there is no way to explain the anxiety that came from trying to live as a male for 35 years. Harry tried to act as macho as possible to overcome the feeling, and even grew a massive beard.

"It was just knowing that what was there didn't belong there," Sheila said. "The pain was so real that I tried to castrate myself three times."

Since Sheila decided to live as a woman, the Reynoldses have been trying unsuccessfully to get a sex-change operation for her. Most doctors require at least two years of psychological testing and hormone treatments before they will do such surgery, and the Reynoldses say, Sheila can't wait that long.

Jean, who realized she was a transsexual seven years ago, says the social trauma was less severe for her. It was easier for her to dress in a masculine way, to attempt traditionally male roles, with less ostracism. She says she can handle being a female for a while longer, that Sheila's condition must be dealt with first.

"I don't want people like myself to have to live in fear," Sheila said. "I want people to know what transsexuals really are. Just because I'm a woman with a problem doesn't mean I'm inhuman.

"I want to believe in something, that somehow I'll get the operation. Then, the worst part of my life would be over."

SOURCE: Joe Rhodes, *Arizona Daily Star,* June 10, 1979.

transsexuals usually want to behave like — and actually *feel* like — a member of the opposite sex. This causes some transsexuals to seek a sex-change operation, in order to bring their sexual identities into line with their physical sex characteristics.

The concept of *gender* refers to the behavioral and psychological differences between men and women which are shaped by one's interaction with the physical and social environment. *Gender roles,* then, are the clusters of culturally prescribed norms (expectations) that define appropriate behavior, privileges, and obligations of people identified as either male or female. According to Diamond (1979:41):

> The *gender (sex) roles* for males and females are sex-appropriate behavior patterns accepted by society as sex-related. Patterns that, in our society, are most often displayed by men are considered *masculine* and those most often displayed by women are considered *feminine.*

As we shall now see, a person's sex is biologically determined, whereas sexual identity, gender, and gender roles are shaped by a combination of biological and social forces working together.

SEX DETERMINATION[1]

An individual's sex is determined by the particular combination of chromosomes which is formed at conception. Chromosomes are the cell structures that carry the *genes,* the material which determines our physical traits and characteristics. Whether we have brown hair or black, blue eyes or brown, are tall or short, have big ears or small are all genetically determined characteristics. Of the 46 chromosomes we inherit from our biological parents, 44 are known as *somatic chromosomes.* These determine bodily characteristics other than those having to do with being one sex or the other. The remaining two chromosomes, known as *sex chromosomes,* will influence the development of either a male or female fetus. The two sex chromosomes are usually referred to as the *X* and *Y* chromosomes, with an *XX* chromosome combination normally resulting in a female offspring and an *XY* combination normally resulting in a male offspring. Whether or not the *Y* chromosome is present is determined by sperm of the biological father,

as approximately half of his sperm will be *X*-bearing and half *Y*-bearing sperm. (A more detailed discussion of human sexual anatomy and the process of conception appears in chapter 5.)

During the first seven or eight weeks following conception, known as the *embryonic stage* of prenatal development, a complex process takes place, which, in almost all cases, will facilitate the normal development of either a female *(XX)* or male *(XY)* geneotype offspring (see Figure 4.1). As late as the fifth and sixth weeks of prenatal development, the sex of the embryo cannot be visually determined. This is known as the *indifferent,* or *undifferentiated, stage.* The embryo in this stage possesses a pair of undifferentiated sex glands, known as *gonads,* which can potentially develop in either direction: male or female. The embryo also possess two sets of ducts, known as *Wolffian* and *Mullerian,* which will eventually develop into internal sex-related organs of the male and female respectively. During the seventh week, substances known as *inducers* are secreted. It is not fully known what these substances are and how they function. They may be a type of hormone which is directed by the combination of *X* or *Y* sperm with the *X* chromosome in the female egg. Some biologists believe that a hormone produced in the mother's placenta, known as *chorionic gonadotrophin,* may stimulate this process. In any event, in an *XY* (male) embryo, the inducers stimulate development of the male *testes* from the previously undifferentiated gonad. The testes are the internal organs that produce sperm and the male hormone *testosterone* in the adult male. In a short time, further development of the Mullerian ducts is inhibited by what is known as a "mullerian-inhibiting substance," and they begin to disappear. The embryonic testes then begin to secrete the hormone *testosterone* (also known as an *androgen*) through the *Leydig cells,* which stimulates the growth and development of the external male genitalia known as the *penis* and *scrotum.* At about the seventh month of prenatal development, the testes begin to move down from the male's abdominal cavity and into the scrotum, although in rare cases the descent may be delayed for several weeks after birth. Testosterone also stimulates other components of the internal reproductive apparatus of the male, including the *vas deferans, seminal vesicles,* and *ejaculatory ducts* (see chapter 5 for a more complete discussion).

In a genotypic female embryo with an *XX* chromosome combination, development of the internal sex organs and external genitalia is marked by the *absence* of hor-

FIGURE 4.1.   Male and Female Prenatal Sex Differentiation by Week of Development.

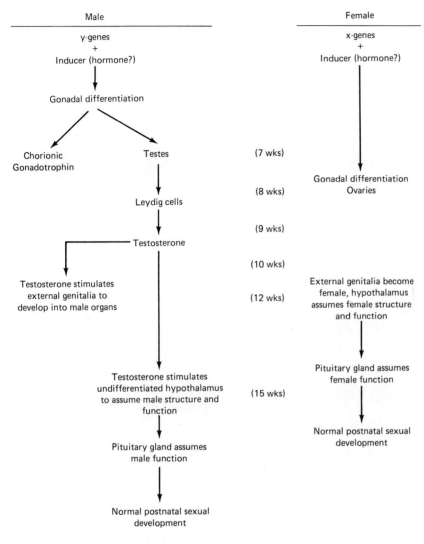

SOURCE: Longstreth (1974:44).

mones. To repeat, until the seventh week of prenatal life, the embryo is equipped with genital ducts capable of producing either a male or female. In the absence of male hormones, normal female development will occur, with the Mullerian ducts stimulating the growth of ovaries from the previously undifferentiated gonads, and the Wolffian (male) ducts disappearing. Further develop-

ment of the Mullerian structure, because of the absence of the male sex hormone, produces the *Fallopian tubes, vagina,* and *uterus;* by the twelfth week following conception, the external genitalia, known as the *labia majora* and the *labia minora* (major and minor lips) and *clitoris,* begin to form.

The growth and development of the *internal sex*

FIGURE 4.2.   Three stages in the differentiation of the sexual system, internal and external.

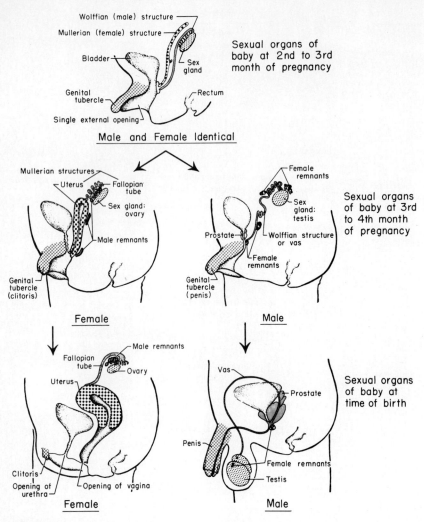

Wolffian (male) structure
Mullerian (female) structure
Bladder
Genital tubercle
Single external opening
Sex gland
Rectum

Sexual organs of baby at 2nd to 3rd month of pregnancy

Male and Female Identical

Mullerian structures
Uterus
Fallopian tube
Sex gland: ovary
Male remnants
Genital tubercle (clitoris)

Female

Female remnants
Sex gland: testis
Prostate
Wolffian structure or vas
Female remnants
Genital tubercle (penis)

Male

Sexual organs of baby at 3rd to 4th month of pregnancy

Male remnants
Fallopian tube
Ovary
Uterus
Clitoris
Opening of urethra
Opening of vagina

Female

Vas
Prostate
Penis
Female remnants
Testis

Male

Sexual organs of baby at time of birth

SOURCE: Money and Ehrhardt (1972:41).

organs of the male and female are pictured in Figure 4.2, and the development of *external* sexual genitalia is pictured in Figure 4.3. The fact that male and female prenatal sexual development emerges out of a previously undifferentiated gonadal structure means that each part of the male's anatomy has its counterpart in the female's anatomy, and vice-versa. These are known as *male-female homologies* (see Table 4.1).

Of particular importance to the process of prenatal sex differentiation is that the development of the normal male depends *not only* upon the XY chromosome combination, but also upon the inducer substances, the sex hormone testosterone, and the Mullerian-inhibiting substance. Without the intrusion of these substances and hormones, typical female development will occur *regardless of whether or not* the chromosome combination is XX or XY. In almost all cases, an XY combination will actually result in the intrusion of these substances to stimulate

FIGURE 4.3. Comparison of external male and female genitalia from undifferentiated through completely differentiated stages.

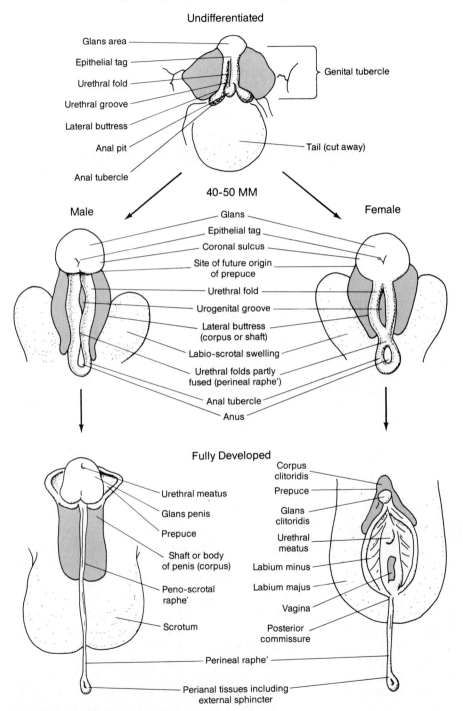

SOURCE: Adapted from Witters and Jones-Witters (1980:21).

TABLE 4.1. *Homologies Between Male and Female Sex Structures*

Male Derivative	Primordial Structure	Female Derivative
	Gonad	
Testes	Indifferent gonad	Ovaries
Spermatogonia → sperm	Primordial germ cells	Oogonia → ova
	Genital ducts	
Efferent ducts of the testes, epididymis, vas deferens, seminal vesicles, ejaculatory duct	Wolffian duct	Vestigial structures
Vestigial structures	Mullerian duct	Fallopian tubes, uterus, vagina (upper portion)
	External genitalia	
Penis: glans and corpora cavernosa	Genital tubercle	Clitoris: glans and corpora cavernosa
Corpus spongiosum	Urethral folds	Labia minora
Scrotum	Labioscrotal swellings	Labia majora
Bulbourethral glands, prostate	Urogenital sinus	Bartholin's glands, vagina (lower portion)

SOURCE: From *Human Sexuality: A Biological Perspective,* by W. L. Witters and P. Jones-Witters. Copyright © 1980 by Litton Educational Publishing, Inc. Reprinted by permission of Wadsworth Health Sciences Division, Monterey, California 93940.

the growth of testes and inhibit the further development of the Mullerian ducts. However, the research of John Money (Money and Ehrhardt, 1972) at Johns Hopkins University, and others (e.g., Jost, 1958; 1972), has shown that in the rare instances where these substances have been abnormally low or absent, the fetus will develop with primarily female anatomical characteristics. The reasons for the failure of an *XY* chromosome combination to produce and interject these substances are not fully understood, although it is believed that some *XY* embryos contain a nonsex chromosome (known as an *autosome*) which produces insensitivity to male hormones. On the other hand, genotypic females *(XX)* whose mothers ingested drugs containing androgens (male sex hormone) during the critical stage of sex differentiation (the sixth through tenth weeks), usually in order to prevent a miscarriage and to carry the fetus to term, are sometimes born with typical male genitalia, including a penis and scrotum. Hence, determination of one's anatomical sex is not simply a matter of *XX* or *XY* chromosome combinations. If a normal male is to develop from an *XY* chromosome combination, as it *almost always* does, male hormones and other substances must be triggered. Without the intrusion of these hormones and other substances, as is *almost always* the case with an *XX* chromosome combination, a

normal female will develop (Money and Ehrhardt, 1972:24).

SEXUAL IDENTITY AND GENDER ROLES

Whether one is a genotypic male *(XY)* or female *(XX),* and thereby manifests the bodily features typically associated with one sex or the other, there exists considerable room for variability in the degree to which one *identifies* the self as either male or female. In addition, there is considerable variability in the propensity of a person to *think* and *behave* in ways that our culture typically defines as masculine and feminine. An important question is, "To what extent are behavioral and social differences between males and females biologically and genetically determined, rather than culturally conditioned?" This question is important because the answer will determine to what extent individuals are able to *change* their behavior in order to live a more satisfying life, or to accommodate to another person in an intimate relationship such as marriage.

The research evidence suggests that the interaction between our biological sex and the social environment determines the degree to which we identify ourselves as either male or female, which is considered *sexual identity*. The extent to which we behave in ways that are consistent with cultural expectations regarding what is appropriate and acceptable behavior for males and females is considered *gender role* (Diamond, 1976). The general process of *gender socialization* occurs from the moment of birth, as we interact with parents and other adults, siblings, the schools, and the mass media of television, magazines, and movies. These environmental influences are powerful in shaping our identities as basically male, female, or some combination of the two, and our behavior as either typically masculine or typically feminine, according to culturally defined gender roles.

How Sexual Identity and Gender Roles Are Learned.

The process of gender-role socialization, as we have said, begins early in life. In fact, it begins with the name given to us by our parents which, in most cases, pushes us in the direction of either masculinity or femininity. The way parents handle infants, play with them and talk to them, the type of toys given to children, and the games they play all contribute to the foundation of sexual identity and gender roles that the child assumes. Boys, for example, are often dressed in trousers and the color blue, girls in dresses and in the color pink. By the age of three, most children have a well-developed sense of masculinity and femininity, which expands in subsequent years of life (Kagan, 1964).

There are many theories about how children accept a particular sexual identity and assume certain gender-specific roles. The most viable theories are: (1) social learning theory, (2) cognitive development theory, and (3) social power theory (Diamond, 1979; Longstreth, 1974). *Social learning theory* suggests that a child is rewarded by others, particularly parents, for behaving in ways that are viewed as appropriate for the child's sex. That is, young boys are rewarded in tangible ways (such as toys or presents) and in intangible ways (such as praise) for behaving in masculine ways. Girls are similarly rewarded for feminine kinds of behavior. Boys are rewarded for assertive, competitive, rough-and-tumble, muscular kinds of activities, and girls are more likely to be rewarded for quiet and passive behavior, and for simply being "cute." Eventually, children of either sex identify with the same-sex parent and other same-sex adult role models, and imitate the already established gender-role behavior of those models without having to be directly reinforced with rewards for doing so. However, peers can certainly replace parents when it

Gender roles in our society are learned in a number of ways, with boys more often being rewarded for rough-and-tumble play. *(Photo by Alvin Snider.)*

comes to being rewarded and reinforced for gender-appropriate behavior.

Cognitive development theory begins with the premise that self-identification as a "boy" or a "girl" takes place prior to any reinforcement process. Owing primarily to the work of Kohlberg (1966, 1969), this theory posits that a child will only become interested in appropriate gender-role behavior after he or she identifies himself or herself as "boy or girl," which is the result, in part, of biological (genotypic) factors:

The social learning syllogism is: "I want rewards, I am rewarded for doing boy things, therefore I want to be a boy." In contrast, a cognitive theory assumes this sequence: "I am a boy, therefore I want to do boy things, therefore the opportunity to do boy things is rewarding." (Kohlberg, 1966:89)

Social power theory assumes that the child will imitate the behavior of others who are perceived as powerful and who are able to do things that the child cannot do. This theory is closely related to the social learning theory in that the powerful adult usually has control over any rewards that may be acquired for behaving in gender-appropriate ways. There is less emphasis on rewards in social-power theory, however, and more emphasis on the child's motivation to imitate those who have special privileges, such as parents.

As might be expected, research on social determinants of gender-role learning has shown that each theory has some validity (Hetherington and Frankie, 1967). Gender-role learning, then, is probably a product of many factors in the social environment, including the affection and love received from parents; being rewarded for behaving in masculine or feminine ways; identifying oneself as either a boy or girl; and imitating a more powerful person in one's environment.

Gender roles are also learned and reinforced outside the home and family setting. For example, elementary and secondary schools promote gender-role differentiation with sex-segregated classes, such as physical education, home economics, and vocational and trade-skills education (Hobson, Skeen, and Robinson, 1980; Naffziger and Naffziger, 1974). Team sports are also segregated along sex lines in schools. In addition, textbooks, literature, and readers at preschool, grade school, and high school levels promote gender-role differences by placing females in traditional feminine roles (such as homemaking, care-giving, and expressive roles), and depicting males in traditional masculine roles (work outside the home, being active and assertive, making decisions, and other instrumental behaviors) [Kolbe and LaVoie, 1981; Weitzman, 1979]. In regard to women, Naffziger and Naffziger (1974:255) noted:

A recent study of thirteen popular texts conclude with what by now must seem a refrain: women in such texts are "passive, incapable of sustained organization or work, satisfied with [their] role in society, and well supplied with material blessing." There is no mention of the struggle by women to gain entrance into higher education, of their efforts to organize or join labor unions, of other battles for working rights, or of the hundred-year-long multi-issue effort that ended, temporarily, in the Suffrage Act of 1920.

There are many other areas of life in which gender roles are learned. For example, such messages are communicated through the mass media in the form of television advertisements for floor wax, laundry soap, and bathroom cleaners, in which women are almost always shown using and evaluating these products. On the other hand, automobile repair and maintenance, car wax, beer, and tire commercials picture men (Osofsky and Osofsky, 1972; Walum, 1977; Williams, LaRose, and Frost, 1981).

Biology versus Culture.   One of the most stimulating debates in the social and biological sciences today is the question of which forces — biological, or social and cultural — have the greatest influence on the development of sexual identity and gender roles in the individual person. To demonstrate how powerful the cultural transmission of sexual identity and gender roles is, we can again turn to the work of John Money and his associates at Johns Hopkins University. Recall the androgen-induced *hermaphrodites* mentioned previously. These are genotypic females *(XX)* whose mothers, while pregnant, took a drug with chemical compounds similar to the male sex hormone. Although they were born with the external genitalia of a male, they grew to identify themselves and behave as either a male or female according to the way they were socialized in their families, especially in the first few years of life. If the problem was surgically corrected, and the child was raised as a girl, feminine gender identity and role behavior followed; some, however, showed evidence of "tomboy-ism," and developed intense interests in competitive sports and outdoor activity, and expended high levels of muscular energy (Money, 1971:206). Evidently, the influence of biological makeup persisted, despite the heavy dose of social influence these individuals received throughout childhood. If the problem was not corrected surgically (that is, the male genitalia were left intact), and the XX child was raised as a male, he would develop a male identity and adopt gender-role patterns toward the masculine end of the continuum. Longstreth (1974:43–44) summarized Money's research on genetic versus cultural determination of sexual identity and gender roles by stating:

> In almost all cases, androgen-induced hermaphrodites develop the sex (gender) role assigned to them by their parents; and it is exceedingly hard to change this identity after the first few years. It may be concluded, therefore, that although behavioral differentiation in childhood is influenced by the fetal hormonal environment, the human organism at birth is capable of sex-typing in either direction, male or female. The environment appears to make the final decision.

Sexual identity and gender-role preferences therefore seem to be acquired primarily as a result of socialization in one's family and in the broader sociocultural milieu.

It is apparent that social and cultural forces strongly influence the development of sexual identity and gender roles. However, recent scientific evidence shows the non-trivial role of biological, or innate, forces, mainly in the form of sex hormones such as estrogen in females and testosterone in males. Carefully conducted studies of animals injected before birth with hormones of the opposite sex showed that they would demonstrate significantly altered sexual preferences as adults, and would behave in ways more typical of the opposite sex (Diamond, 1979). However, it was realized that animal studies may or may not generalize to human beings. Consequently, scientists have taken great interest in studies of human transsexuals, who identify themselves as members of the opposite sex in spite of extensive childhood conditioning to the contrary. That is, transsexual males are born and raised in their families as males, yet persist throughout their childhood and adult years in identifying themselves as females. The same pattern is observed in studies of transsexual females, who persist in identifying themselves as males despite being reared as females (see Feature 4.1). It seems, then, that sexual identity has a strong biological component, which is carried into the world at birth, and which, at least in the case of many transsexuals, is unaltered by social experiences.

Other evidence supporting the role of biological forces has been accumulating. For example, Diamond (1979:49) describes the results of medical research on children in the Dominican Republic, who actually changed their sexual identities and gender-role behaviors at puberty when their bodies underwent a hormonal change: testosterone levels increased suddenly.

In a small community in the Dominican Republic, due to a genetic-endocrine problem, a large number of males were

born who, at birth, appeared to be females. These males had a blind vaginal pouch instead of a scrotum and, instead of a penis, had a clitoris-like phallus . . . The uneducated parents were unaware of anything unusual and these males were raised as typical females in the community. There was no reason to do otherwise. At puberty, a spontaneous change in their biology induced a penis to develop and their psychological orientation to change. These males, born years ago and raised as females, nevertheless, at puberty individually gave up their living as females and assumed life as males.

Hence, the question of which has a greater impact on sexual identity and gender-role preferences — biological make-up at birth, or cultural and social experiences — is unanswerable at this time. It is probable, as Diamond (1979) concluded, that biological and sociocultural forces are inextricably bound together, such that one is born with certain *biological predispositions* to identify with a particular sex and to behave along predominantly masculine or feminine lines. The person will seek out, and be particularly sensitive to, social experiences that are consistent with these biologically preprogrammed sex and gender preferences, but experiences in the family and with friends and other social influences (TV, teachers, movies) can significantly inhibit or promote whatever biological predispositions one has. The result is that the relative impact of biological and cultural forces, and the potential for conflict between them, can vary considerably from one individual to the next.

GENDER-ROLE STEREOTYPES

Recall our definition, in chapter 2, of a social *role*. Roles are clusters of norms that define a given activity for an individual, defining wl.at we and others expect from us in terms of behavior, duties, and obligations, as well as what rights and privileges we are entitled to as a result of playing that role. In view of the preceding discussion, we can say that one's biologically determined sex is an *ascribed status,* because we can do nothing (short of a sex-change operation, of course) to alter the physiological characteristics that we share with others of the same sex category. *Gender roles* are also ascribed, to the extent that the individual is socialized strictly along traditional masculine (for boys) or feminine (for girls) lines without being provided the opportunity to think or choose otherwise. According to Duberman (1975:25–28), society tends to equate biological sex with gender roles, giving people the false im-

Experiences in the family join those with friends and other social influences (TV, movies, teachers) to shape gender-role preferences.   *(Photo by Mark Rogers.)*

pression that they *must* behave and think in certain ways *because* they are male or female.

The problem is that sex status and gender role are frequently confused. In our society, men are thought of as biologically (inherently and unchangeably) aggressive and women as biologically nurturant. Male and female children are treated differentially from birth. They learn very early to accept the relationship between their sex status and their gender role as defined by the society, and forever after the concepts remain intertwined. It should be clear . . . that gender-role differences are not based in biology. To be born male does not guarantee masculinity. To be born with a penis does not ensure that one will be brave. The male learns how to act as if he were brave because he believes that such behavior is a display of masculinity. To be born female does not guarantee femininity. Having ovaries does not assure a girl that she will love housework. She will be socialized to act as if she loves housework because that is the behavior socially accepted as feminine. Masculinity and femininity must be learned within a social context.

What, then, are the traditional views of masculinity and femininity held in our culture? We have alluded to some of these already, such as aggressiveness and competitiveness, passivity and dependence, and intellectual abilities. In addition, there are many dimensions of social life in which gender roles have an influence: in intellectual pursuits through education; dating and courtship; marriage and family relations; on the job and in the place of work; and in politics and religion. An excellent list of stereotypical gender-role differences between men and women is provided by Chafetz (1974) [see Table 4.2]. These *traits* are called *stereotypes* because they represent typical ways of viewing men and women, regardless of each individual's actual characteristics. It is unfortunate that people tend to categorize others, often unfairly, on the basis of sex alone. Moreover, people who have learned gender-role stereotypes also learn to *want* to behave according to that stereotype; they do not fully understand that they do not have to do so.

The gender-role stereotypes in Table 4.2 were compiled by asking college students, "What kinds of words or phrases do you think *most Americans* use to characterize males and females, or 'masculinity' and 'femininity'?" A useful feature of this table is that it demonstrates how gender-role stereotypes can influence our views of people across a broad spectrum of behavior and thought, from the physical, sexual, and emotional to the intellectual. A close

DOONESBURY

by Garry Trudeau

examination of Table 4.2 will also show some apparent contradictions within both the male or female columns of gender-role traits. For example, in the intellectual area, males are expected to be *objective and rational* but at the same time *dogmatic*. In the sexual area, females are expected to be *sexually passive* and *uninterested* but at the same time *seductive* and *flirtatious*. These expected behaviors appear to be at odds with each other, and could place people in uncomfortable binds if they feel others expect them to conform to both expectations in a given situation.

Another way to look at gender-role stereotypes is to examine the actual *norms* that people attach to male and female roles. Osmond and Martin (1975) developed a scale composed of 32 statements designed to tap an individual's norms regarding gender-appropriate roles (see Table 4.3). As with the gender-role traits described in Table 4.2, the various norms associated with gender roles have been grouped according to various aspects of social life: (1) family and marriage; (2) nonfamily roles; (3) stereotypes of male/female nature and behaviors; and (4) beliefs about social change related to sex roles. This

gender-role-questionnaire was given to nearly 500 undergraduate college students (225 males and 255 females), and the researchers found that

1. Males and females were in greatest *agreement* about marital and family roles and the social-change issues.

2. Males and females were in greatest *disagreement* over the roles of women and the norms relating to male/female nature and behaviors.

3. Both men and women were the most *traditional* in the area of marriage and familial roles.

4. Both men and women were most *equalitarian* (modern) regarding the social-change issues.

The Osmond and Martin study provides further evidence that males and females in our society are differentiated along culturally defined traditional gender roles. In addition, this differentiation is made by *both men and women*. However, there is also evidence of equalitarianism in some areas which may, in the future, expand.

95

TABLE 4.2. *Gender-Role Stereotype Traits*

Characteristics	*Masculine Traits*	*Feminine Traits*
I. Physical	Virile, athletic, strong Sloppy, worry less about appearance and aging Brave	Weak, helpless, dainty, nonathletic Worry about appearance and aging Sensual Graceful
II. Functional	Breadwinner, provider	Domestic Maternal, involved with children Church-going
III. Sexual	Sexually aggressive, experienced Single-status acceptable; male "caught" by spouse	Virginal, inexperienced; double-standard Must be married, female "catches" spouse Sexually passive, uninterested Responsible for birth control Seductive, flirtatious
IV. Emotional	Unemotional, stoic, don't cry	Emotional, sentimental, romantic Can cry Expressive Compassionate Nervous, insecure, fearful
V. Intellectual	Logical, intellectual, rational, objective, scientific Practical Mechanical Public awareness, activity, contributor to society Dogmatic	Scatterbrained, frivolous, shallow, inconsistent, intuitive Impractical Perceptive, sensitive "arty" Idealistic, humanistic
VI. Interpersonal	Leader, dominating Disciplinarian Independent, free, individualistic Demanding	Petty, flirty, coy, gossipy, catty, sneaky, fickle Dependent, overprotected, responsive Status-conscious and competitive, refined, adept in social graces Follower, subservient, submissive
VII. Other Personal	Aggressive Success-oriented, ambitious Proud, egotistical, confident Moral, trustworthy Decisive Competitive Uninhibited, adventurous	Self-conscious, easily intimidated, modest, shy, sweet Patient Vain Affectionate, gentle, tender, soft Not aggressive, quiet, passive Tardy Innocent Noncompetitive

SOURCE: Reproduced by permission of the publisher, F. E. Peacock Publishers, Inc., Itasca, Illinois.

TABLE 4.3. *Gender-Role Norms, from Traditionalism to Modernism**

I. Familial Roles
 *(1) Women with children in grammar school should, if at all possible, stay at home rather than work.
 *(2) Women with preschool children should not work—if at all possible.
 (3) Whoever is the better wage-earner, wife or husband, should be the breadwinner.
 *(4) It is possible for women to satisfy their needs for achievement through their husbands.
 (5) Men should have more freedom to do such things as cook and care for children, if they so desire.
 *(6) A man's self-esteem is severely injured if his wife makes more money than he does.
 (7) Men should take the same amount of responsibility as women in caring for home and children.
 *(8) A husband who is the breadwinner in the family should make all the important decisions.

II. Extrafamilial Roles
 *(9) I would feel uncomfortable if my immediate supervisor at work was a woman.
 *(10) To a great extent, women are less able to make a career commitment than men are.
 (11) Females should be encouraged to plan for a career, not just a job.
 (12) I would vote for a woman for President of the United States.
 *(13) Women are less capable of making important decisions than men are.
 *(14) Men are more capable of assuming leadership than women are.

III. Stereotypes of Male/Female Nature and Behaviors
 *(15) Women generally prefer light conversations over rational discussions.
 *(16) There is considerable evidence that men, in general, are a "superior species" to women.
 *(17) Women really like being dependent on men.
 *(18) Career women generally are neurotic.
 *(19) Females should go ahead and pamper males—"Tell him how great he is"—because that's a useful way to get what they want.
 (20) Men should stop appraising women solely on the basis of appearance and sex appeal.
 *(21) Either consciously or unconsciously, most women would like to be men.
 *(22) The way men and women behave is more a result of their genetic make-up than of the way they were brought up.
 (23) Women are as capable as men of enjoying a full sex life.
 *(24) Since men have a natural urge to dominate and lead, women who challenge this actually threaten the welfare of society.

IV. Social Change As Related to Sex-Roles
 *(25) Unlike the race riots, the "battle between the sexes" will never involve violence on any large scale.
 (26) There should be low-cost, high-quality child-care centers for working women.
 (27) Men need liberation equally as much as women do.
 (28) Men's clubs and lodges should be required to admit women.
 (29) Women should get equal pay with men for doing the same jobs.
 (30) Women should have equal job opportunities with men.
 (31) Women can attain true equality in this country only through a really drastic change in the social structure.
 (32) The Equal Rights Amendment related to sex should be ratified as soon as possible.

Response Categories: Strongly Agree; Agree; Neutral; Disagree; Strongly Disagree.
* Items where a *Strongly Agree* response indicates a traditional gender-role norm.

SOURCE: Osmond and Martin, "Sex and Sexism." Copyrighted 1975 by the National Council on Family Relations, Fairview Community School Center, 1910 West Country Road B, Suite 147, St. Paul, Minnesota 55113. Reprinted by permission.

Consequences of Gender-Role Stereotypes for the Individual

Because we know that gender roles are both learned and biologically influenced, and that people often make assumptions and judgments about others solely on the basis of their biological sex, it is important to develop some understanding of the *consequences* of gender-role stereotypes for the development of the individual.

GENDER-ROLE PRIVILEGES AND OBLIGATIONS

Gender-role stereotypes place different kinds of burdens on men and women, and also grant different privileges and rewards (see Table 4.4). In Table 4.4, characteristics of traditional male and female gender roles are categorized according to their perceived advantages and disadvantages. Each characteristic is also identified according to the aspect of that role which is relevant to the individual, whether it is a normative *proscription* (prohibitive); an *obligation* (an expected duty or *prescription*); a *right* (privilege); or a structural *benefit* (reward). In analyzing this table, Chafetz (1974:59) concluded:

Masculine disadvantages consist overwhelmingly of obligations with a few proscriptions, while the disadvantages of the feminine role arise primarily from proscriptions, with a few obligations. Thus females complain about what they can't do, males about what they must do. Females complain that they cannot be athletic, aggressive, sexually free, or successful in the worlds of work and education; in short, they complain of their passivity. Males complain that they must be aggressive and must succeed; in short, of their activity. . . .

Clearly, gender-role stereotypes impose limitations on both sexes when society defines what is appropriate behavior, and what are the acceptable rights, privileges, and obligations for males and females (Friedan, 1963; Bernard, 1972; Pleck, 1976; Levine, 1974).[2]

GENDER ROLES AND ADULT DEVELOPMENT

Other researchers have examined the *objective* consequences of gender-role stereotypes for individual development, as opposed to the perceived or *subjective* consequences. A study conducted by Mussen (1961, 1962), for example, examined boys with highly masculine interests as teenagers and their coping abilities and personal development in adulthood. Mussen studied adolescent boys who expressed strong attraction toward traditionally masculine interests and occupations (such as engineers, construction workers, and mechanics), and compared them with those boys who had fewer masculine vocational interests (such as authors, musicians, and teachers). Although the more "masculine" boys seemed more exuberant, self-confident, relaxed, independent, and carefree as teenagers, by age 30 to 35 the *less* "masculine" males demonstrated more positive self-concepts; greater self-acceptance; were more carefree and happy; had more poise; and were less likely to have problems related to social functioning. Apparently, highly masculine interests promote better personal adjustment during the teenage years, when athletics, physical strength and competition, and other action-oriented activities gain status among peers. However, less masculine interests, such as those relating to concern for others, sociability, aesthetic interests, and outgoingness, promote social and occupational success as adults. It is likely that these more feminine traits are conducive to coping with the strains and challenges of adult roles, because the traditional masculine traits are insufficient in and of themselves (Rosenberg and Sutton-Smith, 1972:85).

The Economics of Gender Roles. Certain *combinations* of "helpful" masculine and feminine traits are most likely to yield payoffs for success in adult roles (Chafetz, 1974). For example, consider the combination of such masculine gender-role traits as decisiveness, ambition, leadership, and objectivity with such feminine-role traits as compassion, intuitiveness, perceptiveness, and patience. This combination of traits would seem to be an excellent one for occupational success in our modern *Gesellschaft* type of society—a society which seems to blend the impersonal and distant with the close and personal modes of relating to one another. For example, the more adjusted males in Mussen's study (previously described) did not show an *absence* of traditional male-gender characteristics. Rather, they showed more feminine traits *in relation* to the highly masculine boys and men.

Although we have little direct scientific evidence relating to the impact of various combinations of masculine and feminine gender-role characteristics on success in adult role performances, research evidence supports the

TABLE 4.4. *Male and Female Views of Gender-Role Disadvantages and Advantages*

Disadvantages of Same-Gender Role and Advantages of Opposite One, As Perceived by Males*

Male Disadvantages	*Female Advantages*
Can't show emotions (P)	Freedom to express emotions (R)
Must be provider (O)	Fewer financial obligations; parents support longer (S)
Pressure to succeed, be competitive (O)	Less pressure to succeed (P)
Alimony and child support (O)	Alimony and insurance benefits (S)
Liable to draft (O)	Free from draft (S)
Must take initiative, make decisions (O)	Protected (S)
Limit on acceptable careers (P)	
Expected to be mechanical, fix things (O)	
	More leisure (S)
	Placed on pedestal; object of courtesy (S)

Disadvantages of Same Gender Role and Advantages of Opposite One As Perceived by Females*

Female Disadvantages	*Male Advantages*
Job opportunities limited; discrimination; poor pay (P)	Job opportunities greater (S)
Legal and financial discrimination (P)	Financial and legal opportunity (S)
Educational opportunities limited; judged mentally inferior; opinion devalued; intellectual life stifled (P)	Better educational and training opportunities; opinions valued (S)
Single status stigmatized; stigma for divorce and unwed pregnancy (P)	Bachelorhood glamorized (R)
Socially and sexually restricted (P)	More freedom sexually and socially (R)
Must bear and rear children; responsible for birth control (O)	No babies (S)
Must maintain good outward appearance; dress, make-up (O)	Less fashion demand and emphasis on appearance (R)
Domestic work (O)	No domestic work (R)
Must be patient; give in; subordinate self; be unaggressive; wait to be asked out on dates (P)	Can be aggressive, dating and otherwise (O)
Inhibited motor control; not allowed to be athletic (P)	More escapism allowed (R)

* Letters enclosed in parentheses refer to a fourfold categorization of roles:
P = Proscription   R = Right
O = Obligation   S = Structural benefit

SOURCE: Chafetz (1974:57–58). Reproduced by permission of the publisher, F. E. Peacock Publishers, Inc., Itasca, Illinois.

idea that children's intellectual ability, as measured by various intelligence test (IQ) scores, is related to gender-role characteristics. Maccoby (1966) found that girls and boys who show elements of *both* traditional masculine and feminine gender-role traits score the highest on intellectual task performance. On the other hand, girls who fall mainly at the traditional feminine end of the continuum, where passivity and dependence are paramount, and boys who fall toward the masculine end, characterized by impulsivity and aggressiveness, do less well on intellectual performance tasks (see Figure 4.4). To the extent that such intellectual performance abilities generalize to the success one has in the world of work, it would appear that a combination of masculine and feminine gender-role characteristics will yield the greatest payoff for occupational pursuits in adulthood.

FIGURE 4.4.   Maccoby's Curvilinear Hypothesis of the Relationship Between Gender Roles and Intellectual Ability.

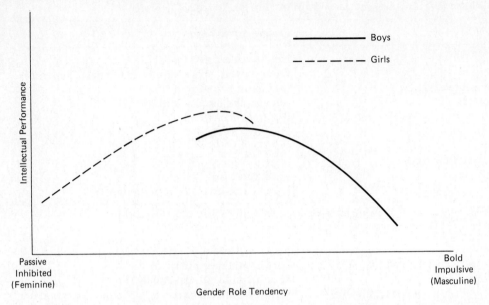

Nonetheless, gender-role stereotypes continue to be a potent force in limiting the ability of women to realize their potential in the world of work. It is true that a disproportionate number of males occupy the higher-prestige and higher-paying occupations in our society (see Table 4.5), although the proportion of women entering such professions as law, medicine, and business has been gradually increasing over the past several years. As also can be seen in Table 4.5, men continue to predominate in all of the professional occupations except those traditionally reserved for women, like nursing and health-related professions, teaching, and librarian work. The ratio of women to men in *all* professional occupations has increased only gradually. In terms of percentage change, women have shown increased movement into some of the more traditional male occupations. The total number of women relative to men in the labor force increased by 5.5 percent between 1972 and 1982, so any percentage increase over that number signals an increase in the number of women in that type of occupation. Significant increases of women in such traditionally male occupations as managers (espe-

cially in banks) and certain types of administrator, craft-worker, and in professional and clerical occupations, can also be seen.

We can conclude that, although we are seeing a trend toward equalization of occupational attainment over the years, the occupational system continues to be markedly differentiated according to sex, and along traditional gender-role lines. For example, women continue to predominate in virtually all clerical-secretarial and service-related jobs. Clearly, even when we look at the *most prestigious* and *highest paying* occupations in our society, women are rare. Presidents, vice-presidents, supreme court and other federal judges, senators, congressmen, financial executives, and religious leaders continue to be exclusively, or almost exclusively, males.

It is reasonable to suspect that women are excluded from these kinds of occupations because they lack the kinds of masculine traits believed to be conducive to competent job performance (being practical, logical, aggressive, ambitious), and have the more "harmful" feminine traits (being emotional, dependent, noncompetitive, easily

Gender-role stereotypes lead us to believe that men and women either do or do not possess certain traits and abilities regardless of whether or not they *actually* possess them. *(Photo by R. J. Hinkle.)*

intimidated). The concept of gender-role *stereotypes,* however, would suggest that women are excluded from such positions because others *perceive* them to possess such traits, regardless of whether or not they actually do. Furthermore, many women may perceive *themselves* along such stereotypical lines and, consequently, may not actively pursue the more prestigious occupations because they view themselves as unable to handle the responsibilities associated with them.

An interesting study by Rosen, Jerdee, and Prestwich (1975) supports the idea that gender-role stereotypes function as structural barriers to prevent women from moving into the more prestigious occupations traditionally reserved for men. These researchers surveyed a national sample of 1,517 male managers and executives drawn from a list of subscribers to a major business magazine. These managers and executives were presented with

five situations depicting an employee or potential employee who was in need of special consideration from the manager/executive.

1. *Travel:* The respondent was to evaluate an applicant for a job requiring extensive travel.

2. *Moving:* The respondent was asked to decide whether or not to make an effort to keep a valuable employee whose spouse was offered a position several hundred miles away, and who was giving serious consideration to moving.

3. *Promotion:* The respondent was asked to decide on the promotion request of an employee who views marriage and family life as having priority over work.

4. *Social Support:* The respondent was asked how to resolve a situation in which an employee's marriage

TABLE 4.5. *Percentage of Women in Selected Occupations: 1972 and 1982*

Occupation	1972	1982	Percent Change 1972–82[1]
Total Percent of Labor Force That Is Female	38	44	6
White-Collar Workers			
Professional, technical, and kindred workers	39	45	6
Accountants	22	39	17
Computer specialists	17	29	12
Engineers	1	6	5
Lawyers and judges	4	15	11
Librarians, archivists, and curators	82	81	−1
Life and physical scientists	10	21	11
Personnel and labor relations workers	31	50	19
Physicians, dentists, and related practitioners	9	15	6
Registered nurses, dietitians, and therapists	93	92	−1
Health technologists and technicians	70	73	3
Religious workers	11	14	3
Social scientists	21	38	17
Social and recreation workers	55	66	11
Teachers, college and university	28	35	7
Teachers, except college and university	70	71	1
Engineering and science technicians	9	18	9
Writers, artists, and entertainers	32	43	11
Managers and administrators, except farm	18	28	10
Bank officers and financial managers	19	37	18
Health administrators	47	51	4
Officials and administrators public administration, n.e.c.[2]	20	29	9
Restaurant, cafeteria, and bar managers	32	41	9
Sales managers	16	26	10
School Administrators	26	36	10
Sales workers	42	45	3
Insurance agents, brokers, and underwriters	12	26	14
Real estate agents and brokers	37	50	13
Sales clerks, retail trade	69	70	1
All other sales workers	13	19	6
Clerical and kindred workers	76	81	5
Bank tellers	88	92	4
Bookkeepers	88	92	4
Cashiers	87	87	0
Estimators and investigators, n.e.c.[2]	43	58	15
Office machine operators	71	75	4
Receptionists	97	98	1
Secretaries	99	99	0
Shipping and receiving clerks	15	25	10
Stock clerks and storekeepers	23	37	14
Telephone operators	97	92	−5
Typists	96	97	1

TABLE 4.5. (*continued*)

Occupation	1972	1982	Percent Change 1972–82[1]
Blue-Collar Workers			
Craft and kindred workers	4	7	3
Electricians	1	2	1
Blue-collar worker supervisors, n.e.c.[2]	0	1	1
Machinists and job setters	1	3	2
Metal craft workers, except mechanics, machinists, and job setters	2	4	2
Mechanics and repairers	1	3	2
Printing craft workers	15	28	13
Plumbers and pipefitters	0	1	1
Telephone installers and repairers	2	11	9
Operatives, except transport	39	41	2
Assemblers	47	54	7
Checkers, examiners, and inspectors, manufacturing	49	54	5
Garage workers and gas station attendants	5	5	0
Packers and wrappers, except meat and produce	61	61	0
Precision machine operatives	10	12	2
Sewers and stitchers	96	95	−1
Textile operatives	55	63	8
Welders and flame cutters	4	5	1
Transport equipment operatives	4	9	5
Bus drivers	34	47	13
Delivery and route workers	3	10	7
Taxi drivers	9	10	1
Truck drivers	1	2	1
Laborers, except farm	6	12	6
Construction laborers	1	3	2
Freight and material handlers	6	10	4
Gardeners and groundskeepers, except farm	2	5	3
Stockhandlers	17	25	8
Farm Workers			
Total	15	15	0
Farmers and farm managers	6	12	6
Farm laborers and supervisors	32	24	−8
Service Workers			
Service workers, except private household	57	59	2
Cleaning service workers	33	38	5
Food service workers	70	66	−4
Health service workers	87	90	3
Personal service workers	72	77	5
Protective service workers	6	11	5
(Firefighters, police, guards)			
Private household workers	98	97	−1

[1] Change computed on the basis of absolute numbers employed in that occupation; all percentages rounded to the nearest whole number.
[2] Not elsewhere classified.

SOURCE: *Statistical Abstract of the United States, 1984,* 104th Ed. Table 696, pp. 419–420, U.S. Bureau of the Census, Washington, D.C., 1983.

was in conflict because of the social requirements of the job (e.g., throwing business-related cocktail parties).

5. *Child Care:*   The respondent was asked to decide whether or not to grant a one month leave of absence to an employee who had urgent (though temporary) needs for care of his/her three children, and who would be impossible to replace for that one-month period of time.

In order to measure the extent to which these business managers and executives were influenced by gender-role stereotypes, the researchers varied the sex of the employee so that in half of the situations he was male and in half she was female. For example, half of the respondents evaluated a "leave of absence" request for a male employee named Ralph Brown, whereas the others evaluated an identical request from a female employee named Ruth Brown. The respondents were given no additional information which would cause them to view a male applicant any differently from the female applicant. The findings of this study demonstrated clearly the existence of gender-role stereotypes that discriminate against women. Rosen, et al. (1975:571) summarized their findings as follows for each of the five situations:

1. *Travel:*   When a married male applicant was considered for a Purchasing Manager position requiring extensive travel, evaluations were more favorable, and decisions to accept more frequent, than when the applicant was a married female.

2. *Moving:*   When the husband in a dual-career marriage had an opportunity to move for a better job, his wife, even though a highly valued employee, was expected to give up her own job for the sake of his career. On the other hand, when the roles were reversed, organizational intervention, in order to retain a valued male employee, was considered much more appropriate.

3. *Promotion:*   When a male candidate for promotion to Personnel Director made the statement, "My first duty is to my family," he was still evaluated favorably for the position. An equally qualified female candidate, who made the same statement, was evaluated much less favorably.

4. *Social Support:*   When a male junior executive's wife objected to attending business cocktail parties, the sentiment among managers was that she should stop making an issue of it and go to the parties. When the

roles were reversed, there was much less sentiment for the husband to sacrifice and to go to the parties.

5. *Child Care:*   When a male accountant requested a one-month's leave of absence in order to care for his three young children, the request was viewed less favorably than when a female made the same request.

Gender-role stereotypes held by such key individuals as executives and managers of major corporations would therefore appear to have more negative consequences for the occupational advancement of women than for men. Women in this study were *perceived* to have certain harmful traits, regardless of what traits they actually might possess.

Another line of research suggests that women also learn to view *themselves* according to gender-role stereotypes, and, as a result, hold back from actively pursuing occupations at the higher end of the prestige and pay scales. The concept of *learned helplessness* explains the reluctance of many women to explore domains outside of those traditionally reserved for women (Radloff, 1975; Seligman, 1974). Learned helplessness is an outcome of socializing women to be dependent, shy, and noncompetitive. Learned helplessness becomes a self-fulfilling prophecy: women do not assert themselves or aspire to the more challenging and responsibility-laden occupations because they have convinced themselves they are incapable of doing so. Their reluctance to act, then, only supports their belief that they are incapable, and they settle for less than their actual abilities would allow them to achieve.

Additional evidence of the negative effects of gender-role stereotypes on the individual development of women in the economic and occupational world is found when comparing the amount of income paid to men and women who have the same level of education (see Figure 4.5). In 1977, employed college-educated women aged 25 years and older earned only 61 percent of what their male counterparts earned, actually *dropping* 2 percentage points during the years between 1970 and 1977! Regardless of age and educational level, the evidence shows that women earn anywhere between 58 percent to 70 percent of what males earn. Not only do women earn significantly less at comparable educational levels, they also earn less than men who are working in the same or similar jobs (see Table 4.6). Note the remarkable consistency across the eleven years covered in this table. Several gains realized between 1970 through 1975 were lost by 1981, as was

FIGURE 4.5.   Female-to-Male Income Ratio for Year-Round, Full-Time Workers, by Age and Years of School
Completed: 1970 and 1977.

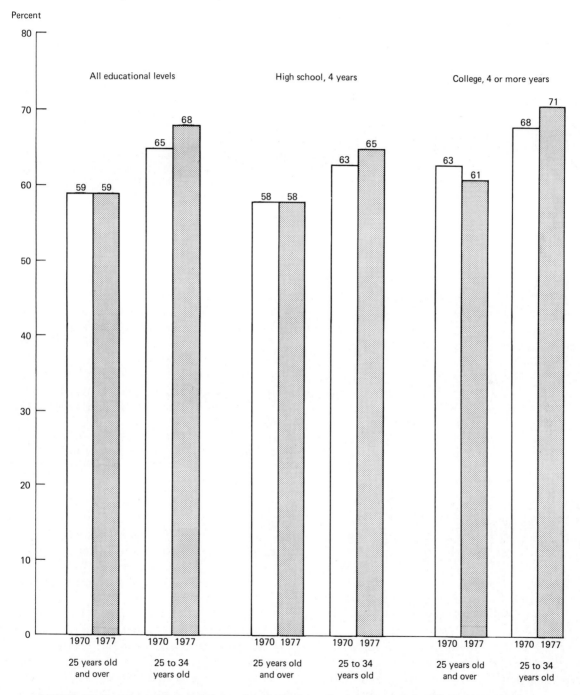

SOURCE: U.S. Department of Commerce, Bureau of the Census, *Current Population Reports,* Series P-60, Nos. 118 and 80.

TABLE 4.6. *Ratio of Female to Male Earnings for Selected Occupational Categories:*
1970, 1975, and 1981

	1970	*1975*	*1981*
Total	0.59	0.60	0.59
Professional, technical, and kindred workers	0.64	0.67	0.64
Managers and administrators, except farm	0.55	0.58	0.58
Sales workers	0.43	0.39	0.50
Clerical and kindred workers	0.64	0.63	0.62
Craft and kindred workers	0.54	0.58	0.64
Operatives, including transport	0.58	0.57	0.61
Laborers except farm	0.68	0.77	0.71
Service workers, except private household	0.56	0.57	0.59

SOURCES: *Current Population Reports,* Special Studies, Series P-23, No. 100, p. 76; U.S. Department of Commerce, Bureau of the Census, February 1980.
Statistical Abstract of the United States, 1984, 104th Ed. Table 715, p. 434, U.S. Bureau of the Census, Washington, D.C., 1983.

the case for "professional workers" and "laborers." All told, women continue to earn between one-half and two-thirds of what men earn for equal work, despite the trend toward the equalization of occupational involvement and the increased awareness of equality of the sexes that evolved in the 1960s and 1970s.

The Politics of Gender Roles.   The differential treatment of the sexes in the occupational world is tied closely to the beliefs of both men and women in our society: masculine gender-role characteristics are more valuable and desirable than female characteristics. These perceptions of gender roles place definite limitations on the individual developmental potential of women in the occupational market place, whether one is referring to the attainment of higher prestige and higher income occupations, or the earning of "equal pay for equal work." Moreover, we have seen that gender-role stereotypes may also have undesirable consequences for the development of men in adulthood.

The different treatment of the sexes on the basis of stereotyped gender roles is pervasive in most aspects of adult life. It is evident in the legal system and in the religious and educational institutions, in the military, and in family relationships. As a result of discrimination based on gender-role stereotypes, a move to amend the Constitution of the United States was begun in the 1970s, in order to put an end to discrimination against people sim-

ply because they happened to be of one sex or the other. Known as the Equal Rights Amendment to the Constitution (ERA), this law would "end the legal support behind traditional sex roles" (Cox, 1978:47). The proposed ERA read as follows:

The Proposed Federal Equal Rights Amendment

Section 1:   Equality of rights under the law shall not be denied or abridged by the United States or by any State on account of sex.
Section 2:   The Congress shall have the power to enforce, by appropriate legislation, the provisions of the article.
Section 3:   This amendment shall take effect two years after the date of ratification.

In effect, the ERA would provide the equitable treatment of both sexes in regard to military service (including the military draft); the criminal justice system; rights and privileges associated with marriage, child custody, child support, and alimony in cases of divorce; and in any federally funded program designed to enhance the occupational skills of individuals.

This idea sounds simple and, on the surface, eminently fair. However, the ERA did not survive. Although 35 of the necessary 38 states ratified the proposed ERA well within the seven-year limit allowed for ratifying amendments to the U.S. Constitution, the time limit expired without any more states voting to ratify. In the late 1970s and early 1980s, a powerful group opposed to the

ERA lobbied in state legislatures to influence them to vote against the ERA. This group was not only successful in blocking the ratification of the amendment in the three additional states needed to ratify, but they played another major role: three state legislatures, which had already passed the ERA, voted to *rescind* the previous ratifications. Meanwhile, a three-year extension of the time period allowed for ratification was granted so that ERA backers could have until March of 1982 to muster the necessary ratifying votes. This deadline too passed without ratification of the ERA, and the proposal died as a result.

It is not entirely clear what the major objection to the ERA is among those attempting to block its passage. Some say that the ERA would wipe out all differences between the sexes, provide a mechanism for requiring unisex bathrooms, and violate the sanctity of marriage and home life. Related to this latter concern is the firm belief that the federal government has no right to interfere in the personal and private relationships of members of the opposite sex, as granted in Section 2 of the ERA, especially when the *potential* exists for carrying the ERA to its extreme by dictating to men and women in families how they can and should run their lives. Other objections to the ERA have strong religious overtones; some view the granting of equal rights and obligations to the sexes as being in violation of Biblical teachings regarding the nature of relationships between men and women. Indeed, the debate over the ERA had become quite heated and, at times, hostile. Regardless of the true reasons, if those who support the ERA are to see it ratified as an amendment to the U.S. Constitution, they must begin all over again, by introducing new legislation in the U.S. Congress.

PROMOTING OR BREAKING GENDER-ROLE STEREOTYPES: TWO EXAMPLES

The Total Woman. Gender-role stereotypes are nurtured in many ways. One of the more explicit attempts to cement traditional gender-role conceptions is a book published in 1973 by Marabel Morgan, *The Total Woman*. After experiencing considerable conflict and lack of fulfillment in her own marriage, Morgan was motivated to write about her strategy for rekindling the flame that had apparently been smothered in her relationship with her husband. Essentially, her book turned out to be a

gender-role manual for women who, like Morgan, needed assistance in rejuvenating marriages turned sour.

Morgan believed that the tone of the marriage relationship is in control of the woman, who has the "power to lift her family spirit or bring it down to rock bottom. The atmosphere in the home is set by the woman (36)." Clearly, the wife's place is in the home, caring for the children, keeping the house in order, and catering to the needs and desires of her husband. According to Morgan, when the romance and fulfillment of marriage dissipate over time, it is usually the woman who has failed in some way to adequately care for the home, or adapt and adjust to the needs of her husband. For example, the breakdown in communication, the increased frequency of arguments and quarrels, and the loss of sexual attraction of the husband for the wife are the result of any one of, or a combination of, the following deficiencies on the part of the wife:

1. She is unable to organize and budget her time efficiently, so the husband comes home from work to a home that is messy or unclean.

2. She nags her husband too much by asking him to do chores around the house, requesting that he communicate with her more frequently and more openly, giving him unsolicited advice, or criticizing him in private or in public.

3. She fails to accept her husband "exactly as he is," and errs by trying to change those qualities that she does not like.

4. She fails to express admiration for her husband to him, which is an important oversight because males have a "natural" need to be "worshipped and admired," both in mind and body.

5. She fails to adapt to him by challenging his God-given power and authority in the home:

> The biblical remedy for marital conflict is stated, "you wives must submit to your husband's" leadership in the same way you submit to the Lord. God planned for woman to be under her husband's rule . . . Unless the wife adapts to his way of life, there's no way to avoid the conflict that is certain to occur . . . God ordained man to be the head of the family, its president, and his wife to be the executive vice-president. Every organization has a leader and the family unit is no exception. (Morgan, 1973:80–82)

When conflict is present, then, it is the the result of the wife's failing to yield to the power of her husband, her "King." She simply has no right to challenge his authority.

6. The wife fails to sufficiently express to her husband her appreciation of him, and does not truly show her gratitude.

7. The wife fails to keep herself sexually attractive to her husband, both in terms of her physique and dress.

8. The wife's attitude toward sexual intercourse is too negative, and she fails to do all she can to be sexually appealing in any way necessary to please her husband.

Morgan states that women who have let their marriages fall apart by allowing these problems to develop can "instantly" reverse this trend toward conflict and unhappiness by completing specific tasks, or "assignments." Following are some examples of what women can do to rekindle their husband's lost love and affection (Morgan, 1973:106–107, 163–171).

1. Accept your husband just as he is. Write out two lists—one of his faults and one of his virtues. Take a long, hard look at his faults and then throw the list away; don't ever dwell on them again. Only think about his virtues. Carry that list with you and refer to it when you are mad, sad, or glad.
2. Admire your husband every day. Refer to his virtue list if you need a place to start. Say something nice about his body today. Put his tattered ego back together with compliments.
3. Adapt to his way of life. Accept his friends, food, and life-style as your own. Ask him to write the six most important changes he'd like to see take place at your house. Read the list in private, react in private, and then set out to accomplish these changes with a smile. Be a "Yes, let's!" woman some time of every day.
4. Appreciate all he does for you. Sincerely tell him "Thank you" with your attitudes, action, and words. Give him your undivided attention, and try not to make any telephone calls after he comes home, especially after 8:00 P.M.
5. Be an atmosphere adjuster in the morning. Set the tone for love. Be pleasant to look at, be with, and talk to. Walk your husband to the car each morning and wave until he's out of sight.
6. Once this week call him at work an hour before quitting time to say, "I wanted you to know that I just crave your body!" or some other appropriate tender term. Then take your bubble bath shortly before he comes home.
7. Thrill him at the front door in your costume. A frilly new nighty and heels will probably do the trick as a starter. Variety is the spice of sex.
8. Be prepared mentally and physically for intercourse every night this week. Be sure your attitude matches your costume. Be the seducer, rather than the seduced.
9. In order to re-open closed lines of communication, follow these instructions: (a) be a good listener; (b) don't give your husband unsolicited advice; (c) don't criticize your husband or put him down; (d) understand your husbands' frame of reference; (e) be sensitive to your husband's moods; and (f) be interested in his interests.

It is obvious, from these instructions, that the Total Woman is one who cares for the home, children, and husband. She makes every effort to assume traditional feminine-gender roles. According to Morgan's philosophy, marriages suffer because the wife has violated one or more of these gender role "rules," and the burden is upon her to correct the situation. The husband bears no responsibility for such marital problems. It is the wife who must change by moving toward the feminine extreme of the gender-role continuum to restore the marital relationship to health. It is the woman who must change in order to adapt to the partner, with no expectation of reciprocity on the part of the husband. His primary roles are to earn the money and make decisions, and the Total Woman is simply repaying him for those investments of himself.

Morgan's philosophy of solving marital problems has worked for some. However, it may come at a great cost to the woman. She must sacrifice certain aspects of her own personal development, such as a career or an independent identity, if she follows this plan of gender-role change. Moreover, for some couples, such a gender-role pattern may lead to individual stagnation and increased problems for a marital relationship, depending upon their particular role expectations and situation. For example, husbands who want their wives to be companions and full partners in decision-making and leadership in the family are likely to object to a Total Woman in the house. In addition, wives who embrace the Total Woman concept, but regret the personal sacrifices made in order to do so, may be causing more problems than were solved by their becoming more traditional in gender-role orientation.

The Inexpressive Male. With the concept of the *Total Woman*, Marabel Morgan sought to *promote* feminine-masculine gender-role stereotypes. Another stereotype, which several have tried to change, is known as the

Inexpressive Male. The *Inexpressive Male* syndrome is viewed as limiting the potential for development among adult males as well as their female partners.

According to Balswick and Peek (1971), who took the first critical look at this concept, males in our culture are taught to avoid expressing their emotions, feelings, fears, thoughts, and other personal aspects of themselves.

> In learning to be a man, the boy in American society comes to value expressions of masculinity and devalue expressions of femininity. Masculinity is expressed largely through physical courage, toughness, competitiveness, and aggressiveness, whereas femininity is, in contrast, expressed largely through gentleness, expressiveness, and responsiveness. When a young boy begins to express his emotions through crying, his parents are quick to assert, "You're a big boy and big boys don't cry . . ." What parents are really telling their son is that a real man does not show his emotions, and if he is a real man he will not allow his emotions to be expressed. These outward expressions of emotions are viewed as a sign of femininity, and undesirable for a male. (Balswick and Peek, 1971:364)

There are two basic types of Inexpressive Males: the *cowboy type* and the *playboy type.* The cowboy type is based on the stereotype portrayed in the Hollywood movies, in which the male is a "strong, silent, two-fisted" type who does not show tenderness or any sort of emotions to women because it would be incompatible with his masculine image. Although he may have feelings for "his woman," the contemporary cowboy type male does not express them because it would be a sign of weakness.

> As the cowboy equally loved his girlfriend and his horse, so the present day American male loves his car or motorcycle and his girlfriend. (Balswick and Peek, 1971:364)

The *playboy type* of Inexpressive Males is portrayed in Hollywood films by the James Bond character. He is similar to the cowboy type in that he interacts with women by remaining emotionally detached and "playing it cool." Unlike the cowboy, however, the playboy really has no internal feelings to hide. He is a person who is emotionally "dead inside," who views women as "consumer commodities" to be "manipulated and exploited." The playboy type, then, is not only inexpressive, but also nonfeeling.

The concern over the Inexpressive Male centers upon the potentially harmful consequences for a long-term relationship such as marriage. Balswick and Peek (1971:365) noted that American society has become "increasingly

mechanized and depersonalized" (see chapter 1). As a result, primary-group relationships are handled mainly in marriage and the family, and the burden of supplying the intimacy necessary to meet individual needs for companionship and affection has become a major task of the marriage and family institutions. To the extent that males today are unable to express their feelings, emotions, and fears, the ability of modern marriage to meet the intimacy and companionship needs of adult members is seriously threatened.

> When the inexpressive male marries, his inexpressiveness can become highly dysfunctional to his marital relationship . . . When the husband and wife no longer find affection and companionship from their marriage relationship (due to the husband's inability or unwillingness to express his feelings and emotions), they most likely question the wisdom of attempting to continue in their conjugal relationship. When affection is gone, the main reason for the marriage relationship disappears. (Balswick and Peek, 1971:365)

Research on communication in marriage has tended to substantiate the claim that males are significantly more inexpressive than females, and that such inexpressiveness often inhibits the ability of married couples to function effectively and experience a satisfactory level of mutual fulfillment and gratification (Rubin, 1976; Komarovsky, 1962; Rainwater, 1960; Derlega and Chaikin, 1975; Jourard, 1971). Male inexpressiveness is also related to gender-role stereotypes that have been learned in childhood and adulthood (Balswick and Averett, 1977; Balswick, 1979). For partners in intimate relationships who value the open exchange of feelings and emotions in order to meet each other's needs for warmth, intimacy, companionship, and love, male inexpressiveness is one aspect of gender-role stereotypes that seriously impairs their efforts to realize the fulfillment of these needs (Balswick, 1980; Scanzoni, 1979).

TOWARD ANDROGYNY?

In strict biological terms, *androgyny* refers to the "condition of showing some male and female characteristics in body build" (Money and Ehrhardt, 1972:280). However, social scientists have broadened this concept to denote freedom from the burdens and rigidity imposed by traditional gender-role stereotypes, allowing people of both sexes to "feel free to express the best traits of both men and women" (Bem, 1977:165). As Bem (1977:165–166) notes further, *androgynous* people should be "more flexible in meeting new situations, and less restricted in what they can do and how they can express themselves." Bem (1974:161–162) questions the belief that traditional gender-role stereotypes are conducive to healthy psychological functioning, and challenged the

traditional assumption that it is the sex-typed individual who typifies mental health and to begin focusing on the behavioral and societal consequences of more flexible sex-role self-concepts. In a society where rigid sex-role differentiation has already outlived its utility, perhaps the androgynous person will come to define a more human standard of psychological health.

The most important feature of androgyny is that masculinity and femininity are not mutually exclusive dimensions. Being more masculine does not have to be associated with being less feminine, and vice veresa (Bem, 1974). Masculinity and femininity can more reasonably be viewed as *independent* dimensions of gender roles (Constantinople, 1973). The relevant question, then, is not, "How masculine *or* feminine are you?" Rather, the question is, "How masculine *and* feminine are you?" The idea that gender roles are independent dimensions is graphically illustrated in Figure 4.6. Individuals who possess significant levels of *both* masculine and feminine gender-role characteristics are considered androgynous (Spence, Helmreich, and Stapp, 1975). These individuals have behavioral abilities which are adaptable to a given situation. They can draw upon either masculine or feminine qualities, whichever is the most conducive to reaching their goals. Perhaps this is why Maccoby (1966) found that the highest levels of intellectual performance were evident among children who demonstrated both masculine and feminine traits.

Indeed, a considerable number of research studies have shown that androgyny has advantages over traditional gender roles when it comes to adult development and day-to-day functioning. Independence and gentleness, leadership and compassion, and assertiveness and cheerfulness represent combinations of stereotypically masculine and feminine traits that enhance adult development by providing the individual with an expanded behavioral repertoire to meet the diverse and complex situations posed by our modern *Gesellschaft* type of society (Hirsch, 1974; Hobson, Skeen, and Robinson, 1980; Naffziger and Naffziger, 1974). Traditional gender-role

FIGURE 4.6.   Androgyny as a Combination of Masculinity and Femininity.

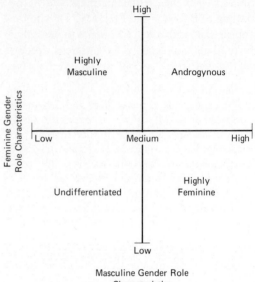

stereotypes impose unnecessary restrictions on the behavior of men and women, discouraging men to enter the more "gentle" world of "women's work" and women to enter the more "assertive man's world." Androgynous people do not view such behavior as inappropriate for their sex.

They are not limited by labels. They are able to do whatever they want, both in behavior and in their feelings. (Bem, 1977:166)

Bem's (1976, 1977) studies comparing androgynous men and women to highly feminine women and masculine men found that the androgynous were more flexible and better able to cope with the different kinds of situations one is likely to encounter day-to-day in the workplace, as well as in more intimate relationships with marriage partners, family members, or other loved ones. She found the following:

1. Highly feminine women display far less independence of judgment, less assertiveness, and are more likely to conform to group norms than either masculine or androgynous people.

2. Highly masculine men demonstrate less helpful behavior, less sympathy, and lower responsiveness in relation to the needs of others.

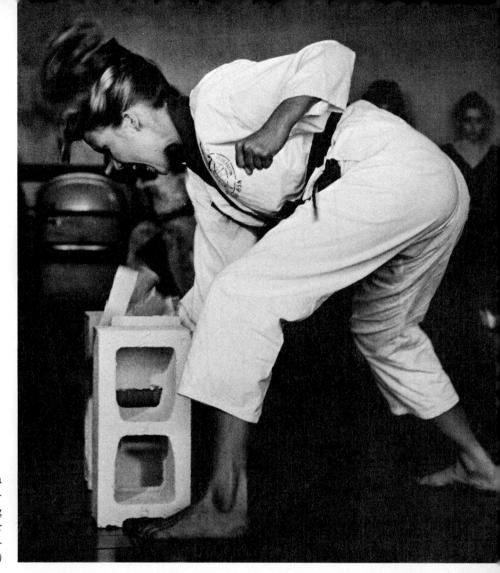

Androgynous people possess a combination of desirable masculine and feminine traits, leading to greater flexibility in behavior across different types of situations. *(Photo by Mark Rogers.)*

3. Whereas highly masculine men respond well in situations requiring assertiveness or independence of judgment, they do not respond well in situations requiring warmth, responsiveness, and sensitivity to the needs of others; highly feminine women, on the other hand, performed poorly in the former and well in the latter types of situations. Androgynous persons of both sexes performed well across all situations, being "independent and assertive when they needed to be, and warm and responsive in appropriate situations."

Androgyny therefore appears to have many benefits for personal development and for the development of intimate relationships, such as marriage. But how androg-

ynous are we as a culture, and how likely is it that we will move toward greater androgyny in gender roles in the future? Let us now take a closer look at these questions.

Traditional Gender Roles: Change or Stability?

Given the limitations imposed by traditional gender-role stereotypes on individual development, as well as the adverse consequences they can have for the development of intimate relationships between men and women, it is important to examine the potential for change in traditional gender roles that might exist today. There is no doubt that revolutionary changes in gender roles of women have taken place in the past two decades (Cherlin and Walters, 1981). The trend is away from traditional views of women's roles and toward male-female equality. These changes toward gender-role equality have, however, been more pronounced in regard to feminist issues and the economic, political, and legal status of women. Gender-role preferences in marriage, family relationships, and general behavioral expectations of men and women continue to remain relatively traditional, as you will see in Table 4.3 (Osmond and Martin, 1975; Parelius, 1975; Roper and Labeff, 1977). Traditional gender-role preferences are even prevalent on college campuses, where one might expect to find less gender-role stereotyping, and traditional role preferences are found in generations of both older and younger adults (Bayer, 1975; Albrecht, Bahr, and Chadwick, 1979). Despite the major trends away from traditional gender roles over the past several years, this evidence suggests that it may take several generations of rather slow-paced social change if traditional gender-role stereotypes are to be removed in favor of equalitarian and flexible views of male and female roles.

CAN GENDER ROLES BE CHANGED? THE ISRAELI EXPERIENCE

Given that an individual's gender role-identity and behavior are shaped by cultural forces as well as heredity, we might expect that people would be able to alter their cluster of gender roles in order to better meet their goals and objectives as adult members of society. However, gender roles become internalized early in life, as early as three years old (Kagan, 1964). They become quite deeply ingrained over the years as one is socialized by family members (parents and siblings), peers, and the mass media. Indeed, research has shown how difficult it is to alter gender-role clusters among adults, particularly if those attempting to change are not fully committed to doing so.

The best example we have of an attempt to change the structure of traditional gender roles on a large-scale basis is that of the Israeli *kibbutz*. The *kibbutzim* began early in this century as small agricultural collectives that

were designed to obtain equal work participation from all their members, as well as equal distribution of food, clothing, housing, and money, all available as a result of the collective efforts of the entire community. A major part of this highly socialistic system was the equalization of men and women by means of eradicating traditional gender-role stereotypes. Such stereotypes were viewed as competing with the ideology of equality. These stereotypes would also interfere with the needs of the *kibbutz* for equal work contributions of *all* members, in order to survive as a self-contained unit. Thus, every effort was made to remove the traditional sources of gender-role stereotypes from the society. In order to foster gender-role equality, for example, nurseries were constructed, and children were removed from their parents' home at an early age (usually by one or two years of age), allowing women to work and not be burdened by the nurturant and caretaking roles traditionally ascribed to women with infants and young children. In addition, every attempt was made to socialize the children in nonstereotypical ways in the nurseries so that future generations of *kibbutz* residents would develop with androgynous rather than stereotyped gender-role identities and behavioral patterns.

Contrary to this plan, however, research has shown that *kibbutz* residents have resisted the movement away from gender-role stereotypes (Spiro, 1956; Talmon-Garbor, 1959). If anything, gender-role differentiation seems to have increased in the *kibbutz* in recent years (Schlesinger, 1977). Many women have moved out of the fields and factories back to more traditional housekeeping roles or female occupations where nurturance and caretaking are required—such as teaching in the nurseries, kitchen chores, child care, nursing, taking care of clothing needs, and other traditionally feminine household chores. What happened to the plan for gender-role equality?

Although researchers have been unable to provide any definitive answers, the evidence suggests that a combination of factors might be involved. First, in simple agricultural types of economies which demand considerable amounts of hard physical labor, men are typically socialized throughout life to assume the responsibility for the tasks requiring physical strength (Barry, Bacon, and Child, 1957). Women in the *kibbutz* found much of the traditional males' work to be more strenuous than they were willing to accept, and they tended to settle in occupations that were viewed as more compatible with their feminine gender-role identities. Second, gender-role socialization is a powerful process. Gender roles are deeply rooted, and efforts to impose change from outside the individual are likely to meet stiff resistance if people lack total commitment and motivation to change. Although some in the *kibbutz* had that level of commitment, many others did not. Finally, even self-contained agricultural collectives such as the *kibbutz* are not totally isolated from the broader society. So long as traditional gender-role stereotypes are depicted as desirable by others, these values and expectations will find their way into subcultural units such as the *kibbutz*.

Making Your Own Decisions about Gender Roles

The major purpose of this chapter has been to illustrate the wide spectrum of possible gender-role clusters—from the highly masculine to the highly feminine, to the androgynous, or anywhere along a continuum between these extremes. Our knowledge about the diverse range of gender-role possibilities leads to the following summary points that the reader may find useful in making decisions affecting his or her future as an adult member of society and as a partner in marriage.

1. Behavioral and psychological differences between males and females are learned, and this learning process is closely related to genetic differences between the sexes.

2. Gender roles are deeply ingrained and can only be changed when a person is highly motivated to do so.

3. There is no intrinsically "best" gender role arrangement; that is, the value of one's gender-role identity and behavior can only be measured according to a person's goals, aspirations, and needs at any given time in relation to one's own development and the development of an intimate relationship with a person of the opposite sex.

4. Androgynous gender roles are compatible with the demands of our contemporary *Gesellschaft*-type of society, where both men and women are expected to engage in instrumental and expressive types of activities on the job, in marriage, and in the family. For many men and women, androgyny allows flexibility to adapt to and cope with the multiple and complex demands of contemporary society.

Summary

Gender roles are an important feature of relationships between people, both within and outside of marriage and the family. In this chapter we detailed several possible types of gender-role perceptions, and identified some of the economic, social, and political consequences of various types of gender-role perceptions for the development of the individual. Gender-role stereotypes influence people to react to others, and to perceive themselves in masculine or feminine terms, solely on the basis of their biological sex and regardless of their actual characteristics. Because gender roles are primarily learned in a particular social and cultural milieu, however, there exists the possibility for changing them if they do not appear to meet one's personal needs, goals, and expectations at a given time. However, gender roles and role stereotypes are internalized quite strongly and are resistant to attempts to change. If change in gender roles is to occur, a minimum requirement would be that the person be highly motivated and committed to change. The concept of *androgyny* was introduced to illustrate that people of either sex can possess desirable characteristics that would be considered traditionally feminine or masculine. Combining masculine and feminine traits may facilitate psychologically and socially healthy adult development, because the individual would then be equipped with a behavioral repertoire capable of meeting the demands of a variety of situations. It is also important to understand that no single cluster of gender roles is intrinsically *better* or *best* in relation to any other cluster of gender roles. The value of any specific person's gender-role cluster depends upon several factors, including that person's priorities, needs, goals, and expectations at the moment, as well as any expectations, needs, or goals of his or her partner in an intimate relationship. For example, although an androgynous female may enjoy a high degree of personal development in adulthood, as a result of possessing both masculine and feminine characteristics, that same cluster of gender roles might not provide the best fit with those of her highly masculine fiance or husband who would prefer a more traditional gender-role arrangement. A result of this misfit of gender-role clusters may be considerable conflict, disagreement, or perhaps even dissolution of the intimate relationship. We will return to this issue—the consequences of various *combinations* of gender roles in the development of intimate *relationships*—in chapter 9, when the premarital stage of development in marriage is discussed.

Questions for Discussion and Review

1. Think of your parents' marriage and the type of gender-role patterns you have observed in their relationship. How are their gender roles the same as or different from the gender-role patterns you expect to have in your marriage?

2. Re-read the list of gender-role attitudes presented in Table 4.3. Write down whether you agree or disagree with each one. Based on your answers, determine those areas in which you are traditional, those in which you are more egalitarian ("modern"), and those for which you are in between these two extremes. How do your gender-role attitudes correspond to those of your best friends? To those of someone in an intimate relationship with you?

3. Identify and discuss ways that traditional gender-role stereotypes are promoted in our society. Consider such influences as movies; television shows and commercials; schools, colleges, and universities; employers. Also think of ways in which one or more of these influences has recently presented less traditional gender-role behaviors.

4. Discuss the concepts of the Total Woman and the Inexpressive Male, which were presented in this chapter. What evidence of each of these have you seen among people you know? What consequences have these kinds of behaviors had for relationships in which these people are involved?

5. What are your views about a Constitutional amendment, such as the ERA, which would remove legal bases for sex discrimination? If such an amendment is unacceptable, what might be a more acceptable alternative for eliminating discrimination on the basis of sex?

6. Recently, the United States Supreme Court ordered insurance companies to make monthly payments to surviving female spouses (widows) that are equal to payments to surviving males (widowers), despite the fact that women live, on the average, six to seven years longer than men. This may have created a situation of equality, but it also has forced insurance companies to raise their rates in order to compensate for the higher monthly payments to widows. Is this fair?

7. Are there any jobs or occupations that should not be assumed by women? by men? Explain your answer.

8. What are the benefits and rewards of being female in our society? What are the disadvantages and problems? What are the benefits and rewards of being male in our society? What are the disadvantages and problems of being male?

Notes

1. This section is based largely on the work of Longstreth (1974), Money and Ehrhardt (1972), and Witters and Jones-Witters (1980).

2. It must be pointed out that the overall level of male and female satisfaction with traditional gender roles cannot be determined from Table 4.4, because only half of the picture is presented. What this table does not show are females' perceptions of the *advantages* of traditional feminine roles and the *disadvantages* of traditional male-gender roles. Also, we do not know what males' perceptions are regarding the *advantages* of traditional masculine-gender roles, and the *disadvantages* they see in regard to traditional feminine roles.

Human Sexuality

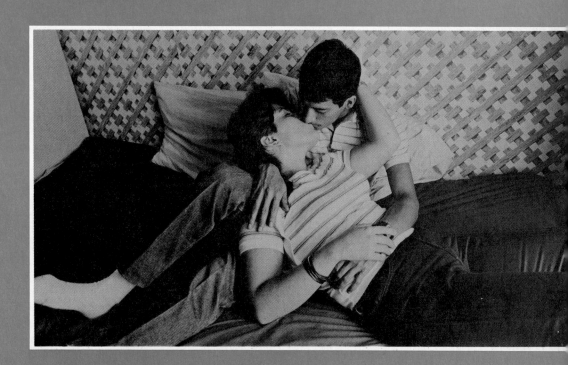

may i feel said he

e. e. cummings

may i feel said he
(i'll squeal said she
just once said he)
it's fun said she

(may i touch said he
how much said she
a lot said he)
why not said she

(let's go said he
not too far said she
what's too far said he
where you are said she)

may i stay said he
(which way said she
like this said he
if you kiss said she

may i move said he
is it love said she)
if you're willing said he
(but you're killing said she

but it's life said he
but your wife said she
now said he,
ow said she

(tiptop said he
don't stop said she
oh no said he)
go slow said she

(cccome? said he
ummm said she,
you're divine! said he
(you are Mine said she)

Marriage functions as a socially approved context for the satisfaction of human sexual needs. Throughout history, societies the world over have recognized the powerful nature of the human sexual drive. All known cultures have instituted some sort of mechanism for defining, controlling, and regulating the legitimate means by which sexual needs can be satisfied. Typically, human sexual behavior has been closely associated with pregnancy and childbearing, which are viewed as necessary for a society to replenish its population and to survive as a viable unit of social organization. The interpersonal commitment and stability implied by marriage have served to legitimate childbearing by ensuring, as much as possible, that any children born of the union receive the emotional and physical support of two parents. It follows, then, that human sexual behavior also has been granted legitimacy in a context of commitment and stability such as that provided by marriage.

However, modern *Gesellschaft* society has departed from these historical precedents that have regulated sexual behavior by defining marriage as the only legitimate context for sexual intercourse. Social norms prohibiting sexual intercourse before marriage, sexual relations with others outside the boundaries of marriage, and any sort of homosexual relations among men or women have weakened considerably. In the last two decades in the United States there have been significant increases in the proportion of young people who have had *premarital* sexual intercourse at least once. Many of these individuals have experienced several episodes of sexual intercourse, either in an ongoing sexual relationship with one partner, or in relationships with two or more partners. In fact, there are more men and women today who enter their first marriages having had sexual intercourse (nonvirgins) than there are those who enter marriage without previous sexual experience (virgins) [see chapter 9]. The frequency of *extramarital* sexual relationships has also increased. The increasing divorce rate has resulted in a growing number of individuals who are sexually active *between* first and later marriages, yielding yet another group of people who seek satisfaction of sexual needs outside of a marital context.

All in all, although marriage continues to be a major context within which sexual interaction between men and women takes place, societal *norms* that traditionally placed a taboo on premarital and extramarital sex have become more relaxed and permissive over the past several years. Sexual *behavior* patterns have also become more liberal in regard to the context in which sexual intercourse actually takes place.

There is, however, more to human sexuality than physical contacts between people. Also important to note are the *social* aspects of human sexual behavior. The probability that a given individual will participate in sexual relationships in one context or another is influenced by prevailing norms and values of the culture at any given time. Also, the very way one expresses his or her sexuality in seeking to give and receive sexual gratification is *learned role behavior,* shaped by the experiences one has had in growing up, and by the people from whom one has learned to behave and relate to in sexually intimate ways. Parents and other family members play a key role in

shaping one's definitions and expectations relating to sexuality. Ours is also a society where sex has become a cultural theme—commercialized, and used as a vehicle for profit-making among entrepreneurs. Sex sells toothpaste, cars, mouthwash, shaving cream, liquor, and perfume. Sexual themes, both explicit and implicit, and sexual scenes are now common on the television and movie screens, playing a major role in soap operas, dramatic productions, and situation comedies—available for all to watch, both young and old. We are continually bombarded by sexual messages on billboards and through the mass media channels, as sexually explicit magazines and books have assumed a legitimate position in the casual reading available to the consumer. These, too, are sources of sexual learning that are inescapable in a society which has become increasingly sex-oriented. Clearly, human sexuality is a complex phenomenon shaped by a powerful combination of biological, psychological, and social forces.

Human Sexual Anatomy

In chapter 4 we discussed the remarkable similarities that exist between male and female sexual anatomy in the embryonic stages of human development. Even after full sexual differentiation takes place, there remain significant similarities between male and female sexual structures, such that some of the components of the anatomy of one sex have counterparts in the anatomy of the other. Bearing these similarities in mind, let us examine the distinctive features of female and male sexual anatomy which emerge in adolescence and into adulthood. These features give human sexuality a quality that is unique in relation to the sexuality of other animal species.

SEXUAL AND REPRODUCTIVE ANATOMY OF THE FEMALE

The internal sex-related organs of the female are depicted in Figure 5.1, and a view of the external sexual organs is depicted in Figure 5.2. The development of the internal sex organs and external genitalia occurs as a result of the *XX* chromosome combination that was formed at the time of conception. As she matures in adolescence, usually between the ages of 9 and 15, the sex organs reach

FIGURE 5.1.   Front and Side Views of Internal Sexual Anatomy of the Female.

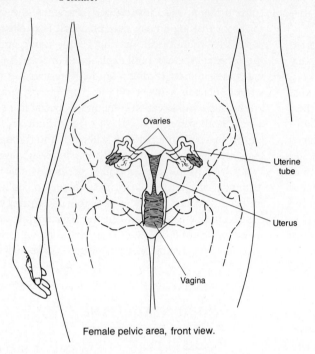

Female pelvic area, front view.

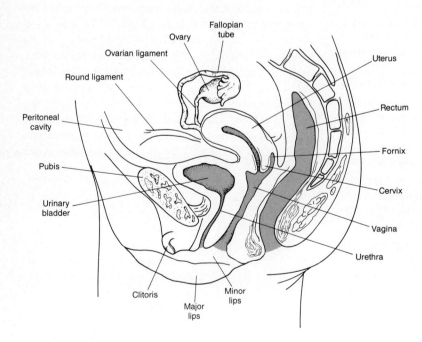

Female pelvic area, side view.

FIGURE 5.2. External Genitalia of the Female.

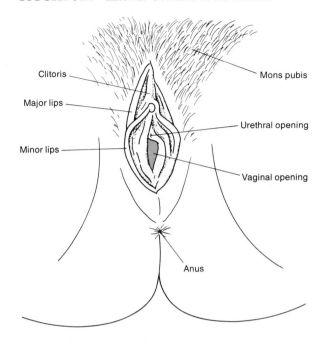

Clitoris

Major lips

Minor lips

Mons pubis

Urethral opening

Vaginal opening

Anus

their full growth potential as particular combinations of hormones are released during the process of *puberty*. The *hypothalamus*, which is located at the base of the brain, increases its activity during pubescence by stimulating the *pituitary gland* to release *gonadotrophic hormones*. This activity causes the release of the female hormone *estrogen*, which eventually becomes regularly released on approximately a monthly cyclical schedule. In combination with other hormones that are released at puberty, some of which lead to a rather dramatic growth spurt during adolescence, the sex hormones influence the growth and development of such secondary sex characteristics as pubic hair, broadening of the pelvic region, and the breasts. The primary sex characteristics of the female have been present from birth, such as the *uterus, Fallopian tubes, vagina,* and *vulva*, but are given final adult size and form during the process of pubescence. But there is perhaps no puberty-related change which is a stronger sign of movement toward adult sexuality than *menarche*, or the onset of *menstruation*. Menarche is a clear signal that *ovulation*, or release of mature eggs for potential fertilization by the male sperm cell, is about to begin — usually within one year from the first menstrual period.

Internal Sex Organs. In regard to the internal sexual organs of the female (see Figure 5.1), it is important to note the interrelatedness of the *ovaries, Fallopian tubes* (also known as *oviducts* or *uterine tube*), *uterus, cervix,* and *vagina*. At birth, the human female possesses sex organs known as *ovaries,* one attached to each side of the pelvic wall by ligaments. The ovaries contain follicles that lie dormant until pubescence. As the process of puberty gets underway, the pituitary gland releases a follicle-stimulating hormone, known as FSH. Every month, FSH causes at least one follicle to develop the egg cell it contains into a mature egg, or *ovum*, which is released into the *Fallopian tube* through long, finger-like projections known as *fimbria*. The ovaries usually alternate from month-to-month as to which one will release the mature egg. In actuality, then, the female is equipped with her life supply of *ova* at birth, and she is likely to release anywhere from 400 to 500 mature eggs over the course of her lifetime. Because the egg is released on roughly a monthly schedule, the process known as *ovulation,* the female is capable of becoming impregnated if the egg should be fertilized by a male sperm cell.

As the mature egg is released from the ovary, it travels through the *Fallopian tube,* taking anywhere from one to three days to reach the *uterus*. The Fallopian tube is a thin strand of tissue, similar in diameter and shape to a strand of spaghetti (about 4 inches, or 10 cm, long). It is in this tube that fertilization of the ovum by a sperm cell, if it is to occur, usually takes place. The egg, either unfertilized or fertilized, is transported through the tube by means of vigorously moving, tiny hair-like projections known as *cilia* (see Figure 5.3). If the egg has been fertilized en route, the thick mucous lining of the Fallopian tube provides an adequate environment for the *zygote* (fertilized egg) to thrive until it reaches the *uterus*.

The *uterus* is a pear-shaped organ which is positioned between the urinary bladder (in front) and the rectum (in back). It is composed of three layers of tissue, which have important functions if a pregnancy should occur. The inner layer, or *endometrium,* develops a thick rich layer of blood during the days prior to *ovulation*. If the ovum released in any given month is *not* fertilized by a male sperm cell, the egg travels into the uterus, but does not become implanted in this uterine lining of blood. In the absence of a pregnancy, then, the uterus sloughs off this rich lining of blood, and other tissue fluids, about 14 days after ovulation has taken place. This is the process of

FIGURE 5.3.   The Menstrual Cycle: (1) Egg matures in ovary and endometrium thickens in early stage of cycle; (2) mature ovum is released several days after menstruation ends, and endometrium thickens further; (3) egg moves through Fallopian tube, uterine lining engorges with blood and fluids, and corpus luteum evolves out of ruptured ovarian follicle; (4) if egg is not fertilized by male sperm, lining of endometrium is sloughed off by means of menstrual bleeding.

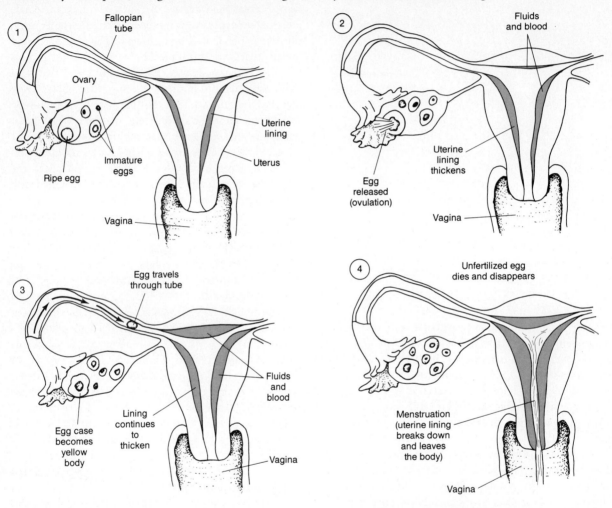

SOURCE: Adapted from McCary, 1973: p. 94.

menstruation, which occurs for most women on a more or less monthly basis. The actual span of time between menstrual periods can be quite irregular, and can vary between 21 and 40 days or more. If a pregnancy should occur, the fertilized egg travels into the uterus and becomes implanted in the enriched lining of the endometrium. Known at this point as the *embryo,* the fertilized egg begins its approximately 9-month period of nourishment from the mother. The uterus expands considerably as the embryo develops into a fetus over this period of time, causing some pressure on, and displacement of, the other internal organs of the woman. The middle layer of the uterus, or *myometrium,* and the outer layer, or *perimetrium,* contain the connective muscle tissue that eventually will help to expel the fetus during childbirth. During the pregnancy, the muscle fibers of the uterus increase nearly ten times their normal length, and new muscle fiber is added to assist in the process of expelling the fetus at birth (see chapter 11).

The *cervix* is composed of fibrous tissue that produces a mucous secretion. It is located at the lower base of the *uterus*. The cervix protrudes into the vagina roughly one-third to one-half inch, and yields an extremely small opening between the uterus and vagina. If pregnancy has taken place, the mucous secreted by the cervix forms a plug that remains in place during the pregnancy. This protects the uterus from infection and assists in keeping the uterine fluids, which support the fetus, in place. At childbirth, the cervix dilates to a diameter of 10 cm, to allow room for the passage of the infant's head and body into the vaginal, or birth, canal.

The *vagina* is a cylindrical, muscular canal which extends from the cervix to the external sexual genitalia (about 3 to 4 inches). It is here that the male's penis is inserted during sexual intercourse, and where sperm cells are deposited following ejaculation. The muscular walls of the vagina are capable of considerable expansion and elongation during intercourse, and, of course, during the childbirth process in order to function as the birth canal for the fetus. The walls of the vagina actually have only a few scattered nerve endings, and, consequently, sensation during sexual excitement is quite minimal in this area. A major function of the vagina during sexual intercourse, other than serving as a repository for sperm cells, is to secrete a mucous substance that enhances the level of sexual pleasure for both the male and female; this substance also creates an environment conducive to the survival of the male's sperm cells.

Sometimes referred to as the "maidenhead," the *hymen* is a fold of connective tissue which partially extends across the outermost opening of the vagina. In most cases, the hymen tissue is naturally perforated in order to allow passage of the bloody fluid sloughed off during menstruation. This tissue often is fully ruptured during the first sexual intercourse, but it is also susceptible to rupture by bicycle or horseback riding, by the use of tampons to absorb the menstrual flow, or by some sort of accident involving the genital area. As McCary (1973:86) points out, however, an intact hymen at marriage has long been considered in many cultures to be an essential ingredient in matrimony.

A ruptured hymen is certainly not *prima facie* evidence that a girl is not a virgin. On the other hand, rare cases exist in which the hymen is so flexible or pliable that coitus (intercourse) can take place repeatedly without rupturing the tissue. The importance of an intact hymen to some women at the time of marriage is attested to by the fact that a Japanese gynecologist not long ago performed for the ten-thousandth time a surgical operation creating an artificial hymen for a prospective bride.

Because breaking of the hymen at first intercourse can be quite painful for the woman, it is possible for a physician to cut or dilate an intact hymen, after anesthetizing the area for a woman.

External Sexual Genitalia.   The external sex organs of the female are known collectively as the *vulva*. The *mons pubis* (also called *mons veneris*) is a fatty cushion of tissue that rests upon the woman's pubic bone and which is covered by pubic hair. This area is quite sensitive to the touch, and is a source of considerable sexual stimulation for many women.

The *labia majora*, or major lips, correspond anatomically to the scrotum of the male. They consist of fatty tissue that have some nerve endings, thereby providing some degree of pleasure during sexual contact. The outer portions contain some pubic hair, whereas the inner folds contain none.

Contained within the labia majora are the *labia minora*, or minor lips. During sexual excitement, the labia majora flatten out to expose the labia minora, which are susceptible to considerable sexual stimulation as the result of becoming engorged with blood with increased excitement. The folds of the labia minora fuse at the upper end to form a protective sheath for the *clitoris*. The clitoris is actually the primary locus of sexual excitement for the woman, as is the penis for the male. The clitoris is an extremely sensitive organ that becomes enlarged and erect during sexual excitement. The pleasurable sensation provided by the clitoris is significantly enhanced by some sort of lubricant, either the mucous secreted by the vaginal walls of the female, the male's pre-ejaculatory emission, or an artificial lubricant. Without the presence of a lubricant, direct pressure and rubbing of the clitoris can be quite uncomfortable or irritating for the female. Unlike the male's penis, which hangs freely from the body, only the end (or *glans*) of the clitoris extends from the female's body. The remainder of the comparatively small shaft of the clitoris is covered by the skin folds of the vulva. Erection of the clitoris, as with the penis, is a result of the shaft becoming engorged with blood during sexual stimulation, and can increase to twice its unstimulated size.

Because of the anatomical placement of the clitoris, the shaft of the penis often does not come into direct contact with it during conventional episodes of sexual intercourse. For many women, therefore, some other form of direct stimulation to the clitoris is needed in order to produce peak sexual pleasure and orgasm. This stimulation is often provided by hand or finger contact by the male, by the female herself, or by movement of the tip *(glans)* of the penis directly over the clitoral area.

The Menstrual Cycle.   Menstruation takes place as the uterus sloughs off the rich lining of blood that builds up in preparation for a fertilized egg. Menstruation follows when the process of ovulation in the female occurs without the released egg being fertilized. However, it is important to understand the hormonal determinants of menstruation and the timing factors involved in order to understand how it might be utilized as a method of birth control.

Figure 5.4 describes what is happening over the course of a normal 28-day menstrual cycle. Although most women have menstrual cycles that last from 25 to 32 days with considerable regularity, many experience shorter cycles, longer cycles, or cycles that vary considerably from one to the next. The duration of bleeding usually spans a 3- to 7-day period, lasting an average of 4 days. In addition, the regularity and duration of menstrual cycles is highly susceptible to psychoemotional stress, nutrition and diet, and physical activity. Even air travel or a cold virus can cause women to delay or miss a menstrual period. This is because menstruation is guided by the release and eventual balance of hormones in the woman's endocrine system, a process which is clearly affected by psychological, emotional, and physical states of the woman.

Figure 5.4 shows that the menstrual cycle is divided into three stages: the menstrual, postmenstrual, and premenstrual. During the menstrual stage (days 1 through 5), the endometrium (lining) of the uterus is discharging the blood which has been building up since the previous menstrual flow. In the ovary, several follicles containing egg cells are beginning to develop as a result of the gradual

FIGURE 5.4.   Changes in Hormone Levels, Ovary, and Endometrium (Uterine Lining) over a 28 Day Menstrual Cycle.

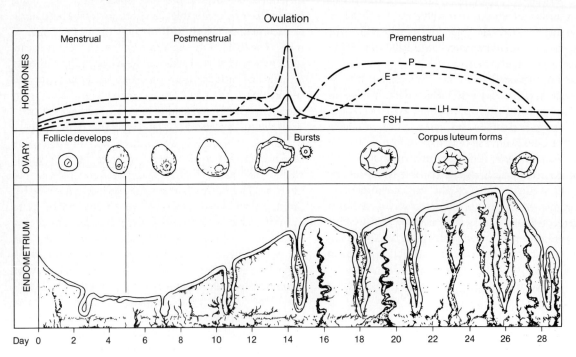

SOURCE: Adapted from Witters and Jones-Witters (1980:91).

increase of the *follicle-stimulating hormone,* or *FSH,* caused by activity of the hypothalamus and pituitary gland. This occurs because the hormone *estrogen,* which normally inhibits the secretion of FSH, is at a relatively low level in the system at this time.

As the follicles develop through days 5 to 14, estrogen levels continue to build. This hormone inhibits any further release of FSH. Estrogen is actually released by the follicles of the woman's ovaries. Just before ovulation occurs in this postmenstrual stage of the cycle, the level of estrogen reaches its highest concentration. At this point, the pituitary gland releases *luteinizing hormone,* or *LH,* which functions in combination with estrogen to promote the actual release of one of the eggs by the ovary, approximately 16 to 24 hours later.

After the mature egg bursts through the wall of the follicle, it begins its travel through the Fallopian tube toward the uterus, during the premenstrual stage of the cycle. This period of time, between ovulation and the onset of menstrual bleeding, is approximately 14 days, regardless of the total length of the entire menstrual cycle. Stated another way, the reason for the differences among women in the length of their menstrual cycles is related to the menstrual and postmenstrual stages, during which the follicle is maturing and the rich blood lining of the uterine wall (endometrium) is beginning to build. But once ovulation occurs, the approximately 14-day period of time until the next menstrual bleeding begins is standard for all women. Hence, one can count back 14 days from the time menstruation begins to determine the approximate time ovulation actually took place. However, it is difficult to determine in advance when ovulation will occur because few women's cycles are perfectly regular in the duration of the menstrual and postmenstrual stages. Shortly after release of the ovum, the ruptured follicle continues to secrete estrogen as well as another hormone, *progesterone.* Progesterone is produced in the cells of this follicle, which is known as the *corpus luteum* (yellow body), and this hormone functions to maintain and enhance the development of the rich lining of the endometrium.

If after 12 to 14 days a fertilized egg has not implanted in the uterine wall, the corpus luteum begins to break down and the amounts of estrogen and progesterone in the system rapidly decrease. Consequently, the elements necessary to maintain the build-up of blood in the lining of the endometrium are no longer present. This signals the onset of the menstrual stage, where the blood lining of the uterus is discharged over a period of a few days. Then, the level of estrogen again reaches a low level in the woman's system; the pituitary gland is again stimulated to produce FSH; a new follicle begins to develop an egg cell—and the cycle begins anew. However, if pregnancy does occur after ovulation, the fertilized ovum travels into the uterus and becomes implanted in the blood-rich endometrium, where it receives the nourishment essential for its survival. Within three days, the implanted ovum itself begins secreting a hormone that maintains intact the corpus luteum, allowing the continued release of progesterone and small amounts of estrogen in order to maintain the nourishing, thick lining of the uterus. Because the lining is not sloughed off when pregnancy occurs, the pregnant woman is not likely to experience a menstrual flow of blood until after the pregnancy has ended.

SEXUAL AND REPRODUCTIVE ANATOMY OF THE MALE

Because the male does not undergo a process analogous to menstruation in the female, the male reproductive system is somewhat less complex. However, as with the female, sexual development and functioning of the human male are guided by hormonal secretions in the endocrine system. The development of the male sexual apparatus, and the hormonal secretions that guide it, are determined initially by the *XY* chromosome combination established at conception. A view of the adult male sexual and reproductive organs is presented in Figures 5.5 and 5.6.

Although the penis is the center of sexual excitement and orgasm for the male, the actual reproductive functions take place elsewhere, in the male's internal anatomy. Actually, the main reproductive organs of the male are the *testes* (or testicles), and all other components of the system (including the penis) are generally considered to be *accessory* structures (Hubbard, 1977). The testes produce male reproductive cells, called *sperm,* as well as the male sex hormone *testosterone.* Unlike the female, who is born with her full complement of ova, the male continuously produces sex cells and does so only after puberty. Approximately 300 million sperm are generated in a 24-hour period for the average male (Witters and Jones-Witters, 1980:26). Just the same, it takes only one sperm to fertilize the released ovum of the female.

The male has two testicles, located within a protec-

FIGURE 5.5.   (a) Side View of the Male Sexual and Reproductive Anatomy, (b) Cross-Section of the Male Testicle.

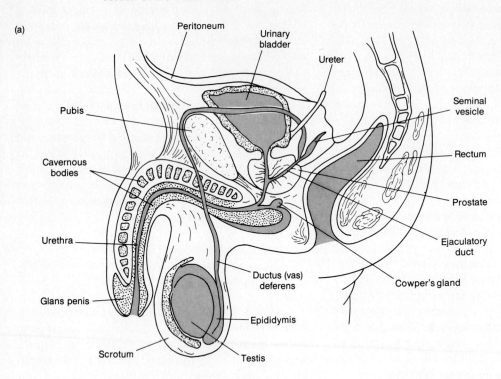

(a)

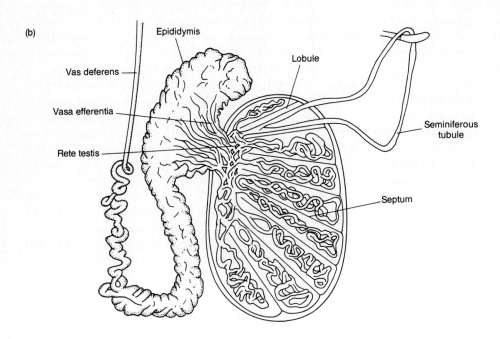

(b)

FIGURE 5.6.   Longitudinal Section of the Penis and Connecting Tissues.

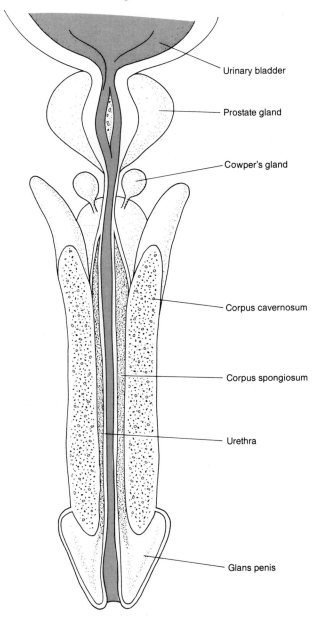

- Urinary bladder
- Prostate gland
- Cowper's gland
- Corpus cavernosum
- Corpus spongiosum
- Urethra
- Glans penis

ment for sperm production. As the external temperature drops below the ideal level, as would happen in a cold bath or shower, or even during periods of emotional stress, the skin of the scrotum contracts and wrinkles, drawing the testicles upward in order to hold them closer to the warm body. Conversely, when the external temperature is warmer than the ideal level for sperm production, the skin of the scrotum expands and the thin muscle fibers relax, causing the testicles to extend from the body in order to release body heat.

Each testicle contains approximately 1,000 *seminiferous tubules,* where sperm cells are actually produced. The sperm cells are then stored in a network of tubes known as the *epididymis,* in order to mature. In addition, many weak or mutated sperm cells which are unlikely to survive after ejaculation are selected out and absorbed by the epididymis. This is probably a natural way of reducing birth defects and disorders. From this storage area, the sperm are then transported for storage through a tube known as the *vas deferens.* This tube serves also to transport the sperm cells up into the abdominal cavity and into two *seminal vesicles,* which are situated between the rectum and bladder, and near an organ known as the *prostate gland.* When ejaculation occurs, a thin, milky, and alkaline substance called *semen* (or seminal fluid), which has been produced both in the seminal vesicles and the prostate gland, is combined with the sperm as they are transported through the *ejaculatory ducts* and into the *urethra.* The urethra is a tube that extends the entire length of the penis, through which the male's urine also is discharged from the urinary bladder. Because of the control exercised by certain nerves in the prostate area, however, the semen and urine are kept separate and cannot be discharged at the same time.

In order to facilitate the ejaculation of the sperm-bearing semen, two small *bulbourethral glands,* called *Cowper's glands,* lubricate the urethra with a thick alkaline fluid during sexual excitement. These glands are located at the upper base of the penis, one on each side of the urethra. Normally, this fluid contains no sperm, although scientists have been able to observe sperm in approximately 25 percent of samples examined (McCary, 1973). Hence, a pregnancy can occur even if the penis does not fully penetrate the vagina and if ejaculation of the full volume of semen does not occur. The alkalinity of the semen is thought to contribute to the survival of the sperm cells, which must remain alive in the relatively acidic environment of the woman's vagina if they are to reach the Fallopian tubes and fertilize the released ovum.

tive skin pouch called the *scrotum.* Internally, the scrotum is divided in two halves, which are separated by a thin membrane, or *septum.* An important function of the scrotum is to regulate the temperature in the sperm-producing environment, which must be somewhat lower than normal body temperature in order to provide an ideal environ-

Although the total volume of ejaculate is quite small, weighing only a few grams and being only 3 to 5 millimeters in volume, there are anywhere from 100 to 400 million sperm cells in the ejaculate of the average male. Ejaculation is caused by contraction of the muscle tissue surrounding the upper end of the urethra as the erect penis is stimulated. The muscular contractions and the pleasurable sensations associated with them comprise the male *orgasm*. If orgasm occurs during sexual intercourse, the sperm contained in the semen are deposited in the female's vagina. This begins the journey of sperm cells through the cervix, uterus, and Fallopian tubes. The possibility of pregnancy exists only if an egg is present in a Fallopian tube, and if a sperm cell survives the journey and fertilizes the egg.

The *penis* is the organ which is the locus of sexual excitement. In addition to containing the urethra, through which urinary wastes are passed and ejaculate expelled, the penis is composed of three columns of spongy tissue known as *erectile tissue*, which contain an extensive network of blood vessels and sensitive nerves. The flaccid (nonerect) penis varies in size from male to male, although the average range is 2.5 to 4 inches long, and just over 1 inch in diameter (McCary, 1973). The erect (tumescent) penis results from a massive inflow of blood that fills the spongy erectile tissue when the penis is stimulated. When erect, the average penis extends from 5.5 to 6.5 inches and becomes approximately 1.5 inches in diameter (McCary, 1973). The upper end of the penis connects to the body's pubic bones by means of rods called *crura*. The end of the penis contains the *glans*, an extremely sensitive area. Although the shaft of the penis is quite sensitive as well, the glans constitutes the center of sexual excitement for the male. The tip of the penis, where the urethral opening is located, is called the *meatus*.

The Role of Hormones in Male Sexuality and Reproductive Anatomy.

As is the case with females, the development of males' sexuality and reproductive capacities is guided by hormones released by the endocrine system. At puberty (around 11 to 13 years of age), the hypothalamus directs the pituitary gland to disperse several hormones into the male's system. Although they do not have ovaries, males also have the *follicle-stimulating hormone* (FSH). In males, FSH stimulates the growth of the testes, and also stimulates the

seminiferous tubules to begin forming and developing sperm cells. At the same time, the pituitary releases the *interstitial cell-stimulating hormone* (ICSH), which is identical to the *luteinizing hormone* (LH) in women, in order to stimulate the interstitial (Leydig) cells of the testes to produce more of the male hormone *testosterone*.

The development of the male's secondary sex characteristics, such as deepening of the voice, facial and pubic hair growth, sudden spurt in height, and increase in muscular strength are primarily the result of the influence of testosterone during the years of puberty. Testosterone also fosters the growth and development of the penis, seminal vesicles, and prostate, as well as the male sex drive. The male sex drive is sharply reduced in the event that castration (removal of the testicles) should occur.[1] If castration occurs prior to puberty, moreover, males will not develop such characteristic features of adult men as deepening of the voice, development of the musculature, and growth of facial and pubic hair. For women, on the other hand, the sex drive is not significantly influenced by removal of the estrogen-producing ovaries, although their removal *is* associated with the loss of elasticity of the vagina, lubrication ability, and secretions (Witters and Jones-Witters, 1980:103).

The Sex Researchers

Our knowledge of human sexual activity and the nature of human sexual response is based, to a large extent, on the pioneering work of several researchers who have asked questions and observed a large number of people. The major research efforts will be briefly described here, and the results of these studies will be reported at various points in this chapter and throughout the remainder of the book. As you will see, every one of these major studies of human sexual behavior suffers as a result of sampling problems inherent in research on so sensitive and personal a topic as sex.

THE KINSEY REPORTS

Beginning in 1937, Alfred Kinsey and his associates at Indiana University began what has become the benchmark of all research on human sexual behavior. Kinsey, a zoologist, joined forces with Wardell Pomeroy (a psychologist), Paul Gebhard (an anthropologist), and Clyde Martin (a statistician), in interviewing 8,603 male and 7,789 female respondents about several aspects of their sexual lives. The final reports were published in 1948 *(Sexual Behavior in the Human Male)* and in 1953 *(Sexual Behavior in the Human Female),* under the auspices of the Institute for Sex Research at Indiana University. The uniqueness of Kinsey's research at the time it was conducted lies in the fact that he focused on the actual *sexual behavior* of people, rather than their attitudes and beliefs about sex. Among the many topics covered by Kinsey's interviewers were premarital sexual behavior, marital sex, extramarital sex, homosexual behavior (both pre- and postadolescent), nocturnal sex dreams, sex with animals, sexual response and orgasm, and various methods of sexual foreplay. Because Kinsey was working with such a large sample, he was able to make interesting comparisons across educational, age, social class, and religious categories.

As large as Kinsey's sample was, however, the representativeness of his respondents has been called into question. Kinsey's respondents all volunteered to participate in this research on sexual behavior, raising the question of whether or not volunteers in such a study reflect accurately the types of sexual behavior characteristic of those who refuse to participate. In addition, Kinsey sought the cooperation of research subjects through social groups in various communities, such as fraternal and service clubs, colleges, PTAs, and church groups; and only 28 percent of the groups asked to participate had all of their members agree to become involved in the study. Partly as a result of the sampling problems posed by a study of such a personal and sensitive topic as sex, Kinsey's lower-class male sample is overrepresented with ex-convicts, and the female sample has a larger than representative number who had attended college.

Despite these serious questions of representativeness, the scope and detail of Kinsey's study has rendered it the most widely cited and referenced research ever conducted on human sexual behavior. It is the Kinsey report to which contemporary sex researchers continue to compare and contrast their findings, a tribute to a group of researchers who had the courage to ask questions about a central feature of human life that others had thought was a taboo subject.

MASTERS AND JOHNSON

In contrast to the interviews conducted by Kinsey and his associates on the range and diversity of human sexual experience, William Masters and Virginia Johnson studied the actual physiological reactions of males and females to sexual excitement and orgasm (Masters and Johnson, 1966). In order to do this, Masters and Johnson made actual observations of the anatomical and physiological responses of research subjects to sexual stimulation. A total of 312 male and 382 female subjects agreed to engage in self-stimulation (masturbation), mechanical stimulation (e.g., female use of a vibrator), and sexual intercourse while their physiological responses were being monitored by sophisticated electronic equipment. Masters and Johnson supplemented their machine-assisted observations with in-depth interviews of the subjects in regard to their subjective perceptions of various stages of the sexual-response cycle.

As with the Kinsey studies, however, the composition of the Masters and Johnson sample is biased in certain ways. Both male and female subjects tended to be more educated and from higher socioeconomic backgrounds than the population in general. In addition, the laboratory environment in which sexual behavior was observed introduced questions of artificiality, which could potentially alter sexual-response patterns. Nonetheless, the obvious care taken by these researchers in the conduct of the research, and the rare quality of their observations, are generally accepted by other scientists in the field as valid, providing the primary basis for our understanding of human sexual response. Therefore, the Masters and Johnson study merits our serious consideration.

THE HUNT STUDY

In order to provide a contemporary comparison to the reports on sexual behavior provided by Kinsey, Morton Hunt (1974) had 2,026 men and women complete a questionnaire on their sexual activities both inside and outside of marriage. Many of Hunt's questions paralleled those of Kinsey, so that direct comparisons could be made, even though the questionnaire format was far less detailed than Kinsey's intensive interviews. Again, however, the old nemesis of sample bias crept in: more than 80 percent of those potential subjects asked to participate refused to do so.

THE *REDBOOK* STUDY

In order to find out more about the sexual lives of American women, *Redbook* magazine published a questionnaire in one of its 1974 issues. Approximately 100,000 women responded to the questionnaire, which covered frequency of sexual intercourse, orgasm, types of foreplay, and communication with husbands or other male partners about the sexual relationship. The findings were published by Tavris and Sadd (1977), and several of them were found to be remarkably consistent with those reported by Hunt. Despite the tremendous number of responses in this survey, however, the non-scientific sampling method prevents us from concluding that we have a representative picture of the sexuality of American women. These respondents were *self-selected* into the survey, and are highly overrepresentative of younger and more educated women.

THE HITE REPORT

Published as a "nationwide study on female sexuality," Shere Hite (1976) was able to obtain only a 3 percent response rate from the 100,000 questionnaires distributed through various magazines and newspapers. The 3,000 participants were responding to questions relating to masturbation, orgasm, sexual activities, relationships with partners, and general attitudes toward sexuality. The real value of Hite's study is in the fact that actual comments of the respondents are published, so that we are able to gain a more descriptive picture of each woman's feelings, thoughts, and attitudes. Hence, the data from Hite's study, although statistically difficult to generalize, provide a nice complement to the more statistical reports of Kinsey, Hunt, Tavris and Sadd, and Masters and Johnson.

Human Sexual Response

As stated earlier, the primary sexual-response mechanism for males is the penis, and for females it is the clitoris. However, there are other sensitive parts of the body, known as *erogenous zones,* that can also contribute to the enjoyment of sexual play. For example, Kinsey and his colleagues found that ears, eyebrows, buttocks, feet, and other body parts, when touched in gentle and pleasing ways, can create considerable sexual excitment for both males and females (Kinsey, Pomeroy, and Martin, 1948; Kinsey, Pomeroy, Martin, and Gebhard, 1953). In fact, actual physical contact between two individuals need not even take place, because some men and women respond sexually to such stimuli as films, pictures, on-stage performances of nude persons, and even to the power of their own ability to fantasize.

Research has shown that there exists a broad range and diversity of stimuli that people find sexually arousing, and which are capable of producing a sexual response. Given this variability from person to person, in terms of which body parts are sexually sensitive and which stimuli are sexually arousing, it should be clear that human sexuality is part of the *socialization process* in our lives. That is, we *learn* to be sexual beings: what stimuli we find sexually pleasing, and how to give to and receive sexual pleasure from another person (Calderone, 1974). Some of us learn part of our sexuality from parents, although many people rely on friends, sexual partners, and such media as books, magazines, and films to shape sex-related expectations and response patterns. These socialization agents also help to determine what external stimuli are most likely to arouse us sexually.

In view of the central role that sexuality plays in the development of the marriage relationship, it is important to understand that human sexuality is a *learned* set of physiological and behavioral responses. As such, there exist a number of possible *sexual scripts* in marriage. These scripts may vary between husband and wife, and, as a result, may be mutually satisfying or acceptable to the partners to varying degrees. As in other areas of intimate relationships, sexual fulfillment of both the male and female partners is more likely to occur if mutuality and reciprocity are involved in the sexual relationship.

SEXUAL ROLE SCRIPTS IN MARRIAGE

For most people, there is far more to human sexuality and sexual behavior than a penis entering a vagina and producing an orgasmic response for both partners. There are *scripts of norms* that define (1) when, how often, and under what conditions sexual intercourse is appropriate; (2) what positions in sexual intercourse provide the greatest pleasure for each partner; (3) what kinds of sex play, other than intercourse, provide pleasure and are appropriate; and (4) how much and what sorts of *foreplay* (or pre-intercourse touching and caressing) are most conducive to sexual enjoyment. A man and woman whose sexual scripts are in agreement will find that their sexual relationship provides a greater level of mutual enjoyment and fulfillment than if they have incompatible scripts. However, gender-role differences between males and females often result in sexual scripts with conflicting expectations. When sexual scripts do not mesh, the sexual relationship may develop in a disappointing manner.

Timing, Frequency, and Situational Norms.   Research on sexual interaction both before and after marriage shows that partners may have conflicting expectations in regard to the appropriate times, frequency, and situational conditions under which sexual play takes place. In regard to frequency, for example, Hunt's (1974) large national survey found that about 80 percent of the husbands expressed a desire to engage in sexual intercourse with their wives more frequently, whereas only one-third of the wives expressed the same desire. In another study of middle-class marriage, Levinger (1970) found that the average husband *desired* to have intercourse between 9 and 10 times per month, but reported that the *actual* frequency was 7 times. Their wives, on the other hand, reported identical *desired* and *actual* frequencies of intercourse—about 8 times per month. In addition, husbands tended to *underestimate* their wives' desired frequency for sexual intercourse, and wives tended to *overestimate* their husbands' desired frequency. Such conflicts in the sexual scripts of husband and wife create the potential for misunderstanding and disappointment in the sexual relationship (Reiss, 1980; McCary, 1973).

Any of a number of factors may cause conflict in the sexual scripts of marriage partners. For example, the role clusters of wives with young dependent children are often heavy compared with those of their husbands, especially if the wives are also working outside of the home (see chapter 8). Employed wives often continue to perform the bulk of household tasks and child-care responsibilities, despite the fact that they are involved in outside occupational pursuits. Such gender-role arrangements can lead to greater

fatigue, mood swings, and depression, all of which are emotional and physical conditions that can dampen the desire for sex. In addition to their energy levels being influenced by heavy marital, parental, and occupational role demands, the sex drive of women is less constant, and they are more tolerant than men of extended periods of abstinence from sexual relations (Zehv, 1968). Clearly, the sexual roles of married partners are subject to conflict as a result of role expectations and demands in other areas of the marriage relationship.

Other factors may cause conflict in the sexual scripts of marriage partners. One is the general level of satisfaction in the marriage. The desire for sexual intercourse, and satisfaction with the sexual relationship, vary according to how satisfied one is with the communication, power, and affection-exchange patterns in the marriage. Dissatisfaction with these or other aspects of a marriage can dampen one's desire to engage in the intimate kinds of physical contact that are part of the sexual relationship. The importance of communication cannot be overemphasized, because conflicts in sexual scripts can best be resolved when partners are able to discuss their different expectations.

Sexual scripts of marriage partners may also vary according to each person's definitions of appropriate and inappropriate situations in which sexual intercourse may occur. For example, a common belief is that sexual intercourse during the female's menstrual period is either unappealing, harmful, or both. Actually, sexual relations during menstruation pose no danger to either the man or woman. Some women maintain that they have an even greater sex drive during this time. Masters and Johnson (1966) found that women who experienced orgasm during menstruation actually "increased the rate of (blood) flow, reduced the pelvic cramping (when present) and frequently relieved their menstrually associated backaches" (p. 123). As in other cultures around the world, many of which demand total avoidance of sexual intercourse during menstruation, people in our society are conditioned to avoid sexual contact at this time because it is too "messy," "dirty," or "unhealthy." Problems resulting from incompatible sexual scripts may arise when one partner believes that sexual intercourse is acceptable during menstruation, but the other finds it unacceptable.

Other norms regarding appropriate situational conditions for sexual relations may also be in conflict. For example, what is the proper mood and environment for sexual relations? Lights on, or lights out? Children in bed and asleep, or up and about? An extended period of foreplay, or a quick sexual episode? When marriage partners find conflicting sexual scripts in terms of the conditions under which sex play is appropriate, misunderstandings and dissatisfaction with the sexual relationship can result. Again, only open and honest communication about each person's sexual expectations will increase each others' awareness of any conflicts in sexual scripts, and reveal areas where expectations might be brought more into line with those of the other partner (see chapter 7).

Positions in Sexual Intercourse.   Another important aspect of sexual role scripts concerns the body positions that partners find to provide the greatest mutual enjoyment of the sex act. There are a number of possible positions during sexual intercourse and other kinds of sex play. However, as with other aspects of human sexuality, the preferred position is part of our sexual learning, and mutual sexual gratification of the partners depends upon agreement in sexual role scripts. There is no intrinsically "best" way, other than the one that best meets each partner's needs and goals for sexual fulfillment.

The most common position in sexual intercourse is the "face-to-face, man above" position.[2] This is probably the position preferred by many males in our culture because it allows maximum freedom of movement and the most pleasurable feeling for the male partner. This is also known as the "male superior" position; and many men who hold traditional gender-role expectations may be more comfortable in this position because it allows them to maintain control of the sexual act. However, the position of the female's clitoris is often too high on the vulva to allow the male's penis to make direct contact, and, as a result, the sexual pleasure the female experiences in this position is often less than the male's (Hite, 1976).

In order to facilitate direct stimulation of the clitoris, many couples prefer the "face-to-face, woman above" position. Many find that this position enhances the pleasure of the sexual act for the woman without reducing it significantly for the male. In this position, the woman is in direct control of her pelvic movements and is not as restricted as she is under her partner's weight in the "man above" position. The nature of a couple's sexual scripts may make this position less satisfying, however, if the

male is not comfortable in sacrificing his "male-superior," more "aggressive" position above the woman. Again, cultural conditioning plays a role here, in that gender roles defining appropriate male and female behavior can influence the sexual scripts of partners who are seeking to give sexual pleasure to one another.

The third common position in the sexual repertoires of many couples is the "face-to-face, side" position. Because the weight of one partner is not on the other, this position can provide considerable freedom of movement for *both* partners. It is the most satisfactory position during pregnancy because of the more even weight distribution of the partners. Masters and Johnson (1970) reported that this position is preferred by many couples because it provides mutual enjoyment for both partners as a result of the greater flexibility and freedom of sexual expression allowed to each during the sexual act.

The fourth common position for sexual intercourse is *rear entry,* in which the male places himself behind the woman and enters the vagina from the rear. The woman is normally positioned on her stomach or in an "all fours" kneeling position, although rear entry may also be accomplished in a "side-by-side" position. This is another satisfying position during the advanced stages of pregnancy, and can provide the male with maximum freedom to caress various parts of the woman's body that are sexually-sensitive.

Many people in our culture believe that the male-superior sexual position is the "normal" or "natural" one. However, research on the preferred sexual role scripts in other cultures shows that this is the preferred position primarily in North America and in European societies. In Malinowski's (1929) study of the Trobriand Islanders in the South Pacific, and in wall drawings found among the ruins of the ancient Greeks, Indians, and Romans, the "female superior" position was found to be far more typical. Indeed, the Trobrianders were so surprised by the European pattern promoted by the missionaries that the male-superior position came to be called the "missionary position." In comparing the results of their research on married couples with that of Kinsey, Hunt (1974) and Tavris and Sadd (1977) found that contemporary couples employ a much greater variety of sexual positions than was true in past years, despite the continuing popularity of the male-superior position in our culture.

The male and female partners must discover which positions, or combination of positions, provide the greatest mutual enjoyment. It is up to them as well to find sexual behavior and varieties of sexual play other than intercourse to enhance their sexual enjoyment. In this way, it is possible to expand sexual role scripts to increase the range and variety of sexual behavior so that the sexual relationship remains vital and alive over time. This is *role reciprocity* that involves open and honest communication about what each partner finds most pleasurable.

Alternative Means of Satisfying Sexual Needs.

Sexual intercourse in marriage is not the only means of satisfying sexual desires, and the sexual-role scripts of marriage partners may reflect quite different expectations and behavioral patterns in this regard. Kinsey's research (Kinsey, et al., 1948; Kinsey, et al., 1953) identified several distinct methods of attaining orgasm among never-married and married men and women (see Figures 5.7 and 5.8): masturbation, petting, coitus (intercourse) in marriage, premarital coitus, extramarital coitus, homosexual contacts, and nocturnal orgasms. When these various behaviors are compared across age levels of married men, it appears that the frequency of experiencing orgasm by means of sexual intercourse with one's marriage partner *decreases* over time, relative to other sources of attaining orgasm. Extramarital intercourse tends to increase, and masturbation (self-stimulated orgasm) remains about the same with increasing age. For single men, on the other hand, the relative frequency of attaining orgasm by means of masturbation decreases over time, whereas orgasm by intercourse with female companions and homosexual contacts tend to increase with age. For married women (see Figure 5.8), attaining orgasm by means of intercourse with the spouse also shows a tendency to decline with age, and extramarital intercourse and masturbation show some increase over time. For single never-married women, attaining orgasm by means of masturbation is greatest for the youngest and the oldest women. Orgasm by means of intercourse with a male companion tends to increase relative to other means, but the frequency of homosexual contacts increases steadily up to a point (36- to 40-year-olds), then sharply declines.[3]

Clearly, problems in the sexual relationship of married partners can be caused by spouses who embrace different sexual scripts regarding appropriate methods for seeking and attaining sexual satisfaction. For example, a wife may find masturbation or extramarital affairs to be acceptable methods of sexual gratification although her husband may view intercourse only with one's marriage partner as legitimate sexual behavior.

The Duration and Type of Foreplay.

The sexual-role scripts of partners may also conflict in regard to the means of achieving sexual excitement with each other, or *foreplay*. Foreplay is an extremely critical aspect of the sexual relationship because it sets the stage for sexual intercourse and influences the level of tension-release and gratification that intercourse will provide.

The ability of partners to engage in mutually stimulating foreplay is one aspect of the sexual-role script that requires considerable skill. Knowledge concerning what kinds of touching or talking will stimulate a partner sexually does not come naturally. Over the course of repeated sexual experiences with the partner, we learn what "works" and what does not. (See Table 5.1 for the most common methods of foreplay.) As stated earlier, both men and women vary in terms of which body parts are sexually sensitive and capable of contributing to sexual gratification. Hence, no matter how much we have learned from our peers, movie stars, or various kinds of reading material about how to excite a person of the opposite sex, individual variations require that we learn the unique combinations of foreplay behavior specific to the needs and desires of our partners, if the sexual relationship is to be mutually fulfilling.

Again, communication skills are essential if the partners' sexual scripts differ in terms of *how long* foreplay should take place before actual intercourse begins, what kinds of foreplay are desirable, and if *foreplay-to-orgasm* (without intercourse) is acceptable or preferred. In a study of American and Canadian women, for example, DeMartino (1970) found that the major criticism of the sexual behavior of male partners is that they do not take the time to properly stimulate and prepare the woman for intercourse. Women complained that their male partners are overly concerned with their own sexual gratification, and are in too much of a hurry during foreplay to satisfy the woman's needs. Indeed, women generally require a longer period of foreplay than do men in order to attain orgasm (Hite, 1976). This point is illustrated by the following quote, which is typical of those from respondents in Hite's survey of the sexual behavior of American women. This woman was responding to the question, "Are your

FIGURE 5.7. Sources of orgasm among (a) single men and (b) married men, all with some college education, expressed as relative percentages of total sexual outlet.

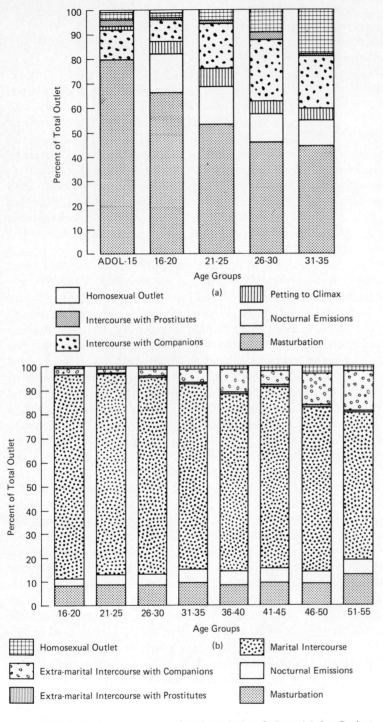

SOURCE: Reprinted by permission of The Kinsey Institute for Research in Sex, Gender & Reproduction, Inc.

FIGURE 5.8. Sources of orgasm among (a) single females, and (b) married females, expressed as relative percentages of total sexual outlet.

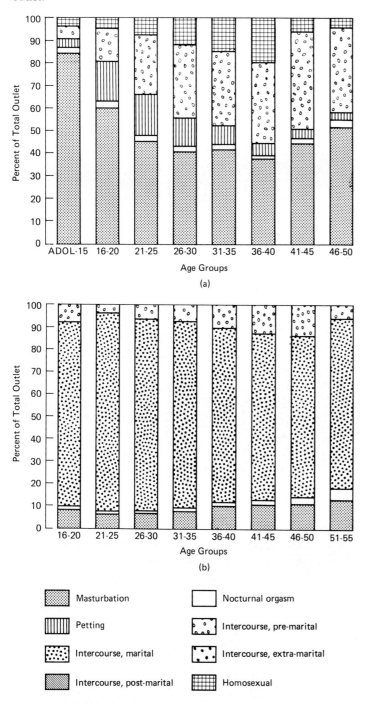

(a)

(b)

Masturbation

Nocturnal orgasm

Petting

Intercourse, pre-marital

Intercourse, marital

Intercourse, extra-marital

Intercourse, post-marital

Homosexual

TABLE 5.1. *Most Common Methods of Foreplay, Arranged According to Decreasing Frequency of Use (1 = most frequent)*

1. General body contact — hugging and caressing.
2. Simple kissing.
3. Tongue kissing (French kissing).
4. Manual manipulation of the female breast.
5. Manual manipulation of the female genitalia.
6. Oral stimulation of the female breast.
7. Manual stimulation of the male genitalia.
8. Oral stimulation of male genitalia (fellatio).
9. Oral stimulation of female genitalia (cunnilingus).
10. Oral stimulation of the anal area (anilingus).

SOURCE: From *Human Sexuality: A Biological Perspective,* by W. Witters and P. J. Witters. © 1980 by Litton Educational Publishing, Inc.

partners well-informed, and are they sensitive to the stimulation you want?''

Most partners seemed to think that I would be automatically aroused by two minutes of kissing and touching and then would be just as ready for intercourse as they were. I have had to tell them or show them what I wanted. No one has ever asked me, or known already what would turn me on. It hasn't been embarrassing exactly, but it's hard to strike the right tone; showing lovingly what pleases without suggesting that the man is an ill-informed selfish animal (unless, of course, he is!!).

In regard to the kinds of foreplay necessary to achieve a maximum level of sexual gratification, variety and imagination are of critical importance. Particularly in marriage, where partners are expected to limit their sexual contact to each other (and *only* each other) for many years, boredom with sex is likely to follow if foreplay techniques have become mechanical and ritualistic over time. According to McCary (1973:151):

Variations in sexual approach and setting can add considerable spice to marriage. Too often sexual acts become ritualized, stale and unimaginative, engaged in only to provide relief of physical urgency. Couples who wish to preserve delight and vigor in their sexual interaction will work as consistently on this aspect of their marriage as on any other.

Ideally, partners will agree on the kinds of experimentation to be engaged in and will share a mutual interest in engaging in varieties of foreplay which provide the greatest amount of satisfaction for each.

ORGASM

Because it is experienced as the peak of sexual intensity and pleasure, most people hold as the ultimate goal of sexuality the achievement of orgasm. However, the extreme importance placed on the orgasmic experience by some men and women can cause them to overemphasize this aspect of sexual behavior at the expense of others (such as foreplay, mutual affection, and sexual excitement). The result can be serious disappointment and frustration in the sexual relationship.

The physiological nature of orgasm was carefully studied in the laboratory by Masters and Johnson (1966), who were able to monitor the internal and external responses of both males and females to the orgasmic experience. The attainment of orgasm is actually only part of a pattern of sexual arousal for both men and women, what Masters and Johnson referred to as the "sexual response cycle" (see Figure 5.9). The four stages of the response cycle are (1) excitement; (2) plateau; (3) orgasmic; and (4) resolution. Although individual variations abound in terms of intensity and duration of sexual response, Masters and Johnson found these patterns to be the most commonly observed among their research subjects.

The excitement phase involves the process of sexual arousal, either through fantasy or physical contact. This phase can be either brief or extended in time, depending upon the situational constraints and sexual scripts of the partners involved. The plateau phase is reached near the peak of sexual excitement and, if stimulation continues, will lead to orgasm. Following orgasm is the resolution phase, which involves a rather dramatic decrease in sexual tension and a return to an unstimulated state. During resolution, males undergo a *refractory period*. During this time, which varies among males from a few minutes to an hour or more, they are unable to reach an erection of the penis and generally are not interested in re-engaging in another episode of sexual intercourse, as the result of the drop in sexual tension following ejaculation. Women, on the other hand, are capable of responding to restimulation much more quickly than males, and many are able to attain multiple orgasms during any given sexual episode. Males report that the first orgasm is more pleasurable than any that might follow, whereas females often find subsequent orgasms to be more pleasurable than the first. The multiple-orgasmic capacity of women is a major difference in sexual response capability compared with that of the male.

FIGURE 5.9.   The Sexual Response Cycles of (A) Females and (B) Males.

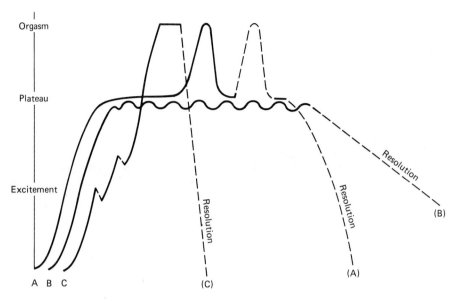

(A) The Female Sexual Response Cycles (3 types)

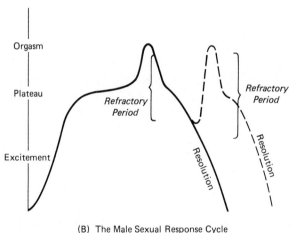

(B) The Male Sexual Response Cycle

SOURCE: Masters, W. H., and Johnson, V. E. *Human Sexual Response.* Boston: Little, Brown and Company, 1966.

Male Orgasm.   During orgasm, a series of pleasurable contractions in the testes and tissues of the penis occur as the sperm-containing semen is ejaculated. The heartbeat and rate of breathing reach a maximum level, and the male loses voluntary control of the sexual apparatus. The greater the volume of fluid ejaculated by the male, which is generally determined by the amount of time that has elapsed between orgasms, the greater the experience of sexual pleasure associated with ejaculation. Although many parts of the male's body are reacting in some way to the orgasmic experience, the focus of feeling and attention is on the pelvic region, particularly the penis.

Female Orgasm. Unlike males, females are capable of experiencing multiple orgasms in any single sexual encounter, and subsequent orgasms after the first can be more pleasurable. The female orgasmic experience begins with a focus of feeling in the clitoris, then radiates upward through the pelvis. Many women then experience a feeling of warmth radiating through the rest of the body, followed by a feeling of pelvic throbbing focused in the vagina and lower pelvic region. This throbbing sensation is related to rhythmic contractions of the uterus and lower portions of the vaginal canal. The heartbeat may double its rate during orgasm, and the rate of breathing extends two to three times its normal level.

It is important to note that the experience of orgasm for both males and females can vary considerably from person to person and from one sexual episode to the next. The experience varies both in terms of intensity and duration. For males, the experience of orgasm depends largely on the volume of ejaculate that has developed between orgasmic experiences, but is also related to age, general health, and degree of sexual stimulation. For women, the experience of orgasm is much more influenced by social and psychological factors, such as feelings for the partner, previous sexual experiences, daily nervous tension and anxiety, fear of pregnancy, guilt about sexual activity, and duration and type of foreplay. Perhaps these male-female differences in regard to influences on orgasmic experiences account for the finding of Kinsey, et al. (1953), that over 95 percent of all men reported attaining orgasm on a regular basis (2 to 3 times per week), but only 63 percent of all women reported attaining orgasm at all by the end of the first year of marriage. More recent studies have found that nearly 40 percent of wives experience orgasm during intercourse only occasionally, and 7 percent never have experienced orgasm (Hunt, 1974; Tavris and Sadd, 1977). The experience of orgasm is simply another manifestation of differences that can develop in sexual scripts in the process of socialization, differences which may require open and honest communication if partners are to realize a reciprocal and mutually fulfilling sexual relationship.

Homosexuality

A *homosexual* person is one whose preferred sexual partner is the same gender (male-male; female-female), in contrast to the heterosexual person whose preferred sex partner is of the opposite gender (female-male). Although more than simply a matter of sexual choice, homosexuality today has become a relatively visible, open, and increasingly acceptable life-style in many cultures around the world, including our own. Such has not always been the case. Until the 1970s the homosexual life-style was far more subdued and hidden as a result of strong negative attitudes in "straight" society toward homosexuals. Often, these negative attitudes were expressed in the form of sanctions, or punishment: homosexuals were persecuted by laws that made many of their sexual activities illegal; policies of employers prevented homosexuals from being hired for work they were fully qualified to do; governmental regulations prevented them from gaining custody of children after divorce, or adopting children, even if they were capable of effective parenting; and friends and relatives rejected their "deviant sexual behavior" and excluded them from social activities. Although homosexuals have made great strides toward removing the legal and social stigma attached to their life-style, many of the negative attitudes and sanctions still exist. These are barriers that reduce the homosexual person's chances for realizing fulfillment of individual growth needs and human intimacy throughout adulthood.

In this section we will examine homosexuality as it relates to the broader area of human sexuality in general. We will consider the social and psychological aspects of the homosexual life-style and homosexual relationships more fully in chapter 16, when marriage and family careers of the future are discussed.

HOMOSEXUAL BEHAVIOR

The most common kinds of sexual scripts among homosexual men include kissing, mutual penis stimulation to orgasm, anal intercourse, and oral-genital contact (fellatio) [Witters and Jones-Witters, 1980; Wilson, Strong, Robbins, and Johns, 1980]. Among homosexual women, or "lesbians" (note that the comparable acceptable term for male homosexuals is "gay"), sexual play most often involves mutual petting of the breasts, tongue and lip kissing, mutual masturbation of the genital area to orgasm, and oral-genital contact (cunnilingus). Contrary to popular belief, lesbians do not typically use simulated penises (dildos) or other objects that penetrate the vagina.

The objects of their erotic mental images are women, not men, and such male substitutes are usually viewed as undesirable. For both homosexual men and women, the same general pattern that is seen in the heterosexual population seems to hold: sexual scripts that involve variety, creativity, and taking adequate time in sexual expression are associated with sexual fulfillment and satisfaction.

Homosexuals of either sex sometimes adopt different role scripts in their sexual relationships, as do heterosexuals. These roles usually reflect the preferences of partners to be either sexually dominant and aggressive *vis à vis* their partners, or passive and submissive. The dominant lesbian role is known as the "butch," and the submissive role is the "fem." Among gay men, the dominant role is the "bull," and the submissive role is the "queen." However, research has shown that most homosexuals can and do play either role, depending on the sexual partner and the circumstances surrounding the sexual episodes (Bell and Weinberg, 1978). In addition, many in the homosexual community today encourage the rejection of these roles as harmful stereotypes modeled after the traditional "straight" heterosexual sexual pattern of male dominance-female submissiveness (Wilson, et al., 1980). This more contemporary norm encourages sexual mutuality and equality in the homosexual relationship.

INCIDENCE OF HOMOSEXUALITY IN THE UNITED STATES

Both male and female homosexual behavior has been observed in nearly all mammal species, including cats, dogs, sheep, cattle, horses, rabbits, rats, mice, pigs, monkeys, and chimpanzees (Godow, 1982; Ford and Beach, 1953). Humans, however, are the only species in which individuals prefer homosexual contact exclusively (Reiss, 1980; Beach, 1977). In addition, homosexual behavior has been found to exist in cultures all around the world. In some, homosexuality has been a common and accepted pattern of sexual partner preference. In ancient Greece, for example, homosexual unions were not only tolerated, but they were encouraged (Witters and Jones-Witters, 1980). Homosexual unions have also been accepted in various cultures in Africa and South America (Ford and Beach, 1953). In most other cultures where homosexuality has appeared, however, strong social pressure and punishment of those involved in homosexual relationships have kept visible evidence of such behavior at a minimum (Godow, 1982).

For a number of reasons, it is impossible to estimate with any degree of precision the incidence of homosexuality in contemporary American society. First is the problem of *definition*. Should we define as homosexual two 16-year-old adolescents who experiment with their emerging sexuality by engaging in one or two homosexual encounters? What if neither engages in homosexual behavior again? And what about the person who is married, and satisfied with the heterosexual relationship with the spouse, who has only occasional desires for homosexual contacts? Is a person homosexual who desires sexual contact with others of the same sex, yet does not act on his or her fantasies?

In addressing the question of defining homosexuality, Kinsey, et al. (1948), in their study of sexuality in the human male, concluded that homosexuality is really not an "either-or" phenomenon. Rather, homosexuality and heterosexuality are a matter of degree, accurately viewed as nonmutually exclusive dimensions of the same continuum (see Figure 5.10). In Figure 5.10, an individual could be placed at any point along the homosexuality-heterosexuality continuum. The 6 point on the scale represents a person who is exclusively homosexual, with no desire for sexual contact with a person of the opposite sex. Conversely, point 0 on the scale is the exclusively heterosexual individual, one who desires sexual contact with opposite-sex persons only. Between these extremes are varying shades of *bisexuality*, a person who is sexually interested in either males or females. Point 3, for example, is the person who is equally desirous of homosexual and heterosexual activity. Because of this continuum of varying degrees of homosexual and heterosexual choice, it is difficult to identify a specific number of people who can be defined as homosexual.

Beyond this issue of defining what homosexuality is and what it is not, there are other problems in generating reliable estimates of the incidence of homosexuality in our society. As stated previously, the punitive attitudes and practices of society toward homosexuals have kept many "in the closet," where they cannot be counted by routine methods. Also, some individuals who have homosexual tendencies, which result in one or more homosexual episodes, repress their urges and refuse to adopt an identity or self-concept as a homosexual person. Such individuals,

FIGURE 5.10.   Heterosexual-Homosexual Rating Scale. (Alfred C. Kinsey, et al., *Sexual Behavior in the Human Male* [Philadelphia: Saunders, 1948]), p. 63. Based on both psychological factors and actual behavior:

0-exclusively heterosexual with no homosexual
1-predominantly heterosexual, only incidentally homosexual
2-predominantly heterosexual, but more than incidentally homosexual
3-equally heterosexual and homosexual
4-predominantly homosexual, but more than incidentally heterosexual
5-predominantly homosexual, but incidentally heterosexual
6-exclusively homosexual

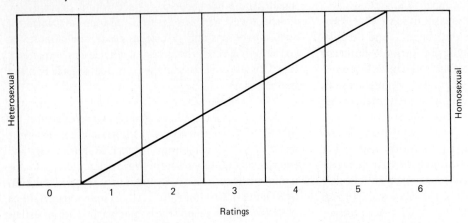

too, are likely to elude the scientist attempting to estimate homosexuality incidence.

Bearing these problems in mind, it is interesting to see the variation in estimated homosexual incidence reported by the various sex researchers identified earlier in this chapter. Kinsey, et al. (1948), for example, reported that 37 percent of the males in his sample had experienced at least one homosexual encounter (most often an incidental or isolated experience in adolescence), and another 13 percent had at least fantasized about homosexual contact with a positive response. Only 50 percent of his sample did Kinsey and his colleagues consider to be a *0,* exclusively heterosexual, on his homosexuality scale (see Figure 5.10). Eighteen percent of Kinsey's males reported having had at least as much homosexual as heterosexual experience over a 3-year period (a *3* on the Kinsey scale), and 8 percent reported exclusively homosexual experience and mental response for at least a 3-year period during adolescence and adulthood (a *6* on the scale). In the Kinsey, et al. (1953) study of females, the reported incidence of homo-

sexuality was far less than it was for males. The sample was divided into unmarried, married, and previously married (divorced and widowed) women, and Kinsey, et al. found that from 8 to 20 percent had experienced at least one homosexual experience; between 1 and 7 percent had experienced at least as many homosexual as heterosexual encounters (*3 – 6* on the scale); and only 0.3 to 3.0 percent reported exclusively homosexual experience in their lives (*6* on the scale).

Subsequent studies conducted in the 1970s reported substantially lower estimates of male homosexuality than Kinsey's. Hunt (1974), for example, found that only 10 percent of his male sample had at least one homosexual encounter after age 15, and only 4 percent rated themselves as predominantly or totally homosexual. Hunt's estimates for females are more consistent with Kinsey's, however, in that 7 percent of his single respondents, and 2 percent of his married respondents, reported more than incidental homosexual experience after age 19. (Kinsey's estimates ranged from between 2 and 14 percent for the same categories.) Hite (1976) found that 8 percent of her respondents reported at least one homosexual experience, but Tavris and Sadd (1977) reported that 3 percent of the married women in their sample had homosexual experience.

Three conclusions can be drawn from these various studies. First, the American population is not as exclusively heterosexual as many people believe. A substantial number have at least bisexual tendencies. Second, the incidence of male homosexuality is significantly greater than that of female homosexuality, perhaps twice as great. This difference probably reflects the more permissive atmosphere that surrounds male sexuality in general, because female sexuality historically has been more suppressed (and limited to a marital context) than that of males (Godow, 1982). Third, most males who report some homosexual experience had isolated or incidental encounters as adolescents and lived the remainder of their lives in predominantly heterosexual relationships. Clearly, many humans are capable of engaging in a variety of sexual experiences, whether with a person of the same sex or of the opposite sex.

CAUSES OF HOMOSEXUALITY

Theories attempting to explain the origins of homosexual preferences abound in the medical and social science literature. However, research comparing predominantly or exclusively homosexual and heterosexual people have yielded inconsistent, and at times contradictory, results. Sexual-partner preference is a complex aspect of human existence, and scientifically valid explanations are simply lacking at the present time.

Part of the difficulty in finding adequate explanations lies in the propensity of some to consider heterosexuality "healthy," "normal," and "functional," while homosexuality is considered "sick," "abnormal," or "dysfunctional" for the individual. Some believe that homosexuality is caused by hormonal or genetic defects in the person. According to these theories, homosexuality is rooted in deficient female or male sex hormones in the fetus during the prenatal stage of development, or by a genetic predisposition to behave in a homosexual way, given favorable circumstances in childhood or adulthood. Other theories target the origin of homosexuality in the

dynamics of the child's family. According to one psychoanalyst (Bieber, 1962), gay males have an intense fear of women because of mothers who were overly protective and "smothered" them as young children. Their fathers, Bieber says, were indifferent and uncaring about them as children, and simultaneously projected an extremely masculine role image. Lesbians, on the other hand, had overly protective fathers, and distant, weak, and uninterested mothers. This pattern, the theorist claims, would lead to the seeking of intimate relationships with other females, to fill the void left by the girl's mother.

Still other theories point to the role of the child's experiences in the family and with peers while growing up. In this view, some people develop homosexual tendencies when they feel that they are unable to live up to the culturally defined expectations for their gender. Traditionally, these are achievement and success in the educational and occupational worlds for men, and marriage and motherhood for women. Also included in this perspective are the child's sexual experiences while growing up. The results of Kinsey's and other researchers' studies have shown that during childhood one is likely to have a number of opportunities to engage in sexual play and discussion about sexuality with peers of the same or opposite sex. Playing "doctor" or "house," expressing curiosity about one's own and another's gentalia, and engaging in "touching" of one another's body parts are all normal and rather common childhood experiences. Whether one develops a sexual preference that is homosexual, heterosexual, or both depends upon which experiences are perceived to be rewarding and which ones are not. In addition, sexual orientation is influenced by reactions of peers and parents to one's emerging sexuality. Satisfying homosexual experiences are likely to be reinforced when peers or parents warn the child of the "evils" of sex and the danger of becoming sexually involved with a person of the opposite sex (e.g., loss of reputation, pregnancy, sexually transmitted disease, and so on). Heterosexual encounters that are satisfying, on the other hand, are more likely to be reinforced when family members or friends encourage the more usual progression of heterosexual involvement found in our culture. As Reiss (1980:159) notes, heterosexual experiences more often receive positive reinforcement from peers and parents than do homosexual ones:

Starting at very early ages one learns to fall in love and to have crushes on members of the opposite gender. Then one learns, by senior high school, to go to movies with someone of the opposite gender, to dance, and to date. Each step helps in the learning processes involved in the next step. Related to this overall process is a constant passing down from older and similar age peers of the lore of sexual and romantic relationships. Beliefs concerning the glories of romantic attachments are passed down more often in the female peer group and stories of the wonders of sexual excitement are more often passed down in the male group. These cultural attitudes also prepare one for choosing a partner of the opposite gender. Often, there is open ridicule or hostility toward homosexuality incorporated in the youth culture which further pressures toward heterosexual choices. Parents, too, pass down, often through indirect comments about sexuality, a perspective that supports heterosexual behavior.

It is likely that any one (or a combination) of these theories explains sexual partner preference for a particular individual. Genetic or horomonal predispositions may either be reinforced, or overridden, by learning experiences in the context of one's family and friends. Whatever the case, it is generally agreed upon, in the scientific and medical communities, that homosexuality is not indicative of a "sick" or pathological person. The American Psychiatric Association and the American Psychological Association have both removed homosexuality from their lists of mental illness. Today, homosexuality is viewed as an alternative expression of one's sexuality rather than as a pathological mental condition or physical disturbance.

Myths about Human Sexuality

In responding to questions he had received from his students and members of his lecture audiences, the late psychologist and sex educator James Leslie McCary wrote a book entitled *Sexual Myths and Fallacies* (McCary, 1971). A selection of the various myths discussed by McCary follows. Some have already been identified in this chapter. The interested reader is encouraged to consult McCary's book for a more thorough listing and discussion.

MYTH ONE: NOCTURNAL EMISSIONS ("WET DREAMS") ARE INDICATIONS OF SEXUAL DISORDERS.
It is estimated that nearly 85 percent of all males have experienced orgasm as a result of erotic

dreams. Although the frequency of such dreams decreases in adulthood, they can continue as a normal outcome of a person's imagination in combination with a certain level of sexual tension. Women, too, experience nocturnal orgasm as a result of erotic dreams, although the frequency of such dreams *increases* with age, for women. For both men and women, however, nocturnal orgasm accounts for a very small percentage of their total number of orgasms.

MYTH TWO: WOMEN EJACULATE, AS MEN DO.
Although women secrete a mucous substance in the vagina during sexual excitement, there is no female counterpart to the ejaculation process in males.[4]

MYTH THREE: SIMULTANEOUS ORGASMS ARE MORE SATISFACTORY THAN THOSE EXPERIENCED SEPARATELY BY THE MALE AND FEMALE.
Although the goal of the two partners experiencing orgasm at the same moment may be important for some couples, it is often more pleasurable if the male attempts to delay his own orgasm until the female has been fully satisfied.

MYTH FOUR: WOMEN ARE INCAPABLE OF MULTIPLE ORGASMS.
We have already discussed the fallacy of this statement in reviewing the survey research of Kinsey and the clinical observations of Masters and Johnson.

MYTH FIVE: THERE IS A DIFFERENCE BETWEEN VAGINAL AND CLITORAL ORGASMS.
The clinical research of Masters and Johnson (1966) demonstrated that women experience one type of orgasm regardless of the source of sexual stimulation, whether it is indirect, through penile penetration, or direct clitoral stimulation.

MYTH SIX: IT IS DANGEROUS TO HAVE SEXUAL INTERCOURSE DURING MENSTRUATION.
As already stated, the aversion people have to sexual relations during the female's menstrual period is culturally conditioned and has no basis in physiological fact. As McCary pointed out: "Life is short enough as it is, so why shoot down three or four days out of each twenty-eight?" (1971:13).

MYTH SEVEN: THE BEST HEALTH IS ENJOYED BY THOSE WHO ABSTAIN FROM SEX.

Despite the sense of fatigue that some may experience after sexual intercourse, there is no evidence to suggest that sex is unhealthy. Related to this myth is the misconception that athletes should refrain from sexual relations the night before competition because it may diminish their performance ability. It is the long hours of "wining, dining, and sleeplessness" that might accompany having sexual relations, not sex itself, that can diminish an athlete's performance the next day.

MYTH EIGHT: A LARGE PENIS IS IMPORTANT TO A WOMAN'S SEXUAL GRATIFICATION, AND THE MAN WITH A LARGE PENIS IS MORE SEXUALLY POTENT THAN THE MAN WITH A SMALLER PENIS.

With only a few exceptions, where the penis may be so large that it causes pain or discomfort for the female, or is so unusually small that penetration cannot be maintained, the size of the penis has no bearing on the female's level of satisfaction. The outer tissues of the vagina are quite elastic and can accommodate well to just about any size penis.

MYTH NINE: SEXUAL INTERCOURSE SHOULD BE AVOIDED DURING PREGNANCY.

There are no sound reasons to avoid sexual relations during pregnancy, at least until three to six weeks prior to the baby's due date. If there is no pain associated with sex, if the uterine membrane is intact, and if the woman's health and pregnancy are otherwise normal (e.g., no bleeding or spotting), then sexual relations *should* be maintained if both partners so desire (see chapter 11). Pregnancy and childbirth are associated with so many changes and tensions for a couple that sex may play a valuable role in maintaining the emotional bond between husband and wife during this time of heightened stress. However, because recent studies have found a small increase in the chance of infection in the woman as the result of sex within six weeks of the due date, and because the uterine contractions resulting from female orgasm can initiate the process of labor within three weeks of the due date, the best advice is to consult a physician before engaging in sexual relations during the final six weeks of pregnancy.[5]

MYTH TEN: EACH INDIVIDUAL IS ALLOTTED JUST SO MANY SEXUAL EXPERIENCES, AND WHEN THEY ARE USED UP, SEXUAL ACTIVITY IS FINISHED FOR THAT PERSON.

The root of this myth lies in the belief that the male can produce only so much semen or so many sperm cells in a lifetime, so that his ejaculate eventually becomes exhausted. However, the male is continually producing ejaculatory material, replacing that which is "used," regardless of how many orgasms are experienced in his lifetime.

MYTH ELEVEN: ALCOHOL IS A SEXUAL STIMULANT, AND INCREASES THE ENJOYMENT OF SEXUAL PLAY.

Although alcohol may reduce one's inhibitions about sex, too much alcohol can reduce sexual enjoyment for both men and women. Alcohol is a depressant that anesthetizes and deadens nerve endings. When neural pathways are blocked, erection of the penis may become a physical impossibility for the male, and the female may not even *feel* the contact made by her male partner. Orgasm is unlikely under either of these conditions.

MYTH TWELVE: ONCE A MAN OR WOMAN IS STERILIZED, THE SEX DRIVE DIMINISHES.

Neither tubal ligation (female sterilization) nor vasectomy (male sterilization) inhibit sexual response mechanisms. If anything, the fear of pregnancy that is removed as a result of sterilization has been found to *enhance* sexual enjoyment for many couples.

MYTH THIRTEEN: MASTURBATION IS KNOWN TO CAUSE LUNACY, ACNE, AND A CONSTELLATION OF OTHER PHYSICAL AND PSYCHOLOGICAL PROBLEMS.

The results of Kinsey's research, and that of Hunt, Hite, and others in more recent years, has shown that almost all men and the majority of women have masturbated (self-stimulated) to orgasm at some point in their lives. Experts on human sexuality agree that masturbation is a perfectly normal mode of sexual expression, and the only harm that is caused by it are the feelings of guilt aroused by believing in this myth.

MYTH FOURTEEN: VAGINAL-PENIS INTERCOURSE IS THE ONLY NORMAL METHOD OF SEXUAL RELATIONS.

The normal range of human sexual behavior is quite broad. Most people today experiment with any of a number of sexual techniques, none of which is intrinsically harmful or perverted. Again, variety and experimentation in sexuality only seems to enhance the sexual bond between partners, allowing them to realize the potential for fulfillment that sex is capable of providing.

Sexual Dysfunctions

There are a number of problems that can plague a sexual relationship. Sexual problems, or dysfunctions, are sometimes rooted in biological or physical abnormalities. Usually, however, sexual dysfunctions are related to conflict in sexual-role scripts, psychological problems, or emotional "hang-ups" in regard to one's sexuality. Hence, sexual dysfunctions can be treated and cured by modern methods of sex therapy. Therapy often focuses on enhancing the skills of partners to communicate about their sexual needs and preferences, thereby increasing their abilities to devlop a mutually fulfilling sexual relationship. We will examine three such dysfunctions here, acknowledging that others do exist.

IMPOTENCE

According to Masters and Johnson (1970), impotence is the inability of the male to achieve or maintain an erection. Impotence thereby prevents the male from engaging in sexual intercourse. Although impotence may be related to a physical problem in the man's central nervous system, the cause is usually related to emotional or psychological barriers. Impotence is the diagnosis when the man's failure rate approaches 25 percent of all occasions in which he attempts to engage in intercourse. Occasional failure to achieve an erection because of overindulgence in food or alchohol, illness, or fatigue should not be viewed as indicative of impotence.

Impotence sometimes stems from early sexual experiences of the adolescent male, or experiences in his family (Masters and Johnson, 1970:137–138). Impotence can also develop when one of the normal occasions of a failure to achieve an erection undermines the man's self-confidence, and he begins to have doubts about his ability to perform sexually. The anxiety caused by these doubts leads him to experience difficulty in achieving an erection on the next occasion for sexual intercourse, and the initial self-doubts are reinforced, the anxiety heightens, and so on, until he finds himself totally unable to engage in sexual behavior. To make matters worse, the female partner may blame the male or herself for his problem; the morale of the relationship is threatened, and conflict can erupt. This only increases the male's anxiety level and further complicates the problem.

The major treatment goal of the sex therapist working with an impotent male is to remove his anxiety about sexual performance. The therapist also works to relieve the female's fears about her partner's inability to perform sexually (Masters and Johnson, 1970:196). The couple is taught how to communicate sexually, using the foreplay techniques that each finds most stimulating. Once the partners learn this skill, the impotent male and his partner are better able to relax and enjoy each other. The ability to achieve an erection increases under these more relaxed conditions. Therapy with impotent males is highly successful with today's modern methods of treatment.

PREMATURE EJACULATION

Masters and Johnson (1970:92) define premature ejaculation as the male not being able to "control his ejaculatory process for a sufficient length of time during intercourse to satisfy his partner in at least 50 percent of their sexual encounters." A serious problem for a sexual relationship emerges when the male repeatedly is unable to delay his orgasm until the female partner has been sexually satisfied. Recall that the *refractory period* following ejaculation causes the male to lose his ability to maintain an erection and, usually, to lose his interest in further sexual intercourse for several minutes, or even several hours. The female partner is therefore likely to view the repeated instances of premature ejaculation with great frustration and perhaps even anger, accusing the male of selfishness or of being uninterested in her sexual satisfaction. She may feel that she is "being used sexually, rather than loved," and major conflicts can arise.

For some men, having a sexual-role script that allows for their own gratification without regard to that of the female partner (as is usually the case in male sexual contacts with prostitutes), leads to a pattern of quick ejaculation (McCary, 1973). Other males develop premature ejaculatory habits as teenagers or young adults who begin experimenting with sex under less than ideal circumstances. According to McCary (1973:343):

These experiences usually took place in a parked car, in the imminent danger of being spotlighted by the police; or on a couch in the living room of the girl's parents, where at any moment her father was liable to bound into the room, shotgun in his hand and blood in his eye. The anxiety engendered by these settings served to condition many younger men to the pattern of quick ejaculation.

Premature ejaculation, therefore, emerges as a pattern of sexual response that is learned and reinforced as a habit over time.

As with treating impotence, the sex therapist works to help the partners establish open channels of communication relating to their sexual behavior. It usually takes both the male and female partners in therapy to learn techniques of controlling the male's ejaculatory process.

Any form of sexual inadequacy is a problem of *mutual* involvement for partners in a marriage. With a wife's full cooperation, her willingness to learn and to apply the basic principles of ejaculatory control, and the warmth of her personal involvement expressed openly to her mate, reversal of this crippling marital distress is essentially assured. (Masters and Johnson, 1970:113)

In their own work in sex therapy, Masters and Johnson (1970:113) reported a 97.8 percent success rate for the 186 premature ejaculators they attempted to help.

Recently, sex therapists have been focusing on the opposite problem among some men — *ejaculatory incompetence* (Razani, 1978). This is the inability of the male to experience an orgasm and ejaculate, despite the fact that he is able to achieve and maintain an erection and otherwise engage in sexual intercourse. Sometimes ejaculatory incompetence is assocated with a low level of sexual desire, but this is not generally the case. Because this sexual dysfunction has only recently been recognized as one deserving study, treatment for it is still in an experimental and tentative stage.

FEMALE ORGASMIC DYSFUNCTION

Whereas impotence and premature ejaculation are sexual dysfunctions that focus on the male's sexual response, orgasmic dysfunction relates to the female's response patterns and capabilities. Masters and Johnson (1970) define orgasmic dysfunction as the inability of a female to move beyond the plateau stage in the sexual response cycle (see Figure 5.9).

Female orgasmic dysfunction usually is a result of psychological and emotional factors, not physical ones. Some women have learned sexual-role scripts stating that sex is "a man's pleasure and a woman's duty." Certain cultural values regarding sexuality dictate that women should not enjoy the feelings and sensations of sex. If they do, they are behaving in animal-like and undisciplined ways. This sexual double standard is ingrained in the minds of young girls who grow up thinking that sex is "bad," "dirty," or that "good girls don't do it." This repressive atmosphere shrouding the development of sexual scripts among young women can carry over into adulthood, so that even when engaging in sexual behavior in marriage, the feeling that they are doing something "wrong" leads to guilt, anxiety, and consequently, lack of sexual responsiveness. In addition, females with partners who ejaculate early, or those with partners who do not take the time to engage in sufficient foreplay to set the tone for stimulating the female to orgasm, are also unlikely to experience orgasm or "feel anything" as a result of sexual intercourse. Some experience pain because they become tense at the dreaded thought of intercourse, possibly as a result of early sexual encounters involving conditions of fear, force, or violence.

Orgasmic dysfunction may also result from placing *too much* emphasis on orgasm. Some women get caught up in what they believe "modern sexually liberated women" should feel as a result of intercourse: rockets exploding, lights flashing, and multiple orgasms with each sexual encounter (Ellis, 1961). In a sense, these women try too hard to achieve orgasm but do not really enjoy the act of sexual intercourse with their partners for the purpose of providing *mutual* pleasure to each other.

Therapists recognize two types of orgasmic dysfunction: *primary,* in which the woman has never in her life had an orgasmic experience as a result of any method of sexual stimulation; and *situational,* in which the woman has reached orgasm on at least one occasion by any means of stimulation (masturbation or intercourse, for example), but can no longer do so. Just as is true in the treatment of male sexual dysfunctions, the therapy for orgasmic dysfunction among women involves the establishment of open and honest lines of communication between the male and female partners. For example, Masters and Johnson (1970:229) found in their clinical sample of married couples, a high correlation between females complaining of orgasmic dysfunction and partners who were premature ejaculators. If orgasmic dysfunction is more directly related to negative learning experiences in the female's past, the emphasis is placed on getting the female to accept her own sexuality as valid and legitimate. She must learn that sexual response is a healthy and normal type of behavior for a woman, and she must develop a realistic set of expectations in regard to what a sexual relationship can and cannot provide. In addition, she must learn that orgasm cannot be *forced* or *willed*.

Love, Sex, and Gender Roles

There are many possible connections between the concepts of love, sex, and gender roles. First, they are all, to varying degrees, composed of *normative scripts* that partners bring into intimate relationships such as marriage. As a result of our interactions with parents, friends, siblings, and others in our social environments, we learn what to expect from ourselves and others when it comes to loving, gender-appropriate behavior, and modes of sexual expression. Second, regardless of how thorough and detailed these scripts may be when we enter intimate relationships on the path to marriage, there is always room for improvisation in any of them. Premarital and marital partners help to shape normative scripts in areas that have not been fully established for our roles as lovers and sex partners. In addition, new experiences may force us to re-evaluate our role scripts in these areas.

LOVE AND SEX

Several experts agree that sexual intercourse is a far more fulfilling and gratifying experience when it takes place in a context of commitment and affection for the partner, such as that provided by love (May, 1969; McCary, 1973). Researchers have found that premarital

sexual relations are most likely to occur when partners believe that they are in love, feel a strong sense of affection for one another, and are committed to the future of the relationship (Reiss, 1967; Sorensen, 1973; Thompson and Spanier, 1978). The same is true for sexual relations in marriage—spouses often report satisfaction with sexual relations when they have open communication channels, mutual respect, affection, and commitment (Hine, 1980). It is interesting to note that satisfaction with sex in marriage is primarily a *result,* not a cause, of satisfaction with other aspects of the relationship, such as reciprocal exchanges of affection and understanding between the partners. This does not rule out the possibility that satisfaction with sex can have a positive effect on marriage as a whole. However, sexuality in marriage must be considered in the total context of the marital relationship, being influenced by the level of intimacy, warmth, and mutuality experienced by the marriage partners at any one time.

GENDER ROLES AND SEX

Recall that in chapter 4 we stated that gender roles prescribe the privileges, obligations, and appropriate behavior of males and females. Sexual scripts of both men and women are influenced by gender roles, in terms of favored positions in intercourse, attitudes toward foreplay, the experience of orgasm, and the desired frequency of sexual relations. However, sexual equality among men and women has increased over the years, along with the general shift toward gender-role equality in our society. There has been an increased interest of both males and females in the female's sexual responsiveness and attainment of orgasm, as well as more permissive attitudes toward the female's sexuality both before and within marriage. These changes have occurred as a result of modern gender-role expectations among women: women are more dominant and assertive in their relationships with men, and less submissive and powerless than traditional gender roles would prescribe (Hunt, 1974; Reiss, 1980). For example, in a sample of employed professional women, Whitley and Paulsen (1975) found that female assertiveness was significantly related to sexual satisfaction and diversity of sexual activity. Mutual sexual satisfaction is also more likely when the male partner is expressive, understanding, and supportive, rather than dominant, all-powerful, and inexpressive—male traits more characteristic of traditional gender-role behavior (Rainwater, 1965; Rubin, 1976). The way we view ourselves as men and women, that is, our gender-role identities, as well as our feelings of love for another person, are closely related to our sexual scripts: to whom, when, where, and in what ways we express ourselves sexually.

Summary

Human sexuality is a complex phenomenon. Whether heterosexual, homosexual, or bisexual, it includes a unique combination of powerful biological, emotional, and social drives. Humans are capable of a wide range of sexual expression. The fact that human sexual relationships comprise such an important part of marriage means that partners should establish a fundamental understanding of the biological, emotional, and social aspects of sexuality so that this aspect of the marriage is allowed to develop in a satisfactory way. Ideally, this understanding would be acquired prior to marriage, or in the earliest stages of the marital career, before dysfunctional or unsatisfying patterns of sexual interaction are allowed to develop. Some male and female partners in a sexually intimate relationship have learned, and bring to marriage, quite conflicting sexual-role scripts. Because people learn their scripts relating to sexual expression from a diverse set of socialization agents—parents, friends, sex partners, books, and movies—norms relating to the frequency, timing, duration, foreplay techniques, and appropriate means for sexual expression may vary significantly from one person to the next. These potential differences in sexual-role scripts underscore the importance of *communication* between partners if the sexual relationship is to grow in a satisfying direction. So much of partners' ability to communicate about their sexuality depends upon the degree of *role reciprocity* that has previously emerged in the relationship; that is, the degree to which each partner's fulfillment of role obligations satisfies the expectations and perceived rights of the other. This fact is especially evident in the discussion of sexual dysfunctions and their treatment by sex therapists, who have found that only when partners are able to communicate effectively, and reciprocate warmth, support, and understanding, are they able to overcome the very serious barriers to sexuality posed by impotence, premature ejaculation, and female orgasmic dysfunction. Finally, there are definite linkages between the concepts of love, gender roles, and sexuality. To develop an adequate understanding of one of them, in any particular marriage relationship, requires placing it in the context of the other two. Clearly, the potential of marriage to foster the personal and mutual development of the partners depends, to a large extent, on the nature of each partner's definitions of love and the combination of gender-role and sexual-role scripts that are brought to the relationship.

Questions for Discussion and Review

1. What were your major sources of learning about sex? Parents? Friends? Books and magazines? A class in school? Did you find that one or more of these sources of sexual learning was more reliable than others in terms of providing accurate information? If so, which ones were they?

2. What myths about human sexuality did you believe prior to reading this chapter? What questions do you still have that need answering?

3. As stated in the text, our society has become more open and explicit about sex in the mass media of television, movies, books and magazines, and commercial advertising. Do you believe that this trend is good or bad? To what extent, if at all, should society regulate the availability of sexually explicit materials? Who should be responsible for setting the standards of what sexually explicit materials can or cannot be made available to the consumer?

4. To what degree is sex an important aspect of day-to-day life on the college campus? What are the major issues and problems facing today's college student in regard to sexual behavior? How might these problems be resolved to the benefit of both males and females on campus?

5. In what ways do males and females view sex differently? What problems arise as a result of male-female

differences in attitudes and expectations relating to sexual behavior?

6. Would our society be better off if we placed less emphasis on sex? If so, in what ways?

7. What is your attitude toward homosexuality? How open is the homosexual life-style in your community? Should it be more open? Less open? Explain your responses.

8. Should homosexual individuals be allowed to legally marry? Should either single or married homosexual be allowed to adopt children? Are there any occupations or positions in society which homosexuals should *not* occupy? In each case, explain your response.

Notes

1. Male castration is also possible by means of injection with a powerful hormonal drug. Depo Provera is a drug containing high levels of the female hormone progesterone, and was developed as a means of long-term birth control for women who would need only a single injection to provide several months of contraceptive protection (see chapter 6). In males, Depo Provera sharply reduces the male sex drive by reducing the level of the male hormone testosterone that is produced. A stormy legal controversy has recently emerged over the use of Depo Provera as a treatment for certain men convicted of rape. Courts in a number of states have given some rapists the option of long prison terms or castration by injection of Depo Provera. The controversy centers on the ethical issue of whether or not the legal system has the right to castrate a male in this or any other manner, and whether or not rapists should be be set free and "cured" by medical treatment rather than punished for their crimes. To date, the treatment has been used only on men whose rape-related crimes are attributed to an uncontrollable sex drive, and not on those whose crimes are rooted in a violent personality or feelings of hatred toward women. What do you think? What is the most ethical approach to this problem?

2. See McCary (1973) and Witters and Jones-Witters (1980) for a more complete description of the four typical patterns of sexual intercourse in our culture. In addition, a number of excellent books describe and illustrate a variety of sexual techniques that may expand the sexual-role scripts of partners who are willing to experiment. For example, see Alex Comfort's *Joy of Sex* (1972).

3. The reader must be aware that Kinsey's studies were conducted many years ago, and that the patterns he discovered may or may not be found today if attempts to replicate his findings were to be made. The important point, despite the "age" of his results, is that American adults satisfy sexual needs in a number of different ways—from one individual to the next, and even for a given person from one stage of adulthood to the next.

4. Recent scientific research has shown that some women (the percentage yet undetermined) may experience a type of ejaculation through an opening in the wall of the vagina. Usually referred to as the *Grafenberg Spot,* microscopic photography has shown the emission of a milky fluid at the time of orgasm for women who have such an opening. The spot is particularly sensitive to sexual stimulation, as well. Research is continuing in order to determine the source and nature of this response, the percentage of women who are capable of experiencing it, and any similarities it may bear to the nature and intensity of ejaculation in the male (Addegio, et al., 1981).

5. The research of Dr. Richard Naeye of Milton S. Hershey Medical Center of Pennsylvania State University, at Hershey, PA., has linked sexual intercourse during the last month of pregnancy to the occurrence of infections of the amniotic fluid. The thousands of records he examined showed that 156 infections per 1,000 births occurred among women who engaged in sex during the last month of pregnancy. The rate for those who abstained from sexual relations was 117 per 1,000 births. The frequency of infant death and illness was also somewhat greater among women experiencing intercourse and infection during the last month of pregnancy (*Arizona Daily Star,* August 14, 1980).

CHAPTER 6

Planning Families:
Current Contraceptive Methods and Issues

In this chapter, the methods of birth control available today will be explored, focusing on their relative effectiveness, costs, advantages, and disadvantages. In addition, contraceptive methods showing potential for use at some point in the future will be discussed. Current abortion techniques and their associated risks and costs will also be detailed. Sexually transmitted diseases (STD's) will also be examined, as they can have devastating effects on the sexual and reproductive lives of both men and women.

Reasons for Effective Family Planning

As the status and roles of men and women have changed over the past several years, so too have the goals and expectations of marriage partners changed in terms of the timing, number, and spacing of children. Indeed, a growing number of couples have decided to limit their families to one or two children, or have decided to remain permanently childless in marriage (see chapter 16). Let us look briefly at two trends that have influenced the family planning goals and behavior of married couples today.

WOMEN AND WORK: THE COSTS OF HAVING CHILDREN

Trends in the American birthrate show a marked decline in the average number of children born to women of childbearing age since the mid-1960s (see Feature 6.1). At least in part, this trend is the result of the rather dramatic movement of married women and mothers into the world of work and careers (see chapter 8). Traditionally, it has been the wife/mother who stays at home and cares for the children who are born, even if she had previously been employed outside the home. Children, however, are costly in terms of the time, energy, and money expended on them (see chapters 11 through 13), and many couples have realized the value of having smaller numbers of children, spaced in a way that will not interfere with the wife's employment outside the home. Effective family planning is therefore critical to those marriages

FEATURE 6.1 National Polls Show Increase in Number of Mothers Working
While Preferred and Actual Family Size Declines

Two national opinion and behavior polls conducted in 1980 have shown that the number and percentage of mothers employed in the labor force continue to increase while both the preferred and actual number of children continues to decrease. Citing that 95 percent of Americans feel that it is "important to use your mind and abilities," and that 81 percent believe that it is "highly important to have a good self-image," a 1980 Louis Harris survey concludes that these values

> are most significant these days to women who are now embarking on permanent work careers. The percentage of women working has risen from about 35 percent to 50 percent over the past 20 years and is likely to continue to rise during the next decade.

Another 1980 survey, conducted by George Gallup (*The Gallup Poll*), has found a concomitant decline in the preference of American adults for four or more children.

> Clear evidence that large families are going out of style in the United States is seen in a recent Gallup Survey which shows only 11 percent of Americans favoring families with four or more children, the lowest percentage in 44 years . . . In the 35 years since the 1945 measurement, an overall downward trend has been recorded in the proportion favoring large families, although as recently as 1968 no fewer than 41 percent of Americans said the ideal family size includes four or more children. From 1968 to the present, however, the number in favor of

such large families has plunged 30 percentage points. . . . The high cost of rearing children and uncertainty regarding the world situation are undoubtedly factors in the trend away from large families.

In addition, the *actual number* of children born to the average family has declined right along with these shifting preferences in the same time period, so that by 1982 the average number of children expected to be born per married woman was just under 2.0. In 1960, the average number was nearly 4 per married woman. Moreover, the increasing number of women in the labor force has been most marked for those with preschool (ages 1–5) and school-age (ages 6–12) children.

Taking all of this information together, it is reasonable to conclude that American husbands and wives are managing to effectively plan their families in order to meet the growing demand for women to enter the occupational world, whether they do so for reasons of financial necessity or to just "use their minds and abilities" and "to have a good self-image." Effective family planning behavior, then, appears to be a critical aspect of achieving financial stability in contemporary families, both by allowing women to enter the occupational world and by reducing the overall cost of childrearing.

SOURCE: *Arizona Daily Star,* January 1, 1981.

where the wife's employment is essential for the economic well-being of the family; where parenthood would threaten her career involvement and success; and where adding children would be more than the family could afford, regardless of whether or not the wife is employed outside the home. Despite small annual increases in birth rates since 1978 (see chapter 1), in 1982 the average number of children expected to be born per adult woman of childbearing age was slightly less than two — 1.8 (National Center for Health Statistics, 1984d).

SEXUAL EQUALITY AND
CONTRACEPTION: SEPARATING
SEX FROM PREGNANCY

The trend toward sexual equality in our society means that women are no longer content to be the "givers" of sexual enjoyment to their partners. Along with their male partners, women too wish to experience the pleasurable aspects of human sexuality without feeling guilty about it (see chapter 5). In addition, advances in the technology and effectiveness of birth control methods have helped to divorce the concepts of sex and pregnancy. No longer do men or women have to fear the risk of pregnancy when they engage in sexual intercourse. This fear has been a major source of anxiety in past years, especially for women; anxiety which has inhibited their ability to relax during sexual relations and to derive sexual gratification.

So long as sex and unwanted pregnancy remain related in the minds of sex partners, anxiety and tension are likely to result in a lack of sexual gratification. This fact is poignantly expressed in the following quote of a wife and mother of four children who participated in Rainwater's (1960) classic study of sexuality and family planning. This woman was asked how she felt about her sexual relationship with her husband:

We do it (have sex) less now and I enjoy it less. He enjoys it more, I do less because I'm afraid every time I'll get a baby for sure. We do it once a week now. It used to be two or three times. I put him away from me now because I'm afraid I'll get pregnant again. I don't enjoy it because I might get stuck with another baby. If I could do it and not get a baby it would be better. (Rainwater, 1960:136)

With the advent of effective contraceptive methods, both women and men now have the means to derive sexual gratification without adding children that are not wanted.

Fertility and Fecundity

Before discussing various methods of family planning, it is important to understand the definitions of two frequently confused concepts. *Fertility* is a measure of the actual number of children that a woman or group of women bear in their lifetimes. The *fertility rate* refers to

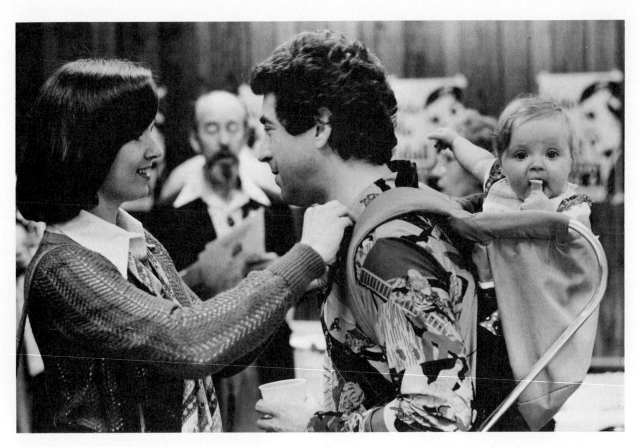

Compared to past generations, contemporary couples are better able to time and space the arrival of children in ways that meet their family planning expectations and career goals. *(Photo by Owen Franken.)*

the number of children born per 1,000 women of child-bearing ages, generally considered to be 15 to 44 years, in the population. *Fecundity,* on the other hand, refers to the biological capability of a married or unmarried couple to conceive a child.

In 1982, only 51 percent of all married couples were considered to be *fecund* (Mosher and Pratt, 1985) [see Figure 6.1]. Six percent were defined as *subfecund,* meaning that although it was possible for a couple to conceive a child, they had difficulty in doing so. Subfecundity also refers to women who, for some reason, are unable to carry a pregnancy to term. Subfecundity-related impairments might include a wife with one or both Fallopian tubes blocked, who releases an egg only infrequently or irregularly, or who has a disorder in the uterus. Husbands, too, can contribute to subfecundity if they have unusually low sperm counts. Another 2 percent of all married couples were identified as *long interval,* meaning that for three continuous years in marriage, prior to being interviewed, no contraception was employed and no pregnancy occurred. Thirteen percent were defined as *noncontraceptively sterile* as a result of a sterilizing operation conducted for health reasons; sterility because of illness or an accident;

or simply being unable to conceive a child because of a lack of egg or sperm production or blocked Fallopian tubes. Finally, 28 percent of all couples were identified as *contraceptively sterile,* those in which the husband or wife voluntarily had a sterilizing operation.

Birth Control Today: Effectiveness and Popularity

There are several types of contraceptive methods in use today. These methods range from those considered to be medically safe and effective to those viewed as ineffective and potentially harmful to the health. In addition, the various methods of birth control vary considerably in terms of their advantages, disadvantages, and financial cost. The major objections which people may have about using any particular contraceptive method, and whether or not they will actually use that method, relate directly to the perceived advantages, disadvantages, and costs involved. A method is more likely to be avoided if it is perceived to

FIGURE 6.1. Percent of All Currently Married Couples with Wife 15–44 Years of Age, by Fecundity Status: United States, 1982.

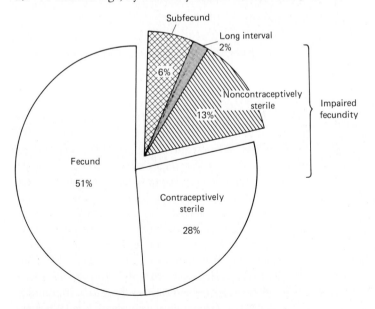

SOURCE: Mosher, W. D. and Pratt, W. F. Fecundity and Infertility in the United States, 1965–82. *Advance Data,* No. 104, Washington, D.C.: National Center for Health Statistics, Feb. 11, 1985.

have the disadvantages of being messy or unnatural; if it interferes with the spontaneity and enjoyment of sexual intercourse by requiring that the partners take time during foreplay to apply the method; if it involves health risks or adverse side effects; if it is too costly; or if it has too high a failure rate. *It is important to note that the perfect contraceptive method has not yet been discovered.* Actually, every method of fertility control has certain disadvantages, and the likelihood of any particular method being used depends largely upon its ratio of advantages to disadvantages. Finally, given the relative advantages and disadvantages associated with any method of birth control, the method of choice often varies over time in a relationship. For example, birth control pills may be used in the early years of marriage when a couple wishes to postpone the arrival of children. In later years, after the couple has had the number of children they desire, a more permanent method such as surgical sterilization may be used. As with other aspects of marriage and family life, family planning behavior changes as the context and circumstances of the marriage and family change over time.

The methods of birth control to be discussed here fall into one of three categories:

1. *Chemical methods,* such as the pill, which alter the body's hormone balance to prevent pregnancy.

2. *Barrier methods,* such as the diaphragm, creams and jellies, foams, and condoms, which prevent the sperm from entering the woman's uterus by providing an impenetrable shield. (Foams, creams, and jellies also have a *spermicidal* quality, meaning that the male's sperm cells are killed as they come into contact with the contraceptive.)

3. *Action methods,* such as surgical sterilization, withdrawal (coitus interruptus), rhythm, and lactation (a woman nursing a child), none of which provide an artificial barrier or introduce a chemical into the body, and all of which require some kind of effort on the part of the male, female, or both partners to prevent a pregnancy.

DEFINING CONTRACEPTIVE EFFECTIVENESS

In discussing the *effectiveness* of the various contraceptive methods, we will be referring to two concepts:

theoretical effectiveness and *actual effectiveness* rates. Theoretical effectiveness refers to the number of women out of 100 who would experience a pregnancy in one year's time while employing a particular contraceptive method in a complete and effective manner. This can also be described as applying the method in "textbook" fashion, following the instructions provided with the method "to the letter." *Actual user effectiveness,* on the other hand, refers to the number of women out of 100 who actually experience a pregnancy in one year's time while using any particular method. This is a more realistic estimate of a contraceptive's effectiveness because it takes into account the situational factors and unanticipated circumstances which people encounter. These would include failure to understand or follow the instructions provided with the method; not employing the method every time sexual intercourse takes place; carelessness in applying the method after one too many Margaritas; or not wanting to interrupt the excitement being experienced in sexual foreplay to apply the method.

Both theoretical and actual effectiveness rates for the various contraceptive methods to be discussed here are presented in Table 6.1. The various advantages, disadvantages, and costs of each method are summarized in Table 6.2. The reader should refer to these tables as we discuss each method.

POPULARITY OF CONTRACEPTIVE METHODS IN THE UNITED STATES

As can be seen in Table 6.3, voluntary surgical sterilization is today the most popular contraceptive method in the United States. These statistics are based on a large national survey of married and unmarried women, ages 15 to 44, in 1982 (Forrest and Henshaw, 1983). Of the 33.4 million women whose current circumstances placed them at risk of unintended pregnancy (sexually active, not pregnant or wanting to get pregnant), nearly one in three were either sterilized or had male sex partners who were sterilized (11.6 million, 32 percent). Among those couples using sterilization as a method, in 58 percent the female was sterilized (6.8 million), and in 42 percent the male was sterilized (4.9 million). In 1980 alone, more than 1 million American men and women chose to be sterilized as their method of birth control, representing a 19 percent increase over the number of sterilization operations in

TABLE 6.1. *Theoretical and Actual Effectiveness Rates of Various Contraceptive Methods. (Number of pregnancies during the first year of use per 100 nonsterile women initiating method)*

Method	Theoretical Effectiveness (used correctly and consistently)	Actual User Effectiveness (typical use patterns)
Surgical sterilization		
Tubal ligation	0.04	0.04
Vasectomy	0.15	0.15
Injectable progestin	0.25	0.25
Oral contraceptive (combined pill)	0.5	2.0
Condom plus spermicidal agent (foam)	Less than 1	5
Low-Dose oral progestin (minipill)	1	2.5
Intrauterine device (IUD)	1	5
Condom	2	10
Sponge with spermicide	a	10–20
Diaphragm with spermicide	2	19
Cervical cap	2	13
Spermicidal foam, cream, suppositories, jellies	3–5	18
Coitus interruptus (withdrawal)	16	23
Fertility-awareness techniques (basal body temperature, mucous method, calendar)	2–20	24
Chance alone	90	90
Douche	?	40

[a] There are inadequate data for determining the lowest observed failure rate of this new method of birth control.

SOURCE: Hatcher, et al. (1984:3).

1979 (Arizona Family Planning Council Newsletter, 1982b). From 1971 through 1982, nearly 13 million people in the United States underwent contraceptive sterilization operations. However, the tremendous popularity of sterilization seems to have peaked, as the number of such operations in 1982 dropped to 968,000 (a 15 percent decrease from 1981) [*Family Planning Perspectives,* 1984b]. Nonetheless, it is expected that the popularity of surgical sterilization as a method of birth control will remain quite high for years to come.

The second most popular method in 1982 was the oral contraceptive (pill), used by 27 percent (10 million) of those seeking to prevent a pregnancy. The condom is a distant third choice, with the remainder of the methods somewhat evenly distributed. It is also worthy of note that

more than 3 million women at risk of unintended pregnancy in 1982, or 8 percent of the total, were using *no* contraceptive method at all to prevent a pregnancy.

Preferences regarding contraceptive methods vary according to certain characteristics of the woman or the couple. Forrest and Henshaw (1983) found that women in their thirties and forties are more likely than others to rely on surgical sterilization, and women in their teens and twenties are far more likely to use the pill. Condoms are most frequently used by teenagers. Women at lower-income levels rely on sterilization, particularly of the female, more so than higher-income women. Higher-income women rely on the pill and sterilization about equally. In regard to race, Black women more often rely on the birth control pill than do white women, but the latter are more

TABLE 6.2. *Summary of Advantages and Disadvantages Associated With Various Contraceptive Methods*

Method	Advantages	Disadvantages
Surgical Sterilization Vasectomy	Highly effective; no chance for user error; does not interfere with sex act; minor surgical procedure requiring short recovery period; postoperative complications rare; repeated application of mechanical or chemical method not required; less costly than other sterilization procedures on females; inexpensive after initial surgery.	Nuisance effects of surgery (soreness, some pain); irreversible (a problem only if more children are wanted).
Tubal Ligation	Highly effective; no chance for user error; does not interfere with sex act; minor surgical procedure with short recovery period; postoperative complications rare; repeated application of mechanical or chemical method not required; inexpensive after initial cost of surgery.	Nuisance effects of surgery (soreness, some pain); irreversible (a problem only if more children are desired); more expensive than vasectomy.
Birth Control Pill	Highly effective; little chance for user error if routine followed; convenient; does not interfere with sex act; inexpensive; safe for most women.	Health risks to some groups of women (over 30 years of age, smokers, those prone to blood clots or high blood pressure, and those prone to certain cancers); not safe for diabetics or obese women; nuisance side effects (weight gain, nausea, breast tenderness, etc.); increases susceptibility to certain STD's (gonorrhea and trichomoniasis).
Intrauterine Device (IUD)	Highly effective; no chance for user error; does not interfere with sex act; repeated application of mechanical method not required; inexpensive; safe.	Difficult for some women to maintain in place; sometimes expelled unknowingly; nuisance effects (heavier menstrual flow and cramping); potential for an ectopic (tubal) pregnancy increases slightly; potential for pelvic infection or uterine perforation increases slightly.
Condom	High theoretical effectiveness; more convenient than other barrier methods; widely distributed and easy for anyone to obtain; inexpensive; safe; prevents or limits the spread of STD.	Potential for user error because of inconvenient features; interferes with foreplay; easily punctured and heat-sensitive; may reduce sensitivity for some men.
Diaphragm	High theoretical effectiveness when inserted properly with spermicidal jelly; can be inserted prior to intercourse, so it does not interefere with sex act; inexpensive; safe.	Potential for user error because of inconvenient features; requires skill and motivation by user; can become dislodged during intercourse; must be left in place for several hours after intercourse; some may find it messy, or are uncomfortable in touching genital area; easily punctured and heat-sensitive (must be regularly inspected for holes or tears); must be fitted by a physician.

TABLE 6.2. *(Continued)*

Method	Advantages	Disadvantages
Spermicidal Foam	High theoretical effectiveness when properly inserted; user effectiveness increases when used in combination with condom; widely distributed in pharmacies and easily obtained (no prescription necessary); inexpensive; safe.	Potential for user error because of inconvenient features; some may find it too messy; foreplay interrupted in some cases; must be left in vagina for several hours after intercourse; may cause allergic reaction (some brands).
Contraceptive Sponge	Can be inserted prior to intercourse; inexpensive; safe; can be purchased over the counter; one size fits; spermicide reduces risk of cervical cancer; can be left in place for 24 hours after insertion.	Potential for user error as result of improper insertion; requires skill and motivation of user; some might be uncomfortable in touching genital area; may lead to vaginal irritation or dryness.
Cervical Cap	High theoretical effectiveness; can be inserted prior to intercourse; inexpensive; safe; can be left in place for 36 to 48 hours after insertion.	Potential for user error as result of improper insertion; requires fitting by a medical professional; requires skill and motivation by the user; some might be uncomfortable in touching genital area; sizes vary, and some may not be able to be properly fitted; may lead to irritation of cervix or surrounding tissue or, possibly, pelvic infection.
Coitus Interruptus	Inexpensive; safe; does not require repeated application of a chemical or mechanical method; available for use at any time.	Low theoretical and user effectiveness rates; sex act must be interrupted prior to male orgasm; requires high level of self-control for male; may present psychological problems for some if enjoyment of sex act is reduced.
Fertility-awareness Techniques	High theoretical effectiveness (BBT and mucous methods); does not require repeated application as with a chemical method; inexpensive; safe; does not interfere with sex act.	High potential for user error (especially calendar method); requires motivation, knowledge, and patience by users; BBT influenced by many extraneous factors; restricts number of days during cycle when intercourse may take place.
Lactation	Does not interfere with sex act; safe; inexpensive; theoretically effective for several weeks.	When women will resume ovulation is unpredictable; effectiveness drops sharply as woman reduces breast-feeding; back-up method required after first several weeks of lactation.
Douche	Safe; inexpensive; easily available.	Low theoretical- and user-effectiveness rates; may actually increase risk of pregnancy.

TABLE 6.3. *Percentage and Number of Women in the United States Using Various Birth Control Methods in 1982.* (Married and unmarried women included)*

Method	Percent Using	Number Using (in millions)
Sterilization	32%	11.6 Million
(Female)	(19)	(6.8)
(Male)	(13)	(4.9)
Pill	27	10.0
IUD	6	2.3
Condom	12	4.5
Spermacides (foams, suppositories)	4	1.5
Diaphragm	5	1.9
Withdrawal	3	.9
Rhythm	2	.6
Other (douche)	0	.2
No method used	8	3.1
TOTAL	100%	33.4 Million

* Only women who were exposed to the risk of an unintended pregnancy in 1982 were included in this Table. Another 18.1 million women in the survey were not exposed to unintended pregnancy, for a number of reasons (never had sex; had gone through menopause; had a hysterectomy for medical reasons; were not fecund; were pregnant; or were trying to get pregnant). These women were not included.

SOURCE: Forrest and Henshaw (1983).

likely to rely on male or female sterilization. Blacks are also more likely than whites to be using no method at all. Of particular interest is the fact that religion makes little difference in contraceptive choice. Catholics, Protestants, and Jews rely on sterilization, pill use, and the other methods more or less equally (Forrest and Henshaw, 1983).

Modern Contraceptive Methods

SURGICAL STERILIZATION

There are two primary methods of surgical sterilization, each of which should be considered as permanent. *Vasectomy* is a surgical procedure to sterilize men, and *tubal ligation* is a surgical procedure designed to sterilize women. As can be seen in Figure 6.1 and Table 6.3, these methods have become quite popular relative to other contraceptive methods in use. These methods are the most effective both in terms of theoretical and actual user effectiveness rates (see Table 6.1).

Vasectomy. The purpose of a vasectomy is to sever the male's *vas deferens,* the tubes which connect the testes and seminal vesicles (described in chapter 5). This prevents any sperm cells from reaching the ejaculatory duct and mixing with the semen that is produced by the prostate gland, seminal vesicles, and bulbourethral glands (see Figure 6.2). The semen which is ejaculated during orgasm, therefore, contains no sperm cells. The male is unable to inpregnate a female, as a result.

The surgical procedure for a vasectomy is simple and quick. It can be completed in the physician's office, on an out-patient basis. A local anesthetic is used to numb the scrotum area, and two small incisions are made on each side of the scrotum to allow the physician access to the vas tubes. The tubes are then cut, and a small portion removed in order to reduce the chances of the tubes eventually reconnecting. The ends of the tubes are either crushed with a forceps or cauterized (burned) with an electroneedle in order to encourage scarring, thereby increasing the sperm-blocking potential of the operation. Each tube is then tied back on itself to further assure that the tubes will not reconnect or in any way allow sperm cells to pass through during ejaculation. The incisions are then stitched with sutures which automatically dissolve after the incisions have healed.

One advantage of the vasectomy method is that it is a reasonably fast and efficient surgical procedure which involves relatively little time taken out of one's daily activities. Medical complications, such as blood clotting or infection are rare. Although there is some scientific evidence to suggest that vasectomy may lead to long-term cardiovascular disorders in monkeys and baboons, such as heart disease or hardening of the arteries, there is even stronger evidence to suggest that no such long-term risks exist for human males (*Family Planning Perspectives,* 1984c). Some physical discomfort is almost certain to follow the operation, such as swelling, soreness, and some black-and-blueness, as the result of localized bleeding. However, the pain is minimal and can be alleviated by taking aspirin. Another major advantage of this contraceptive method is that it is *highly effective* (see Table 6.1). The chances of the

FIGURE 6.2.   Male Vasectomy, Showing Vas Deferens Before and After Surgery.

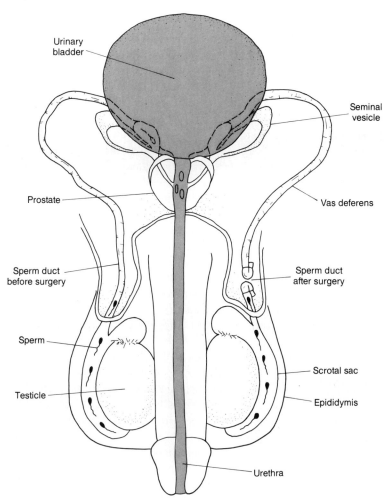

surgery being followed by a pregnancy in the male's partner are miniscule, even less than those associated with the birth control pill. Finally, vasectomy has the advantage of not involving application of a contraceptive device each time intercourse takes place. The spontaneity and enjoyment of sex are not reduced, as they are by methods that are perceived to be messy, unnatural, or interruptive of the sexual act. In addition, the fear of pregnancy is effectively eliminated. The volume of ejaculate and resultant pleasure experienced at orgasm are unaltered, because the male's semen continues to be produced at the normal rate. Sperm

also continue to be produced, but they are absorbed into the body by the action of white blood cells.

The disadvantages of vasectomy as a contraceptive method are few, although certain conditions may make this a highly undesirable method for some men. Perhaps the greatest potential disadvantage is that vasectomy is considered irreversible. This can be a serious problem if the male changes his mind about not wanting any more children. A change in childbearing intentions can occur for any of a number of reasons: death of a wife, death of a child, divorce, and remarriage are a few of the reasons. Although modern methods of microsurgery have realized some degree of success in reconnecting severed *vas deferentia* in order to restore fertility, these methods fail, in most cases, to either reconnect the tubes or allow enough sperm to be released to cause a pregnancy. Hence, vasectomy should be considered as a *permanent* contraceptive method, to be used only when the male is certain that his childbearing career is completed.

Tubal Ligation.   This procedure is analogous to the vasectomy for the male, and is a far simpler and more complication-free operation than is a hysterectomy.[1] A tubal ligation involves the severing of both Fallopian tubes so that the egg released each month is prevented from uniting with a sperm cell (see Figure 6.3). Although more than 100 variations of tubal ligation surgery have been identified (Hatcher, et al., 1978), only the three most commonly utilized procedures in the United States will be discussed here: *culpotomy, laparoscopy,* and *mini-laparotomy.*

The *culpotomy,* known also as "vaginal tubal ligation," involves no incisions or scarring of the outer skin.

FIGURE 6.3.   Tubal Ligation, Showing the Fallopian Tube Before and After Surgery.

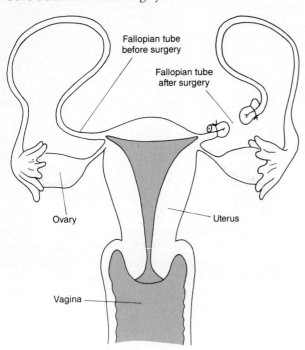

Fallopian tube before surgery

Fallopian tube after surgery

Ovary

Uterus

Vagina

The physician gains access to the Fallopian tubes through the vagina by making a small incision in the abdominal wall. The Fallopian tubes are then located, tied off, and cut. The incision is stitched with a self-dissolving suture. A portion of each tube is removed (known as the Pomeroy method) in order to prevent the severed ends of the tube from rejoining. The severed ends of the tubes may be cauterized (burned) in order to promote scarring. In the absence of postoperative complications, the woman who has had a culpotomy may go home on the same day as the operation.

The *laparoscopy* is accomplished by making a small incision just below the navel, and usually requires a general anesthetic and at least a one-day stay in the hospital. The surgeon uses an instrument, called a *laparoscope,* which has a long tube containing a high intensity beam of light and magnifying lens. The laparoscope is inserted through the abdominal incision to allow the surgeon to view the Fallopian tubes and surrounding tissues. A second incision is then made lower on the abdomen to allow a surgical blade and electric cauterization device to be inserted. Each tube is then cauterized and severed, causing the ends of the severed segments to scar and form a permanent blockage. The incision is then closed with stitches.

Another technique that is quite popular is the *mini-laparotomy.* This method requires only one incision, and can be done with a local anesthetic. Each Fallopian tube is located, after a careful infiltration of each layer of tissue is accomplished, and the cutting and tying off (or cauterizing) follows.

These tubal ligation operations are often performed shortly after pregnancy and childbirth, because the woman is already hospitalized, the Fallopian tubes are more accessible, and the abdominal area is more relaxed than normal. As with vasectomy, the risk of postoperative complications is quite small (Hatcher, et al., 1984).

The advantages of tubal ligation as a contraceptive method parallel those of vasectomy. It is a highly effective method that does not require application of a contraceptive device during each act of sexual intercourse (see Table 6.1). It does not interfere with the spontaneity or naturalness of intercourse, and the pleasurable aspects of sex are unaffected. Although an egg continues to be released each month, it is absorbed into the body and deteriorates through normal physiological processes.

The disadvantages of tubal ligation are also few. Postoperative complications are somewhat more frequent than for vasectomy, although they are generally minor nuisances that can be controlled. This surgery should be considered *permanent* and *irreversible,* as is the case with vasectomy. However, somewhat greater success in reversing tubal ligations has been realized with modern methods of microsurgery, especially if the scarring and tissue destruction resulting from the surgery has been minimal. The success rates for reversal operations varies between 10 and 90 percent, depending on the method used and the amount of scarring following surgery (Hatcher, et al., 1984:221).

THE BIRTH CONTROL PILL (ORAL CONTRACEPTIVE)

The development of the oral contraceptive pill in the 1950s and 1960s revolutionized the field of contraceptive technology. Because of its ease of use and extremely high effectiveness rates (see Table 6.1), the pill became, by the early 1970s, the most popular method of contraception. According to the results of the 1970 National Fertility Study, approximately 6 million women were taking the pill in 1970, comprising over 34 percent of all contraceptive use by the fecund population (Ryder, 1973). However, specific health risks associated with use of the pill, and the development of modern methods of surgical sterilization, have reduced somewhat the overall popularity of the pill as the contraceptive method of choice in our society (see Table 6.3).

The birth control pill works by means of the artificially produced hormones it contains. These hormones have the same effect as naturally produced estrogen and progesterone, and operate on the body's endocrine system by affecting the normal functioning of the hypothalamus and the pituitary gland (refer to the section on the menstrual cycle, in chapter 5). Recall that the pituitary gland causes the woman to ovulate by releasing the hormone FSH. This hormone is only released when estrogen levels in the blood are low. However, a woman who takes a pill containing estrogen for 20 or 21 days out of every month never has a low estrogen level. As a result, FSH is not released and ovulation does not occur. After 21 days of taking the pill, the woman "rests" for approximately seven days by either taking a placebo (inert) pill or taking no pill at all during that time period. Because most birth control pills also contain a synthetic version of the hor-

mone progesterone, the lining of the uterus becomes engorged with blood over the course of the month, and menstruation occurs as usual.[2] The menstrual flow may be lighter or heavier than normal, depending upon the hormone dosages contained in the particular pill in use. In any event, the menstrual flow will be quite *regular,* in view of the "21-day on, 7-day off" schedule routinely followed by pill users.

The major advantages of the oral contraceptive are its effectiveness rates and its ease of use. If a woman follows the instructions provided to her by her physician, and remembers to take the pill daily, the user-effectiveness rate is extremely high (see Table 6.1). Even if she forgets to take a pill one day, there is a safety margin which allows the woman to take two pills the following day and still be protected from pregnancy. (A physician should be consulted for the proper dosage, should more than one day's pill be forgotten.) There is no interference with the sexual act, and the spontaneity and enjoyment of intercourse are not affected by this method. Finally, birth control pills are a relatively inexpensive contraceptive method.

The major disadvantages of pill use by women have only been realized over the past few years. The disadvantages have to do exclusively with the potential health risks involved with pill use. It is important for any woman contemplating pill use to realize that the oral contraceptive is a *drug,* and should be approached with caution and in close consultation with a physician. Most physicians will conduct a thorough physical examination and take a detailed medical history of the woman and her family before prescribing oral contraceptives.

A number of severe health risks have been associated with use of the oral contraceptive containing estrogen: abnormal blood clotting and strokes (thromboembolism); high blood pressure; heart attacks; some cancers in the breast and reproductive-tract areas; and abnormal uterine bleeding. Women who have ever had tendencies to experience these health conditions, or who have someone in their immediate family who has experienced any of them, are usually advised to avoid taking the pill. The potential risks of the pill increase significantly for women who smoke, have high blood pressure or high blood cholesterol levels, who are overweight, who have diabetes, or who are 35 years of age and older. One study found that cigarette smoking among women over 30 years of age sharply increased the chances of having a heart attack if they were using oral contraceptives (*Family Planning Perspectives,*

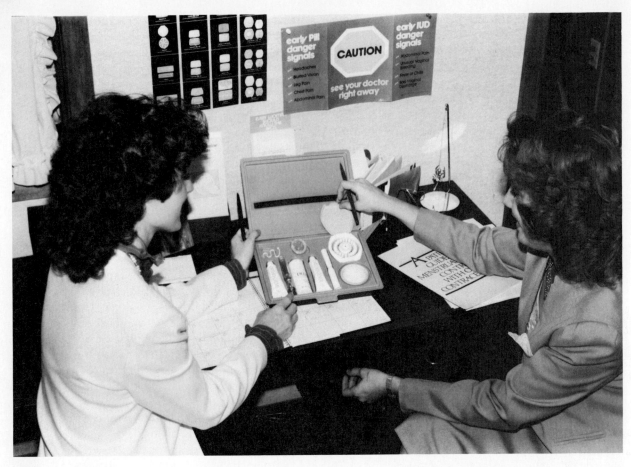

Couples today have a wide variety of birth control methods available to them, each with its own advantages, disadvantages, and effectiveness potential.   *(Photo by Carl Hill.)*

1977). The effect of *minipills,* which contain a synthetic progesterone only, has not yet been determined because their recent development has not allowed for the kind of long-range study necessary to determine the risk factors (Hatcher, et al., 1984:75).

Although estrogen-containing pills have been associated with these serious health complications, it is necessary to place the risk factors in proper perspective. When mortality rates of women using the birth control pill are compared to those of pregnant women, the probability of being placed in a life-threatening situation is far greater for the woman who is pregnant. In addition, birth control pills have been found to *reduce* the risk of other health problems among women, such as benign breast disease; cysts of the ovaries; pelvic inflammatory disease (PID); cancer of

the endometrium (uterus lining); and iron deficiency anemia (Ory, 1982). Therefore, the decision of whether or not to use the pill must be made by placing the risk factors in perspective, weighing them against the risks associated with pregnancy and childbearing. For the great majority of women—and with proper medical screening—the oral contraceptive is a safe and highly effective method of family planning.

THE INTRAUTERINE DEVICE (IUD)

An intrauterine device, or IUD, is a small object that is placed inside the female's uterus in order to prevent a pregnancy. For nearly 2,000 years, the contraceptive effect of placing a foreign object in the uterus of an animal has been well known. Prior to embarking on long safaris across Asian deserts, for example, merchants would prevent pregnancies among their camels by placing pebbles in the female camel's uterus. By the middle of the nineteenth century, this idea had been applied to humans, and the first "made-for-human-use" IUD's (consisting of silk and silver rings) were used. After considerable controversy regarding use of the IUD emerged in the 1930s (primarily because of the problems of cramping, infection, and abnormal bleeding sometimes associated with IUD use), their popularity declined rapidly. After modern medical technology and sterilization procedures were developed, by the early 1960s there was renewed interest in the IUD as a feasible method of contraception.

Several types of IUD's were developed in the 1960s and 1970s, each with a rather distinct shape (see Figure 6.4). They are made of a soft, pliable plastic; all are approximately the same size, and all are equally effective. Some IUD's have a thin wrapping of copper wire around them, because it is believed that copper may have contraceptive properties.

Insertion of an IUD in the woman's uterus requires a visit to her gynecologist's office, and is usually a simple and painless procedure. The physician will select an IUD that is best for a particular woman, on the basis of whether or not she has ever been pregnant; the size of the uterus; whether or not she has a history of painful or unusually heavy menstruation; and other situational or social factors which might prevent her from using a particular IUD (Hatcher, et al., 1984). The IUD should definitely *not* be inserted when a woman is pregnant, when she has an active or recurrent case of infection in the pelvic region, when a pre-insertion examination reveals an abnormal Pap smear, or when the uterus itself is unusually small.

The IUD has several advantages as a contraceptive method. First, it is a highly effective method which has a user-effectiveness rate approximately equal to its theoretical effectiveness rate (see Table 6.1). Although pregnancy can occur with the IUD in place, these occurrences are rare. Of course, pregnancy can also occur if the device is unknowingly expelled. Despite its high effectiveness rate, however, scientists still do not know for sure *why* the IUD is an effective contraceptive device. One possibility is that the presence of a foreign object in the uterus causes the accumulation of antibodies which will attack any foreign object, thereby preventing a fertilized egg from being implanted in the uterine wall. Another possibility is that the device causes the fertilized egg to move through the Fallopian tube much more rapidly than usual, causing it to arrive in the uterus before the blood-rich lining of the uterine wall (endometrium) has had a chance to be built up. More recently, it has been thought that the copper wire surrounding some IUD's creates a chemical environment in the uterus that is hostile to sperm cells and to the female's ova.

FIGURE 6.4.   IUDs Approved by the U.S. Food and Drug Administration, 1976.

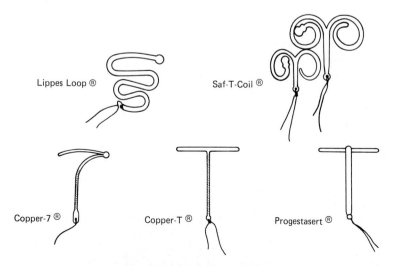

Lippes Loop ®   Saf-T-Coil ®

Copper-7 ®   Copper-T ®   Progestasert ®

A second advantage of the IUD method of contraception parallels the use of the oral contraceptive and sterilization. Once in place, there is no need for application of a contraceptive method at each sexual encounter. The IUD does not interfere with the spontaneity and enjoyment of sexual intercourse. In addition, there is no need to remember to take a pill, with the potential health risks associated with altering the body's chemistry by the infusion of a drug.

Finally, the IUD is a safe and economical method of contraception for many women. The health risks and discomfort associated with its use are rare and usually quite minor; and women of any age (except some very young women) can use it. The insertion procedure is a simple one, as is the monthly process of checking to verify that the device is in place (by feeling for the thread protruding into the vaginal canal). The procedure to remove an IUD (which for some devices should be done every two to three years) is also a simple one, requiring only a visit to the physician's office. The IUD is also a relatively inexpensive method of birth control.

Despite the advantages associated with IUD use, it has not become one of the more popular methods of birth control (see Table 6.3). As of 1982, only 6 percent of fecund married women in the United States were employing this method. This reflects the fact that there are some disadvantages to the use of the IUD, some of which may be more perceived than real. For example, many women cannot accept the thought of having a foreign object lodged inside their bodies. Others may be uncomfortable with the thought that the effectiveness of the IUD is the result of preventing a fertilized egg from being implanted in the uterine wall, which may run counter to their beliefs regarding abortion.

There are some very real nuisance side effects, and potentially serious health risks, however, which prevent some women from being able to employ this method. Most women will experience greater menstrual flow and more irregular bleeding patterns for the first several weeks after the IUD is inserted. Cramping is also likely to be heavier during this time, which is too much for some to handle. These nuisance side effects are more severe for women who have never had a baby (perhaps because the cervix is less pliable, or because the uterus has never been expanded by a pregnancy), and these women are more likely than others to have the device voluntarily removed during the first year.

Another potential disadvantage is that some women will unknowingly expel an IUD, usually during menstruation in the first several months of use, and an unwanted pregnancy can occur. If a pregnancy should occur while the device is in place, although a rare occurrence, it is a potentially serious health complication, one that requires immediate medical attention and removal of the device. Finally, IUD use is associated with higher than normal rates of pelvic infection and perforation of the uterus, both of which are potentially serious medical complications that require immediate attention. A physician should be consulted as soon as the IUD user notices any fever, pelvic pain or tenderness, severe cramping, or unusual vaginal bleeding (Hatcher, et al., 1984:104). The combination of pregnancy and pelvic infection with an IUD in place is especially dangerous, and may result in a life-threatening situation.

All things considered, however, we must place the risk factors in proper perspective. The risk of pregnancy among IUD users is extremely low, with perhaps 1 or 2 women out of every 100 experiencing a pregnancy during the first year when the IUD is in place (Hubbard, 1977:71). The risk of being placed in a life-threatening situation is actually less than that associated with either pill use or pregnancy, occurring to approximately 2 women out of every 100,000 users. With proper medical screening, and relevant information provided by the physician to the potential IUD user, the IUD is a safe, effective, and convenient contraceptive method for many women.

THE CONDOM

The *condom,* also known as a *rubber,* is a thin, latex rubber sheath that is worn over the erect penis during sexual intercourse, acting as a barrier to prevent the passage of semen from the penis into the vagina. Although many brands and types of condoms are sold over the counter in drug stores, health clinics, gas stations, and elsewhere, they are all about the same length (7 inches) and width (1 inch). Condoms can be purchased in various colors and shapes. They come unlubricated or prelubricated, textured (thought to increase the female's sexual pleasure) or untextured, and round-ended or nipple-ended to catch the ejaculate. Condoms of one type or another have been in use for over two thousand years. The ancient Egyptians and Romans, and, more recently, the

Renaissance French and Italians, used sheaths made of linen or sheep intestine to prevent pregnancy as well as venereal disease.

Prior to the development of surgical sterilization and the pill, the condom was probably the most popular method of contraception employed in our society. However, its popularity has declined, and it is no longer the primary contraceptive method in use by contemporary married couples (see Table 6.3). The condom is *theoretically* a highly effective contraceptive method, ranking close to the IUD (see Table 6.1). However, as you will see in Table 6.1, it is the method for which the *actual* user effectiveness is significantly less than its *theoretical* effectiveness. For every 100 couples employing this method for one year, only 2 should experience a pregnancy. In reality, however, errors in application of the method yield an actual pregnancy rate of 10 per 100 couples over a year's time.

There are four major advantages to employing condoms as a contraceptive method. First, the condom is capable of providing excellent contraceptive protection if employed consistently during each act of intercourse. Second, compared with the other barrier methods (i.e., spermicidal foam and diaphragm), the condom is the easiest and most convenient to apply. Condoms are widely distributed in drug stores, clinics, and other places and are easy for anyone to obtain without a prescription from a doctor. Third, condom use is an inexpensive contraceptive method. Finally, the condom is the only contraceptive method that can prevent the spread of some sexually transmitted diseases, provided that it is properly used. Because of this feature—which was the reason for its development centuries ago—condom use may also diminish the likelihood of cancer of the cervix among some women (Hatcher, et al., 1984:128).

The disadvantages of condom use generally account for the user errors, which reduce its actual effectiveness rates. Some men complain that the condom reduces the pleasurable sensations of intercourse—and comment that it is like "wearing a raincoat in a shower." A dry condom can be an irritant to the female's vaginal tissues, and lubricated condoms may be viewed as too messy. Use of the condom requires that foreplay be interrupted in order to put it on, and some men do not have the degree of self-control to do so in the advanced stages of foreplay. As pointed out in chapter 5, some sperm cells are contained in the fluid produced by the bulbourethral (Cowper's)

glands during sexual excitement, and these sperm can enter the vagina and cause a pregnancy, if the condom is put on too late in the foreplay process.

THE DIAPHRAGM

Whereas the condom is a barrier method used by the male, the diaphragm is a barrier method employed by the female partner. The diaphragm is a dome-shaped cup made of latex rubber; it is inserted into the vaginal canal prior to intercourse (see Figure 6.5). It has a flexible rim that allows it to fit snugly in the upper end of the canal so that it covers the opening to the cervix. The contraceptive effectiveness of the diaphragm is increased when it is covered with a spermicidal cream or jelly prior to insertion. Like the condom, the diaphragm was at one time one of the more popular methods of birth control, especially in the 1930s, 1940s, and 1950s. Since the development of the oral contraceptive, IUD, and modern sterilization procedures, however, its popularity has declined considerably (see Table 6.3). When used with a spermicidal cream or jelly, the diaphragm has an excellent theoretical effectiveness rate, equal to that of the condom and close to that of the IUD (see Table 6.1). However the high potential for user error associated with diaphragm use yields an actual user-effectiveness rate which is substantially lower.

Because the sizes of the vaginal canal and cervical opening vary from one woman to the next, diaphragms are made in different sizes in order to provide the best possible fit. This means that a woman must see her physician to be measured and fitted for a diaphragm that provides the best possible coverage of the cervical canal. The physician should provide detailed instructions on how to insert the diaphragm, after the proper size has been determined. The woman is encouraged to practice inserting it herself several times, before she leaves the physician's office.

The major advantage of the diaphragm is that it is a highly effective method of contraception when used in combination with spermicidal cream or jelly. Once the diaphragm is in place, the woman is free to move about as she pleases. The diaphragm may be inserted up to two hours prior to sexual intercourse, as long as the woman checks to be sure it is properly placed just before sexual activity begins. If the diaphragm is in place for more than two hours, a reapplication of spermicidal cream or jelly is required. In addition, the diaphragm does not have any

FIGURE 6.5.   (a) Insertion and Placement of the Diaphragm, (b) Types of Diaphragm.

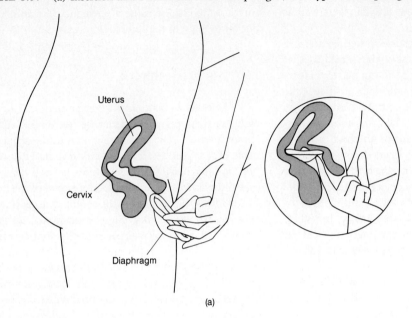

(a)

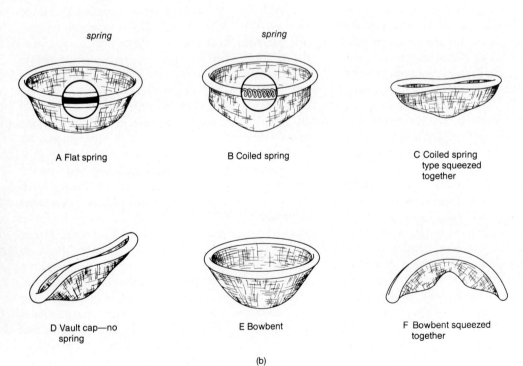

(b)

undesirable side effects which pose a threat to the woman's health. Another advantage of this method is that it is relatively inexpensive.

The disadvantages of this method of contraception relate primarily to its inconvenience. It requires a relatively high level of motivation, knowledge, and manipulative skill on the woman's part, each of which can vary considerably from one woman to the next. The diaphragm must be properly inserted prior to each act of sexual intercourse. Accidental pregnancies resulting from improper insertion of the diaphragm usually result within the first several months after diaphragm use is initiated, before the woman has been able to develop the level of proficiency and skill necessary for maximum contraceptive effectiveness (Hubbard, 1977). Because the vaginal canal actually changes shape during sexual arousal, the diaphragm may become dislodged, allowing sperm cells to pass into the cervical canal. Other situations, such as weight gain or loss of 10 to 20 pounds, or discomfort caused by diaphragm insertion, require that the woman return to the physician's office to have the fitting checked and, if necessary, a new diaphragm prescribed.

Because a diaphragm should be left in place for at least six hours following sexual intercourse (to allow time for the spermicide to kill all sperm cells) the woman may forget it is in place, or find it inconvenient to remove at that time. In any event, the diaphragm must be carefully removed to prevent any loss of the ejaculate that it contains. Some women may find that using spermicidal cream or jelly is messy, or they may feel uncomfortable by having to touch the genital area in the ways necessary to assure proper diaphragm insertion. Finally, care must be taken to assure that the diaphragm is kept clean and dry when not in use. Because it is made of latex rubber, the woman must keep it away from any heat source, and avoid accidentally scratching or puncturing it with a fingernail or other sharp object. Inspection for leaks, holes, and cracks (by filling the diaphragm with water) must be done periodically. Some may find such caretaking procedures to be too inconvenient to justify the use of the diaphragm as the primary method of contraception.

Although the diaphragm has decreased in popularity over the past several years, and the potential for user error is high, it remains a viable contraceptive method for women who are unable to use the pill or an IUD. The diaphragm is highly effective when properly used with a spermicidal agent, and the risk of pregnancy as the result of user error can be greatly reduced when combined with another barrier device, such as the condom.

CONTRACEPTIVE SPONGE AND CERVICAL CAP

In April of 1983, the U.S. Food and Drug Administration approved for general use the *contraceptive sponge*. This device was designed to provide the advantages of the diaphragm but eliminate some of the diaphragm's disadvantages. Natural sponges have been used as a barrier method of birth control for hundreds of years in preindustrial cultures. The sponge in use today, however, is a small, doughnut-shaped disc made of polyurethane, and contains a spermicidal agent (nonoxynol-9) (Hatcher, et al., 1984). The sponge has a concave dimple on the side that fits over the woman's cervix. It comes in only one size, but is flexible enough to conform to the anatomical size and shape differences of different women. The woman soaks the sponge in water prior to insertion, which should be done before intercourse begins. It can be left in place for 24 hours, and will provide continuous contraceptive protection during that time. However, the sponge should be removed and thrown away no more than 24 hours after insertion.

The advantages of the sponge parallel those of the diaphragm. While it is slightly less effective than the diaphragm in preventing pregnancy, based on early studies of its use (Hatcher, et al., 1984:118), it does not interfere with the spontaneity of sexual foreplay or intercourse, it is considered safe to use, and it is inexpensive. The spermicide in the sponge decreases the likelihood that sexually transmitted diseases, such as gonorrhea and trichomoniasis (see Figure 6.7), will be passed from the male to female partner (Hatcher, et al., 1984:119). Another benefit is that the sponge is available for over-the-counter purchase, so a visit to a medical professional is unnecessary. The disadvantages of sponge use appear to be mainly of the nuisance variety. For example, a few women develop a vaginal irritation in reaction to the spermicide. Some have difficulty in properly inserting and removing the sponge, which is sometimes torn as a result of this problem. Still others experience vaginal dryness, as the sponge absorbs vaginal secretions that enhance sexual pleasure.

Although there is a remote possibility that use of the

sponge will cause *toxic-shock syndrome,* a serious and potentially fatal disease, medical evidence to indicate that this is any more than a small risk is lacking at this time (*Contraceptive Technology Update,* 1984).

During its first year on the market, the contraceptive sponge was used by more than 500,000 women, and 17 million were distributed in the United States alone (*Contraceptive Technology Update,* 1984). Thus, it has become the most popular over-the-counter female contraceptive method and, with continuing evidence of its safety and effectiveness in pregnancy prevention, may eventually become the most popular barrier method of birth control.

Another barrier method currently being tested is the *cervical cap.* Although it has not yet been approved for general use in the United States, cervical caps are widely used in Great Britain and other European countries. The cap comes in various shapes and sizes, each a dome-like soft rubber device with a firm, yet somewhat flexible, rim that fits over the cervix. The cap is held in place by suction created when it is inserted. The insertion guidelines for the cervical cap, like those of the diaphragm, call for the insertion of a spermicidal cream or jelly inside the device; removal within 36 to 48 hours after insertion; and careful cleaning before it is reinserted. As with the diaphragm and contraceptive sponge, the cervical cap functions as a barrier to prevent sperm from entering the cervix. The spermicide, which should be applied, also destroys sperm cells that might somehow cross the barrier.

The effectiveness of the cervical cap is approximately the same as that of the diaphragm (see Table 6.1), although additional research is needed to provide reliable estimates of its effectiveness. The cervical cap has the same benefits as the diaphragm. Because they come in various sizes and must be fitted with the assistance of a medical professional, however, the cap lacks the advantages of the contraceptive sponge (available over-the-counter; one size). Preliminary reports of the cap's disadvantages indicate that some women (1) are allergic to the latex rubber or to the spermicide; (2) have anatomical abnormalities that prevent any cap from fitting properly; (3) do not learn the proper insertion technique; (4) irritate the cervix and surrounding tissue by improper insertion, or by leaving the cap in place for too long (Hatcher, et al., 1984:122–123). Cap use has also been associated with pelvic infection, and theoretically could cause toxic-shock syndrome. However, more research is needed before we can judge

with any degree of accuracy the chances that any of these adverse effects will occur.

FOAMS AND SUPPOSITORIES

Contraceptive foams and suppositories combine certain elements of the other barrier methods and provide effective contraception. Not only do they form a barrier to the cervical opening, to help prevent the passage of sperm into the cervical canal, but they also have spermicidal properties. As with the other barrier methods, however, the actual user effectiveness rate is significantly less than the theoretical effectiveness rate (see Table 6.1), which means that the potential for user error is high.

Foams are sold over the counter at drug stores, meaning that a prescription from a physician is unnecessary for this method. Each container of foam is sold with an applicator, and contains approximately 20 applications. Some foams are available in pre-filled applicators, a convenience feature such that the container does not require shaking or filling. It is best to wait to apply the foam until shortly before sexual intercourse begins, because the foam bubbles begin to dissipate shortly after insertion. This means that foreplay often must be interrupted in order to apply the foam in the proper manner.

In addition to contraceptive foam, suppository contraceptive capsules are now available. Following insertion of the suppository, it effervesces, blocks the cervical opening, and spreads a spermicidal agent throughout the upper portion of the vaginal canal. At least 20 minutes must be allowed for the effervescence to take place, prior to sexual intercourse. The effectiveness of the suppository is about the same as that of contraceptive foam.

The major advantages of foams and suppositories relate to their theoretical effectiveness rates and their being relatively inexpensive methods of contraceptive protection. Their potential effectiveness is identical to that of the diaphragm and condom, and approaches that of the IUD. The effectiveness of combining foam with another barrier method, such as the condom, increases its effectiveness to the level obtained for oral contraceptives (see Table 6.1). Another advantage of the foam method is that it is easy to obtain from the local drugstore—without a visit to the doctor and without a doctor's prescription.

As with the diaphragm, the major disadvantage of

the foam method is the high potential for user error. This potential is reflected in the user-effectiveness rate, which is substantially lower than the theoretical effectiveness rate (see Table 6.1). User error can result from failing to shake the foam container sufficiently prior to application; measuring the improper amount (which can easily occur in a darkened room); failing to interrupt foreplay to apply the foam before intercourse actually begins; not realizing that the foam container is empty or near-empty; and not inserting the foam close enough to the cervical opening. Some couples find that foam and suppositories are too messy, causing them to reject this method altogether. Suppositories require several minutes to fully effervesce prior to intercourse, and some couples are unwilling to wait that long. Use of some foams and suppositories may create an allergic reaction, although this can usually be handled by switching to another brand. Again, the potential for user carelessness is great enough to support the recommendation that foams be used in combination with the condom.

COITUS INTERRUPTUS (WITHDRAWAL)

This method involves the male withdrawing his penis just prior to ejaculation. Perhaps the oldest method of contraception employed throughout history, withdrawal is not recommended as a contraceptive method today because of its high rate of ineffectiveness relative to more modern contraceptive alternatives (see Table 6.1). Again, as with other methods requiring repeated application and conscious behavior on the part of the sex partners, user error is largely a result of carelessness in employing the method.

The withdrawal method does have certain advantages, most of which make it particularly appealing to teenagers or young adults experimenting with sexual intercourse. It costs absolutely nothing and has no harmful side effects. There are no devices or chemicals involved, and it is "available" for use at any time.

The ineffectiveness of the withdrawal method is its major disadvantage, and its use cannot be justified when other contraceptive methods are available. Because the male waits until the instant before ejaculation to withdraw the penis from the vagina, it is possible for some sperm cells to enter the vagina in the seminal fluid that is released

from the bulbourethral (Cowper's) glands prior to ejaculation. This method is also risky because it demands a rather high level of self-control on the part of the male. Ejaculation involves a series of involuntary reflexes, once it begins. The natural tendency during ejaculation is to thrust deeper into the vagina, but the male must be able to draw back. Some men are not able to do so just prior to ejaculation, or wait too long and deposit the ejaculate on the outer portions of the female's genitalia. It is entirely possible for sperm cells deposited anywhere on the female's pelvic region to survive long enough to work their way into the vaginal canal and eventually cause a pregnancy. There are psychological consequences of the withdrawal method as well: each partner is focusing on when the male is going to withdraw, rather than concentrating on the mutual fulfillment and gratification that the sexual union is expected to bring. The enjoyment of the sexual act will be diminished even further if the partners fear a pregnancy. In view of these considerations, it is no wonder that this method is not recommended for contraceptive purposes.

FERTILITY-AWARENESS TECHNIQUES

Fertility-awareness techniques involve abstaining from sexual intercourse during the ovulation phase of the menstrual cycle, when pregnancy can occur. Many couples practice these methods for religious reasons. For example, the Roman Catholic Church forbids the use of the pill or any other artificial or unnatural means of contraception, but allows Catholic couples to practice *rhythm* to control family size. Because of the uncertainty of when ovulation occurs, and the resulting high potential for user error associated with the rhythm method, the failure rate is often higher for this contraceptive method than for most others.

The calendar method, or *rhythm,* requires that the woman monitor the duration of her menstrual cycles for at least 8 months, and preferably 1 year, in order to determine the days during the cycle which should be considered "unsafe" for intercourse to occur. Recall (chapter 5) that women vary considerably in the duration of the *postmenstrual* phase of the menstrual cycle (the time elapsed between the last day of menstrual bleeding and ovulation). Because of this, a *range* of days considered to be unsafe must be determined on the basis of her shortest and longest cycles. We know that all women ovulate approximately 14 days (plus or minus 2 days) prior to the next menstrual period. This helps to establish the range of unsafe days, because it is possible to count back 14 days from the onset of menstrual bleeding to determine when ovulation occurred for any given cycle. Counting the first day of menstrual bleeding as Day 1, the earliest time that the woman is fertile is calculated by subtracting 18 from the length of the shortest cycle experienced in the 8-month to 1-year monitoring period. She then subtracts 11 from the number of days in her longest cycle, to determine the last day of her fertile, or unsafe, period. The numbers *18* and *11* are used to calculate the unsafe period because they allow for the facts that (1) an egg cell (ovum) can survive as long as 24 hours after release from the ovary; (2) the release of the egg can vary by as much as 2 days from the theoretical 14 days prior to the next menstrual period; and (3) the male's sperm cells can survive in the uterine environment for 48 hours (sometimes longer).

The range of unsafe days, which is established after monitoring cycles for several months, should therefore be broad enough to compensate for these contingencies. For example, if a woman's shortest cycle is 22 days and her longest cycle is 30 days, she should abstain from sexual intercourse from Day 4 (22 minus 18) through Day 19 (30 minus 11) of her menstrual cycle (see Table 6.4). The contraceptive effectiveness of the calendar method increases for women who have regular cycles from one month to the next, an attribute of fewer than 10 percent of all women of childbearing age (Hatcher, et al., 1978:99). In addition, women who are approaching the end of their reproductive years (say 35 to 44 years of age, when a pregnancy is definitely not wanted by most women), experience increasingly irregular and unpredictable menstrual cycles and ovulation patterns. The rhythm method rapidly loses its effectiveness among women in this age category, and alternative methods of pregnancy prevention should then be considered.

Two variations of the calendar rhythm method also are based on the ability of sex partners to estimate accurately when ovulation takes place. The *basal body temperature* method, or *BBT,* requires careful monitoring of the ever-so-slight body temperature changes that occur in the woman just before and just after ovulation (see Figure

TABLE 6.4. *Calculating the "Safe" Period by the Calendar Rhythm Method*

Duration of Shortest Menstrual Cycle in a One-Year Period	First Fertile (Unsafe) Day[1]	Duration of Longest Menstrual Cycle in a One-Year Period	Last Fertile (Unsafe) Day
20 Days	Day 2	20 Days	Day 9
21 Days	Day 3	21 Days	Day 10
22 Days	Day 4	22 Days	Day 11
23 Days	Day 5	23 Days	Day 12
24 Days	Day 6	24 Days	Day 13
25 Days	Day 7	25 Days	Day 14
26 Days	Day 8	26 Days	Day 15
27 Days	Day 9	27 Days	Day 16
28 Days	Day 10	28 Days	Day 17
29 Days	Day 11	29 Days	Day 18
30 Days	Day 12	30 Days	Day 19
31 Days	Day 13	31 Days	Day 20
32 Days	Day 14	32 Days	Day 21
33 Days	Day 15	33 Days	Day 22
34 Days	Day 16	34 Days	Day 23
35 Days	Day 17	35 Days	Day 24
36 Days	Day 18	36 Days	Day 25

[1] Day 1 is the first day of menstrual bleeding.

FIGURE 6.6. Variation in Basal Body Temperature (BBT) for a 28 Day Menstrual Cycle.

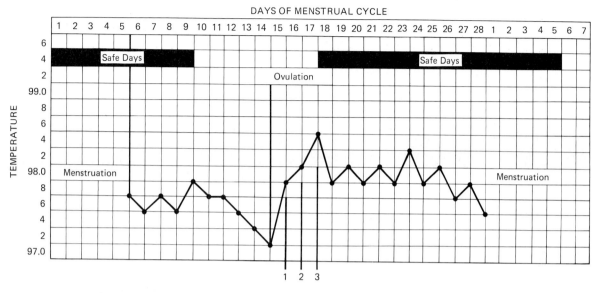

SOURCE: Hatcher, et al. (1978:97).

6.6). Ovulation can be determined only with a specially designed thermometer, used under carefully controlled conditions — after hours of rest or sleep and prior to moving about, drinking coffee or water, urination, or even smoking tobacco. The *cervical mucous method,* or *Billings method,* requires careful monitoring of the mucous secreted by the woman's cervix prior to ovulation. The mucous changes color and consistency when ovulation is about to occur. Usually it requires some practice before such changes in cervical mucous can be accurately identified on a consistent basis.

As with all other methods of contraception, the fertility-awareness methods have both advantages and disadvantages. The major advantages are that no chemicals, health hazards, special devices, or artificial barriers are associated with its use. Foreplay and the sexual act itself are therefore allowed to occur spontaneously and in an uninterrupted manner. It is one of the least expensive methods a couple can use. Although the calendar method has been found to have a high failure rate (anywhere from 25 to 40 pregnancies per 100 women years), the BBT and cervical mucous methods, especially when combined, have been found to be extremely effective in preliminary studies of highly motivated and consistent users of these methods

(from 2 to 3 pregnancies per 100 woman years) [Hatcher, et al., 1984:144]. This combination of the BBT and mucous monitoring method is known as the *sympto-thermal* method.

The major disadvantage of calendar rhythm is in the relatively high failure rate. Failure rates for all three fertility-awareness methods are higher among those women with irregular menstrual cycles; those who happen to miss ovulating in any given month (which happens occasionally, for many women); and those couples who do not have the motivation, patience, or knowledge required to establish an accurate program of rhythm over a several month period before actually relying on it as the major contraceptive method. The BBT method is especially problematic for many couples because several factors can influence body temperature other than the ovulatory process. For example, an infection, anxiety, irregular sleeping patterns, or even the use of an electric blanket can alter basal body temperature enough to totally confound the accurate monitoring of temperature changes related to ovulation. In some women, the BBT simply does not change enough to detect when ovulation occurs. Women who are uncomfortable in touching around and inside the genital area will have difficulty in using the cervical mucous method.

Finally, a disadvantage of all three fertility-awareness methods is that these are the only contraceptive methods that restrict the number of days in a given month or menstrual cycle during which sexual intercourse may take place. If a couple does not feel comfortable in having sexual relations during the female's menstrual period, only the number of days between ovulation and the onset of menstruation are available for engaging in intercourse. For a 28-day cycle, there may be only ten "safe days," a tough situation for many who find it difficult to abstain from sexual intercourse for 18 days or more at a time. Under these conditions, a couple practicing rhythm may desire to seek alternative sources of sexual gratification, such as masturbation, mutual petting to orgasm, or oral sex.

OTHER METHODS: LACTATION, DOUCHE, AND CHANCE

Lactation. Women who are breast-feeding a child (lactating women) can delay ovulation a year or more. In developing societies around the world, lactation has probably prevented more pregnancies than all organized family-planning programs put together (*International Planned Parenthood Federation Bulletin,* 1976). As a contraceptive method, lactation has all of the advantages: it does not interrupt or interfere with the sexual act; it is free of health hazards; it costs absolutely nothing. However, failure rates tend to be high among those who rely on this method exclusively over a long period of time. There are two reasons for this. First, although menstruation is usually delayed 8 weeks or more if the new mother is breast-feeding, ovulation can occur any time before the onset of an actual menstrual period. In addition, women demonstrate considerable variability in terms of when ovulation will resume. Hence, it is impossible to predict exactly when ovulation will occur for the first time. Second, if lactation is to prevent ovulation for a year or more, the woman must continue a full schedule of breast-feeding for that entire period. However, at some time during the first year, breast-feeding mothers usually begin supplementing the infant's diet with formulas and solid foods, thereby reducing the level of breast-feeding. The chances of ovulation increase dramatically as soon as this occurs. It is generally recommended that a reliable method of con-

traception be employed once intercourse resumes after childbirth. Because birth control pills can reduce the breast-feeding mothers's normal milk supply, another method of contraception should be used if lactation is to continue.

Douche. After sexual intercourse, some women attempt to prevent a pregnancy by rinsing the vaginal canal with either water or a mild solution, such as vinegar and water. This is known as *douching*. This method is often used by teenagers experimenting with sex, women who are unaware of other more reliable methods, or who have nothing else available at the time. Although it is better than nothing, the failure rate of douching is among the highest when compared with other methods (see Table 6.1). This is because sperm cells can pass through the cervix and into the protective environment of the uterus in a minute or less after ejaculation. Douching is unlikely to totally rid the vagina of sperm, and may actually aid the entry of sperm into the cervical canal, because of the force of the water. In short, douching is an unreliable method, and a poor substitute for simpler and far more effective contraceptive methods.

Chance. Relying on chance, or fate, to prevent pregnancy is the most popular method among the sexually active teenage population. As seen in Table 6.1, it is extremely unreliable. The 90 pregnancies that would occur to 100 women employing this method for one year can be viewed as a baseline by which to compare the effectiveness of other methods. A popular, but true, saying is that "Chance is not a method."

Contraceptive Methods of the Future

Researchers in the field of contraceptive technology continue to search for a birth control method that will be free of any of the disadvantages of the methods just described. It would be 100 percent effective, totally free from harmful side effects, easy to use, divorced from the sexual act, acceptable to people of different moral and religious persuasions, and inexpensive. If such a method is ever invented, developed, and approved for general use, it may replace all others currently in use. However, some experts believe that we will never find a perfect contraceptive method.

By now it is generally recognized that there can never be such an ideal contraceptive method, and that an array of methods is needed for people who live under different circumstances and have differing preferences and requirements. Each method has its unique advantages and drawbacks, and it is likely that there will always be some trade-off between effectiveness and risk. (Atkinson, et al., 1980:173)

We have already discussed (pp. 165–166) the recent development of the contraceptive sponge and the cervical cap. Although some other promising new methods are beginning to appear on the horizon, it is doubtful that any of them will be the "perfect" contraceptive.

MORNING-AFTER PILLS

A pill taken the day *after* sexual intercourse has occurred may simplify matters for many partners who fail to contracept when ovulation is likely. Such a pill has already been approved and marketed in the United States: *diethylstilbesterol* (DES).[3] DES is a highly concentrated synthetic estrogen derived from coal tar. Taken for five days, as soon as possible after unprotected intercourse, DES is 97 to 98 percent effective in preventing implantation of a fertilized ovum. However, because of recently discovered health risks associated with DES use, it is now used only under extreme emergency conditions, such as when attempting to prevent a pregnancy for a woman who has been raped. With DES, not only are the nuisance side effects associated with the normal birth-control pill use more extreme — nausea and vomiting, dizziness, high blood pressure, and headaches — but the male and female offspring of women who have taken DES are more likely than others to contract cancer and other abnormalities in their reproductive systems. Hence, the search for a "morning-after" pill that is safe for general use continues.

INJECTIONS AND IMPLANTS

Researchers are currently experimenting with contraceptive vaccines and implants that can be injected into the female to provide several months of contraceptive protection. A major problem that continues to hinder efforts to develop acceptable vaccine methods, however, is that it often takes a long period of time for fertility to return if the woman should desire to become pregnant (Atkinson, et al., 1980). One version consists of a hormone that would cause the body to stop producing progesterone, thereby preventing a fertilized egg from being maintained by the walls of the uterus. This vaccine continues to undergo rigorous testing in order to determine if it has any serious health risks or side effects. At this point, its potential seems to be great.

Another vaccine for females would prevent the occurrence of menstruation altogether, by releasing small amounts of a steroid hormone into the body on a time-release basis. The effectiveness of this vaccine would last for six months. Although the initial trials for this method show that it works as expected, more extensive testing is necessary to establish whether there are any health risks. Because the active contraceptive ingredient is gradually released over time rather than in highly concentrated doses, it is hoped that the health risks will be significantly less than those associated with pill use.

A third type of female contraceptive vaccine, *Depo Provera,* is currently in use in more than 70 countries around the world, although it has not been approved by the Food and Drug Administration (FDA) for general use in the United States. The effectiveness of Depo Provera lasts for three months or more, because the synthetic progesterone it contains prevents pregnancy by inhibiting ovulation, thickening the cervical mucous, and hastening the movement of the ova through the Fallopian tubes. This particular vaccine has started a raging controversy within the scientific community, and between researchers and government officials (Maine, 1978). At issue is whether or not Depo Provera increases the risk of breast cancer, causes abnormal bleeding, and leads to birth defects and deformities among children born to women who use the vaccine. Until more definitive clinical evidence of health risks associated with Depo Provera use can be obtained, the debate will continue for some time to come (Gold, 1983).

Scientists are also seeking to develop a capsule that could be implanted under the female's skin and provide up to six years of contraceptive protection. Tests of *norgestrienone,* or *d-norgestrel,* have demonstrated that contraceptive implants are effective. However, more extensive testing is required before this drug is considered safe for general use.

MALE PILLS

Research on a birth control pill for men is progressing. Such a pill would work by eliminating the male's sperm production while he is taking the hormones contained in the pill. Because the follicle-stimulating hormone (FSH) and the luteinizing hormone (LH), released by the male's pituitary gland, combine to trigger the production of sperm cells, it makes sense to attempt to repress the production of FSH and LH in the pituitary.

Initial attempts to produce the male pill involved giving men estrogen and, later, testosterone (Stokes, 1980). Although each worked to reduce the sperm count, they both had highly undesirable side effects: estrogen caused breast enlargement and higher voices, and testosterone caused excessive weight gain, acne, and metabolic disorders. More recently, Chinese scientists have claimed great success with a male pill containing a derivative of cottonseed oil, called *gossypol*. The precise mechanics of its action are unknown at this time, but gossypol is believed to inhibit the sperm production and maturation process (Atkinson, et al., 1980; Stokes, 1980). Clinical trials indicate that it has a 99 percent effectiveness rate. However, preliminary evidence from the thousands of Chinese men involved in tests of gossypol indicate that it may lead to physical weakness, a result of lowering the body's level of potassium. Although it is not a hormone, gossypol accumulates in the body, meaning that the likelihood of health problems associated with its use increases over time.

Other substances for reducing male fertility have shown promise, although scientists are currently only in the beginning stages of clinical development and testing. However, a major problem faced by researchers seeking to develop a safe and effective male pill is that many of the pills developed to date have been found to reduce the male sex drive. In addition, after blocking or inhibiting sperm production with any of the substances discovered so far, long time periods have been required before the male recovers his normal rate of sperm production — anywhere from four months to a year or more — after he stops taking the pill. As a result of these problems, as well as those associated with finding a male pill that is free of harmful side effects and that approximates 100 percent effective-

ness, it now appears that a male pill will not be available on the market for 10 or possibly 20 more years (Stokes, 1980:25).

NONSURGICAL AND REVERSIBLE STERILIZATION

Researchers are seeking to eliminate the discomfort of current female sterilization procedures by developing safe, effective, and less costly methods of blocking ovulation. One involves introducing a substance, known as a *sclerosing agent*, into the Fallopian tubes. This substance would irritate the tubes, causing them to scar and permanently close. Because the sclerosing agent could be inserted through the vagina and uterus, no surgery or long recovery period would be required.

Another promising method of nonsurgical female sterilization that would be reversible involves implanting a small silicone plug in each Fallopian tube. Inserted through the vagina and uterus, the silicone hardens in five minutes after it is inserted. In order to restore fertility, the plug can be easily removed. No anesthetic is required, and the woman is able to resume her normal activities immediately (*Arizona Family Planning Council Newsletter,* January 1982a).

Abortion

Perhaps there is no human behavior that inspires more political, social, and emotional reaction than abortion. In 1973, the Supreme Court of the United States decided that pregnant women have the right to choose whether or not to continue a pregnancy anytime during the first trimester (3 months) of pregnancy. During the second trimester, the authority to make the decision was given to the woman and her physician, although the state was given the right to intervene if there was a question of the woman's health being jeopardized by the procedure. During the final trimester of pregnancy (after approximately 24–26 weeks), the state can regulate abortion in any manner, and even prohibit it in all cases, except where continuation of the pregnancy would pose a threat to the life of the woman.

Since the landmark Supreme Court decision on abortion was made in 1973, repeated attempts have been made to override the decision by individuals and groups who are against abortion on moral and religious grounds. Organized oppositon groups, known as "right-to-life" groups, have lobbied state legislatures in order to effect an amendment to the U.S. Constitution that would ban all abortions except in extreme situations, such as when the woman has been raped or when her life is threatened by the pregnancy. Arguing that abortion is murder and infanticide, and that women who wish to terminate a pregnancy have no complaint because use of effective contraception would have prevented the pregnancy in the first place, these groups claim to speak on behalf of the more than one million fetuses that are voluntarily aborted each year. Human life begins at conception, the right-to-live groups believe, and voluntarily terminating that life is a murderous act which should be outlawed.

On the other side of the issue are groups, known as "pro-choice" groups, who believe that women have the right to control their own reproductive destinies. This right includes the right to choose abortion if a pregnancy is not wanted. Arguing that unwanted pregnancies result in unwanted and potentially abused or neglected children, and that it is impossible to determine at what point during a pregnancy a fetus becomes a viable human life deserving the full protection of laws against murder, pro-choice groups continue to speak in support of the Supreme Court's 1973 decision. They do so in order to prevent the decision from someday being overturned or reversed.

Despite the years of controversy and debate that the abortion issue has raised, these and other legal and moral issues remain unresolved. For example, what are the rights of *fathers* when the abortion decision is being made? When *does* human life begin — at conception? When the fetus first moves? When it could survive on its own if born? Should taxpayers' money be used to pay for abortions of women who cannot afford them? Can doctors or private hospitals refuse to perform abortions? Should women be allowed to have repeated abortions, as if considering abortion to be a birth control measure? If abortion is made illegal, how many women would turn to hazardous self-induced methods or "back room" abortionists, where the nonsterile and primitive instruments used would lead to infection and possibly death?

While these questions continue to inspire vigorous, and often heated, debate between "pro-choice" and "right-to-life" groups, the 1973 Supreme Court decision permitting abortion continues to stand. Somewhere between 1 and 1.5 million abortions are performed yearly in the United States, and over 90 percent are performed within the first 12 weeks of pregnancy. Around one-third of all abortions are performed on teenagers, and another one-third are performed on women in the 20- to 24-year age group (Witters and Jones-Witters, 1980:251).

The purpose of discussing abortion here is not to resolve the complicated legal and moral issues which continue to spark the emotional controversy over abortion. Rather, the purpose is to provide information about the various types of abortion procedures available, indicating their risks and costs. The decision to have an abortion is very personal, and one must make one's own decision after carefully evaluating the issues and arguments on each side of the abortion controversy.

SPONTANEOUS ABORTION

Not all abortions are induced, that is, occurring as a result of a voluntary choice. Those that occur involuntarily are known as *spontaneous abortions,* or *miscarriages*. Often the fetus that is aborted spontaneously is one with a congenital or chromosomal abnormality that would have resulted in a subsequent birth defect or disease after the infant was born (Carr, 1972). Spontaneous abortion, then, may be nature's own "quality control mechanism," mercifully terminating the lives of some of those who would be born retarded, severely deformed, or otherwise diseased.

INDUCED ABORTION

There are three types of voluntary abortion, which account for nearly all abortions performed. As with certain methods of birth control, each has its advantages, disadvantages, and health-related risks. The type of abortion to be performed by the physician usually depends upon the *period of gestation* (amount of time the woman has been pregnant). After the 12th week of pregnancy, the potential for medical complications rises sharply, however. First trimester abortions, then, are considered to be relatively safe and free of harmful complications, compared with abortions in later stages of pregnancy.

Vacuum Curettage.

This method of abortion can be performed in a clinic or physician's office, with the aid of a local anesthetic. The vacuum method is normally performed before the 12th or 13th week of pregnancy. The ease with which it is performed, and its relative safety, make this the most popular method during the early stages of pregnancy.

The cervix is first dilated with special dilating instruments. After dilation, a small tube, called a *vacuum curette,* or *vacurette,* is then inserted through the cervix and into the uterus. The vacurette is connected to a small pump, which creates enough suction to draw the entire contents of the uterus out in one to two minutes.

Dilation and Curettage (D & C).

Before the perfection of the vacuum curettage method, the D & C was probably the most popular. Rather than using vacuum suction to remove the fetus and uterine lining, the D & C involves gentle scraping of the lining of the uterus with a sharp metal curette. Compared with the vacuum curettage method, the D & C is usually more painful and requires a general anesthetic, and it involves a greater loss of blood. The cervix must first be dilated, then the curette is inserted through the cervical canal and into the uterus so that the lining can be scraped and the contents removed. After the 12th week of pregnancy, a woman should expect to undergo the D & C procedure because the size of the fetus would prevent the more convenient vaccum method from being used.

Intraamniotic Solution.

This method is also known as "salting out." The physician may choose this nonsurgical method, in which a saline solution (salt and water) is injected directly into the uterus after the 14th to 16th week of pregnancy. This procedure is used when the pregnancy has reached such an advanced stage that the vacuum curettage and the D & C methods are no longer tenable for removing the fetus and the surrounding placental tissues. Fluid is actually withdrawn from the *amniotic sac,* the membrane which encases the fetus, and is replaced with the saline solution. After 24 to 48 hours, the solution has killed the fetus and the woman goes into labor to expel the fetal tissues. This procedure requires hospitalization for two or three days, just as is true when a full-term baby is delivered; and the woman is likely to experience cramps and bleeding for several days after the abortion.

MAKING THE ABORTION DECISION

As stated at the outset, the decision to have an abortion is a highly personal one, which can be complicated by one's conscience, career or educational plans, and family planning ideals. The decision is one the woman may wish to make in consultation with her husband, male partner, or personal physician. The moral issues involved must be carefully weighed so that the final decision is one that is acceptable, and one with which the individual can live. An additional consideration in the abortion decision is the degree of health risk involved in the type of abortion procedure to be performed. It must be emphasized that first trimester abortions, those that are performed within the first 12 or 13 weeks of pregnancy, are quite safe for the woman and highly effective if conducted by a trained physician, under the most sterile of conditions. After the first trimester, however, abortion becomes an increasingly complicated and risky operation (Cates, Schulz, Grimes, and Tyler, 1977).

Sexually Transmitted Diseases (STD's)

Of all infectious diseases that exist today, none is more prevalent than those associated with sexual contact (see Table 6.5). The two most widely known sexually transmitted diseases, or STD's, are *gonorrhea* and *syphilis.* These diseases are also known as *venereal diseases—* probably named after the Roman goddess of love, Venus. Three other venereal diseases that are rare these days are *granuloma inguinale, chancroid,* and *lymphogranuloma.* Because of the shame and dishonor that have come to be associated with people who are unfortunate enough to contract venereal disease, and because a variety of other diseases are now known to have the capability of spreading by means of sexual contact, health experts today apply the more neutral term *STD* to all diseases that spread from one person to the next as a result of sexual contact.

CAUSES AND RATES OF STD's

STD's can be caused by any of a number of microorganisms, including viruses, bacteria, and fungi, a fact that has made identification and treatment somewhat difficult for medical professionals. Although some STD's are easily recognized and treated with modern antibiotics, such as tetracycline and penicillin, others are as yet incurable. Many STD's are capable of causing severe damage to the reproductive systems of men, women, and the unborn children of infected women if not detected and treated in their early stages. The warm and moist environment of the mucous membranes in both the male and female reproductive systems provide a perfect environment for the growth and spread of STD microorganisms. The nose and mouth are also conducive to the growth of STD fungi and bacteria.

The frequency of occurrence of these STD's varies (see Table 6.5). By far the most common type in the 1970s was gonorrhea, a disease which alarmed public health professionals because of its rapidly increasing incidence in that decade. From 1970 to 1979, the number of gonorrhea cases reported to public health clinics increased 40 percent. However, it must be pointed out that gonorrhea and other STD's are often reported to private physicians, who do not relay the information to public health officials. Also, many people who have contracted the disease fail to report it. Therefore, the figures presented in Table 6.5 are *underestimates* of the actual frequency of these diseases. In actuality, there may be closer to 2.5 million new cases of gonorrhea and 100,000 new cases of syphilis occurring each year (Witters and Jones-Witters, 1980; Yarber, 1978).

If gonorrhea was the disease of major public health concern in the 1970s, then the STD drawing the most attention during the 1980s is Herpes Simplex II, or genital herpes. Herpes is a viral infection that has no known cure. Estimates of the frequency of herpes in our population vary widely, but the number of new cases each year probably ranges between one-half million to one million or more. The herpes virus remains in the person's system even after the symptoms have disappeared, and can recur at a later time (see Figure 6.7). Although several painful sores and blisters are common in women infected with this disease, males often experience only one or two blisters, and therefore may be unaware that they are infected until the sores have disappeared. In the meantime, the disease can be spread to sexual partners, unknowingly. Researchers are vigorously searching for a cure for the herpes virus, but until one is found, the incidence and adverse long-term effects of the disease continue to be a major public health problem.

Another disease that has recently drawn the attention of public health officials is *acquired immune deficiency syndrome,* or AIDS. This disease, although not always spread by sexual contact, is most common among male homosexuals who engage in sexual relations with a number of partners. AIDS is also found among drug users who inject drugs through the skin, hemophiliacs, and among Haitian immigrants who, for some unknown reasons, appear to be susceptible to the disease. AIDS is a disorder of the blood that causes the body's natural disease-fighting mechanisms to break down. Without this protection, the afflicted person has no resistance to common viruses and bacteria, and death is often a result. AIDS was first reported in 1979. Although only 11,500 cases of this disease in the United States have been officially reported as of 1985, a determined, all-out search for its cause(s) and cure by biological and medical scientists is underway. This is because of its deadly nature, its increasing rate of incidence, and its apparent spread to heterosexual partners of homosexuals (Hatcher, et al., 1984). In 1984, great progress was made in combatting this dreaded disease. Scientists isolated the cause of AIDS as a tiny virus of the type related to leukemia in humans — *Human T Lymphocyte Virus III (HTLV-III).* This virus attacks and immobilizes the nucleus of white blood cells, which constitute the body's disease fighting mechanism. Now that the cause of AIDS has been identified, and a blood-screening test devised to detect its presence, it is hoped that a cure for AIDS will soon be discovered.

REASONS FOR THE INCREASE OF STD RATES

There are a number of possible reasons for the increasing rate of STD over the past several years, an increase of considerable concern to public health officials. Saxton (1980:166–168) lists five logical reasons for explaining the rising incidence of STD in our society:

1. The increasing rate of premarital sexual activity has placed a greater number of young people "at risk" of

TABLE 6.5. *Incidence of Certain Sexually Transmitted Diseases in the United States Compared With Other Infectious Diseases: 1970–1979*

Disease	1970	1971	1972	1973	1974	1975	1976	1977	1978	1979
1. Gonorrhea	600,072	670,268	767,215	842,621	906,121	999,937	1,001,994	1,000,177	1,013,436[1]	1,003,958[1]
2. Syphilis:										
Primary & Secondary	21,982	23,783	24,429	24,825	25,385	25,561	23,731	20,362	21,656[1]	24,874[1]
All stages	91,382	95,997	91,149	87,469	83,771	80,356	71,761	64,473	64,875[1]	67,049[1]
3. Chancroid	1,416	1,320	*	*	*	*	*	*	521[1]	840[2]
4. Granuloma inguinale	736*	781*	2,251*	1,635*	1,386*	1,113*	1,064*	878*	72[1]	76[1]
5. Lymphogranuloma venereum	*	*	*	*	*	*	*	*	284[1]	250[1]
6. Chicken pox	—	—	164,114	182,927	141,495	154,248	183,990	188,396	154,089	199,081
7. Hepatitis										
(a) Infectious	56,797	59,606	54,074	50,749	40,358	35,855	33,288	31,153	29,500	30,407
(b) Serum	8,310	9,556	9,402	8,451	10,631	13,121	14,973	16,831	15,016	15,452
8. Measles (Rubeola)	47,351	75,290	32,275	26,690	22,094	24,374	41,126	57,345	26,871	13,597
9. Mumps	104,953	124,939	74,215	69,612	59,128	59,647	38,492	21,436	16,817	14,225
10. Rubella (German Measles)	56,552	45,086	25,507	27,804	11,917	16,652	12,491	20,395	18,269	11,795
11. Tuberculosis	37,187	35,035	32,932	31,015	30,210	33,554	32,105	30,145	28,521	27,669

* Listed together as "other."

[1] Civilian cases only.

[2] Provisional data only.

SOURCE: Morbidity and Mortality, Annual Supplement, Summary, Center for Disease Control, 1970, V. 19 (53); 1971, V. 20 (53); 1972, V. 21 (53); 1973, V. 22 (53); 1974, V. 23 (53); 1975, V. 24 (54); 1976, V. 25 (53); 1977, V. 26 (53); 1978, V. 27 (54); 1979, V. 28 (54).

FIGURE 6.7.   Summary of the Most Important Sexually Transmissable Diseases in the U.S. (Developed in cooperation with the American Social Health Association, Palo Alto, Calif.)

Disease	**GONORRHEA*** (gon″o-re′ah)
Also Called	GC, dose, clap, drip
Cause	Bacterium: *Neisseria gonorrhoeae* ("gonococcus")
Incubation	Males: 2–8 days; Females: uncertain
Typical Symptoms	Pus discharge from penis; burning on urination; (women) pain in or around genitals or lower abdomen; occasionally no symptoms in males; about 80% of females have no early signs
Infectious	All stages
Diagnosis	Microscopic observation of discharge; culture from possible infection site
Treatment	Curable with antibiotics
Complications	Pelvic inflammatory disease; sterility, arthritis, blindness, meningitis, endocarditis, ectopic pregnancy; eye damage in newborns
Notes	Number 1 reportable infectious disease in U.S.A.; nearly 50,000 involuntary sterilizations in young women yearly; a strain resistant to penicilin has emerged

Disease	**SYPHILIS*** (sif′i-lis)
Also Called	Syph, pox, bad blood, lues
Cause	Spirochete: *Treponema pallidum*
Incubation	10–90 days
Typical Symptoms	First stage: painless chancre at site of entry (usually genitals). Second stage: rash, sores, hair loss, flulike illness, swollen joints. Latent stage, no symptoms
Infectious	First and second stages, up to two years; pregnant woman may transmit for much longer period
Diagnosis	Blood test; microscopic slide from chancre
Treatment	Curable with antibiotics
Complications	Severe damage to nervous system or body organs possible after many years; brain damage, insanity, heart disease, death, blindness; severe damage to or death of baby
Notes	Symptoms may imitate those of other diseases; damage by spirochetes permanent; treatment of syphilitic pregnant woman before fifth month prevents damage to fetus

Disease	**NON-GONOCOCCAL URETHRITIS*** (non-gon″o-kok′ al u″re-thri′tis)
Also Called	NGU, non-specific urethritis, NSU, gleet
Cause	Bacteria: *Chlamydia trachomatis; Mycoplasma hominis;* others(?)
Incubation	7–28 days
Typical Symptoms	Genital discharge, painful and frequent urination in male; discharge or cervical bleeding in females, although many do not show any symptoms
Infectious	Uncertain
Diagnosis	Microscopic observation of discharge; culture from possible infection site; blood tests
Treatment	Curable with tetracycline, erythromycin, sulfonamide
Complications	Uncertain; infection of male's bladder or prostate gland; female sterility; *chlamydial*-caused eye infection in newborn infant

Notes	May be inaccurately diagnosed as drug-resistant gonorrhea; does not respond to penicillin; less well-defined in females; as prevalent as gonorrhea; some cases may spontaneously cure themselves

Disease	**HERPES SIMPLEX GENITALIS*** (her′pez)
Also Called	Herpes genitalis, herpes, HSV-2, genital herpes
Cause	Virus: *Herpes virus hominis.* Type 2
Incubation	2–20 days
Typical Symptoms	Minor genital rashes or itching at first, developing into painful blister-like, fluid-filled lesions or sores, with flu-like illness and swollen lymph glands
Infectious	During active flare-up when lesions are present
Diagnosis	Pap smear, examination, culture
Treatment	None considered completely safe or effective; treatment for pain and ointments for sores are used
Complications	Women with HSV-2 of cervix are eight times more likely to develop cervical cancer (no cause and effect established); secondary infection during active stage; spontaneous abortion, premature delivery; meningitis in baby acquired during birth, infant death at birth
Notes	Cannot be cured—person may have recurrences of lesions throughout life; only 30% of active cases are new infections

Disease	**CANDIDIASIS*** (kan″di-di′ah-sis)
Also Called	Moniliasis, vaginal thrush, yeast
Cause	Yeast or fungus: *Candida albicans*
Incubation	Uncertain
Typical Symptoms	Female: odorous, cheesy vaginal discharge, itching. Male: possibly urethritis. Infants: patchy sores in mouth and diaper areas
Infectious	Uncertain
Diagnosis	Microscopic slide and culture from possible infection site
Treatment	Local treatment with Nystatin
Complications	Not significant except in rare cases; secondary infections; oral infections in infants
Notes	Many people have organism without developing disease; antibiotic therapy, other bacterial infections, poor nutrition, diabetes, pregnancy, use of birth control pill, for example, may trigger infection

Disease	**HEPATITIS B** (hep″ah-ti′tis)
Also Called	Serum hepatitis, Australian antigen hepatitis
Cause	Hepatitis B virus
Incubation	2–5 months
Typical Symptoms	Fever, loss of appetite, tiredness, jaundice; none specific to this disease; many persons are asymptomatic
Infectious	Uncertain
Diagnosis	Lab test of blood serum
Treatment	None known to be effective; most cases recover eventually without treatment
Complications	Severe illness; death possible; severe liver damage
Notes	Penile-oral or penile-anal transmission appears to be most common

continued on next page

FIGURE 6.7.   *(Continued)*

Disease	**PEDICULOSIS PUBIS** (pe-dik″u-lo′sis pu′bis)
Also Called	Crabs, cooties, lice
Cause	Louse: *Phthirus pubis*
Incubation	Begin to multiply from infestation
Typical Symptoms	Intense itching, pin-head blood spots on underwear; eggs or nits on pubic hair
Infectious	Uncertain
Diagnosis	Examination
Treatment	Insecticide lotions, creams, and soaps; cleaning bed linen or clothing
Complications	None
Notes	Very common

Disease	**CYTOMEGALOVIRUS*** (si″to-meg″ah-lo-vi′rus)
Also Called	CMV
Cause	Virus: *Cytomegalovirus* (herpes family)
Incubation	Uncertain
Typical Symptoms	Fever, swollen glands, and sore throat in adults; disease may be CMV mononucleosis; few or no symptoms in most adults; signs of nervous system damage in babies
Infectious	Uncertain; pregnancy
Diagnosis	Lab test of blood serum; culture test
Treatment	No known cure
Complications	Usually not harmful to adults; severe birth defects (e.g. mental retardation, blindness, deafness) in infants
Notes	Most important viral cause of mental retardation; 25% of all serious infant retardation and cerebral palsy is caused by congenital (CMV); acquired by 80 percent of the population by age 40; responsible for about 10 percent of adult cases of mononucleosis; no damage in 90 percent of infected fetuses

Disease	**GROUP B STREPTOCOCCUS*** (strep″to-kok′us)
Also Called	
Cause	Bacteria: *Beta hemolytic streptococcus*
Incubation	Varies from days to weeks in young children
Typical Symptoms	Most adults do not show symptoms
Infectious	Uncertain; pregnancy
Diagnosis	Lab culture from possible infection site
Treatment	Curable with antibiotics
Complications	No particular complications in adults; high death and incapacitating rate in infected infants
Notes	Maternal infection fairly common; estimated attack rate of 3 to 4 per 1000 live births. About 50% of 12,000 annually infected newborn infants die from disease—many survivors suffer damage to brain, sight, and hearing

Disease	**TRICHOMONIASIS*** (trik″o-mo-ni′ah-sis)
Also Called	Trich, TV, vaginitis
Cause	Protozoan: *Trichomonas vaginalis*
Incubation	4–28 days
Typical Symptoms	Female: heavy, odorous vaginal discharge, vaginal itching or soreness, burning urination. Male: slight discharge and painful urination. Usually produces symptoms in females but rarely in males
Infectious	Always
Diagnosis	Microscopic slide of discharge; culture; examination
Treatment	Curable with Flagyl
Complications	Does not lead to severe organ damage; chronic inflammation and resulting damage to cervix may predispose tissue to cancer
Notes	Costly in terms of increased health care expenses and time loss from work or school; approximately 3 million cases annually

Disease	**SCABIES** (ska′be-ez)
Also Called	Itch
Cause	Mite: *Sarcoptes scabiei*
Incubation	4–6 weeks
Typical Symptoms	Intense itching; raised gray lines where mite burrows
Infectious	Uncertain
Diagnosis	Examination
Treatment	Same as pediculosis pubis
Complications	May infect hands, elbows, breasts, and buttocks as well as genitals
Notes	Very common

Disease	**VENEREAL WARTS***
Also Called	Genital warts, condylomata acuminata
Cause	Virus
Incubation	Unknown
Typical Symptoms	Local irritation, itching, warty growths around genital and anal areas
Infectious	Uncertain
Diagnosis	Examination
Treatment	Caustic chemicals or surgery
Complications	May spread enough to interfere with birth passage; may spread to newborn
Notes	Very contagious

Pronunciations from: *Dorland's Illustrated Medical Dictionary.*

* = can be transmitted to babies before, during or shortly after birth

SOURCE: Yarber (1978); based on the work of Chiappa and Forish (1976), Zarate (1977), Knox (1977), and National Institute of Allergy and Infectious Diseases (1976).

contracting STD. The greatest incidence of STD occurs in the teenage and young adult population, a population which is experiencing increasing rates of sexual intercourse with a greater number of sex partners (Zelnik and Kantner, 1980).

2. The development of the oral contraceptive pill has contributed to the rising incidence of STD, for two reasons. First, the popularity of the pill reduced the popularity of the condom. Because the condom is the contraceptive method which best prevents the spread of STD, a significant number of people began leaving themselves open to contracting an STD. Second, use of the birth control pill alters the vaginal environment of the female, increasing its alkalinity and decreasing its acidity. A more alkaline environment renders the mucous membranes of the vagina more amenable to the growth of certain STD fungi and bacteria, especially gonorrhea.

3. Some of the major STD's, like gonorrhea and syphilis, are difficult to detect. As many as 80 percent of women who are infected with gonorrhea bacteria may not experience enough of the symptoms to prompt them to go to a physician for an examination. Yet, they are just as infectious as others who experience the painful symptoms of this STD. Syphilis goes through stages where the disease is latent and no symptoms are present, which may mean, to the infected person, that the disease has gone away. However, the person with syphilis may be at the *most* infectious stage before any major, or easily recognized, symptoms appear. In addition, syphilis often mocks other diseases, such as chicken pox and heat rash, therefore it may be misdiagnosed or misidentified.

4. Many people are ignorant of the prevalence of STD's and of their highly infectious nature. This ignorance results in the failure of many to recognize the symptoms and the serious health effects of STD. They fail to seek immediate treatment when telltale symptoms appear, and do not take the available steps to prevent the spread of STD to themselves.

5. The social stigma, or shame, that many people attach to the term *venereal disease* leads them to believe that those who contract an STD are bad or immoral. Consequently, these individuals are reluctant to admit that they might have contracted an STD, simply because they are not prepared to consider themselves to be "one of those sorts" of people. This belief, then, leads to unnecessary delays in seeking diagnosis and treatment when symptoms do occur.

Figure 6.7 gives a brief summary of the symptoms, common names, complications, and treatment regimens for some of the more commonly occurring STD's. The reader should also take the STD Test (Feature 6.2) to see how much you know about sexually transmitted diseases.

Making Your Own Decision about Contraception

In this chapter, we have reviewed the currently available contraceptive methods which allow partners to limit and space their childbearing, according to their desires. Every contraceptive method reviewed has associated with it at least some advantages and disadvantages. The perfect contraceptive method, one that has no disadvantages and has all of the advantages of convenience, low cost, effectiveness, noninterference with the spontaneity and enjoyment of the sexual act, and freedom from health-related risks, has yet to be invented.

In making a decision about which contraceptive method or combination of methods to use, many people take into account what they perceive to be an acceptable balance of advantages and disadvantages. For example, some would be willing to accept the inconvenience and potential user-related problems associated with the diaphragm in order to avoid the potential health risks of the more effective birth control pill. Others may perceive the health risks of the pill to be so slight as to make the less effective and more inconvenient aspects of the diaphragm a sufficient basis for choosing the pill as their primary contraceptive method. However, if a given individual is *unaware* of the advantages and disadvantages of various contraceptive methods, or if they are unaware that certain effective methods are available for use, the chance of selecting a contraceptive method that best meets their needs is limited. An effective decision in regard to contraception, that is, a decision which leads to the choice of the most

1. Sexual intercourse is the only way of spreading STD.

    _____ True

    _____ False

2. Once a person has had an STD, he or she is immune to that particular disease.

    _____ True

    _____ False

3. Syphilis and gonorrhea may cause sterility.

    _____ True

    _____ False

4. Use of a diaphragm with spermicidal jelly or foam will help prevent spread of STDs.

    _____ True

    _____ False

5. Unless treated, a syphilis sore on the penis will become seriously infected and cause pain and swelling in the groin.

    _____ True

    _____ False

6. Some STD's are caused by viruses.

    _____ True

    _____ False

7. The condom is an effective contraceptive device which can also prevent the spread of STD.

    _____ True

    _____ False

8. Symptoms of gonorrhea usually begin one day after sexual contact.

    _____ True

    _____ False

9. At the present time, there is no specific cure for genital herpes (Herpes Simplex II).

    _____ True

    _____ False

10. Syphilis and gonorrhea are the only serious STD's in the United States.

    _____ True

    _____ False

11. Teenagers and young adults account for most STD incidence.

    _____ True

    _____ False

12. The signs of an STD often go hidden or unnoticed.

    _____ True

    _____ False

13. Once the signs of an STD disappear, the person is cured.

    _____ True

    _____ False

14. A sexually active person can take preventive measures to reduce the likelihood of contracting an STD.

    _____ True

    _____ False

15. A minor can be examined and treated for an STD without parental consent.

    _____ True

    _____ False

16. A person is required to name his or her sexual contacts when being treated for an STD.

    _____ True

    _____ False

17. The primary victims of the STD's are women and unborn or newborn babies.

_____ True

_____ False

18. A person who contracts an STD is "bad."

_____ True

_____ False

Answers to this quiz may be found on pp. 185 – 186.

SOURCES: University of Arizona Student Health Service information materials, and Yarber (1978).

effective method, as well as the method one finds is the most comfortable to use, depends upon knowing the pluses and minuses of several different methods.

Each contraceptive method was also discussed in terms of both its theoretical and actual user-effectiveness rates. Clearly, some methods realize a significant gap between these two measures of effectiveness because of the skills and conscious behavior necessary to put them into effect. As sophisticated as we have become in terms of contraceptive technology, and even though highly effective contraceptive techniques have been made available to our population, millions of people (both married and unmarried) experience unintended or unwanted pregnancies each year (National Center for Health Statistics, 1980b; Vaughan, et al., 1977). In 1976 alone, 8.1 million, or 12 percent of a total of 67.8 million live births to mothers 15 to 44 years of age, were unwanted at the time of conception. A certain percentage of these unwanted pregnancies was undoubtedly a result of carelessness or some other user error in applying a particular contraceptive method. Perhaps, too, some of these unwanted pregnancies were a result of insufficient knowledge about effective contraceptive methods and their advantages and disadvantages. In 1982, as we have seen, 3.1 million women in the United States were risking an unintended pregnancy by using no birth control method whatsoever (see Table 6.3). A major task in choosing a contraceptive measure, therefore, must be to estimate the potential for user error associated with the preferred method. The contraceptive user must be reasonably certain that the necessary skills, information, and motivation to use a particular method are in hand before that method is adopted.

It is important to note that user errors are often the responsibility of *both* partners in the sexual relationship. Even the choice of the best contraceptive method must often be made with the needs and feelings of both the male and female partner in mind. There are relatively few methods that require the participation of the male (withdrawal, condom, and male sterilization), in comparison to those that the female could handle on her own (foams, pill, IUD, rhythm, diaphragm, and female sterilization). Contraceptive user effectiveness depends to a large extent on the ability of partners to communicate to each other openly and honestly about how comfortable each is with the various devices and techniques available. To a certain extent, both partners must be comfortable with their own and the other's sexuality and sexual needs. Is the female willing to undergo any of the health risks associated with pill use? Is she willing to experience the discomfort of having an IUD inserted, or a diaphragm fitted? Does the male feel comfortable about wearing a condom, or does it reduce the sensation of sexual intercourse too greatly? Is the male willing to undergo the discomfort of a vasectomy? If not, is the female willing to undergo the discomfort of a tubal ligation? If fertility awareness is the method of choice, do both partners have the patience to spend several months charting cycle length and basal body temperature? And is each willing to cooperate in following the rhythm plan to the letter, once it is established? These questions are a few that confront couples seeking an effective contraceptive method which provides an acceptable ratio of advantages to disadvantages, and which is unlikely to result in an unintended pregnancy because of user error. The potential for user error is reduced and effectiveness of contraception is enhanced when both the choice of a contraceptive method and its implemen-

Although unintended and unwanted pregnancies each year number in the millions, modern methods of contraception provide the means of assuring that pregnancies and children born today are *wanted* by their parents.
(Photo by Stephen R. Jorgensen.)

tation over time are shared by both partners (Rainwater, 1965).

Summary

The range of contraceptive devices available today requires that those in sexual relationships ponder carefully the advantages and disadvantages, the benefits and risks, of each method prior to deciding on one. Effective family planning is an important aspect of sexual relationships both in and out of marriage. Family planning errors are costly to the couple, to society, and to the child who is conceived when the parents neither intended nor wanted a pregnancy to occur. Effective family planning also involves prevention, awareness, and care regarding sexually transmitted diseases. STD's continue to be a major public health problem in the United States despite the fact that many people could prevent their spread with proper precautions and prompt medical attention. Finally, family planning decisions require the joint participation of both the male and female partners in order to be most effective. Joint decisions are also most likely to lead to family planning methods that are mutually acceptable to each partner.

Questions for Discussion and Review

1. After reading about the various methods of birth control in this chapter, which do you find to be most acceptable to you? Which are the least acceptable? Explain your answer in terms of the advantages and disadvantages discussed.

2. What are your opinions and attitudes relating to abortion? Under what circumstances is abortion acceptable?

3. Why do you think more male methods of birth control have not been developed for general use? Are more male methods, such as a male pill or injections, necessary in order to make the responsibility for birth control more equal between men and women?

4. What can be done to stem the epidemic of sexually transmitted diseases in our society? What preventive measures can and should be taken?

5. Do you think that current abortion laws should be changed in any way? If so, what changes would you support?

Notes

1. A hysterectomy involves the removal of the woman's uterus, and in some cases, the ovaries. At one time, this surgical operation was conducted routinely as a permanent contraceptive measure. This is not the case today. After considerable controversy, and the development of far less drastic surgical procedures for female sterilization (i.e., tubal ligation), many physicians no longer will perform hysterectomies for other than urgent medical reasons: the presence of malignant and nonmalignant tumors, high cancer potential, abnormal uterine bleeding, or some other type of serious health disorder. Moreover, hysterectomies are costly, require extensive hospitalization, and carry the usual risks of major surgical procedure requiring general anesthesia.

2. Two other types of pills have been marketed in the past, although the problems associated with their use have either reduced their popularity significantly or have caused them to be withdrawn from the market. First, the *minipill* contains no estrogen, only progesterone. Because estrogen is the most likely cause of the health risks associated with pill use, it was once thought that a progesterone-only pill would be a safer but equally effective substitute. Research has shown, however, that user effectiveness rates are slightly lower for the minipill (about the same as the IUD; see Table 6.1), and that some of the by-products produced as the minipill is metabolized become active estrogens (Hubbard, 1977). Menstrual bleeding also follows a more unpredictable and irregular pattern, reducing further the popularity of this method. Second is the *sequential pill* regimen, in which the first 15 or 16 pills taken in a month contain estrogen only, and the last five contain both estrogen and progesterone. It was thought that this sequence would more closely parallel the natural order in which the woman releases these hormones during the menstrual cycle, and would therefore be better. Research has shown, however, that pregnancy rates were considerably higher for women using this type of pill regimen, and that the probabilities of blood clotting and uterine cancer were greater with this method of oral contraception. This contraceptive package is no longer marketed.

3. From 1950 through 1969, DES was used extensively to prevent spontaneous abortions among women who had experienced problems in carrying a fetus to term (Hatcher, et al., 1978). Children born to such women have been found to have reproductive health problems when they move through adolescence and into their early twenties. Some female offspring of DES women have developed cancer of the vagina, and some male offspring have experienced lower than normal semen and sperm production, as well as cysts within the scrotum. As a result of these findings, women who maintain a pregnancy even after DES use as a "morning-after" birth control measure often consider having a voluntary abortion. The pregnancy can continue if DES is taken too long after fertilization and implantation have occurred, if an insufficient dosage is taken, or simply if the drug fails to have the desired effect. Children of DES users should inform their physicians that such is the case, and they should be regularly checked for any of the health problems that have been found to be associated with DES. For these reasons, DES use

should be reserved only for medical emergencies or under certain extreme circumstances (such as rape), and certainly only under the orders of a qualified physician.

Answers to the STD Quiz

1. *False* Though sexual intercourse is a common way of spreading STD, it can also be spread by a person touching infectious genitals and spreading it to disease-free genitals and/or through oral-genital contact. Almost any mucous membrane or body opening can be susceptible to an STD infection. Some STD's (for example, syphilis, genital herpes) can enter the body virtually anywhere, particularly if the skin is broken.

2. *False* Immunity to these diseases does not occur. A person can get an STD again and again. A person can have more than one STD at a time, and treating one may not get rid of the other.

3. *True* Unless treated in time, syphilis and gonorrhea can advance to a stage where they can cause permanent sterility (and other serious complications).

4. *True* Although the condom is the most certain means of preventing the transmission of STD, contraceptive foams, jellies, and sponges have been found to reduce the chances of spreading certain types of STD by action of the spermicide they contain. Trichomoniasis and gonorrhea, in particular, appear to be checked, at least in some instances, by use of these contraceptive methods.

5. *False* A chancre from syphilis is a painless, pimple-like bump which goes away in a couple of days. Females may not even know the chancre exists. Though a man may see the chancre on his penis, it is entirely possible that the chancre is on the underneath side and may go undetected. After the chancre disappears, other symptoms won't appear for several weeks, and they too may not be detected.

6. *True* Herpes Simplex Type II (genital herpes), genital warts, mollescum, lymphogranuloma venereum are all diseases caused by a virus. (A virus might remain dormant in the person's body and reappear, depending upon the individual's circumstances.)

7. *True* A condom is the method of birth control that can best prevent the spread of STD, other than total abstinence.

8. *False* For men, gonorrhea usually appears 3 to 5 days after sexual contact with an infected person. He will probably notice a mucous discharge from his penis and a burning sensation while urinating. Most females infected with gonorrhea don't even know they have it for the first few weeks or months; some do show signs within a few days of infection, usually in the form of a discharge which is irritating to the external genital area.

9. *True* There is no curative treatment for Herpes Simplex Type II or cytomegalovirus, at the present time. There are methods which help lessen the pain and discomfort, but results in eliminating the symptoms are inconsistent and at best temporary.

   A person with an STD should be treated as soon as possible, before any permanent damage results (for example, sterility, insanity, blindness, arthritis, or heart disease). A person with an STD should not try to cure himself or herself. Only a physician can administer the proper tests and prescribe the right drugs.

10. *False* Many STD's are quite common—for example, genital herpes affects at least one-half million persons annually; trichomoniasis (trich) occurs in approximately 3 million cases yearly; nonspecific urethritis affects an estimated 2.5 million men annually; and cytomegalovirus (CMV) is contracted by 80 percent of the population by age 40. Other common STD's are: candidiasis (yeast, moniliasis); hepatitis B; Pediculosis pubis (lice, crabs); scabies (itch); venereal warts; and Group-B streptococcus.

11. *True*   About 65 percent of STD incidence occurs in the 15 to 24 age group.

12. *True*   Because of the external nature of their sex organs, males are more likely than females to detect an STD; males, therefore, typically represent an "early warning system" for medical care and for notifying female contacts. But the signs of an STD can often be hidden, unnoticed, or absent in both men and women. In this case, notification that an STD may have been contracted would probably come from an infected partner. The first sign of an STD may be a sore, burning or uncomfortable urination, drip or ooze from sex organs or eyes, persistent itch, or swollen glands. Later signs, which may appear anywhere on the body, can include a rash or blotches, a sore, abdominal pains, swollen glands, or hair loss.

13. *False*   Occasionally, some STD's are cured by the body's natural defense system. In the vast majority of cases, however, the germs remain present, in the body—even though visible symptoms may disappear—and may cause permanent damage.

14. *True*   Abstinence and fidelity are the best ways to avoid STD's. The more people with whom a person has intimate contact, the greater the risk of exposure. Though no method is fail-safe, a sexually active person can reduce the chances of getting an STD by not having sex with persons not well known, or potentially infected with an STD; by using a condom; by douching after intercourse; by looking for sores or discharge, and washing exposed areas after contact; and by urinating after contact.

15. *True*   Every state in the U.S. now permits minors to be examined and treated for an STD without parental or guardian knowledge or consent. In some states, the law applies to persons 12 years of age and over; in others it is 14 years of age.

16. *False*   One is not required by law to name sexual contacts. However, a person would be helping greatly to control STD's by getting infected persons to treatment. Individuals should give the names of their sexual partners to the physician or public health officer, or take them to the clinic as soon as possible.

17. *True*   STD's can pose greater danger to females than to males, because the early symptoms are not obvious in females. Females and babies, therefore, run a greater risk of medical complications from a prolonged infection.

18. *False*   A person who contracts an STD is ill, not bad.

CHAPTER 7

Communication and Conflict Management

I Know
You Believe You Understand
What You Think I Said,
But I Am Not Sure You Realize
That What You Heard
Is Not What I Meant

(Hunt and Rydman, 1979:23)

Communication is a major part of each of the other bases of marriage and the family discussed in this book. For example, falling in love and establishing a mature relationship (chapter 3) involve the ability to communicate feelings of intimacy and warmth to another person. Also, we are far more likely to love another who we believe communicates well with us than someone with whom we have difficulties in communicating our thoughts and feelings. The phrase "We just don't seem to relate to each other" is commonplace among ex-lovers and former spouses, a clear indicator of love relationships gone awry as the result of communication difficulties. Our knowledge of male and female gender roles (chapter 4) shows that men and women differ in their methods of communicating to members of the opposite sex: women tend to be more expressive than men when it comes to revealing personal aspects of themselves, including their ideas about love and intimacy. Gender roles not only provide guides for what constitute appropriate topics of communication between the sexes, at least as viewed by

the partners, but they also help to determine the appropriate *contexts* and *styles* of communicating in any given relationship. Finally, human sexuality and family planning (chapters 5 and 6) involve extensive communication between male and female partners in order to attain the most rewarding patterns in these realms of marriage. Indeed, the sexual aspect of intimate relationships such as marriage may be viewed as one special *type* of communication between partners — communicating the intensity of one person's love and affection for another. In brief, there is no component of marriage that is left untouched by *what* partners communicate about and *how* they go about communicating with each other.

The Process of Communication

On the surface, the word *communication* appears to represent a rather simple concept: just talking to another person. In fact, it is not that simple. There are a number of component parts which, taken all together, comprise the *process of communication*. "Failure to communicate," "communication breakdown," "inability to relate," and "ineffective communication" are phrases suggesting that the communication process is deficient in one or more of these component parts.

DEFINING EFFECTIVE COMMUNICATION

The concept of *effective communication* is important for intimate relationships such as marriage. *Effective communication is the exchange of information between two or more individuals in a relationship, such that the message sent by one (the sender) is accurately interpreted and understood by the other (the receiver), and vice versa.* Effective communication means that the message that is sent equals the message that is received. However, this concept does *not* imply that effective communication between any two individuals is in any sense "good" or "healthy" in that it promotes growth and development in the relationship. For example, one marriage partner might effectively communicate hatred and contempt for the other quite effectively by saying, "you are a disgusting person and I despise the very sight of you." Such a message would in no way be viewed as a sign of a relationship wherein the partners are meeting each other's goals for intimacy and emotional comfort. Effective communication implies that "message sent equals message received," regardless of the *style* of the communication and its *effects* on the development of the intimate relationship.

COMPONENTS OF THE COMMUNICATION PROCESS

Every time we are in the physical presence of another person, or when we are making contact via another mode (e.g., telephone or letter writing), we are engaged in some form of information exchange with the other. The act of communication may be accomplished verbally (e.g., talking) or nonverbally (body language), intentionally or unintentionally. No matter what *form* the effort to communicate takes, however, the basic components of the communication process are the same from one situation and context to the next.

The model of the communication process that will guide us here is borrowed from Bormann and Bormann (1972) and Gordon (1970) [see Figures 7.1 and 7.2]. The model applies to any of a number of interpersonal relationships, whether intimate (such as marriage) or nonintimate (such as communicating with a sales clerk or service station attendant). In Figure 7.1, we see that the *sender,* or *source,* of the initial message transmits the intended message through some sort of medium or channel

to a receiver of the message. Telephones, talking, writing, and body language are all types of communication channels. The sender has a particular *goal* or *objective* in mind when he or she sends the message to the receiver. This may be simply to make his or her thoughts clearly understood by the receiver. The communication process involves a "step-by-step, give-and-take interaction between source and receiver by which the source reaches the desired goal," the goal being that which inspired the effort to communicate (Bormann and Bormann, 1972:25). The role of the receiver is to send *feedback* information to the source. In this way, the sender can determine the degree to which the goal of making himself or herself understood by the other has been attained (see Figure 7.2).

Communication problems can arise, however, because of a variety of conditions. For example, both parties may attempt to be the sender, and thereby seek to control the flow of the discussion by attaining their own personal goals without regard to the other. Also, neither party may be willing or able to provide feedback information to the other so that the receiver's level of understanding can be determined. One party may also choose, either consciously or unconsciously, to hear what they want or expect to hear from the other, rather than hear what the other actually has to say. Another kind of communication problem may arise when the source is sending inconsistent messages to the other, either verbally, nonverbally, or both. In this case, the receiver may have difficulty in determining precisely what message the source is attempting to get across. Thus, effective communication is hampered.

Two other concepts will aid in our understanding of the communication process: *encoding* and *decoding* (see Figure 7.2). When one person has an idea, message, or other mental image to be communicated to another, the idea must be put into a form that can be understood, interpreted, and evaluated by the other. This is the process of *encoding,* whereby the source places the idea in a communicable form. Generally, in our society, we rely on the English language as the code by which we send messages and share information with others. Other codes may be used, such as body and other nonverbal language, mathematical symbols, Morse code, or other languages (e.g., Spanish, French, or German), which allow us to put our mental images into a form that can be taken in by another. *Decoding,* then, is the process by which the receiver breaks the code, or develops an interpretation and understanding of the message which the source is attempting to transmit.

FIGURE 7.1.   Components of the Interpersonal Communication Process.

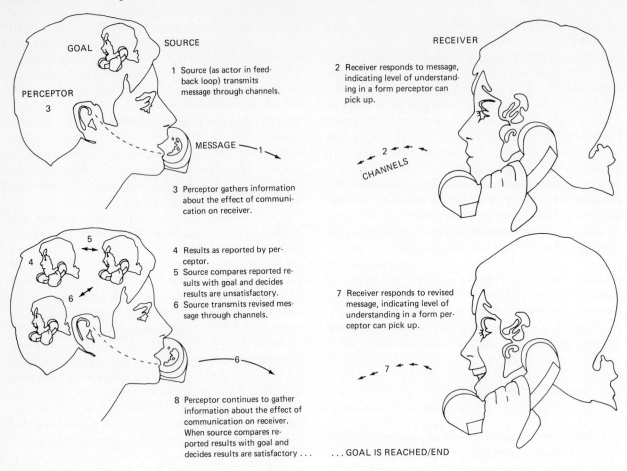

SOURCE: Adopted from Bormann and Bormann (1972:26–27).

As long as two parties share the same code and have open communication channels between them, communication proceeds rather smoothly and effectively by a reciprocal process of encoding and decoding.

However, anyone who has enrolled in an advanced English or mathematics class, or who has been scolded for misbehavior by a parent, knows quite well that communication is hampered when one party uses words or symbols in his or her code that are not shared by the other, or which are defined differently by the two parties. For example, if a parent scolds a child for misbehaving, the parent may intend to communicate (encode), "What you did was wrong, and you should be punished so that you will not try

it again." This may stem from a genuine concern for the child's welfare and safety, as in the case of the child who insists on running into the street against the parent's orders. The child, on the other hand, may decode the message by interpreting the scolding thus: "I hate you and I want you to be miserable." This difference in the encoding-decoding process is the kind of communication breakdown that may lead to more extensive misunderstandings if the parent fails to explain to the child why he or she was scolded. The more two parties agree on the meaning of words and other symbols, the greater the probability that they will be able to communicate effectively in their relationship with one another.

FIGURE 7.2. Encoding and Feedback in the Communication Process.

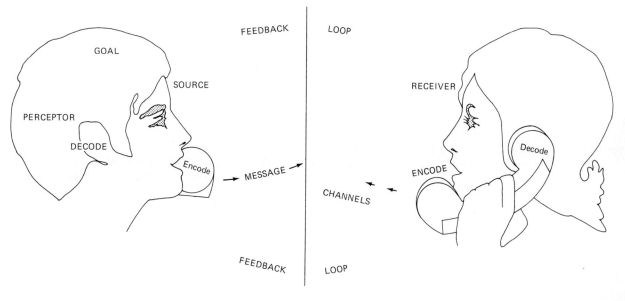

SOURCE: Bormann and Bormann (1972:30–31).

As an example of how feedback and the encoding and decoding processes operate in intimate relationships, refer to the discussion of love in chapter 3. Recall that the words "I love you" may mean one thing to the male (such as affection and caring for another), yet be interpreted quite differently by the female (such as commitment to marriage). Serious misunderstandings can develop when the male says "I love you" to the female (encoding), meaning that he cares a lot for her, and the female interprets (decodes) the message to mean "I want to marry you." Ideally, these two partners will put into play feedback processes whereby they verbally exchange their respective definitions of what the concept of "love" means to each of them. If feedback messages do not follow, unnecessary misunderstanding and possible conflict may ensue at a later time. The major problem here is that neither partner was aware of the breakdown in the encoding-decoding process at the time that the initial "I love you" message was sent (Gordon, 1970). It is up to the receiver to *feed back* verbally what she feels the sender *meant* by his message. She might say, "Does that mean you wish to marry me?" This allows the sender to either verify that, indeed, his message was accurately decoded,

or, as is the case here, inaccurately decoded. When the feedback process shows that inaccurate *understanding* (interpretation) has taken place, the sender is able to clarify his *actual meaning* for the receiver, thereby preventing the misunderstanding before it causes conflict later on. In our example, the male might say, "No, I only meant that I really care for you and hope to see you on a more regular basis."

Concepts and Principles Relating to Communication

The study of communication among human beings is vast. Research has focused on just about every aspect of communication imaginable: what people communicate about; with whom they communicate; why they say what they do; how they communicate; when and under what conditions they communicate to others; how men and women differ in their communicative behavior; how people learn communication skills; what constitutes effective communication; what role communication plays in the development of the individual and social relationships, ad infinitum. We will rely upon a number of concepts and principles of human communication to help organize this information.

COMMUNICATION AND MARRIAGE AS A SYSTEM

It is useful to view the marriage relationship as a *system* (Kantor and Lehr, 1975; Watzlawick, Beavin, and Jackson, 1967; Lederer and Jackson, 1968). Marriage is one type of *social system* in that there are two elements, husband and wife, who influence each other in a more or less stable, or structured, way over time. Just as in other types of systems — the engine in your automobile, a computer, your stereophonic system, or the heating and cooling systems in your house — social systems such as marriage are characterized by three features.

First, all systems require some sort of *information input* and *information exchange* in order to operate efficiently and effectively. Communication, then, involves the exchange of information within a system in order to keep it operating as was intended. Partners in any kind of lasting intimate relationship, including marriage, depend upon information from outside sources, such as friends, relatives, workmates, television, and newspapers, in order to function effectively on a day-to-day basis. These outside contacts provide an abundance of information relating to role expectations, beliefs and opinions, the nature of daily events, and values. People today are literally bombarded by a massive amount of information on any particular day, information which is carried into a relationship and discussed between the partners. On any given day, for example, a husband and wife may find themselves exchanging information about each person's day at the office or on the job; what the boss had to say; whether or not to accept a dinner invitation from friends for Saturday night; what a child's teacher had to say about his or her behavior at school; which television programs they will view that evening; and even the nature of world events read about in that morning's newspaper. The list could go on indefinitely. When we add the information exchanges that might emanate primarily from *within* the couple, such as their views on how they communicate and relate to each other; their feelings and emotions toward each other at a particular time; their preferences about where to go on

vacation that year; and what to plan for dinner, it becomes clear that the average married couple must process a tremendous quantity of information, on a continuing basis, in order to function smoothly and effectively.

A second aspect of all social systems, including marriage, is that they are *selectively open* to outside influences. The concept of *selective boundary maintenance* (chapter 2) is useful in this regard. Married couples have the ability to control the kinds of information allowed to cross the boundaries established by the couple, as well as the sources from which such information will flow. This is all part of the married pair's efforts to establish a *couple identity* which separates them from others outside of the relationship. A major aspect of any marriage's communication structure, then, is the degree to which each partner can *selectively* choose *which* information will be brought into the relationship to provide a basis for discussion between the partners, and how, and under what conditions, that information will be discussed. Generally, the more open a married couple is to new information flowing in, and the greater the willingness of both partners to *share* such information with each other, the greater their chances of mutual growth and fulfillment by means of new and varied experiences. Partners in such marriages are more capable of experiencing the fullness and richness of experiences that life has to offer because they have available a wider variety of information from which to selectively map and guide their lives together. However, marriage partners who are relatively *closed* to the introduction of new information are more prone to stagnation and lack of growth. Nena and George O'Neill refer to those who are open to new information as having "open marriages."

Open marriage is a non-manipulative relationship between man and woman . . . Being individuals, both are free to develop and expand into the outside world. Each has the opportunity for growth and new experiences outside the marriage . . . Because each one is growing through freedom toward selfhood, adding new experiences from the outside and at the same time receiving the incremental benefit of his mate's outside experiences, the union develops in an upward spiral. . . . Therefore their union thrives on change and new experiences. . . . Marriage must be based on an openness to one's self, an openness to another's self and an openness to the world. (O'Neill and O'Neill, 1972:39–40)

Marriage systems in which the partners are relatively closed to new information, or in which the communication structure does not allow for the sharing and exchange of

Communication in an intimate relationship helps to establish a couple identity, as information is selectively filtered into the relationship and discussed by the partners. *(Photo by Carl Hill.)*

information with which both partners come into contact on a daily basis, are unlikely to experience the growth necessary to meet the needs of each partner on a continuing basis over the years of the marital career.

A third feature of marriage as a social system is that this type of relationship is *goal-directed.* As pointed out in chapter 1, most people hold as important goals in marriage the fulfillment of the basic human needs for intimacy, warmth, and companionship. We also have a driving need for self-confirmation, for someone to tell us we're "O.K.," so that our existence is acknowledged as meaningful and relevant. Conversely, we have a need to avoid rejection, humiliation, and failure. In our society, where marriage is usually based on romantic attachment, we more or less consciously select marriage partners in hopes of satisfying these needs and attaining these goals. Attainment of these goals is rewarding, but failure to attain them is psychologically and emotionally painful, for most of us (Knox, 1971; Patterson, 1975).

The primary means by which marriage partners establish their goals and seek the rewards of reaching them is, of course, through communication. Marriage partners must be able to communicate their individual needs and goals to each other in order to know just what it is each one is hoping to accomplish in the marriage. As Patterson (1975) points out, an important aspect of both giving and receiving satisfaction in intimate relationships is *role reciprocity* (chapter 2): being aware of what you can do to reward the other person, and making the other aware of what they can do to reward you. Being able to effectively communicate about each other's needs and goals in marriage will allow the partners to exchange the kind of behaviors that will reinforce their commitment and promote satisfaction in the relationship.

Much seemingly complex human behavior can be understood in terms of a person's efforts to maximize rewards and minimize pain. . . . There are many things which can function as a reward, or "reinforcer," and they all have one thing in common. *When a behavior is followed by a reinforcer, the behavior is strengthened.* This means that the behavior is more likely to occur again in the future . . . The "little things," *the close attention of another person, a touch, words of approval, a smile, a glance, or a kiss, are all examples of social reinforcers* . . . Observations of real people in real social settings show that *the individual who gives the most reinforcement receives the most reinforcement and that the person in the family who gives the most punishment receives the most punishment from other family members. You get what you give.* (Patterson, 1975:9–10; 11; 20)

Marriage partners must be able to communicate their dissatisfaction when needs are being unfulfilled and goals are not being attained, just as they must communicate the fact that needs and goals *are* being met. This is especially challenging when each person's needs and goals change over the years of marriage, as we shall see in chapters 9 through 14.

Despite the tremendous importance of communication in promoting development in marriage, research has also shown that it is the most problematic realm in marriage for most couples. In fact, it is the breakdown in communication which is most often identified by divorcing couples as the underlying reason for dissatisfaction with marriage (Knox, 1971; Brown, 1979). According to Thomas (1977:1):

Communication difficulties are probably the most common type of problem encountered in couples who seek assistance to improve their interpersonal relationships. Among the frequently heard complaints are that partners argue, quarrel, nag, insult or put each other down; that they talk past each other, don't say what they mean, mislead, talk out of both sides of their mouths, or lie; that they can't or won't understand what is said, or ignore each other; that they talk too much, too little, too softly, or too loudly; that they never offer praise or acknowledgement for doing a good job; that there is too much gloomy talk and too little that is pleasant.

PRINCIPLES OF INTERPERSONAL COMMUNICATION

The following are basic principles of interpersonal communication. They apply to intimate relationships, such as marriage, as well as nonintimate relationships.

PRINCIPLE 1. ONE CANNOT *NOT* COMMUNICATE.

It is easy to grasp the meaning of this principle if one can accept the fact that communication, the sending and receiving of information between people, is one type of *behavior*. Clearly, it is impossible to *not* behave in some fashion. No matter what we are doing—sleeping, talking, listening, watching television, playing tennis, or engaging in a long and tender embrace with another—we are *behaving* in some way. When we are awake, and in the presence of another person, we are communicating something to that person regardless of how hard we try not to. According to Lederer and Jackson (1968:98–99):

People in our culture believe that the most important communications are spoken or written. This view is erroneous. Scientists have estimated that fifty to a hundred bits of information are exchanged *each second* between individuals communicating actively. Everything which a person does in relation to another is some kind of message. There is no *not* communicating. Even silence is communication.

Try it for yourself. See if you are able to *not* communicate with someone who happens to be with you at the moment.

PRINCIPLE 2. PEOPLE COMMUNICATE NONVERBALLY AS EFFECTIVELY AND EXTENSIVELY AS THEY DO VERBALLY.

One of the more interesting lines of research on human communication has to do with the nature of nonverbal communication, sometimes referred to as *body language*. Communication researchers have estimated that the average person consumes only 10 minutes per day speaking words—the typical spoken sentence takes only 2.5 seconds to complete. In a normal conversation between two people, only 35 percent of the social meaning of the situation is carried by verbal messages, and 65 percent is nonverbal (Knapp, 1972). Facial experessions; body posture; hand gestures; movement of the brow and eyebrows; eye glances; placement of the arms and legs; and the style, color, and volume of clothing are all methods by which human beings communicate with each other without talking. In intimate relationships such as marriage, nonverbal communication is probably just as important as verbal communication for sending information about one's thoughts, feelings, and intentions relative to another.

Herr von Osten purchased a horse in Berlin, Germany in 1900. When von Osten began training his horse, Hans, to count by tapping his front hoof, he had no idea that Hans was soon to become one of the most celebrated horses in history. Hans was a rapid learner and soon progressed from counting to addition, multiplication, division, subtraction, and eventually the solution of problems involving factors and fractions. As if this were not enough, von Osten exhibited Hans to public audiences where he counted the number in the audience or simply the number of people wearing eye glasses. Still responding only with taps, Hans could tell time, use a calendar, display an ability to recall musical pitch, and perform numerous other seemingly fantastic feats. After von Osten taught Hans an alphabet which could be coded into hoofbeats, the horse could answer virtually any question — oral or written. It seemed that Hans, a common horse, had complete comprehension of the German language, the ability to produce the equivalent of words and numerals, and an intelligence beyond that of many human beings.

Even without the promotion of Madison Avenue, the word spread quickly and soon Hans was known throughout the world. He was soon dubbed "Clever Hans." Because of the obviously profound implications for several scientific fields and because some skeptics thought there was a "gimmick" involved, an investigating committee was established to decide, once and for all, whether there was any deceit involved in Hans' performances. Professors of psychology, physiology, the director of the Berlin Zoological Garden, a director of a circus, veterinarians, and cavalry officers were appointed to this commission of horse experts. An experiment with Hans from which von Osten was absent demonstrated no change in the apparent intelligence of Hans. This was sufficient proof for the commission to announce there was no trickery involved.

The appointment of a second commission was the beginning of the end for Clever Hans. Von Osten was asked to whisper a number into the horse's left ear while another experimenter whispered a number into the horse's right ear. Hans was told to add the two numbers — an answer none of the onlookers, von Osten, or the experimenter knew. Hans failed. And with further tests he continued to fail. The experimenter, Pfungst, discovered on further experimentation that Hans could only answer a question if someone in his visual field knew the answer. When Hans was given the question, the onlookers assumed an expectant posture and increased their body tension. When Hans reached the correct number of taps, the onlookers would relax and make a slight movement of the head — which was Hans' cue to stop tapping.

The story of Clever Hans is frequently used in discussions concerning the capacity of an animal to learn verbal language. It also seems well suited to an introduction to the field of nonverbal communication. Hans' cleverness was not in his ability to verbalize or understand verbal commands, but in his ability to respond to almost imperceptible and unconscious movements on the part of those surrounding him. It is not unlike that perceptiveness or sensitivity to nonverbal cues exhibited by a Clever Carl, Charles, Frank, or Harold when picking up a girl, closing a business deal, giving an intelligent and industrious image to a professor, knowing when to leave a party, and in a multitude of other common situations.

SOURCE: Reprinted from Knapp (1972:1–2)

Knapp (1972) has categorized different types of nonverbal communication, according to the role and function of such behavior in a given situation (see Table 7.1). Think of someone you know well, try to visualize the last time you interacted with them, and then categorize them according to each of these forms of nonverbal communication. How is your overall impression of that person shaped and conditioned by your perceptions of his or her nonver-

TABLE 7.1. *Types of Nonverbal Communication*

Body Motion or Kinesic Behavior: Gestures, movements of the body, limbs, hands, head, feet and legs, facial expressions (smiles), eye behavior (blinking, direction and length of gaze, and pupil dilation) and posture. Within this broad category are several subtypes, based on the specificity and purpose of the communication.

1. *Emblems:* These include nonverbal acts which have a direct verbal translation, usually a word or two or a phrase. Included are the sign language for the deaf, nodding, or signals used by underwater swimmers, shaking of the head ("yes" or "no"), an umpire's gestures, and hand gestures, such as those representing "A-OK" and "Hello."
2. *Illustrators:* These are nonverbal acts which accompany or are directly related to speech, for example, giving emphasis to a word or phrase, pointing to an object being discussed, and illustrating a bodily action.
3. *Affect displays:* These are facial configurations which communicate feelings and emotions, such as disappointment, sorrow, anger, pain, happiness, joy, and satisfaction.
4. *Regulators:* These are nonverbal behaviors which seek to maintain or regulate the process of speaking and listening between two or more communicants by telling the speaker to continue, repeat, elaborate, hurry up, or give the other a chance to talk; for example, head nods, eye movements, and hand motions which are equivalent to the verbal "mm-hmm," "oh boy," and "let's get on with it," respectively.

Physical Characteristics: In contrast to the body movements mentioned in the previous category, this category includes such nonmovement characteristics as physique, body shape, physical attractiveness, body or breath odors, height, weight, hair length and color, and skin color or tone, each of which communicates something about one person to another, be it interests, values, nationality, or intentions.

Touching Behavior: This category includes such gestures as stroking, hitting, greeting and farewell embraces, holding, or guiding another's movements, any of which can communicate something about one's true feelings, intentions, or goals relative to another.

Paralanguage: This relates primarily to *how* something is said, rather than the actual content of the verbal message. For example, the following sub-types of paralanguage can be distinguished.

1. *Voice qualities:* These include pitch range, pitch control, tonal quality, rhythm control, tempo, articulation control, resonance, and lip control.
2. *Vocalizations:* These include vocal characterizers such as laughing, sighing, yawning, belching, swallowing, heavy inhaling or exhaling, coughing, throat clearing, hiccupping, moaning, groaning, whining, yelling, whispering, sneezing, snoring, and stretching. In addition, there are such *voice qualifiers* as intensity (overloud to oversoft); extent (extreme drawl to extreme clipping); and *vocal segregates,* such as "uh-huh," "uh," and "ah."

Proxemics: This category relates to the use and perception of physical and social space when communicating with another. For example, seating arrangements (at dinner, in a group, in a parked or moving car, and so on); conversational distance, which varies according to sex, status, and cultural background (e.g., Latin Americans stand much closer to each other in a casual conversation than do North Americans); and the tendency to stake out personal territory or untouchable space. All these contribute to the nonverbal communication process between people.

Artifacts: These are objects attached to, or associated with, two individuals who are communicating. For example, perfume or cologne, lipstick, eyeglasses, clothing, false eyelashes and fingernails, wigs, make-up, and the whole repertoire of falsies and "beauty" aids.

Environmental Factors: These include objects in the immediate surroundings which provide cues as to the nature and background of one with whom another is interacting. For example, the furniture, interior decor, lighting, colors, smells, temperature, and arrangement of other material objects in an apartment communicate something about the occupant and contribute to the formation of one's impression of another.

SOURCE: Adapted from Knapp (1972:5–8).

bal cues? Do they contribute to or detract from a favorable impression of that individual?

Research on nonverbal communication has shown that people tend to like another more when the other is standing close rather than at a distance; leaning forward, when seated, rather than back; facing them squarely rather than from the side; touching them; sharing eye contact; offering bodily contact, as in a handshake or embrace; and prolonging goodbyes (Mehrabian, 1971:22). For example, the degree to which we maintain eye contact during a conversation with another communicates much about our intentions and feelings at the time. Eye contact is usually maintained when we seek feedback from another; when we wish to tell the other that the channels for communication are open and that they are invited to speak; and when we wish to reduce the physical and psychological distance between one another. In addition, eye contact with another, accompanied by a smile, indicates an interest in affiliating with or becoming involved (for the moment) with the other. People are more likely to make eye contact when they are being socially rewarded by another. Conversely, avoiding eye contact is indicative of either a negative attitude, or a problem in the relationship with another: dislike, fear, anxiety, or shyness.

Consider also the importance of physical attractiveness as a first filter in the dating and courtship process. People tend to like, make contacts with, and seek to date and marry those perceived to be physically attractive and sexually appealing (Bersheid and Walster, 1969; Murstein, 1970). A major nonverbal way of communicating the fact that we find a person attractive is by gazing at them. Both males and females tend to gaze at attractive opposite-sex persons significantly longer than they gaze at less attractive ones (Coutts and Schneider, 1975). Knapp (1972:17) applies this principle to the singles bar scene:

On a purely intuitive level, we know that there are some men and some women who can exude such messages as "I'm available," "I'm knowledgeable," or "I want you" without saying a word. For the male it may be such things as his clothes, sideburns, length of hair, an arrogant gaze, a thrust of his hips, touch gestures, extra long eye contact, carefully looking at the woman's figure, open gestures and movements to offset closed ones exhibited by the woman, gaining close proximity, a subtleness which will allow both parties to deny that either had committed themselves to a courtship ritual, making the woman feel secure, wanted, "like a woman," or showing excitement and desire in fleeting

facial expressions. For the woman, it may be such things as sitting with her legs symbolically open, crossing her legs to expose a thigh, engaging in flirtatious glances, stroking her thighs, protruding breasts, using appealing perfume, showing the "pouting mouth" in her facial expressions, opening her palm to the male, using a tone of voice which has an "invitation" behind the words, or any of a multitude of other cues and rituals. . . .

One has only to enter a singles bar or campus nightspot in order to observe firsthand the tremendous volume of nonverbal communication. Nonverbal communication usually precedes any sort of verbal effort in the courtship ritual that many young people in our society go through to make social contact with members of the opposite sex.

Touching is one of the most powerful means of nonverbal communication, particularly in marriage and other intimate relationships (Frank, 1957; Montagu, 1971). The importance of tactile stimulation begins early in life, as early as the months before birth, while the child is in the mother's uterus. The vibrations of the mother's heartbeat and body motions are magnified through the amniotic fluid and stimulate the fetus. After birth, infant and early-childhood development are retarded if there is no tactile stimulation from other human beings, or if the tactile explorations by the young child are restricted (Bowlby, 1969; Harlow and Harlow, 1977). During adolescence and young adulthood, touching behavior takes on added significance as heterosexual relationships are formed and nurtured. Touching is a primary means of communicating affection, intimacy, and love for another person. Conversely, touching of another kind is a primary means of communicating hatred and disrespect for the other: hitting, slapping, and other forms of physical violence can and do occur in marriage and other intimate relationships (Straus, 1974; Makepeace, 1981).

PRINCIPLE 3. INTERPERSONAL COMMUNICATION INVOLVES SIMULTANEOUS CONTENT AND RELATIONSHIP COMPONENTS.

Effective communication between two people does not depend exclusively on *what* is said; it is heavily dependent on *how* it is said, and in what *kind of context* it is said. Saying "I love you" to another in a soft voice, with the lights turned low in a romantic setting, conveys quite a different message than the same words uttered with anger in one's eyes and a tensed body. In intimate relationships we often exchange messages with a particular content, or surface meaning, as well as a meaning relative to the nature of the relationship between the partners. Watzlawick, et al. (1967) refer to these two aspects of communication as the *content* and *relationship* components of communication.

The most serious communication problems between partners in intimate relationships such as marriage often occur at the *relationship* level, not the *content* level. Regardless of whether you disagree about who works harder, what to have for dinner, and whether or not the Dodgers are a better baseball team than the Yankees, the real issue often boils down to who has the control in the relationship, and who is defined as being "right." As Watzlawick, et al. (1967) point out, communication involves a continual definition of the "self-other" relationship, and involves three possible functions: *confirmation, rejection,* and *disconfirmation. Confirmation* implies that each accepts the other person as valid and worthy of respect and concern. It is a way of saying, "I accept you and confirm your worth as an equal human being." As these authors point out, confirmation through communication with others is essential for mental health.

confirmation of *P*'s view of himself by *O* is probably the greatest single factor ensuring mental development and stability that has so far emerged from our study of communication. (Watzlawick, et al., 1967:84)

Rejection, on the other hand, means that when communicating, one or both partners refuse to accept the other's view of himself or herself as valid. It is like saying, "I know that you think you are that way (good, powerful, intelligent, competent, handsome, etc.), but you are wrong." *Disconfirmation* in communication is a serious problem because one partner denies the other's existence. It amounts to trying to relate to a person while that person continually ignores you. Both *rejection* and *disconfirmation,* then, are types of relationship definition which can result in serious communication problems and devastating blows to the person who is being either rejected or disconfirmed.

Problems in effective communication also arise when the content and relationship aspects of a verbal message are in conflict, or when partners attempt to solve a problem or resolve a conflict which exists on one level (relation-

ship) by focusing on the other (content) level. Consider, for example, the following discussion of a husband and wife, married for 14 years, about how much money to spend for food each week.

Dave: The major problem in this house is that you spend too much money on food.
Ellen: Yes, I have to spend less dear. But you have to make more, dear.
Dave: Ellen, I make plenty of money. But you spend more than we can afford.
Ellen: I don't spend what I should on food at all. Have you noticed now inflation has raised food prices?
Dave: You spend more than we can afford. We eat lamb chops, steaks, turkey, hamburgers . . . . these are *expensive* things to eat!
Ellen: But food is not an item that we should be cheap about. For health purposes, we have to eat those things.
Dave: (raising his voice) Ellen, you can't get healthy eating broiled steaks!
Ellen: You get healthy eating good food, believe me.
Dave: (voice raised) But good food is not expensive!
Ellen: (voice raised) It is too!
Dave: It is not.
Ellen: It is too.
Dave: Ellen, why are you arguing with me? I decide how much to budget for different things in this house, not you.
Ellen: Since when?
Dave: Ellen, the issue is that you spend too much on food, and you know it. Let's stick to the issue.

In this dialogue, the *content* of the communication between these partners is the cost of food and excessive food expenditures. However, toward the end of the conversation it becomes evident that the real issue is on the *relationship* level: *who has the right to tell who how much to spend* on anything in their household? The actual problem lies in their disagreement over who has the power in the relationship, each rejecting the other's view. Yet, they insist on keeping the discussion at the *content* level without discussing their differing views of their *relationship.*

Communication about the nature of the interpersonal relationship, including how the partners communicate with each other, is *metacommunication* (Watzlawick, et al., 1967). Because much communication between married partners and others involved in intimate relationships is charged with some degree of feeling and emotion, it is important to recognize that both content and relationship aspects are present, and that they may be incompatible: for example, saying "I love you, can't you see that, you fool?" with a scowl. Only *metacommunication* can resolve issues and problems at the relationship level.

PRINCIPLE 4. COMMUNICATION IS RULE-GUIDED.

Each partner in a marriage or other intimate relationship brings to it an implicit set of communication rules. These *relationship rules* define *who* can do or say *what,* to *whom, where, when, how,* and for *what length of time* (Miller, Corrales, and Wackman, 1975:147; Watzlawick, et al., 1967:132–134). Each person's rules are learned during the childhood socialization process (observing and interacting with parents and siblings), as well as through direct experiences with others during adolescence and early adulthood. Following is only a partial list of rules that an individual might have regarding communication with another person in marriage. These rules, or norms, guide the nature and direction of communication in a relationship. They also shape the consequences such communication will have for the development of the relationship over time, as in marriage. It is expected that you will disagree with some of these and agree with others.

1. Married partners should communicate openly and honestly about all aspects of their lives all of the time.

2. When one partner is upset about something the other has done, it is best to just keep it inside and forget about it.

3. It is inappropriate to hold hands, kiss, or hug in public.

4. It is all right for women to talk about their feelings and problems, but it is a sign of weakness and personal inadequacy for men to do so.

5. It is wrong for a married person to talk to a person of the opposite sex for any length of time, while at a party.

6. Arguments and quarrels should be avoided whenever possible.

7. Talking about problems in your marriage is inappropriate when friends or relatives are present.

8. Each partner in marriage is entitled to at least one hour of privacy and silent meditation every day.

9. It is unfair to bring up past disagreements or issues when resolving a conflict in the present.

10. Physical violence (slapping, pushing, hitting, etc.) is inappropriate behavior for married partners.

Of course, there are many other communication rules that people could embrace. Each partner in an intimate relationship such as marriage has an agenda of rules, either conscious or unconscious, for communicating. Problems can ensue when the rules are broken by one or both partners, or when partners disagree on the nature and meaning of the rules that should be in force.

PRINCIPLE 5. COMMUNICATION CAN FOLLOW A VARIETY OF STYLES.

Many styles of communication are possible. Communication styles may vary according to family background, ethnicity, gender roles, sex, social class background, and educational level, meaning that two individuals in marriage may not follow the same set of communication styles and rules. For example, one partner may rely primarily on nonverbal messages to communicate feelings, desires, and intentions, and the other may rely on talking. Although a relationship involving such radically different communication styles may operate quite smoothly for a time, the chances are that the nonverbal partner may come to view the other as a "nagging complainer," and the verbal partner may eventually view the other as "secretive and mistrusting" (Cutler and Dyer, 1965).

PRINCIPLE 6. INDIVIDUALS VARY ACCORDING TO THE LEVEL OF COMMUNICATION SKILLS THEY HAVE ACQUIRED OVER THE COURSE OF THEIR LIFETIMES.

Effective communication is a *skilled* behavior. That is, some people are better at communicating than others, but this ability does not come naturally. One must *learn* these skills, if effective communication is to take place. Moreover, the effectiveness of communication depends on the skill levels of *both* partners in the relationship. If one partner lacks specific skills, or is deficient across a variety of skills, communication breakdown is likely to occur regardless of the other partner's skill level. Effective communication is a team effort, and requires the skilled contribution of *both* partners if the communication structure is to be one that will promote mutual growth and development in the relationship over time.

Styles of Communication

As stated in Principle 5, communication in marriage and other intimate relationships may be one of a variety of styles. Furthermore, we can say that particular styles of communicating characterize each partner as an *individual,* as well as the *pattern* of communication that develops between two individuals in a relationship.

INDIVIDUAL COMMUNICATION STYLES

People differ in their characteristic way of talking and relating to others. Think of one or two others who are close to you — parents, friends, roommates — and think of how they typically communicate with you. Would you characterize them as basically open, willing to share freely of themselves, or closed and somewhat private? Are they quite verbal, or do they rely more on nonverbal messages and body language to communicate with you? Do they concentrate mainly on idle chitchat and discussions of mundane events, or do they communicate more deeply about their feelings, emotions, and personal thoughts? Do they ever initiate communication about your relationship with them and the ways in which you communicate with each other? Do they give negative criticisms to others, verbal rewards and reinforcement, or both? Now try to compare yourself with those you have just characterized. In what ways are you like them? Different? Do you communicate as effectively with them as you would like to? Do you feel rewarded when communicating with them, or do you get impatient, or possibly angered, more than you would like?

These are important questions to ask in order to understand a person's communication style. Individual styles may vary greatly. The quality of any intimate relationship depends to a large degree on the particular combination of individual styles that are present. A person's style is highly dependent on the *kinds of statements* that are typically made in a variety of situations (see Table 7.2). According to the authors who developed this classification in Table 7.2 (Hunt and Rydman, 1979; Gordon, 1970), the typical response styles a person may follow are catego-

TABLE 7.2. *Individual Response Styles in Communication*

Negative	Examples:	Positive	Examples:
1. Ordering, directing, commanding	"Stop ordering me around." "You can't buy that." "Don't talk to me like that."	1. Providing self-direction and choice	"You appear very disappointed." "Let's discuss whether that would be a good purchase." "When you talk like that, I feel frightened."
2. Warning, admonishing, threatening	"Listen to me or else." "If you won't, then I'll find someone who will."	2. Seeking causes for differences	"What did I say that turned you off?" "Help me to understand why you don't want to . . ."
3. Exhorting, moralizing, preaching	"You should tell your boss you want that raise."	3. Choosing one of several alternatives	"Which do you think would be best for you, . . . for us, . . . for all involved?"
4. Advising, giving solutions or suggestions	"Why don't you try . . ." "You ought to stay home more."	4. Exploring possibilities	"What could you try?" "Would it help you if . . ."

TABLE 7.2. *(Continued)*

Negative	Examples:	Positive	Examples:
5. Lecturing, teaching, giving logical arguments	"It makes more sense to do it this way." "The Browns are happy and they don't have a new car."	5. Considering consequences	"Which way seems to get better results for you?" "Let's think about what would result from each decision."
6. Judging, criticizing, blaming	"You are wrong." "It's all your fault." "What a stupid idea!"	6. Sharing responsibility	"Those two statements seem to conflict." "Let's do what we can to solve it." "Let's see if that idea will work."
7. Praising, agreeing, evaluating	"I think you are absolutely correct." "You do so many good things."	7. Expanding openness	"This seems like a difficult decision for you to make." "You sound discouraged. I'll listen."
8. Name-calling, ridiculing, shaming, categorizing	"You're no good." "You're just like all the other men/women." "You're a liar."	8. Enhancing self-esteem and uniqueness	"I love you." "I appreciate your understanding." "Your interpretation is different from mine."
9. Interpreting, analyzing, diagnosing	"If you weren't so tired you could see my point." "You don't care what I think."	9. Increasing sensitivity	"If you prefer, we can discuss this at another time." "Right now, I'm feeling so alone and left out."
10. Reassuring, sympathizing, consoling*	"Don't worry about that." "All men/women go through that at some time."	10. Expressing care and concern	"What worries you about that?" "This is an especially difficult time for you."
11. Probing, questioning, interrogating	"Where have you been?" "Now, tell me the real reason you feel that way."	11. Giving freedom and privacy	"I've missed you a lot." "You don't need to explain if you would rather not."
12. Withdrawing, distracting humoring, diverting	"You're funny when you are mad." "Why don't you tell me something new!"	12. Accepting, giving attention to the other person	"I understand that you are feeling mad because . . ." "That point is something you haven't mentioned before."

* Praising and reassuring may be negative responses when the other person has a problem because they tend to prevent that person from sharing feelings that are more threatening or painful. It is too quick to reassure. Later, when the partner has sufficiently explored all of the feelings that are associated with the problem, expressing appreciation and confidence in the partner will be positive.

Most of the positive responses are ways of saying to the partner, "Yes, I'm listening." More explicit listening invitations are "I see," "Tell me about it," "This seems important to you," and "Okay, let's work on it together." As you become aware of negative responses in your interaction with your partner, substitute more positive responses which show your care and concern for him or her.

SOURCE: Hunt and Rydman (1979:38–39), based on Gordon (1970:41–44).

rized as either *negative,* in that they seek to control and maintain power over another, or *positive,* in that they express a person's acceptance, warmth, and openness relative to the other. Clearly, the positive response styles are more likely than the negative to promote effective communication. Positive responses keep the lines of feedback open until "message sent equals message received." They are also the most likely to assist partners in reaching such goals as intimacy and reinforcement in a relationship such as marriage.

Negative response styles are often referred to as *aversive communication,* because they seek to create pain, discomfort, or some other negative emotional response in the partner. The following example is taken from Edward Albee's *Who's Afraid of Virginia Woolf?,* in which two married partners strive to jab each other into defeat by means of aversive messages.

George: I'm tired, dear . . . it's late . . . and beside . . .

Martha: I don't know what you're so tired about . . . you haven't *done* anything all day; you didn't have any classes, or anything . . .

George: Well, I'm tired . . . if your father didn't set up these goddam Saturday night orgies all the time . . .

Martha: Well, that's too bad about you, George . . .

George: (grumbling) Well, that's how it is, anyway.

Martha: You didn't do anything; you never *do* anything; you never mix. You just sit around and talk.

George: What do you want me to do? Do you want me to act like you? Do you want me to go around all night braying at everybody the way you do?

Martha: (braying) I don't BRAY!

George: (softly) All right . . . you don't bray.

Martha: (hurt) I do not *bray.*

Aversive messages foster ineffective communication by creating pain and failing to reward the partner. Hence, individual communication styles influence the development of intimate relationships and the ability of each person to experience personal growth with another.

COMMUNICATION PATTERNS OF COUPLES

Each partner brings his or her own style of communicating to an intimate relationship. This makes for more complexity, when we consider that *patterns* of communication emerge over time when two people *combine* their individual styles into one interlocking communication *system.* Watzlawick, et al. (1967) call this the "principle of limitation," because "in a communication sequence, every

exchange of messages narrows down the number of possible next moves" (131).

Raush, Barry, Hertel, and Swain (1974) carefully observed the communication patterns of 46 young married couples. They found that the style of message sent by one partner determined, to a large extent, the style of the partner's response. Communication patterns thereby develop in what these researchers label a *behavioral reciprocity.* Furthermore, these patterns were found to exist quite early in the marriage. After only four months of marriage, couples acted as a "unit," or system, when it came to communication patterns. Whether it involves sharing one's ideas, love, contempt, or hostility with the other, or trying to coerce the other into submission, "What you give to the other is what you tend to get in return."

Others have identified patterns of communication in couples in more general terms. Watzlawick, et al. (1967), identified two basic types of communication patterns that are often linked to serious problems, or *dysfunctional outcomes* in a relationship: *symmetry* and *complementarity.* Symmetrical communication results from each partner seeking to outdo the other and to maintain the upper hand. It is an exercise in *one-upmanship,* as each partner strives to maintain power and control in the relationship. Symmetrical communication can become highly competitive, and may frequently escalate to the point where serious conflicts arise. The following is an example of competitive symmetry, as each person strives to maintain the upper hand in the relationship.

Steve: You're wearing that blue dress again! You always wear that blue dress when we go to the movies.

Sharon: Well, isn't that too bad. You've known for months that I need new clothes, but you refuse to allow me to buy them. This is the only dress I have to wear, and I'll keep wearing it until I get something else.

Steve: Well, maybe if you got a job to earn some money, then you could buy yourself some new dresses.

Sharon: (voice raised) Get a job, is it? I work my fingers to the bone keeping this house in shape, and you tell me to get a job! You don't even have the common decency to voice your appreciation for what I do! Maybe you should get a better job!

Steve: (yelling) Is that so? What do you expect from me? A man can only do so much in this world.

Good jobs don't grow on trees, you know!
You don't have the decency to even give me
credit for what I do!

Sharon: (screaming) We wouldn't be in this mess if
you'd stayed in school and finished your degree. But, no, you had to be a *smart* guy and
take that lousy job. Now look where its gotten
us!

Steve: (screaming) Forget the movie! Just forget it! I
won't take you.

Certainly, not all couples engaging in symmetrical
interaction resort to screaming and yelling. It is entirely
possible to compete for a "one-up" position in more subtle, less dramatic ways. Yet this example illustrates two
important points. First, many couples find themselves in
trouble when this type of communication pattern becomes
dominant in the relationship. So long as neither person is
willing to tolerate losing the competition, sooner or later
the exchanges become increasingly painful and the relationship deteriorates to the point of one or both partners
seeking to end it. Second, this example illustrates the point
made in the foregoing communication Principle 3. Any
effort on the part of this couple to resolve their differences
would probably be handled at the *content* level. Note how
the entire sequence began with a disagreement over a
rather trivial (content) issue—whether or not the wife
should wear her blue dress to the movies. The dialogue
then moved into other *content* areas, such as the wife's
homemaking and occupational roles, and the husband's
income and educational history. However, the far more
serious issue is at the *relationship* level, as defined by the
symmetrical communication pattern: Who has the right to
tell who what to do, and when, and how? Each partner
sought to stay "one-up" by keeping the other "one-
down" in the relationship, yet the competition escalated to
the point of a major conflict. Their inability to *metacom-
municate* (that is, to communicate about their relationship
and to discuss *how* they communicate with each other), can
only lead to further disagreements and conflicts. Watzlawick, et al. (1967:80–81) might say of this couple:

In their attempt to resolve their disagreement this couple committed a very common mistake in their communication: they disagreed on the metacommunicational (relationship) level, but tried to resolve the disagreement on the
content level, where it did not exist, which led them into
pseudodisagreements.

The other major communication pattern identified
by these authors is known as *complementarity*. This is a
"one-up" and "one-down" pattern, which also can result
in long-term problems if allowed to go unchecked. In a
rigid complementarity pattern, one partner continually
maintains the upper hand at the expense of the other.
Complementarity emphasizes and reinforces the differences between the partners in the relationship in terms of
status, power, and personal worth—one partner is high-
status, dominant, and worthy and the other is low-status,
submissive, and, in comparison, worth less. Let us examine the dialogue of the same couple, in which *complementarity* is the pattern instead of symmetry. Note that we
begin with the same statement by the husband.

Steve: You're wearing that blue dress again! You
always wear that blue dress when we go to
the movies.

Sharon: (apologetically) Yes, I know dear, but I just
haven't had time to get out and—

Steve: (interrupting) Time? Is that all? Well, we'll just
have to make time so you can get something
else. I don't work a 40-hour week and bring
home the money I do to have you going
around in the same old clothes all of the time.
Now, do I?

Sharon: (more forcefully) No, dear, you don't. But just
last month you said that we didn't have
enough money even to buy the kids a—

Steve: (interrupting) But that was different! Bicycles
cost more than dresses, now don't they? My
goodness, talking to you would make one
think that you don't appreciate what I do for
others in this family. And furthermore—

Sharon: (timidly interrupting) But you said—

Steve: (interrupting) Stop interrupting me! Don't you
know it's rude to interrupt people?

Sharon: Yes, dear, I do.

Steve: Well, then, stop it.

Sharon: (almost inaudible) O.K.

In this example, the husband maintained his "one-up"
position relative to the wife by talking more, talking
louder, and generally controlling the flow of the conversation to his benefit. The complementary *pattern* could not
have been established, however, without the wife's participation. She routinely defers to his attempts to overpower
her and to coerce her into agreement. She is unwilling, or
unable, to assert herself, even when her partner is being
unreasonable. As was true for competitive symmetry, rigid

complementarity patterns often result in ineffective and unrewarding communication between partners in marriage and other intimate relationships.

Clearly, competitive symmetry and rigid complementarity patterns of communication are dysfunctional in the sense that partners involved in relationships where those patterns exist find them to be unsatisfying, uncomfortable, and even painful. Communication of this kind may lead to a breakdown in the marriage relationship and, ultimately, divorce.

These are by no means the only possible communication patterns that evolve over time in marriage and other intimate relationships. Indeed, each of these have been stated in their extreme form; there undoubtedly exist many different shades and variations of these patterns. The major point is that *patterns* do emerge when the individual communication styles of the partners are combined into a system, and the degree to which the system is able to maintain itself and provide for the fulfillment of personal needs and goals of the partners depends heavily on the types of patterns which develop.

Communication Skills

Communication Principle 6 states that effective communication requires a certain degree of *skill* on the part of the partners involved in an intimate relationship. These skills contribute to what Montgomery (1981) and Bienvenu (1970) refer to as "quality" or "healthy" communication. Skillful communication involves the ability to engage in *effective* communication (message sent equals message received). It also involves the qualities of openness to the partner, confirmation of self and others, adaptability across a variety of situations, and effective management of anger and other emotions.

Communication skills do not come naturally — they must be learned. Communication is one kind of *role behavior* assumed by partners in marriage, defined by particular *normative expectations* and *behavioral skills*. To play any social role effectively, a person must acquire *knowledge* of the norms and behaviors comprising the role; must have the *motivation* to acquire those norms and to behave in an appropriate way; and must have the *ability* to behave accordingly (Brim and Wheeler, 1966). If we are fortu-

nate enough to grow up in an environment where skilled communication role models are available, then we, too, are likely to be skilled at communication. If, on the other hand, we learn from role models who are deficient in such skills, then we are likely to be deficient in our ability to communicate effectively.

The major source of learning how to communicate in intimate relationships is, of course, our families (Hill and Aldous, 1969). It is in the family that we learn the normative expectations and rules that shape our individual communication styles, which we will bring to our subsequent intimate relationships, particularly marriage. Our parents, moreover, are our primary *socialization agents* when it comes to learning communication roles, because it is with them that we have our first and most direct communication in a setting where intimacy and emotions are of paramount importance. However, as Hill and Aldous (1969) point out, our training for *effective* communication skills is often quite limited because of the infrequent opportunities to make direct observations of effective communication in the family setting. This is often the result of a lack of communication skills on the part of parents themselves.

The parental family is not ideally equipped for training its members in the concrete roles of marriage. Their performance requires . . . knowledge about the marital situation and how to perform these roles. The parental family is not a repository of such knowledge about marriage nor is it able to provide practical on-the-job training in the skills of marriage . . . [W]e need to recognize that there are very few opportunities even to simulate marital role-playing in the parental family setting. The family script contains no marital parts for children to play. Moreover, the limited visibility of the marital roles makes for vagueness and lack of clarity in role definitions. The most intimate communication as well as conflict resolution of marriage partners is usually handled behind closed doors and hidden from children. . . . (Hill and Aldous, 1969:895)

Because of the limited communication skills of parents, and the few opportunities for direct observation in the parental family, the learning of communication skills is often supplemented by interactions with friends, siblings, teachers, other relatives, and such mass media influences as television and movies.

Now that we have defined what effective communication is, and have identified the important functions of communication in promoting growth and fulfillment in intimate relationships such as marriage, let us examine some of the skills more directly related to effective communication patterns.

AWARENESS OF SELF

Effective communication skills begin with self-awareness — knowing who you are, what you are about, and what you expect in your relationships with others, both intimate and nonintimate. In order to communicate effectively with another person, and to do so in a way that promotes interpersonal closeness and liking, it is important to be aware of what is going on inside of you. We must be in touch with our own thoughts, feelings, intentions, expectations, and desires relative to the person with whom we are communicating (Miller, et al., 1975). What is it that we mean, or intend to communicate, to the other? How can we best communicate to the other so that the other person interprets our messages in a way that is consistent with our intended meaning? Just what is it that we are feeling toward the other? Do we feel comfortable or uncomfortable? Jubilant? Depressed? Angry? Sad? Lonely? Proud? How can these feelings be communicated in a way that is most conducive to the quality of the relationship we have with that person? Self-awareness in these areas is essential if effective communication is to take place.

Consider the following example of a couple interviewed in Rubin's 1976 study of marriage in the working class. Communication problems, stemming from a lack of self-awareness and of awareness of the other's goals and intentions in the relationship, are evident. Each spouse was interviewed separately; the other was not present in the room:

Husband: She complains that all I want from her is sex, and I try to make her understand that it's an expression of love. I'll want to make up with her by making love, but she's cold as the inside of the refrig. Sure I get mad when that happens. Why shouldn't I? Here I'm trying to make up and make love, and she's holding out for something — I don't know what.

Wife: He keeps saying he wants to make love, but it just doesn't feel like love to me. Sometimes I feel bad that I feel that way, but I just can't help it.

Husband: I don't understand. She says it doesn't feel like love. What does that mean, anyway? What does she think love is?

Wife: I want him to talk to me, to tell me what he's thinking about. If we have a fight, I want to talk about it so we could maybe understand it. I don't want to jump in bed and just pretend it didn't happen.

Husband: Talk! Talk! What's there to talk about? I want to make love to her and she says she wants to talk. How's talking going to convince her I'm loving her?

In sex, as in other matters, the barriers to communication are high; and the language people use serves to further confuse and mystify. He says, "I want to make love." She says, "It doesn't feel like love." Neither quite knows what the other is talking about; both feel vaguely guilty and uncomfortable — aware only that somehow they're passing each other, not connecting. (Rubin, 1976:146–147)

SELF-DISCLOSURE

Related to self-awareness is the concept of self-disclosure. In order for any relationship to be called truly intimate, including marriage, the partners must be able to communicate their innermost thoughts, feelings, beliefs, and fears about themselves, about other people, and about the world around them.

Self-disclosure is a process by which a marriage partner expresses feelings, perceptions, fears and doubts of the inner self to the other partner, allowing relatively private and personal information to surface in the relationship that normally would not be revealed in the course of day-to-day interaction. (Jorgensen and Gaudy, 1980:281–282)

The concept of the *Johari Window* (Luft, 1984) illustrates the range of possibilities in disclosing information about the self to others (see Figure 7.3). In virtually any relationship, there exists a distribution of information across the four boxes of the Johari Window. In a particularly intimate relationship such as marriage, there is likely to be a far greater proportion of information in Boxes I (Mutual Knowledge) and II (Blind Spots), in comparison with more impersonal relationships, such as those with teachers or service station attendants. For those less personal relationships, there is a greater proportion in Box III (My Secrets). Regardless of which type of relationship we might form, however, there is bound to be a certain

FIGURE 7.3.   The Johari Window.

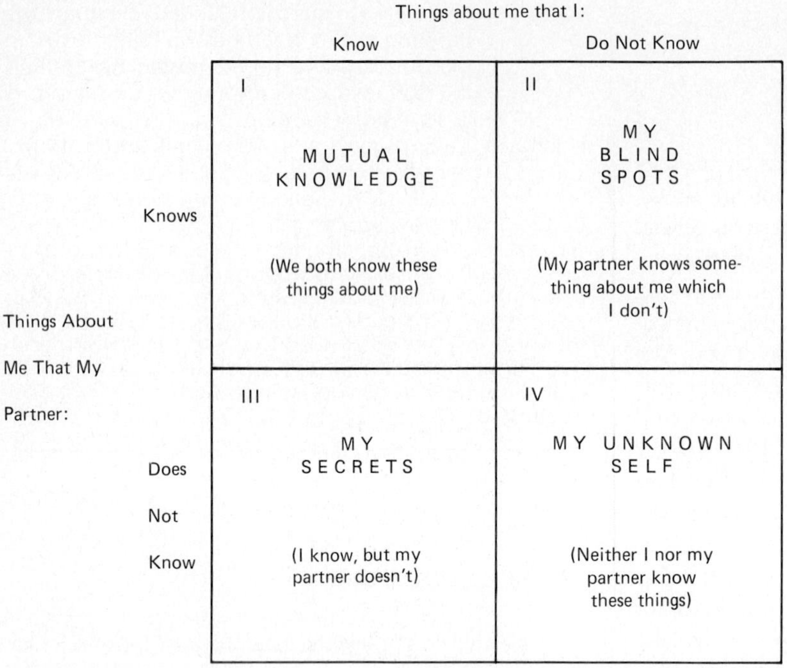

Things about me that I:

	Know	Do Not Know
Knows	**I** MUTUAL KNOWLEDGE (We both know these things about me)	**II** MY BLIND SPOTS (My partner knows something about me which I don't)
Things About Me That My Partner: **Does Not Know**	**III** MY SECRETS (I know, but my partner doesn't)	**IV** MY UNKNOWN SELF (Neither I nor my partner know these things)

SOURCE: Luft (1984).

amount of information about ourselves that neither we nor our partners are aware of (My Unknown Self).

Research on premarital, marital, and other intimate relationships has shown a strong connection between the level of self-disclosure and the degree of satisfaction and fulfillment experienced by each partner in the relationship (Derlega and Chaiken, 1975; Jorgensen and Gaudy, 1980; Jourard, 1971). The more that is disclosed to a partner in a relationship that is defined as intimate, the more satisfied each partner is likely to be with their relationship. *Role reciprocity* (chapter 2) applies to self-disclosure types of communication as well: People who self-disclose to others find those others disclosing themselves as well, resulting in a reciprocal spiraling of mutual satisfaction in the relationship (Jourard, 1959; Jourard and Richman, 1963). The research evidence supports the idea that self-disclosure leads to healthy personalities and reduces the level of stress in our lives (Jourard, 1971). The more we can move into Box I of the Johari Window in our intimate relationships with others, the more personal satisfaction and fulfillment we stand to gain from the relationship (see Feature 7.2).

As Jourard (1971:6) points out, however, a great number of marriages find themselves stuck in Boxes II, III, and IV. Remaining in Boxes II and III means that we do *not* have the motivation, or the skills, to become less of a stranger to our partners. Being in Box IV means that we have not developed a satisfactory level of self-awareness, as discussed in the previous section. In marriage, as well as in other intimate relationships, a primary goal appears to be the development of mutual knowledge between partners. Attainment of this goal brings satisfaction and fulfillment, and is fostered by the ability to self-disclose.

It must be noted, however, that self-disclosure can be *risky*. The more we open ourselves up to another, revealing private and personal information about ourselves, the more vulnerable we become (Chelune, 1979; Gilbert, 1976). That is, the other person may use that information at a later time to take advantage of and hurt us. Self-disclosure may also be viewed as appropriate only in certain situations. For example, most would define an appropriate situation for self-disclosure to be a quiet place where the partners can be alone and where the atmosphere is conducive to this kind of "heavy" communication.

THE SELF-DISCLOSURE QUESTIONNAIRE

Think of someone who is particularly close to you at the present time, such as a boyfriend/girl-friend, fiancé, or good friend. Using the categories below, respond to each statement in this list to determine how much you have self-disclosed to that person in various aspects of your life. Add up the scores for each one. If possible, have the other person do the same exericse by rating how much he or she has self-disclosed to you. In what areas have each of you self-disclosed more or less than the other? Do either of you believe that more or less self-disclosure is needed in any area? If so, why? Is your self-disclosure about equal, or is it one-sided, in your relationship?

Response Categories

0. Have told the other person nothing about this aspect of me.
1. Have talked in general terms about this item. The other person has only a general idea about this aspect of me.
2. Have talked in full and complete detail about this item to the other person. He knows me fully in this respect, and could describe me accurately.
X. Have lied or misrepresented myself to the other person so that he has a false picture of me.

Attitudes and Opinions

1. What I think and feel about religion; my personal religious views.
2. My personal opinions and feelings about other religious groups than my own, e.g., Protestants, Catholics, Jews, atheists.
3. My views on communism.
4. My views on the present government—the president, government, policies, etc.
5. My views on the question of racial integration in schools, transportation, etc.
6. My personal views on drinking.
7. My personal views on sexual morality—how I feel that I and others ought to behave in sexual matters.
8. My personal standards of beauty and attractiveness in women—what I consider to be attractive in a woman.
9. The things that I regard as desirable for a man to be—what I look for in a man.
10. My feeling about how parents ought to deal with children.

Tastes and Interests

1. My favorite foods, the ways I like food prepared, and my food dislikes.
2. My favorite beverages, and the ones I don't like.
3. My likes and dislikes in music.
4. My favorite reading matter.
5. The kinds of movies that I like to see best; the TV shows that are my favorites.
6. My tastes in clothing.
7. The style of house, and the kinds of furnishings that I like best.
8. The kind of party, or social gathering that I like best, and the kind that would bore me, or that I wouldn't enjoy.
9. My favorite ways of spending spare time, e.g., hunting, reading, cards, sports events, parties, dancing, etc.
10. What I would appreciate most for a present.

Work (or studies)

1. What I find to be the worst pressures and strains in my work.
2. What I find to be the most boring and unenjoyable aspects of my work.
3. What I enjoy most, and get the most satisfaction from in my present work.
4. What I feel are my shortcomings and handicaps that prevent me from working as I'd like to, or that prevent me from getting further ahead in my work.
5. What I feel are my special strong points and qualifications for my work.
6. How I feel that my work is appreciated by others (e.g., boss, fellow-workers, teacher, husband, etc.).
7. My ambitions and goals in my work.
8. My feelings about the salary or rewards that I get for my work.

continued on next page

FEATURE 7.2 (*Continued*)

9. How I feel about the choice of career that I have made — whether or not I'm satisfied with it.

10. How I really feel about the people that I work for, or work with.

Money

1. How much money I make at my work, or get as an allowance.

2. Whether or not I owe money; if so, *how much.*

3. Whom I owe money to at present; or whom I have borrowed from in the past.

4. Whether or not I have savings, and the amount.

5. Whether or not others owe me money; the amount, and who owes it to me.

6. Whether or not I gamble; if so, the way I gamble, and the extent of it.

7. All of my present sources of income — wages, fees, allowance, dividends, etc.

8. My total financial worth, including property, savings, bonds, insurance, etc.

9. My most pressing need for money right now, e.g., outstanding bills, some major purchase that is desired or needed.

10. How I budget my money — the proportion that goes to necessities, luxuries, etc.

Personality

1. The aspects of my personality that I dislike, worry about, that I regard as a handicap to me.

2. What feelings, if any, that I have trouble expressing or controlling.

3. The facts of my present sex life — including knowledge of how I get sexual gratification; any problems that I might have; with whom I have relations, if anybody.

4. Whether or not I feel that I am attractive to the opposite sex; my problems, if any, about getting favorable attention from the opposite sex.

5. Things in the past or present that I feel ashamed and guilty about.

6. The kinds of things that make me just furious.

7. What it takes to get me feeling real depressed or blue.

8. What it takes to get me real worried, anxious, and afraid.

9. What it takes to hurt my feelings deeply.

10. The kinds of things that make me especially proud of myself, elated, full of self-esteem or self-respect.

Body

1. My feelings about the appearance of my face — things I don't like, and things that I might like about my face and head — nose, eyes, hair, teeth, etc.

2. How I wish I looked: my ideals for overall appearance.

3. My feelings about different parts of my body — legs, hips, waist, weight, chest or bust, etc.

4. Any problems and worries that I had with my appearance in the past.

5. Whether or not I now have any health problems — e.g., trouble with sleep, digestion, female complaints, heart condition, allergies, headaches, piles, etc.

6. Whether or not I have any long-range worries or concerns about my health, e.g., cancer, ulcers, heart trouble.

7. My past record of illness and treatment.

8. Whether or not I now make a special effort to keep fit, healthy, and attractive, e.g., calisthenics, diet.

9. My present physical measurements, e.g., height, weight, waist, etc.

10. My feelings about my adequacy in sexual behavior — whether or not I feel able to perform adequately in sex-relationships.

SOURCE: Reprinted from Jourard (1971:213–216).

Other situations may be viewed as far less appropriate, such as self-disclosing at parties, or in the presence of friends or relatives. Disclosures at the "wrong time and the wrong place" may actually be embarrassing and lead to *dissatisfaction* with the partner. Dissatisfaction may also result when the disclosing partner shares an imbalance of negative feelings to positive ones. Too much negative disclosure—talking about personal problems, fears, and voicing complaints—may be viewed by the partner as unnecessary complaining or nagging when it is not balanced by more positive messages (Cutler and Dyer, 1965; Gilbert, 1976).

That self-disclosure is risky for some can be seen in the following comments made by a husband in Cuber and Haroff's study of 400 affluent American marriages. This husband, a publishing company executive, is afraid that self-disclosure will unnecessarily "rock the boat."

What's the use in hashing it over? It's done; so why rub it in? Better concentrate on things you can do something about. If you open up a subject like that, the first thing you know the whole matter will get magnified into a federal case and then you've *really* got a problem. (Cuber and Haroff, 1965:74)

Failure to self-disclose is often associated with a lack of self-awareness and awareness of the other's goals and intentions in the relationship (discussed previously). This situation is evident in the following comments made by a husband and wife, interviewed separately in Rubin's (1976) study of working-class marriages:

Wife: I'm not sure what I want. I keep talking to him about communication, and he says, "Okay, so we're talking; now what do you want?" And I don't know what to say then, but I know it's not what I mean . . . I keep telling him that the reason people get divorced isn't *only* financial but because they can't communicate. But I can't make him understand.

Husband: I swear, I don't know what she wants. She keeps saying we have to talk, and then when we do, it always turns out I'm saying the wrong thing. I get scared sometimes. I always thought I had to think things to myself; you know, not tell her about it. Now she says that's not good. But it's hard. You know, I think it comes down to that I like things the way they are, and I'm afraid I'll say or do something that'll really shake things up. So I get worried about it, and I don't say anything. (Rubin, 1976:120–121)

In each of these cases, the affluent and the working-class, failure to self-disclose in the marriage was accompanied by a degree of distress and distance between the marriage partners.

ACTIVE LISTENING AND EMPATHY

Too often people in marriage and other intimate relationships try to communicate with their partners, hear the words that are being said, but fail to really listen, to verify that "message sent equals message received." Effective communication requires the skill of *active listening;* that is, hearing your partner, attempting to understand what he or she is feeling at that moment, and then verbally feeding back in order to verify that you have received the message that he or she intended to send. The concept of *empathy* is critical in this regard. Empathy means being able to place yourself in the shoes of the other person, and striving to see the world, and yourself, as they do. Empathy is a skilled behavior that must be learned, but, as with other communication skills, we have few good role models as we grow up, and little opportunity to put this skill into practice.

O'Neill and O'Neill (1972) refer to these skills of active listening and empathy as *open listening,* which involves more than using your periods of silence (while your partner is talking) to prepare your rebuttal. It also involves comprehending your partner's message, and then confirming that what you heard and understood is consistent with your partner's intentions.

Open listening requires that you become, in effect, transparent, thus letting the other in. You cannot respond properly unless you open yourself completely to what is being said to you. Unless you listen, actively, you cannot hear. (O'Neill and O'Neill, 1972:122)

To be an active listener means focusing on the other person while he or she is talking, and being attentive, concerned, and receptive to their messages. It is a distressing feeling, when communicating with another human being, to find that person staring off into space, or paying attention to something or someone else. It is a signal that they are not really listening, and, worse yet, do not really care what you are saying.

"I" MESSAGES: TAKING RESPONSIBILITY

One of the most difficult tasks to accomplish in communication is taking responsibility for your own intentions, feelings, interpretations, and actions. Compare the following statements, imagining that someone close to you is responding to something you have done.

"You really make me feel terrible when you do that."
or
"I really feel hurt when you do that."

Which would you prefer to hear? In the first statement, the sender is placing the responsibility for his or her own feelings on the receiver, as if to say, "You have control over me and are responsible for the way I feel." In reality, however, only *you* have control over your own feelings, and you must take responsibility for them. In the second statement, the sender is taking responsibility for his or her feelings. Another example will help to illustrate this.

"You're behaving that way just to bother me and make me angry."
or
"When you behave that way, I feel bothered and angry."

In the first statement, the sender is making an undocumented assumption about the other person's intentions. The chances are that those intentions have been misinterpreted, yet the sender is placing the "burden of proof" on the receiver. This kind of attack immediately places the receiver on the defensive. When we put others on the defensive, we are setting a mood of coercion and confrontation in the relationship. In the second statement, on the other hand, the sender takes responsibility for his or her own feelings and seems to be inviting further discussion, perhaps about what it is about the receiver's behavior that causes the sender to feel angry. The problem may not be in the behavior at all, but in the sender's misinterpretation of the intentions that underlie the behavior. By taking responsibility for your feelings, the door is opened for further discussion of the problem, and finding the most agreeable solution.

PROBLEM-SOLVING SKILLS

Effective communication and good problem-solving skills go hand in hand. Despite the fact that people define what a *problem* is in many different ways, it seems that marriage is one type of intimate relationship in which problems arise continually. Problems may arise when deciding which house or car to buy; when establishing a budget so that the family remains out of debt; when disciplining and teaching children acceptable behavior

patterns; when dealing with in-laws, neighbors, and friends; when establishing satisfactory levels of sexual adjustment; when deciding which method of family planning to employ, and how to employ it effectively; when dividing the household tasks (e.g., doing dishes, housecleaning, working outside of the home, and child care); and in many other areas relating to marriage and family life. Effective problem solving is essential if a marriage is to survive over time; and it involves the skills of both partners in order to reach mutually acceptable solutions to problems. *Effective* problem solving, therefore, means that the solution yields a "maximum joint profit" to both partners involved (Scanzoni and Polonko, 1980). If mutually acceptable solutions to certain problems cannot be found, then these problems can turn into major conflicts that may eventually threaten the relationship. Ineffective problem solving may also lead to negative long-term consequences, such as economic problems as a result of failing to budget effectively, or having too many children because of ineffective family planning.

The problem-solving process in marriage involves the following sequence of steps if it is to be effective (Kieren, Henton, and Marotz, 1975).

1. *Recognition of the Problem.* Usually a "problem" is defined when one has a particular goal in mind for which certain barriers or obstacles must be removed or overcome if the goal is to be reached. This step involves *identifying problem ownership* (that is, whose problem it is), which is often somewhat difficult since partners may have different criteria for defining what a problem is.

[I]n marriage, what is important or annoying to one spouse may not be to the other. Take the case of the woman who usually leaves her clothes lying about. Assume that the messy house does not bother her but that it drives her husband up the wall. Since his expectation that she hang up her clothes is not shared by her, it is his problem, not hers. It will become her problem too only if her behavior annoys him so much that it begins to alter their relationship and create an obstacle in reaching one of her [their] goals. (Kieren, et al., 1975:7)

Not only must problem ownership be identified, but the *nature* and *scope* of the problem must be accurately perceived if a satisfactory solution to the problem is to be found.

Good problem-solving skills are an
integral part of effective communication
in an intimate relationship.
(Photo by R. J. Hinkle.)

2. *Involvement in the Problem-Solving Process.* After
a problem is recognized and accurately defined, some
decision must be made as to whether or not one is
motivated to do anything about it. It is extremely difficult to solve any problem effectively if one assumes a
lackadaisical attitude toward searching for a solution.
The greater the motivation to solve a problem, the
greater the chances that a person will become involved
in seeking a solution and, ultimately, the greater the
chances that the solution will be a mutually satisfactory
one (Kieren, et al., 1975:10). Simply ignoring a problem will not cause it to go away; invariably, it will arise
again at a later time.

3. *Generation of Alternatives.* The greater the number of possible solutions to a problem, the greater the
chances of finding a satisfactory solution that is acceptable to both partners. It is critical, therefore, to establish
a list of alternative solutions to which both partners
have the opportunity to contribute before attempting to
settle on one particular solution.

4. *Assessment of Alternatives.* Once a list of alternative solutions is generated, the next task is to evaluate

each one for its relative costs and benefits. Solutions
with the greatest benefit-to-cost ratio are the best ones.
This ratio is determined by (1) the available *opportunities* in the social and physical environment for solving
the problem; (2) the existing *behavioral values* and
standards of the partners that determine acceptable or
inappropriate courses of action; and (3) *the interpersonal
resources* (e.g., communication skills), *material resources*
(e.g., time and money), and *personal resources* (e.g.,
intelligence) that partners have at their disposal. For
example, in solving the family-planning problem of
deciding which contraceptive method is the best one,
the various alternative methods (solutions) must be
evaluated according to (1) the *availability* of the
method and opportunity to obtain it; (2) each partner's
values and *standards* (some methods run counter to
religious doctrine, such as sterilization or the pill); and
(3) *interpersonal resources* (ability of partners to effectively communicate and provide mutual support if
foam or diaphragm are used, so that they are effectively
employed); *personal resources* (some methods may pose
risks to health, such as the pill or surgical procedures);
and *material resources* (some methods, such as sterilization, are more expensive than others, and some, such

as the mucous and the body temperature rhythm methods, require a greater commitment of time).

5. *Selection of the Best Alternative.* Unless two alternatives are equally attractive, the next step is to choose the one that yields the greatest benefit/cost ratio for both partners. If two alternatives are equally attractive, then each should be re-evaluated until one is viewed by the partners as the *best* one.

6. *Action.* The next step involves making a determined effort to implement the solution by behaving in an appropriate way. If the best solution to a person's chronic unemployment problem is considered to be a return to school to obtain further training (assuming, of course, that the time and money resources are available), then the individual must begin the process by making application and registering for the appropriate coursework. It is at this point when social supports become critical, because we often count on others (spouses, friends, relatives) to help us become sufficiently motivated to reach our goal by taking concrete actions.

7. *Assessment of the Solution.* No matter what solution has been adopted, effective problem solving involves an assessment of the degree to which the goal has been reached. A decision must then be made regarding whether to stick with the original solution, or, if it is unsatisfactory, return to the original list of alternative solutions, add any new ones, and select another alternative for implementation.

Effective problem solving also involves such *negotiation* and *bargaining* skills as *mutual flexibility:* each gives in a little to gain concessions from each other; *shared power:* both partners are allowed to be assertive without being coercive or domineering; and both partners behave in ways that each perceives to be *fair* (Scanzoni and Polonko, 1980).

Conflict in Marriage: Issues, Management, and Outcomes

Perhaps the most critical function of communication in marriage is to manage and resolve conflicts. Not only is conflict in marriage inevitable, but conflict is normal and is to be expected. As the saying goes, "Conflict is as natural as loving itself." Conflict, however, can have either positive or negative consequences for the development of the marital relationship, depending upon how it is managed and resolved.

Conflict usually involves some degree of hostility, anger, or other negative feeling. Conflict might be viewed as synonymous with the words *argument* and *quarrel,* and may involve an attempt of partners to psychologically or physically hurt one another (Turner, 1970). This emotion-charged aspect of conflict makes managing it an especially difficult challenge, because emotions often get in the way of the rational application of the communication skills and effective problem-solving techniques already discussed in this chapter. Finally, we cannot speak of marital conflict without also referring to *power* and *control* of marriage partners over each other, as conflict is often viewed as a win-lose situation.

MAJOR CONFLICT ISSUES

Studies of conflict in marriage agree that the most common issue over which partners disagree and argue is *money management* (Blood and Wolfe, 1960; Jorgensen and Klein, forthcoming) [see Table 7.3]. How money is to be budgeted and spent; which expensive items to buy, and when to buy them (e.g., a car, refrigerator, or house); who has the right to decide how much money can be spent on what, when, and where—all are prime subjects for conflicts about money management. Clearly, such conflicts may only be surface manifestations of deeper *relationship issues* in the marriage, such as when partners are involved in struggles for power and control over each other. Money is a powerful force in our society, and marriage is not immune to its effects (see chapter 8).

Children, too, are high on the list of major conflict issues in marriage. Because marriage partners have been socialized in different families of orientation, they often bring to marriage different role scripts and expectations relative to how and when children should be disciplined for misbehavior, and what values and aspirations should be taught to them. Because each has had his or her own parents as primary role models for raising children, husbands and wives may be worlds apart when it comes to the discipline and socialization of their own children.

These are just two of the more common conflict issues in American marriages today. However, conflict can arise over any of a number of possible issues, and at any

TABLE 7.3. *Most Frequent Issues of Conflict in Marriage*

1. Money management.
2. Discipline of children.
3. Household jobs and duties (task allocation).
4. In-law relationships.
5. Being away from home too much (one or both partners).
6. Personalities and habits (smoking, drinking, snoring, and so on).
7. Time spent together as a couple.
8. Condition of house and furniture.
9. Plans for the future.
10. Sexual relationship and general demonstrations of affection.

SOURCE: Jorgensen and Klein (forthcoming).

time. But the particular issues involved are far less important than knowing *how* the conflicts can be managed and resolved.

CONFLICT-MANAGEMENT STRATEGIES

Conflict can be managed in any of a number of ways. We learn to manage conflict just as we learn other styles of communication: by observing our parents, siblings, and others in our social environment as we grow toward adulthood. Other learning occurs as we interact with our partners in marriage and in other intimate relationships. Conflict management in such relationships also tends to become *patterned,* just as in the communication structure in general, because conflicts are handled in relatively consistent ways over time.

The most typical conflict-management behaviors observed by researchers are listed in Table 7.4. They range from the most calm, rational discussions of disagreements, to *quid pro quo* (give something to get something), to hostile and violent interaction (hitting, pushing, slapping, and use of weapons). Spouses may use various combinations of these strategies, depending on the importance of the issue involved and the degree of emotional involvement in the conflict.

It is alarming, indeed, to know that violent exchanges between marriage partners are far more prevalent than anyone ever imagined. Nationwide studies (Straus, 1974; Straus and Hotaling, 1980; Straus, Gelles, and Steinmetz, 1980) show that marriage partners who have been threatened with physical violence, or who have been involved in actual violent behavior with each other, num-

ber in the millions every year. Hitting, slapping, pushing, and the use of guns, knives, or other weapons are only a few of the violent modes of managing marital conflict. Newspaper reports of wife-abuse and husband-abuse, as well as personal knowledge of such cases, are no longer rare in our society. Somewhere between 10 and 15 percent of all married couples engage in threats of violence, or actual violent behavior—not a small number when one considers the devastating personal and social consequences such behavior has for those involved (Straus, et al., 1980). Some estimate that an incident of wife-beating occurs on the average of every 30 seconds, and that almost half of all married couples have had at least one violent episode (*Marriage and Divorce Today,* 1978). Over 15 percent of all murders are commited by the victim's marriage partner (Palmer, 1972). It is difficult to imagine that relationships once built on intimacy, interpersonal warmth, and love can experience conflict so violent that the physical well-being of one or both partners is either threatened or severely damaged. Intimate relationships, however, have the unique quality of blending the concepts of love and hate, intimacy and anger. Perhaps the frequency of violent conflict management is testimony to the complexity of modern life in our fast-paced and highly technological society.

CONSTRUCTIVE CONFLICT MANAGEMENT

Clearly, violence, threats, and confrontations are destructive conflict-management techniques. A relationship between two people suffers when differences are handled

TABLE 7.4. *Common Conflict-Management Styles in Marriage*

Avoidance
1. Brooding, sulking, pouting.
2. Getting confused; telling the partner that you don't understand what they are talking about.
3. Avoiding an issue by keeping the concern to yourself.
4. Joking around and teasing; trying to make the situation seem not so serious.

Destructive Engagement
1. Insulting and blaming the spouse for being at fault in the disagreement.
2. Pushing, grabbing, or shoving the partner.
3. Throwing something at the partner.
4. Threatening to hit or throw something at the partner.
5. Hitting or trying to hit the partner, but not with anything.
6. Hitting or trying to hit the partner with something hard.
7. Lying to the partner.
8. Arguing heatedly or yelling at the partner.
9. Threatening to do something the partner wouldn't like.
10. Throwing something (not at the partner), or smashing something.
11. Refusing to give in, by taking a strong position and stubbornly sticking to it.
12. Walking or stomping out of the room.
13. Begging and pleading with the partner.

Constructive Engagement
1. Looking for some new way to settle the disagreement, one that had not been tried before.
2. Trying to see the partner's point of view and communicating understanding.
3. Seeking an outsider whom both partners trust to act as a mediator in settling the conflict.
4. Discussing the issue relatively calmly and rationally.
5. Seeking to follow each partner's rules of "fairness."
6. Seeking to resolve the disagreement by compromising, doing something for each other that is mutually satisfying *(quid pro quo)*.
7. Promising to change in order to ameliorate the partner's concerns.
8. Communicating feelings by letting the partner know what is bothersome.

SOURCES: Jorgensen and Klein (forthcoming); Straus (1974); Spiegel (1957); Blood (1960).

in these ways. The relationship also suffers when conflict is avoided, because it is only a matter of time before pent-up emotions and feelings surface. Conflict can be avoided for only so long, but it does not go away.

Conflict is, however, a normal and natural part of marriage and other intimate relationships. Nonetheless, it is possible to create conflict-management patterns that yield constructive, rather than destructive, outcomes. Constructive conflict means that both partners (the *relationship*) can win or come out ahead. Destructive conflict, wherein each partner tries to win at the other's expense, usually results in the *relationship* losing in the end (Bach and Wyden, 1969). What is won or lost in a conflict often involves some combination of self-esteem and self-respect: respect and esteem for the partner; satisfaction with the relationship; and learning about how to benefit from future conflict situations.

Following is a useful *Eleven-Point Plan of Constructive Conflict Management,* provided by Hine (1980:195–196). These rules might well be used to handle conflict in any kind of relationship, including marriage.

1. Try to keep in mind what the real issue is and confine the confrontation to this issue. Refuse to get sidetracked into other matters that have little to do with the issue at hand. If you are hassling over finances, don't turn the discussion into a dissatisfaction about one of the in-laws.

Couples can employ any of a number of conflict-management techniques, including constructive and destructive engagement as well as avoidance.   *(Photo by Paul Fortin.)*

2. Keep your partner's point of view and feelings in mind. Keep asking yourself, if I were in my partner's shoes, how would I feel? This is a place for empathy.

3. Keep an open mind. Don't shut out the possibility of considering a point of view other than the one you have. Don't establish a fixed position from which you are unwilling to move.

4. Avoid using highly charged words or phrases. Don't engage in name calling.

5. Don't hit "below the belt." Most people have a level of tolerance below which they cannot accept attacks. Learn what this is for your partner. On the other hand, don't wear your "belt" around your neck. Toughen yourself to be able to accept reasonable aggressive opposition to your ideas.

6. Be conscious of the tone of your voice. Your tonal expression may be more important in communicating your true feelings than the words you use. Your facial expression and body posture are also effective forms of non-verbal communication. Some people exaggerate these forms to a point where they convey meanings that the communicator does not intend, which may block the negotiating process.

7. It has been said that when a person faces an uncomfortable situation he may engage in fight, flight, or a freeze. If you must fight, fight fairly and don't run away, refuse to talk or lock yourself in your room. Also, learn when and where to have conflicts. For example, if possible, do not mix conflict with alcohol consumption, avoid engaging in conflict close to bedtime or when you are tired, and allow enough time so that the issue can be resolved without having to postpone the discussion (that is, don't begin to resolve a conflict as you are rushing out the door to work or an appointment).

8. Give as much time to listening as to talking. Listening means attentively concentrating on what the other is

saying and asking what it means. Let your periods of silence be for more than getting your breath and deciding on how you are going to counter your partner's arguments.

9. The point of your confrontation is not for one to win and the other to lose. It is to arrive at a point you can both live with. The end needs to serve the best interest of both. There would be little gained if you *won* the argument and lost a friend.

10. Show love even if there is no agreement. Agree to disagree if necessary. Remember there is always time later to continue working on your differences. If you cannot arrive at a solution this time, you may be able to do so later.

11. Have patience and continue to work on the art of communication. Bargaining and negotiating make up a skill that no one ever perfects. But as you work to become more skillful, life will become increasingly interesting and fulfilling.

If partners were to follow this plan—establish these as *relationship rules* with which to regulate their conflict—there would be a good chance that the consequences of conflict would be functional for the relationship: productive of self-esteem, personal growth, learning, and continued development of the relationship in a satisfying and rewarding direction.

Summary

The degree to which marriage and other intimate relationships provide for the mutual growth and fulfillment of partners is shaped by the nature of the *communication patterns* that evolve over time. Each partner brings to the relationship an individual communication *style* which combines with that of the other person and becomes a relatively stable communication *system,* one which characterizes the couple as a unit. As a system, communication in marriage has the properties of information exchange, being selectively open to information from outside influences, and being goal-directed (goals of intimacy, interpersonal confirmation and acceptance, and other rewards). *Effective communication* means that the "message sent" by one partner is equivalent to the "message received" by the other, via an elaborate and reciprocal encoding-decoding process. However, effective communication does not assure positive growth

and development in the marriage relationship. Communication is a *skilled role behavior,* requiring knowledge, motivation, and ability on the part of both partners. *Quality communication* promotes relationship development but requires such specific skills as self-awareness; self-disclosure; active listening; taking responsibility for one's own feelings, thoughts, and actions; and effective problem-solving. Marriages and other intimate relationships in which one or both partners are deficient in communication skills are likely to experience problems that will become increasingly difficult to overcome as communication patterns solidify over time. Many marriage partners are deficient in one or more of these skills, and communication is the foremost problem among married couples seeking counseling or a divorce. If marriage is to be viewed by partners as successful, that is, meeting the goals and expectations of both partners over time, then effective and skilled communication is essential. Finally, communication skills are essential if marriage partners are to effectively manage conflicts which arise in the relationship. Conflict is inevitable. Yet frequent conflicts do not necessarily indicate that a couple is in distress. It is the manner in which conflicts are managed and resolved that either promotes or stifles development of the marriage relationship, not the frequency with which conflict occurs. Conflicts can yield either productive or destructive outcomes, depending on how they are managed. Productive conflict involves a maximum of rationality, issue confrontation, compromise, empathy, and effective communication and problem-solving skills. Destructive conflict, on the other hand, involves uncontrollable emotionality, issue-avoidance, tough bargaining, insensitivity to the other, and physical and verbal violence.

Questions for Discussion and Review

1. Pay a visit to a local singles bar, campus night spot, or other place where singles go to meet. Observe the nonverbal communication that goes on. How many of the different types of nonverbal messages, contained in Table 7.1, do you see? Are there differences between the

verbal cues of males and females? How does the non-verbal communication there compare with communication in other settings, such as the classroom or campus cafeteria?

2. Who are the people who are most likely to disclose personal aspects of themselves to you? With whom are you most likely to self-disclose? Do you ever feel that others disclose *too much* of themselves to you? Too little? What steps can be taken to change your own or another's self-disclosure habits, either increasing or decreasing the level of self-disclosure?

3. After reading the section on communication skills, think of your own abilities in these areas. What are your strengths and weaknesses when it comes to communication skills? Do you communicate better with some people than with others? If so, why?

4. Think of a major disagreement or conflict you have had recently with someone who is close to you (e.g., roommate, parent, friend). Was the conflict at the *con-*

tent or *relationship* level? Were there both content and relationship aspects to the conflict? Was the conflict resolved to the satisfaction of both of you? If not, where did communication break down?

5. In reference to the disagreement you identified in Question 4, evaluate the outcome in terms of two processes discussed in this chapter: (1) problem solving, and (2) conflict management. Which of the problem-solving steps did you follow? Which ones were not followed? Was the outcome of the conflict constructive or destructive? Which of the rules in the Eleven-Point Plan for conflict management were you able to follow?

6. Why do you think that the biggest complaint voiced by spouses seeking a divorce is a "failure to communicate?" What is it about marriage that leads to communication difficulties over time? How might two people entering a long-term relationship such as marriage best prevent the emergence of communication problems over the years?

CHAPTER 8

The Economics of Marriage and the Family:

The Work of Husbands and Wives

arriages and families of today exist in an economic climate that can either limit or expand their life chances and life-styles. Ours is a society in which achievement and success in one's occupation are highly valued (Williams, 1970). A certain amount of money also is required to accumulate the assets, luxuries, and "respectable" forms of personal wealth that symbolize success: a nice house, furniture, automobiles (at least one), recreational vehicles, boats, swimming pools, and countless other amenities of modern life. Comfortable levels of living are highly valued for our families, such as that provided by ample clothing, food, and leisure activities. Indeed, compared to other nations in the world, the United States provides one of the highest standards of living for its population.

The importance of money, and the purchasing power it provides in our consumption-oriented economy, is obvious. Income levels determine the degree to which families can share in the reward structure of contemporary society. The usual source of income for families is that which is provided when one or both marriage partners work outside of the home. Work not only provides the income by which families can enjoy a comfortable style of life; we also place an intrinsic value on work — it is an end in itself. To work is "virtuous," "fulfilling," and a sign of our "personal worth." At one time, work was viewed by certain Protestant sects as the only means to achieve religious salvation (Weber, 1958). Idle hands make many Americans feel useless, uninvolved, or even guilty. It is

generally agreed that work provides meaning to existence, and those who voluntarily choose not to work are usually viewed as lazy, unmotivated, or useless to society.

The economic and family institutions of society are mutually dependent. They are connected by the labor that family members provide to produce the goods and services made available to all members of society who can afford them. They are also connected by the *income* paid to those family members, which allows them to enjoy a certain number of the goods and services produced. Occupational involvements — the kinds of work people do — must therefore be considered as we assess the impact that income has on marriage and family relationships.

Not only is money needed to realize the life chances and to enjoy the style of life to which we are accustomed, or to which we aspire; we also tend to judge the personal worthiness and competence of *others* on the basis of their occupational status, the income it produces, and the number and equality of tangible assets they accumulate as a result of their work (Williams, 1970:454–455). "What type of work do you do?" is often the first question one hears at a party or social gathering, or when meeting others for the first time. By knowing what kind of work we do, people make judgments about how to relate to us, what kinds of interests we might have, and whether or not they wish to continue relating to us. Marriage partners also judge each other according to their respective work, economic contributions, and the style of life they are able to afford. Marriage relationships are embedded in a complex

Work is an important feature of adult life in our society, as others make judgments about our personal competence and worthiness based on the type of work we do.   *(Photo by Carl Hill.)*

and complicated web of ties with the occupational system, a system that has a significant impact on the nature of interpersonal bonds between husbands, wives, and children.

The Social Stratification System

Throughout history, all known societies have had some sort of system for allocating the society's goods, services, prestige, and power *unequally* among people. This is known as the system of *social stratification*. This system determines "who gets what and why" (Lenski, 1966:3). Inequity pervades all known societies, as people can be compared and ranked according to the level of valued societal rewards they possess. Lenski (1966:31) points out that the material rewards of society are "in short

supply — that is, the demand for them exceeds the supply." We are limited, to varying degrees, in what we can buy and consume by the amount of money we have. This places us in a competitive position relative to others, as we compete for grades in school, the best available jobs, and the maximum amount of income available from our jobs and the work we do.

SOCIAL CLASS DIFFERENCES

One's ranking in the social stratification system is usually referred to as *social class position*. There are many ways to assess social class position: according to the level of income per year; the quantity and value of tangible assets (house, cars, stocks and bonds, boats, and property, for example); the prestige of one's occupation; or some combination of income, prestige, and level of education (Kahl,

1957). Table 8.1 shows a distribution of the population of American families according to income level. Our society is clearly stratified according to how much money is earned in any given year, and this distribution has remained remarkably consistent for several decades (Chilman, 1975; *Current Population Reports,* 1980). Note also that Black families are overrepresented at the lower-income levels, and underrepresented at the higher levels, relative to white families. These differences, too, have existed for decades.

Some people view the inequitable distribution of income and the goods it purchases as fair, just, and essential. Others view it as unjust, unnecessary, and symbolic of the oppression and domination of the Haves over the Have-Nots. Whatever philosophy is followed, however, it is true that some degree of economic inequality is inevitable (Lenski, 1966). Even in such socialistic societies as the Soviet Union, Cuba, Red China, and the Israeli Kibbutz, where official political doctrine has erased any differences between people based on income, status, and personal and family wealth, clear distinctions between families continue to exist, and parallel those found in the United States,

Canada, and other societies of the industrialized Western world (Porter, 1965; Simirenko, 1972; Spiro, 1979). According to Kahl (1957:119), patterns of social stratification will continue to exist for decades, or even centuries to come:

> Our present economic system is one of capitalistic enterprise based on private ownership of property and competition for the rewards of the market . . . It has always been thus: the value system of a culture defines property and to some degree controls its relative distribution among individuals. Then it permits some freedom of individual action and the resulting distribution of incomes becomes one of the prime causes of invidious distinctions between individuals. These distinctions of income and prestige produce an unequal distribution of consumption goods, or power, and of life chances.

The social stratification system provides a major yardstick by which people compare their personal worth, competence, and success with that of others. People tend to judge, rightly or wrongly, one's position in the social stratification hierarchy in terms of superiority-inferiority and general worthiness. As mentioned before, "Keeping up with the Joneses" was a popular activity in the economically prosperous 1950s, and continues well into the 1980s, where now many strive to keep *ahead* of the Joneses.

DETERMINANTS OF SOCIAL-CLASS POSITION

Precisely where one falls along the social-class continuum is dependent upon several factors: the social class of the family into which one is born; educational attainment; one's values regarding economic achievement and success; the motivation one has to work and to achieve; intelligence; and, to be sure, luck. We refer to a person's social and economic standing that is due to an "accident of birth" as *ascribed status.* That is, being born male or female, Black or white, into a wealthy family or a poor family, or some combination of these, are ascribed to us at birth. Ascribed-status characteristics place limits on economic accomplishments which are extremely difficult, if not impossible, to overcome. For example, only white males have ever been elected to the U.S. presidency, and white males are greatly overrepresented (relative to their number in the population) among business executives,

TABLE 8.1. *Percentage Distribution of Family Income for Blacks, Whites, and All Families for 1982.*[1]

	All Families	Blacks	Whites
Under $5,000	6.0%	17.0%	4.6%
$5,000–$9,999	10.6	20.8	9.3
$10,000–$14,999	12.4	15.7	12.1
$15,000–$19,999	12.1	11.2	12.3
$20,000–$24,999	12.3	10.7	12.6
$25,000–$34,999	19.5	14.1	20.3
$35,000–$49,999	16.0	7.8	16.9
$50,000 and over	10.9	2.6	11.9
TOTAL	99.8%	99.9%	100.0%
Median Income	$23,433	$13,598	$24,603

[1] Totals may not add to 100% because of the rounding of percentages to the nearest one-tenth.

SOURCES: U.S. Bureau of the Census, *Money Income of Households, Families, and Persons in the United States: 1982.* Current Population Reports, Series P–60, No. 142, 1984, p. 39. U.S. Bureau of the Census, *Statistical Abstract of the United States, 1984,* 104th ed. Table 762, p. 463, Washington, D.C., 1983.

judges, doctors, lawyers, and other high-status occupations. Women and racial minorities, on the other hand, are underrepresented in these occupations, because of societal prejudice and discrimination, as well as socialization practices that de-emphasize the value of achievement and success for people in these groups.

Conversely, the social status one attains as a result of one's individual efforts, regardless of one's *ascribed-status* characteristics, are referred to as *achieved status.* Ultimately, the position of most people in the social-class hierarchy results from some combination of ascribed and achieved statuses. For example, research has shown that a male's occupational status is determined by a combination of his own and his father's educational and occupational achievements (Blau and Duncan, 1967). Research has also shown the importance of other characteristics, both ascribed and achieved, for determining social-class position. Included are *birth order* (oldest and youngest children attain higher social-class levels); *aspirations and motivations* to succeed in the world of work; and *family size* (children from smaller families attain higher occupational status). Blacks and other racial minorities attain lower average social-class levels, and consequently, lower average incomes than do whites (see Table 8.1). Because of their ascribed minority status, Blacks have experienced inequality of opportunity, resulting from prejudicial attitudes and discriminatory practices; they have had poorer, and fewer, educational opportunities, and have had inferior career experiences in comparison with whites. Ascribed status, then, is interrelated with various achieved-status characteristics to determine where a given individual or family will be placed along the social-class spectrum.

The Impact of Income on Marriage and the Family

The emphasis on socioeconomic achievement and success in our society is measured by the prestige of one's occupation, the income which that occupation produces, and the tangible rewards provided by the income. These measures are at the core of the American value system. Marital and family institutions are also closely interrelated with the economic system. Therefore, the rather dramatic

social and economic differences between families as the result of the social-stratification system have a profound impact on the course of marriage and family events. This impact can be observed in several areas, including marriage, birth, and divorce rates, as well as in the level of satisfaction with marriage and family relationships at various socioeconomic levels.

INCOME AND GETTING MARRIED

There is a clear relationship between income level and the propensity to marry, although this relationship appears to differ for men and women. For men, income level and the probability of getting married are *positively* related. That is, the proportion of married men increases at increasing levels of annual income (Cutright, 1970). This is true *regardless* of the educational attainment or occupational prestige of the male. Conversely, there is a greater incidence of never-married single men at lower levels of the economic scale. For women, on the other hand, income level and the probability of being married are *inversely* related. That is, there is a greater incidence of never-married single women among those females who earn higher incomes (Havens, 1973; Mueller and Campbell, 1977).

Although researchers have not fully determined *why* income and marriage rates are related as they are for men and women, some interesting hunches have been made. For example, Bernard (1972) speculated on the causes by proposing a concept called the *marriage gradient* (see Figure 8.1). Bernard noted that the prevailing pattern of marriage in our society is that men tend to marry women who are slightly below them in terms of education, age, and occupational status, presumably as a result of seeking to maintain their culturally ascribed "competitive edge." In our society, "the girl wants to be able to 'look up' to her husband, and he, of course, wants her to." (Bernard, 1972:35.) This results in the marriage gradient depicted in Figure 8.1.

The result is that there is no one for the men at the bottom (of the income scale) to marry, no one to look up to them. Conversely, there is no one for the women at the top to look up to; there are no men who are superior to them. The result . . . is that the never-married men (B) tend to be "bottom-of-the barrel" and the women (A) "cream-of-the-crop." (Bernard, 1972:36)

FIGURE 8.1.   The Marriage Gradient.

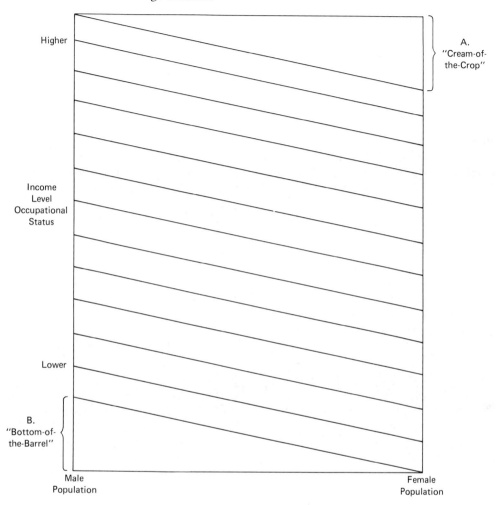

SOURCE: Bernard (1972:36).

According to this explanation, the "pool of eligible mates" is limited for men who are the "down-and-outers" of society, as well as for women who have been successful in attaining the highest levels of education, income, and occupational prestige. Hence, the marriage-gradient concept suggests that being a single never-married person is not a matter of choice or rational decision. These people are more likely than any others to remain single because there are few available partners in the marriage market due to the rules of marital choice, which encourage women to "marry-up" and men to "marry-down."

It is likely that the marriage rate differences for women are also related to a more conscious decision-making process. Successful career women with relatively high incomes have less *need* than others to be married and dependent upon the income and occupational prestige provided by a husband (Mueller and Campbell, 1977; Havens, 1973). For these women, marriage would have too many costs relative to benefits, especially if the prospect of marriage means sacrificing the "ladder of success" to assume the "confining traditional familial sex-role of wife-mother-homemaker" (Havens, 1973:218). Hence, career women may *choose* not to marry because the cost/benefit ratio is too great.

INCOME AND BIRTH RATES

Prior to the development of the birth control pill and modern methods of contraceptive sterilization, income and fertility bore a strong inverse relationship (Cutright, 1971a; Rainwater, 1960). That is, women in higher-income marriages had fewer children. Conversely, women in lower-income families were less able than others to limit their number of children to the desired number (Rainwater, 1960). In addition, because Blacks and Hispanics have been more heavily concentrated among the lower-social-class levels of our society for years, it has not been a surprise to find higher fertility rates in these minority groups.

Since the development of improved contraceptive methods, social-class differences in fertility have been growing smaller (Bahr, Chadwick, and Stauss, 1975; Ewer and Gardner, 1978). Nonetheless, income and occupational involvement continue to be related to the number of children born, particularly for married women. The more highly educated women, and women who work outside of the home, have fewer children than do less educated and nonemployed women (*Current Population Reports,* 1980; National Center for Health Statistics, 1981a). Higher-income working wives also have fewer children than do lower-income wives (Defronzo, 1976; Ewer and Gardner, 1978). In addition, women married to high-income men have lower fertility rates than those married to less educated, lower-income men. Finally, the number of unwanted and unintended pregnancies is about twice as high among those whose total family income falls at or below the poverty level than for others (Anderson, 1981; Westoff, 1981). In 1980, for example, women in families with incomes below $5,000 had 94 births per 1,000 population, whereas women with family incomes of $25,000 or more had only 48 births per 1,000 population. The poverty-stricken, therefore, had nearly double the birth rate of women in higher-income families (Tyrer,

1984). These differences are the result of a complex interaction of skill, knowledge, and motivation in family planning behavior; normative pressures from friends and relatives (to bear children); and gender-role expectations among men and women at different income levels.

INCOME AND DIVORCE

Lower-income marriages have greater rates of divorce than do higher-income marriages. Moreover, moving up the social-class ladder is related to *stability* in marriage, and moving down leads to a greater number of divorces (Glick and Norton, 1977). It appears that higher-income levels allow marriage partners to enjoy more rewarding levels of consumption, in line with typical goals and values in our society. This results in feelings of satisfaction with the marriage, and more satisfied marriage partners are less likely than others to divorce (Cutright, 1971b). Higher income also means a greater accumulation of such assets as savings, investments, homes, automobiles, and furniture. Married couples who have accumulated such assets are not only more likely than others to be satisfied with marriage, but are also less likely to divorce because of the legal and economic problems that would follow the fragmentation of assets through a divorce proceeding.

Again, as with fertility differences according to income levels, Blacks experience greater levels of divorce and separation than do whites at *all* income levels. However, the differences are greatest at lower-income levels, where Blacks and other minorities are more heavily concentrated.

INCOME AND SATISFACTION WITH MARRIAGE

Despite the correlation between income level and divorce, there are many instances of lower-income marriages that are stable and satisfying to both husband and wife. There are also many cases of divorce among the higher-income and higher social-class levels of our society. The influence of income level on each partner's satisfaction with the marriage relationship depends on a number of factors.

1. *Income Expectations.* If the marriage partners' income meets or exceeds their expectations, they are likely to be satisfied *regardless* of how high the income level might be. For example, if a couple's expectations are geared to what their parents or best friends earn, and the style of life these others are able to enjoy, then a married pair may be perfectly satisfied with an income falling at the lower end of the income scale.

2. *Expectations That the Wife Will Work.* In our society, males are taught to be competent breadwinners and providers for their families. The personal worth of an adult male has traditionally been judged according to how much income and social status he can provide. However, the dramatic increase of married women in the labor market over the past twenty years has complicated matters. Many working wives find themselves in the labor force because of economic necessity—their husbands do not earn enough income to provide the family with a standard of living to which they are accustomed or to which they aspire. Hence, although income is being provided by the wife, perhaps amounting to more than that provided by the husband, feelings of injustice and a belief that the husband is inadequate in his role as provider may lead to dissatisfaction of both partners and, possibly, conflict in the marriage. The husband may feel threatened and insecure as a result of his wife's employment. If, on the other hand, the spouses' norms are in favor of the wife's working for as much income as possible, and her employment is not linked to judgments of the husband as a provider, then her financial contribution will enhance marital satisfaction.

3. *Money Management and the Accumulation of Assets.* To be sure, a relatively high income level may result in disappointment and dissatisfaction if it is spent or invested unwisely. No one is immune from excessive indebtedness, poor spending and saving habits, and poor investment decisions. In fact, married couples and others who file for personal bankruptcy are not always from the lowest income groups (Cohen, 1979:355). It is not uncommon today to find doctors, lawyers, business executives, and other professionals among those appearing in court records as having filed for bankruptcy. Conversely, moderate- to low-income levels can provide a satisfying material basis for marriage if partners are able to budget, save, and spend wisely.

Management of financial resources, whether they are plentiful, moderate, or meager, is a key to translating income into satisfying marriage and family relationships (see Appendix).

4. *Occupational-Role Involvement.* Making a substantial income can have negative effects on a marriage relationship if it requires a marriage partner to spend long hours and considerable energy at the office, factory, or other place of work. Some jobs require extensive travel away from home. The net result of such time and energy commitments that many at higher income levels must make is to sharply curtail the companionship and intimate activities that a married couple might otherwise share (Piotrkowski, 1979). Therefore, in an effort to earn an adequate income, one or both partners may be unable to fully participate in the marriage, thus reducing the chances of establishing and maintaining effective communication and conflict-resolution strategies (see chapter 7), working out mutually acceptable gender-role expectations (see chapter 4), and enjoying a satisfying exchange of love and affection (see chapters 3 and 5).

When thinking about the effect that the income contributions of marriage partners have on satisfaction with marriage, consider what some have called the "success constraint theory" (Aldous, Osmond, and Hicks, 1979). As it applies to men, this theory suggests that increasing income levels will lead to marital satisfaction up to a point, beyond which the demands of the job will prevent the husband from adequately participating in the family in his roles as confidant, lover, affection-giver, and sex partner. His ability to share in the household tasks and chores, that is, to help out at home, will also be limited. The business executive, doctor, or lawyer who provides a substantial income for his family may do so at a price to others as he becomes less involved in the family's activities because of extremely heavy job demands.

Too much success in the occupational system . . . limits the man's family participation. His wife must play father as well as mother roles, but without the emotional support her husband is too busy to give . . . The husband's occupational success demands time. The job is also of intrinsic interest—job satisfaction is higher in the professional and managerial occupations—and time spent on an occupation garners men more social prestige than does time spent in the family. As a result, successful men use their family power to avoid family responsibilities. (Aldous, et al., 1979:244–245)

Indeed, research has shown that wives of the highest-income men report less satisfaction with companionship, empathy, understanding, and performance of household tasks and chores, and more disagreement on values and role expectations, than do wives with husbands at other income levels (see Figure 8.2). Hence, although higher-income levels are related to satisfaction with certain aspects

of marriage, the old maxim that "money cannot buy love" appears to have some basis in fact.

BEYOND THE THRESHOLD: POVERTY AND MARRIAGE IN THE UNITED STATES

In 1962, Michael Harrington wrote of the "other America," where poverty-stricken families, lacking adequate food, housing, and medical care, were distinguished from the mainstream working and middle classes who

FIGURE 8.2.   The Curvilinear Relationship Between Income and Marriage Satisfaction.

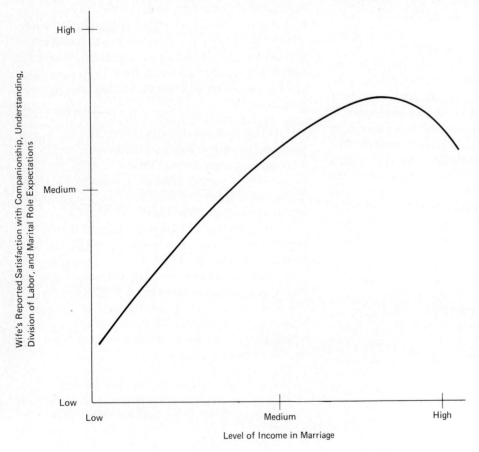

SOURCE: Diagram based on the success constraint theory of Aldous, Osmond, and Hicks (1979) and research of Blood and Wolfe (1960), Dizard (1968), and Scanzoni (1970).

were able to participate more fully in the rewards that our affluent society had to offer. Since that time, the proportion of families living below the officially defined poverty level has not changed significantly, as a sizable number of American families continue to live in the "other America" of the poverty-stricken (Bianchi and Farley, 1979). In 1982, for example, there were 34.4 million people living below the poverty level, constituting 15 percent of the American population (U.S. Bureau of the Census, 1984a). This was an increase of 2.6 million, or 8.1 percent, over the number in poverty in 1981, and the highest rate of poverty recorded since 1966. In 1982, 34.9 percent of all Black families lived below the poverty line, in contrast to 29.2 percent of all Hispanic families, and only 10.6 percent of all white families.

The many causes of poverty are interrelated. Chilman (1975:54) identified eight characteristics that contribute to a family's ability to stay *above* the poverty line. Families lacking several or all of these characteristics are poverty-prone.

1. A white, two-parent family in which both the husband and wife work.
2. A family headed by a person between the ages of 45 and 54 (not a family in which the head is over 65 or under 24).
3. A family with no more than two children.
4. Residence in the northeast or western non-farm regions of the country (particularly not the South).
5. A family with a full-time white male head employed in professional, technical, administrative, skilled craft, or transport employment.
6. Parents with at least some college education, but preferably college graduation or more.
7. Income from money sources besides wages (such as property, inherited income, stocks, and bonds, interest on savings).
8. Excellent physical and mental health.

It is possible, after reading this list, to draw a composite picture of the most poverty-prone families in the United States. They are headed by a Black female with limited education and skills-training; more specifically, a young female who must support two or more children. Women who must "go it alone," because of widowhood, divorce, desertion, or separation (particularly if they are Black and caring for children) find themselves in dire economic straits far more frequently than any other group (Bianchi and Farley, 1979; Payton, 1982). Between 1970 and 1975, there was a 35 percent increase in the number of female headed families below the poverty threshold, primarily because of the dramatic increase in the divorce rate during that time. Moreover, the income gap between single-parent households and those headed by intact married couples actually widened between the years 1970 and 1981 (Bianchi and Farley, 1979; U.S. Bureau of the Census, 1983a) [see Table 8.2]. The average income of households headed by women in 1982 was $11,484. It was $13,496 for white female-headed households and $7,458 for Black female-headed households (U.S. Bureau of the Census, 1984b:32–34). In 1980, 44 percent of all families headed by a single-parent mother were classified as living in poverty, and only 7 percent of married couples with children were so designated (Bureau of

TABLE 8.2. *Average (Median) Income of Families Headed by Married Couples, Males, and Females: 1970, 1975, and 1981*

Family Headed by	Average Income (in 1981 dollars)			Gain Between 1970 and 1980
	1970	1975	1981	
Married Couple	$24,631	$25,123	$25,065	$434
Male, No Wife Present	21,108	21,959	19,889	−1,219
Female, No Husband Present	11,929	11,565	10,960	−969

SOURCE: *Statistical Abstract of the United States, 1984,* 104th ed. Table 767, p. 466, U.S. Bureau of the Census, Washington, D.C., 1983.

Labor Statistics, 1983). Hence, not only does poverty contribute to divorce among those with a low income, but divorce eventually leads to becoming more deeply entrenched among the ranks of the poverty-stricken.

It is here in the "other America" of poverty that the role-reciprocity process in marriage often breaks down. The poverty line constitutes a sort of threshold, beyond which an inadequate income severely erodes a marriage relationship (Brinkerhoff and White, 1978). As Chilman (1975:57) noted:

> Many people erroneously conclude that family breakdown (including illegitimacy) *causes* poverty. It is far more likely that the reverse is true: poverty is a leading cause of family instability . . . Lack of income is related to high rates of unemployment and underemployment, adverse living conditions in deteriorated neighborhoods, poor health, lack of community resources: all of these factors tend to undermine family life.

> These poverty conditions contribute to such attitudes and behaviors as fatalism (feeling out of control of one's future), alienation, distrust between family members, separate male and female worlds, little communication between mates and between parents and children, and punitive and authoritarian methods of child-rearing.

Breakdown of marriage among low-income couples is the result, in part, of chronic unemployment (being out of work) and underemployment (working below one's capacities and level of training) on a continuing basis. Marriage partners tend to evaluate the competency of the provider on the basis of the income and status that are furnished, particularly that of the husband and father. Traditionally, it is the husband's occupational status and income that provide the primary measure of where the family ranks in the social-class system (Sampson and Rossi, 1975). Low-income men who are plagued by unemployment or underemployment are the most likely to be blamed for their poor performance as providers. They are blamed by themselves, their wives, and perhaps even their children, and the marriage is strained as a result (Larson, 1984). To the strain caused by viewing the husband-father as a poor provider, add the stress created by inadequate housing, food, clothing, medical care, and generally substandard living which is the lot of those in the lowest income groups. It is no wonder that marital separation, desertion, and divorce (stemming from lack of communication and dissatisfaction with exchanges of love,

affection, companionship, and other expressive rewards) are prevalent among those near or below the poverty threshold (Chilman, 1975; Larson, 1984; Rubin, 1976).

Work Roles and Development in Marriage

We have already discussed the importance of work in American culture, and the impact that income and status associated with occupational involvements have on marriage relationships. In addition, significant changes have taken place in our society over the past two decades in the relationship between the marriage institution and the occupational system in society. Probably the most important change has been the dramatic rise in the number and proportion of married women and mothers entering the labor force. The working wife and mother is today a common occurrence, as working women are now able to seek fulfillment in work outside of the home and also contribute to the family bank account in a time of economic uncertainty and rising costs of living.

As the news item in Feature 8.1 shows, however, everyone in our society does not approve of women working outside of the home and family environment. Nor is there full support from industry and government, evident by the lack of adequate child-care facilities which are needed for the children of women who choose to, or have to, work outside of the home. Moreover, the prospects for adequate child-care facilities in the next decade or two are uncertain (Hofferth, 1979). Because of the rapidly increasing divorce rate over the past several years, a growing number of working women are single-parent heads-of-households, which means that the entire family must depend upon the income of the mother for food, shelter, clothing, medical care, and any "luxuries" they might be able to afford. Between 1970 and 1979, for example, the number of households headed by women increased 51 percent, making it the fastest growing family structure in the United States. The number of traditional husband-wife headed families grew only 6.6 percent in the same period.

These trends in work patterns have produced a new set of stresses and strains for American marriages and families. In this section, we will take a look at some of the

WICHITA, Kan.—The daughters and granddaughters of the American temperance movement, gathering in Carry Nation territory this weekend, say there is a new threat to family life—the working mother.

"With an increased number of working mothers, the tendency toward a breakdown in family life and discipline, often accelerated by alcohol use, has become a grave concern to us," said Edith Stanley, president of the national Women's Christian Temperance Union, which has headquarters in Evanston, Ill.

About 500 women are on hand for the union's 106th annual convention, which ends today. Representing a national membership of 250,000, the delegates have been praying, singing hymns and talking again of the evils of alcohol, tobacco, gambling, drugs and sinking moral values.

Stanley, who retires today as the 10th president of the group, said the WCTU's "founding mothers' purpose was to fight liquor traffic. It was the No. 1 problem in the home and it still is."

But as more and more young women seek to combine careers and motherhood, the union says it has a new battle to fight. The home may not be a woman's only place, these women say, but it should be the place of top priority.

"A career woman still should remember the home is her first place," Stanley said. "The home is a woman's palace. She should be queen of the home."

Union members acknowledge that some widowed or divorced mothers must work to support their home. And some wives must work to supplement their husbands' incomes.

"But they should know that taking care of their home and family is their first duty," Stanley said.

She worried that many wives and mothers today are working for affluence, rather than necessity.

"We no longer talk about our needs, we talk about our wants," she said. "If a woman wants to get away from the home for a while, there are plenty of worthwhile things for her to do in the community."

Virginia Jarrett, the WCTU's vice president from Richmond, Va., said she admires women who can handle a career and a family.

"But many can't," she said. "For many there's a breakdown in home life that has been caused by working mothers who don't have time for their children."

It is this dedication to home life that makes annual WCTU conventions look like "old ladies' playtime," said Marie Caylor, who handles WCTU public relations. "Our younger members are busy with schoolchildren this time of year."

SOURCE: Scott Kraft, *Arizona Daily Star,* Sept. 1, 1980.

---

pressures brought about by the influx of women into the world of work, and examine some of the effects, both actual and alleged, that changing female employment patterns have had on relationships within the family.

CAREERS AND JOBS

In assessing the impact of working on the marriage relationship, it is important to distinguish two basic types of work: *careers* and *jobs*. Although some degree of overlap exists between the two, it is useful to draw a distinction between them.

Some types of work require relatively little education, training, direct supervision of other employees, and self-direction (Kohn, 1969). They provide quite limited opportunities for advancement up the "company ladder." These we will refer to as *jobs*. Blue-collar work, such as that in a factory, truck driving, machine operating, and manual labor of various sorts, as well as such white-collar jobs as clerical, secretarial, retail sales, and general office work, are examples of occupations in the "jobs" category. They generally involve a standard eight-hour day, and the

Preparation for work roles begins during the childhood socialization process—for females as well as males. *(Photo by Carl Hill.)*

worker is usually paid an hourly wage. When the employee returns home, the job remains at the place of work. That is, there is no carryover work that must be done at home.

Careers, on the other hand, are usually higher-paying and prestigious occupations which require more education and skill-training, involve supervision of others, and require self-direction. There is a "career ladder," which means that it is possible for an employee to advance into the higher ranks of the company or corporation. There usually is no set schedule of hours, although a career frequently involves working an excess of 40 hours per week in order to complete the tasks essential for career advancement. Career employees usually earn a salary— an annual rate of pay, as opposed to an hourly wage. Doctors, lawyers, company administrators and executives,

managers, college professors, several categories of teachers, nurses, and those in business professions are considered to have a *career.* These occupations provide considerably more freedom and flexibility than jobs, in terms of what the employees can do with their time. In jobs, employees are much more structured and closely supervised in terms of what they can do with their time during a working day. According to Rapoport and Rapoport (1971:18), careers are

those types of jobs which require a high degree of commitment and which have a continuous developmental character. The individual develops a career by moving from one job or stage to another, continuously gathering and applying relevant experiences for improved performance in a more senior position or in a more expert role of some kind . . . Careers in professions are thought of as proceeding through stages of cultivation and experience, accumulating expertise.

Jobs are comparatively easy to move into and out of if the family situation demands that one partner (usually the wife) stay at home. Once a person temporarily leaves a career, however, it becomes difficult to "pick up where you left off." That is, it is harder for a person to reenter a career at a level comparable to the one attained when he or she temporarily stopped working.

Compared with being employed in a job, being in a career situation has quite different implications for the marriage relationship, in terms of income, prestige, psychological rewards, and concomitant problems. We will explore some of these more fully after we examine what has been happening in regard to women entering the labor force.

WOMEN IN THE LABOR FORCE

Between 1970 and the end of 1983, the number of female workers (20 years and older) in the American labor force grew from 32 million to 42.3 million, more than one-and-one-half times the increase in the number of male workers (*Current Population Reports*, 1980; *Bureau of Labor Statistics News*, 1983). In 1970, there were 6 female workers for every 10 males in the American work force. By the end of 1983, the ratio had grown to nearly 8 in 10! The number of *married* women in the work force also grew rapidly during the 1970s and into the 1980s. Between 1970 and the end of 1983, the number of *married women* in the labor force grew from 18,383,000 to 25,534,000, with the percentage of all married women working outside of the home growing from 41 percent in 1970 to nearly 54 percent in 1983. Although the majority (54 percent) of wives employed outside the home worked only part-time in 1983, 46 percent were employed in full-time year-round occupations. The U.S. Bureau of the Census estimates that more than two in three of all married women will hold jobs outside of the home by 1990 (*Arizona Daily Star*, September 25, 1979). At present, only 30 percent of all married women are full-time homemakers with children, a number that is expected to drop to around 25 percent by 1990. Clearly, the stereotype of the American family — popularized during the 1950s as comprising a full-time working husband, a wife/mother

As women have increased their average level of educational attainment, they have moved into the labor force at a rapid pace over the past several years, especially those who are married and have children at home.
(Photo by Ed Lettau.)

in the home, and children—actually characterizes only a minority of contemporary families, and this number continues to dwindle with each passing year.

The increasing number of women receiving high school and college diplomas fueled this movement into the world of work; the highest rates of working outside of the home are found for those women with four or more years of college. The lowest rates are found among women who failed to graduate from high school. In addition, more women today are attending college and earning advanced degrees than ever before, and the educational gap between men and women has been closing as a result. For example, the number of women in college increased by 57 percent between 1970 and 1978, but the number of men increased only 16 percent (*Current Population Reports,* 1980). In 1981, more than half of all college students (52 percent) were women, up from 45 percent in 1975 and from 42 percent in 1971 (National Center for Education Statistics, 1981).

Smith (1979) suggested several other changes that have prompted the rapid influx of women into the American labor force:

1. *Double-digit inflation,* which has reduced the buying power of a dollar earned and which has outdistanced average gains in husbands' incomes (see the Appendix). Today, many families require two incomes in order to enjoy a standard of living to which they are accustomed or to which they aspire.

2. *Declining birth rates* of the late 1960s and throughout the 1970s allowed women more freedom to move out of the home and into the world of outside employment.

3. *The number and variety of jobs available to women* have increased dramatically over the past several years, particularly in areas traditionally reserved for men, as legal and social barriers to women in the educational and occupational systems have been breaking down. It is now illegal for qualified women to be discriminated against in seeking an education or an occupation of their choice (although, as we shall see, such discrimination still exists).

4. *Changing gender-role expectations* in our society mean fewer distinctions between the rights, duties, privileges, and obligations of men and women (see chapter 4). There is an increasing range of role options available to women in the educational, familial, and occupational spheres of life, which is the direct result of changing views regarding women's roles. For example, a Gallup Poll conducted in 1980 found that over one in three American women consider an "ideal life-style" to include a full-time job as well as marriage and children. This number undoubtedly would have been higher had these respondents been given the option to choose part-time work (*Parade,* December 28, 1980b).

Perhaps the most striking aspect of this revolutionary movement of women into the world of work outside the home has been the increasing employment of married and divorced *mothers* with young dependent children. In 1981, there were 18.4 million employed mothers in the United States, representing an increase of more than 8 million over the 1970 number (*Current Population Reports,* 1980; *Bureau of Labor Statistics,* 1983) [see Table 8.3]. Nearly half (49 percent) of all mothers below age 35 were employed outside the home in 1984, and 54 percent of all children under the age of 18 in the United States had mothers who were either employed or looking for work. There were also 8.2 million preschool children with employed mothers in 1981, up 500,000 (2 percent) from the previous year. This number included 45 percent of *all* children under the age of six. As Table 8.3 shows, the movement of women into the labor force has been the most rapid among those with young children, ages six and under. It is estimated that by 1990 there will be 10.4 million children under six with mothers in the labor force (Hofferth, 1979), an increase of 27 percent over the number in 1981. The question of what impact the employment of mothers has on the overall development and well-being of their children therefore becomes an important one, because the rate of employment for mothers of young children is projected to continue increasing for at least the next ten to twenty years.

THE STATUS OF WOMEN'S OCCUPATIONS

Although the trend toward women working outside of the home continues, the income and prestige provided by their employment continues to lag behind that of the male (see chapter 4, Table 4.6 and Figure 4.5). Women are grossly underrepresented in the higher-paying and higher-prestige *careers,* and overrepresented in the lower-status and lower-paying *jobs.* Women earn less income

TABLE 8.3. *Labor Force Participation Rates for Women in Various Marital Statuses: 1970 and 1982.*[1]

	1970	1982	Percentage Increase, 1970–1982
Married Women, Husband Present	40.8	51.2	10.4
No children under age 18	42.2	46.2	4.0
Children 6–17 only	49.2	63.2	14.0
Children under 6	30.3	48.7	18.4
Divorced Women	71.5	74.9	3.4
No children under age 18	67.7	71.6	3.9
Children 6–17 only	82.4	83.6	1.2
Children under 6	63.3	67.2	3.9
Separated Women	52.1	60.0	7.9
No children under age 18	52.3	57.5	5.2
Children 6–17 only	60.6	68.4	7.8
Children under 6	45.4	55.2	9.8

[1] Percentage of all women in a category, who are employed outside the home.

SOURCE: U.S. Bureau of the Census, *Statistical Abstract of the United States, 1984,* 104th ed. Table 686, p. 414, Washington, D.C., 1983.

than men at equal educational levels, and this difference actually *increased* during the 1970s. Women earn only one-half to two-thirds of what men earn in the same or a similar type of work. Stated another way, the rate of return realized by working wives and mothers in terms of money earned is far less than that experienced by men, given an equal amount of time and educational training invested in the occupation. In addition, most employed wives make only modest contributions to the social status and prestige of the family, although their contribution increases among those in higher-income and prestige careers (such as doctors, lawyers, and other professionals) [Sampson and Rossi, 1975; Hiller and Philliber, 1978]. The average working wife and mother contributes only 25 to 30 percent of her family's total income (Masnick and Bane, 1980:91).

TO WORK OR NOT TO WORK: THE MARRIED WOMAN'S DILEMMA

The decision of whether or not to work outside of the home is a simple one for some wives and mothers, but is quite complicated for others. There are two factors com-

plicating the decision. First, as we have seen in chapter 4 and in the previous section, women are able to contribute less than men to the family's income because of their lower pay scales and discrimination in the occupational system. For some, the income that could be earned by working may be hardly worth the effort, considering the cost of child care and time spent away from home. This is particularly the case for women who, for one reason or another, can work only part-time. Second, many women today are experiencing internal role conflicts. They may have been socialized to assume the traditional responsibility for care of the home, husband, and children, but recent changes toward gender-role equality encourage them to seek fulfillment and a greater sense of contribution through work and careers outside of the home. These women find themselves in a bind: they may feel stifled in their personal development if they do not seek outside employment, but they may feel guilty if they do.

Hence, the married woman's decision about whether or not to work outside of the home is dependent upon four considerations:

1. The extent to which she views work outside the home as a means for achieving personal fulfillment and satisfaction, providing a certain sense of purpose, con-

NEW YORK (AP) — At current pay rates, the American mother is worth more than $35,000 a year, according to an article in Parents magazine.

In its August issue, the magazine calls for "adequate financial payment for full-time homemakers," and says that an average housewife does work that is worth about $700 a week.

The magazine estimates that house care fetches $3 an hour on the current market, day care costs $4 an hour, on-call care costs $3 an hour, driving costs $5 an hour, and managerial work costs $4.50 an hour.

According to the magazine, a mother with two preschool-age children spends 10 hours of her waking time on child care, and then must be available for on-call care two hours each day and 12 hours each night. Total child care: 70 hours a week, or $280. Add 98 hours of on-call time each week, or $294.

Then there are the other duties: four hours of clothes care, two hours on food shopping, 21 hours on food preparation, and five hours of house cleaning. Total housework: 32 hours, or $96.

Add two hours of budgeting and planning, worth $9, and four hours of driving, worth $20.

Total salary: $699 a week, before taxes.

SOURCE: *Arizona Daily Star,* July 1979.

Other research has shown that homemaking can also be ranked according to the prestige which that "occupation" yields for the woman or, in some cases, the man. In a study of 500 adults, Nilson (1978) asked them to give their idea of the general social standing of a "housewife." Overall, housewives were rated similarly to such occupations as bookkeeper, insurance agent, plumber, auto repairman, radio announcer, newspaper reporter, electrician, and trained machinist. Interestingly, working women and the younger generation tended to rate "housewife" lower on the scale than did others, but housewives and *men* tended to accord higher prestige to this occupation than others.

tribution, and meaning to her life which cannot be obtained in the home.

2. The economic situation of the family, in terms of whether or not the wife's income is necessary for the family to live at or above its desired standard of living.

3. The husband's attitudes and expectations regarding the wife's employment, including his willingness to support the wife's decision to work.

4. Whether or not children are present, and, if there are children, attitudes and expectations of the woman regarding the importance of full-time mothering as opposed to substitute child care (babysitters, day care, and so on).

The decision about whether or not to work outside the home results from some combination of these four considerations. They influence the decision because they determine the *reward/cost balance* for the married wife and mother (Rallings and Nye, 1979; Thomson, 1980). Women enter the labor force if they perceive the rewards of outside employment to significantly outweigh the costs. Caring for children and housekeeping also have a certain balance of rewards and costs to be considered, although financial compensation is not one of the potential rewards (see Feature 8.2). Recalling the distinction between *jobs* and *careers* made previously, women who have *careers* are more likely than others to be motivated by personal fulfillment and satisfaction reasons. Although the money they earn, along with that of their husbands, contributes to a standard of living that is rewarding and comfortable, their primary motivation lies in the "feelings of achievement, competence, and contribution" that they enjoy (Rallings and Nye, 1979:207). The rewards are psychological as well as monetary.

Women who take *jobs,* on the other hand, usually do so for a different set of reasons. They are more likely to be employed because of financial necessity — two incomes are necessary to maintain a minimum, or desired, standard of living for the family. Their husbands usually have lower average incomes than the husbands of career women, and the educational levels of both spouses are likely to be lower than those of marriages where one or both spouses have a career. These women are less likely than career women to be voluntarily childless, and have, on the average, more children than do career women. Still, these women may find that getting out of the house, and being away from the children, along with the nature of the work and friendships formed at the place of work, are rewarding aspects of working which supplement the extra money being earned.

Both types of employed women, those in careers and those in jobs, find that their decision to work outside the home is tempered by the husband's attitudes and expectations, as well as the needs of children and concerns about substitute child care. Rallings and Nye (1979) refer to these as the *costs* which must be figured into the reward/cost ratio. A husband who views himself as the sole provider for the family may feel threatened by the prospect of his wife going to work, particularly if she earns more income than he does. This role conflict may cause him to react negatively, creating problems in the relationship.

A growing number of women today are entering the career world, where personal fulfillment and satisfaction, as well as income, provide the major motivation for working outside the home.

These problems may be viewed by the wife as costs that outweigh the anticipated benefits of outside employment. The net result may be a decision not to work outside the home. In couples where husbands would support their wives' decision to seek outside employment, whether they are motivated by personal fulfillment or economic necessity reasons, the woman is much more likely to enter the labor force.

Decision-making relative to the wife's employment is also tempered by the presence, number, and ages of children. Although they have increased their working outside the home at a faster pace than others, married women with young dependent children (ages 1 to 6) are still less likely than other women to be employed outside the home (Ewer, Crimmins, and Oliver, 1979; *Current Population Reports,* 1980). Many of these women and their husbands expect the wife/mother to stay at home as a full-time parent to children, particularly if they are of preschool age. To work in the home as a full-time parent and homemaker is thereby a conscious and considered *choice*. Their normative expectations will not tolerate substitute child care, such as a babysitter or a day-care center. These alternatives are defined as too costly, if they are viewed as providing less adequate care and attention to the children's needs than the mother can provide. Although fathers are just as capable as mothers of providing nurturance and of taking care of children at any age (Parke and Sawin, 1976; Lamb and Lamb, 1976; Orthner, Brown, and Ferguson, 1976), our gender-role socialization patterns have not changed enough to lead to a noticeable increase in the number of husbands and fathers who stay at home to care for young children while the wife works. Norms in our society denigrate the importance of housework and other aspects of the homemaker's role, and clearly do not consider these kinds of activities to be consistent with traditional concepts of masculinity. A man does not gain status and prestige by performing the drudgery of housework, especially if he thinks his masculinity will be questioned. It is the wife/mother, therefore, who still is expected to stay at home when the couple's norms prescribe full-time parenting as opposed to substitute child care. Although during the 1980s there has been a growing number of husbands and fathers who choose to stay at home, care for the children, and do the routine household chores of cooking and cleaning, these "househusbands" are still a rare breed—the number is still quite small, overall.

For some, the dilemma posed by having young dependent children at home is resolved by seeking part-time employment. Working part-time may allow the woman to spend an adequate amount of time with her children. Part-time work does not drain the woman's energy and psychological reserves to the extent that full-time work does. Part-time employment also helps to avoid the burdensome work overload that often comes to wives and mothers who not only are employed full-time outside the home, but who must also assume the home care responsibilities because their husbands either cannot or will not share them (Walker and Woods, 1976; Pleck, 1979).

Married women are more likely to stay at home to care for young dependent children as their husband's income increases (Ewer, Crimmins and Oliver, 1979; Rallings and Nye, 1979). Research has shown that the primary reason married women with young children enter the labor force is financial necessity of the family (Gordon and Kammeyer, 1980; Hiller and Philliber, 1980). The lower the husband's income and other earning sources for the family, the greater the financial necessity. Under such circumstances, the economic rewards of the job will outweigh the costs of finding substitute child care for the children. Hence, the decision is to work outside the home.

The final consideration in making the decision is the *cost and quality* of the substitute child care that can be arranged. Some couples rely on relatives (mothers, fathers, and siblings) to care for their children, but others must locate preschool or day-care facilities in the community. As the research of Kammerman (1983) has shown, in our society the demand for affordable, accessible, and high-quality day-care programs to meet the needs of two-job and single-parent families will intensify in the future. The greatest current demand for day-care facilities and programs is among families with infants and preschool children, whose mothers have been entering the labor force at a great pace in recent years. Perhaps the biggest issue our society will have to face in the future, as a result of the growth in women's employment outside the home, is the provision of *good quality* day-care for young children of working parents (Hofferth, 1979). For many working parents, the financial necessity of having the wife work outside the home is so strong that they must make some sort of substitute child-care arrangements, *regardless* of how adequate or inadequate they perceive them to be. This can be difficult, because the costs of day-care can consume a good percentage of a working woman's earnings, especially in lower-paying jobs. However, for those couples where the husband's income is high enough to provide some flexibility in the wife's occupational involvement, the inability to find suitable child care may keep the wife and mother at home until satisfactory arrangements can be made for the children. In any event, research has shown that the mothers who are satisfied with the quality of substitute child care are more satisfied than others with their jobs and careers (Harrell and Ridley, 1975). This satisfaction with work, in turn, leads to more satisfying and rewarding relationships between the employed mother and her children.

HUSBANDS' AND WIVES' WORK: IMPACT ON THE MARRIAGE RELATIONSHIP

Working outside the home has an impact on the marriage relationship, whether the husband, wife, or both are employed. In her in-depth study of working-class and lower-middle-class families, Piotrkowski (1978) found three basic "interface patterns" describing the impact of work roles on marriage and family relationships. The first pattern is *positive carryover,* in which a high degree of job satisfaction "spills over" in the family by promoting satisfying relationships with spouse and children. People who enjoy the work they do have more energy when they come home, are in better spirits, and make more attempts to become engaged in activities with family members than do people who dislike their jobs, or find their work to be boring, menial, or physically or emotionally difficult. In describing the situation of one husband and father, a laboratory technician and part-time upholstery repairman, Piotrkowski (pp. 35 – 40) noted the *positive carryover of energy* that his work roles had on interaction with his wife and children.

At the end of the workday I observed, Ezra was in good spirits; he was working alone in his laboratory and just had successfully calibrated a machine. Ezra feels that the enjoyment and gratification he derives from his work extend into his relationship with his family. . . . Using energy metaphors, we could say that Ezra initiated a process of "positive" energy interchanges through his interpersonal availability to family members; he introduced laughter, joking and personal energy for family activities. This energy interchange was

mutually reinforcing. He drove up in a way that invited Isabel (his wife) to joke back, and in working on Patsy's (his daughter) bicycle with her, he helped her to feel important. His approving responses to Charles's (his son) achievement in the track meet helped to enhance his son's self-esteem. These interactions continued throughout the evening. Isabel, Patsy, and Ezra worked in the garden after dinner. While they expended much physical effort, they gained a sense of accomplishment working together, and they laughed over Isabel's timidity regarding a frog that they found. Still later, Ezra and Charles watched a television prize-fight together, keeping up a running dialogue about the relative merits of the fighters.

It should be noted that the energy cycle within a family can be mutually reinforcing. Other family members "charged" Ezra in return by showing him their love and appreciation. Pasty and Charles fueled the family system also through their achievements and development. Thus, "positive" energy was "created." While Ezra's job takes him away from the family, it returns "positive" energy to the family system through the translation of his feelings of well-being — his emotional availability — into interpersonal availability to others. (Piotrkowski, 1979:35 – 40)

The second pattern described by Piotrkowski is *negative carryover.* In such cases, marriage partners experience considerable stress and strain on the job. Such stress is the result of the pressures to achieve in high-income and prestige careers, or the boredom and related tensions experienced by those in lower-level jobs. These strains and stresses are manifested in the form of worry, anxiety, and preoccupation with unfinished work, and carry over into relationships with spouse and children. Communication becomes distant and infrequent; there seems to be less time and motivation to engage in companionship and recreational activities together; and marriage partners establish psychological boundaries which create distance between them. The person who carries home the job-related tensions of the work place is moody and often irritated by relatively trivial matters. Consequently, unnecessary disagreements and open conflict are more likely to erupt than in families where the marriage partners have a relaxed attitude toward work, and who experience gratification from their daily work activities. The researcher presents the following interchange between herself (R), Henry Johnson (HJ), who is a dispatcher and deliveryman, and Henry's wife Betty (BJ), who comments on the negative carryover resulting from Henry's work-related stress.

R: How do you feel about your husband's worries?

HJ: I've probably bored them to death with my work.

BJ: It drives me crazy (stated definitely and tersely) . . . . I try to ignore it, but—he gets too involved. I mean, he brings work home too much.

R: You wish he were able to keep it at work?

BJ: (Indicates yes.)

R: Is that something that you've ever fought about?

BJ: Not in particular. But when he comes home like that it would up—I mean, it would cause tension.

R: When you say "like that," you mean—

BJ: Well, bringing all his work problems home, and he's involved in that. And then if he's mad or upset, then he's mad and upset all night and the next day . . .

R: Do you think people should leave their work at their work?

BJ: Well, sometimes you can't. But I think you can get carried away with it . . . If he had a fight with the driver or something, I mean, he was just very hard —I mean, he was just mad all night.

R: How did he act when he was in a bad mood? How did you know?

BJ: Well, he just walks in and lets everyone know he's had a bad day . . . He walks in and says, "I'm tired." Or he comes in swearing about somebody or something. Then you can ask a question about —I don't care what question it was—and in one sentence it will immediately get back to what had made him upset . . . It bothers me that he gets so involved.

R: What do you do when he gets so involved and so upset?

BJ: There's really nothing—I read. There's really nothing I can do about it.

R: You tried to ignore it, then?

BJ: Yeah. I try. I learn to ignore a lot.

R: What did you do before you ignored it?

BJ: It would bother me. I'd get hurt.

R: You would get hurt?

BJ: Think it was me, or something. Or couldn't understand why he just couldn't forget it. When things would come up about the kids, I couldn't discuss it because sometimes it was just easier not to say something about what I had problems about because he was already so mad. But now I've learned to ignore it a little . . . .

R: Did (the children) react?

BJ: (Nods) To the point where they would come in, like maybe ask a question or something—the poor kids are noisy. Well, Henry didn't like the noise. Everything had to be quiet . . . Well, it's like hard to keep them quiet. And it was hard to explain, "Dad's tired because he's worked all day."

R: It was your job to keep them quiet?

BJ: Yeah. As much as you can to keep four kids quiet. (Piotrkowski, 1979:44–45).

The third pattern relating to the impact of work on marriage is known as the *energy deficit* pattern. Many types of workers, from blue-collar machine operators to white-collar computer operators, experience conditions on the job which deplete physical and psychological energy reserves. These conditions include boring and menial work, unchallenging work duties, and strenuous jobs requiring extensive physical labor. Such conditions lead to physical and mental energy drain, which in turn impacts on marriage and family relationships after a day's work. The energy drain caused by monotonous or strenuous work destroys any motivation a husband or wife might have to be close to other family members, upon arriving home from the work place.

The demands for a worker's energy supplies are often overwhelming, and the only rewards "traded" are the wages and salaries received in return. These rewards come at a cost to the worker and his or her family, however, in the form of moodiness, irritability, physical and mental exhaustion, conflict, and little motivation to communicate or to participate in companionship or recreational activities. Moreover, when job and family compete for a person's energy supplies, it is the job that usually takes priority. This is because of the income it generates, and the lack of any viable alternatives, such as finding a new or more challenging position, or switching career tracks altogether. We are limited by education, family situations, and current economic conditions as to the kinds of work available to us. Few people are able to switch tracks easily enough to make it worth the effort. Marriage and family relationships, therefore, often must suffer because a person has a limited amount of energy, both physical and mental, to spread around.

WHEN HUSBANDS AND WIVES BOTH WORK: DUAL-OCCUPATION MARRIAGES

In the context of more two-earner families in the 1980s, several important questions arise regarding the impact that wife/mother employment has on marriage

Many occupations create strong demands on the energy of husband/fathers and wife/mothers, and "negative carryover" effects can work their way across family boundaries to impact relationships with spouses and children. *(Photo © Gilles Peress.)*

relationships. In this section, we will examine those areas for which valid research data are available.

Division of Labor in the Home.

The egalitarian ideal of many people today would have both husbands and wives being given the option of whether to work or stay at home and raise any children born in the marriage relationship. If both partners are employed outside the home, then egalitarian norms would dictate that work inside of the home, including child care, child rearing, and the homemaking tasks of cooking and cleaning, would be shared equally between husbands and wives. However, this is not usually the case.

Even though employed wives today are the rule rather than the exception, traditional division of labor patterns appear to be persisting (Stafford, Backman, and DiBona, 1977). Although some studies show that employed wives do fewer household chores and spend less time in child care duties than nonemployed wives, employed wives continue to assume the time-consuming chores of cooking, cleaning, laundry, and child care responsibilities *in addition to* working outside the home. According to Stafford, et al. (1977:45):

> The evidence clearly indicates that in contemporary middle-class families, wives are responsible for, and perform a greater share of, the household labor than husbands, even if they are working full time at demanding professional jobs. The division of labor is still stereotyped and traditional.

Why do professionally employed women spend considerably more time and energy than their husbands in performing household and childbearing tasks traditionally assigned to women? Probably because they are products of a social environment that continues to identify womanhood with home and child care responsibilities *in addition to* the contemporary emphasis on seeking gainful employment by means of a career. In describing the attitudes of professional career women, Stafford, et al. (1977:46) note that these women

> felt that to devote themselves entirely to their families would waste their intellectual gifts while to devote themselves entirely to careers would be unfeminine. The resolution of their dilemma seemed to be to maintain a traditional household *and* pursue their careers, an arrangement which left them worn out but happy.

A study of the time-use patterns of married couples found that husbands of employed wives often contribute *less* work on household chores than do husbands of nonemployed wives. For example, in a typical family with one child aged 6 to 11, an employed wife spent an average of 6 hours per day (42 hours per week) on household chores. Her husband averaged 1 hour per day (7 hours per week). In the same type of family, but when the wife was not employed outside of the home, she spent an average of 7 hours per day (49 hours per week) on household chores. The average husband spent 1.5 hours per day on household chores (9.5 hours per week). In other words, nonemployed wives spent 5 hours on household chores for every 1 hour their husbands spent, whereas employed wives spent 6 *hours* for every hour contributed by their husbands (Gauger and Walker, 1980).

> Employed women, then, appear to be on "double duty." They are employed outside of the home but they are still primarily responsible for the more tedious household tasks traditionally assigned to women in the home. And this pattern seems to take a toll on the psychological well-being of the employed wife and mother. Employed wives whose husbands do not assist with the housework report being more "depressed" than those whose husbands lend a hand (Ross, Mirowsky, and Huber, 1983). However, there is some evidence that the division of labor patterns are beginning to move in an egalitarian direction (Pleck, 1979; Lein, 1979). As Pleck (1979:487) suggests, some research is already starting to detect the changing role-perceptions of men.

> Thus, in contrast to earlier time-use studies, it is indicated from this study that men are beginning to at last increase their family work when their wives are employed.

There is no question, of course, that wives continue to hold the primary responsibility for family work. But even as this reality is acknowledged, it is important to recognize that men's behavior is changing on an important social indicator.

Only time will tell if these early indications of husbands' increased sharing of household chores will continue as wives become increasingly involved in work roles outside of the home.

Power in Marriage.   The most consistently documented trend relating to the effects of the wife's employment on the marriage relationship relates to *power*. Whether power is measured in terms of decision-making influence, or getting their way in disagreements with husbands, employed women have more power in marriage than do nonemployed women (Bahr, 1974; Rallings and Nye, 1979). Wives who work for income become more powerful in decisions relating to finances, money management, and various aspects of the provider role in the family (e.g., deciding what jobs the partners will take). The greater power of employed women has also been linked to somewhat higher levels of conflict in marriage. Employed wives appear to be more willing to voice their opposition to their husbands by virtue of the fact that they, too, contribute income to the family bank account (Nye and Berardo, 1973).

Marital Adjustment and Satisfaction.   Citing evidence from six large national surveys, Wright (1978:301) found that employed women are no more satisfied with their lives than are full-time housewives, *in the aggregate.* These findings suggest that both "working outside the home and full-time housewifery have benefits and costs attached to them; the net result being that there is no consistent or significant difference in patterns of life satisfaction." Another national survey, conducted by Locksley (1980), found overall marital adjustment and companionship activities to be unaffected by the wife's employment. For both working wives and their husbands, it appears that satisfaction with marriage can be either greater or less, depending upon a variety of circumstances influencing the balance of rewards and costs attached to the wife's outside employment.

For wives, satisfaction with marriage increases as a result of outside employment if they are (1) satisfied with their job or careers; (2) enjoy the work they do; (3) work for "personal fulfillment" rather than "financial necessity;" (4) receive support from their husbands in their work roles; (5) have help with housework; and (6) are able to find suitable part-time employment while they have children at home (Nye, 1974; Ross, et al., 1983; Piotrkowski, 1979; Rallings and Nye, 1979). For husbands, studies comparing marriages in which the wife is employed with those in which she is a full-time homemaker have found no significant differences in the husbands' stress levels, depression, satisfaction with marriage, or ability to cope (Booth, 1977, 1979; Fendrich, 1984; Locksley, 1980). What appears to make a difference for some husbands of employed wives, however, are the normative expectations for marriage which have been internalized during the socialization process. If a male has been socialized to expect his wife to stay at home and care for the children while he provides the income for the family, her entering the labor force, whether for personal fulfillment or financial necessity reasons, can create considerable distress and anxiety for him (Burke and Weir, 1976; Ross, et al., 1983).

Some husbands of working wives resent their reduced power in the family. They may also be forced to perform some of the traditionally defined "feminine" tasks of housecleaning and child care. This is a challenge to their identities as males, their sense of masculinity. If the wife must work because his income is insufficient to provide a suitable standard of living, his self-concept may be further threatened, as he questions his ability as a provider for his family. However, as gender-role expectations continue to shift toward male-female equality, albeit slowly, we should expect to see fewer husbands whose sense of competency, masculinity, and importance in the family is threatened when their wives pursue careers or other kinds of involvement in the labor force (Spitze and Waite, 1981).

Employed Parents and Their Children. The question of what impact working mothers have on the development of their children assumes increasing importance in view of two trends already discussed: (1) the growing number of working mothers with young dependent children, and (2) the increasing divorce rate, which has produced a growing number of unmarried mothers who must work. The effects on children of a mother's working have therefore been extensively researched (Hoffman, 1974; Harrell and Ridley, 1975;

Rallings and Nye, 1979). Although few significant differences have been found between children of employed and nonemployed mothers, the following have emerged across a variety of studies:

1. Daughters of employed mothers are more likely than daughters of nonemployed mothers to (1) value independence; (2) develop modern (nontraditional) gender-role expectations; (3) evaluate females as competent individuals; (4) identify their mothers as someone they want to be like, and whom they most admire; and (5) value academic and occupational achievement for themselves. (Similar effects on sons of employed mothers have not been detected.)

2. The mother's emotional welfare, as determined by her satisfaction with her work, with substitute child-care arrangements (day-care or baby sitters), and her level of guilt over leaving her children in the care of others, influences her ability to do an adequate job as a parent. Greater satisfaction with work and substitute child care, as well as less guilt over leaving the care of her child(ren) with another, result in more rewarding interaction patterns with children. It is not so much the *quantity* of time spent with children but the *quality* of the time that is important. It appears that the quality of that time is affected, to a great extent, by her morale on the job and her feelings relating to substitute child care.

3. Children of employed mothers are more likely than others to perform household tasks and assume responsibilities in the home. The children of employed and nonemployed mothers show no differences in academic achievement, or in evidence of maternal deprivation.

All in all, the effects of maternal employment on children are highly variable and, as with the marriage relationship, seem to depend on the circumstances of the individual situation.

Relatively little is known about the direct effects of the *father's* employment on the growth and development of children. Because society has traditionally defined the woman's role as being in the home and caring for her children, many research studies have focused on the consequences of deviating from that pattern; that is, the effects of the mother's outside employment on children. Because fathers employed outside the home are merely meeting the expectations of society, that is, that men should be gainfully employed and providing for their families' needs, researchers have been less intrigued by the effects of the father's employment on the children. However, the few studies that do exist have shown that the father's work outside of the home does impact on children.

Studies in the United States and Italy, for example, have shown that the type of work a father does has a direct effect on his child-rearing values and behavior (Kohn, 1969). Fathers in middle-class, white-collar occupations (teachers, businessmen, doctors, lawyers, and so on) are more likely than those in blue-collar, manual occupations to be self-directed and independent on the job. They work with people rather than things, face complex problems requiring creative thinking, and experience, daily, a variety of activities. Blue-collar fathers in manual occupations (custodians, construction workers, factory workers, and so on), in contrast, are more likely to be directly supervised by managers and foremen, to work with objects rather than people, and to experience routine activities that require less complex thought processes. Kohn's research provided convincing evidence that these varying work conditions translate directly into different parenting values and behavior for the middle-class and working-class fathers. Middle-class fathers, for example, were more likely to stress self-direction, independent and creative thinking, curiosity, and dependability in their children. Working-class fathers, on the other hand, stressed obedience to authority, conformity, cleanliness, and being able to defend oneself. Middle-class fathers were more likely to discipline their children's misbehavior based on the child's intent (did he or she break the window on purpose or accidentally?), whereas working-class fathers focused on the severity of the damage done (was it a big, expensive window, or a small, inexpensive one?). Hence, a father's experiences on the job appear to have, to some degree, an impact on the child's experiences in the family.

Dual-Career Marriages

As women have continued to attain higher levels of education and occupational status over the past several years, there has been a growing number of *dual-career marriages*. These represent a special type of dual-occupation marriage, in that *both* partners are involved in a career

line, complete with the pressures for promotion, professional development, and success (see pp. 229–231). Dual-career marriages have a somewhat unique set of gratifications, problems, and stresses, different from those of dual-job or single-provider marriages.

One of the unique features of the dual-career situation is that each partner is located near the high end of the income- and occupational-prestige spectrum. The stage is thereby set for competition and, possibly, conflict as a result of each partner's striving for success and status in his or her career. Husbands in particular may feel threatened by successful career wives who might be perceived as challenging their traditional position of power and dominance in marriage. However, the research evidence suggests that most dual-career couples are able to control any tendency toward competitiveness and conflict (Richardson, 1979). Only in those extreme cases, where career wives are highly achievement-oriented, and their husbands have been unusually successful in their careers relative to others at a comparable educational level, does evidence of competition and psychological stress seem to appear (Hornung and McCullough, 1981).

The stresses, strains, and problems of dual-career couples are related more to career pressures, time and energy demands, and marital roles that must be negotiated in the home, particularly if children are present. Rapoport and Rapoport (1971) identified five areas of strain characteristic of dual-career marriages.

1. *Role overload.* The strain here is the result of both partners managing the pressures of a career, seeking to produce on the job at a level which will result in professional development and promotions up the career ladder, and at the same time handling the domestic roles of housekeeping and child care. To cope with the strain of role overload, spouses must modify their expectations for spending free time together. Free time and leisure activities must be carefully mapped out in the long-range planning of dual-career couples; otherwise, *all* of their time will be consumed by work and domestic roles.

2. *Social stigma and the career wife.* Another source of strain is the negative reaction of friends and relatives that may be directed at a wife and mother who is committed to a career. Gender-role stereotypes also persist in the work place, meaning that career women

may encounter discriminatory attitudes and expectations from those with whom they work (see chapter 4). Some dual-career couples may also be criticized if they decide to remain permanently childless in order to devote their time fully to their careers and to their marriage (Veevers, 1980). To cope with the potential strain associated with negative social reaction to their situation, dual-career couples can choose to not associate with people who hold those views; view the reaction with humor; or select friends who share a similar lifestyle and value system.

3. *Personal identity and self-esteem.* The strain here is associated with self-doubt—wondering whether or not the right choices have been made. The woman might be concerned about her adequacy as a wife and mother, and the man might be concerned about his masculinity if he does more of the domestic housekeeping tasks than he cares to (Keith and Schaefer, 1980). Another concern relates to one partner or the other having to make sacrifices in his or her career, such as moving to a different city or town, in order to accommodate a career-oriented spouse.

4. *Social network dilemmas.* Dual-career spouses each develop a set of friends and colleagues on the job, and the two sets of friends are unlikely to overlap to any great extent. They have fewer ties to relatives than most couples, the result, primarily, of their social and geographic mobility, and because they tend to come from very small families. The strain is caused by meeting obligations to relatives, and from finding suitable friends for social activities, all in the very limited amount of leisure time allowed to dual-career couples.

5. *Dilemmas of multiple-role cycling.* There is a certain amount of strain involved in matching marriage and family roles with career roles so that there will be development in all role areas. The issue here is *timing* and *coordination* of major adult transition points: when and if to marry, and when and if to have children. Should both partners become established in a career prior to marriage? Prior to parenthood? Is it best to get one partner on his or her way in a career, to be followed by the other? If children are desired, is it best to have them *before* the wife becomes established in a career, or afterwards? These questions are quite important, and

we shall address them more thoroughly in chapters 9 through 13, when we examine the orchestration of critical transition points from one stage of the martial career to the next.

There are additional strains confronted by dual-career couples, most of which apply to *any* marriage in which both spouses are employed outside of the home. Finding suitable substitute child care; decision making when one partner is offered a promotion or better job situation in another city where the other may find it difficult to find employment; the compromises made regarding career advancement (usually by the wife) because of the demands of a home and children; and the time demands of the jobs, as well as conflicting work schedules of spouses, which limit their free time together, all contribute to the role strain and psychological stress experienced in dual-career marriages (Skinner, 1980; Hood and Golden, 1979; Keith and Schaefer, 1980).

Despite the role strain associated with the dual-career situation, many couples find effective methods of coping with the stress. Effective planning of time and leisure activities; flexibility and willingness to change plans according to the demands of the situation; effective communication; and compartmentalizing career and family roles (by leaving work and work-related problems at the office), are all effective coping strategies utilized by dual-career spouses (Skinner, 1980). Such couples can also lower their standards for housework and other home-related chores (i.e., not cleaning house as often or as thoroughly as they are accustomed to), or by hiring housecleaning help.

Summary

Economic factors play a major role in the development of marriage and family relationships. Families require an adequate level of income to provide the quality of life, the life chances, that allow them to thrive as independent units in our society. The level of income shapes a number of events in marriage and family life, including marriage, divorce, having children, and satisfaction with relationships between members. The primary means by which families acquire income is through the efforts husbands and wives in the occupational system, that is, their work outside the home. A growing number of families are finding that income contributions of both spouses are necessary to maintain the standard of living they are accustomed to having or to which they aspire. Recent changes in gender roles have facilitated the movement of women into the labor force, resulting in a new set of challenges and rewards, as well as stresses and strains, in marriage and family relationships. The decision of whether or not married women should work outside of the house is a complicated one, conditioned by many variables. There is little leeway in the decision of whether or not the husband will work, because the prevailing socialization patterns for both males and females continue to emphasize the expectation that the husband is a primary provider for his family. On the other hand, married women who must decide about work roles have many things to consider: their needs for fulfillment and satisfaction outside the home; financial necessity; and attitudes and expectations of their husbands. If there are children, decisions must take into consideration the number and ages of children, expectations and attitudes about substitute child care, and the cost and quality of available child-care alternatives. As societal norms have changed in favor of women working outside the home, particularly in higher-income and higher-status careers, making the decision to work has become somewhat easier, because women and mothers today are less concerned about "what others might think." Nonetheless, it remains a difficult, and important, decision for young families today. Whatever pattern of work is arranged for meeting the physical maintenance needs of the family unit, the "long arm of the job" reaches across family boundaries and influences relationships between married partners, as well as those between parents and children, over the years of the marital career.

Questions for Discussion and Review

1. What are your feelings about the social-stratification system and the resulting inequality among people? Should there be more income equality among people in our society? If so, why? How would it be accomplished? If not, why not?

2. What level of family income (per year) is necessary for a husband and wife, with no children present, to live comfortably today? How much income is necessary if they were to have two children? Six children? Would the children's ages make a difference? If so, in what ways?

3. Has the trend toward more mothers with children working outside the home had positive or negative effects on families? Explain your answer.

4. Should business and industry make good quality day-care centers available for the children of female employees? Should male employees have the same benefits for their children? What other steps might be taken in our society to assist working men and women with children to meet the demands of their jobs as well as the demands of parenthood?

5. Should we find some mechanism in our society to pay those who stay at home to handle the child care and housekeeping responsibilities? How would such an effort be accomplished (that is, who would pay)?

6. What steps can be taken by marriage partners to reduce the negative impact of job stresses and strains on the marriage relationship?

7. How do you feel about working wives earning more money, or having a higher-status job, than their husbands? Could you be satisfied with such a situation in your marriage?

PART III

Careers in Marriage and the Family

Love; gender roles; sexuality and family planning; communication and conflict management; and economic functioning are the major bases of marriage and family relationships. In Section III we will examine the ways in which each of these dimensions influences the development of marriage and family relationships over time, beginning with the formation and growth of the premarital relationship, continuing through the various stages when children are present, and ending with the marriage relationship among those in the later years of life. At times we will see a high degree of continuity from one stage of development to the next. At other times, sharp discontinuities and critical transition points will be noted. By placing the several basic dimensions of marriage and the family in the context of time, we will be better able to capture their changing nature than otherwise would be possible.

Life Before Marriage:

The Premarital Stage

Most people who enter marriage today do so with the hope and expectation that the relationship will be a happy and satisfying one that will last for many years. Although the phrase " 'til death do us part" is used far less frequently in the typical marriage ceremony today, the tacit understanding of a *lifetime commitment* to one another remains prominent in the minds of those who marry. Few people enter marriage today expecting divorce, or with the idea that "if it doesn't work out, we'll just get a divorce." Fewer than 5 percent of the 18-year-old respondents in one recent study said they thought it was unlikely that they would remain married to the same person for life (Thornton and Freedman, 1982).

Despite these most noble of intentions, however, there is a tremendous range and diversity of outcomes in marriage. Some partners realize considerable happiness and satisfaction with marriage, others extreme frustration and disappointment, and still others coexist in what are known as "empty shell marriages"—"ho-hum" relationships in which partners are neither satisfied nor dissatisfied. Marriage duration also varies widely; marriage can last anywhere from a few days, weeks, or months to fifty years or more.

The Importance of the Premarital Years

The significance of this diversity of outcomes in marriage relates directly to the topic of this chapter. The period of time before marriage gives shape and direction to how marriage relationships develop after the wedding ceremony. As individuals, we spend years learning role expectations for marriage as a result of our direct observations of other's marriages and our involvements with others of the opposite sex. We also spend this time developing the skills that will eventually contribute to our ability to realize success in marriage, such as communication, decision making, and problem-solving skills.

After we develop a relationship with the person who we will eventually marry, we establish *interaction habits* —patterns of relating to our partners—that will carry over into the marriage and influence the *quality* of the relationship in the future. These habits influence the degree to which the marriage will be satisfying and fulfilling, or dissatisfying and unfulfilling; whether the marriage will remain intact until it is terminated by the death of one of the partners, or whether it will be terminated by a divorce; whether the partners will consider the marriage to be a success, certain that they married the "right person," or whether the partners will define the marriage as a failure or "empty shell," and regret the day they married. In the years before marriage, the foundation is laid for subsequent development in marriage, because it is then that interaction patterns relating to decision making, problem solving, communication, and conflict management are established, and when attitudes and expectations relating to love and sexuality are formed. Although development in marriage is not *fully determined* during the premarital years, these years set the stage and influence the future course of development in the marriage relationship.

The premarital stage is important for the learning of interpersonal skills and role expectations that provide the basis for a longer term relationship in marriage. *(Photo by R. J. Hinkle.)*

Components of the Premarital Stage

The *premarital stage of development* includes all of the time that a person or a couple spend prior to marriage. It is the first stage of the marital career (see chapter 2), lasting until the vows and public commitment are made in the marriage ceremony.

The premarital stage of the marital career is composed of dating and courtship activities, preceded by a history of learning experiences during childhood. It is the premarital stage in which a person begins to make contacts and establish more or less initimate relationships with members of the opposite sex, known as *dating and courtship* activities. Because people in our culture rarely marry the first person they date, and indeed often have a variety of different dating partners and "steadies" on the path toward marriage, it is important to consider the important influences that our dating experiences have on the premarital relationship formed with the person we will eventually marry.

How We Are Socialized for Marriage

The United States is one of the most marrying societies in the world. Well over 90 percent of all American adults marry at least once, and among the more than two million people who divorce each year, about 80 percent will marry again, and will do so in a relatively few number of years (Glick, 1984a). To be so marriage-oriented and favorable in our attitudes toward the institution of marriage, there must be something in the developmental years of childhood, adolescence, and young adulthood that sparks our eagerness to marry. Indeed, research has shown that experiences during these stages of our lives give rise to our motivation to marry.

MARRIAGE ORIENTATION DURING CHILDHOOD

The process actually begins during childhood as we serve as "apprentices" in the parental family (Hill and Aldous, 1969). Whether they know it or not, parents socialize their children for marriage by providing a model of marriage that is observed by the child. Here the first seeds of marital-role expectations are planted as the child observes parents engaging in particular types of role behavior that may come to be viewed as the "correct" or "right" way for marriage partners to behave. How married adults display love and share intimacy; express irritations and resolve conflicts and differences; plan for the future; and make important decisions are just a few examples of role behavior in marriage which can be observed by their children. How a child perceives the parents' relationship with one another also influences the child's attitudes toward marriage and eventual motivation to marry. Children reared in a family where the parents' marriage is functioning effectively, where the parents are happy and well-adjusted in their marriage, and where the child enjoys the childhood experience, are more likely than others to develop a favorable evaluation of marriage (Hill and Aldous, 1969:891). Indeed, a study of more than 10,000 young men and women followed over a 14 year period (between 1966 and 1980) found that whether or not a young person marries at all depends, at least in part, on whether their own parents had experienced a divorce (Kobrin and Waite, 1984). This tendency was most noticeable for black males and white females, who were the most likely to remain single if their parents had divorced while the subjects were growing up.

However, there are limits to one's parents' marriage as a source of learning the motivation and skills for marriage. Parents are often quite limited in their own decision-making, problem-solving, and conflict-resolution abilities; and children usually have little or no practical "on-the-job" experiences that would allow them to practice marriage roles and to develop these abilities. In addition, parents provide only one model of a marriage relationship for their children, which may give the impression that there is only one way to manage in marriage. Finally, in single-parent families, no marital relationship exists, and the child in this situation will have no model of marriage to observe. In view of these circumstances, it is clear that other influences supplement the learning experienced in the parental family.

MARRIAGE ORIENTATION DURING ADOLESCENCE AND YOUNG ADULTHOOD

Young people also become oriented toward marriage because they live in a culture that promotes the idea that marriage is a desirable status. Marriage is viewed by most in our culture as an important goal because of the rewards that most people believe it yields.

The "Romantic Love Complex" and Motivation to Marry. One of the cultural influences on a person's eagerness to marry, for example, are norms emphasizing romantic love and attachment as the major basis for a lifetime commitment between a male and a female. This emphasis on romantic love and involvement (see chapter 3) promotes the desire to make the relationship with the other an exclusive one — "off limits" to those who might potentially attract the loved one. Marriage is the most convenient way, and the *only formalized and legally supported* way, of publicly announcing the romantic attachment each partner has for the other. Marriage is a desirable step in a culture which supports the idea of romantic involvement before and after the marriage ceremony, because of the measure of security and exclusivity it bestows on those who wish to continue in their intimate relationship for many years.

Research on young people in four different cultures has shown that the emphasis on romanticism in a culture is related to young people's motivation to marry (see Table 9.1) [Theodorson, 1968]. Young people in cultures valuing romantic love between men and women (such as the United States) are eager to be married someday. In those cultures where romantic love is less valued (such as in India), the motivation to marry is less intense.

Marriage-Like Experiences. Most people pass through a series of marriage-like experiences during

TABLE 9.1. *Romantic Norms and Eagerness to Marry in Four Cultures: United States, China, Burma, and India*

	Men		Women	
Culture	Average Romanticism Score	Percentage Who Want to Marry	Average Romanticism Score	Percentage Who Want to Marry
Americans	152	85.5%	144	94.4%
Chinese	92	86.9	68	80.5
Burmese	85	81.5	65	75.5
Indians	69	50.0	51	48.5

SOURCE: Theodorson (1968).

the teenage and young adult years which cement further their desire to marry, adding to their eagerness to assume marital roles. These experiences comprise a period of *anticipatory socialization* for the young person, who is actually internalizing the expectations, values, and attitudes related to marriage well before marriage ever takes place. Hill and Aldous (1969) identify some of these:

1. The *mass media* of television, movies, books, and magazines expose young people to many models of marriage, although, for dramatic emphasis and glamour, they often distort reality.

2. Observing the behavior of *same-sex friends* who become involved in dating and intimate relationships with others and who might provide provocative information about the rewards of becoming romantically involved with another of the opposite sex.

3. The *brother-sister relationship,* which "resembles the marriage relationship in its age symmetry, its solidity, its uncircumscribed nature, the propensity to share and support one another in periods of blues and trouble, . . . [and the] steady, sure source of companionship and predictability" (pp. 906–907). Sibling roles are quite similar to the roles a person will eventually adopt as a marriage partner, because in order to "maintain a viable relationship with the cross-sex sibling, [a person] uses many of the competences of empathy, judgment, and creativity, and the same mechanisms of face saving and compromise" required of married mates (p. 907).

4. *Dating experiences and "going steady"* also contribute to the young person's motivation to marry, and is a preparation for assuming the roles of a marriage partner. Dating and going steady provide the opportunity to develop and practice such interpersonal skills as communication, decision making, problem solving, and conflict resolution on a one-to-one basis with a person of the opposite sex, and to search for acceptable means of expressing one's affection for another person in physically intimate ways.

5. *Cohabitation,* or "living together" before marriage, is the marriage-like situation that brings the couple as close to marriage as possible without actually being married. "Living under the same roof" places the cohabiting couple in close proximity and forces them to work out an arrangement for handling household chores and responsibilities, such as cleaning, cooking, and child care, if children are present. Cohabitation usually involves sexual intimacy, which means that family planning measures will have to be taken if pregnancy is not desired.

Experiences such as these provide motivation for getting married and expectations as to what will happen after marriage. They also help to shape the individual's interpersonal skills and behavioral patterns, which will be carried into the marriage relationship. These skills and interaction patterns are known collectively as a person's *interaction habits.* They are forged with the interaction habits of one's eventual marriage partner to form a *system of interaction patterns,* giving shape and substance to the quality of the marriage in the years to come.

Patterns and Functions of Dating

All known societies in the world provide some legitimate means for young people to get together for the purpose of eventual marriage and childbearing. In the Western world, the custom of *dating* has emerged as the primary means for getting to know people of the opposite sex — learning how to relate to them comfortably, and eventually limiting the number of possible marriage choices to one person. For most people in our culture, the first step toward the marital career is taken when they go out on their first date. Indeed, first-time dating and going steady have been identified as ''the beginning of the end'' (Broderick, 1967).

Dating is a general term for describing a wide variety of activities and stages in the ''getting to know one another'' process. The forms and functions of dating in our society have changed dramatically over the course of the twentieth century, and the definitions and meanings that young people attach to dating activities today are quite different from those of years past. Before we take a closer look at the patterns and functions of our contemporary dating system, let us take a brief look at how two other cultures have allowed young men and women the opportunity to meet and come to know one another on the road to eventual marriage.

COURTSHIP IN OTHER CULTURES

The custom of dating is really an invention of the modern Western world, particularly in the United States and Canada. Dating practices as we know them are virtually unknown in some parts of the world, as the following descriptions of courtship in other cultures, provided by Queen and Habenstein (1974), demonstrate.

The Todas of India. The Todas are a small agricultural tribe who live in the mountainous regions of India. They practice a form of multiple-spouse marriage known as *fraternal polyandry,* in which a woman who marries a man also marries his brothers. Toda courtship often involves parents arranging the marriage of their sons and daughters while they are infants or young children. Once the parents of the prospective bride and groom have made the proper arrangements, the boy begins a series of visits to the girl's village, and, on one of the visits, offers a loincloth as a preliminary wedding gift. As he kneels before the girl's parents and her brothers, they touch his forehead with their feet. After several visits, the girl then either returns to the boy's home to live or work until they are wed, or she stays at home until she reaches puberty.

Twice each year, the boy presents the girl with a loincloth gift, until she is 10 years of age. Then, before she reaches puberty, a man from another clan visits the girl during the day. He lies down beside her and both are covered with a cloak for a brief time. Two weeks after this ceremony a young man (*not* the husband-to-be) visits the girl and has sexual intercourse with her. Finally, in one or two years after this *defloration ceremony,* the prospective groom goes, with his parents, to the girl's home, bringing small gifts. After feasting with the girl's parents, he returns to his home with her for the wedding ceremony.

The Baganda of Africa. The Baganda are a large agricultural tribe of about one million people, who reside in the country of Uganda. They are a *polygynous* culture, meaning that the preferred form of marriage is for a man to have two or more wives. Marriage usually occurs between the ages of 13 and 16, and the wife is usually inherited, received as a gift, or purchased by the husband and his family. Nevertheless, a specific courtship procedure must be followed if a marriage is to eventually take place.

The boy begins by contacting the girl's brother and paternal uncle (her father's brother) and making his intentions known. He then presents a small package of salt as a gift, which must be accepted by the girl and her parents. Then, as Queen and Habenstein (1974:80) describe it, a rather interesting courtship ceremony takes place:

The uncle and brother are brought several gourds of beer by the suitor who swears before some of his own relatives as witnesses he will make a good husband. The uncle asks the girl, ''Shall I drink?'' and if she replies, ''Drink,'' and he does so, the marriage is ratified and nothing can afterwards cancel the contract save the husband's consent and his acceptance of the return of the bride-price which he had paid for her. The uncle and brother then report to the parents that the marriage has been arranged and legitimated. All that remains is to settle the bride-price.

Members of the clan will arrange terms and conditions. The price usually involves a number of goats or a cow and several thousand cowrie shells—Baganda money—all of which usually total more than any young man or his parents have been able to accumulate. Thus there may well be a period of several months, or even a year, during which the groom is separated from the bride while he gathers the required amount.

The marriage ceremony is allowed to take place once the bride-price has been collected and distributed among the bride's relatives.

COURTSHIP AND DATING IN AMERICAN SOCIETY

At this point, the reader may be breathing a sigh of relief that our dating practices are as uncomplicated and sensible as they are, compared with the Todas and Baganda, with their elaborate customs and unusual ceremonies. Yet we must exercise caution here and avoid being *ethnocentric*. Ethnocentrism means believing that the practices and attitudes of our own culture are superior or intrinsically better than those of other cultures. Actually, the dating and courtship patterns of people in other cultures are very meaningful and rational *to them,* given their own views about reality, the nature of the world, and their religious beliefs. A most important point is that their courtship customs are such that they satisfy the society's goals for encouraging marriages among their young people. Certainly, our own dating and courtship customs must appear to those in other cultures to be just as odd and awkward to them as theirs might be to us. In many ways, our dating practices and patterns may actually defeat the purposes for which many believe they exist: to prepare us to assume the roles of a married person with confidence and competence, and to select a compatible mate with whom a successful marriage relationship can be developed.

A Brief History of Dating in the United States. Dating practices as we know them today are really a twentieth century innovation. Even during this century, dating behavior and the very meaning of the

phrase "to date" have changed quite dramatically. Prior to the early 1900s, the characteristic means by which young men and women met, got to know each other, and developed intimate premarital relationships that might eventuate in marriage were quite different from those of the 1980s.

The earliest settlers in North America were escaping religious persecution and social oppression in Europe. As a result, during the seventeenth, eighteenth, and early nineteenth centuries, Americans had developed an individualistic ethic, evident in our democratic institutions and system of self-governance. There existed a real desire to move away from the "establishment" European norms that had caused these people to migrate in the first place (Reiss, 1980). European norms governing family behavior in general, and dating and courtship in particular, were viewed as part of this established order. Americans therefore developed courtship practices that were more a reflection of their individualistic values.

In Europe, marriages were typically *arranged by parents,* and little emphasis was placed on romantic attachment or even compatibility between the marriage partners. Arranged-marriage practices in Europe and other cultures around the world thrived as parents maintained nearly complete control over their children's behavior (sexual or otherwise) and marital destinies. Arranged-marriage provided for the merging of wealth, property, and other family assets in order to consolidate family economic power and to ensure the continued economic growth of the family.

The individualistic ethic developed in America, however, rejected the idea that parents should arrange the marriages of their children. Historical studies show that only a small minority of American marriages were ever parentally arranged. These were concentrated among the wealthiest aristocratic families, who stood to gain from the expansion of their financial empires through marriage of their children (Furstenberg, 1966). Compared with the system of parentally arranged marriages found in Europe and most other cultures around the world at the time, American courtship was much more *autonomous* and *participant-run,* with considerably more freedom from parental control (Reiss, 1980).

Nonetheless, parents in past centuries did exercise more control than is the case today. Young men and women often met under far more formal circumstances, usually through church or other family-related functions.

They had to be introduced to each other, either by a mutual friend or by their respective parents. Although parents had no formal or legal control over their children's choice of partners, most maintained a considerable degree of influence, or even veto power, over who a young boy or girl might be seeing or considering for marriage. The same concerns for social prestige, economic status, education, and quality of the family line, which were so important in arranged-marriage systems, persisted even in our more autonomous courtship institution. The use of *chaperones* was common throughout this period — adults, or possibly older siblings, who would be present whenever the young couple was engaged in such courtship activities as dances, dinners, or other social functions — to assure that no precocious sexual hanky-panky took place.[1] In this way, parents could exercise their control without actually having to be present, and the couple was rarely alone long enough to engage in any significant amount of sex play. This is not to say that all couples were virtuously chaste. The illegitimate birth records of the times suggest that couples did find ways to be alone, and that sexual indiscretions did take place. However, such activities were made more difficult than in contemporary society.

From Chaperone to Steady Dating.

By the late nineteenth and early twentieth centuries, the previous level of parental vigilance and involvement in the courtship practices of their children had subsided to a great extent. A new pattern of meeting and getting to know members of the opposite sex emerged: *dating*. Attitudes toward male-female contacts before marriage become more casual. The invention of the automobile and telephone provided the means for more frequent and casual contacts between boy and girl, out of the range of parents' watchful eyes. The growth in the number of women working outside of the home and enrolling in colleges and universities provided more opportunities for such contacts.

Dating differed from the courtship practices of previous times in several key respects (Saxton, 1980). Dates were arranged by the couple, not by their parents, and a date signaled nothing more than an interest on the part of both the man and woman in having fun with each other for the duration of the date. There was no need for the dating partners to know each other well, and certainly no commitment to continue seeing each other, or to maintain the relationship after the date was over. Perhaps most important, however, is the relatively high level of freedom from parental supervision that dating afforded the young couple. This was the result, primarily, of the invention, development, and popularity of the automobile, and to the number and variety of places to go on dates in our modern cities — parties, dances, concerts, movies, and restaurants. Or, one could drive to the beach, or simply park in the moonlight.

FEATURE 9.1 Rating and Dating in the 1930s and 1940s

Even in the 1930s, casual dating had its competitive aspects. A classic example of this is the *rating-and-dating complex* described by Waller (1937), and later by Waller and Hall (1951). By the early 1930s, dating had caught on as the most popular form of meeting opposite-sex others and enjoying recreational activities together, particularly on the college campus. According to Waller, who observed dating behavior on the campus of Penn State University, dating at that time functioned much more as a form of sexual dalliance and fun-seeking than as a means of finding and selecting a future marriage partner. Dating activities followed a predictable pattern that Waller termed "rating-and-dating," a pattern which to Waller served no useful function as far as "true courtship" and mate selection were concerned. Rating-and-dating only functioned to reassert one's status and prestige among the campus student body and to have fun.

Fraternities, sororities, and athletic activities formed the basis for achieving status on the college campus of the 1930s and 1940s, perhaps more so than today. A class-system developed among the male college students, with the highest ranking fraternities having the most members in honorary societies and important campus activities, but most importantly, having the greatest number of players on the football team. For the college co-ed, the most important characteristics of a date were his belonging to a fraternity with a high prestige ranking, having good clothes, being a smooth conversationalist (i.e., having a good "line"), being a good dancer, and most importantly, being considered a popular date by others. A college girl's prestige on the campus thereby depended on the class of her date, and those with all of the desirable characteristics were considered to be in what Waller termed *Class A.*

> Young men are desirable dates according to their rating on the scale of campus values. In order to have Class A rating, they must belong to one of the better fraternities, be prominent in activities (of which some carry vastly more prestige than others), have a copious supply of spending money, be well-dressed, and have access to an automobile. The fraternity membership is particularly important . . . It should be remembered that students on this campus are extremely conscious of these social distinctions and of their own position in the social hierarchy. In speaking of another student, they say, "He rates," or "He doesn't rate," and they extend themselves enormously in order that they may rate, or *seem to rate*. (Waller and Hill, 1951:152, *emphasis added*.)

Those men who did not rate in Class A were placed lower in the campus class system, according to their position on the cluster of dating characteristics — Class B, Class C, and Class D men. The rating-and-dating system meant that Class A boys dated Class A girls, Class B boys dated Class B girls, and so on.

In order to establish and maintain a high prestige rating, the college co-ed had to at least "give the impression of being much sought after," even if she did not actually possess the characteristics of a Class A girl.

It has been reported by many observers that a girl who is called to the telephone in the dormitories will often allow herself to be called several times, in order to give all the other girls the opportunity to hear her paged. Coeds who win campus prestige must never be available for last minute dates; they must avoid being seen too often with the same boy, in order that others may not be frightened away or discouraged; they must be seen when they go out and must have many partners at the dances . . . and, above all, the co-ed who wishes to retain Class A standing must consistently date Class A men. (Waller and Hill, 1951:153)

To Waller, this type of competitive casual dating system was materialistic, hedonistic, and exploitative. It served no useful purpose as far as making a wise selection of a marriage partner. "Serious dating and true courtship," Waller believed, were based more on concerns about family background, companionship, honesty, and friendly personality traits.

Since the time Waller made his observations of the rating-and-dating system, several research studies have been conducted in order to verify the presence of such a system on other campuses. Studies in the 1940s found it to be present (University of New Hampshire, Iowa State University, and University of Wisconsin), and those in the 1950s and 1960s found it to be present, but only a minor influence on the campus dating scene (Purdue University, University of Michigan, and again at Penn State).

More recent evidence suggests that rating people on some type of college class-hierarchy, for the purpose of determining dating desirability, continues to exist (Krain, Cannon, and Bagford, 1977), but in a much watered-down form. This "status grading and status-achieving" function of dating, therefore, appears to have been a far more prevalent feature of the dating system several decades ago than it is today (Gordon, 1981).

By the 1930s, a pattern of dating-based courtship emerged that was to expand through the 1940s, 1950s, and into the 1960s. Beginning at some point in adolescence, young people began to follow a pattern of "playing the field," by casually dating a variety of partners through the high school years, and gradually narrowing down the field to a few special others by "going steady." Whereas the purpose of casual dating most typically was limited to having fun by enjoying the companionship of another in an activity that both partners enjoyed (such as a movie, a dance, or dinner at a restaurant), going steady was a more serious form of dating that implied a certain degree of commitment and exclusivity in the relationship. Going steady meant that a special bond of affection and attachment existed between the partners, and was not to be shared with others. A mutual understanding developed among the two partners, such that dating with others would constitute a breach of their "contract" to go steady; and the desire to date others would provide adequate grounds for terminating the steady relationship. As with casual dating, in no way did going steady imply a commitment to become engaged or married. A person could thereby enjoy steady dating relationships with a variety of partners (at different times, of course), enjoying the relatively exclusive and secure feeling it provided on the path to a more serious and committed kind of relationship, one that might eventuate in marriage.

From "Steady Dating" to "Going Together."   This pattern of courtship, based upon *casual dating* followed by a more serious and committed form of *steady dating,* has persisted in a somewhat modified form through the 1970s and into the 1980s. However, noticeable changes have occurred in the ways that young people usually make initial contacts with each other and proceed to get to know each other better — possibly on the road to a more serious type of dating relationship, or even marriage. A spin-off of the traditional dating system has evolved in the recent past. *Casual group dating* (Reiss, 1980), *hanging around* (Libby, 1977), *getting together* (Melville, 1980; Cox, 1978), and *going out* (Reiss, 1980) are all labels that have been applied to contemporary dating patterns. This pattern is less structured than in previous years, and focuses more on activities with groups of males and females who may or may not be paired-off when the get-together is initially arranged (Murstein, 1980). Of course, this means a less formal concentration on the exclusive one-to-one relationship of a *couple,* at least at the initial contact and "getting to know you" stages of premarital relationship development.

There is little doubt that the traditional "date" in which the male picked up the female at her house at an arranged time, wined and dined her at his expense, and returned her to her residence at an arranged time is rapidly

disappearing. In high schools and colleges, according to informal reports by students, they tend to congregate in groups from which the majority gradually evolve into pairs, although retaining some allegiance to the group. There is less structure as to appropriate male-female behavior, expenses are "dutch treat," and highly structured dating protocol has largely disappeared. (Murstein, 1980:780)

The changing gender roles in our society also mean that females are freer to take the initiative in dating, by telephoning the male to ask him to "go out," by paying for some or all of the expenses of the date, or by asking him to dance at a party or a bar. According to Melville (1980:79–80):

it used to be improper for a young woman to call a male friend and arrange a get-together, but this is a common occurrence today. Whereas a date used to consist of a special occasion planned by the male, with an invitation made days in advance, getting together is a more casual matter. It is common for young people to congregate at parties or movies, perhaps to pair off during the evening.

The process of making contacts with others of the opposite sex today is far more informal and casual than it used to be. It is also more autonomous and free of parental direction than ever, because of the informality of meeting and possibly pairing off in groups of males and females who "get together" at a party, movie, or the beach. Nonetheless, the modified dating system in existence today continues to serve important functions in the overall courtship and mate-selection processes.

THE FUNCTIONS OF DATING

Dating is an integral part of a person's premarital experiences, promoting the "getting together" and "getting to know one another" experiences which are so critical in the process of developing intimate relationships with members of the opposite sex. Dating, then, serves an important function in the process of choosing a marriage partner (Blood and Blood, 1978; Bell, 1979; Winch, 1962). Dating can also serve functions in addition to the selection of a mate.

1. Dating activities of any kind — whether they are casual, with a variety of dating partners, steady dating relationships, or just getting together and pairing off in groups of friends — contribute to a person's *motivation*

to either marry or remain single. In addition, a person's expectations of marriage, and the eventual marriage partner, are influenced by dating experiences.

2. Dating functions as a popular form of *fun and recreation,* and thereby is an end in itself, with no obligation for future interaction among the dating participants.

3. Dating has a *status-achieving function*. A person seeks to gain recognition from one's friends, and prestige by dating those with such desirable characteristics as good looks, a popular personality, money, or a nice car. Dating a person one's friends would like to date if they could is especially rewarding because of the envy it inspires.

4. As mentioned earlier in this chapter, dating has a *socialization function.* It allows young people an opportunity to develop and practice the interpersonal skills important for relating to a member of the opposite sex. Although dating experiences are limited in the learning they provide, they do function to eliminate some of the "mystery" about members of the opposite sex (Winch, 1962). Dating also allows a person to associate with a variety of personality types, and to see how others react to one's own personality characteristics. The kind of person with whom one tends to get along—whether they are talkative and with an active sense of humor; quiet and pensive; domineering or submissive; oriented toward an active, athletic life-style; or physically reserved and intellectual—is the kind of person who will

FEATURE 9.2

"WELL, LET ME SEE WHAT WE HAVE HERE..."

contribute to one's comfort and security in a longer term intimate relationship such as marriage. In other words, dating functions *to promote the wise choice of a marriage partner.*

PATTERNS OF DATING TODAY

Desirable Qualities of a Date.

Research indicates that *what a person looks for in a dating partner can differ significantly from what that same person would look for in a marriage partner.* For example, a survey of more than 1,100 college students asked the respondents to name three qualities they considered to be most important for a date, and then to name three qualities considered most important for a spouse (see Table 9.2). Such *extrinsic* characteristics as physical attractiveness, sense of humor, and being fun and conversational are the more important qualities for a date, and such *intrinsic* qualities as being loving and affectionate, honest, ambitious, and loyal are the more desirable characteristics of a spouse. This pattern was found for both males and females. This evidence suggests that young people tend to look for somewhat different qualities in a date than in a spouse, a fact that may hinder the selection of a compatible marriage partner.

Dating Activities.

As mentioned earlier, the range of possible activities available to dating partners has expanded tremendously as we have become a more urbanized and technologically advanced society. Movies, restaurants, sporting events, and social gatherings are only a few of the many possible activities from which dating partners can choose. Also, the use of such recreational drugs as alcohol and marijuana have become more commonplace among dating partners of all ages. Knox and Wilson (1981), for example, found that more than half of the 334 college students they surveyed in North Carolina consumed alcohol on their last date, and nearly one in four reported having smoked marijuana on their last date.

The freedom our culture grants to dating participants also makes sexual intimacy a central concern among most dating partners. As we shall see later in this chapter, premarital sexual intercourse rates among both adolescents and college-age youth have increased over the past several years. Hence, the issue of how sexually intimate one should become with one's date is an important one for many dating couples. The issue of sexual intimacy on a date is closely tied to gender-role prescriptions in our society. Because of gender-role expectations, the male is encouraged to move as far as he can on the path of increasing sexual intimacy — from kissing to petting and caressing, and eventually to sexual intercourse — if the opportunity should present itself. But the female is encouraged to

TABLE 9.2. *Rank Order of Desirable Qualities in a Date and in a Spouse for 1,134 College Students*

Most Important Qualities of a Date	*Most Important Qualities of a Spouse*
1. Physical Attractiveness	1. Loving and Affectionate
2. Congenial Personality	2. Honest
3. Sense of Humor	3. Congenial Personality
4. Intelligence	4. Respectful
5. Manners/Being Considerate	5. Intelligent
6. Sincere, Genuine	6. Mature/Responsible
7. Compatible Interests	7. Ambitious
8. Conversational Ability	8. Loyal and Trustworthy
9. Fun to Be With	9. Physical Attractiveness

SOURCE: Unpublished Survey of University of Arizona Students, 1976–1982.

TABLE 9.3. *Percentage of 227 Women and 107 Men University Students Indicating Appropriateness of Various Sexual Behaviors, by Number of Dates*

Sexual Behavior	Number of Dates						
	0	1	2	3	4	5	6 or more
Kissing	W = 14%	W = 55%	W = 23%	W = 6%			
	M = 14%	M = 69%	M = 14%	M = 1%			
Petting	W = 3%	W = 4%	W = 5%	W = 9%	W = 3%	W = 15%	W = 58%
	M = 12%	M = 19%	M = 13%	M = 7%	M = 11%	M = 15%	M = 22%
Intercourse	W = 8%	W = 4%	W = 1%	W = 1%	W = 1%	W = 8%	W = 69%
	M = 8%	M = 11%	M = 9%	M = 8%	M = 2%	M = 10%	M = 52%

(M = Men; W = Women)

SOURCE: Knox and Wilson (1981).

only gradually move down this path, without discouraging her male partner altogether.

Knox and Wilson's (1981) survey of 334 university students provides evidence that such a gender-role pattern exists in college-age dating activities. Asked how many dates with a particular person it would take before kissing, petting (hands placed anywhere), and sexual intercourse would be appropriate, these students gave the responses summarized in Table 9.3. The differences between the sexual norms of college men and women are readily seen in the petting and intercourse comparisons. More than three-fourths (77 percent) of the men stated that petting (hands anywhere) is appropriate by the fifth date, but nearly three-fourths (75 percent) of the women stated that petting should be *delayed* until after the fourth date. Indeed, nearly one-third (31 percent) of the men stated that petting is appropriate *on or before the first date!* In regard to sexual intercourse, men again expressed an interest in sexual intimacy earlier in the dating relationship. Nearly one-half (48 percent) of the men, but only one-fourth (23 percent) of the women, stated that sexual intercourse was appropriate by the fifth date.

Dating As a Progression of Stages. Dating practices in our culture proceed through a series of stages as the individual moves through adolescence and into early adulthood. There is a process of narrowing-down the field of eligible and desirable dating partners.

The process of dating tends to move from dating *extensity* to dating *intensity* (Blood and Blood, 1978). A young person typically begins by casually dating an extensive number of partners, in order to "play the field," and along the way develops more intensive and serious relationships with one or a few particularly attractive others with whom special feelings of exclusivity, affection, and commitment are shared. Some time during the high school years, but often later, one of these "going steady" relationships progresses through more advanced stages of courtship as the partners come to believe that they are "in love" and that this person is the "right one" for marriage. Engagement would be the next step in the courtship process, and then, if all went satisfactorily during the engagement period, marriage between the partners would follow (see Figure 9.1).

DATING-RELATED PROBLEMS IN PREMARITAL-RELATIONSHIP DEVELOPMENT

There are a number of problems that can hinder one of the basic goals of dating held by many: to meet another person with whom one can develop a strong and compatible interpersonal relationship that might eventuate in a successful marriage. These problems are the result of having a courtship system that is based on the individual's

The progression of dating relationships today is one of moving from extensity, or playing the field, to the intensity of an exclusive relationship with one person.   *(Photo by Stephen R. Jorgensen.)*

freedom to control his or her dating activities. The problems are made even more complicated because dating, and then making a wise choice of a marriage partner, are confounded by our *romantic-love complex* (see chapter 3). Romantic love has the potential to blind one to the realities of another's personality, and to the meaning of another's behavior in an intimate relationship. We will now look at two distinct, yet closely related, problems associated with our dating customs.

Personal Dating Objectives.   At any stage of one's dating activities — during the early adolescent, high school, or college-age years — the personal goals of the dating partners may be quite different. Recall the discussion on dating functions: one person might be seeking to achieve status or prestige in the eyes of peers, but the other might be hoping to develop a close relationship, one that moves along a normal course of increasing sexual intimacy. Others date solely to have fun, to enjoy the companionship of another but with no intention of be-

coming "involved"; but those they date may seek and expect full sexual relations on the first or second date, without first developing an emotional attachment or falling in love (Knox and Wilson, 1981). Still others date with an eye toward selecting a marriage partner. Whatever the combination of different dating objectives might be, misunderstandings, conflicts, and broken relationships between dating partners can occur once the discrepancy in dating goals surfaces.

At the heart of many conflicts in dating objectives are the twin problems of *deception* and *exploitation*. The intentions of dating partners often revolve around the control and direction of sexual activities. Deception and exploitation enter as dating becomes a sort of game, where strategy, move-countermove, and cunning determine who in the dating relationship, male or female, will reach their dating goals. More than three decades ago, for example, Waller and Hill (1951) recognized the usefulness to the male of the *line*. In trying to win her affection, and possibly progress to advanced levels of sexual play with her, the

FIGURE 9.1.   Stages of Dating: Seriousness and Range of Partners.

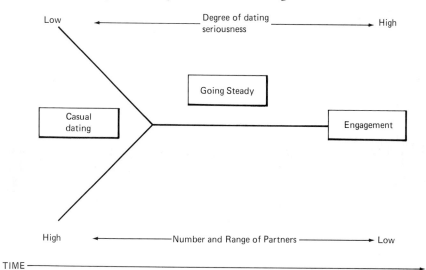

male hands the female a "line," telling her "how beautiful, charming, and possessed of incomparable graces she is."

The "line" is often a first step toward exploitation. The young man does not, of course, suppose that the girl will take what he says altogether seriously; and if she does he will probably be frightened away. But if she does take him seriously, interesting possibilities are suggested. And in any case, the "line" enables him to talk interestingly and is an effective device for covering up his own embarrassment and shyness and passing himself off as a man of experience. The "line" has a further function of covering up a real emotional involvement by exaggeration. Both sexes use the "line," although conventionally the man takes the initiative. (Waller and Hill, 1951:184)

The "line" continues to be an important weapon in the dating arsenal of some today. As we mentioned, males and females continue to have somewhat different ideas of how fast one should move up the ladder of sexual intimacy in dating relationships (Knox and Wilson, 1981; see Table 9.3). The "line" comes in handy for those who wish to move faster than their dating partners, gaining sexual pleasures at the other's expense, provided that the partner is willing to "buy" the line or is genuinely deceived by it.

Deception in dating relationships also occurs when partners play stereotyped roles that they really do not endorse. Many people in the dating system wear "masks," concealing their true identities and personalities in order to impress others by behaving in a way they *think* meets with the other's expectations. Many males behave in traditionally masculine ways — being dominant, sexually and socially aggressive, and not expressive of genuine feelings and sentiments — in order to impress a female, even though the males may, *"beneath the surface,"* embrace less traditional role expectations. Females may also play the traditional role — the submissive, nurturant, and emotionally expressive woman, when they really *wish to be* more assertive and decisive in their relationships with men. The opposite patterns are also possible: females and males who are truly traditional (beneath the surface) pretend to be modern and egalitarian in their behavior with others because that is what they believe is expected of them. These are patterns of relating called *pluralistic ignorance:* each partner pretends to be something they are not, in order to "be" what they believe the other expects them to be.

The propensity of people to employ deception and exploitation in dating promotes *superficiality* in relationship development. The dangers here are twofold. First, those who wear an "identity mask" (play stereotyped gender roles) may miss developing a relationship with a person who is highly compatible. Second, wearing masks prevents both partners from delving beneath the surface of the other's personality. Delving is necessary, if genuine attempts to develop communication and other interpersonal skills are to be initiated *prior* to an eventual marriage. Although dating experiences can provide opportunities for practicing interpersonal skills, in reality the practice sessions may turn out to be quite poor because neither person's true personality is revealed, nor are one's role expectations about behavior in an intimate relationship made apparent to the other.

Gender-Role Conflicts.

The traditional dating pattern is modeled after twelfth century values on "courtly love" (see chapter 3). This pattern closely follows traditional gender-role scripts: the male takes the initiative in contacting the female, asking her out for a date, picking her up, opening every door for her, paying for her meal or movie ticket, asking her to dance with him, initiating any sexual advances, and going as far on the kissing-petting-intercourse spectrum as the female will allow him to go. The female, in this pattern, is truly "wooed and courted," as the male strives to win the female's affection and commitment.

However, in the context of changing gender roles in our society over the past two decades (see chapter 4), role expectations in premarital relationships have become less scripted and, consequently, more ambiguous. A survey conducted over a six-year period found a watered-down pattern of male dominance in dating patterns (see Table 9.4). Although male initiative in dating is no longer the preferred pattern, more than one in four males *and* females still prefer this tradition. Fewer than 1 percent stated that females should take the lead in dating activities. The majority of respondents expressed a preference for *both* dating partners to take initiatives in dating activities.[2] That is, females should also be expected to ask the male to dance, ask him for a date, pay for his evening, initiate

sexual activities, and take other dating initiatives traditionally prescribed for the male.

One potential problem created by this shift toward equality in initiative-taking is that young people today may be uncertain about who has responsibilities in the relationship, and this might possibly create misunderstanding and conflict. One person may subscribe to the traditional pattern of male initiative, but the other is more oriented toward gender *equality*. In the eyes of more traditional men and women, females asking males to dance or offering to pay for a dinner may create the impression that she is "fast," "easy," or "overly aggressive." She may scare off more tradition-oriented males with whom she may be trying to initiate a casual, or possibly a dating, relationship if she decides to take the initiative. Some males actually feel threatened by women who assume this posture, and will seek women who share their traditional point of view but will avoid those who "come on too strong."

However, the increased emphasis on initiative-sharing is welcomed by many contemporary males. The fear of being rejected is a serious problem, in their eyes, and consequently they may be reluctant to initiate contacts or otherwise develop intimate relationships with women. The more contemporary pattern of sharing the initiative means that men now find themselves in the position of either accepting or rejecting the advances of *females,* rather than always running the risk of being rejected themselves. Men may be flattered, not threatened, by the attention they receive from women who take the lead in dating activities. Initiative-sharing is also a welcome feature of premarital relationships for many young women, because they are no longer forced by traditional role prescriptions to wait for interested males to call for a date or to initiate a conversation at a dance or party. Hence, the modern norm on sharing the initiative in dating activities can actually work to the advantage of many, despite the potential for role confusion.

TABLE 9.4. *"Who Should Take the Initiative in Dating,"* *According to 1,134 Undergraduate Students, 1976–1982*

Male	27.0%
Female	00.5%
Both	72.5%

SOURCE: Unpublished Survey of University of Arizona Students, 1976–1982.

ALTERNATIVES TO STANDARD DATING PRACTICES

In view of the potential problems associated with contemporary dating practices just discussed, a variety of modern alternatives to standard dating practices have been developed (Jedlicka, 1980). One of these involves a most important twentieth century invention: the *computer*.

Computer dating services have been developed to bring a higher degree of scientific accuracy to the marriage-partner-selection process than might otherwise be possible in the random dating system. Computer dating services require that their members supply a volume of information about themselves so that a compatible match can be arranged. Occupation, religion, age, education, race, ethnicity, height, weight, history of previous marriages, personality traits, selected attitudes, interests, hobbies, and values are all part of a large volume of data that members provide to the computer (for a *fee,* of course!) [Wallace, 1959]. The computer then searches for the most compatible pairs among the male and female records that have been entered, and "matches" those individuals with the greatest "fit."

However, it must be noted that computer-generated compatibility ratings are based upon what are believed to be the most important variables for predicting a successful relationship both before and after marriage. Unfortunately, our ability to predict the future of relationship success (or failure) in this way — by examining cultural background characteristics, attitudes, and values — is still in a primitive stage (Spanier and Lewis, 1980). It is extremely difficult to predict with any significant degree of accuracy whether or not two individuals matched by a computer will realize happiness and success in a long-term relationship such as marriage. Computer match-ups, therefore, are great for getting dating partners together, but they have limited utility in locating male and female couples who will "make it" in longer term relationships or marriage (Jedlicka, 1980).

So long as we continue to develop increasingly sophisticated technology, inventors will continue to develop novel ways of getting people together in hopes of forging compatible matches (see Feature 9.3). More modern techniques include the use of videotape libraries. A member of

FEATURE 9.3 Miniature Matchmaker Gives Odds for Happiness

PHOENIX — Some people spend a lifetime getting to know each other. For Ed White, seven seconds is long enough.

His gimmick is Alter Ego, a computer jammed into a plastic pendant half the size of a match book. For $74.95 two people can clasp their computers together for seven seconds and come up with a lighted-dial readout of the odds for a compatible relationship.

"It was partly inspiration, but it began in my college days," and White, an engineer who founded Bowmar Instrument Corp. in Fort Wayne, Ind., and developed the first hand-held calculator. So far, he has sunk $250,000 into his plastic matchmaker.

"It takes so much time and energy to get acquainted," said White. "I've often wished people would go around with a number on their belt or something."

Alter Ego is programmed by punching a tiny stylus into four numbered holes, recording answers to 96 attitude questions. Topics range from "falling in love" to sexual arousal, disciplining children, table manners, religion, astrology and careers.

C. M. Whipple, professor of psychology at Central State University in Edmund, Okla., developed the questionnaire as "an effective way of calculating your chances for a compatible relationship." He also said it "shows where the difficulties in a relationship are most likely to occur."

Instead of using the "What's your sign?" approach, people should ask, "Where's your Alter Ego?," White said.

Endorsed by Dr. Joyce Brothers, Alter Ego is made by Arizona Digital Corp. and marketed in department and computer stores in Phoenix with plans for sales in California.

"It's too early to guarantee a blissful relationship because of a high score on the computer's tiny light-up dial," White said.

"But it's a great interaction thing," he said.

SOURCE: Mike McCloy, *Arizona Daily Star,* August 20, 1979.

the dating service has a videotaped interview and casual conversation, which is placed on file along with a one-page autobiography (profile) and a still photograph. In one of the largest of such videotape dating services, Great Expectations (based in California), each of the more than six thousand members can read the various files of opposite-sex members and select certain videotapes for viewing (*Parade,* May 18, 1980a). Arrangements to meet are made after the male and female have seen each other's videotapes, and like what they have seen.

Another method of making initial contacts prior to dating appears to be gaining in popularity: the use of newspaper and magazine advertisements (Cameron, Oskamp, and Sparks, 1977; Murstein, 1980; Bolig, Stein, and McKenry, 1984). The research of Cameron, et al. (1977) on personal ads in singles newspapers found a pattern of self-advertising, which they labeled a "heterosexual stock market," because advertisers "seek to strike bargains which maximize their rewards in the exchange of assets (28)." The more recent research of Bolig, et al. (1984) found that both men and women who place ads in singles magazines seek responses from those who are physically attractive and who have desirable personality characteristics (warm, honest, open-minded, sensitive, and with a sense of humor). In exchange, these "profilers" offered attractiveness, intelligence, education, and career rewards. The only notable difference between male and female profilers was age preference: males preferred younger women, while females preferred older males. Readers of the ads are able to "comparison shop" and make "offers and bids" among the various available alternatives (as in the stock market) [see Feature 9.4]. Whether or not such advertising yields a percentage of "successful" dating or marriage relationships, beyond that afforded by more conventional dating practices, is as yet undetermined by social science research.

Sex Before Marriage: Trends in Attitudes, Behavior, and Consequences

Throughout the preceding discussion of dating stages and problems, references were made to a major concern of most, if not all, young people in dating activi-

ties: *the control of sexual interaction between the partners.* Throughout our history, young people have been confronted by the moral, social, and religious issues relating to premarital sexual relationships: Should I have sexual intercourse? How far can I go sexually before I have done something wrong? What difference will it make if I have sex before marriage? Are there certain conditions under which sex before marriage is all right? These questions are made all the more important by certain negative consequences that are attached to premarital sexual intercourse, some of which are the result of societal norms regarding this behavior: guilt and anxiety, accusations of immoral behavior, unwanted premarital pregnancy, venereal disease, and exploitation of one partner by the other.

Despite the warnings about the dangers of premarital sexual involvement, young people are presented with a seemingly contradictory message — that sex is a beautiful experience and the most important sign of one person's love for another. It is no wonder, therefore, that many teenagers and young adults have developed a highly ambivalent attitude about sex before marriage. Advertisers of perfume, toothpaste, clothing, shaving cream, and even automobiles tell everyone, married or not, to be "sexy, seductive, and stimulating," at the same time that others decry sex between unmarried persons as "dirty," "bad," or "sinful."

PREMARITAL SEXUAL STANDARDS: NORMS AND BEHAVIOR TODAY

The research on premarital sex focuses on two distinct, yet related, areas: premarital sexual *norms* and premarital sexual *behavior.* Norms are the sexual standards, or code, to which people subscribe and which dictate what kinds of sexual behavior are considered *acceptable.* Norms, as defined in chapter 2, constitute the *guides* for behavior — the "should's" and the "ought to's" that shape our beliefs about what is right and wrong in our behavior. Studies of premarital sexual *behavior,* on the other hand, focus on what people *actually do,* which may or may not coincide with what their norms indicate is acceptable.

Premarital Sexual Norms. At one time, it was thought that chastity in the form of abstinence from any form of serious sex play before marriage was the single

WANTED:
Divorced, white female, 37, seeks prosperous, compassionate, stable, educated, financially secure man. Must be handsome and into children, cuddling by the fire, sharing, togetherness, skiing, and sailing. Ages 30–45 preferred. Reply to Box 4132, xxxxxxx.

WANTED:
Single, black female, 5'7", 120 lbs., and 32 beautiful years old desires secure relationship with older man who is sensitive, caring, and does not smoke. I love horseback riding, beaches, tennis, honesty, and independence. Send photo and reply, only if you dare, to Box 470, xxxxx.

WANTED:
Can you believe that a single white male, 28, blond, and handsome as Tom Selleck is available today for a lasting relationship? I am shy and sensitive, but also dominating and extroverted at the right times. I love photography, ballet, fine restaurants, and penthouses on the 48th floor. I am looking for warm, well-built, attractive non-smoking female, 29–35, who wants to share in my fantasy for play, romance, travel, and outdoor frolicking. Send photo and reply to Box 212, xxxxx.

WANTED:
Single black male, 42, has craving for older black female (45–50) who can cook, take care of my 7 bedroom villa in the Bahamas, and be my companion for a long time. Marriage is a distinct possibility for the right woman. I am caring, generous, well-bred, strong, muscular, athletic, handsome, and

built for comfort, not speed. No children. The right woman must be vulnerable, gorgeous, competent, intelligent, and not hung-up on sexual inhibitions. Come play with me. Reply with photo to Box 2799, xxxxx.

WANTED:
Single white male, 28, 5'10", strong, and well-packaged desires meaningful relationship with slim, pretty, blue-eyed blond, 25 to 35. Must be into Zen, movies, sharing, long walks, Mozart, and any type of outdoor activities. If you are a stunning and vivacious lady with these traits, apply NOW to Box 22771, xxxxx. Photo essential.

WANTED:
Divorced white female, 42, successful, attractive, brunette who loves jazz, fireplaces, white wine, bicycling, and the Los Angeles Dodgers wants tall, strong, caring male for companionship, travel and *fun!* Must be financially independent and willing to make a commitment to a meaningful relationship. Send reply to Box 27, xxxxx.

WANTED:
Divorced white male, 50, intellectual, handsome, professional, and secure (emotionally and financially) desires companionship of younger woman (under 45) who loves nature, chess, sports, making love, Brandy Alexanders, beaches, and psychology. Must be uninhibited, sexy, tallish but not too thin, and willing to explore exotic places and things. Send photo and reply to Box 2777, xxxxx.

sexual standard that applied to all. The only distinction made was between those who remained chaste (abstaining from heavy petting and certainly avoiding sexual intercourse before marriage) and all others who happened to fall victim to certain sexual indiscretions and deviate from the single sexual norm of the society. Imagine the surprise,

then, when contemporary researchers found that four basic premarital sexual standards comprised the sexual code of our society (Reiss, 1967; 1980). These include

1. *Abstinence.* Sexual intercourse before marriage is not acceptable *under any conditions* for men or women.

The control of sexual interaction between partners before marriage has been an age-old issue with religious, social, and moral overtones.   *(Photo by James D. Anker.)*

2. *Double Standard.* Sexual intercourse before marriage is acceptable for males, but *not* for females.

3. *Permissiveness With Affection.* Sexual intercourse before marriage is acceptable for both males and females *only if* the partners are engaged, in love, or feel strong affection for one another.

4. *Permissiveness With or Without Affection.* Sexual intercourse before marriage, for both males and females, is acceptable under *any* conditions, regardless of the degree of relationship intimacy.

The proportion of people endorsing *abstinence* has declined significantly over the past several years, most noticeably among females. Five national surveys, conducted by the National Opinion Research Center between 1972 and 1978, show that the number of adults sub-

scribing to the abstinence standard has dropped below 30 percent (Singh, 1980). In addition, a three-wave study conducted at the University of Georgia in 1965, 1970, and again in 1975 (King, Balswick, and Robinson, 1977) found a decreasing number of college students agreeing with the statement, "I feel that premarital sexual intercourse is immoral." Among male respondents, 33 percent agreed in 1965, 14 percent in 1970, and 19.5 percent in 1975. Among females, 70 percent agreed, in 1965, that premarital intercourse is immoral, but the figure dropped to 34 percent in 1970 and to 20 percent in 1975.

The Double Standard, which holds that sex before marriage is acceptable for males but not for females, has also declined in popularity. The Double Standard is strongly rooted in the long history of traditional gender-role expectations that have existed, both in our society and in others, for centuries. Both males *and females* have sub-scribed to the Double Standard. Sex has usually been viewed as a male's privilege before marriage, and many societies (including our own) gave legitimacy to a male's finding premarital sexual outlets. The use of prostitutes has not been uncommon, as Kinsey et al. (1948) found in their study of American males: 22 percent had bought the services of a prostitute by 21 years of age. Many societies have created distinctions between "good girls" and "bad girls," in order to provide a sexual outlet for males before marriage and to maintain a sufficient number of female virgins for those men to marry. "Bad girls" were to be found in the lower classes and were usually from "the other side of the tracks," or, possibly, "houses of ill re-pute," and were to be used by males for sexual release and then discarded. A common source of a young boy's or man's prestige in his peer group was to be able to "score" with such women, and then brag about it to his friends. The more scores he made, the higher his prestige. Con-versely, women who admitted to premarital intercourse, or whose sexual activities were somehow discovered, ac-quired "bad reputations" among friends, not prestige. Yet, the ideal, according to the Double Standard, was for the man to find a nice young virgin to marry when it was time to settle down — a "good girl" who had not been "violated" by sexual intercourse with any previous male partners. In brief, "bad girls" were for a male's legitimate need for sexual release, and "good girls" were for marriage and motherhood.

Probably the *most* popular of the four standards of premarital sexual permissiveness in the 1980s is *permis-siveness with affection* (Reiss, 1980:187). According to this standard, premarital sex should be accompanied by strong affection or love for the partner. The same standard applies to men and women equally. Although males are still more sexually permissive before marriage, the male-female gap has narrowed considerably in recent years. This suggests a convergence of premarital sexual standards toward one standard that applies equally to men and women — a standard that assigns equal responsibilities for emotional attachment and commitment, and equal privi-leges in the enjoyment of sexual relations, to both the male and female partners in a premarital relationship.

The *permissiveness with or without affection* standard has never been a popular one in our society. The idea that young people today are engaging in sex whenever they want, and with whomever they want, simply has no basis in scientific fact (Reiss, 1967; 1980).

Premarital Sexual Behavior. Premarital sexual norms and behavior may or may not be consistent with each other, for any given person. Research on the incidence of premarital sexual activity has documented three trends: (1) *an increase in the proportion of people engaging in sexually intimate behavior* of all types before marriage, but especially sexual intercourse; (2) *an increase in the average number of sex partners* a sexually experienced person has before marriage; and (3) *a decrease in the average age* at which premarital intercourse begins (Clay-ton and Bokemeier, 1980). Clearly, the increasing permis-siveness in sexual norms has been accompanied by an increase in the permissiveness of sexual behavior before marriage.[3]

Recent evidence shows a gradual increase in the inci-dence of premarital sexual intercourse on the college campus in the 1970s and 1980s. The research of King, et al. (1977), depicted in Figure 9.2, was conducted in three waves on the campus of a large university, in 1965, 1970, and again in 1975. By 1975, nearly three-fourths of the males and over half of the females reported having had premarital sexual intercourse. These percentages are simi-lar to those found in a study of college students and young adults not in college (DeLamater and MacCorquodale, 1979). These results show the *more conservative* sexual behavior of college students in comparison with the gen-eral population as a whole. They found that 75 percent of the college student males and 79 percent of the nonstudent males reported premarital intercourse, and 60 percent of the college student females and 72 percent of the nonstu-dent females in the study reported premarital sexual expe-rience. Reiss (1980:188) estimated that among today's young adults entering marriage, 75 percent of all females and 90 percent of young males do so having had premari-tal sexual intercourse. In any event, the great majority of people in our society enter marriage today with prior sex-ual experience. Contrary to what was probably true years ago, the minority are those who enter marriage as virgins.

Do these trends, then, signal a sexual *revolution* in premarital relationships? Certainly, the answer to this question depends on one's own definition of the term *revolution*. Most experts, however, would not call these changes revolutionary (Diepold and Young, 1979). Reiss

FIGURE 9.2.   Incidence of Premarital Sexual Intercourse: 1965, 1970 and 1975.

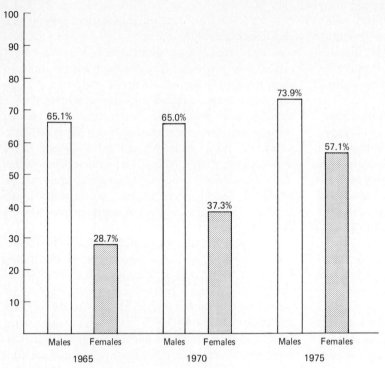

SOURCE: King, Balswick, and Robinson (1977).

(1980) believed that the changes we have seen in females' premarital sexual behavior are a result of "an increase in what (sexual) choices are viewed as legitimate for people to make" (188). According to Bell and Coughey (1980), the increased incidence of premarital sexual experience among women does *not* mean that a new uniform set of values that promote premarital sex has emerged.

It doesn't appear that there are any particularly strong and new sanctions *for* premarital coitus. The experience is not part of a clearly articulated value system common to the college female. What seems to have happened is that the sanctions *against* it have been greatly reduced. Therefore, the reasons that could effectively restrict premarital coitus in the past have much less impact today (357).

Despite the trend toward greater sexual permissiveness before marriage, it is still true that most premarital sexual experiences occur in a context of love and strong affection

between the partners, who many expect to marry some day (Reiss, 1980; Bell and Coughey, 1980).

REASONS FOR THE INCREASE IN PREMARITAL SEXUAL PERMISSIVENESS

A number of factors account for the increase in sexually permissive norms and premarital sexual activity over the years, as several researchers have concluded (Clayton and Bokemeier, 1980; Chilman, 1980; Reiss and Miller, 1979). These relate to significant social changes that have swept our society over the past several years.

1.   There is *greater freedom from parental controls* over high school and college dating activities. Adolescents and young adults today have considerable autonomy in choosing who they date, what they will do while dating,

and how to manage the pressures toward increasing sexual intimacy in premarital-relationship development.

2. There is *an extended period of adolescence and young adulthood* prior to marriage. The average age at marriage has gradually increased over the past 20 to 30 years (Glick, 1975), meaning that there is a longer period of time when young people are psychologically and physically ready for sexual intercourse.

3. There is an *increasing openness and frankness about sex in our society,* which has been prompted by increasingly permissive sexual norms among older married adults. Sex is now viewed as "recreational rather than procreational," an activity that can be enjoyed in its own right, with no other obligations or greater purposes.

4. *Changing gender roles* prescribe an increasing amount of equality between the sexes. If males can enjoy the rewards of premarital sexual experience, then females too should be able to enjoy them, under the new code of gender role and sexual equality.

5. The development of *modern, effective methods of contraception* has removed the fear of premarital pregnancy for many, and has separated the recreational aspects of sex from the procreational.

CONSEQUENCES OF PREMARITAL SEXUAL INVOLVEMENT

Given these trends in premarital sexual permissiveness, the obvious question arises, "So what?" What difference does it really make if a person has sexual intercourse before marriage? What effect does it have on the quality of subsequent sexual relationships either before or after marriage? Although researchers have not yet provided adequate answers to all of these questions, we do know that under certain conditions premarital sexual involvement can have adverse consequences for the subsequent development of the person and on an eventual marriage relationship (Juhasz, 1975). When deciding upon one's own level of sexual activity, each of these potential consequences must be weighed against the perceived rewards that premarital sexual activity will bring. If the perceived rewards outweigh the perceived costs, then sexual intimacy is likely to occur, given the right person

and circumstances. If, on the other hand, the potential risks are perceived to outweigh any benefits that might be realized, then a person should think long and hard about the decision to become sexually involved.

Guilt, Remorse, and Enjoyment of Sex. One possible consequence of premarital sex is a feeling that one has done something wrong, something that one should feel ashamed of doing. This is most likely to occur in a situation where one's sexual behavior has violated his or her sexual norms.

There are potentially adverse effects that sexual guilt and remorse can have on the future development of a sexual relationship in marriage. The inability to experience orgasm, or to be incapable of deriving any enjoyment from sexual intercourse in marriage, can result from early sexual experiences which induced guilt or anxiety (see chapter 5 on female orgasmic dysfunction).

It is important to human sexual enjoyment, most especially for women, that sex-oriented guilt be reduced to a minimum. Studies have shown that the more guilt over sex that an individual feels, the less the desire for sex, the fewer the orgasms experienced, and the less sexually responsive he (she) is. (McCary, 1973:287)

Females are more inclined to feel guilty about premarital sexual activity, because of the more repressive societal norms regarding female sexuality. Also, it is the female who is risking a pregnancy, and she will fear that outcome if no adequate contraceptive measures are taken. Indeed, in a recent study on a large college campus, 51 percent of the 18- and 19-year-old sexually experienced females had *never* experienced orgasm (Bell and Coughey, 1980).

Sexually Transmitted Disease. Most cases of such sexually transmitted diseases (STD's) as gonorrhea and Herpes Simplex II occur among the younger population, many of whom are engaged in premarital sexual activity (see chapter 6). These are among the most prevalent of STD's, and are likely to occur under the conditions one might find among those engaged in premarital sexual activity: more than one sex partner, and lack of knowledge about STD's and their prevention. Genital herpes is of particular concern because it is incurable—once one contracts it, the virus continues to live somewhere in the central nervous system after the symptoms disappear. Although the symptoms may never reappear, they can recur after months or even years. If a person should contract the disease from a partner in a premarital sexual relationship, then marry someone else, the disease can be transmitted to the marriage partner years after the initial contact with the disease. This situation can cause a negative climate—one of blame and conflict—which will cloud the early years of the developing marriage relationship.

Pregnancy. Another possible outcome of premarital sexual intercourse is an unintended pregnancy. Unintended pregnancy rates are far greater for those who are sexually active before marriage than they are for married couples. In the early 1980s, the annual number of *pregnancies* among unmarried women under age 20 was close to 1,500,000. Nearly one-half of all premarital pregnancies among teenagers are aborted every year (Baldwin, 1982). In 1980, approximately 30 percent of the 1,593,890 abortions in the United States were on females 19 years of age and younger. Between 1970 and 1979, the number of out-of-wedlock births in the United States climbed nearly 50 percent, from 399,000 in 1970 to 597,800 in 1979 (*Arizona Family Planning Council,* Dec., 1981). In 1970, 10.7 percent of all births were out-of-wedlock, and in 1979, this number accounted for 17 percent of all births.

According to Juhasz (1975), the decision to become sexually active before marriage leads to a "chain reaction" of sexual decision making for the young person. The chain is either broken or perpetuated, depending on the decision made at each step (see Figure 9.3). For example, to engage in a sexual relationship introduces the question of whether or not to have children. This decision then leads to the decision of whether or not to seek birth control. If pregnancy occurs, then decisions must be made about whether or not to keep the baby, and whether or not to marry. At each step the person is confronted with a complex array of issues which must be considered in order to make the "best decision." The person must weigh the costs and benefits of each decision—each link in the chain—then decide accordingly.

The increase in premarital pregnancies and out-of-wedlock births is somewhat puzzling, given the advent of modern means of effective contraception and the availability of abortion services (see chapter 6). In regard to pregnancies, research has shown that, although more teenagers and college-age youth are sexually active before marriage,

they have lagged far behind in their willingness to seek out and employ effective contraceptive methods (Jorgensen and Alexander, 1981; Zelnik and Kantner, 1980). In fact, between 1976 and 1979, teenage and college student sexual activity continued to increase, but the use of the most effective contraceptives (such as the pill) *declined,* and the use of ineffective methods (such as withdrawal) *increased.* The net effect has been a significant jump in the number and rate of unintended premarital pregnancies to teenagers. Taking all 15- to 19-year-old teenagers into account (including the sexually experienced as well as the inexperienced), Zelnik and Kantner (1980) estimated that one in six (16 percent) in 1979 had already experienced one or more pregnancies. This is up from one in eight (13 percent) in 1976, and one in eleven (9 percent) in 1971.

The negative consequences of pregnancy and childbirth for those under 20 years of age have been thoroughly documented by medical and social science research (Nye and Lamberts, 1980; Bolton, 1980). These consequences can affect the fetus or infant, the pregnant teenaged girl, the teenaged father, and society at large. Sometimes the consequences are severe (see Table 9.5). The younger the girl or boy at the time of the premarital pregnancy, the greater the chances are of experiencing one or more of these consequences.

MAKING YOUR OWN DECISIONS ABOUT PREMARITAL SEX

Ultimately, all people must decide for themselves about their premarital sexual behavior. We have seen that premarital guilt, anxiety, negative sexual experiences, sexually transmitted disease, and unintended pregnancy are all possible consequences of premarital sexual intercourse. Having had extensive premarital sexual experiences with a number of partners may also contribute to a suspect reputation, rendering a person less desirable as a potential marriage or dating partner, in the eyes of others (Istvan and Griffitt, 1980). These consequences are complicated by the fact that premarital sexual intercourse often takes place under less than ideal conditions, such as in an automobile or in one partner's home while parents are away. Zelnik and Kantner (1977) found that teenagers are most likely to have their first sexual experience in the girl's home. As Cox (1981:126) noted:

FIGURE 9.3.   A Chain of Sexual Decision-Making.

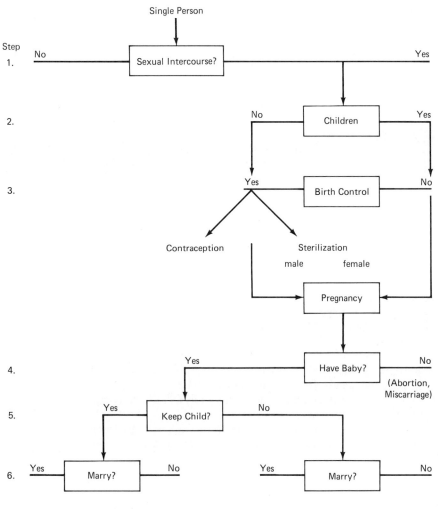

SOURCE: Juhasz, 1975:45.

[T]he environment in which these early clandestine experiences take place is almost always negative and is seldom, if ever, conducive to relaxed, uninhibited sexual contact. Many of these contacts take place in the automobile; having to duck each time a car passes hardly helps the boy or girl relax and feel secure. Relaxation and security are both important psychological attributes to the successful sex act. The general environment is especially important to the girl's ability to find satisfaction.

What tends to follow is a cycle of disappointment and anxiety. There is disappointment because the sexual experience did not produce physical "fireworks" (the total sensual fulfillment that movies and friends have promised); this leads to anxiety, which leads to disappointment, and so on.

We can add to this list two other possible consequences: the potential for exploitation, as discussed earlier in this chapter, and becoming prematurely committed to one person.

Apart from these negative consequences, sexual activity before marriage does have its rewarding aspects. (If it did not, then we certainly would not be seeing the increas-

TABLE 9.5. *Physiological, Psychological, and Social Consequences of Teenage Pregnancy*

I. *Physiological/Medical Consequences*
   A. To the pregnant teenage girl
      1. Anemia.
      2. Abnormal delivery.
      3. Uterine dysfunctions.
      4. Infections relating to pregnancy and childbearing.
      5. Postpartum hemorrhage and abnormal bleeding.
      6. Premature rupture of the uterine membranes.
      7. Maternal mortality (death at childbirth).
   B. To the fetus or infant
      1. Premature birth.
      2. Low birth weight.
      3. Physiological and neurological abnormalities, such as epilepsy, spinal injuries, head injuries, mental retardation, low IQ, blindness, deafness, and nervous disorders.
      4. Still birth.
      5. Spontaneous abortion.
      6. Infant death.
      7. Voluntary abortion.

II. *Psychological Consequences*
   1. Stress, perceived helplessness, depression.
   2. Suicide and suicidal attempts (pregnant teens have suicide rates 7 times the national average).
   3. Low self-esteem; perception of self as a failure, bad, or immoral.

III. *Social Consequences* (affecting both the girl and, if they marry, the boy).
   1. Child abuse and maltreatment as the result of:
      a. Unrealistic expectations and norms regarding normal patterns of child growth, behavior, and development.
      b. Stressful ties to kin, spouse, employers, and society (e.g., the welfare system).
      c. Frustrations because of having to modify one's life script by lowering educational and occupational aspirations.
      d. Economic insecurity and lack of sufficient economic resources.
      e. Isolation from meaningful and rewarding social contacts, particularly the kind of peer relationships which are so critical for building self-esteem and shaping one's personal identity during the adolescent years.
   2. High possibility of dropping out of high school.
   3. Not receiving a college education.
   4. Lower-paying jobs and lower lifetime earnings.
   5. More frequent unemployment.
   6. Childbearing histories marked by more children than desired, and less control over child-spacing.
   7. Much higher rates of marital conflict and divorce among those who choose to marry.

IV. *Societal Consequences* (economics and loss of human resources)
   1. Billions of taxpayers' dollars spent on food stamps, cash support payments, social and medical services, and other welfare outlays are the direct result of teenage pregnancies (over $8 billion in 1979).
   2. Children of adolescent parents perform more poorly in school, have lower educational aptitude scores, and have lower career and educational aspirations than do other children.
   3. Children of adolescent parents are more likely than others to become adolescent parents themselves.

ing rates of premarital sexual activity already noted.) As Kelly (1979:116) has pointed out, premarital sex provides the satisfaction of physical needs and desires, which are very real during our extended period of adolescence. It is also a way of responding to peer pressure—gaining status through conformity with one's friends. Finally, it is the ultimate physical expression of one person's love and affection for another, and therefore may solidify the interpersonal relationship of the two partners.

Clearly, the decision of whether or not to become

sexually active before marriage is important, and should not be taken lightly. It would be wise to take the time to ponder the pluses and minuses carefully, because one must be willing to accept the responsibilities and consequences of whatever decision is reached.

Cohabitation: Living Together Before Marriage

Another significant change in premarital dating and courtship activities has been the increased popularity of living together before marriage, or *premarital cohabitation*. For many young people today, cohabitation is simply one more stage of courtship: dating extensively; narrowing the range of dating partners to a few special steady relationships; living together for a period of time; and then either marrying or breaking the relationship and returning to the dating system. Almost all premarital cohabitation relationships include sexual relations between the partners as part of the arrangement.

THE POPULARITY AND ACCEPTABILITY OF PREMARITAL COHABITATION

Cohabitation before marriage, particularly that on the college campus, began rising in popularity since the middle 1960s. The social upheaval associated with the Vietnam war, women's liberation, and changing definitions of human sexuality all contributed to the popularity of cohabitation. Perhaps most important, though, was the increased freedom of college students who were no longer under the watchful eye of parents, and the decreasing role of the college or university as the parent surrogate (*in loco parentis*) for the college student. The development of coeducational dormitories and increased popularity of off-campus apartment living also facilitated the increase of cohabitation.

Studies conducted on college campuses estimate that somewhere between 25 to 35 percent of all college undergraduates will cohabit at least one time (Bower and Christopherson, 1977; Macklin, 1980). Males are more likely than females to report having cohabited, and males are also more likely to repeat the cohabitation experience after the first one has ended. However, these figures estimate

the total percentage of college students who will *ever* cohabit. The actual percentage cohabiting at *any one time* is probably much smaller—around 6 percent (Glick, 1984b; Clayton and Voss, 1977). This is because of the rather short-term nature of most premarital cohabiting relationships (Macklin, 1980).

The number of cohabiting couples as a percentage of all *couples* in United States households continues to be rather small—about 4 percent in 1983 (Glick, 1984b). This number includes couples of all ages and previous marital statuses—elderly couples living together outside of marriage; divorced or widowed people living together, either as an alternative to marriage or as a step on the path toward remarriage; and young college-age adults.

Despite the small percentage of *all* "couple households" headed by an unmarried pair, the sheer *number* of unmarried living together partners increased dramatically during the 1970s and 1980s. The number doubled between 1970 and 1978, going from 530,000 *couples* (1.1 million individuals) in 1970 to 1,137,000 *couples* (2.3 million individuals) in 1978 (Glick, 1979). By 1983, the number of cohabiting couples reached nearly 2 million (4 million individuals), showing annual increases of 19 to 22 percent in the late 1970s (Glick, 1984b). More than four in five cohabiting couples in 1978 were under 45 years of age. About 16 percent of all divorced men under 29 years were cohabiting outside of marriage in 1983, while 17 percent of divorced women in the same age category were cohabiting in that year (Glick, 1984b).

Further evidence of the increasing popularity of premarital cohabitation can be seen in the norms people hold regarding the *acceptability* of cohabitation. Clearly, norms today are more accepting of premarital cohabitation than in previous generations. For example, in a survey of over 1,100 college students between 1976 and 1982, most agreed that living together before marriage is acceptable for people in general, either unconditionally or given the right conditions (see Table 9.6). Only one in four stated that cohabitation is not an acceptable alternative to a more traditional dating and courtship pattern. More than one third (38 percent) of the respondents, however, would have no qualms about living together before marriage, and another 18 percent stated that they would cohabit given the right circumstances. Hence, premarital cohabitation seems to have developed a certain degree of legitimacy among the college student population today. Although only a minority will ever actually cohabit, the majority believe that cohabitation is acceptable—either

TABLE 9.6. *College Student Norms on Cohabitation for Others and for Self (numbers in parentheses)*

Question 1: Do you think that living together before marriage is all right?

Yes	52% (541)
It Depends	23% (232)
No	25% (261)

Question 2: Would *you personally* live with someone before marriage?

Yes	38% (397)
It Depends	18% (190)
No	43% (450)

SOURCE: Unpublished Survey of 1,134 University of Arizona Undergraduates.

under the proper relationship conditions or without reservation.

REASONS FOR COHABITING

Young people live together before marriage for a variety of reasons: sexual convenience; to facilitate the growth of the relationship; to solidify the bonds of affection and mutuality; to prepare for marriage by having a "trial run" at living under the same roof and engaging in marriage-like roles; or to satisfy certain psychological and emotional needs for intimacy with another person without making the lifelong commitment of marriage. The pooling and sharing of expenses is also viewed by many as a major reason for cohabiting (Arafat and Yorburg, 1973).

COHABITING AND NONCOHABITING COUPLES: ARE THEY DIFFERENT?

The duration and nature of cohabiting *relationships* are remarkably similar to noncohabiting dating and "going steady" relationships. In fact, one researcher has noted these similarities and coined the phrase *going very steady* to describe cohabiting couples (Macklin, 1974). Following is a brief summary of research findings comparing cohabiting and noncohabiting relationships on the college campus.

Relationship Duration. Cohabiting relationships seem to fare about the same as noncohabiting "going steady" relationships in terms of endurance over time and rate of breakups (Risman, Hill, Rubin, and Peplau, 1981). Both types of relationships can last anywhere from a few weeks or months to a year or more.

Orientation Toward Marriage. After beginning its rapid climb in popularity during the 1960s, it appeared that cohabitation would become a substitute for marriage for many young people. It provided the psychological and sexual rewards of intimacy previously reserved for marriage, and avoided the legalistic and formal commitments of marriage that would "tie the partners down." The "no strings attached" convenience of cohabitation was seen as allowing partners to enjoy the *privileges* of marriage without being legally obligated to assume the *responsibilities* of marriage. This meant, to some, that marriage would soon lose its popularity, and that marriage would be made obsolete by a more convenient alternative.

However, research has shown that nothing could be further from the truth. Just as is true of the population of dating couples in general, over 90 percent of those in cohabiting relationships intend to marry some day (though not necessarily to the current cohabiting partner) [Bower and Christopherson, 1977]. Cohabitors are just as likely to believe that they will marry their current partner as are noncohabiting "going steady" partners (Risman, et al., 1980). Both types of arrangements yield a range of possible "levels of commitment" to the current partner — ranging from *casual and noncommitted* to *intending to marry* (Macklin, 1980; Peterman, et al., 1974).

In view of these findings, researchers agree that, for some, cohabitation is another step in the courtship process. It is part of the progression of interpersonal intimacy that evolves in the premarital lives of many young people today (Newcomb, 1979). Rather than being a *permanent alternative* to marriage, therefore, cohabitation more typically represents a legitimate courtship choice which makes a special kind of contribution to the variety of heterosexual experiences one has during the premarital stage.

The Quality of Cohabiting versus Noncohabiting Relationships. The research of Risman, et al. (1981) found noteworthy differences between cohabiting and noncohabiting couples in terms of the quality of their relationships. In terms of *gender roles,* cohabiting men were found to be less traditional (more egalitarian) than noncohabiting men, but women were likely to be nontraditional regardless of cohabiting status. However, cohabiting women were more likely than the others to report male dominance in the relationship, viewing themselves to be at a "power disadvantage" vis à vis their partners.

This discrepancy between egalitarian norms and male-dominant behavior did not affect the cohabiting woman's *satisfaction* with her relationship to her partner. In fact, they reported *more satisfaction* with the relationship, as did their male cohabiting partners, in comparison with noncohabiting men and women. This finding is consistent with the results of other studies, in which cohabitation is reported by the participants to have "rewards which outweigh the problems," to be "both maturing and pleasant," and to have contributed to "individual growth" (Macklin, 1972:469).

In terms of *commitment* to their partners, cohabiting and noncohabiting "going steady" men were equally likely to believe that they would marry their current partner. However, cohabiting women were *more* likely than other women to predict that they would marry their current partner. Cohabiting women are often more committed to marrying than are their male partners (Arafat and Yorburg, 1973; Lyness, et al., 1972). In some cases, at least, partners bring different motivations, meanings, and intentions to the cohabiting relationship — one partner counting on a long-term relationship in marriage after cohabitation, the other a shorter term relationship without eventual marriage. In many cases where discrepant intentions exist, moreover, the partners are unaware of their different views.

Although cohabiting couples report about the same number of relationship problems that noncohabiting couples do, the *kinds* of problems experienced by cohabiting couples tend to be somewhat different (Macklin, 1972; Bower and Christopherson, 1977). The following are problem areas more common to the cohabiting experience, as delineated by Macklin (1972) and Risman, et al. (1981):

1. *Emotional problems,* such as feelings of being trapped or being used; guilt; jealousy of partner's other involvements; overdependency; and overinvolvement.

2. *Sexual problems,* such as differing degrees or periods of sexual interest; fear of pregnancy; and lack of

sexual gratification, all of which are more common to cohabiting couples because of the greater frequency of sexual intercourse than is true for sexually active "going together" couples who are not cohabiting.

3. *Living situation problems,* such as lack of money, space, and privacy; disagreement over how money should be handled; fear of parents finding out about the situation; and difficulty in keeping the situation a secret from parents.

COHABITING AND YOUNG MARRIED COUPLES

In many respects, cohabiting couples are more similar to young married couples than they are to noncohabiting "going together" couples. Living together thrusts the cohabiting couple into a more contained and continuous structure of face-to-face interaction, decision making, and problem solving. They are consequently brought closer to marriage-like roles, such as cooking, housecleaning, household repair and maintenance, family planning, and budgeting and money management. Whether one or both partners are employed outside of the home, division of labor in the home is equally traditional among cohabitors and young marrieds, with the women "bearing the brunt" of the household chores (Stafford, Backman, and DiBona, 1977). Thus, despite their liberal sexual ideology and more egalitarian gender-role norms, cohabiting couples tend to embrace the more traditional role patterns characteristic of young marrieds. Stafford, et al. (1977:55) concluded that the increased popularity of cohabitation alone is not enough to break down the traditional gender-role patterns often found in modern marriages:

> We would have expected that the traditional sex role ideology would be eroded among cohabiting couples. This would seem especially true for the women since many of them believe they are in the forefront of the women's liberation movement . . . However, the more research that is done, the more the cohabitants seem like ordinary students and the more their relationships, at least in regard to the household division of labor, seem like ordinary marriage.

In sum, it seems that cohabitation and marriage are quite similar experiences. The most significant difference is the legal one — marriage is a license granted by the state, with legal rights, responsibilities, and obligations in regard to the social and economic relationship of the partners. No such body of law and licensing procedure exists for those who wish to cohabit before marriage. However, as we shall see in chapter 10, recent court cases bearing on the rights and mutual responsibilities of cohabiting partners show that the "no strings attached" arrangement previously thought to exist among cohabitors is rapidly changing to one where *many* strings are attached. Even in the eyes of the law, therefore, cohabitation and marriage are looking more and more alike.

COHABITATION AS SOCIALIZATION FOR MARRIAGE: DOES PRACTICE MAKE PERFECT?

Theoretically, at least, it seems that premarital cohabitation *should* result in marriages that are more satisfying, better adjusted—more "successful"—than those where the partners did not cohabit. Being able to explore each other's role expectations, personalities, and values before marriage allows those cohabitors who eventually marry a chance to practice and develop their interpersonal skills in the areas of communication and decision making. They also get experience in budgeting and economic cooperation, which, over the course of the marital career, become so important. Living together before marriage imposes certain constraints on a couple, and these may have significant long-term effects—they must adjust to each other's needs and preferences, if the relationship is to be a satisfying one. Cohabitors should, therefore, develop more realistic expectations for marriage, and not suffer the romantic delusions that the superficiality and game playing of more traditional dating patterns tend to create (Jacques and Chason, 1979). Also, one would think that the increased popularity of cohabitation would yield a more successful set of marriages, because it allows incompatible couples a chance to discover their differences *before* marriage, and such couples would break up before they commit themselves to each other in marriage. This is known as the "filtering function," the notion that cohabitation might be the process that filters out the incompatible couples—those who never would have made it as a married pair anyway.

As logical as this all sounds, several studies have revealed virtually no differences in the success of married couples, based upon whether or not cohabitation had taken place (Newcomb, 1979). In one study, Jacques and

Chason (1979) found no significant differences between those who had cohabited premaritally and those who had not—in terms of commitment to the marriage; conflict; communication and self-disclosure patterns; sexual behavior and adjustment; or need fulfillment.

One important question, then, is "*Why* aren't those who cohabited before marriage at an advantage?" There are three reasons. First, cohabitors and noncohabiting "going together" couples have been found to have similar breakup rates before marriage (Risman, et al., 1981). This means that the "filtering function" of cohabitation works equally well (or poorly) for "dating and going together" partners who do not cohabit. Poor matches and incompatible partners are therefore just as likely to be filtered out of the system, or eventually marry, regardless of whether or not cohabitation has taken place.

Second, research comparing cohabiting couples with married couples has found so many similarities between the two that cohabitation is probably most accurately viewed as a *type of marriage*—one without the legal document and public announcement that traditional marriage involves. Cohabitors and young marrieds experience similar problems in relating effectively to each other, in terms of working out differences in role expectations, role behavior, communication, conflict management, and decision making, as well as in managing financially and coping with a lack of space and privacy in their house or apartment. Division of labor in the home also follows along traditional gender-role lines among both groups.

Third, and perhaps most important, is the wide range of intentions and relationship goals that partners bring to the cohabiting experience. We have already seen that males and females tend to differ in their intentions and goals. Males are more likely than females to cohabit for sexual gratification and convenience purposes, and females are more likely than males to view long-term commitment and a desire for eventual marriage with the cohabiting partner as part of the decision to cohabit. As in other areas of the dating system, this leaves one partner vulnerable to being deceived or exploited by the other, a situation that surely will not prove advantageous later on in marriage (Ridley, Peterman, and Avery, 1978).

Summary

In this chapter, we have seen the many ways in which the premarital stage of development can have a significant impact on subsequent stages of the marital career. The motivation to become married and to assume the roles that married people play involves a gradual process of premarital socialization, best described as *anticipatory socialization*. This process begins in childhood and extends through the adolescent years of individual growth and development, as the person observes those role models of marriage that are visible: parents, friends, siblings, and such media influences as movies, television, and literature. The learning that occurs during the premarital stage will be limited to the extent that those models are romanticized and idealized (as in the media). Also, these models often lack the skills and personality traits necessary for developing a satisfying and fulfilling relationship over time (as in the case with parents, friends, and dating partners).

Dating experiences provide opportunities for exploring different personalities of opposite-sex others; comparing and contrasting one's own attitudes, values, and interests; and practicing the behaviors that will eventually evolve into rather stable and predictable *interaction habits* that the person or couple will carry into a marital relationship. Yet the superficiality, deception, and exploitation which often characterizes the dating system means that this, too, is a time of limited learning. The learning that occurs in dating can even have a *harmful* effect on subsequent marital relationships, if corrective measures are not taken.

The interaction habits and interpersonal skills that are shaped by our anticipatory socialization and dating experiences become behavioral patterns that are carried into marriage. Poor communication habits, as well as effective ones, may be learned during the premarital stage when one is observing and interacting with others. Gender roles have changed over time, from the traditional and scripted roles to more egalitarian and ambiguous behavioral guidelines for the two sexes to follow before marriage. This has had the effect of making expectations in male-female relationships before marriage more ambiguous in terms of initiative-taking, self-disclosure, and sexual behavior, and has introduced a certain degree of uncertainty and "role strain." However, the relaxing of gender-role differences can also mean a wider *range of choices* for many, particularly females, who now can take the initiative in making contacts with males rather than having to wait to be asked; and males need no longer bear the full burden of taking the lead in initiating and developing premarital contacts with females, each time risking rejection.

A person's feelings about sexuality and sexual behavior patterns are influenced during the premarital stage, especially in a society where the great majority of young people enter marriage having had premarital sexual intercourse. Early sexual experiences, whether they are rewarding, or painful and guilt-inducing, influence sexuality later in marriage. This increase in premarital sexual permissiveness also emphasizes the importance of family planning and the proper use of contraceptives. Adolescent pregnancies and out-of-wedlock births have increased sharply over the past decade, meaning that effective family planning behavior has lagged behind the trend toward greater sexual intimacy before marriage, particularly among young women. The popularity of premarital cohabitation, or "living together" before marriage, has grown, along with increased sexual permissiveness before marriage. Although cohabitation might be expected to enhance a couple's success in an eventual marriage, research has found few significant differences between marriages preceded by cohabitation and others. Cohabitation has become, for some, another step in the normal progression of courtship stages, but it has not evolved as a permanent alternative to legal marriage for the vast majority of cohabiting couples.

Questions for Discussion and Review

1. Think back to observations you made of your parents' marriage, while you were growing up. Did they have any influence on your own attitudes toward marriage? What aspects of their marriage would you like to carry into your own marriage? What aspects would you like to avoid, if possible?

2. Do parents today have any control or influence over the dating activities of their young adult children? If so, how is this influence exercised? Do parents have any influence over who one chooses for a marriage partner? If so, in what ways?

3. What do you believe are the most desirable qualities of a dating partner? How do these compare to your idea of desirable qualities in a marriage partner?

4. Who should take the initiative in dating and meeting members of the opposite sex — males or females? Is it acceptable for females to take the initiative by asking the male for a date? By asking the male to dance? By paying for his dinner? How would most males feel about such initiative-taking by females?

5. Do deception and exploitation still exist in dating relationships today? Have you observed such behavior in your own relationships or in those of your friends? What are the most typical "masks" that people wear when meeting and dating members of the opposite sex? Is superficiality a problem in developing meaningful relationships with others?

6. What are your attitudes toward cohabitation? Would you ever consider cohabitation before marriage? Under what conditions would cohabitation be acceptable for you? What would you hope to accomplish, should you decide to cohabit?

Notes

1. The chaperonage custom has maintained its popularity in the Western world well into the twentieth century, mainly among Hispanics in the United States, Mexico, and other parts of Latin America.

2. There were no differences in the responses of males and females in this survey. That is, males and females were equally likely to say that males should take the initiative in dating.

3. Although no definitive answer can be found for which change preceded the other — norms or behavior — Reiss (1980) argues that *behavioral permissiveness* actually *preceded* the changes in premarital sexual norms:

> I believe that it has been sexual behavior which has changed first and sexual attitudes which have gradually caught up. Although clearly once the attitudes have caught up to the behavior, the attitudes themselves have helped precipitate another increase in sexual behavior (168).

This relates to the findings of Reiss (1967) and others, that older respondents, those who are married, and those with children, are less permissive than others, all other things being equal. This probably means that young people today, who are high on normative and behavioral sexual permissiveness, will become more *conservative* in their views toward premarital sex as they get older, marry, and have their own children (about whose sexual activities *they* will be worried, in the future).

Engagement and the Transition to Marriage

The transition to marriage, and the exit from the premarital years, is officially marked by the civil or religious ceremony that legally assigns the status of "married" to each person in the relationship. Recall, in the discussion of cohabitation in the last chapter, that *legal* marriage and *pyschological* marriage are two distinct concepts that may or may not coincide with each other. For example, partners in a cohabiting relationship who subsequently marry may have *felt* like they were married to each other all along, and legal marriage is merely a formality that really does not significantly affect their feelings for each other, or the nature of their relationship. The way chores are divided in the home, who provides the income, and the interaction habits developed in regard to communication, decision making, and conflict resolution may all carry over from the cohabitation experience into marriage. On the other hand, other people may marry and spend a year or more without ever really *feeling* married to one another. Clearly, *legal* marriage does not guarantee *psychological* marriage, and such partners might eventually divorce and return to the premarital "field of eligibles" for a possible remarriage. However, they might also remain in the legal marriage relationship indefinitely, without a genuine feeling or belief that they are psychologically married.

For these reasons and many others, we will view getting married as a *critical role-transition point* (see chapter 2) which is negotiated with varying degrees of difficulty. The choice of a particular marriage partner, the engagement period, and other experiences in the premarital stage (see chapter 9) combine with events in the first several months after marriage to determine the degree of difficulty and stress experienced in the transition to marriage. In this chapter, we will explore in greater detail the most important of these factors which shape and give direction to marriage in the transition to marriage stage of the marital career. We will also see that events during this stage, particularly as they relate to the partners' ability to negotiate conflicts and manage the stress and strain common to this stage, influence the development of the marriage relationship in subsequent stages of the marital career.

Marriage As a Critical Role-Transition Point

Marriage satisfies all of the criteria for a *critical role-transition point* defined in chapter 2. It is a normal and expected event for which a person or couple can plan ahead. Yet, it represents for most people a significant shift in life style and behavior, compared with the premarital years. A person's *role cluster* is likely to be expanded to the extent that the new roles of sex partner, provider, and housekeeper are added. Financial planning and budgeting, decision making, communication, and affection-giving and receiving patterns are also role behaviors required of newlyweds. The expanding *role clusters* of the partners means greater complexity and, consequently, more potential problems and stress in the relationship. An acceptable level of *role reciprocity* must be established if the marriage is to be viewed as successfully meeting the instrumental and emotional needs of both partners over time. The set of role expectations that each partner carries into marriage, including both the obligations and privileges of each, will probably be compatible in some areas but will conflict in others. The *interaction habits* in the areas of communication, power, and affection exchanges developed in the relationship before marriage may not be adequate to meet the needs of one or both partners *after* marriage. Finally, circumstances may be such that a couple is unable to satisfactorily establish and maintain effective *boundaries* — keeping out influences that are viewed as undesirable and allowing desirable influences to penetrate the couple's boundaries. For example, friends, in-laws, and old flames can be the source of serious marital problems in this early stage of the marital career, if ties with them are not adequately modified or broken.

The transition to marriage can therefore be quite a stressful experience for many couples because of the increased complexity in role relationships, potential role conflict between the partners, and problems in selectively maintaining boundaries. The best evidence to support this conclusion can be found by examining the probability of divorce in our society, in relation to the number of years married. The *most divorce-prone years of marriage* are the *first two or three* (U.S. Bureau of the Census, 1976), which suggests that many couples in this stage of the marital career find it to be a stressful transition experience.[1] Some choose never to experience this transition, however, as we shall see in the next section.

Permanent Singlehood: Is There a Choice?

The percentage of all adults in American society who never marry has always been small in comparison with other societies. Ours is a marriage-oriented society, in which those who never marry may be looked upon as deviant or different in some way. There "must be something wrong with someone who does not marry," is a typical reaction to those who violate this powerful norm.

In the depression years of the 1930s, the singlehood rate was near an all time peak, as 9 per cent of all women 50 years of age and older had never married (Glick, 1975). This was primarily the result of economic conditions that prevented the marriage of many who otherwise would have preferred to be married. Although marriage rates continued their gradual ebb and flow through the 1940s, 1950s, and 1960s (see chapter 1), the percentage who were to remain permanently single gradually dropped as economic conditions improved. By the 1950s, only 4 or 5 percent of American adults remained permanently single. However, in the 1970s, the rate of permanent singlehood began to creep up again as more young people modified their attitudes toward marriage, delayed marriage decisions until later ages, and began to *voluntarily choose* singlehood over marriage as their preferred lifestyle. It is estimated that 10 to 12 per cent of young adults in the 1980s will remain permanently single — most by choice (Glick, 1984a).

WHO ARE THE SINGLES?

Some people remain permanently single because they prefer it that way, and make that choice; other singles would rather be married. The evidence suggests that single females are more likely than single males to choose this life-style.

According to research conducted by Spreitzer and Riley (1974), single females tend to have a history of positive relationships with fathers and siblings, and have higher than average intelligence, education, and occupational attainment. They tend to be upwardly mobile and successful. These are females who do not need to depend on a husband to provide the economic and social status rewards of his work or career. They are relatively independent and self-supporting. These females, therefore, are clearly undeserving of the derogatory labels placed on unmarried women in our society, such as "old maid."

Single males, on the other hand, are more likely to have a history of poor interpersonal relationships with parents, brothers, and sisters. This raises the possibility that such males have difficulty in forming and maintaining intimate relationships that might eventuate in some degree of permanence, such as marriage. Single men also tend to be at the lower end of the education and occupational ladders, being "unmarriageable" because there are so few women below them who are willing to risk depending on them for economic support and intimacy (Bernard, 1972; see also the discussion of the marriage gradient, chapter 8). This picture of the single male, therefore, is a far cry from the attractive "swinging single bachelor" picture painted by our society.

CONSEQUENCES OF SINGLEHOOD: ADVANTAGES AND DISADVANTAGES

The advantages of singlehood tend to accrue to those who *voluntarily choose* this life style over marriage. Historically, these have been females. We have already discussed (chapter 1) research showing that single never-married women fare as well or better than married women on a number of mental health, physical health, and life-satisfaction indicators (Verbrugge, 1979; Bernard, 1972; Gove, 1972; 1973; Kobrin and Hendershot, 1977). Single never-married men, on the other hand, fare much worse than married men or single women in terms of physical illness, depression, mental illness, mortality, and other disabilities.

As Stein (1975:489) noted, the decision to voluntarily remain single is a relatively new phenomenon in our society, and is including males as well as females who enjoy its rewards:

There is an emergent new style of singlehood that opposes the generally held view that single people are not single by right or by choice; rather, that single people do indeed have a choice and a growing number of them are exercising that choice consciously and voluntarily, in order to pursue life styles that will meet their needs for human growth and supportive interpersonal relationships. The emergence of singlehood as a life style is seen as a developmental phenomenon in response to the dissatisfaction with traditional marriage. As such, it represents a significant change in the cultural expectations underlying many of our social values.

Stein compared the various "pushes and pulls" of deciding to remain single to those of marrying (see Table 10.1). Freedom and independence are keys to the decision to remain single—being able to come and go without having to be concerned about what a spouse is doing; being able to do what one pleases without the interference of a

wife or husband; forming intimate and/or sexually active relationships with others without the worry of having violated vows to maintain sexual exclusivity (which one usually makes to a marriage partner).

Singlehood has its disadvantages, too, even for those who choose it. One danger is the negative social context in which singles live. Social norms, which dictate that marriage and parenthood are virtues, and that singlehood denotes character deficits or personality flaws, can complicate the single life style. Social disapproval is leveled at singles, often in the form of stereotypical images of them as "sexual swingers," or "jet-setters," who desire only to fulfill their own selfish needs and who avoid responsibility. Their parents, relatives, colleagues at work, and their own married friends may continually needle them about their singlehood, and push them toward marriage by setting up blind dates, joking, or even expressing anger and hostility (perhaps jealousy?) at their single status. Singles may be viewed as sexual threats to friends' or acquaintances' marriages, and they may be excluded from social events as a result. Others may be excluded for another reason— singles are often suspected, rightly or wrongly, of being homosexual. As more and more of their previously single friends marry, singles may experience even more social isolation and loneliness. This is why Stein (1975) found in his research on singles that their "greatest single need" is for social "networks of human relationships that provide the basic satisfactions of intimacy, sharing, and continuity" (p. 501). Without good friends or solid relationships with parents or other family members, the single life style can be a lonely, confusing, and frustrating existence, causing a void that fleeting relationships formed in single bars or singles apartments cannot fill.

As the number of people who delay marriage or who choose to remain permanently single continues to climb, however, the available support networks for singles will grow. Such networks will be beneficial because one factor contributing to the comparatively high number of divorces in our society is that so many people marry in the first place (see chapter 15). Deciding to remain single is a legitimate choice of life styles today.

Finding the One and Only: The Process of Marital Choice

Of all the potential marriage mates in the world, how do we manage to find the *one person* to whom we are

TABLE 10.1. *Pushes and Pulls Toward Marriage and Toward Singlehood*

Toward Marriage

Pushes	*Pulls*
Economic security	Influence of parents
Influence from mass media	Desire for family
Pressure from parents	Example of peers
Need to leave home	Romanticization of marriage
Interpersonal and personal reasons	Love
Fear of independence	Physical attraction
Loneliness	Emotional attachment
Alternatives did not seem feasible	Security, Social Status, Prestige
Cultural expectations, Socialization	
Regular sex	
Guilt over singlehood	

Toward Singlehood

Pushes	*Pulls*
Restrictions	Career opportunities
Suffocating one-to-one relationships,	Variety of experiences
feeling trapped	Self-sufficiency
Obstacles to self-development	Sexual availability
Boredom and unhappiness and anger	Exciting life-style
Role playing and conformity to expectations	Freedom to change and experiment
Poor communication with mate	Mobility
Sexual frustration	Sustaining friendships
Lack of friends, isolation, loneliness	Supportive groups
Limitations on mobility and available experience	Men's and women's groups
Influence of and participation in	Group living arrangements
Women's Movement	Specialized groups

SOURCE: Stein, *Single* (Englewood Cliffs, N.J.: Prentice-Hall), p. 65, 1976.

willing to commit ourselves (at the outset, at least) to a lifelong relationship in marriage? Is it a matter of luck, or chance? Or are there "guiding forces" operating to narrow down the field of eligibles *for us,* so that we have only a relatively small number of potential partners from which to choose? The answer to both of these questions is yes. Being at the right place at the right time in order to meet our future partners does involve a measure of chance or luck. On the other hand, because of a number of forces, the chances of meeting that particular person, rather than one of a million others, are significantly increased so that there is also a certain measure of predetermination in the mate-selection process. The process actually begins during the dating phase of the premarital stage (see chapter 9), where both chance and societal influences begin to narrow the range of acceptable marriage partners.

THEORIES OF LOVE AND MARITAL CHOICE

Social scientists have proposed several theories about how people meet, fall in love, and eventually marry. In addition, a number of research investigations have been conducted in order to see which of these theories, if any, allows us to predict with accuracy who will marry whom.

The Love Theories of Marital Choice. The theory of *role reciprocity and love* developed by Orlinsky (1972) [see chapter 3] suggests that people fall in love when they satisfy each other's needs for personal growth and development, such as the needs to be understood, respected, and trusted. Partners respond positively to having their growth needs fulfilled by the other, thereby fulfilling the other's growth needs, and so on, in a reciprocal, spiraling fashion, toward a deeper level of intimacy, interpersonal attraction, and love.

Reiss (1960) and Borland (1975) took a similar *cycle* approach toward defining how love relationships develop, although they label the components differently. The *Clockspring theory of love* (also known as the *wheel theory*) postulates that love will develop between two people as their relationship progresses through a series of related and mutually reinforcing stages (see Figure 10.1). Love begins with partners establishing a certain level of rapport, which leads in turn to self-revelation, mutual dependency, and personality-need fulfillment, which then builds rapport further, and so on, in a positive, spiraling fashion.

Rapport means that the two partners are comfortable with one another; believe that they understand each others' feelings, values, and expectations; and feel free to talk to each other. Once rapport is established after meeting, the two individuals are likely to feel comfortable in communicating deeper, more intimate aspects of themselves in the process of *self-revelation*.[2] Personal ambitions and goals, fears, worries, and feelings are likely to be shared among those who feel comfortable in each other's company. Once the self-revelation process is underway, the partners develop "interdependent habit systems" whereby each partner's behavior becomes interlocked and *mutually dependent.*

One becomes dependent on the other person to fulfill one's own habits: e.g., one needs the other person to tell one's ideas or feelings; one needs the other person to joke with; one needs the other person to fulfill one's sexual desires. When

FIGURE 10.1.   *The Clockspring Theory of Love.*

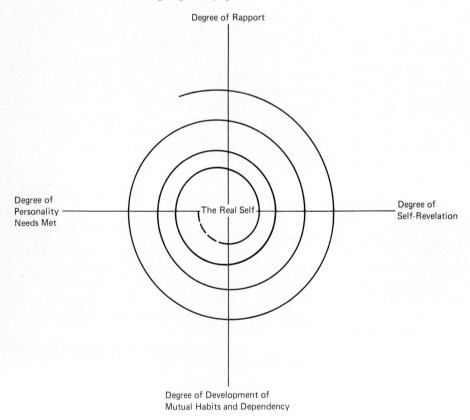

SOURCE: Borland (1975:290).

SOURCE: © United Features Syndicate, Inc., 1956.

such habitual expectations are not fulfilled, loneliness and frustration are experienced. (Reiss, 1960:142)

Personality-need fulfillment follows as feelings of rapport, self-revelation, and mutual dependency combine to satisfy each partner's needs for intimacy, encouragement, respect, and recognition. Having these needs filled by another in a close relationship contributes further to rapport, and the *clockspring* of love grows tighter as the partners find themselves falling more deeply in love over time, and as they grow closer to each other's "real selves."

Of course, the clockspring can unwind, as well, prompted by a serious disagreement or conflict in the relationship. People can "fall out of love" by reversing the processes that caused them to fall *in* love in the first place. For example, increasing self-disclosure means that partners are aware of each other's vulnerabilities and sensitive areas (see chapter 7). There is less superficiality in the relationship as a result. This can be uncomfortable or even threatening to some, who might suddenly break off a relationship that gets "too close," particularly if the other person actually takes advantage of this knowledge. They may "hit below the belt" in a conflict, or possibly share their intimate knowledge with a third person, in violation of the partner's trust. Falling *out* of love, then, occurs as the clockspring *unwinds,* whether it does so quickly or only gradually, over a period of time.

The Sociocultural Theories of Marital Choice. Life presents numerous places and situations for meeting others of the opposite sex with whom we might fall in love, and eventually marry: childhood friendships, high school, dances, religious or church-related events, singles bars, dating services, blind-dates arranged by mutual friends, the office or work place, and simply chance meetings, such as those on a subway or bus, are the possible ways and places where we might meet our "one and only." There is far more to it than this, however. Research has identified several social and cultural forces that limit the marital-choice process. These forces narrow the field of eligible partners to a point that leaves us with a rather limited range of potential mates with whom we will fall in love and eventually marry.

1. *Residential Propinquity.* You are likely to meet, fall in love with, and marry someone who lives within a mile or two of your residence (Katz and Hill, 1958). This is known as *residential propinquity,* meaning that the pool of eligible marriage mates is limited by geographic location: you must live in or near a person's neighborhood, town, or college campus in order to meet them and initiate the steps of rapport-building essential to the relationship development process. Geographic proximity also contributes to racial endogamy and sociocultural homogamy, to be discussed next.

2. *Racial and Religious Endogamy.* A cultural norm stating that marriage should occur between people within a certain social group is known as *endogamy.* The strongest type of endogamy in our culture has to do with racial background. That is, the field of eligible marriage partners is limited, to a great extent, to those with the same skin color and generic physical features: whites marry whites, Blacks marry Blacks, Orientals marry Orientals, American Indians marry American Indians, and so on. Another less stringent form of en-

dogamy has to do with religion: Jews marry Jews, Protestants marry Protestants, Catholics marry Catholics, and Mormons marry Mormons. Some religions consider marriages between church members and nonmembers to constitute a breach of the person's contract with the church and a serious violation of religious doctrine. Evidence that racial endogamy is a stronger norm than religious endogamy is provided in Table 10.2. A survey of over 1,100 college students shows that only 17 percent would consider marrying interracially, but 57 percent would consider marrying outside of their religion. However, a better measure of the strength of these norms of endogamy is given by the *actual behavior* of people when it comes to marrying within their racial or religious group. Only about 1.4 percent of all marriages in our society occur between Blacks and whites, or between whites and other racial categories (U.S. Bureau of the Census, 1983a). Interreligious marriages involving Protestants, Jews, and Catholics comprise an estimated 15 to 20 percent of all marriages (Glenn, 1982). Although the evidence in Table 10.2 would suggest that people may be quite tolerant in their beliefs about the general acceptability of interracial and interreligious marriage, racial and religious endogamy continue to function as rather strong cultural practices, narrowing one's field of eligible marriage partners.

3. *Social and Cultural Homogamy.*   For many years it has been observed that "likes marry likes" in regard to

TABLE 10.2. *Norms Relating to Racial and Religious Intermarriage of 1,134 Undergraduate Students*

Response to the Question, "Would You Ever Consider Marrying Someone of a Different Race (Religion) Than Yourself?"

	RACE
YES	16.6%
IT DEPENDS	30.6%
NO	52.8%
	RELIGION
YES	56.9%
IT DEPENDS	28.3%
NO	14.7%

SOURCE: Unpublished survey of 1,134 University of Arizona Students.

certain social characteristics, such as age, education, and social class background. This process is known as *social homogamy,* whereby people are likely to meet, fall in love, and eventually marry another who is approximately the same age (within a year or two), has completed about the same level of education, and whose parents have a similar level of income and standard of living. Social homogamy is believed to lead to more compatible matches because it promotes *cultural homogamy*—similarities between partners in terms of major life values, role expectations for marriage, and interests. Research has shown that people who share similar values and role expectations are attracted to one another, and are more likely to fall in love and marry than are those who do not agree in these areas (Coombs, 1966; Murstein, 1970). Residential propinquity, racial and religious endogamy, and being socialized for marriage in similar socioeconomic environments are likely to foster value, role, and interest similarities, thereby narrowing the range of acceptable marriage partners.

The Personality Theories of Marital Choice.   Some authors claim that within the broad sociocultural guidelines which are created by norms of endogamy and homogamy, partners will meet, fall in love, and marry if they possess certain combinations of personality characteristics. According to a classic study conducted by Winch (1958), *personality* factors are the major cause of people falling in love and deciding to marry at some point after they first meet each other. Winch postulated that "opposites attract," and that only those partners who complemented each other's psychological and emotional needs would actually fall in love and eventually marry. Winch's *Theory of Complementary Needs,* then, was based on his belief that love evolves in a relationship in which the partners have *different* personality traits. For example, a person who has strong needs for achievement and dominance is likely to fall in love and marry a person who does *not* have strong needs in those areas. Also, a person who has need to dominate others will marry someone who has a need to give deference to others.

Although Winch's own research on 25 married couples showed some evidence of need complementarity (1955a; 1955b; Winch, Ktsanes, and Ktsanes, 1954; 1955), at least a dozen studies conducted later found *no evidence of need complementarity* among dating, engaged, or married couples (Murstein, 1980). If fulfillment of complementary needs is a factor in marital choice, then, it seems that it is true of only a small number of couples. Perhaps, too, need complementarity is overshadowed by other forces which contribute more to the decision of whom to marry.

The Filter Theories of Marital Choice.

More recent research indicates that a series of *filtering stages* determines "who will fall in love with and marry whom." Usually the filter theories combine certain elements from the other viewpoints just discussed, stating the *each* is important. They claim that endogamy, homogamy, and even need complementarity can all be observed in couples who fall in love and marry, if we look at them in their proper sequence in the relationship-development process. Two individuals are likely to develop an intimate relationship, fall in love, and eventually marry if they are able to pass through the sequence of filtering stages.[3]

One filter theory is called S-V-R, which stands for *Stimulus-Value-Role* (Murstein, 1970). The S-V-R theory views *physical attractiveness* as a major factor influencing the development of relationships toward increased intimacy and possibly toward marriage. Physical appearance influences who we meet and eventually marry. There is strong evidence to show that our impressions of another person, upon first meeting them, are influenced by their physical appearance (Berscheid and Walster, 1969). The research suggests that we like people more, and prefer their company, if we find them to have an attractive appearance. Also, physically attractive people *know* that they are attractive, and believe that they have better personalities and are more outgoing and popular than are those who are less attractive (Walster, Aronson, Abrahams, and Rottman, 1966). For example, singles bars and other locations frequented by young people are so popular because they provide a legitimate opportunity to "size-up" others according to their facial looks and body build. People who usually go to singles bars or parties for singles expect to examine the physical attributes of others, just as they themselves expect to be examined. Two people who like what they see may give a look or other cue to show that they are interested in striking up a conversation. Their talk usually focuses on their interests and occupations, or more superficial topics that will build rapport but will not reveal too much about their "real selves" (see Figure 10.1, p. 286). Physical attractiveness is certainly an important influence in the teenage and high school dating

system as well, and has probably replaced fraternity membership in the "rating and dating" practices of the contemporary college campus. Cute girls, beautiful women, and handsome men "rate"; homely, plain, or chubby men and women do not "rate." No stronger evidence to support this contention can be provided than the multibillion-dollar-a-year diet, cosmetics, and personal grooming businesses, which are developing and marketing their products while keeping in mind our contemporary values on youth, beauty, and attractive appearance.

Research has also shown that men and women are more likely to make an effort to meet each other and begin a relationship if they are *similar* in terms of physical attractiveness level. A recent movie, "*10*," popularized the idea of rating others on a scale of 1 to 10, with 10 being the highest possible physical appearance rating. In reality, women who rate toward the top of the physical attractiveness scale — say, 8, 9, or 10 — tend to meet and initiate relationships with men who rate 8, 9, or 10. Women who rate low or medium tend to associate with men with a rating similar to theirs.

However, the astute person would ask, "Isn't 'beauty in the eye of the beholder?' " "Isn't what is considered attractive, beautiful, or handsome a purely subjective experience?" "If so, how can researchers say, with any objectivity, who is attractive and who is not, and that men and women who rate at a similar level of attractiveness will tend to pair off in the dating and courtship process?"

Remarkable as it may seem, researchers have found that people do agree about what is and what is not attractive in women and men (Walster, et al., 1966; Murstein, 1970). And if one partner should be noticeably more attractive than the other, there is usually some kind of *compensating quality* possessed by the less attractive person, such as money and other material possessions, or an unusual ability to share affection or to be self-sacrificing (Berscheid, Walster, and Bohrnstedt, 1972).

Once a young male and female move through this *Stimulus Stage* of physical attraction, S-V-R theory states that they will begin to explore each other's values and interests. During the *Value Stage,* each person's philosophy of life, political views, religious beliefs, attitudes toward sex, and values relating to their marriage and family plans are usually explored and tested for compatibility. If they are found to be compatible, then the relationship bond is strengthened, and the couple will probably move on to the next stage of the process. If, however, the partners realize that they do not share compatible attitudes and values, they are likely to "filter out" of the process, and return to the *Stimulus Stage* — that of finding another person of comparable physical attractiveness.

If value compatibility is established, the couple will then progress toward exploring each other's role expectations and behavior in the *Role Stage*. During this stage, partners begin to realize a genuine liking, or perhaps even love, for each other as a result of disclosing more and more of their "real selves" and their feelings for each other. They strive to establish a degree of "role fit," after they gradually come to see each other as the kind of person they would like to marry. They then acquire a basic understanding and acceptance of the partner's role expectations and motivations in the relationship. They begin to evaluate the adequacy of each other's personalities, and courtship progress is made if the partners are similar in terms of emotional stability, maturity, and sex drive. In regard to sex drive, Murstein (1970:475) noted that differences between partners can influence each person's perception of the other's personality and commitment.

The stereotyped response of the low sex-drive woman to the insistence of the high sex-drive male partner is "you are just using me for my body." The high sex-drive male may perceive his partner, however, as "cold" or indifferent.

Courtship progress is therefore in jeopardy if different sexual expectations cause mutual feelings of insensitivity or misunderstanding between the partners.

The reader should be able to detect the similarities that exist among all of these theories of marital choice, although each may emphasize somewhat different aspects of relationship development. Also, note the importance each places on the *gradual building* of a relationship *over time*. Certain problems after marriage, such as conflict, disappointment with the partner, and even divorce, might be avoided if partners were to take the time necessary for building a solid relationship *before* marriage, by moving gradually through the stages of relationship development. The choice of a marriage partner is a critical one, and should not be taken lightly or be made in haste.

The Engagement Process

The engagement period can function as an important means of *anticipatory socialization* prior to making the transition to marriage. If partners take advantage of the opportunities that the engagement period provides for applying and sharpening their communication, decision making, and conflict-management skills, the engagement can greatly ease the transition to marriage by reducing the level of stress associated with taking on marriage roles.

ENGAGEMENT DEFINED

In past years, a male and female were said to "be engaged to be married" after the male proposed to the female, offered her an engagement ring, the female accepted his "offer," and an announcement of their betrothal was made publicly. As with so many other aspects of contemporary male-female relationships before marriage, however, this traditional type of engagement has undergone dramatic changes. Changing gender-role expectations, and a more casual attitude of today's young people toward the marital institution, have greatly broadened the meaning of the concept of engagement.

At least two types of engagement characterize most couples (Hicks, 1970). The *formal engagement* involves the more traditional pattern of offering and accepting of a ring, coupled with a public announcement that engagement has taken place. The formal engagement involves a "firm commitment to marry" each other. This pattern was far more common years ago, when engagement signaled a high degree of public commitment between the partners, making it quite difficult to break. A broken engagement was nearly as serious as a marriage broken by divorce. Therefore, engagements were far more binding, and less frequently broken, than they are today.

The *informal engagement* pattern seems to characterize the majority of relationships today. This type of engagement is more of "a decision to think about marriage and test the relationship," rather than a firm commitment to marry. "When we first seriously considered getting married someday" is a typical phrase which describes entry into an informal engagement; it is a sort of "tentative pact or agreement" between the two partners (Hicks, 1970:60).

For our purposes here, engagement is defined as follows:

Engagement is the period of time in an intimate relationship beginning when each partner intends and fully plans to marry the other and makes these intentions known, and ending either when the marriage takes place or when at least one partner decides that they do not intend to marry the other.

To be engaged means that each person must intend to marry the other and must communicate those intentions, at least to the partner. However, this does not necessarily mean making a public announcement. *All couples* who eventually marry spend at least *some* time being engaged —whether it is the few minutes elapsing between the decision to marry and the Las Vegas wedding chapel marriage, or the years that might pass between a formal proposal and the marriage of two people who have been somewhat reluctant to take the last big step. Of course, each type of engagement is dissolved when one or both partners change their intentions to marry.

THE FUNCTIONS OF ENGAGEMENT

The principal function of the engagement period is to allow time for the partners to prepare for the transition into marriage, making the transition a smooth one. Specifically, the engagement may serve the following functions, if the partners allow it to.

1. To Adjust to Differences in Each Other's Values, Role Expectations, Goals, and Interests.
One of the benefits of marrying a person from a similar sociocultural background (homogamy) is that it increases the chances for agreement on major life goals and values. The chances for compatibility in role expectations are also increased, and it is more likely that the partners will enjoy the same kinds of activities for personal recreation and enjoyment. However, it is highly unlikely that two individuals will match each other in *all* of these important areas, and differences will exist. For example, one might like sports and athletic events, and the other might prefer the arts and cultural events (and may even dislike athletic events). One might expect to have a few nights out every week with friends, but the partner might expect more time together. One partner might be expecting to buy a home, and to start a family within a year after marriage, and the other partner might be planning to rent an apartment, and to delay having children for an indefinite period of time. Whatever the case, partners can take advantage of the engagement period to explore

their differences, and to take action to compromise on them.

2. To Develop Skills for Relating to Each Other in Mutually Satisfactory Ways.
The concept of *interaction habits* (discussed in chapters 2 and 9) implies that two people in an intimate relationship develop consistent patterns of relating to each other in terms of communicating, making decisions, solving problems, and exchanging affection. These patterns become comfortable habits over time. As such, they are difficult patterns to change if they are found to be unsatisfactory by one or both partners. For example, two partners may find that avoiding conflicts is the easiest way to handle them. They do this in order to avoid rocking the boat; they hope that the problems will just fade away if they pretend that they don't exist. Once they get into this habit, they may discover that they are avoiding serious problems that should be discussed and resolved. However, it is usually best not to delay resolving serious conflicts for the sake of long-term stability in the relationship (see chapter 7). The engagement period is an excellent time to recognize this pattern and its unsatisfactory nature. If the partners do not change this pattern in engagement, the habit will only get stronger, and more difficult to change, at some point after they have married.

The engagement period, then, allows time to develop skills for relating to each other in more satisfying ways. It is here that partners should review how they make decisions, talk to each other, resolve their differences, and exchange affection with each other. Does one partner always make the important decisions without regard to the other's wishes? Does one partner have difficulty discussing feelings or personal problems? Are both partners happy with the frequency and ways of showing their affection for each other? If there are problems in these areas, it is best to resolve them *before* marriage.

3. To Adjust to Each Other's Needs and Limitations by Gaining a Satisfactory Level of Mutual Knowledge.
One of the characteristics of our romantic love complex (see chapter 3) is that love often blinds people to the realities of the loved one. This is known as *idealization,* which can give partners a false sense of adjustment to each other (Schulman, 1974). They believe that they know each other well when, in fact, they only know the "image" that the other has

been projecting in the "best possible light." The classic example is that of the two people who date each other, fall in love, and become engaged but never see each other in any other way than nicely dressed, made-up, and neatly groomed. They each see an idealized picture of one another because they never *allow* themselves to be seen as they really are. The man has never seen the woman in her curlers, cold cream, tattered nightgown and robe, or in her semiconscious state after waking in the morning. The woman has not seen the male's unshaved stubble, uncombed hair, or grumpiness in the morning. After marriage, there might be considerable *reality shock* when, for the first time, they see each other as they really are (Waller and Hill, 1951).

Idealization, however, goes beyond just physical appearance. More important are the personality traits and needs that might be hidden from each other, in order to keep the other interested in continuing the relationship, and eventually, in marrying. One person may have a terrible temper, or may be a chronic complainer. One might be an extremely competitive person, who is afraid of letting others get the upper hand. Still another might be an extremely critical person, always looking for faults in what another says or does. If these traits are hidden before marriage—as they may be in order to avoid threatening the future of the relationship, then they are likely to reveal themselves after marriage and the "knot is tied." The reality shock that results can cause severe problems. Indeed, one major reason that divorce rates are highest in the first year or two of marriage is that many partners rarely get to know one another well enough before marriage, and experience a high degree of disillusionment after marriage. Many people are simply unable to adjust to the new reality they discover in their partners after marriage.

Engagement can be a useful time for acquiring knowledge about each other's personality needs and traits, as well as about one's major life values, role expectations, and interests. Couples who are likely to overcome the problem of idealization during engagement are those who have multiple and varied experiences with each other. They search out and confront situations that force them to make difficult decisions, solve problems, resolve conflicts, or make plans for the future. They are couples who communicate effectively and who are unafraid to engage in self-disclosure activities during this time (see chapter 7). In sum, two partners must develop a *realistic* understanding of each other before marriage, and quite often this means

making a deliberate, conscious effort to delve beneath the surface of the other's personality.

4. To Terminate the Relationship If One or Both Partners Finds That He or She Is Better Off Not Being Married to the Other.

According to Landis and Landis (1977), roughly one half to two thirds of all engagements are broken before the marriage takes place. There are several common reasons for breaking engagements, which these authors refer to as "danger signals." These include

(a) *A loss of interest* in getting married to the other, especially if the relationship up to the engagement has been of the superficial "love-at-first-sight" variety, and the novelty of the romance has worn off.

(b) *Separation of the partners and subsequent maturing of each,* which often occurs when they attend different colleges or work in different cities.

(c) *Incompatibilities in values, role expectations, and personal interests,* which cannot be resolved, and which were not recognized or confronted when the pair was dating prior to engagement.

(d) *Cultural differences,* as the result of engagement to a person from another social class, or from a different racial, religious, or educational background, and finding that these differences cannot be reconciled.

(e) *Friends and family* who react negatively to a young couple's decision to marry. This can place a heavy burden on the relationship, because economic and emotional support from these important people might be lacking in time of need.

One would hope that one or more of these danger signals will prompt an engaged couple to reconsider their plans. Broken engagements, although emotionally distressful and at times traumatic, are far less painful, and less costly—both economically and psychologically—than divorce. The recognition of any of these signals ought to be taken seriously, and the problem resolved to the mutual satisfaction of the engaged partners, *before* the wedding occurs.

DEVELOPMENTAL TASKS OF ENGAGEMENT

We saw in the preceding section that engagement can serve useful functions by preparing partners to make a smooth transition into marriage. However, a couple must be willing to take enough time to work on their relationship during engagement, if they have not already done so. That is, if they accomplish certain *developmental tasks* prior to marriage, the transition into marriage will be less complicated and stressful (see chapter 2 to review the nature of *developmental tasks*).

Rapoport (1962) identified several developmental tasks that are important for engaged couples to consider. Three are tasks that the individual undertakes, and seven are tasks that both partners must work on as a couple. Accomplishment of these tasks is important if engagement is to have the favorable outcomes outlined in the previous section.

Engagement Tasks of the Individual.

Each person in the relationship should prepare to make the transition to marriage by attaining a certain amount of psychological readiness. This can be done in the following ways.

1. *Making oneself ready to take over the new roles of husband or wife.* This means that a person should imagine what married life will be like: living in close proximity with another; the role responsibilities and obligations that must be assumed (e.g., earning a living, sharing intimacies, family planning, keeping a house, and so on); and being supportive of one's partner. These are all dimensions of marriage with which one should come to grips beforehand. For those who are unable to do so before marriage, the chances for disillusionment and disappointment with these less romantic aspects of marriage are increased.

2. *Disengaging from, or modifying, close relationships that would compete or interfere with commitment to the newly formed marital relationship.* Close ties with others before marriage can interfere with the subsequent marital relationship, if a person is not careful to subordinate them to a lower priority. Parents, siblings, other relatives, a former girlfriend or boyfriend, other close friends, and workmates fall into this category. This is *not* to say that a person should totally cut off important relationships to other people after marriage. On the contrary, it is important to maintain a rich network of relatives and friends for personal growth and development throughout adulthood. Rather, this task means that, if a person starts to neglect or ignore the marriage partner-to-be by continually seeking fulfillment of intimacy and social needs from others, then the significance and meaning of the marriage relationship

will be impaired. For example, feelings of resentment and jealousy can be sparked, unnecessarily, by the marriage partner who keeps close contact with a former dating partner, or who stops at his or her parents' house every night after work, to discuss the day's events.

It is during the engagement period that a person should examine such relationships with others and prepare, psychologically at least, to modify them if necessary. Research shows that such a disengagement process does actually occur, but mainly in regard to friendship ties. Johnson and Leslie (1982) studied 750 young adults in different stages of relationship intimacy — from occasional dating, regular dating, and exclusive dating of the partner to engagement and marriage — and found that the number of close friends, and the importance attached to friends' opinions, decreased consistently at each step on the intimacy ladder. In regard to relatives, on the other hand, some reported increased involvement, but others reported decreased involvement as the relationship became increasingly intimate. Relatives, especially siblings, parents, and parents-in-law, maintain a greater level of importance than do friends for many engaged and newly married couples. One negative result is that there is a greater possibility that these relatives will interfere with one's commitment to the marriage relationship. If possible, such potential problems should be averted.

3. *Accommodating the competing gratifications of premarital life to the new "couple" (marital) relationship.* Marriage often means that a person is asked to give up certain activities or "freedoms" because they are not acceptable to the other partner. Going out with friends several nights a week, and the card club, the dances and dinners, the sports events, and the flattering attentions from the opposite sex — all so much fun for a single person — must now be accommodated, if necessary, to the desires of the marriage partner. The important question here, of course, is how much should a person be expected to sacrifice in order to please the partner? Because one's very self-concept is related to activities enjoyed for fun and relaxation, to change them might imply losing a certain amount of self-identity and individuality.

This question has no good answer that would apply to all. Fortunately, the filtering process of the premarital stage (described earlier in this chapter) means that there will be a certain degree of similarity in interests and values among engaged partners. For most people, then, only one or two such interests may present a problem. Such disagreements should at least be addressed during engagement, and this should result in a compromise solution satisfactory to both partners. If the weekend football games on TV are a sore spot, then the football fan may have to reduce the number of hours in front of the TV set, or the critic may have to change the negative views toward football, or sit in anyway. However, if engaged persons are *unwilling* to change their expectations or behavior regarding recreational and leisure activities, then the marriage plans ought to be reconsidered until a satisfactory compromise can be reached. Clearly, some engaged partners expect to spend all of their free time in "couple" types of activities, and others expect more of a balance between time spent together as a couple and time spent alone or in activities with others. Each couple must find its own balance—activities that involve both partners versus those enjoyed individually. This balance can only be achieved by making a conscious effort during engagement to understand each other's preferences and expectations, and seeking a compromise in areas of serious disagreement.

Engagement Tasks of the Couple.

The three developmental tasks just discussed relate to what each person in the engagement relationship can do to make the transition to marriage a smoother one. Rapoport (1962) also identified seven *interpersonal, or couple,* tasks involving the joint efforts of both partners in order to improve the degree of *role adjustment* and make the relationship a more harmonious one.

1. *Establishing a couple identity.* This means that it is important for two partners to be viewed as a unit rather than as two "loosely related" individuals. Not only is it critical that they view themselves as a unit, but it is also important for others in their social network (such as friends and relatives) to view them as a unit. This helps the partners to cement the bond between them, developing a comfortable feeling with the idea that they belong to each other and with each other (Lewis, 1973). This task is a prerequisite for partners who wish to develop a harmonious relationship built on mutual support, rather than one in which each person "goes their own way" or "does their own thing."

2. *Developing a mutually satisfactory level of sexual adjustment.* It is important for engaged partners to begin communicating about the nature of their sexual relationship. As we have seen in chapters 5 and 9, sexual behavior

Establishing a "couple identity" and learning to adjust satisfactorily to each other in a number of areas are important tasks of engaged partners.   *(Photo by R. J. Hinkle.)*

before marriage plays a key role in the development of premarital relationships, and unsatisfying sexual patterns can develop into sexual problems and dysfunctions if they continue over time. These problems may persist into the marriage relationship and may have adverse long-term effects if sexual communication does not occur. What are each person's sexual expectations during engagement? Are the partners engaging in sexual behavior that is more intimate than one, or both, really desires? Are the partners satisfied with their current level and frequency of sexual contact? If they are engaging in sexual intercourse during engagement, is an effective family planning method being employed regularly? If not, what steps will be taken if the female becomes pregnant? These are just some of the questions that confront engaged couples. Therefore, this task can be accomplished only if the partners are willing to make a conscious effort to communicate with each other about their sexual behavior, expectations, and needs at this point in the development of their relationship.

3. *Developing a mutually satisfactory agreement regarding family planning.* Sexually active engaged couples should be concerned about birth control measures to prevent a premarital pregnancy, but *any* engaged couple would benefit by discussing their future family planning expectations and plans. Will they have any children at all? If so, how many does each person desire? Which of the partners will take responsibility for contraception after marriage? What will be the preferred birth control method? If children are desired, when will the woman begin her childbearing years, and how will children be spaced (years between children)? It is expected that engaged partners will disagree over one or more of these matters. However, it is best if these disagreements are discovered, and attempts made to resolve them, at this early stage in the relationship rather than after marriage, when spouses might surprise each other with their family planning goals and expectations. Such surprises can result in serious conflicts, which are difficult to resolve if the partners have never taken the time to discuss their family planning intentions.

4. *Establishing a mutually satisfactory system of communication between the partners.* As with the other aspects of premarital relationship development, patterns of communication that are established at this time become *habits* that carry over into the marriage. It is desirable that effective and mutually satisfying communication habits be established during engagement so that the ensuing marriage will begin on a sound foundation. If, on the other hand, communication problems that develop before marriage are not resolved during engagement, they can develop into negative habits that become increasingly difficult to break over time. It is important to remember that the communication structure underlies and influences nearly every other aspect of the relationship: conflict management, affection exchange, sex, decision making, problem solving, and family planning. How do partners talk to each other? What are their expectations regarding communication, in terms of frequency, topics, and mode

(body language, verbalizing, and so on)? What are appropriate areas for self-disclosure? Feelings? Problems? Fears? Are partners able to talk to each other *about* their communication (that is, *metacommunication*)? Are there male-female differences in communication frequency, style, or topic? For example, is the male reluctant to discuss problems or feelings he is experiencing? Do partners view each other's talking about problems as nagging or unnecessary complaining? Does "message sent equal message received" most of the time, or do the partners experience difficulty in effectively communicating their intentions, thoughts, and feelings? It is critical that communication problems be confronted during engagement, before they become nagging habits in marriage. Engagement is a good time to begin *metacommunication* — communicating about each other's communication habits.

5. *Establishing a mutually satisfactory pattern with regard to friends and relatives.* We have already discussed the importance of each person's mentally preparing to either terminate or modify any social relationships that might compete with the marriage. This task should also be addressed by the couple: partners should communicate their feelings and expectations about their relationships with friends and relatives (particularly parents and in-laws-to-be), those which are likely to continue after marriage. Marriage does not exist in a social void. Friends and relatives can be useful sources of emotional and social support, advice, and economic assistance. They can also be a burden and interfere with the marriage relationship. Engaged partners should recognize this, and seek agreement about how these continuing relationships will be managed, and what impact they might be expected to have on the future marriage.

6. *Developing a mutually satisfactory agreement regarding work plans.* As we saw in chapter 8, the survival of marriage depends heavily on the economic functioning of the married pair. The basic needs for food, clothing, and shelter must be met. More than this, though, is the fact that people usually have a desired or ideal standard of living to which they aspire. What kind of house, car, or other material things one wants varies from one individual to the next, as do one's preferences about leisure time and entertainment activities. In view of these preferences, and the amount of money they will cost, engaged partners should attempt to come to some understanding of whether one or both partners should work after marriage, whether or not their expected level of income will provide for their

basic needs, and how they will go about earning enough income to purchase the "extras" they want.

This task also involves family planning. How will the arrival of children influence the wife's career involvement? Is she willing to step out of the labor force, at least temporarily, to give birth to a child and care for it until she is ready to return to work? Will the husband be willing to stop working to care for the child(ren) while the wife continues in her career? How does each partner feel about substitute child care? Should one parent be expected to care for the child full time, until the child reaches a certain age? If so, what age?

The blending of marital- and parental-role responsibilities is a critical one for women today. It is a dilemma for the married couple who want the woman to establish herself in a career and who also want to have one or more children. Although the issue may not be resolved during engagement, the couple should at least address it, identify alternative courses of action, and begin planning for the future. In doing so during engagement, communication channels should remain open until the time when these decisions *must be* made during marriage.

7. *Developing mutually satisfactory patterns regarding decision making.* Marriage involves a certain amount of power and influence of one partner over the other when it comes to making key decisions. We have seen how important some of these decisions are during engagement: decisions about children, family planning, careers, friends, and relatives. In addition, we must also be concerned with the *process* of how decisions are made. Does one partner make all of the decisions on his or her own? Does one make all of the *important* decisions, leaving only the trivial matters up to the other partner? Do partners share equally — a mutual give and take — when making important decisions? Do partners have separate domains, in which each person makes decisions with little or no involvement of the other ("separate but equal")? Whatever the case, it is important that the decision-making pattern in the relationship is recognized, and that any dissatisfaction with the pattern be addressed during engagement. A sore spot in many marriages is the question of who has the right to make decisions, and whose decision will prevail, in the case of a disagreement. This is why it is best to resolve any differences *before* marriage, and before *any* unsatisfactory decision-making patterns become habits that are difficult to break years later.

JUDGING THE SUCCESS OF ENGAGEMENT

In defining engagement as a time when certain *developmental tasks* should be accomplished, it is implied that those couples who are able to accomplish these tasks are more likely to make the early years of marriage more successful, in terms of reaching the goals they have set for themselves. A successful engagement, then, would be one in which the partners prepare for the transition to marriage by working to complete these developmental tasks.

Success in engagement can be gauged in other ways, however. First, it is unlikely that many couples are able to accomplish all seven of these tasks satisfactorily. The important point is that engaged partners at least make an *attempt to work* on those areas viewed as troublesome in the relationship. Even if the agreement is not reached and the differences of opinion remain, at least the key issues have been brought out into the open. The problem can therefore be more readily addressed at a later point than otherwise might be possible. The rule of thumb here would be to accomplish as many of these tasks as possible before marriage, and continue to "keep the book open" on troublesome ones that cannot be completely resolved.

Second, a successful engagement is also one where the partners recognize too many "danger signals" (see page 292) and realize that either the marriage should be delayed or the engagement broken. Broken engagements are just as *successful* as those in which the developmental tasks of engagement are completed. To filter out poor matches is an important function of the engagement process, and the breaking of an engagement should not be viewed as a failure on the part of either person.

There is no magic formula for how long engagements should last in order to promote a smooth transition into marriage. It depends entirely upon what the partners *do* with their time during the engagement. Here, the *quality* of the time spent together in developing the relationship is far more important than the *quantity* of time spent. Engagements of 6 months or more duration will yield favorable outcomes for the transition to marriage if partners use this time to work on developing the relationship, and focus on performing key developmental tasks. Such an amount of time also allows a greater opportunity for filtering out those couples who probably should not get married in the first place (Landis and Landis, 1977). Longer engagements will *not* have such a favorable impact if the time is spent avoiding conflicts and dissatisfactions with various aspects of the relationship. Short engagements—a few weeks or months—are often too brief to successfully accomplish developmental tasks. Such engagements are more likely than longer engagements to result in marriages between "strangers" who never really got to know one another well enough before entering marriage. In general, then, duration of the engagement is only important to the extent that partners are able to use the time wisely by preparing for marriage in a conscientious manner.

Marriage and the Law: Rights and Obligations

Marriage is a civil contract entered into by the two partners and the state. In this way, society expresses through the legal system its concern for the integrity of the family. Husband-wife, parent-child, and sibling relationships, along with other aspects of family life, are governed by laws designed to protect the rights and well-being of all family members. Marriage laws, in particular, are designed to specify the rights and obligations of each partner in marriage.

In many ways, marriage contracts are like any other contracts. In order to be valid, all contracts must satisfy the following conditions:

1. Consent to the agreement by both parties, as evidenced by the signature of both partners on a legally valid contractual agreement (such as a marriage license);

2. Absence of duress, coercion, or undue influence on either partner entering the contract;

3. The signature of a legally recognized witness and, in the case of marriage, the presence of a legally acceptable person to officiate (justice of the peace, minister, etc.).

There are several features of marriage laws that are important to know. First, marriage laws vary considerably from one state to the next. Each state government has full control over the laws governing marriage contracts of its residents. This has resulted in widespread confusion and misunderstanding, because little uniformity exists from one state to the next. The criteria for a valid marriage contract in one state might not be considered valid in another. As the information contained in Table 10.3 indicates, laws vary in terms of age guidelines, medical examination requirements, parental consent rules, adultery, property ownership, recognition of marriages in other states, and waiting periods. It would be wise for anyone considering marriage to know and understand the body of marriage laws of the state in which the marriage is to take place, as well as those of the state in which one is to take up residency.

Second, because marriage involves a legally binding agreement between the two partners and the state, only the state can legally change or dissolve the contract. It is reasonably simple to satisfy the conditions *to enter* a marriage contract, given the mutual consent of age-eligible partners, their willingness to wait the required time period and to pay the modest license fee, and the presence of an approved person to officiate. However, marriage is unlike other contracts in that the two parties involved cannot change any of the conditions of the agreement. Only the state can do that, through its legislative system. Also, the *dissolving* of a marriage contract, or divorce, is far more complicated and expensive than entering a marriage. It requires legal petitions, legal assistance of a lawyer (in many cases), a court hearing, and a decision by a judge or magistrate to terminate a marriage contract. The presence of children, property accumulation, and the individual rights and obligations of partners seeking to dissolve a marriage contract all mean that the judicial system will become involved, in an effort to bring justice and fairness to divorce cases. The state is interested in protecting the well-being of those involved, children as well as adults. Even with the easing of contemporary divorce laws and the creation of alternative divorce procedures (see chapter 15), divorce is usually a more complicated affair than marriage.

Third, there are some laws that are consistent from one state to the next. For example, all states require that only two individuals can be married at any one time. Moreover, they must be of the opposite sex; homosexual unions do not carry the legal status and protection available in marriage. The same can be said for laws prohibiting marriage between members of the same family; these are

TABLE 10.3. *State-by-State Legal Guidelines Relating to Marriage*

State	Legal Age for Marriage Without Parental Consent		Legal Age for Marriage With Parental Consent		Medical Tests Required [2]	Common-Law Marriage Allowed	Property	Status of Out-of-state Marriages	Waiting Period	Adultery A Crime?	Cohabitation Legal?
	Males	*Females*	*Males*	*Females*							
Alabama	18	18	14	14	Blood test	Yes	Separate	Valid if valid in state where marriage occurred	None	Yes, if combined with cohabitation	No
Alaska	18	18	16[1]	16[1]	Blood test	No	Separate	Valid if valid in state where marriage occurred	3 days	No	Yes
Arizona	18	18	16[1]	16[1]	Blood test	No, but recognized if valid in state where marriage occurred	Community	Valid if valid in state where marriage occurred	None	Yes (misdemeanor)	No
Arkansas	18	18	17	16	Blood test and physician's certificate	No	Separate	Valid if valid in state where marriage occurred	3 days	No	No
California	18	18	Not Fixed	Not Fixed	Blood test and physician's certificate	No, but recognized if valid in state where marriage occurred	Community	Valid if in state where marriage occurred	None	No	Yes
Colorado	18	18	16[1]	16[1]	Blood test for venereal disease, rubella, and ph factor, and physician's certificate	Yes	Separate	Valid if valid in state where marriage occurred	None	No	Yes

State					Medical requirement	Common law marriage	Property	Validity of marriage from other jurisdiction	Waiting period	Criminal penalty	
Connecticut	18	18	16[1]	16[1]	Blood test and physician's certificate	No	Separate	Recognized unless contrary to strong public policy	4 days	No	Yes
Delaware	18	18	16		Blood test and physician's certificate	No, but recognized if valid in state where marriage occurred	Separate	Valid, unless prohibited by Delaware law	24 hours for residents, 96 hours for non-residents[6]	No	Yes
District of Columbia	18	16	16		Blood test and physician's certificate	Yes	Separate	Void if prohibited in D.C. and entered into another state by a D.C. resident	3 days	Yes; fine and/or jail[3]	Yes
Florida	18	Not Fixed	Not Fixed		Blood test and physician's certificate	No, unless entered into before 1968	Separate	No provision, but presumably valid if valid in state where entered into	3 days	Yes (misdemeanor)	No
Georgia	16	Not Fixed	Not Fixed		Blood test and physician's certificate	Yes	Separate	Valid, if valid in state where marriage occurred	3 days unless both over 18	Yes (misdemeanor)	Yes
Hawaii	18	16[4]	16[4]		Blood test	No	Separate[5]	Valid, if valid in state where marriage occurred	30 days	No	Yes
Idaho	18	16[1]	16[1]		Blood test and physician's certificate	Yes	Community	Valid if valid where marriage occurred	None	Yes (misdemeanor)	No

(continued)

299

TABLE 10.3. (*Continued*)

State	Legal Age for Marriage Without Parental Consent		Legal Age for Marriage With Parental Consent		Medical Tests Required?[2]	Common-Law Marriage Allowed	Property	Status of Out-of-state Marriages	Waiting Period	Adultery A Crime?	Cohabitation Legal?
	Males	Females	Males	Females							
Illinois	18	18	16	16	Blood test and physician's certificate	No	Separate	Void if prohibited in Illinois; otherwise valid if valid in state where marriage occurred	3 days	Yes, if open and notorious	No
Indiana	18	18	Not Fixed	Not Fixed	Blood test and physician's certificate	No	Separate	Invalid if done with the intention of avoiding Indiana law	3 days	No	Yes
Iowa	18	18	Not Fixed	Not Fixed	Blood test and physician's certificate	Yes	Separate	Valid if valid in state where marriage occurred	3 days	No	Yes
Kansas	18	18	Not Fixed[1]	Not Fixed[1]	Blood test	Yes	Separate	Valid if valid in state where marriage occurred	3 days	Yes (misdemeanor)	Yes
Kentucky	18	18	Not Fixed	Not Fixed	Blood test	No, but recognized if valid where marriage occurred	Separate	Valid if valid in state where marriage occurred	3 days	No	Yes
Louisiana	18	16	Not Fixed	Not Fixed	Blood test and	No	Community	Valid if valid in state	3 days[6]	No	Yes

State				physician's certificate			where marriage occurred			
Maine	18	18	16[1]	Blood test and physician's certificate	No, but valid if valid in state where marriage occurred	Separate	Valid unless done to avoid Maine law	5 days	No	No
Maryland	18	18	16[1]	No	No, but valid if valid in state where marriage occurred	Separate	Valid if valid in state where marriage occurred	2 days	Yes, nominal fine	Yes
Massachusetts	18	Not Fixed	Not Fixed	Blood test and physician's certificate	No	Separate	Void if Massachusetts resident enters a marriage in another state that would not be valid in Massachusetts	3 days	Yes; fine or jail term	No
Michigan	18	Not Fixed	Not Fixed	Blood test	No	Separate	Valid if valid where marriage occurred	3 days	Yes; felony[8]	No
Minnesota	18	18	16[1]	No	No	Separate	Valid if valid where marriage occurred	5 days	Yes; fine and/or jail term	Yes
Mississippi	18	17[1]	15[1]	Blood test and physician's certificate	No	Separate	Valid if valid where marriage occurred	3 days	Yes[8]	No

(continued)

TABLE 10.3. (*Continued*)

State	Legal Age for Marriage Without Parental Consent		Legal Age for Marriage With Parental Consent[2]		Medical Tests Required[2]	Common-Law Marriage Allowed	Property	Status of Out-of-state Marriages	Waiting Period	Adultery A Crime?	Cohabitation Legal?
	Males	Females	Males	Females							
Missouri	18	18	15	15	Blood test and physician's certificate[7]	No, but recognized if valid in state where marriage occurred	Separate	Valid if valid where marriage occurred	3 days	No	Yes
Montana	18	18	15[1]	15[1]	Blood test for syphilis and rubella immunity and physician's certificate	Yes	Separate	Valid if valid where marriage occurred	3 days	Yes (misdemeanor); fine or jail term	No
Nebraska	18	18	Not Fixed	Not Fixed	Blood test for syphilis and rubella immunity and physician's certificate	No, but recognized if valid in state where marriage occurred	Separate	Valid if valid where marriage occurred	2 days	Yes; jail term	No
Nevada	18	18	16[1]	16[1]	None	No, but recognized if valid in state where marriage occurred	Community	Valid if valid in state where marriage occurred	None	No	Yes
New Hampshire	18	18	14[9]	13[9]	Blood test and physician's certificate	No[10]	Separate	Valid if valid in state where marriage occurred	None	Yes (misdemeanor)	Yes
New Jersey	18	18	16[1]	16[1]	Blood test and physician's	No, but recognized if valid in	Separate	Valid if valid in state where	3 days	No	Yes

State					certificate	state where marriage occurred		marriage occurred			
New Mexico	18	18	16[1]	16[1]	Medical examination	No, but recognized if valid in state where marriage occurred	Community	Valid if valid in state where marriage occurred	None	No	No
New York	18	18	16	16	Blood test and gonorrhea test	No	Separate	Valid if valid in state where marriage occurred	1 day[6]	Yes (misdemeanor) fine and/or jail term	Yes
North Carolina	18	18	16	16	Medical examination[11]	No, but recognized if valid in state where marriage occurred	Separate	Valid if valid in state where marriage occurred	None	Yes (misdemeanor) fine and/or jail sentence	Yes
North Dakota	18	18	16	16	Medical examination[12]	No	Separate	Valid if valid in state where marriage occurred unless same marriage would be prohibited in North Dakota	None	Yes (misdemeanor)	No
Ohio	18	16	Not Fixed	Not Fixed	Blood test, physician's certificate, and laboratory statement	Yes	Separate	Valid if valid in state where marriage entered	5 days	No	Yes

(continued)

TABLE 10.3. (*Continued*)

State	Legal Age for Marriage Without Parental Consent		Legal Age for Marriage With Parental Consent		Medical Tests Required[2]	Common-Law Marriage Allowed	Property	Status of Out-of-state Marriages	Waiting Period	Adultery A Crime?	Cohabitation Legal?
	Males	Females	Males	Females							
Oklahoma	18	18	16	16	Blood test, physician's certificate, and laboratory statement	Yes	Separate	Valid if valid in state where marriage entered	3 days (only if either partner is under age)	Yes; fine or jail term	Yes
Oregon	17	17	Not Fixed	Not Fixed	Blood test, physician's certificate, and laboratory statement	No, but recognized if valid in state where entered into	Separate	Valid if valid in state where marriage entered	3 days	No	Yes
Pennsylvania	18	18	16[1]	16[1]	Blood test and physician's certificate	Yes	Separate	Valid if valid in state where marriage entered	3 days	No	Yes
Rhode Island	18	18	Not Fixed	Not Fixed	Blood test for venereal disease and rubella	Yes	Separate	Valid if valid in state where marriage entered	None	Yes; fine or jail term	Yes
South Carolina	18	18	16	14	No	Yes	Separate	Valid if valid in state where marriage entered	1 day	Yes; fine and/or jail term	No
South Dakota	18	18	Not Fixed	Not Fixed	Blood test and physician's certificate	No	Separate	Valid if valid in state where marriage entered	None	No	Yes

State											
Tennessee	18	18	16	16	Blood test and physician's certificate	No, but recognized if valid in state where marriage occurred	Separate	Valid if valid in state where marriage entered	3 days	No	No
Texas	18	18	14[1]	14[1]	Blood test and physician's certificate	Yes	Community	Valid if valid in state where marriage entered	None	No	Yes
Utah	18	18	14	14	Blood test and physician's certificate	No, but recognized if valid in state where marriage occurred (except Utah residents)	Separate	Valid if valid in state where marriage occurred	None	Yes (misdemeanor)	Yes
Vermont	18	18	14	14	Medical examination	No	Separate	Valid, unless entered into with the intention of avoiding Vermont law	5 days	Yes; fine and/or jail term	Yes
Virginia	18	18	Not Fixed	Not Fixed	Blood test and physician's certificate	No, but recognized if valid in state where marriage occurred	Separate	Valid, unless entered into with the intention of avoiding Virginia law	None	Yes (misdemeanor)	No

(continued)

305

TABLE 10.3. (*Continued*)

State	Legal Age for Marriage Without Parental Consent		Legal Age for Marriage With Parental Consent		Medical Tests Required[2]	Common-Law Marriage Allowed	Property	Status of Out-of-state Marriages	Waiting Period	Adultery A Crime?	Cohabitation Legal?
	Males	Females	Males	Females							
Washington	18	18	17	17	No[13]	No, but recognized if valid in state where marriage occurred (except Washington residents)	Community	Valid, unless entered into with the intention of avoiding Washington law	3 days	No	Yes
West Virginia	18	18	18	16	Blood test and physician's certificate	No, but recognized as valid in state where marriage occurred	Separate	Valid, if valid in state where marriage occurred, and not contrary to public policy of W. Va.	3 days	Yes; fine	No
Wisconsin	18	18	16	16	Blood test and	No	Separate (will become	Valid, if valid in state	5 days	A legal felony	No

				physician's certificate		"community" in 1986	where marriage occurred, and not contrary to public policy of Wisconsin	None	No	No
Wyoming	18	18	16¹	16¹	Blood test and physician's certificate	No, but recognized as valid if valid in state where marriage occurred	Separate	Valid if valid in state where marriage occurred	None	No	No

1. Younger ages can be approved by court.
2. Maximum number of days test is required before issuance of marriage license varies from state to state, from between 10 and 45 days.
3. Adultery between married woman and unmarried man, both are guilty; between married man and unmarried woman, only man is guilty.
4. Written approval of family court required at age 15; marriage not permitted under 15.
5. Modified community-property system in effect.
6. Counted between issuance of license and ceremony.
7. Certificate from physician stating that female applicant is not pregnant; or that either applicant is not on their deathbed and unlikely to consummate marriage.
8. Extends to those who cohabit (live together) after divorce.
9. Approval of judge of probate or superior court required for any marriages to those under 18 years of age.
10. Statute provides that individuals who cohabit, acknowledge each other as husband and wife, and who are generally thought to be married for at least three years are thereafter considered legally married.
11. Must show absence of venereal disease, tuberculosis, mental incompetence, and have rubella immunity (for females).
12. Must show applicant is not feebleminded, imbecile, insane, a drunkard, or infected with venereal disease.
13. Affidavit must be filed showing applicant not infected with venereal disease.

SOURCE: Sonenblick (1981). The reader should note that these laws were in effect in 1981. Some may have changed since that time. Current state statutes may therefore vary somewhat from those noted in this table.

known as *incest laws*. All states have outlawed marriages between close *consanguineal* relatives, or those "related by blood," such as a mother, father, grandparent, cousin, sibling, aunt, or uncle. However, states vary widely in regard to incest laws which apply to second and third cousins, as well as to *affinal* relatives (related *by marriage, not by blood*).

Fourth, although some marriage laws may exist, they are only rarely enforced. Examples of this are the laws relating to extramarital sexual intercourse, or adultery (see Table 10.3). Some states prohibit sexual intercourse outside of marriage (fornication), and several have outlawed cohabitation. Some states even outlaw certain sexual acts of consenting adults, married or unmarried, such as oral or anal sex. However, unless such activities are deemed "lewd and lascivious," and were to be conducted in an "open and notorious" manner in violation of a community's antiobscenity policies, they would rarely come to the attention of the legal authorities for eventual prosecution. As one legal expert has pointed out, in regard to anticohabitation, antiadultery, and antifornication laws:

> No one, least of all the law-enforcement community, is seriously interested in enforcing them, in part because the police know that the citizenry is in greater danger from muggers, murderers, and traffic violators . . . , and partly because prosecutors are aware of the shaky constitutional foundations of such laws and the difficulty of getting convictions without treading on the now-protected privacy rights of individuals. (Sonenblick, 1981:30)

COMMON-LAW MARRIAGE

Thirteen states and the District of Columbia allow a male and female to be granted full legal marriage status without ever going through a state-authorized ceremony (see Table 10.3). These are known as *common-law marriages*. The law usually requires that both individuals agree to be married, that they live together as husband and wife, and that they present themselves in the community as a married couple (Sonenblick, 1981:445). There is no set limit on the number of years a couple must live together to qualify for common-law-marriage status.

PROPERTY RIGHTS

One of the basic ingredients of marriage contracts in all states is that they assure both partners certain rights in regard to property acquired in the marriage. In the event of a divorce, the distribution of such property between the ex-spouses is a task that the state assumes through a divorce court judge. There are only two types of property distribution systems in the United States: (1) community property and (2) separate property (see Table 10.3).

Community Property. Eight states have marital property laws stating that "all property accruing from the labor of either spouse during the marriage belongs equally to both; this includes all wages, salaries, and income from property or investments acquired with such monies" (Sonenblick, 1981:80). The community-property-law states are Arizona, California, Texas, Nevada, Idaho, Louisiana, New Mexico, and Washington.

The major benefit of community-property laws is for the spouse who does not work outside of the home, and who, as a result of this position of dependency, has never actually earned the money that has purchased a home, car, clothing, appliances, and other material possessions in the marriage. Upon divorce or death of the spouse, one half of the value of all property acquired during the marriage automatically is given by the state to the dependent or surviving spouse. However, it should be noted that the nature of community property law varies across all states having such laws. Some (California and Arizona) apply such laws to new residents who were married in a separate-property state, and others do not. Some states give judges considerable leeway in dividing community property in a way that is fair and equitable, though not necessarily equal. For example, a judge might decide that a divorcing wife deserves more than half of the community property, if she receives custody of the children and must pay for their care.

In community-property states, *separate property* is that which was acquired by either spouse *before* the marriage took place, or was received by a spouse by means of gift or inheritance after the marriage. It should be noted, however, that separate property can become *community* property very quickly if it is *comingled* by the spouses. This means that if such separate property or wealth is ever placed in the names of both partners, or made accessible to both (such as in a joint checking or savings account, or by securing joint title to a piece of land, or car), then the court may decide that it is owned equally by both spouses and subject to equal distribution upon divorce.

Another point in regard to community-property laws deserves mention. Debts and other financial obligations acquired by one spouse during a marriage become a burden shared equally by the other spouse. That is, in community-property states one is legally liable for debts incurred by a spouse. By the same token, debts incurred by a spouse *before* the marriage are his or her sole responsibility, and any separate or community property one might have in the marriage cannot be touched by legal action taken by creditors.

Separate Property.   Forty-two states and the District of Columbia have *separate-property* laws. This means that "all income or property acquired before or during the marriage belongs to the acquiring spouse" (Sonenblick, 1981:83). However, all but five of the separate-property states provide for fair and equitable property settlements in the case of divorce, regardless of who is in possession of the separate property. As Sonenblick (1981:83) points out, any divorcing spouse may place a claim upon and receive some or all of the separate property of the partner.

The five states which do *not* provide judges with this leeway in distributing separate property are Florida, Mississippi, South Carolina, Virginia, and West Virginia. In these locations, spouses can be denied access to any property, income, or wealth whatsoever if they were dependent upon the other and did not earn any income during the marriage. Because of such laws, an individual, usually the wife, may be left penniless, unless the partner decides to "share the wealth" after divorce. In any event, being the nonemployed partner in a single-earner marriage can create severe postdivorce financial problems, if one lives in one of these five separate-property states.

PERSONAL MARRIAGE CONTRACTS

During the 1970s, it became popular in some circles for married partners to draw up individualized marriage contracts, specifying the rights and obligations of each spouse—those which are not addressed in the regular marriage laws of the state. Such contracts had great appeal for some because they listed in black and white what each person's expectations were regarding self and other, and because they acquired a certain level of credibility in the eyes of the spouses who actually signed their names to them. However, such contracts were criticized because of the formality and legalistic jargon they introduced into a relationship that is based on romantic feelings and emo-

tional considerations. Marriage contracts have touched on such areas as these: who will handle domestic chores and household duties (washing dishes, housecleaning, ironing, repairs, and so on); who is responsible for contraception; whether or not children will be born to the married couple; how the children will be raised; how finances will be handled (joint versus separate bank accounts, financial planning, and decision making); property rights, obligations, and special arrangements; and career priorities and decisions bearing on where the partners will live (domicile agreements).

In actual court tests of such contracts, it has been made clear that the courts will uphold and honor them, *provided that they are legally valid contracts and do not conflict with existing marriage law or public policy.* Contracts stating that a couple will not bear children, that the parents are not responsible for child-support, or that sexual privileges can be exchanged for financial support are considered *invalid* and *nonbinding* because they run counter to existing law or public policy. Other contractual agreements, such as household maintenance and career decisions, are enforceable if contained in a legally drawn contract. The best advice regarding whether or not to formalize a special marriage contract with your spouse is, learn the marriage laws in your state and seek the assistance of a qualified attorney. This can make the difference between formulating a valid and binding contract, or an unenforceable document which is worth no more than the paper on which the "agreement" is written.

MARRIAGE VERSUS COHABITATION: WHAT DIFFERENCE CAN A PIECE OF PAPER MAKE?

In chapter 9, we discussed the social and psychological aspects of living together before marriage, or cohabitation. However, the legal aspects of cohabitation have been left unaddressed until now, in order to compare them directly with the legalities of marriage.

One of the primary forces underlying the popularity of cohabitation is the belief that "living together" constitutes a "no strings attached" arrangement. Whereas marriage implies commitment and legal obligations, unmarried cohabitation allows the freedom to leave the partner when it is determined that the relationship is no longer fulfilling each other's needs. Divorce means legal hassles and court battles; ending a cohabitation relationship involves little or no "muss or fuss," at least legally. Although it is true that, in many ways, marriage and cohabitation are viewed differently by the courts, several recent court cases point to one stark conclusion: *The differences between cohabitation and legal marriage are diminishing in the eyes of the law.* This conclusion is particularly applicable where property, wealth, and children are involved.

The Marvin vs. Marvin Palimony Case.

The event that first brought the legal issues of cohabitation to national attention was a lawsuit filed in 1976 by Hollywood actor Lee Marvin's former live-in mate, Michelle Triola Marvin. She claimed that she and Marvin cohabited for nearly six years before he left her for another woman. During that time, Michelle claimed, Lee agreed to give half of his earnings to her and support her for the rest of her life, in exchange for her valued affection and services. She functioned as his housekeeper, sex partner, and nursemaid after she gave up a career as a singer-actress to be his "permanent," but unmarried, companion. When he left her, Michelle sued for half of Lee's earnings during the time that they cohabited—about $1.5 million worth of "palimony"—claiming that Lee's verbal statements constituted an implicit contract that he was legally and morally bound to keep. The case went to court, and established important legal precedents in regard to the rights and obligations of unmarried cohabitants.

The legal rulings made in the *Marvin vs. Marvin* case have had profound implications. First, the California Supreme Court ruled that oral and written agreements between cohabitants constitute enforceable contracts, if documentation that they were made can be provided. As a result, cohabitors were given the legal right, previously reserved exclusively to the married population, to make claim to each other's possessions, earnings, and property. Although sex-for-economic support agreements are invalid, exchange of household duties and companionship for economic support were declared valid in the eyes of the California law.

Second, the California courts ruled that "tacit (unspoken and/or implied) understandings" of commitment and support between cohabitants, as evidenced in their behavior with each other and the ways in which they present themselves publicly, could be used to determine the property rights of unmarried cohabitants. If those in a couple have "an understanding" that they are to support each other and relate to each other "as if they were married" or "as married people would," one of them could find that they are subject to losing some or most of their property after the relationship has ended. The casual kind of cohabitation, such as that which lasts for a few months on a college campus, where there is little or no commitment or promise of support for the future, is *not* included in such property-rights decisions.

In sum, cohabitation is no longer viewed as a "no strings attached" relationship—in the eyes of the law. To the contrary, the strings can be quite substantial, and just as strong as those attached to marriage, when it comes to property rights.

COHABITATION AND MARRIAGE: THE DIFFERENCES

In the previous section, we saw how cohabitation is becoming more and more like marriage in the eyes of the law, especially when it comes to property rights. There are still some key differences, however, between the two statuses of "married" and "cohabiting." Following is a list of only some of these differences, which vary from one state to the next.

1. *Economic Benefits.* Marriage confers the right to gain access to the spouse's pension, Social Security benefits, Workman's Compensation, and some insurance policies, but cohabitation does not. Married persons may also pay lower insurance premiums because they are defined as "better risks" by insurance companies. A married person can also claim a spouse as a dependent on federal and state income tax forms, whereas a cohabiting individual can claim a dependent live-in mate as a dependent only in states where cohabitation is legal (see Table 10.3). Finally, spouses are normally granted generous inheritance rights when a spouse dies, particularly when no last will and testament has been made (known as *intestate succession*). Cohabitants usually lose out to the blood relatives of the deceased partner when it comes to inheritance.

2. *Testimonial Privilege.* A married person may not be forced to testify against the spouse in a court of law. However, one spouse may *voluntarily* testify for or against the other. Cohabitants do not have the right to avoid testifying against the partner in court.

3. *Lawsuits.* Most states prohibit one spouse from suing another for wrongdoing. However, there is nothing to prevent cohabitants from suing their partners.

4. *Domicile.* A person's domicile is the state in which one claims residence. In many states, a wife's legal domicile must be the same as her husband's (but not vice versa). In Iowa, Kentucky, Minnesota, Montana, New York, Vermont, West Virginia, and Wisconsin the husband is given the right to determine the place of legal residence. This is an important issue when dual-career spouses live apart for a time because of career demands, or when one commutes to work between states. Domicile determines where one can vote, become a candidate for public office, or be called for jury duty. There are no such rules for cohabitants.

5. *Husband's Support of Wife.* Many states legally obligate the husband to provide the "necessaries" of food, clothing, and shelter for the family. In only six states does the law require spouses to support each other. No such laws applying to cohabitants exist.

6. *Responsibility for Debts.* In community-property states, a married person is held liable for the debts and financial obligations incurred by the spouse. Cohabitants, on the other hand, are not liable for each other's debts, even in community-property states. This fact may have a bearing on the greater difficulty experienced by cohabitors in acquiring loans and other kinds of credit, and in securing a favorable credit rating.

The Early Years of Marriage: Making it Through the Transition

A number of factors contribute either to strength or difficulty in the early years of marriage. Entry into this stage constitutes a critical transition point in the marital career. Because nearly one in four divorces occurs in the first two years of marriage, it is clear that for many there is substantial stress and strain during this time.

PERSONALITY FACTORS

The kind of person one is, and the kind of person one chooses to marry, influences the degree of success in the early years. The term of *marriageability* means that marriage may suit the needs, goals, and abilities of some more than others.

Some people are definitely more marriageable than others. They would have a better than average probability of making a success of any marriage they might enter. Others would have difficulty no matter whom they married. (Landis and Landis, 1977:75–76)

A number of behavioral and personality traits foster marriageability in the individual. These traits assume their importance as a result of the newness of marriage to the partners, the unanticipated twists and turns that marriage is likely to entail, and the normal sorts of stress and strain involved in being married to an individual who may possess quite different values, habits, and expectations (Landis and Landis, 1977).

1. *Adaptability.* The ability to adjust to new situations, to be flexible in the face of change, and to relate to a variety of other sorts of people in different settings are all characteristics of adaptability. People who have rigid personalities, who are unwilling to tolerate change or challenges to their points of view, and who are inflexible and uncomfortable in situations that might be different from what they are used to, are poor marriage risks. Adaptability is an important quality while the newly married is seeking to adjust to a new situation with another person (Kieren and Tallman, 1971).

2. *Empathy.* The ability to accurately perceive the attitudes, role expectations, and feelings of other people is an important aspect of marriageability. Recall that empathy is an important component of the communication process in a relationship (chapter 7), and that effective communication is more likely to occur if partners are not only able to express accurately their own thoughts and feelings, but to understand those of the partner as well.

3. *Problem-Solving Ability.* A marriageable person is one who is able to maintain a certain level of calm and cool in the face of problems. This means being able to identify accurately the nature and scope of a problem, consider the available alternative solutions, and select the alternative most likely to yield constructive results. Marriageable people are not overwhelmed by problems in early marriage, whether they relate to in-law relation-

ships or money matters, and they do not confront problem situations with a defeatist attitude.

MARITAL-CHOICE FACTORS

Recall the concept of *homogamy,* which was discussed earlier in this chapter. We stated that partners who are similar in terms of age, education, race, and social class are more likely than others to share similar values, role expectations, and goals for marriage. For example, if one marries a person similar in age, or one from a similar educational background, there is more likely to be a compatible match in gender-role expectations — what each expects from the other in regard to exchanging affection, communicating, doing household chores, and earning income.

Presumably, homogamous marriages will have less stress and strain than nonhomogamous, or *heterogamous,* marriages, because disagreements and conflict over these important aspects of marriage are likely to be minimal. Indeed, research evidence gathered between 1940 and 1960 supported this conclusion (Burgess and Cottrell, 1939; Roth and Peck, 1951; Blood and Wolfe, 1960; Landis, 1949). These studies found that homogamous marriages were less divorce-prone, and were better adjusted than others.

However, more recent research has cast some doubt on the generalization that homogamy leads to a smoother transition into marriage and more successful adjustment to the early years of marriage (Glenn, Hoppe, and Weiner, 1974; Jorgensen and Klein, 1979). Most heterogamous couples today are just as likely to agree with each other

Contemporary society has grown more accepting of interracial dating and marriage; however, interracial couples still experience the stress and strain caused by prejudicial attitudes and discrimination.
(Photo by Stephen R. Jorgensen.)

about important marital values and role expectations as homogamous couples. This is true regardless of whether they are heterogamous along age, educational, religious, or social-class lines. Other studies have found that although divorce rates are slightly higher than average for interreligious and age-discrepant marriages, the differences are small and the majority of such marriages survive without divorce (Bumpass and Sweet, 1972; Landis, 1949). More recent research has found that spouses in interreligious marriages and those in religiously homogamous marriages report about equal levels of satisfaction with marriage (Glenn, 1982).

The exception is interracial marriage, particularly between Blacks and whites. Divorce rates in these marriages run significantly higher than in racially homogamous marriages (Heer, 1974). Apparently, the stresses and strains in interracial marriages are far greater than those in other kinds of heterogamous unions. Societal attitudes — prejudice and discrimination — reactions of friends and family members, and the uncertain status of children born in racially-mixed marriages, all contribute to making such marriages difficult to negotiate successfully. Nonetheless, the majority of such marriages survive without divorce, indicating that many such couples are able to weather the storm of negative social reaction.

At this time, there is simply no convincing evidence to suggest that a person should avoid marrying someone from a different socioeconomic, religious, or cultural background. As long as potential value- and role-conflicts are recognized during the premarital and engagement stages, as long as partners are able to adjust to their differences, and as long as the partners are willing to work to resolve their differences, the outcome in the early years of marriage should be about the same for both homogamous and heterogamous couples: a successful transition into this stage of the marital career.

TIMING FACTORS

Research shows that the timing of marriage, in terms of the *age* at which it occurs, is an important aspect of marital adjustment in the early years. The median age of marriage today is approximately 25 for males and 23 for females (that is, half of all marriages occur by those ages) [(U.S. Bureau of the Census, 1984c)]. This means that many people are not marrying until they have accom-

plished certain things. As can be seen in Table 10.4, the average age at first marriage has steadily increased in the United States, since 1960.

First, waiting until this age allows both partners enough time to complete the education they want, particularly if college is involved; and there is also enough time for one or both to secure employment. In view of the significance of income in promoting marital stability (see chapter 8), it is important to have developed a solid economic base before marriage. Much stress in these early years can be avoided if there is adequate income to pay for the monthly bills; to meet the expenses involved in purchasing a home or renting an apartment, buying a car, furniture, and appliances; to purchase adequate life, health, and household insurance; and to meet the numerous incidental expenses associated with being married. Delays in the timing of the first marriage have been fostered by the rapid movement of women into advanced levels of educational and career pursuits over the past two decades (Glick, 1979).

Second, waiting to marry allows time to develop a mature love relationship that will last after the marriage (see chapter 3). A period of time is necessary to allow a satisfactory level of trust, security, and mutual knowledge to develop in the relationship. A closely related concept is that of emotional maturity, which is strongly associated

TABLE 10.4. *Median Age at First Marriage in the United States, 1960–1983*

Year	Males' Age	Females' Age
1983	25.4	22.8
1982	25.2	22.5
1981	24.8	22.3
1980	24.7	22.0
1979	24.4	22.1
1978	24.2	21.8
1977	24.0	21.6
1976	23.8	21.3
1975	23.5	21.1
1970	23.2	20.8
1965	22.8	20.6
1960	22.8	20.3

SOURCE: U.S. Bureau of the Census, Marital status and living arrangements: March 1983. *Current Population Reports,* Series P–20, No. 389, Washington, D.C., 1984, P. 1, Table A.

with adjustment success in the early years of marriage (Dean, 1966; Cole, Cole, and Dean, 1980; Quinn and Dennis, 1982).

Third, proper timing allows an opportunity for partners to accomplish the developmental tasks important for making a smooth transition into marriage (as discussed earlier in this chapter). Research evidence shows that couples who are better at accomplishing developmental tasks before marriage make a smoother transition into marriage, and experience fewer disagreements and misunderstandings because they meet each other's role expectations more fully (Aldous, 1978). They are more likely to be mature enough to have developed realistic expectations for the marriage, and of each other's roles in the marriage. A major part of this process is dispelling romanticized notions of what marriage is — taking off the "rose-colored glasses." This is the best way to avoid postmarital reality shock, a devastating experience for those who marry without really knowing each other very well. A study of young married couples, conducted by Cutler and Dyer (1965), shows that many such couples experience disappointment when communicating and attempting to resolve conflicts. When the wife in this study did something that violated the role expectations of the husband, he tended to adopt a "wait and see" strategy, hoping that the conflict would disappear. Wives, on the other hand, tended to vocalize their complaints freely. Neither wives nor husbands were satisfied with the way their partners reacted in conflicts. Wives thought the husbands were trying to avoid resolving the issue, and husbands perceived their wives as nagging. All this is strong evidence that this stage of the marital career is difficult to negotiate if partners have not taken the time to establish effective and mutually satisfying patterns of communication and conflict-management beforehand.

FACTORS RELATING TO ROLE RECIPROCITY

Role reciprocity contributes to the morale of both marriage partners and helps to motivate them to make their relationship a growth-oriented and dynamic one. Daily patterns must be established for household chores and duties, as well as for such routine activities as sharing the bathroom; spending free time together; awake-sleep cycles; meal schedules; frequency and interest in sexual activity; television viewing; and entertainment. Role reciprocity is established when both partners view the other's behavior in these realms as meeting their expectations. For many couples in this stage, companionship activities are particularly important for the partners' morale and successful marital adjustment (Lowenthal, Thurner, and Chiriboga, 1977; Quinn and Dennis, 1982). Going to movies, plays, sporting events, restaurants, having fun together, or simply enjoying free time with each other strengthens the marital bond. The blending of *joint* versus *individual* time is no easy task, however, and differences between partners in this area may lead to serious conflict. The goal is to find a balance, or compromise, between the two partners, one that meets the companionship needs of each.

To realize fulfillment by means of a satisfactory sexual adjustment is also important for building strength and stability in this stage of the marital career. The sexual relationship is an important part of the role-reciprocity process, especially at this stage, because of its relative novelty for many. Even for those who are sexually active before marriage, enjoyment of sexual activity is a high priority during the early years of the marital career. For those who may have experienced some guilt over premarital sexual activity, sex in the marriage context may prove to be more rewarding and enjoyable than ever before, because of the legitimacy that marriage is perceived to bestow on the sexual act.

FACTORS RELATING TO SELECTIVE BOUNDARY MAINTENANCE

Research has also shown that establishing and maintaining effective *couple boundaries,* and doing so on a *selective* basis, promotes a smooth transition to marriage during these early years (Minuchin, 1974; Solomon, 1973). Central to this effort is making an effective separation from one's own friendship network and family, shifting one's primary loyalty to the newly formed marriage relationship. We referred to this earlier as establishing a "couple identity." This does not mean disengaging completely from friends or family. Rather, it means redefining relationships with these significant others so that the needs of the marriage take priority, making the marriage partner the primary source of gratification for intimacy needs. Friends, relatives, and in-laws will continue to be an important source of support over the years, perhaps helping the couple by providing financial assistance or participating as companions in social events and recreational activities. The spouse who spends time each day on the telephone with a parent, or who has to visit with a particular friend or relative several times a week, may be one who has been unable to "cut the cord." As a general rule, only those influences which are welcomed by both partners should be allowed to cross family boundaries.

An important aspect of developing couple identity involves the *physical boundaries* established in finding, furnishing, and maintaining the first residence (Duvall, 1977). However, this is a stage when income is lower than in later stages, and debts and obligations are beginning to increase rapidly. The cost of housing and of borrowing money in the 1980s makes it extremely difficult, if not impossible, for many young couples to purchase their own home. The costs of outfitting a home with furniture, dinnerware, appliances, and cooking utensils have also soared, adding to the economic burden of many young couples making the transition to marriage. As Duvall (1977:196) points out, the young couple often brings to marriage unrealistic expectations regarding the standard of living they hope to enjoy, as personal fantasies, romantic myths, and hard-sell advertising outstrip the young couple's economic resources to pay for them. This can lead to financial difficulty if great care is not taken in spending and financial planning.

The young couple may risk spending more than they earn, buying too much on credit, and getting into debt with monthly payments for things they bought on the installment plan. Before they realize how much their regular costs will be for food, rent, utilities, fuel, car expenses, and all the rest, they are over-committed. (Duvall, 1977:196)

It is at this point that the issue of selective boundary maintenance often comes in. Many young couples find that they must open their boundaries by accepting financial assistance from parents or in-laws during this stage. Some may even have to live in the parents' home until they can afford their own house or apartment. If, for some reason, parent and in-law relationships with the couple are strained, then the offer of financial aid may not be forthcoming. A young couple might also be too proud to accept an offer of assistance from outside. In regard to taking up residence in the home of parents, the task of disengaging from, or modifying, premarital ties would, under these

circumstances, be made extremely difficult, if not impossible. Hence, if the couple is able to establish *physical* boundaries by affording their own house or apartment, and the furnishings that go with it, they will find it easier to accomplish the developmental task of establishing a couple identity: neither partner will rely unduly on friends and/or parents.

Summary

This chapter has focused on the ways in which intimate relationships formed during the premarital stage move toward increased mutual commitment between the partners. Social scientists have developed many theories of how any two people meet, fall in love, and decide to marry each other. The research has been inconclusive because many factors appear to be involved, in complex ways, in the marital-choice process. Also, these theories do not take into account the factors of luck or chance in meeting "the one and only," and moving toward a more intimate, loving relationship. What we can say with confidence is that the choice of a marriage partner proceeds through a series of stages, each one taking the partners closer to feeling secure and comfortable enough in the relationship to decide to marry. At any point in the progression of stages, however, the two partners may realize that marriage is not the best path to take, and they filter back into the "pool of eligibles" once more. The amount of time it takes to move through the stages of relationship development varies widely from one couple to the next, as do the points in the filter process when couples decide to breakup and seek another marriage candidate.

Engagement is that stage in the process when the two partners have decided that they intend to marry one another. Engagement can last anywhere from a few hours to several years, and is the last stage before the partners make the transition into marriage. The amount of time spent in engagement is less critical than what the couple does with the time that they have. In order to facilitate a smooth transition into marriage and, one would hope, create a situation of minimal stress and strain for the couple in the early years, engaged partners should consider working on the developmental tasks of the engagement stage. Working on these tasks will not only help to create realistic expectations of one another and for the marriage (thereby preventing "reality shock" after marriage), but will help to develop healthy patterns of relating to one another. It is during engagement that the interpersonal skills of communication, decision making, and conflict management can be improved. Interaction habits established in this stage carry over into the marriage and can be difficult to break later on.

In this chapter we also detailed many of the legal aspects of marriage. Marriage is a legally binding contract which two partners enter into with each other and with the state. State laws vary quite significantly, and anyone contemplating marriage would be wise to learn what the laws are in their state of residence. It is also important to remember the similarities and differences between marriage and cohabitation in the eyes of the law. Although cohabitation is becoming viewed more and more like marriage in terms of property rights, significant differences between these statuses will continue to exist for several years to come.

Finally, we examined the factors relating to making a smooth transition into the early years of marriage. Successful adjustment during this very critical and often stressful stage of the marital career is promoted by several things. Included here are personality factors (marriageability), timing factors (age and maturity at marriage), marital-choice factors (homogamy and heterogamy), role reciprocity (companionship and sexual fulfillment), and selective boundary maintenance (couple identity, modified ties with family of origin and friends). We also noted the importance of entering this stage with realistic expectations of the partner—avoiding overly romanticized visions of life after marriage.

Questions for Discussion and Review

1. At what age do you plan to enter your first marriage? Is this the best age for you? Explain your answer.

2. What are your attitudes toward those who choose to remain permanently single? Do you think that the average single person is better off than the average married person? Is singlehood better for men or for women? Explain your answers.

3. Based on your own experiences in the dating and courtship system, which statement would you say has more validity: (1) "opposites attract," or (2) "Likes marry likes?" Can you think of specific friends or acquaintances who might fit either or both of these statements?

4. When choosing a dating partner, how important is physical attractiveness? How important is physical attractiveness in choosing a marriage partner? Do you think that physical attractiveness is overemphasized in our culture as an important characteristic for evaluating the worth or value of another person?

5. How important is it that a person give up an activity or interest when the marriage partner does not share that interest? How much of marriage should involve interests and activities enjoyed together by both partners, as opposed to those enjoyed by each person separately? What is the proper balance between "togetherness" and "separateness" in marriage?

6. What are the laws regarding marriage in your state?

7. Would you ever marry someone of a different religious persuasion? From a different racial or ethnic background? If your answer is, "It depends," upon what conditions does it depend? What are the major forces operating against such heterogamous marriages?

Notes

1. The higher divorce rate during this stage may also be the result, in part, of fewer "external constraints" on the relationship. The effects of children, economic assets, and friends seem to build over time. This creates a pressure for marriages not to break up, even if they are *not* viewed as "happy" or "satisfying" (Jorgensen and Johnson, 1980; Levinger, 1965). Divorce among younger couples married only a short time is also more likely; they have not been out of the premarital stage for very long and would find reentry easier because of their youth and marriageability. Nonetheless, the fact that

being divorce-prone is greatest during this stage of the marital career is a signal that for many the transition to marriage can involve a significant degree of stress in the relationship.

2. Reiss's concept of *self-revelation* is identical to the concept of *self-disclosure,* discussed in chapter 7.

3. This sequence parallels that described in regard to dating, in chapter 9. As we move from dating *extensity* to dating *intensity,* in terms of singling out one or a few partners with whom particularly intimate relationships are developed, we also begin to move through the series of filters that push us closer to the decision that we wish to marry one particular person. At any point along the way, however, a stage may be unsuccessfully negotiated, and the couple is *filtered out* of the marital-choice system. Each person returns to the *dating extensity* phase and begins anew the search for a suitable marriage partner.

CHAPTER 11

The Making of a Family:
Pregnancy and Childbirth

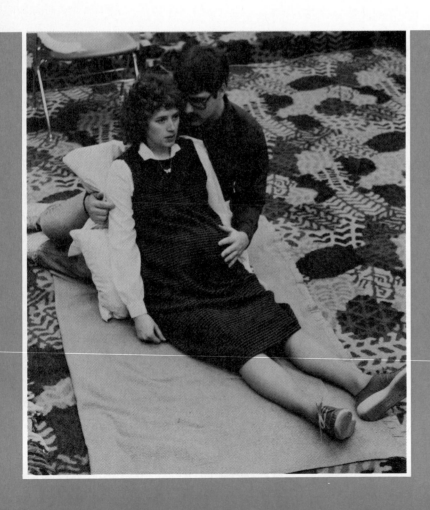

At one time in our history, it was a fact of life that sex, marriage, and parenthood all went together in harmony. If any of these was missing, a person was considered to be living an incomplete life — at least until the missing component was added. However, we have seen (chapter 9) the degree to which contemporary society has separated sex from marriage, given the high rates of premarital sexual activity that have evolved over the past several years. In chapter 6, we discussed the fact that sex and parenthood are no longer so closely linked because the development of modern contraceptive technology has freed men and women from the fear of pregnancy, replacing the norm of *sex for reproduction* with the norm of *sex for pleasure*.

The concepts of marriage and parenthood, however, are still closely related. It is still true today that the vast majority of married couples have children, either by their own reproductive processes or by adoption, and that most children are wanted and planned for. Although the number and percentage of married couples choosing permanent childlessness have increased over the past several years, the proportion of married couples having at least one child is likely to remain at about 85 to 90 percent for some time to come (Masnick and Bane, 1980; Veevers, 1979). Parenthood, therefore, remains a popular choice among married couples, and it appears that it will remain so in the future.

Childbearing in World Perspective

The survival of a society depends upon the replenishment of its population by means of human reproduction. Throughout history, men and women have been encouraged to conceive many children, as evidenced by such norms as "Power in numbers," and "Be fruitful and multiply." However, this is no longer the case in most societies today, where the concern is for having *too many* people to support, given our limited economic resources, natural resources, and food supplies.

THE THREAT OF OVERPOPULATION

Runaway population growth, in several countries, is a serious threat to their survival now and in the future. The world now has more than 4.5 billion inhabitants (4.8 billion in 1984), and more than 1 million new inhabitants

319

are added every week (Weeks, 1978). The world's population actually *doubled* between 1945 (the end of World War II) and 1984. It is expected to grow to 5 billion inhabitants by 1987, and to 6 billion by the year 2000 (*Family Planning Perspectives,* 1984a). Of particular concern is the rapid population growth in areas of the world that are economically underdeveloped and lack the natural resources for food production. In Latin America, the population is expected to grow by 45 percent between the years 1980 and 2000. In Africa, the expected growth is 70 percent, and in Asia, 39 percent during this time span. These growth rates are high compared with the 12 percent and 5 percent rates projected for North America and Europe, respectively (*Arizona Family Planning Council Newsletter,* January 1983a).

Such countries as Mexico, India, and China are among several that would probably double their total population in 20 to 30 years, if concrete measures to limit family size were not taken. These societies have been caught in the middle of what is known as the *demographic transition* — rapid population growth as a result of people living longer, combined with high fertility rates. Less advanced agricultural societies than these have a rather stable population level because fertility and mortality (death) rates are both high. Among fully industrialized and economically developed societies, such as the United States, Great Britain, and Canada, population size is relatively stable because birth rates have dropped along with the decline in mortality. In developing countries like China, Mexico, and India, however, people are living longer because of modern medical technology but their preferences for larger families remain strong. The result is rapid population growth.

As a result of population pressures, these societies are currently involved in a dedicated effort to reduce the average number of children each female will have. In India, a massive campaign of surgical sterilization of more than 8 million people in 1975 and 1976 reduced the fertility rate there. Also, abortion on demand in India has further reduced the birth rate. Indians also face the prospect of losing salary increases, leave, and travel benefits if they have more than three children. In Mexico, the government has developed and implemented a public relations campaign to encourage people to employ effective contraceptive methods in order to limit the number of children to no more than they can reasonably afford. They have backed this up with a network of family planning health care facilities in many parts of the country, so that access to birth control and surgical sterilization is easier for Mexican couples. In China, the measures taken to reduce fertility are even more stringent than in Mexico and India. China's population is now over one billion, and is still growing. Chinese couples are rewarded for having one child and then having one of the partners sterilized. Such couples receive a monthly income subsidy; the child receives priority in admission to nursery school or kindergarten; and tuition is free for the child through the middle years of school. Retirement benefits are also greater for government employees who have only one child. Chinese couples who have *more* than one child, however, are penalized with the "more children fee." Couples with three children, for example, are fined approximately 10 percent of their wages and work points.

The economic incentives in China and India appear to be effective in reducing population growth. The effects of Mexico's public relations campaign also seem to be favorable. Whereas having many children may once have been viewed by a society's leaders as a symbol of strength, this is no longer the case today as the concern about overpopulation and the drain of the earth's natural resources has spread around the world.

CHANGES IN REASONS FOR BEARING CHILDREN

According to Peterson (1969), we have seen a dramatic shift in reasons for bearing children as societies have moved from the *Gemeinschaft* type of rural, agricultural societies to the *Gesellschaft* type of modern postindustrial and technological societies (see chapter 1). Families in agricultural societies find it useful to have as many hands and strong bodies as possible, working the fields and helping with the chores necessary for maintaining a home-based agricultural enterprise. Bearing several children is one means of providing the labor necessary for these arduous tasks. Hence, children in agricultural societies are viewed as economic assets for maintaining the family business. Women in such cultures often have more children than is necessary because the risk of infectious disease and childhood mortality is quite high. When children die, they need to be replaced in order to continue filling the need for physical labor. Having children in these societies is often consistent with religious doctrine as well, because fertility is viewed as godly, or as a means of attaining grace and salvation.

As modern societies have moved away from agriculturally based economies, the need for child labor in families has diminished. Family units are no longer the major *production* units of society; rather, families are now the primary *consumption* units of society. As such, children of today are viewed more in terms of their *costs* than for their potential contribution to the productive output of the family group (Heer, 1968). Moreover, social norms no longer promote the idea that a woman should have many children as a symbol of her adult status. A greater sense of control over family size has emerged, along with the development of modern industrial societies.

> Children were no longer seen as facts of nature, as gifts of God, but rather as the consequence of acts that could be regulated, within limits, in order to bring about families of a larger or smaller size. (Peterson, 1969:13)

What happened as a result of this shift in attitudes toward having children was a reduction of the average family size in contemporary society, combined with a tremendous broadening of the reasons why adults of today decide to have children. We have moved from a time, one hundred years ago, when five or more children born to each woman was the norm, to a point where wanting two children is the norm (Buckhout, 1972; *Arizona Family Planning Council Newsletter,* January 1983a). National polls in the United States have shown that the number of adults preferring to have four or more children is at its lowest point in over forty years. Only 11 percent of American adults favored having four or more children in 1980, compared to 49 percent in 1945 and 41 percent in 1968 (*Arizona Daily Star,* January 1, 1981). In 1957, the *Total Fertility Rate* (TFR), which is a measure of the average number of children women of childbearing age would have if they continued bearing children at that year's rate, was 3.8 children per woman. By 1975, the *TFR* had dropped to below 1.9 (Glick, 1975). The *TFR* has remained below 2 since then, although it has shown small up-and-down fluctuations since 1978. A *TFR* this low will allow for eventual *zero population growth* (ZPG), meaning that the number of children born will be counterbalanced by the number of people who die. By the years 2020–2040, we will see no population growth in the United States, or perhaps even a *decline* in population, if currently low birth rates are maintained.

INDIVIDUAL REASONS FOR HAVING CHILDREN

There are a number of reasons for having children. However, many people never need to give reasons for their decision to have children, and perhaps will decide to have them without ever seriously asking themselves, "why?" Having children, for some, is as automatic as getting married.

Bereleson (1972) discussed six general reasons why people want children. First is the *biological.* Are people biologically driven to want children?

> In psychoanalytic thought there is talk of the "child-wish," the "instinctual drive of physiological cause," the innate femaleness of the girl directing her development toward motherhood," and the wanting of children as "the essence of her self-realization," indicating normality. From the experimental literature, there is some evidence that man, like other animals, is innately attracted to the quality of "babyishness." (p. 19)

Although humans clearly have many personal reasons for bearing children, scientists have not discarded the possibility that certain biological drives contribute to the decision to become a parent.

Second are the *culturally induced* reasons for having children. Cultural norms prescribe rewards for those who have children in the right numbers—not too many and not too few—and punish those who deviate from the acceptable pattern. For example, Polit (1978) studied people's attitudes toward families of varying size. The most negative attitudes were found to be toward people who choose to be childless, or who have decided to have only one child. Such people tend to be viewed as selfish, unfriendly, immature, and rebellious. Males with more than eight children were also viewed in negative terms, probably as the result of the belief that such men are impractical. People who are involuntarily childless, and women with more than eight children, on the other hand, tended to receive favorable reactions from others. Presumably, this is a "sympathy vote" from those who feel sorry for others who are infertile; and there are those who sympathize with women who are burdened with so many children. Those in the "normal" family size range, between two and four, also received favorable evaluations. Clearly, then, society seems to have a built-in system of expectations when it comes to bearing a certain number of children.

Third, Berelson (1972) identified *political* reasons for having children. "To perpetuate the species"; for the sake of "national glory or competitive political position"; to supply "workers and soldiers for the country"; and ethnic minorities and churches struggling to build their power by increasing their numbers, are just some of the political motivations for having children. In the war-torn Soviet Union during the 1940s, for example, mothers were given medals of honor and declared national heroines for bearing more than eight children. This was done in order to replace the millions of young men—nearly one out of every three—who perished in World War II.

Fourth are the *economic* reasons. These are related to the trends in economic development discussed before. In agricultural areas, children can contribute valuable labor in the fields; they are to hunt, fish, and care for animals; they can also care for other children in the home, and support family members in later life. However, children in contemporary society are viewed more in terms of their costs—the valued commodities that must be forgone in order to have them. Children today tend to be viewed as "consumer durables."

another child or a trip to Europe, a birth deferred in favor of a new car, the *n*th child requiring more expenditure on education or housing. But observe the special characteristics of children viewed as consumer durables: they come only in whole units, they are not rentable or returnable or exchangeable or available on trial, they cannot be evaluated quickly, they do not come in several competing brands or products, their quality cannot be pretested before delivery. . . . (Berelson, 1972:22)

The fifth category of reasons for having children is the *familial*. "To extend the family life or family name," or to satisfy one's ancestors, are, for some, important reasons for bearing children. Other familial reasons are to strengthen a marriage, or to strengthen existing ties with the immediate family or other relatives. Potential grandparents-to-be, for example, are known for their propensity to apply pressure to young couples who decide to delay their transition into parenthood beyond the "normal" time.

Finally, Berelson identified several *personal reasons* that people often give when pressed to answer the question of why they want children. These can be grouped into six categories:

1. *Extension of the self.*   Having children perpetuates one's own biological line by creating descendants

who will live on after the parent has died. This is one form of immortality. Maintaining the family name for future generations is also part of this concern. And others simply want to see the results of his or her own reproductive abilities.

2. *Prestige and status.*   For some, bearing children is a sign of full entry into adulthood. One becomes a "real man" or a "real woman" upon becoming a parent. We have seen that it confers certain social rewards for the parent from other family members and in-laws, and permits one to be viewed as being on an equal level with others.

3. *Power.*   Some people have children because they derive satisfaction from being able to control and influence them. Having children can also be a source of economic power. Upper-class families often arrange marriages between their offspring in order to consolidate economic resources.

4. *The parenthood experience.*   People may decide to have children simply in order to have the experience, part of their lifelong process of learning. Parenthood also provides the opportunity to relive, vicariously, one's own childhood. There is also the thrill of creativity involved in producing a child—shaping the child's personality, values, and behavior.

5. *Competence.*   Being able to conceive and bear children is a symbol of individual competence in an important adult role. If infertility or subfecundity (see chapter 6) are perceived as measures of personal inadequacy, then fertility is an indication of one's personal adequacy.

6. *Parental pleasure.*   Becoming a parent, for some, means taking pleasure in loving another and being loved, and in caring for a dependent being who is not capable of taking care of himself or herself.

Of course, there are several other possible reasons for having children. These may be *religious* ("having children is a sign of grace and salvation"), *social* ("all of my friends are having children"), or *purely personal* ("I will create a child to fill a need for loving someone in my life"). The personal reasons for having children are closely tied to one's experiences in the family of origin (such as the number of siblings, and the parents' values); the marriage partner's values relating to children; and one's current life

Parenting continues to be a popular choice among adults of the 1980s, many of whom take pleasure in loving another and being loved in return.

situation (employment status, costs of having children, and personal readiness).

Permanent Childlessness: Is There a Choice?

The sharp decline in birth rates among American women in the 1970s (see chapter 1) led some observers of the family institution to predict that permanent voluntary childlessness would become a popular choice — perhaps among 40 to 50 percent of all women — by the late 1980s. It was predicted that this increase in voluntary childlessness would be caused by the rapid movement of women into colleges and universities, and by their expanding career opportunities and aspirations.

However, it is difficult to predict with any accuracy how many women of childbearing ages in the 1970s and 1980s never will have children. First, it is necessary to consider the fact that a number of women who *want*

children will be *involuntarily* childless because of fecundity problems in their marriages (see chapter 6). Second, intentions and plans can change, as can social values regarding bearing children; those who, at one point, intend to have no children might change their minds later on when life circumstances change. Finally, many women in the 25 to 40 year range today are only *delaying* the birth of a child, because of educational and career pursuits (Glick, 1979). Recent increases in the birthrate among older women show that many are having children before their advancing age "makes it too late" (Ventura, 1982). Hence, this delay in parenthood today gives the impression that the rate of permanent childlessness is greater than in fact it will turn out to be.

Because of these unknown factors, predictions of how many women today will remain voluntarily childless vary tremendously. Some say that fewer than 5 percent of all married women will remain permanently childless (Mosher and Bachrach, 1982), but others estimate the percentage of voluntary childless women to be as high as 10 to 15 percent (Veevers, 1980), or even 25 to 30 percent (Bloom, 1981; Westoff, 1978). Whichever estimate turns out to be accurate, it is clear that there is a choice today — between a life with children or without them.

THE DECISION TO BE CHILD-FREE: VOLUNTARY CHILDLESSNESS

The advantages and disadvantages of choosing a child-free life-style, along with the reasons for doing so, are quite similar to those for choosing permanent singlehood (see chapter 10). The most extensive research and writing about the child-free decision has been that of Veevers (1979; 1980), who has documented the problems and rewards of such a life-style.

Advantages of Choosing Childlessness: Reasons for the Decision. There are a number of reasons to choose the child-free life-style. Some make up their minds and are committed to childlessness before they even marry — the *"early articulators"* (Houseknecht, 1977) — and others decide to be childless after a series of postponements following marriage. After years of thinking about it, those in the latter category decide that they are better off without children, and make the decision to remain that way (Veevers, 1973).

Permanent childlessness has the following advantages, according to those who choose this life-style (Veevers, 1979; 1980; Movius, 1976).

1. *There are couples who like a feeling of freedom, of keeping their options open.* Those who opt for childlessness are more inclined than others to seek experiences in traveling and recreational activities, as well as spontaneous pleasures, with which children might interfere. They tend to feel that children will interfere with the growth and development of the marriage relationship.

2. *Some couples have negative views of parenting, based on their observations of friends and relatives who have children, including their own parents.* The decision to remain child-free is more common among those whose parents' and/or friends' marriages were unhappy and conflict-ridden; they believe that the presence of children contributed to that unhappiness.

3. *Some believe that being a parent is a demanding task, one that must be done well.* A number of child-free individuals feel that children are valuable human beings who demand, and deserve, a parent's undivided love and attention. They believe that one cannot be a good parent and also work outside the home. Day care is a poor substitute for full-time parenting, in their eyes, and they believe that taking a "casual attitude" of "raising children in one's spare time" is wrong (Veevers, 1979:15). Because they feel they do not have the qualities essential for competent parenting — patience and understanding, for example — and they know that competing interests in work, career, or other outside activities would interfere with their roles as parents, such individuals make the choice of remaining childless.

4. *There are those with negative attitudes toward children they have known, whom they perceive to be "brats, spoiled, or generally unlikeable."* Some people have a genuine dislike for children, and therefore have little difficulty in deciding to remain childless. And some, who have known children who were retarded, disabled, deformed, or emotionally disturbed, have acquired negative feelings about children in general.

5. *Some couples want career mobility, and few family commitments, so as not to deter their professional development.* Many career-oriented women know how the demands of parenthood can interrupt their career mobility. Taking time off from a career to have a baby and nurture it during the early weeks or months of its life can break the continuity in one's profession, and possibly cause one to fall behind. As the child grows, and perhaps as other children are born, the parent's life is complicated even further with the demands of the school, the child's friends, and activities (see chapter 13). Because they know that few husbands today are willing or able to take time out of their own careers to care for children, many career-oriented women are not willing to risk having children, and decide not to.

Consequences of Voluntary Childlessness: What Difference Does it Make? Just as is true for permanent singlehood, the decision to remain childless goes against the grain of societal norms: "women, married women in particular, should have children if they are to be considered in compliance with their adult role obligations." In other words, a woman is not really a

Couples who choose to remain childless are more inclined than others to believe that children would interfere with their valued companionship and recreational activities. *(Photo by Michael Kagan.)*

woman until she fulfills her biological destiny of motherhood. Consequently, the voluntarily childless tend to be looked upon as selfish, irresponsible, immature, rebellious, less friendly, and less "wholesome and good natured" (Polit, 1978). Voluntarily childless husbands tend to be viewed as less psychologically healthy than men with children; childless wives are liked less, and are viewed as having more negative personality traits than are mothers (Calhoun and Selby, 1980). Parents, friends, and workmates can make life difficult for the childless by criticizing or placing pressure on them to have children.

Research has shown that these are stereotyped views of childless marriages, with no basis in fact (Veevers, 1979; Houseknecht, 1979; Polonko, Scanzoni, and Teachman, 1982). Voluntarily childless people are no more likely than others to experience emotional problems, maladjustment, or mental disturbances. Those who have *unplanned* or *unwanted children,* on the other hand, more often have psychological problems and undue stress in their families than do the childless. Childless women have fewer distractions, and are able to maintain greater continuity in their career pursuits, than women who interrupt their careers to have children. This factor appears to contribute to somewhat higher levels of occupational success among the childless. Voluntarily childless wives also report somewhat higher levels of satisfaction with their marriages than do mothers married the same number of years. Their level of satisfaction with the marriage relationship is because of the more equalitarian relationships they have with their husbands. As we will see in chapters 12–14, children impact on marriage as they add role strain, tensions, and financial burdens.

INVOLUNTARY CHILDLESSNESS

The married couple who want to have children, and discover that they cannot, have a totally different set of problems. Unfortunately, we know less about the full range of these problems, and the long-term consequences of involuntary childlessness, than we do about those who choose to remain childless.

Estimates of the number of married couples who are involuntarily childless because of a fecundity problem of one or both spouses, range from 2.2 percent (Mosher and Bachrach, 1982) to 4 percent (Rao, 1974). Particularly for those individuals who have a genuine and deep-rooted desire to become parents, finding out that they cannot conceive or carry a child to term can be traumatic. This discovery is usually preceded by a number of medical tests to determine whether it is the male or female who has the fecundity problem (see pp. 330–331).

The major problem for the involuntarily childless couple is the conflict that might arise when it is discovered that they cannot bear children (Chester, 1972). A process of "blaming and shaming" might produce a destructive conflict situation for the couple, if one or both spouses is compelled to point the "finger of fault" at the other. The person who does have the fecundity problem may feel guilt or shame for not being able to fill what society has taught them is an important social role: parenthood. The sexual relationship can be adversely affected as a result, and negative feelings and communication barriers may evolve (Elstein, 1975). In these cases, professional counseling may have to accompany the medical treatment of any reproductive disorders which might be discovered. Because of the wonders of modern technology, such as artificial insemination, corrective surgery, and *in vitro* (test tube) fertilization, many couples are bearing children today who, in years past, would have been unable to.

Conception

In this section, we will deal with special problems and concerns relating to pregnancy and childbirth. Let us begin with a brief view of the physiology of conception and the symbiotic relationship that develops between the pregnant woman and the growing fetus.

THE CONCEPTION PROCESS

In chapter 5, we saw which hormonal changes in the adult female promote the release of an egg *(ovum)* from the ovaries, and then create a receptive environment in the uterus in preparation for a fertilized egg, or *zygote*. Fertilization can only take place during an approximately 24-hour period after ovulation. The average male ejaculation contains several hundred million sperm cells, and are capable of fertilization for a period of 48 to 72 hours after ejaculation. If an egg is present in the woman's Fallopian tube, several of the surviving sperm cells will swim, by means of whip-like movements of their tails, directly toward the ovum. If no egg is present, sperm cells swim about in a more or less random pattern. However, only several thousand sperm are likely to survive the journey through the female's reproductive system. Several will simultaneously press their heads against the outer wall of the ovum, releasing a hormone *(hyaluronidase)*, which begins to break down the coating of the egg. As soon as one sperm cell is able to penetrate the shell, usually in the upper portion of the Fallopian tube, the egg becomes impervious to penetration by any other sperm cells. After fertilization, the zygote is propelled toward the uterus by means of wave-like movements of tiny hairs, known as *cilia*.

If all goes well during this journey, the zygote will become implanted in the blood-rich lining of the uterus, where it will receive nourishment and protection during the course of its development into a fetus. By the time the single-cell zygote reaches the uterus for implantation, usually within 5 to 7 days after the ovum was first released, it has grown and divided into a 32-cell organism, known as a *blastocyst* (Witters and Jones-Witters, 1980:151). (See Figure 11.1.) The center of the blastocyst is hollow, and its outer wall is comprised of a more rapidly dividing cluster of cells known as the *trophoblast*. The trophoblast cells actually implant themselves in the uterine wall within two to three weeks following conception, marking the beginning of the *embryonic stages* of pregnancy. The trophoblast cells then evolve into what eventually will be the life-support system for the developing

FIGURE 11.1.   Development of the Blastocyst and Implantation in the Uterine Wall.

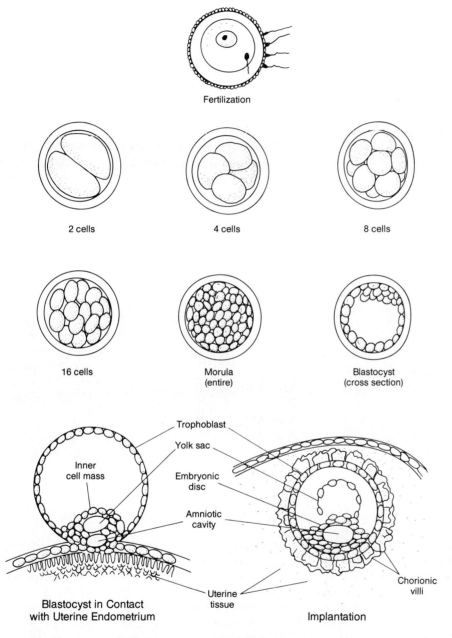

SOURCE: Adapted from E. B. Steen and James H. Price, *Human Sex and Sexuality*. New York: Wiley, 1977.

embryo: umbilical cord, placenta, and amniotic sac. But if fertilization does not occur, the unfertilized egg distintegrates and is absorbed into the body, or is sloughed off during menstruation.

THE GENETIC BASIS OF LIFE

Conception entails a combining of genetic material from the two parents. Each cell, the sperm and ovum, contains a set of genetic material that is carried on 23 *chromosomes.* The two sets of chromosomes combine at conception, forming a single-cell zygote with the 46 chromosomes (23 pairs) that are necessary for a human cell to develop. The genes in each chromosome are comprised of molecules known as *deoxyribonucleic acid,* or *DNA.* First discovered by Nobel Prize laureates Francis Crick and James Watson in 1953, DNA molecules are complex, strand-like structures composed of billions of atoms called *nucleotides.* These nucleotides form genetic codes which direct the growth and division of human cells after conception. These codes will determine the physical features of the individual, including hair color, height, growth rate, eye color, facial features, skin color, sex, and other characteristics of the person. As such, it can be said that DNA molecules are the most fundamental building blocks of human life. DNA-directed cell division, known as *mitosis,* results in duplicate cells, each of which contain the same 46 chromosomes, which, in turn, contain the same DNA code, which directs further cell division, and so on, in a complex and fascinating process of human growth.[1]

SEX DETERMINATION

The sex of the child is determined by certain chromosome combinations (see chapter 4). One pair of chromosomes, the twenty-third, determines the sex of the child. The female's sex chromosome pair are both designated as X, because they resemble that letter of the alphabet. Each ovum of the adult woman contains an X sex chromosome. Males, on the other hand, have a sex chromosome pair that is different. As sperm cells are developed through meiosis, half of the new sperm are of the X type and half are of the Y type. The sex of the child is thereby determined by the type of sperm cell, X or Y, which fertilizes the ovum. An XX combination will result in a female, and an XY combination will become a male (provided, of course, that the normal hormonal processes, discussed in chapter 4, take place).

The probability of a male being conceived is higher than that of a female — roughly 135 to 140 males will be conceived for every 100 females conceived. However, the number of males which will actually reach term and be born is roughly the same as that of females. Prenatal survivability of males is therefore less than it is for females. In 1980, there were 105.3 males born for every 100 females, a rate that has remained quite constant since 1940 (U.S. Bureau of the Census, 1983a). Males are the weaker sex, therefore, when it comes to survival (See age-specific death rates in Table 11.1) (National Center for Health Statistics, 1984c). At every age level, the male death rate exceeds that of the female rate. At this time, there is no firm understanding of the genetic basis of these

TABLE 11.1. *Age-Specific Death Rates for Males and Females, United States 1981*[1]

	Females	Males
All Ages	775	955
Under 1 year	1,077	1,332
1–4 years	53	67
5–9 years	24	34
10–14 years	22	37
15–19 years	50	130
20–24 years	59	186
25–29 years	67	191
30–34 years	191	191
35–39 years	122	241
40–44 years	191	353
45–49 years	315	576
50–54 years	493	921
55–59 years	744	1,428
60–64 years	1,125	2,171
65–69 years	1,697	3,294
70–74 years	2,589	4,936
75–79 years	4,044	7,219
80–84 years	6,985	10,884
85 years and over	14,203	18,138

[1] Rates per 100,000 population in specified group; decimals rounded to nearest number.

SOURCE: National Center for Health Statistics. Advance report of final mortality statistics, 1981. *Monthly Vital Statistics Report,* Vol. 33, No. 3, June 22, 1984.

sex differences in survivability. It is especially puzzling because the differences appear both before and after birth.

MULTIPLE BIRTHS

The normal course of events in human pregnancy is for the woman to conceive, bring to term, and deliver *one* child. However, this is not always the case. Twins, triplets, quadruplets, and quintuplets, all known as *multiple births,* can further complicate the transition to parenthood by adding to the parents' child-care responsibilities. Relatively few parents-to-be either want or plan to have multiple births, so it is usually a surprise—and an expensive one at that. Whether in terms of extra expenses, or the added burden of feeding, clothing, and caring for two or more infants at the same time, multiple births can add stress to an already stressful stage in the parent's lives.[2]

Multiple births occur quite infrequently. There were 71,434 multiple birth deliveries in the United States in 1981, 98 percent of them twins (National Center for Health Statistics, 1983d). Twins occur in about one out of every 80–90 cases; triplets are born once in every 7,000–8,000 cases; quadruplets are born once in every 700,000 cases; and quintuplets only once per 41 million births (Witters and Jones-Witters, 1980:192). For every 1,000 live births in 1981, 19.7 were live multiple births (National Center for Health Statistics, 1983d). Multiple births are more common among Black women (24.2 multiple births compared with 18.6 per 1,000 for white women), and they are more common among older women (26.6 per 1,000 live births for women aged 35–39 years, compared with 13.1 per 1,000 for mothers 15–19 years of age).

Multiple-birth babies are usually born prematurely and weigh less than single-birth babies. This means that they are somewhat less viable at birth, especially among quadruplets and quintuplets. Multiple births have become more common because the so-called *fertility drugs* are now more frequently prescribed by physicians for women who ovulate infrequently or irregularly. Most of these drugs stimulate the woman to produce healthy ova on a regular basis. In some cases, overstimulation can occur; many eggs are released simultaneously, and multiple conceptions can take place.

Twins that are conceived by sperm cells fertilizing

Although uncommon relative to single births, multiple births pose an extra strong challenge to the parents' resources of time, energy, and patience.
(Photo by Stephen R. Jorgensen.)

two separate eggs are known as *fraternal,* or *dizygotic,* twins. Fraternal twins receive different sets of genetic material, or DNA, as a result of being conceived by two different ova and two different sperm. They are no more alike physically than other brothers and sisters, and can be of the same or opposite sex.

Some twins are conceived when a single fertilized egg (zygote) divides into two parts, and these twins develop the same physical characteristics. These are *identical,* or *monozygotic,* twins, because their chromosomes carry the same genetic material (one egg plus one sperm). Identical twins account for only 1 in 3 of all sets of twins, and are always of the same sex because of the single sperm cell (X or Y) that fertilizes the egg.

Triplets and higher-order multiple births can evolve from any combination of monozygotic or dizygotic conceptions. One set of triplets may derive from a single fertilized egg that divides into three parts, in which case all three children would be physically identical. All three triplets may be fertilized from three different eggs; or two of the triplets may be monozygotic twins, formed from the division of one egg, and the third may be conceived from a second egg.

FECUNDITY, SUBFECUNDITY, AND STERILITY

In chapter 6, we examined the concepts of fecundity and fertility. *Fecundity* refers to the physiological ability to reproduce, whereas *fertility* is the "realization of this potential, the actual birth performance as measured by the number of offspring" (Peterson, 1969:173). The fecundity of married couples varies across a wide spectrum—from low to high. The available statistics show that in 1982, 51 percent of the married couples (wife age 15–44) in the United States were defined as *fecund*. Another 28 percent had been surgically sterilized for contraceptive reasons (either the husband or wife), indicating that they had been fecund at one time but desired to have no more children. Nine percent were defined as *impaired fecundity*—able to conceive, but with some degree of difficulty. Thirteen percent were categorized as *noncontraceptively sterile*—unable to conceive at all. Hence, roughly 22 percent of all married couples in 1982 found it impossible or difficult to bear children of their own (Mosher and Pratt, 1985).

Medical science today has made it possible for couples to bear children, who in the past would have found it difficult or impossible to do so. Before discussing these modern methods of treating sterility and subfecundity, however, it is important to understand their causes. These causes vary from psychological and emotional to anatomical and physiological (Guttmacher, 1973; Witters and Jones-Witters, 1980).

Causes of Subfecundity and Sterility in Men. Male fecundity depends primarily upon the quantity and quality of sperm production. There is dis-

agreement, however, over the number of sperm per ejaculate necessary to consider a man fecund. The American Fertility Society states that 60 to 100 million sperm per ejaculate is the minimum number for normal male fecundity, but other estimates vary from 10 million to 25 million sperm per ejaculate as the minimum necessary for a man to impregnate a woman (Witters and Jones-Witters, 1980:409). As important as the number of sperm, though, is the *quality* of the sperm produced. When placed under a microscope, they should be seen to be active (motile) and free of structural abnormalities (heads missing, two heads or tails, or incompletely formed).

Low rates and poor quality of sperm production might relate to disorders of the testes, including a failure of the testes to descend during childhood, tumors, or enlarged veins in the testicle region. Low sperm production can also result from diseases, such as mumps, sexually transmitted diseases, gland disorders, or conditions that cause temperatures to be abnormally high within the scrotum. Inadequate nutrition, or the failure to absorb key minerals, vitamins, and proteins, may depress sperm production by affecting the seminal fluids which give sperm their vitality and motility. Studies have shown that exposure to certain industrial chemicals can also reduce sperm count, as can cigarette and marijuana smoking.

Blocked or obstructed sperm ducts and channels leading from the testicles through the urethra can also be sources of male subfecundity. Infections, sexually transmitted diseases, diabetes, or enlarged prostate glands can cause such obstructions. Infections and diseases do so by creating scar tissue in the *vas deferans* or in the *epididymis* (testicles).

Male impotence—the inability to develop or maintain an erection long enough to deposit sperm in the female's vagina—is another source of male subfecundity. Impotence may be a result of several things, including alcohol consumption, disease, psychological and emotional problems, and aging (see chapter 5).

Causes of Subfecundity and Sterility in Women. Problems related to conception difficulty are more common among women. Some conditions prevent the uniting of sperm and ovum; and others cause women to spontaneously abort the fertilized egg before it is implanted in the uterine wall. Tumors, cysts, disease, or infections may cause a failure to ovulate consistently, or possibly, at all. Irregular hormone release from the hypothalamus and the pituitary, thyroid, or adrenal glands may also restrict the production of healthy ova. Disorders in the uterus because of hormone-release problems, physical defects, or disease, all may lead to female sterility or subfecundity by failing to create a sufficiently nurturant environment for implantation of the fertilized egg. Sexually transmitted diseases, particularly gonorrhea, and other infections can create sterility by scarring and closing off the Fallopian tubes. Some women have difficulty in conceiving because of overly acidic vaginal secretions which are hostile to sperm cells. Other women have even been found to develop antibodies which attack sperm cells, as if they were hostile invaders of the female's body.

Subfecundity in women may also be the result of psychological factors. It is possible that a deep-rooted fear of pregnancy, or apprehension about assuming the burden of parental responsibilities, can reduce fecundity. Emotional problems and upheavals are known to alter a woman's normal menstrual cycle, by delaying or preventing ovulation. It is also possible that a woman might try *too* hard to conceive thus beginning a cycle of disappointment, frustration, and anxiety, leading to more fervent attempts to conceive, and so on.

Methods to Overcome Fecundity Problems.

There are a number of methods for overcoming fecundity problems (Zimmerman, 1982). One major source of female sterility is failure to ovulate, or to do so on a consistent basis. There are available a variety of *drugs* which promote the development and release of a healthy, viable ovum. Most of these drugs promote ovulation by altering the hormone levels and hormone-regulating functions of the pituitary gland.

The problem of blocked Fallopian tubes can be overcome by a variety of methods. First, it is possible in some cases *to remove the obstruction surgically*. Second, it is now possible to fertilize an ovum in the laboratory, and implant the fertilized egg in the uterus of a woman who has Fallopian-tube scarring which cannot be surgically repaired. This is known as *in vitro fertilization,* or "test-tube pregnancy." This method was developed and first carried through by English physicians Robert Edwards and Patrick Steptoe, in 1978. John and Lesley Brown, then 30 years of age, became parents of the first documented case of a baby conceived in a laboratory. After trying to conceive for nine years, the Browns discovered that Lesley had severely scarred Fallopian tubes. Drs. Ed-

wards and Steptoe first administered an ovulation-stimulating hormone to Mrs. Brown. Then they removed one of her eggs, and placed it with a sample of John's sperm in a culture dish specially prepared with a nutrient solution. After fertilization took place, the physicians observed the process of *mitosis* occur over the next four days. When the zygote had divided and grown to an eight-cell blastocyst, it was transported through the cervix and implanted in Mrs. Brown's uterus, which had been chemically prepared to promote the implantation and nourishment of the embryo. The pregnancy was a normal full-term one, and Louise Brown was born—a healthy, 5-pound 12-ounce baby—on July 25, 1978. Several *in vitro* babies have since been born in Australia, Canada, the United States, and Europe, including the first set of test-tube twins. In January of 1984, the first baby was born by means of artificial insemination in the uterus of one woman, the "surrogate," with the father's sperm and then transplanted into the uterus of his wife, the "mother," who then carried the baby to term and delivered it. The success of pioneers Steptoe and Edwards, and those who have followed them, has given hope to thousands of couples who previously would have been unable to conceive their own children because of dysfunction in the female's reproductive system.

Other methods of overcoming fecundity problems are being developed. One in particular seems to be gaining in popularity and acceptability—the use of *surrogate mothers* (Zimmerman, 1982). If a couple finds it impossible to conceive a child of their own, they may hire a woman to be impregnated with the husband's sperm, by means of *artificial insemination*. The surrogate mother then carries the pregnancy to term and delivers the child—normally for a sizable fee. The child is then turned over to the couple.

This procedure is bound to have long-term ethical and legal ramifications—if, for example, a surrogate mother decides to keep the child after it is born, if she or the child experience medical complications during the pregnancy and labor, or if the surrogate mother wishes to see or make contact with the child while it is growing up. Issues of legitimacy and inheritance rights might also arise in the practice of surrogate mothering. And then there are the religious and moral questions about altering the course of nature in human reproduction. For example, a case in 1982 involved a child with severe mental and physical defects, who was born to a surrogate mother. The man whose sperm was used to impregnate her refused to accept the defective child as his own offspring. At the same time, the woman and her husband refused to take responsibility for the child. For a time, the case was in court, to determine just who should bear the economic and legal responsibility for the child. After definitive medical tests, however, it was determined that the woman hired to be the surrogate mother was actually impregnated by her own husband. Subsequently, they voluntarily accepted parental responsibilities for the child.

If the man is the source of a couple's fecundity problem, the most popular method in use is *artificial insemination*. The number of pregnancies by artificial insemination probably now number in the millions, in the United States alone. There are two types of artificial insemination. One involves use of the husband's sperm, which are refined to increase the sperm count. The sperm are then inserted into the uterus, through the wife's cervix, with a long syringe-like instrument. The other method involves the use of an anonymous doner's sperm, which have been stored in a sperm bank under ultra-cold conditions (−320° Farenheit). An attempt is made to match as closely as possible the genetic characteristics of the donor with those of the husband (hair color, blood type, height, and body build). Between 10 and 20 attempts at artificial insemination may be made before a pregnancy occurs, especially with the less effective frozen sperm. The same kinds of ethical and legal questions that are associated with surrogate mothers may arise regarding artificial insemination: legal status of the child, inheritance rights, and interference with the natural reproductive process. There is also the potential for misuse of this modern reproductive technology, and some fear that, in the wrong hands, such techniques could be used to create either a group of "superhumans" or a group of criminal types. One sperm bank in California, for example, has collected sperm samples from Nobel Prize winners and other highly intelligent males, and several women have already been artificially inseminated (*Time Magazine,* March 10, 1980). Whether or not such a practice will violate any basic principles of ethical human conduct remains to be seen.

Finally, if a couple does not choose to use any of these methods of overcoming sterility or subfecundity, another option is open to them: *adoption*. If adoption is their choice, a couple has the option of selecting the child they want in terms of age, sex, and genetic characteristics. However, adoption is usually a long, drawn-out process

for the prospective parents, who have to demonstrate to the adoption agency their financial, psychological, and emotional stability. Also, because of liberalized abortion laws, improved contraceptive methods and practices, and the increasing propensity for unwed mothers to keep their babies, there is a shortage of babies with certain characteristics — healthy, free of birth defects or physical anomalies, and white (Caucasian) [Duvall, 1977].

PREGNANCY AND AGE OF PARENT

It is possible for women across a wide age range to conceive a child. Records indicate that conception has occurred as early as 5 years of age and as late as 60. The normal fecundity range is considered to be between the ages of 15 and 44. However, research has shown that the ideal age for motherhood, measured by the absence of adverse medical and physiological problems in pregnancy and delivery, is between the ages of 20 and 30. Clearly, the timing of pregnancy in terms of the parents' age should be a consideration in making the transition to parenthood.

Medical researchers have found a relationship between the age of parents at the time conception occurs and the possibility of medical complications during pregnancy and childbirth. Both teenagers and older mothers are more likely to experience adverse consequences than are mothers between the ages of 20 and 35, and evidence is building to suggest that the age of the father can also be a critical variable.

Teenage Parents. The adverse medical, psychological, and social consequences of teenage pregnancy were reviewed in chapter 9. Clearly, mis-timing a pregnancy can have undesirable effects when it occurs in a teenager. The medical complications stem primarily from the teenager's lack of physical maturity, such as having an underdeveloped reproductive system and pelvic bone structure, which will not accommodate the delivery of a full-size infant. Teenagers often have poorer than average self-care habits, and may not maintain an adequate level of nutrition and personal hygiene. Such adverse consequences are more severe, and are more likely to occur, among younger teenagers. Moreover, the social and psychological consequences tend to reinforce each other in a complex, vicious cycle. For example, teenagers are more likely to physically abuse their children, as a result of the stress and strain created by *financial insecurity* (low-paying jobs, unemployment, and lack of education); *stressful ties to relatives, spouse, employers, and society* (which may also stem from financial problems); *social isolation* as the result of being removed from the activities of one's friends, who are still in school and free from the responsibilities of child care; *frustration* because of having to lower educational and occupational goals; and *unrealistic expectations* regarding normal patterns of child growth, behavior, and development, which lead to further frustration.

Older Parents. Research has also shown that older parents and their infants run a greater risk of medical problems, although the risks are not as great as those associated with teenage childbearing.

Most women will have completed their childbearing careers by 35 years of age, although it is possible for many to conceive and bear children through ages 45–50. However, a definite increase in medical complications has been detected for women who bear children past the ages of 34 or 35. For example, older mothers are somewhat more likely than those in their twenties or early thirties to undergo a cesarean section delivery (surgical removal of the fetus), and to have a child that is defined as "low birth weight" (under 5 lbs. 8 ozs.) [Ventura, 1982]. They are also more likely to conceive a baby with *Down's Syndrome* (mongolism), a relatively severe form of mental and physical retardation caused by a chromosome defect (Witters and Jones-Witters, 1980). For mothers under the age of 30, the chance of bearing a Down's Syndrome baby is one in 500. The chances increase to one in 200 for mothers between 35 and 40, and climb to one in every 50 to 75 births for women over the age of 40. Researchers have not yet discovered the cause of this problem, but speculate that it is the result of the aging process of either the mother or father (Witters and Jones-Witters, 1980). As the female's ova age, cells may divide less effectively than at earlier ages. And because older males ejaculate less frequently, it is possible that the sperm that have been generated between orgasms begin to deteriorate, thereby increasing the chances that an imperfect sperm cell will impregnate the woman.

Concern about parental age has increased as the number of older parents has increased. In 1979, there were 115,000 births to women in their thirties who were having their first child, compared with 68,000 in 1975 and only 54,000 in 1970 (Ventura, 1982). This represents an increase of 73 percent and 110 percent, respectively. The reason for this dramatic rise in the number of older mothers is the fact that women today are delaying marriage and parenthood in order to seek higher levels of education and to pursue careers (see chapter 8). However, the fact that older mothers are increasingly well educated means that they are the most likely group to seek prenatal care from a physician or other medical professional. This functions to *reduce* the risk of adverse birth outcomes for these women, which would undoubtedly be higher if they were not so careful to obtain prenatal care.

[R]eceipt of prenatal care is highly correlated with educational attainment of the mother. Therefore, it is not surprising that older first-time mothers, better educated than their younger counterparts, seek prenatal care very early in their pregnancies. Although women in their thirties face a higher risk of bearing infants with certain congenital anomalies than younger women do, . . . delayed childbearing, because it is associated with principally well-educated women, carries fewer health risks now than perhaps was true a decade or more ago. (Ventura, 1982:5)

Pregnancy

With conception, there begins a period of time that can be both exciting and stressful for the male and female partners. Although most people view pregnancy as lasting nine months, a normal pregnancy *(gestation)* period can last anywhere from 240 to 300 days. The average length of time is 266 days (Delora and Warren, 1977).

SIGNS OF PREGNANCY

When a woman becomes pregnant, her body usually gives off clear signals. However, these signals can sometimes be delayed or misleading. Therefore, the only definitive evidence that conception has occurred is to have a reliable pregnancy test.

The earliest signs of pregnancy can begin two to three weeks after the fertilized egg has become embedded in the uterine wall. The most common signal to a woman that she is pregnant is to have missed a menstrual period. However, emotional stress, or other disruptions in her normal routine, such as extended travel or illness, can also cause a woman to miss her period. Moreover, some pregnant women experience one or two brief "spotty" periods after conception has taken place (Delora and Warren, 1977:390).

If a woman has missed a period and believes that she might be pregnant, she may look for other symptoms. First, she may notice a number of changes in her breasts. The breasts may increase in size and fullness, and become somewhat tender. The *areolae,* the darker pigmented tissue around the nipples, become darker, and veins in that area become more pronounced as the flow of blood increases. She may experience some throbbing, or a slight discomfort because of the swelling of the breasts. Second, many women experience nausea, usually in the morning, as a result of the changes in hormone balance associated with pregnancy. Such "morning sickness" may be mild or severe, resulting in vomiting and much discomfort. Usually these symptoms dissipate by the eighth week of pregnancy. A third early sign of pregnancy is an increased frequency of urination, caused by pressure on the bladder from the expanding uterus. Hormonal changes may also alter the body's metabolism so that fluids are more rapidly passed through the system. This symptom will also disappear over time as the growing uterus moves up into the abdomen and out of the pelvic region. A fourth symptom of pregnancy is increased fatigue and an urge to sleep. The woman may find that occasional naps during the day, and longer periods of sleep at night, are required to alleviate the fatigue.

It must be noted that the extent and severity of these symptoms vary widely from one woman to the next, and may even vary for one woman from one pregnancy to the next. In any event, whenever a woman believes that she may be pregnant, it is important that she obtain more definite evidence by means of a reliable pregnancy test. If she is pregnant, the woman should initiate appropriate prenatal care as soon as possible.

PREGNANCY TESTS

At one time, it took several days for the results of a pregnancy test to become known. Laboratory animals, such as a mouse, rabbit, frog, or rat were injected with a sample of the woman's urine. After the second week of a woman's pregnancy, the developing embryo secretes *HCG (human chorionic gonadatropin),* a substance that will appear in the pregnant woman's urine. This hormone will cause the laboratory animal to release eggs, if female, and sperm, if male. However, the time and expense involved in this procedure made it a rather cumbersome and impractical one.

Recently developed pregnancy tests are more rapid, efficient, and accurate. Most common are the *immunological* tests, whereby a few drops of the woman's urine are mixed on a slide with chemical agents that contain, among other things, particles of latex rubber. The mixture is then placed under a microscope. If the woman is not pregnant, the particles will clump together (agglutinate) after two minutes. If she is pregnant, the substance will have a smooth, milky appearance, after two minutes. Another test, known as the *latex agglutination inhibition* test, will yield just the opposite reaction. That is, agglutination will occur if the woman is pregnant (Delora and Warren, 1977; Witters and Jones-Witters, 1980). These tests are between 95–98 percent accurate, and can be reliably performed approximately seven days after the first missed menstrual period.

A second modern pregnancy test is known as a *radioimmunoassay.* This accurate test requires a small sample of the woman's blood, which yields slightly higher levels of HCG earlier in the pregnancy than does the urine. It can be reliably conducted by the sixth day after fertilization has occurred, and takes about one hour to obtain an accurate reading.

A reliable pregnancy test is important because of the need to initiate proper prenatal care early in the pregnancy. In view of the fact that harmful environmental influences on the embryo and fetus cause their greatest damage during the first three months of pregnancy, a woman should be aware that she is pregnant as soon as possible. When pregnancy tests are inaccurate, it is usually because they have been given too early in the pregnancy, or because the HCG level is too low to detect. This is known as a *false negative* test. Only rarely does one hear of a *false positive* test — a test indicating that a woman is pregnant when she really is not. Occasionally women experience *false pregnancies (pseudocyesis).* They show all of the physical symptoms of pregnancy, but chemical tests accurately indicate that no pregnancy has occurred. It is most commonly a psychological problem stemming from an intense desire to either become pregnant or to *not* become pregnant. The woman may experience nausea, missed menstrual periods, weight gain, breast tenderness, and may even secrete milk.

Witters and Jones-Witters (1980:168) describe one extreme case of false pregnancy:

> In one case, a 16-year-old girl reached an estimated 38 weeks "gestation." She had experienced fetal movements, morning sickness, breast tenderness and enlargement, and was producing a milky discharge from the nipples. Her abdomen was the size expected for a near-term pregnancy. When no fetus could be felt by manipulating her abdomen, and no fetal heart sounds were detected, the physician had an ultrasound scan made to see what the enlargement might be due to. The sonography showed a normal sized, nonpregnant uterus. The distended abdomen was entirely due to retained intestinal gas, which she passed within 30 minutes of being told she was not pregnant.

Males, too, can experience the symptoms of pregnancy — psychologically at least. A fascinating psychological syndrome, known as the *couvade,* has been identified in cultures all over the world, including our own. Morning sickness, abdominal cramps when the wife is in labor, bloating, and appetite loss can all plague the male mate of the pregnant woman. In some cultures, particularly in Africa and Latin America, the male is expected to take on as his duty his wife's "pain and suffering" during pregnancy, labor, and delivery. Although the *couvade* is a psychological phenomenon, the perception of pain and discomfort is quite real among men who experience it.

THE STAGES OF PREGNANCY

Pregnancy normally is divided into three stages of approximately three months (12 – 13 weeks) each, called *trimesters.*

The First Trimester. The early signs of pregnancy just described occur during this first stage of pregnancy. The greater the number and severity of these symptoms, the greater the likelihood that the woman will be irritable and more sensitive to others in her environment, particularly her husband. It is at this point that the marital relationship realizes its first changes as a result of parenthood, as the pregnancy begins to have an effect on the couple's normal patterns of sharing affection and communicating with one another. The degree of sexual interest on the part of the wife is also likely to be depressed during this trimester, especially for first-time mothers.

During this stage, the fertilized egg (0.15 millimeters or 0.005 inch) has developed into the 32-cell blastocyst (0.3 millimeters or 0.01 inch) that implants itself in the uterine wall approximately five to seven days after fertilization (see Figure 11.1). It does so by means of tiny, fingerlike projections, known as *chorionic villi,* which burrow into the uterine wall and begin to draw nourishment from tiny blood sacs. As the blastocyst continues to grow, this "food supply" is digested and waste material is exchanged through the villi into the mother's system. The cells of the blastocyst, by the end of the third week, begin to differentiate (Godow, 1982), marking the beginning of the *embryonic stage.* During the embryonic stage, the development of the skeletal, muscular, nervous, circulatory, and excretory systems begins. Skin tissue begins to form, as do the basic components of the digestive and respiratory systems. The umbilical cord develops, in order to provide a means for oxygen and nourishment to pass to the growing embryo from the mother. The umbilical cord contains two arteries and one vein for transporting nourishment to, and waste material from, the embryo. The *placenta* is an organ that also develops at this time. It is embedded in the wall of the mother's uterus by a complex system of blood vessels and villi, and is the exchange point for nourishment and waste materials which move back and forth through the umbilical cord and the mother's system.

Between the sixth and eighth week after conception, the embryo moves into a new stage of development — the *fetal stage.* By this time, the major body organs have begun to take shape: the brain, muscles, blood vessels, and heart (week 3); eyes, arms, and legs (weeks 4 and 5); upper and lower limb buds (arms and legs), buttocks, and ears (weeks 6 and 7); and chin, fingers, and toes (week 8). Although internal sexual differentiation into a male or female is beginning in the embryonic stage, it is not possible to detect the sex by visual examination of the external genitalia until sometime after the tenth week. During the embryonic stage, the embryo has developed from a length of 1.5 millimeters (week 2), to 11 – 14 millimeters (about a half inch) by week 6, and 30 millimeters by week 8. Although it still weighs less than one ounce, the embryo's mass has increased by about 10,000 times during this stage!

The Second Trimester. The second trimester spans the 13th to the 26th week of pregnancy. The woman begins to notice a swelling in the abdominal area as the growing fetus begins to expand the uterus beyond its normal size. The woman is also likely to experience weight gain at this time. She will first notice the fetus moving sometime between the 18th and 22nd week. This is called the *"quickening"* of the fetus, and will be perceived as a fluttering sensation caused by arm or leg movements of the fetus. The woman may notice some nuisance symptoms during the second trimester, such as increased salivation and perspiration; leg or foot cramps, indigestion, and constipation; skin dryness; and water retention in the hands, wrists, face, and ankles (known as *edema*) [Godow, 1982]. The breasts will also become even more enlarged, as the body makes a natural preparation for nursing the baby; and the discharge of a thin yellow fluid from the breasts, known as *colostrum,* may begin during the second trimester. Much to her relief, the morning sickness she might have felt during the first trimester is likely to have disappeared by this time. Interestingly, during the second trimester the pregnant woman often experiences a significant increase in her level of sexual drive, presumably because of the shifting balance of hormones in her body. This is particularly true for first-time (primiparous) mothers (Masters and Johnson, 1966). This, then, may have the benefit of bringing her closer to her husband than was possible during the uncomfortable first trimester of pregnancy.

The fetus continues to grow at a remarkable rate during the second trimester. The average length at the end of the 14th week (approximately 3 months) is 87 millimeters (3.5 inches) and the fetus weighs about 45 grams (1.6 ounces) (Witters and Jones-Witters, 1980). It will be about 14 centimeters (5.5 inches) and 200 grams (7 ounces) after 18 weeks (4 months); and 19 centimeters (7½ inches) and 460 grams (one pound) by the end of the 21st week. All basic body structures and functions evolve by the second trimester, and the fetus takes on a definite human appearance. The sexual genitalia begin to take form during this time, and it is possible to determine the sex of the child by means of *amniocentesis* — withdrawing amniotic fluid from the uterus by inserting a needle through the woman's abdomen, and then analyzing the structure of skin cells sloughed off by the fetus. Definite sucking motions of the fetus's lips can be detected during this stage, as can swallowing motions. The fetal heartbeat can be detected by means of a stethoscope, sometime during the fourth or fifth month of pregnancy, and hand and foot movements become increasingly strong and frequent by the end of the sixth month.

The Third Trimester. This period lasts from the 27th week until the fetus is born (after about 38 weeks). It is likely that this trimester will be the most uncomfortable one for the pregnant woman because of the weight gain and the enlargement and stretching of the abdomen. Common effects of these changes include lower back pain, indigestion, constipation, frequent and urgent need to urinate, and shortness of breath, caused by the expanding uterus pressing against the internal organs of the body (stomach, bladder, bowels, and lungs). At this time, the expectant first-time mother may experience a drop in the level of sexual interest, as occurred in the first trimester. Furthermore, some physicians advise sexual abstinence during the last weeks of pregnancy, because of the increased risk of infection (see chapter 5).

The uterus is now beginning to prepare for the actual childbirth. Brief painless contractions may occur several times a day (known as *Braxton Hicks* contractions) [Godow, 1982]. Also, the head of the fetus may descend in the uterus in order to make contact with the cervical opening, sometime between 2 to 4 weeks prior to childbirth, an event known as *engagement* (see Figure 11.2).

The fetus doubles its length and weight during the last two months of pregnancy, gaining approximately a half pound a week during the final weeks of this stage (Witters and Jones-Witters, 1980). The central nervous system, with its capability of regulating important body functions, develops rapidly at this point, so a fetus born prematurely — after eight months of pregnancy — has an excellent survival potential. Its "kicks and punches," and even its hiccupping, can be felt through the abdominal wall during the entire third trimester; and there is evidence that the fetus begins to respond to sounds emanating from outside the uterus, and to being touched from outside the mother's abdomen, from the beginning of the third trimester. A healthy, full-term baby may be born up to two weeks on either side of the physician's estimated "due date" for the woman, because of the imprecision in determining exactly when conception occurred, and variations in rates of fetal development.

MEDICAL ISSUES IN PREGNANCY

A number of concerns arise in regard to the physical health of the pregnant woman and the developing fetus. Although some of these concerns are beyond the direct control of the woman, most can be directly controlled with

FIGURE 11.2. Fully Developed Fetus in Third Trimester of Pregnancy.

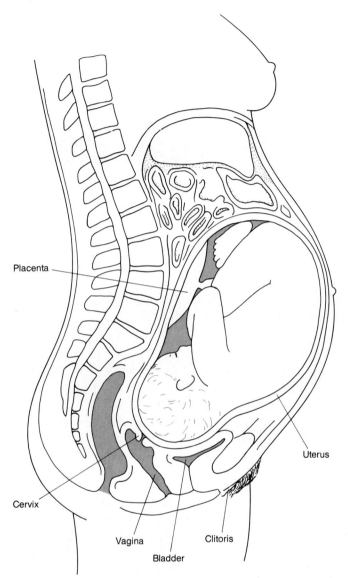

Placenta

Cervix

Vagina

Bladder

Clitoris

Uterus

proper self-care and regular consultations with a physician during all stages of pregnancy. We will discuss the most typical ones here.

Drugs and Alcohol.   Because of the physical bond that exists between the pregnant woman and her unborn child, compounds and chemicals ingested by the mother cross the placental barrier and are absorbed by the fetus. Recent medical evidence has shown that cigarette smoking, alcohol consumption, and the ingestion of such drugs as marijuana, heroin, and other opiates can have harmful effects on the fetus. The effects of such agents are the most severe and frequent during the first trimester of pregnancy, although equally severe consequences may result if the pregnant woman ingests them at a critical developmental stage for the fetus at *any* time during the pregnancy. *Cigarette smoking* has been associated with low birth weight and premature babies, conditions which contribute to higher rates of fetal and infant medical complications, and even death. In addition, there is increasing evidence to suggest that the father's cigarette smoking can damage the sperm-development process, thereby contributing to the occurrence of birth defects in the child. In addition to these adverse effects on the fetus, cigarette smoking can lead to nicotine concentrations in the breast-milk of mothers who are nursing their infants (Petrakis, et al., 1978), and may also increase the likelihood of spontaneous abortion and medical complications in the pregnant woman.

Alcohol consumption can have even more devasting effects on the fetus. *Fetal alcohol syndrome* is a severe nervous disorder of the fetus whose mother is a heavy consumer of alcohol during her pregnancy. These children are not only physically addicted to alcohol when born, but they are more likely to have such birth defects as facial deformities, eye and ear problems, small head size, mental retardation, and heart defects (Godow, 1982). Even occasional heavy bouts of drinking by the pregnant woman (3 ounces or more of liquor per day) can sharply increase the chances of fetal alcohol syndrome and related birth defects.

Although they are used less frequently in our population then either alcohol or cigarettes, certain *recreational drugs* have also been found to have adverse effects on the developing fetus. Marijuana, heroin, morphine, amphetamines, and barbiturates are some of the drugs which cross the placental barrier and are absorbed in the fetus's system. Even prescription and nonprescription ("over-the-counter") remedies can create problems if not used with caution. These include aspirin, sedatives and tranquilizers, muscle relaxers, cortisone, antihistamines, certain antibiotics, vitamins C, D, and K, and insulin (Godow, 1982; Witters and Jones-Witters, 1980). The best advice for the pregnant woman is to moderate or eliminate her use of any such substances, and to keep in close consultation with a medical professional regarding what is ingested while pregnant.

Household Compounds.

Many everyday household products can be harmful to the pregnant woman who is not cautious when using them. The fumes of certain cleaning fluids, paints, and pesticides can reach the fetus, if the mother uses them with inadequate ventilation. It is best to avoid use of such products, if at all possible, particularly during the first trimester of the pregnancy.

Disease.

Several diseases may be contracted by the pregnant woman which can seriously affect the normal development of the child. Herpes Simplex II (see chapter 6) can cause blindness or death to the fetus if the mother has an active case during childbearing. Rubella (German measles) virus can have severe effects on the fetus, particularly during the first trimester. Cataracts, deafness, mental retardation, and heart disease are possible effects of the rubella virus on the infant (Godow, 1982). Syphilis (see chapter 6) is a particularly hideous disease which is easily transmitted to the fetus, causing severe malformations and lesions.

The adverse effects of these and other diseases can be prevented by early and regular prenatal check-ups by a qualified midwife, nurse practitioner, or physician. It is important that a woman who believes she is pregnant begin visits to a physician as soon as possible.

Radiation.

If at all possible, a woman should avoid having x-rays taken if she is pregnant. Radiation at any level penetrates the body and can harm the developing embryo or fetus.

Toxemia.

Toxemia is a general term describing a set of interrelated health problems that can occur during the latter stages of pregnancy. These are problems that affect the woman directly, and thereby affect the fetus indirectly. Toxemia affects between 5 percent and 10 percent of all pregnant women in our society, being most common among pregnant teenagers and first-time mothers. When the first symptoms of toxemia are evident, the woman is said to be in a condition of *pre-eclampsia*. These include headaches, blurred vision, *edema* (fluid retention in hands, feet, face, arms, and legs), *hypertension* (high blood pressure), and *proteinuria* (excess protein in the urine). If not treated early, these symptoms can worsen to the point of causing *eclampsia*: convulsions, coma, and death in 15 percent of all cases (Witters and Jones-Witters, 1980). Regular medical exams and careful monitoring of the pregnancy by a qualified medical practitioner, as well as sound nutritional habits, can help to prevent toxemia.

Nutrition and Weight Gain.   Beyond helping to prevent toxemia, proper nutritional habits are essential to a healthy pregnancy for both the mother and unborn child. A properly balanced diet will provide the nutrients essential for a healthful pregnancy. A physician might also prescribe multiple vitamin or iron supplements to assure an adequate intake of these compounds. The pregnant woman should limit her intake of sugar, salt, fats, and starches, which, in excess quantity, have little or no nutritional value and can contribute to excess weight gain or fluid retention during the pregnancy. The amount of weight a woman should gain is determined by her medical advisor. See Table 11.2 for an approximate distribution of normal weight gain associated with a full-term pregnancy. However, a physician or other qualified medical consultant is in the best position to judge the normal *range* of weight gain for a particular woman.

Ectopic Pregnancies and Miscarriages.   Occasionally a fertilized ovum will become implanted in the Fallopian tube rather than following the normal course of travel into the uterus. This is known as an *ectopic pregnancy,* and is potentially dangerous for the woman. Between the 8th and 12th week of pregnancy, the growing embryo will begin to press on the walls of the Fallopian tube, causing extreme pain or cramping (Delora and Warren, 1977). If left untreated, the Fallopian tube will burst, and the woman will be in a life-threatening situation. Immediate medical treatment is essential to prevent death as a result of shock or hemorrhaging. Fortunately, ectopic pregnancies are rare.

In approximately 10 to 15 percent of all pregnancies,

a woman experiences a *miscarriage,* or *spontaneous abortion* (Godow, 1982). The embryo or fetus is expelled from the body, usually during the first trimester, and is accompanied by a heavy bloody discharge. It is believed by medical scientists that some miscarriages occur when the fetus is defective in some way, and that this is nature's reproductive "quality control" among humans. Maternal illness or inadequate implantation in the uterine wall can also contribute to the chances of miscarriage, which in most cases can be followed by a normal full-term pregnancy.

Maternal Stress.   There is a growing body of evidence pointing to the adverse effects on the fetus of prolonged psychological or emotional stress of the mother (Ferreira, 1960; Lugo and Hershey, 1974). Women who experience stress and anxiety during pregnancy are more likely than others to have babies who are irritable, ill, have difficulty sleeping, or who cry more than is normal. A baby may also have become accustomed to the mother's daily routine while she was pregnant; these infants demonstrate consistent, and otherwise unexplainable, irritability at meal times or at other times when the mother is typically under stress.

Rh Blood Factor.   An important feature of human blood is known as the *Rh type.* There are two types: *Rh-positive* and *Rh-negative.* The combination that can be dangerous to the fetus occurs when the mother is Rh-negative, the father is Rh-positive, and the child conceived is Rh-positive.

The Rh factor is actually a substance attached to the red blood cells. Roughly 87 percent of Americans have this substance in their blood (Rh-positive), and the remaining 13 percent are Rh-negative. If an Rh-negative mother delivers a child that is Rh-positive, the result of her blood mingling with that of the fetus (caused by the separation of the placenta from the uterine wall) is that she will develop antibodies to fight the Rh factor introduced by the fetus's blood. Although this is never a problem with a woman's first pregnancy, it can be for subsequent pregnancies involving an Rh-positive fetus. The antibodies produced in the mother's blood after the first pregnancy will penetrate the placental wall and attack the red blood cells of the Rh-positive fetus conceived in a subsequent pregnancy, leading to severe anemia, retardation, or even death for the unborn child (Godow, 1982).

TABLE 11.2. *Normal Sources of Weight Gain for a Woman Carrying a Fetus Weighing 7½ Pounds*

Fetal Tissues (Baby)	7½ lbs.
Placenta	1 lb.
Amniotic Fluid	2 lbs.
Organ Growth (Uterus)	2 lbs.
Breast Growth	1½ lbs.
Increase in Blood Supply	3½ lbs.
Tissue Fluid and Stored Body Fat	6½ lbs.
TOTAL	24 lbs.

SOURCE: Guttmacher (1973:125).

Until the late 1960's, the only way to prevent this problem was to transfuse the infant's blood. However, a vaccine known as *RhoGAM,* which was developed in 1969, prevents the development of these antibodies if injected within 72 hours after an Rh-positive childbirth, abortion, or miscarriage. The risks associated with Rh incompatability increase with each pregnancy following the initial Rh-positive pregnancy to an Rh-negative woman, therefore a RhoGAM injection should be taken the first time such a pregnancy has ended. A RhoGAM injection is recommended for *all* Rh-negative women who have an abortion or a miscarriage, because it is not always possible to determine the fetal blood type.

THE IMPORTANCE OF PRENATAL CARE

At several points in this section, it has been suggested that immediate and regular prenatal check-ups by a qualified medical consultant will help to prevent problems associated with pregnancy. In the first several months of pregnancy, such a check-up is necessary only once every 3 to 4 weeks. Most medical practitioners recommend a weekly visit during the last month of pregnancy. It is important to have a thorough physical examination early in the pregnancy to verify that the mother is free of disease or physical problems which might impair her ability to have a normal pregnancy and a healthy baby.

Beyond seeking medical care, it is critical that the pregnant woman embark on a good self-care program. Proper nutritional habits along with adequate daily rest and sleep at night are important. Regular exercise is also important in order to keep in shape for the rather strenuous childbirth and delivery process that she faces. The husband can be an excellent source of support, if he is willing to assume some of the routine household responsibilities of the wife and help her to structure her daily routine to include an adequate amount of rest and physical activity.

Childbirth and Delivery

The childbirth process, or *parturition,* is also divided into three stages. The first of these is preceded by the fetus's head dropping several inches down and engaging with the cervix. This is most likely to occur a few days prior to the onset of labor. Engagement of the head is likely to be accompanied by contractions of the strong uterine muscles, or Braxton-Hicks contractions. This is really *false labor* in that the mother's body is not yet ready to give birth. It is believed that these early contractions are the body's way of physically preparing for the strenuous task of child delivery that lies ahead. False labor may be experienced for several weeks prior to the actual childbirth, and is often the cause of couples making futile trips to the hospital.

The first stage of actual labor is marked by one or more of the following: expulsion of the mucous plug from the cervix, breaking of the uterine "bag of waters" (amniotic fluid), and the onset of uterine contractions which occur with increasing strength, frequency, and regularity. The cervix begins to dilate, and will continue to do so until it reaches 10 cm dilation just before delivery of the child. The woman is encouraged to relax and avoid eating. A woman can be in the first stage of labor for several hours, on the average of 7 to 10 for first-time (primiparous) mothers and 4 to 6 for women who have previously given birth (multiparous) [Guttmacher, 1973]. One in nine primiparous mothers are in labor more than 24 hours. A woman is usually instructed to leave for the hospital when contractions occur regularly every 5 to 10 minutes.

After arrival in the hospital, the woman's and infant's vital signs will be carefully monitored by the medical staff. When the cervix reaches a diameter of 7 to 9 cm., the woman is said to be "in transition" to the second stage of childbirth. She will feel an urge to push on the fetus to expel it from the uterus, but must avoid doing so in order to avoid damaging the cervical area. She must wait to push until the cervix reaches a full 10 cm. dilation. It is this transitional stage of labor that is often the most uncomfortable but also the shortest. The husband or others in the labor room can be most supportive and helpful in assisting the woman through the transition phase of childbirth.

When full cervical dilation is reached, the woman is encouraged to push the baby into the birth canal during contractions. This, then, begins the second stage of childbirth. If she is in the hospital, she may be moved into the sterilized environment of the delivery room at this time. Some hospitals are equipped with "birthing rooms"— labor rooms furnished like a home, with comfortable chairs, TV, and bed — where the woman delivers her child in a more comfortable environment. If they have not done

The husband is an important source of support for the woman at all stages of pregnancy, including the labor and delivery process (parturition).   *(Photo by Carl Hill.)*

so already, the membranes holding the uterine fluids will rupture as the child's head presses hard against the cervical opening.

During this stage of labor, the baby will have gradually moved from the upper to the lower portion of the birth canal. The top of the head will be visible through the vaginal opening, which is known as the "crowning," and will most often be in a face-down position (see Figure 11.3). With each contraction of the uterus, which by now have reached their peak in frequency and intensity, the baby's head will push further down the birth canal, stretching the elastic tissues in the pelvic floor region until the head eases through the vaginal opening. In order to prevent tearing of this delicate tissue, the physician may make an incision at the base (rectal side) of the vagina to allow the baby's head to pass through with less stress. This procedure is known as an *episiotomy,* and is made painless by the injection of a local anesthetic which numbs the surrounding tissue. Once the head emerges, the child can be gently eased out of the birth canal.

The third stage of labor and delivery begins after the baby has been expelled from the mother's body. The baby's head is held in a downward position so that the mucous in the mouth and nose can be easily sucked out by means of a rubber syringe-type bulb. The child begins to breathe spontaneously (without assistance) and many cry for the first time at this point. The umbilical cord is then cut to about 2 to 3 inches from the infant's abdomen, and a clamp is applied in order to prevent infection. The baby will then be given a rating, known as an *Apgar score,* to indicate to the medical personnel the degree to which the child is viable and healthy at this early stage of life. This method of scoring (see Table 11.3) is based on a 10-point scale developed in 1952 by a physician, Virginia Apgar, to assess the physical condition of the infant one to five minutes after birth (Querec, 1981). A score of 0 – 3 indicates that the infant is "severely depressed"; scores of 4 – 6 indicate "moderate" depression; and 7 – 10 indicate "good" to "excellent" condition (Querec, 1981). The great majority of infants score in the 7 – 10 range; only 9 percent score lower after one minute of life, and 2 percent score lower after five minutes.

The episiotomy, if done, is then sutured with self-dissolving stitches, which do not have to be removed at a later time. The labor and delivery are thereby complete, and the mother and child are sent to rest and recuperate from what has been, in all likelihood, a tiring and strenuous, yet exhilarating, experience for both.

Special Issues Relating to Child Delivery and Birth

A number of other considerations enter into the labor, delivery, and birth process. These are far too numerous to list here. For more detail, the interested reader

FIGURE 11.3. The Birth Process: Stages One through Three.

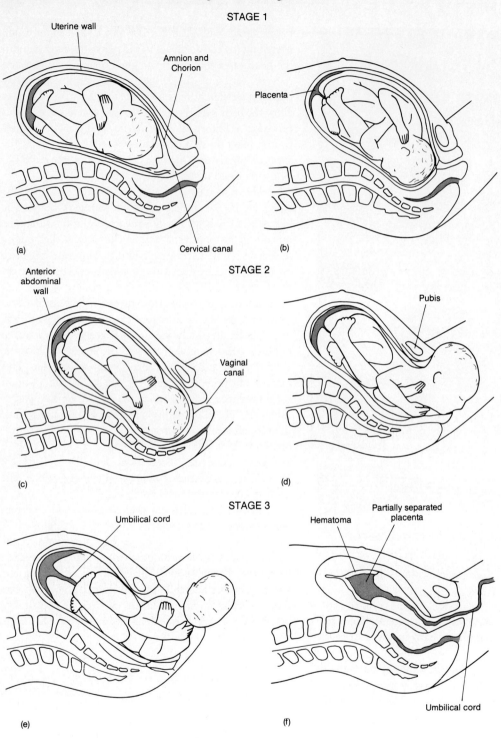

STAGE 1

Uterine wall

Amnion and
Chorion

Placenta

(a)

(b)

Cervical canal

STAGE 2

Anterior
abdominal
wall

Vaginal
canal

Pubis

(c)

(d)

STAGE 3

Umbilical cord

Hematoma

Partially separated
placenta

(e)

(f)

Umbilical cord

SOURCE: Adapted from Witters and Jones-Witters (1980).

TABLE 11.3. *The Apgar Method for Rating the Health and Viability of Newborns*

Sign	Score		
	0	*1*	*2*
Heart rate	Absent	Slow (less than 100)	100 or more
Respiratory effort	Absent	Weak cry; hypoventilation	Good; strong cry
Muscle tone	Limp	Some flexion of extremities	Well flexed
Reflex irritability	No response	Some motion	Cry
Color	Blue; pale	Body pink; extremities blue	Completely pink

SOURCE: Querec (1981).

should consult other excellent sources of information on this general topic, such as Alan Guttmacher's (1973) *Pregnancy, Birth and Family Planning,* or Tracy Hotchner's (1979) *Pregnancy and Childbirth: The Complete Guide for a New Life.* However, there are a few issues which we should discuss here.

BREECH BIRTHS

Not all fetuses engage the cervix in a head-first, or *cephalic,* position as the first stage of labor begins. Although it is rather common for the fetus to be in a feet-first or buttocks-first position well into the third trimester of pregnancy, most rotate spontaneously into a head-first position by four to six weeks before labor actually begins. However, the physician may attempt to manually rotate the fetus into a head-first position during the later stages of pregnancy or during early labor, a procedure that is not always successful. About 4 percent of all labors begin with the child in some sort of *breech* position, with one or both feet or the buttocks presenting first in the birth canal. Breech births usually are no more difficult or complicated than cephalic deliveries, with modern medical techniques for examining and monitoring the fetus during labor. However, if the fetus shows signs of distress during labor,

or if the baby is a larger size than the mother's pelvic region can easily handle, the physician will decide to remove the baby surgically by a procedure known as *Cesarean section.*

CESAREAN SECTION

A Cesarean section, or C-section, is a surgical procedure for removing the child from the uterus by first making a horizontal or vertical incision through the abdominal wall. This procedure is named after the Roman emperor, Caesar, who is thought to have been delivered by this method. The fetus's head is eased through the incision and the remainder of the body is born as in a normal vaginal delivery. The estimates of how many babies in the United States are delivered by C-section vary, from 6 to 7 percent (Guttmacher, 1973) to 10 to 15 percent (Witters and Jones-Witters, 1980). It is required in those cases where the mother's pelvic region is too small to handle the passage of the baby; when either the mother or child show signs of distress during vaginal delivery; where certain fetal positions render vaginal delivery untenable; when the cervix does not fully dilate after 24 hours or more of labor; or when the mother has severe toxemia. A Cesarean birth is a major surgical operation, requiring the sterile environment of a hospital surgery room, a qualified physician, and an extended recovery period for the mother. Under proper conditions, such a birth is a safe procedure which prevents what could have been serious complications with a vaginal delivery.

ALTERNATIVES TO TRADITIONAL CHILDBIRTH

The Leboyer Method. The French obstetrician Federick Leboyer believed that it is a physical and emotional shock for an infant to be born into the cold, bright, and noisy environment of the hospital delivery room, after enjoying nine months of the warm, dark, gently swaying environment of the mother's uterus. He therefore developed a procedure (Leboyer, 1975) to allow for "birth without violence" and a reduction in the birth-related trauma experienced by the infant. The procedure involves dimming the lights in the room; keeping the room as quiet as possible; warming the room to above normal temperatures; laying the infant on the mother's abdomen, where it can be gently stroked (whereby mother-infant bonding can take place); then immersing the baby in a tub of warm water and swaying it gently, to imitate the uterine environment as much as possible. Leboyer reasoned that, by following these procedures in the delivery room, the baby's sense of security would be increased and the trauma of birth decreased. Although there is some evidence that babies born by the Leboyer method fare better by age 3, in terms of psychomotor skills, sleep habits, and eating problems, we lack the necessary large-scale controlled studies necessary to draw any firm conclusions at this time (Godow, 1982).

Midwives. There is a growing trend in the United States and Canada for specially trained nurses to attend the childbirth, rather than a physician. They are known as *certified nurse-midwives.* These professionals can often spend more time with the woman during the pregnancy, labor, and delivery than a physician does (Coombs, 1980; Guttmacher, 1973). Given their technical training and their concern and support for the individual patient, nurse-midwives are likely to become an important aid to the physician whose time and energy might otherwise be unduly taxed by an overload of patients. There are more than 2,000 certified nurse-midwives in the United States, and their number continues to grow despite some unfounded criticism by the medical community (Coombs, 1980). Still, the percentage of infants delivered by midwives in the United States falls far short of the worldwide percentage, where 80 percent of all infants are delivered by midwives.

Home Births. Also increasing in prevalence are couples who choose to give birth to their infant at home. For whatever reason — whether it is to involve the entire family in experiencing the birth and supporting the mother, or to provide the familiar and comfortable home environment to which the mother is accustomed — home births are viewed as a viable alternative to the traditional procedure of driving to the hospital, staying for hours in a strange and unfamiliar labor room, delivering the child in a sterile delivery room, and then paying a handsome price to use the hospital facilities both during and following the birth of the child. However, it is important to recognize that home births must be an option only for pregnancies with no suspected complications. Should complications arise, it is critical that appropriate medical facilities and equipment be nearby. Therefore, it is important that couples considering home births be carefully pre-screened by a qualified medical professional, and that a physician or nurse-midwife be present throughout the labor and delivery.

PARENT-INFANT ATTACHMENT

During the 1970s, an idea known as "parent-infant bonding" became popularized (Klaus and Kennell, 1976). According to this theory, there is a critical period of *bonding* that must take place immediately following birth. It was believed that bonding increases the chances that a parent would develop positive parenting skills, such as holding and other physical signs of affection, maintaining eye-to-eye contact, and talking to the child. It was said that mothers and infants for whom early bonding took place would demonstrate a number of desirable characteristics months, even years, after the birth of the child, compared with mothers and infants who, for some reason, were unable to undergo an adequate period of bonding immediately following birth (Brazelton, Koslowski, and Main, 1973; Klaus and Kennell, 1976). Bonding, it was believed, must occur in the first few hours after childbirth if such positive effects were to be realized. For these reasons, many obstetricians would place the infant on the mother's abdomen soon after birth so that she could begin stroking it, talking to it, and realizing the pleasures of skin-to-skin contact with her newborn child that was to expedite the bonding process and its predicted long term effects.

However, research has shown that the concept of bonding is an oversimplification, and is not a true reflection of reality (Lamb, 1982; Lamb, et al., 1983). It does not appear that attachment between a mother and child depends on any one "critical period" following birth. Nor is it true that positive long term effects in parenting behavior or in the child's development hinge on whether or not "bonding" types of behavior take place soon after the infant's birth. Rather, the evidence suggests that mothers, as well as fathers, and their infants develop a sense of mutual *attachment* during the early months and first few years of the child's life. This attachment is shaped over an extended period of time by a complex array of variables, including the infant's temperament, caretaking arrangements, the parenting attitudes and skills of the mother and father, and the life circumstances of the family (social class, education, family size, etc.), and does not depend on a single event in one "critical period" shortly after the child's birth. Nonetheless, skin-to-skin contact between mother and infant, along with other types of "bonding" behavior following birth, is an excellent way to begin the longer term attachment process. Hence, such delivery room practices are a welcome addition to the birthing process and are to be encouraged (Lamb, 1982).

BREAST-FEEDING OR BOTTLE-FEEDING

A controversy that has raged for years centers on which method of infant feeding is preferable. The advantages and disadvantages of both breast and bottle feeding must be considered prior to making a decision (*Consumer Reports,* 1977). Most experts would agree that the parents should choose the method with which they are most comfortable.

The percentage of mothers breast-feeding their infants increased during the 1970s, and 35 percent of all new infants were breast-fed in 1975 (National Center for Health Statistics, 1980c). Although this number is higher than in the 1960s, it is lower than the more than 50 percent of mothers who breast-fed their infants during the

1940s. Breast-feeding has the following advantages over bottle-feeding:

1. It is convenient not to have to heat formula milk, refrigerate it, clean and sterilize bottles, and go to the store to replenish the food supply.

2. Breast milk contains protein and antibodies not found in infant formula, promoting immunity to some diseases in the infant.

3. The physical contact of nursing facilitates the attachment and security of the infant and mother.

4. Breast-feeding can be psychologically gratifying to the mother, increasing her bond with the infant and her general sense of satisfaction with life.

5. Breast-feeding is less expensive than bottle feeding.

Bottle-feeding, on the other hand, has advantages over breast-feeding.

1. Nursing may be inconvenient in certain situations, such as when the mother works outside the home, goes to a restaurant or social event, or otherwise must be separated from her child.

2. Bottle-feeding allows the father the opportunity to be in contact with the infant at feeding time, as well as relieving the mother of the full burden of the feeding process.

3. Breast milk carries, in small amounts, substances ingested by the mother, such as drugs, alcohol, caffeine, antibiotics, and nicotine, whereas bottle milk is free of such substances.

4. Breast-feeding mothers may experience cracked nipples, engorged breasts, and breast infection and inflammation as a result of the regular contact of the infant's mouth, and sometimes hands, with the breast area. Milk production is also influenced by several factors, including the emotional state, tension, anxiety, and diet of the mother.

Breast-feeding also delays the return of ovulation for many women, and thereby serves as a sort of natural child-spacer. However, this effect is by no means universal, and this alone should not be relied upon as a birth control method once sexual intercourse resumes (normally between 3 to 6 weeks following childbirth). It is best that breast-feeding mothers avoid use of the birth control pill, however, because the hormones in the pill reduce the available milk supply in many women (Hatcher, et al., 1984). Many physicians recommend a condom-foam combination as the best method of contraception after childbirth (see chapter 6).

The decision of whether to feed by breast or bottle is an individual one, and a woman should not be pressured into adopting a method with which she is uncomfortable. It depends on the parents' own feelings, attitudes, and life circumstances, and the decision must be made in that context.

POSTPARTUM DEPRESSION: THE "BABY BLUES"

It is natural for the majority of new mothers to experience a period of mild to severe emotional depression for several weeks, or even months, following the birth of a child. She may be fatigued from the childbirth, and may have had inadequate rest and help with household tasks and child care when she returned home from the hospital. Her body has undergone dramatic hormonal adjustments during the pregnancy and following delivery, which can affect her mood states. Also, the enthusiastic anticipation of the new baby is now over, and the "reality shock" of assuming new parental roles, with their attendant stresses and strains, has set in. The net result may be alternating periods of crying, depression, or happiness, with no apparent explanation for abrupt changes in mood. This situation requires an extra degree of caring, understanding, and patience on the part of the husband-father until the "baby-blues" pass. In most cases, they are a temporary state of only mild to modest severity (Godow, 1982).

Summary

Parenthood will continue to be a popular choice for the vast majority of people in our society for years to come. Parenthood, however, entails a demanding set of roles for both parents; these require a high degree of patience, skill, knowledge, caring, and responsibility. The human infant is a delicate and relatively helpless organism that requires constant care and nurturance if it is to grow, thrive, and survive. Many people who become parents may not be adequately equipped to assume these roles, and some have children that are neither planned nor wanted.

In this chapter we examined in some detail the wonderful and fascinating workings of nature in the processes of conception and fetal growth and development. There exist a myriad of possible influences on these processes, making every conception and eventual birth of a child a genuine "miracle unto itself." Whereas many of these influences are beyond the control of the parents-to-be, scientific research has shown conclusively that several influences—such as health, diet, environment, and stress—are within our control, if we maintain the proper level of self-care and seek attention from modern medical experts.

As we shall explore in greater detail in the next chapter, the transition to parenthood brings with it a profound impact on the marriage relationship. The changes in marriage brought on by parenthood are, in most cases, permanent ones. A marriage will never be quite the same once children enter the picture. In this way, children add substantially to the dynamic, ever-changing nature of marriage as it develops across stages of the marital career.

Questions for Discussion and Review

1. Do you plan to have any children? If so, how many? What is the ideal family size? When do you plan to have your first child? How will any subsequent children be spaced?

2. What are your attitudes toward those who choose to be permanently childless? What pressures are placed on people in our society to bear children? Are children essential to a happy marriage? Why or why not?

3. If you plan to have children, what are your own personal reasons for doing so? If you plan to remain childless, what are your reasons?

4. What are your views concerning current methods of overcoming fecundity problems, such as artificial insemination, test-tube pregnancy, and surrogate

mothers? What ethical issues arise with such practices? Are they useful tools for helping people realize their desire to be parents, or are they simply the tinkering of scientists with the sacred laws of nature?

5. What are your attitudes regarding pregnancy and childbirth? Are they events eagerly anticipated and looked forward to, or are they dreaded? (Both males and females can answer this question.)

Notes

1. The process of *mitosis* exists in all types of human cell division, with one exception. When sperm and ova are created, the process of *meiosis* occurs. Meiosis involves the division of the primary sex cells into two equal parts, each containing 23 chromosomes. Whereas mitosis results in an exact duplicate of the original cell, complete with its full complement of 46 chromosomes, meiosis in sex-cell division involves two new cells (either sperm or ovum), with only 23 chromosomes each.

2. In May, 1985 only the fourth known birth of live sextuplets (6 children) in the world occurred, to a California couple. The wife had been taking a fertility drug (Perganol) due to previous difficulty in getting pregnant. All weighed less than 2 pounds at birth, and were delivered by Cesarean Section after the 28th week of pregnancy.

CHAPTER 12

And Baby Makes Three:
The Transition to Parenthood

In this chapter we will take a closer look at changes in marriage and family life caused by the arrival of children. The *quality* of the marriage relationship is influenced by the arrival of children and other factors converging at this stage of the marital career, including the marriage partners' work outside the home and changes in the marriage relationship brought on by the passage of time.

Parenthood As a Critical Role-Transition Point

Just as is true for the transition to marriage, the transition to parenthood presents the couple with a new situation for which they have had little or no preparation or training. It is a period of *discontinuity* in the development of a couple's *marital career*. The addition of a child to the lives of a married couple means that the marriage relationship will be confronted with entirely new problems and concerns, stress and strain, and of course, joy and gratification. In brief, the marriage relationship will never again be as it was before the transition to parenthood. In

this sense, parenthood constitutes a "point of no return" to the way life was before.

The transition to parenthood increases the *role complexity* of the family. A husband and wife now occupy modified positions in the home—husband-*father* and wife-*mother*. With these modified positions comes a tremendously expanded *role cluster* for each partner, as compared with the years before children. Not only must they continue to perform the numerous *marital* roles effectively if they are to maintain satisfaction in the marriage, but they must also perform *parental* roles, and do so effectively if they are to view themselves and be viewed by others as competent parents. A partial listing of important parental roles is contained in Table 12.1. It should also be noted that there is an increase in the number of interpersonal relationships in the family (see Figure 12.1).

With new roles added to their role clusters, marriage partners contend with a number of norms that come with the arrival of children. Not only must they perform child-care and child-socialization roles, but the normative expectations which guide each partner's view of *how* the roles should be performed, and *who* should perform them, assume prime importance as the transition to this stage of development in the marital career is made. For example,

TABLE 12.1. *Role Demands for Parents*

1. Caretaker of child (diapers, feeding, clothing, and so on)
2. Affection-giver
3. Teacher of values and childhood roles
4. Disciplinarian
5. Companion
6. Confidant
7. Guide
8. Link with external agents (new grandparents, school)
9. Nurse/doctor, when child is ill

who should be responsible for changing diapers? For feeding the infant or young child? Disciplining when the child misbehaves? Should these duties be handled primarily by the husband? Wife? Or should partners share equally in these duties? What if only one partner is working outside of the home? Should the other bear the full brunt of the child-care responsibilities? What if both partners work outside of the home? Beyond questions of how the new role responsibilities will be shared is the question, *what is the appropriate behavior* in each role? What is the preferred way to care for a child? To discipline a child? Or to teach a child values that are considered by the parents to be important?

It should be readily apparent that there is great potential for *role ambiguity* for first-time parents; that is, simply not knowing *what* to do, from the time the child comes into the home as an infant, through the subsequent

stages of child development—toddlerhood, middle childhood, and adolescence. In addition, there is a strong potential for *role conflict* between husband and wife, who may bring to the parenting situation different expectations about how parenting roles should be played. There may be role conflict, for example, if the spouses have heterogamous family backgrounds (see chapter 10). They may have experienced different parenting styles from their own parents, or may have observed different gender-role arrangements between their respective sets of parents. For example, the father of one spouse may have shared the child-care responsibilities, and the other's father may have avoided those duties. Even homogamous couples experience role conflicts when it comes to parenting, and such conflicts can add significantly to the stress that a young couple experiences as they enter the transition to parenthood stage.

The transition to parenthood also means changes in the normative expectations and role behavior in the marriage relationship. Certain *interaction habits* developed in the premarital and early marriage stages (see chapters 9 and 10) must be modified in order to accommodate the transition from a married couple to a family. Among the role sequences sparked by the transition to parenthood are those involving companionship, sex partner, communication, decision making, and affection giving-receiving roles. Household task performance roles are also affected because the addition of a child adds to the daily household chores and responsibilities. The transition to parenthood means that much of the time which marriage partners once had to lavish attention upon each other is suddenly shifted to the child. An infant is a full-time, 24-hour-a-day responsibility for new parents, and the amount of time and energy infants require necessarily cuts into the time marriage partners previously shared with each other.

FIGURE 12.1.   Plurality Patterns of the Childless Couple and the Childbearing Couple.

2 one-way relationships

1 two-way relationship

6 one-way relationships

3 two-way relationships

1 three-way relationship

The Marriage Relationship During Pregnancy

The changes brought about in marriage by making the transition to parenthood actually begin during the wife's pregnancy. These changes touch each of the major bases of the marriage relationship: love, gender roles, sexuality, communication, and economic functioning.

LOVE AND AFFECTION

The exchange of love and affection in marriage is affected by the wife's pregnancy, in several respects. This is primarily a result of physical and psychological changes occurring in the pregnant woman, but it also relates indirectly to effects on the husband because of these changes in his wife's appearance and psychological state.

The early years of marriage, before the arrival of children, are marked by a high degree of *role reciprocity*. Companionship, doing things together as a couple — going to movies, plays, restaurants, and sporting events — comprise a major basis for a satisfying marriage in this early stage. Sharing feelings of love and affection for each other contributes a great deal to this experience. However, the wife's pregnancy can either enhance this reciprocal exchange of affection or it can detract from it, depending upon a variety of circumstances.

Psychological Effects of Pregnancy.
Studies of pregnant women have shown that the psychological reaction to pregnancy affects attitudes and behavior toward the husband and, consequently, the marriage relationship. A detailed longitudinal study of more than 80 pregnant women and their husbands (Grossman, Eichler, and Winickoff, 1980) traced the psychological effects of pregnancy on affection exchange in marriage over the nine months of pregnancy, during the labor and delivery, and over the first year of the infant's life. The factors most strongly related to the wife's willingness and ability to continue exchanging affection with her husband were (1) an ability to keep anxiety and uncertainty about the future to a minimum by coping with the physical and emotional changes associated with her pregnancy; (2) a willingness to mentally prepare herself for the emotional and physical stresses of pregnancy, labor, and delivery; (3) accepting an increase in her level of dependency on her husband, as evidenced by her desire to ask for help, and receiving a favorable response from her husband; and (4) avoiding the feeling of being isolated, unsupported, and vulnerable by drawing on her husband's ability to assist her. A favorable attitude toward the pregnancy, and a genuine desire to become a mother, were also related to lower anxiety levels, which, in turn, contributed to the woman's ability to relate intimately with her husband.

A different set of factors contributed to the husband's expression of love and affection during pregnancy. Many expectant fathers in this study became more protective toward their wives over the course of the pregnancy, but at the same time they became increasingly worried about possible complications in the labor and delivery. Some of the husbands found that their ambivalent feelings about the wife's pregnancy had a negative influence on their ability to relate to their wives in an intimate way. However, most of the expectant fathers reported a high level of satisfaction with the marriage because their anxieties tended to focus more on their concern about being good fathers than with the exchange of love and affection in the marriage. It is important to note that these, and other effects we will discuss relating to the effects of pregnancy on the marriage, are the most pronounced for first-time *(primiparous)* parents, and they fade with each succeeding pregnancy.

Physical Effects of Pregnancy.
As we discussed in chapter 11, the hormonal changes and changes in body size and shape, brought about during pregnancy, are significant. Pregnancy can increase the woman's feelings of self-consciousness and can adversely influence her self-concept. In an in-depth study of 55 expectant mothers, Leifer (1980) found that their physical changes tended to interfere with their ability to view themselves in a positive light. As we saw in chapter 3, it is difficult to express love and affection for another when the person does not hold herself or himself in high regard. Leifer concluded from her study that

[T]here was a growing sense of anxiety about the bodily changes that were occurring. For some women who had gained weight rapidly, there was concern about being able to regain their appearance once the baby was born . . . The rapidly growing abdomen continued to evoke anxiety, and women reported feeling like Alice in Wonderland, upon taking the magic pills: growing and growing, with no end in sight . . . The added size and weight of the body led to feelings of awkwardness and clumsiness. The women repeatedly used the term "cowlike" to describe their feelings about their bodies during the last weeks of pregnancy. (Leifer, 1980:34–35)

As might be expected, these self-images became more negative as the pregnancy progressed, reaching a low point during the third trimester. The discomfort associated with any nausea, backache, dizziness, or fatigue during pregnancy may also affect the pregnant woman's motivation to exchange love and affection with her spouse. Husbands, too, can react to the physical changes in their wives in a way that would reduce their motivation to give affection. Because of her changing appearance, and also because of the emotional stress and mood swings that accompany hormonal changes during pregnancy, a husband may be discouraged from drawing close to his wife in his usual intimate and loving way. According to the results of Leifer's study, the wife's mood tone can have a real impact on the exchange of affection in the marriage:

> The events of pregnancy and motherhood evoke considerable change in customary mood tone, and for most women, the change is of a predominantly negative nature. The general trend toward negative affect was shown by most women regardless of their characteristic mood before pregnancy, although some who reported a relatively positive mood tone prior to pregnancy experienced less disruption in affective life during pregnancy and post partum. (Leifer, 1980:43)

The key is for the woman to avoid being *overwhelmed* by the anxiety; to work together with her husband to cope with the anxiety, channeling it in productive directions. The fears and uncertainties of pregnancy, and the anxiety they provoke, can thereby function as a catalyst for *enhancing* the reciprocity in affection-giving and -receiving roles in marriage. Unless partners take active measures to prevent these psychological and physical factors from threatening the satisfying affection structure built up during the early years of marriage, this important basis of marriage may begin to cause problems, by failing to meet the spouses' continuing need for emotional nurturance afforded by the exchange of love and affection.

THE SEXUAL RELATIONSHIP

The sexual aspect of marriage is important for most couples, as sexual enjoyment and fulfillment are central goals of the relationship. As we discussed in chapter 11, many couples are able to maintain their prepregnancy levels of sexual activity for nearly the entire course of the pregnancy. However, the sexual relationship can be adversely affected during pregnancy because of the aforementioned fear, anxiety, and uncertainty about the pregnancy. In one study of 400 couples expecting their first

child, the average frequency of sexual intercourse during the second trimester was three times a week (Meyerowitz and Feldman, 1967). However, the frequency dropped off to an average of one time every two weeks during the last trimester of the pregnancy. The physical changes associated with pregnancy can also reduce the sexual interest levels of the wife and husband. If the wife experiences headaches, nausea, backache, or general discomfort during any stage of the pregnancy (usually in the first and third trimesters), she is likely to have a reduced level of sexual drive. Some husbands are uncomfortable with the physical changes in their wives, most importantly the expanding abdomen, and find their wives to be less sexually attractive as the pregnancy develops. Often adding to the wife's anxiety about the health and well-being of herself and the fetus, is her fear of losing her husband's sexual attentions, and, possibly, of his seeking sexual release outside of the marriage (Masters and Johnson, 1966; Leifer, 1980). Yet, despite their concerns about their husband's sexual interest, many women "hold back" sexually, out of fear for what physical effects intercourse and orgasm might have. Summarizing from Leifer's study:

> More than half of the respondents expressed concern that sexual intercourse might either harm the fetus or provoke a miscarriage. For some women this fear decreased their readiness to initiate lovemaking or to respond to their husband's initiations. The experience of orgasm often evoked fantasies of harming the fetus, and many women continued to have sexual intercourse but refrained from reaching orgasm. (Leifer, 1980:48)

Such fears, however, are usually unfounded. Sexual intimacy can be maintained during pregnancy for as long as *both* partners find it to be a pleasurable and rewarding experience. This fact should emphasize the importance of accurate information and knowledge on the part of marriage partners.

Masters and Johnson (1966) studied the sexual interest of pregnant women during each trimester, and found an interesting pattern of change (see Figure 12.2). First-time *(primiparous)* pregnant women experienced a sharp decline in sexual interest during the first trimester, but those who had previously given birth *(multiparous)* experienced relatively little change in sexual drive. However, both groups of women realized a notable *increase* in sex drive during the second trimester, reaching a higher level than previously known for many. The third trimester

FIGURE 12.2. Sexual Interest Levels of Women During Pregnancy.

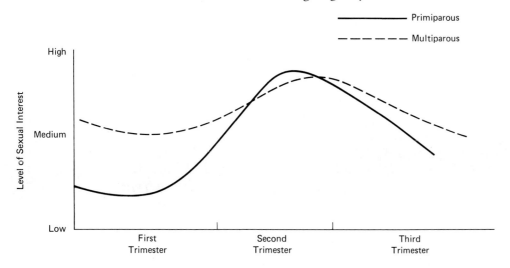

saw another drop in sexual interest for both groups, because of the physical discomforts normally associated with that stage of pregnancy—backache, abdominal pressure and discomfort, and general fatigue.

Clearly, the maintenance of satisfaction and fulfillment in marriage at this time hinges to a large extent on the couple's ability to maintain a satisfactory level of sexual adjustment. This requires a degree of coping with the psychological and physical stresses normally associated with the woman's pregnancy. The sexual relationship is an important foundation in most marriages, reaffirming as it does the bond of love and affection; therefore partners must strive to understand each other's needs and feelings in the sexual realm, and attempt to satisfy them in a mutually acceptable way.

GENDER ROLES

We have already seen that many husbands take a protective attitude toward their pregnant wives, and some develop a higher than normal level of anxiety because of the uncertainties of the pregnancy, childbirth, and parenting processes (Grossman, et al., 1980). Many husbands gradually assume a greater share of the household chores and heavier work around the home (Feldman, 1971). For those couples more oriented toward traditional gender-role expectations, this may be the closest they ever come to an equal division of labor around the home. In fact, the degree to which the husband is willing to share or assume the burden of household tasks normally done by the wife —whether it includes child care, housecleaning, preparing meals, or running errands—is positively related to the satisfaction that the wife feels toward the pregnancy and her marriage *if she interprets her husband's assistance in a positive light.*

Our data show that the (pregnant) woman's acceptance of her new dependency (on others) can best be accomplished if she is able to ask for help and if her husband is able to hear that request and to respond appropriately. If he is unable to do so, she feels isolated, unsupported, and vulnerable—a situation that cannot but add to her psychological burden. (Grossman, et al., 1980:43)

Pregnancy, then, can have a profound impact on gender roles in marriage. Wives tend to become more dependent, psychologically and physically, on their husbands, whereas husbands tend to assume more of the tasks normally undertaken by their wives. The pregnancy experience tends to shift the traditional masculine-feminine gender role distinctions in marriage toward greater male participation. Pregnancy tends to be a particularly burdensome and stressful experience for women when such a shift does not occur.

COMMUNICATION AND CONFLICT MANAGEMENT

Perhaps the most important reason for effective communication at this time is the fact that the pregnant woman is often going through mood swings, and is also experiencing one or more uncomfortable "nuisance" effects of pregnancy — fatigue, backache, irritability, nausea, and weight gain. She may be having ambivalent feelings about her future as a mother. This situation increases the potential for conflict and misunderstanding, as the husband may have difficulty understanding his wife's state of mind and body. He may feel that she is insensitive or uncaring about *his* needs — that she is overly concerned for the baby and herself. Some pregnant women tend to withdraw from the external world, and go through a process of "psychological disengagement" in order to find peace, quiet, and privacy (Leifer, 1980). Although this process of disengagement from the spouse and social activities probably plays a functional role in allowing the expectant mother to psychologically prepare for the baby, it can lead to misunderstandings and conflict with the husband. It is therefore important that spouses try to communicate their feelings to each other — whether it is the wife's feeling a need to disengage, or the husband's feeling left out and abandoned. By communicating, misunderstandings and unnecessary conflicts may be avoided.

Research on conflict management during pregnancy offers some interesting insights into the ways in which gender roles, love and affection, and communication patterns interact with one another. Raush, Barry, Hertel, and Swain (1974) observed a group of married couples in which the wives were pregnant, and compared them with another group of couples married approximately the same number of years, but in which the wives were not pregnant. When having disagreements or conflicts, husbands of pregnant women were much more likely than other husbands to compromise with their wives or give in to them. Because these husbands were so accommodating of their wives' wishes, the researchers referred to them as the "lambs" of the study.

Pregnancy, therefore, appears to usher in a period of protectiveness and accommodation on the part of many husbands who are taking care of their wives during a time when they are vulnerable and dependent. Some men even define their wives' pregnancy as a kind of illness or disease, causing them to assume care-giving roles relative to their "sick" wives.

Although pregnancy and its effects may increase the number of disagreements in marriage, many couples insulate themselves from the conflict situation simply by the husband's accommodation to his wife's wishes and needs. In any event, this situation demands open, two-way communication, a continuing exchange of love and affection, and flexibility in gender-role expectations, if unnecessary conflict and the stress it produces are to be avoided. In brief, continuing the process of *role reciprocity* is critical at this point in the marital career.

ECONOMIC FUNCTIONING

Pregnancy and the delivery of a child take a definite toll on a couple's budget. Pregnancy requires an increased intake of good, nutritionally balanced foods on the part of the wife. This is necessary in order to support herself as well as the developing fetus. There are a number of supplies to be purchased in preparation for the new baby. Visits to the doctor increase in frequency with each trimester of the pregnancy. Vitamins or medications that the woman must take during pregnancy add even more to the expenses.

An important issue facing many couples at this time concerns the wife's work outside the home. Many women are physically able to work on a full-time basis during the entire pregnancy. Moreover, some couples may need to have the wife employed as long as possible in order to accumulate enough savings to absorb the expenses following the baby's birth. However, if the wife should have to leave work early (by two or three months) because of medical complications relating to the pregnancy, can the couple survive financially? Although such complications are unlikely to occur, the couple must satisfy themselves that they have a sufficient financial cushion to absorb the costs of an unexpected loss of income because of the wife's leaving her job.

Families With Infants

Children have an impact on the shape and quality of marriage across the entire marital career (Lerner and Spanier, 1978). At all stages of their growth and development, as we shall see in subsequent sections of this chapter, children make a difference in the ways in which partners exchange love and affection, communicate and resolve conflicts, and manage economic resources. As infants, children are an intriguing, interesting, and challenging addition to family life.

PHYSICAL AND MOTOR DEVELOPMENT DURING INFANCY

Human infants are one of the few species of animals that are totally dependent upon adult nurturance and care at birth. They require a good deal of attention to their physical needs for food, warmth, and touching. They are immobile, and require the assistance of others in order to move them about.

Newborn infants differ markedly from each other in terms of birth weight, length, hair fullness and color, skin coloration, awake and sleep cycles, and activity level. Although newborns weigh an average of 7.5 pounds at birth, anywhere from 6 to 9 pounds is considered normal. Many babies sleep about 75 percent of a 24-hour day (18 hours), but others may sleep only 10 to 12 hours or less.

The physical growth of an infant is guided by three principles: (1) *cephalocaudal development;* (2) *proximodistal development;* and (3) *differentiation and hierarchic integration* (Hall, 1975). *Cephalocaudal* (from the Greek for *head* and the Latin for *tail*) development means that growth proceeds from the head downward to the feet. The more complex functions and structures of the brain and nervous system develop first, followed by the less complex structures of the limbs and torso. The proportionate size of head-to-body is greatest during infancy, and decreases steadily as the child grows older. Boys and girls differ very little in length and weight averages during infancy (Papalia and Olds, 1978).

The second principle of infant physical development, *proximodistal,* refers to the fact that growth progresses "from the center of the body toward the periphery" (Hall, 1975:107). For example, shoulders can be physically controlled before the arms and fingers. Also, the upper leg comes under the infant's control before the lower leg, feet, or toes.

The third principle of infant growth is *differentiation and hierarchic integration.* Differentiation means that the infant's reflexes and movements progress from general responses to more specific and distinct responses.

For example, a baby may react to a shoe that is too tight with his whole body, wiggling, thrashing, crying, and gener-

ally creating a ruckus. As the baby grows older, his movements become more specific, so that his response to a tight shoe is to thrash about only the offending foot. Eventually he learns to make very specific responses; for example, he may ultimately say, "Foot hurt." (Hall, 1975:107)

Hierarchic integration is the infant's ability to develop complex skills by combining more basic movements previously mastered. It may involve learning to sit, which requires a combination of basic arm movements for bracing, abdominal muscle control for strength, and neck muscle coordination for head control. A more complex type of hierarchic integration is involved in learning to drink with a cup, which requires a combination of many more basic skills: reaching out; locating the object; coordinating visual information with body information relative to the position of head, mouth, arms, and hands; tilting the cup at the proper angle, reversing the tilt before it spills; and, at long last, swallowing (Hall, 1975:108).

The development of *motor skills* — such as physical coordination, limb movement, and eye-hand coordination — parallels the physical growth and development of the infant. The developmental norms for accomplishing various motor feats are described in Table 12.2. Motor skills develop in a stage-wise progression, following the proximodistal and differentiation-integration principles of development. Although motor development is influenced by the child's inherent biological timetables, others in the infant's environment (especially parents) must work to stimulate the infant.

As Table 12.2 indicates, the first motor skills an infant learns relate to head movement and head control (recall the principle of cephalocaudal development). The *average* age for sitting alone is 8 months, although sitting with some support can occur at 4 months. Infants learn to roll from stomach to back at approximately 5 months, and from back to stomach at around 7 months. They begin to creep and crawl along the floor at around 10 months, and can stand with some assistance at about the same age. The average age an infant can walk with help is 9 to 11 months, usually preceded by a series of trial-and-error falls and repeated attempts to walk one, two, or three or more steps at a time. By age 15 months, the average infant can walk alone; at 18 months, can run stiffly, and also climb stairs with assistance; and at 20 months, can jump (Papalia and Olds, 1978; Hall, 1975). Remember, though, these are *average* guidelines, around which there is considerable variation from one child to the next.

The infant's *fine-motor skills,* such as grasping and

TABLE 12.2. *Patterns of Normal Infant Development by Age in Months*

Age in Months*	Motor	Social	Hearing and Speech	Eye and Hand
1	Head erect for few seconds	Quieted when picked up	Startled by sounds	Follows light with eyes
2	Head up when prone (chin clear)	Smiles	Listens to bell or rattle	Follows ring up, down, and sideways
3	Kicks well	Follows person with eyes	Searches for sound with eyes	Glances from one object to another
4	Lifts head and chest prone	Returns examiner's smile	Laughs	Clasps and retains cube
5	Holds head erect with no lag	Frolics when played with	Turns head to sound	Pulls paper away from face
6	Rises on to wrists	Turns head to person talking	Babbles or coos to voice or music	Takes cube from table
7	Rolls from front to back	Drinks from a cup	Makes four different sounds	Looks for fallen objects
8	Sits without support	Looks at mirror image	Understands "No" and "Bye-bye"	Passes toy from hand to hand
9	Turns around on floor	Helps to hold cup for drinking	Says "Mama" or "Dada"	Manipulates two objects together
10	Stand when held up	Smiles at mirror image	Imitates playful sounds	Clicks two objects together in imitation
11	Pulls up to stand	Finger feeds	Two words with meaning	Pincer grip
12	Walks or side-steps around pen	Plays pat-a-cake on request	Three words with meaning	Finds toy hidden under cup
13	Stands alone	Holds cup for drinking	Looks at pictures	Preference for one hand
14	Walks alone	Uses spoon	Recognizes own name	Makes marks with pencil
15	Climbs up stairs	Shows shoes	Four to five clear words	Places one object upon another
16	Pushes pram, toy horse, etc.	Tries to turn door knob	Six to seven clear words	Scribbles freely
17	Picks up toy from floor without falling	Manages cup well	Babbled conversation	Pulls (table) cloth to get toy
18	Climbs on to chair	Takes off shoes and socks	Enjoys rhymes and tries to join in	Constructive play with toys
19	Climbs stairs up and down	Knows one part of the body	Nine words	Tower of three bricks
20	Jumps	Bowel control	Twelve words	Tower of four bricks
21	Runs	Bladder control by day	Two-word sentences	Circular scribble
22	Walks up stairs	Tries to tell experiences	Listens to stories	Tower of five or more bricks
23	Seats self at table	Knows two parts of body	Twenty words or more	Copies perpendicular stroke
24	Walks up and down stairs	Knows four parts of body	Names four toys	Copies horizontal stroke

* These are median averages, meaning that one half of infants reach these levels by the stated age, and half afterward. In reality, there is a wide range around these averages which is considered normal.

SOURCE: Wood (1974); Papalia and Olds (1978).

manipulating small objects with the fingers and hands, are progressing along with the *gross-motor skills,* just described. The improvment of hand-eye coordination during the 4th to 6th months allows the infant to grasp objects purposefully by seven months. Most objects will find their way into the infant's mouth, regardless of how clean or how dangerous they are. The fine-motor skills become increasingly refined with each passing month, so that by 14 months, the walking, talking, and grasping infant is a genuine force to be reckoned with by the new parents.

INTELLECTUAL DEVELOPMENT DURING INFANCY

Cognitive development refers to how the child acquires knowledge, and the mental processes involved in acquiring and using information to help solve problems in the environment around him or her (Lerner, 1976). According to the late Swiss psychologist Jean Piaget (1952), cognitive development in childhood takes place in four basic stages: (1) the *sensorimotor* (ages 0–2); (2) the *preoperational* (2–6 years); (3) the *concrete operational* (7–12 years); and (4) the *formal operational* (13 years through adulthood). The sensorimotor stage finds the infant moving from primarily reflex types of behavior to an ability to organize and direct sensory and motor abilities in a purposeful way, to manipulate the environment (including *parents!*). Much of this progress is a result of the infant's trial-and-error learning about what is rewarding—what satisfies needs (e.g., needs for comfort, touching and being held, and food). By age 2, infants can anticipate the consequences of their actions, plan and carry out complicated activities, use resources effectively, and focus on a task while maintaining an awareness of goings-on around them (White, 1975:182–184).

The development of sensory abilities, and the amount of learning during the first two years of life, occur at an astonishing rate. Yet the rate and pace vary markedly from one child to the next, depending both on the child's inborn developmental timetable and abilities and on the parents' efforts to stimulate and teach the child. All this while, the child is developing language skills (see Table 12.2), which begin with crying, cooing, and babbling (birth to four months). Then the baby progresses to imitating adult sounds (words) [10 months]; one-word sen-

tences (one year); multi-word sentences (24 months); and grammatically correct verbal utterances (three years) [Papalia and Olds, 1978; White, 1975]. Rapidly, the infant becomes a full, participating member of the family. They are curious: they explore, and continually learn about pleasant and unpleasant aspects of their environment. They become goal-directed and purposeful, and quickly add a new dimension to the marriage relationship of the parents (Bromwich, 1977).

SOCIAL AND EMOTIONAL DEVELOPMENT IN INFANCY

Social development refers to the process by which the child learns to relate to other people—adjusting to them, learning to know their expectations and needs, what pleases them and displeases them, and learning how to behave in acceptable ways. The learning of such social skills as communication, conflict management, and empathy is a key part of social development. By two years of age infants are able to engage in "make-believe" activities and "role playing"; express affection and annoyance to parents, siblings, and other children; show pride in personal accomplishments; and use adults as resources when a task is too difficult for them to handle (White, 1975). Emotional development is a closely related process; it refers to the child's ability to experience and manage in healthy ways the emotions of joy, anger, happiness, disappointment, frustration, envy, fear, trust and mistrust, hurt, and sadness. As with physical, sensorimotor, and cognitive development, children vary widely, within a normal range, in terms of their rate of social and emotional development.

The primary feature of the infant's socioemotional development during the first two years of life is that of *attachment* (Ainsworth, 1964; Bowlby, 1973). We have seen (chapters 3 and 11) that mother-infant contact following birth can provide a basis for developing mutual attachment as the child grows older. Social and emotional development in the infant is impeded if a strong sense of attachment with a nurturing caretaker is not realized during this early stage of life.

According to Erik Erikson (1980), the human life span can be divided into eight stages of psychosocial growth and development. Each stage has a specific "crisis"

Infants require the stimulating touch and attention of a loving caregiver if they are to develop and grow in a healthy way—socially and intellectually as well as physically.

associated with it (see Table 12.3). The person makes a smooth transition into subsequent stages only when the crisis of the present stage is resolved and negotiated successfully. During the infancy stage, for example, the major crisis facing the person is *trust* versus *mistrust*. If infants can develop a sense of trust in other people, and in the predictability of events, then they will develop the "psychosocial strength" of *hope*. Attachment of the child, in the form of warmth, touching and cuddling, food and shelter, and comfort, all foster *trust*. Mistrust follows the experience of pain, abandonment, delay of satisfaction, and unpredictable behavior of others in the environment. This can lead to estrangement from other humans in later stages of life. As with our concept of *developmental tasks,* achieving a sense of trust will help the person negotiate the

crises of subsequent life stages more successfully, whereas mistrust generated during infancy may lead to difficulty and problems in successful crisis resolution later on.

Although newborns exhibit reflex smiles and vocalizations, they depend upon the caretaker to teach them how to respond to *social stimuli,* such as a smile or the human voice. Meanwhile, the cooing, smiling, clinging, and "cute" behaviors of newborns are likely to have attachment value for the parents. It is not until 2 or 3 months of age that infants actually begin to behave "socially" by responding to particular people and demonstrating their attachment to them. Research has shown that children are born with a certain personality predisposition, or *temperament,* that can either contribute to, or detract from, the parent-infant attachment process

TABLE 12.3. *Erikson's Eight Stage of Life*

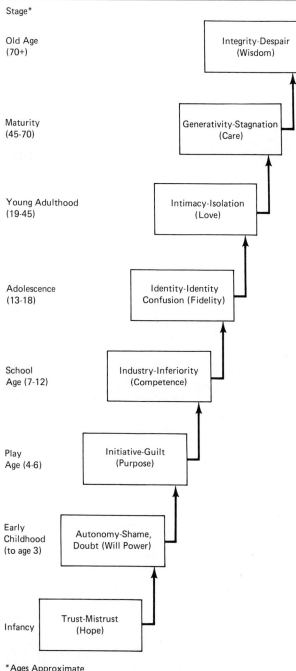

Stage*

Old Age (70+) — Integrity-Despair (Wisdom)

Maturity (45-70) — Generativity-Stagnation (Care)

Young Adulthood (19-45) — Intimacy-Isolation (Love)

Adolescence (13-18) — Identity-Identity Confusion (Fidelity)

School Age (7-12) — Industry-Inferiority (Competence)

Play Age (4-6) — Initiative-Guilt (Purpose)

Early Childhood (to age 3) — Autonomy-Shame, Doubt (Will Power)

Infancy — Trust-Mistrust (Hope)

*Ages Approximate

CRISIS THAT MUST BE RESOLVED
AND PSYCHOSOCIAL STRENGTH THAT RESULTS

SOURCE: Erikson (1980).

(Thomas, Chess, and Birch, 1968). Some children are "naturally easy" children, and others are "naturally difficult" or "slow-to-warm-up." Some infants are generally cheerful and happy, and others are relatively unhappy. Some are adaptable to new people and events, but others resist new experiences. Some have regular sleeping, eating, and elimination habits, but others do not. Some engage the world and the environment around them; others withdraw and isolate themselves. The temperament of infants is also evident as the child grows into later childhood and adolescence, and these traits often persist regardless of the parents' method of child rearing or the parents' own temperaments. Parents have an easier time attaching to infants who cuddle and who respond with pleasure to being held and talked to (Schaffer and Emerson, 1964). Attachment is more difficult with infants who tend to withdraw from physical contact, whose dispositions are rather negative, who cry much of the time, or who have irregular sleep/wake cycles (Lamb, 1978). This latter group presents a challenge to their parents' patience and reserves of energy. The outcome, in terms of social and emotional development of the child, depends in part on how the parents respond: with patience, caring, and concern—or with anger, hostility, and impatience.

Because of the attachment process during infancy, infants normally demonstrate two types of behaviors at about 8 or 9 months of age: *separation anxiety* and *stranger anxiety.* In the case of *separation anxiety,* the infant will cry or fuss when it loses sight or contact with the caretaker, and will do what it can to regain contact immediately. Often this involves clinging and burying its head in the caretaker's shoulder, in order to regain the security it needs when encountering novel situations or strange environments. *Stranger anxiety* refers to the infant's negative reactions to being around strangers, including obvious fear of and withdrawal from them. Both stranger anxiety and separation anxiety vary in the degree of intensity from one child to the next. However, it appears that infants who are least likely to exhibit these behaviors are those who have developed a secure and trusting attachment to the caretaker (mother or father, in most cases) [Hall, 1975; Papalia and Olds, 1978].

In sum, social and emotional development begins in infancy, and both depend on the nature of the parents' attachment behaviors and the infant's own temperament and attachment behaviors. Parents, therefore, cannot take all of the credit for a child who develops a healthy personality and who grows into a well-adjusted individual. Nor should parents take all of the blame when children develop into "problem kids" who always seem to be in trouble, or who have difficulty in getting along with others.

When Baby Comes Home: New Parents

A loving and nurturant caretaker for the infant is essential to ensure healthy growth and development. Early studies focused on the effects of *maternal deprivation* on young children raised in institutional settings, such as hospitals, orphanages, and foundling homes (Spitz, 1945; Rheingold, 1956; Bowlby, 1960; Rutter, 1971). Each one found that children suffer mentally, emotionally, physically, and socially when deprived of sensory stimulation and nurturant caretaking.

Here we will examine the different ways in which mothers and fathers can provide the nurturant care-giving that is needed by the child at this stage of life. Let us first take a brief look at typical reactions mothers and fathers have to their new roles.

MOTHERS AND INFANTS

Our culture has traditionally assigned the role of primary caretaker of children to the mother rather than the father. It is the mother who gives birth to the child, nurses it, and usually stays home to care for it in its early months or years, while the husband-father continues to provide income by means of his work outside the home. However, this traditional gender-role pattern has changed over the past several years as the levels of education, labor force participation, and career-orientation of wives and mothers have changed. Today, more women than ever before are combining work outside the home with motherhood.

Motherhood can have any of a number of consequences for the first-time mother, depending upon many factors. Motherhood can isolate the woman from the outside world, which may lead to feelings of loneliness, helplessness, and depression, or it can give her a heightened sense of self-worth and a new purpose for living.

The effects of first-time motherhood depend on three factors: (1) having realistic expectations of the motherhood experience prior to the child's birth; (2) favorable responses of the husband to the woman's role as a mother, wife, and worker in or out of the home; and (3) priority of their new status as mother relative to other statuses, such as wife, housekeeper, and income provider outside of the home (Leifer, 1980; Grossman, et al., 1981). Women usually experience a combination of gratifications and stresses associated with becoming mothers, and their overall sense of satisfaction and well-being in mothering a new infant depends on the balance of the "pluses" and "minuses." In one study, most first-time mothers reported that the benefits outweighed the costs, despite the turmoil and disorganization parenthood caused, as motherhood fulfilled one of their major life goals.

The fact that for most of the group, motherhood was associated with a heightened sense of self-esteem and maturity is quite striking, in view of the fact that these women were simultaneously experiencing considerable emotional disequilibrium in confronting the stresses of the maternal role. It appears that the lifelong socialization to bear children culminates in a feeling of having achieved one's major life goal and a concommitant enhancement of one's sense of self. The early months of motherhood are, thus, experienced as a time in which one's sense of fulfillment as a woman is at a peak. To some extent this is quite functional, since a heightened feeling of self-worth can cushion a woman against the exhausting work of caring for a new infant and provide sustenance throughout the lonely and difficult early months of motherhood. (Leifer, 1980:177)

Although many mothers suffer from the stress and turmoil introduced by new infants, it often dissipates by the time the baby is one year old. Families have a way of adjusting to the new set of "patterns and routines," and life gets on an even keel again as the new child becomes "integrated into the family system" (Grossman, et al., 1981). However, not all women experience a heightened sense of emotional maturity with parenthood; some experience problems in incorporating their new roles of motherhood into their identities. According to one study, some women

find the task of motherhood too great for their emotional resources; they seem less stable, less able to cope well with their life situations than before pregnancy. Not surprisingly, a very complex intertwining of factors determines the kind of adaptation that a woman makes: her psychological

The stress and strain often experienced by first-time mothers usually dissipates by the time the infant has reached one year of age, when the rewards and gratifications of parenthood take over.

health, her husband's psychological health, their marital adjustment, and their sociocultural assets and liabilities — all these interact to influence the mother's adaptation. (Grossman, et al., 1980:140)

FATHERS AND INFANTS

Because tradition has assigned to mothers the status of "primary care-giver" to children, the role of fathers relative to their young children has long been ignored by researchers. However, recent research has shown that fatherhood is an important and valued status for men today, and that fathers in our society play a key role in infant and child socialization, a role which mothers usually do not play. The traditional role of "father as breadwinner and power figure" in the family has given way to a new, modern view of "father as companion and nurturant care-giver" to his wife and children (Grossman, et al., 1980).

If both a mother and father are present and involved in caring for the child, infants become attached to both parents about the same time (Lamb, 1978). However, they tend to exhibit a preference for their mothers by about one year of age, especially in stressful or unusual situations (such as in the case of stranger anxiety). Research shows that fathers engage in different kinds of interaction with their infants than mothers (Lamb, 1978; Parke and Sawin, 1976; Lamb and Lamb, 1976; Rendina and Dickerscheid, 1976):

1. Fathers are more likely than mothers to play with their children in physically stimulating, unusual, or unpredictable ways, and mothers more often engage infants in more conventional games (such as pat-a-cake).

2. Fathers are more likely than mothers to hold their infants just to play with them or because they want to be held, whereas mothers more often hold infants to restrict them or to take care of them (such as feeding).

3. Fathers have a greater effect than do mothers on male children in terms of appropriate gender-role learning and the socialization of morals and values. Mothers, in turn, have a larger impact on daughters.

4. Fathers spend more time in social activities, such as playing games, rough-and-tumble activity, talking to, and in just watching their infants, whereas mothers spend more time in infant caretaking (diapering, feeding, and bathing).

Most experts agree that the kinds of contact fathers usually provide for their infants are important for the development of the child. Fathers are encouraged to take as much time as they can in relating to their infants on a one-on-one basis. The father-infant relationship can function to complement the more caretaking sorts of activities that mothers more often perform.

EFFECTIVE PARENTING FOR INFANTS

Infants are complex and curious little creatures who bring into the world their own personality predispositions and unique qualities. For this reason, there is no "recipe" to follow for effective parenthood. But there are a number of general parenting guidelines which appear to promote infant development in all areas.

Providing a predictable and secure environment during infancy contributes to healthy social and emotional development in subsequent stages of childhood. (Photo by Paula Deering.)

Promoting Physical and Motor Development. Paramount in this developmental area is the need to provide adequate nutrition for the infant. Growth of brain cells and development of the central nervous system require adequate nutrition for the infant throughout this stage. If it is lacking, irreversible brain damage to the child can occur (Longstreth, 1974). Parents should be sure that an infant receives a nutritious diet containing the essential vitamins, protein, and minerals. Starches and sugars are best avoided, in order to prevent the all-too-common problem of infant obesity. The infant's pediatrician is a good source of information regarding nutrition, and should be freely consulted by parents.

Other aspects of physical development, including motor development, are primarily directed by the internal maturational timetables of the child (White, 1975). There is little a parent can do, or should do, to "strengthen" a child or make it more "coordinated" during infancy. Infants and older children vary widely within a normal range, and so long as parents provide an average environment of physical stimulation and care for the child, physical and motor development should proceed on schedule with the child's own hereditary "clock."

Promoting Cognitive Development. A parent can do much more to stimulate development of the infant in this realm. After several years of studying infants and their parents, psychologist Burton White (1971; 1975) developed a number of suggestions for parents who wish to facilitate their infant's cognitive development during six "phases" of the infancy stage.

Phase I (Birth to 6 weeks)
1. Encourage interest in the outside world by providing occasional changes in scenery or a good mobile hung over the crib.

2. *Do not* feel the need to provide an elaborately "enriched" environment at this time. Fancy and colorful toys and gadgets are of little use to the infant who sleeps much of the time and whose intellectual capabilities are too primitive to put such items to use.

3. Verbalize and talk to the child.

Phase II (6 weeks to 3½ months)
1. Continue fostering curiosity and interest in the outside world by use of appropriate mobiles for the crib, small mirrors, an infant seat, and changes of scenery.

Money-wasters in this phase are rattles and most crib devices, which "provide negligible amounts of play value and have very little educational merit." (White, 1975:56)

2. Provide opportunities for interesting visual experiences, as well as for hand-eye activities (again, with the use of a mirror or appropriate crib mobile, or by elevating the child in an infant seat).

3. Verbalize and talk to the child.

Phase III (3½ to 5½ months)
1. Continue fostering curiosity in the outside world as in previous stages, including mirrors (nonglass), infant seats, mobiles, and various age-appropriate crib toys. Expensive toys or fancy "enrichment" gadgets are of little value, and the money spent on such items would be better spent on something else.

2. Continue talking to the baby, particularly about the events or goings-on of the moment, because interest in socializing with people is beginning to accelerate during this phase.

3. Continue providing a change of scenery periodically; avoid leaving the infant in a crib or playpen for extended periods of time.

Phase IV (5½ to 8 months)
1. Continue talking to and verbalizing with the child in concrete, not abstract, terms. Concentrate on the here and now. Read aloud to the child just before nap-time or bedtime.

2. Provide small objects and mechanisms that can be dropped, banged, thrown, or manipulated (rattles, jack-in-the-boxes, balls, etc.). Be sure that the objects are large enough to avoid being placed in the infant's mouth, and possibly lodged in the throat.

3. Continue to foster curiosity and interest in the outside world with crib devices, stuffed toys, and stacking toys (such as plastic doughnuts, cups, or blocks). A "walker on wheels" is appropriate, to allow the child greater mobility, provided that parents are prepared to monitor the child and take care that it does not pull objects down onto herself or himself, or move out of sight for more than a few moments at a time.

Phase V (8 to 14 months)
1. Provide toys that are unlikely to bore the child. Toys that permit water play, especially bath toys, are good for this age. Various colors and sizes of balls are excellent toys, as are blocks and containers of varying shapes, colors, and sizes.

2. Help to nurture his or her curiosity by providing a safe accident-proof environment in the home. Be especially careful of sharp or breakable objects, stairs and steps, poisons, sharp utensils, extremely small objects, paint, and electrical outlets. Attempt to reduce as much as possible restrictions on the child's ability to move about.

3. Continue verbalizing to the child, and reading to him or her.

4. *Avoid forced learning* in the form of commercial "reading kits" to "get children on the road to reading at eight and nine months of age." Such efforts are likely to bore the child and will have a "negative influence on his basic curiosity and interest in learning." (White, 1975:146)

Phase VI (14 to 24 months)
1. Help to facilitate the child's ever-growing interest in the outside world by providing objects of various shapes, sizes, and functions. These do not have to be elaborate and expensive toys; they may be such common items as ping-pong balls, pots and pans, plastic containers, water, or paper. Playing on the swings and slides of the local playground is, of course, appropriate.

2. Try to balance the child's interest in exploring the world and in practicing new motor skills, with interest in you — the parent. The major problem at this stage is either too much, or too little, involvement of the parent in the child's world.

3. Continue interacting verbally with the child, including reading aloud to him or her at bedtime. Try to begin conversing with the child *as a peer,* or friend.

4. Avoid pushing the child into early educational activities, such as reading or writing, which may jeopardize other aspects of development, such as social or motor-skill development.

Promoting Social and Emotional Development. During *all* the phases of infancy, what will help to strengthen the bond of attachment and trust between parent and child is *giving the infant a feeling of being loved and cared for.* This means holding and cuddling the infant; talking to him or her in caring and affectionate ways; responding to his or her needs and desires; and valuing and respecting his or her individual qualities. These are all means by which a parent communicates love to the child, and in this way creates an atmosphere of security and trust in which healthy socioemotional development can take place.

Gonzalez-Mena and Eyer (1980) offer ten "principles of care-giving," which, if followed by the parents, should contribute to this healthy environment.

Principle 1: Involve infants in things that concern them. This involves paying attention to the infant and "working together" in play activities as a team, rather than generally ignoring the infant and pacifying it with a toy or other object in order to turn your attention to other matters.

Principle 2: Invest in quality time. This means spending time with the infant that is focused on responding to him or her. This is particularly important for parents who work outside of the home. In terms of parent-infant attachment, *quality* time can compensate for a reduced *quantity* of time because of job demands.

Principle 3: Learn infants' unique ways of communicating, and teach them yours. This principle includes talking naturally to the baby, "teaching it to listen rather than tune out." Parents should avoid repeating words over and over, or using baby talk, but should respond to the baby's forms of communication (sounds, facial expressions, and body movements) in similar ways.

Principal 4: Invest in time and energy to build a total person. This relates to a point raised earlier. Infants' development occurs in a number of domains—physical, motor, sensory, intellectual, cognitive, social, and emotional—and care should be taken not to over-emphasize one to the exclusion of others.

Principle 5: Respect infants as individuals. Infants bring unique personalities into the world. These core personality elements are difficult to change, and it is usually undesirable to attempt to do so. Parents should attempt to modify their own role expectations and behavior in order to create a workable adjustment, or "fit," with the child's temperament.

Principle 6: Be honest about your feelings. Children become confused and frustrated when parents feel angry or hurt but mask their true sentiments with a "honeyed voice." Be forthright with a child about feelings, without blaming, accusing, judging, or belittling. Be sure to let a misbehaving two-year-old know that you disapprove of his or her *behavior,* and not that you disapprove of him or her as a person.

Principle 7: Model the behavior you want to teach. Children, especially young ones, are like sponges: they soak up what they see going on around them. Because parents are such a major part of their lives, children are likely to imitate those behaviors and values they observe in their parents. Children imitate such parental-role behaviors as cooperation and conflict; respect and disrespect; and communicating feelings honestly and openly. Children then incorporate these observed patterns into their own role-behavior repertoires.

Principle 8: Let infants learn to solve their own problems. To the extent possible, infants should be allowed to solve the problems they encounter in their environment. This will help to create a sense of independence and self-reliance early in life, which will provide a basis for development in subsequent stages of the life span. As Gonzalez-Mena and Eyer (p. 24) point out:

> Infants can probably solve more problems than many people give them credit for. The caregiver's role is to give them time and freedom to work on them. That means not responding to every frustration immediately. Sometimes a bit of facilitating will move a child forward when he gets stuck on a problem, but the facilitating should be the least help necessary, leaving the child free to work toward his own solution. Problems are valuable learning opportunities.

Principle 9: Build security by teaching trust. Parents should be dependable, offering strength and support for the child. Don't lie to, or trick, even infants. Many parents do this when they "sneak out" when leaving a child with a babysitter. Parents should demonstrate to the child that they can be trusted: one way is to make certain that the child always knows whether his or her parents are at home or away.

Principle 10: Be concerned about the quality of development in each stage. Infant development is a continuous process. Parents should not be too eager to push their young children along from phase to phase before their children are ready to move ahead. Each phase should be enjoyed and appreciated in its own right. Gonzalez-Mena and Eyer (p. 25) phrase it well when they state:

> Many of us have the idea that faster is better. Some people chart milestones and cheer when their child gets to one early. In the care of people with this attitude, babies are propped up before they can sit on their own, they are walked around by the hand before they can stand by themselves. The important learnings come only when the baby is ready to learn, however, not when the adult is ready to teach.
>
> Each baby is a unique individual who develops in his own way at his own time. Rather than try to push him ahead in his development, caregivers ought to concentrate on broadening his experience in the stage where he is. . . . The question to ask is, not is the baby reaching milestones with great speed, but rather, *how well* does the baby do what it is that he *is doing*?

The Marriage Relationship After the Transition to Parenthood

Although pregnancy, childbirth, and caring for the infant can prove to be stressful experiences for first-time parents, they also have rewarding aspects that make them worthwhile and exciting experiences for many couples. Especially if the child is a wanted and planned child, and if the husband is an active participant in the process of preparing for the childbirth, the transition to parenthood can be relatively smooth.

In this section, we will focus on the first year or two immediately following the transition to first parenthood. This is a critical period for the married couple, as the addition of a child often has its most profound effects on the husband-wife relationship during this stage of the marital career (Lamb, 1978).

LOVE AND AFFECTION

Some studies have shown that first parenthood is viewed by most parents as a *crisis* in their lives (Lemasters, 1957; Dyer, 1963). Often parents who view parenthood as a crisis feel that they are ill-prepared for the demands and challenges of parenthood, having romanticized parenthood to a large degree. Parenthood can have a serious negative impact on the reciprocal exchanges of love and affection in marriage if it is a crisis in the lives of a husband and wife.

Despite the fact that parenthood is a normal and expected life event in the context of marriage, it appears that children can disrupt a marriage as parents shift their focus from themselves to the demands, responsibilities, and gratifications that come with a new baby. A child can be like a wedge between husband and wife because of the necessary reorganization of life; and there is the potential for jealousy, as the child competes for the affection and attention of one or both parents.

> [T]hey (the spouses) find that living as a trio is more complicated than living as a pair. The husband, for example, no longer ranks first in claims upon his wife but must accept the child's right to priority. In some cases, the husband may feel that he is the semi-isolate, the third party in the trio. In other cases, the wife may feel that her husband is more interested in the baby than in her. If they preserve their pair relationship and continue their previous way of life, relatives and friends may regard them as poor parents. In any event, their pattern of living has to be radically altered. (Lemasters, 1957:355)

More recent studies of the effects of first-time parenthood on the marriage relationship have found that the transition to parenthood is no more than "stressful," "difficult," or "bothersome" for most spouses (Russell, 1974; Waldron and Routh, 1981; Hobbs and Cole, 1976; Grossman, et al., 1980; Leifer, 1980). The major causes of stress and difficulty in marriage following the transition to parenthood are summarized in Table 12.4. As this table indicates, the stress of parenthood can flow from a number of sources both *within* the marriage (e.g., household chores or sexual relationship) or *outside* of the marriage (e.g., change in work involvement or in-laws and relatives). Some reflect the physical and emotional condition of the wife, such as fatigue and postpartum depression.

Although parenthood has its problems and stresses it also has *gratifications* and *rewards* (see Table 12.5). These

TABLE 12.4. *Factors Contributing to Stress in Marriage Following the Transition to Parenthood*

1. Loss of sleep because of infants' waking up at night.
2. Fatigue and tiredness.
3. Being confined to home and curtailing social involvements (decreased companionship).
4. Wife sacrificing psychological and economic benefits of employment outside the home.
5. Additional household tasks (washing, ironing), and difficulty in keeping up with it.
6. Concern about competency as parents.
7. The 24-hour-a-day, 7-days-a-week demands of the infant, and the new routine.
8. Wife's concern about her appearance (weight, muscle tone, etc.) following pregnancy and childbirth.
9. Interruption of the sexual relationship.
10. Additional expenses associated with the child.
11. Worry about a second (unwanted) pregnancy in the near future.
12. Postpartum depression (baby blues) or emotional "edginess."
13. Conflicts or competition with relatives and in-laws relating to new baby.
14. Husband's not paying enough attention to the wife, or reducing the level of attention paid while the wife was pregnant.
15. Wife's losing power relative to the husband when disagreements arise.
16. Wives feeling guilty about neglecting their husbands, not providing enough companionship, attention, or love, and being too tired to spend time together during the evening.

SOURCE: Lemasters (1957); Dyer (1963); Russell (1974); Hobbs and Cole (1976); Ryder (1973); Grossman, et al. (1980); Leifer (1980); Waldron and Routh (1981).

TABLE 12.5. *Gratifications and Rewards of Parenthood for Mothers and Fathers*

1. Pride in the baby's development.
2. Fewer periods of boredom.
3. Closer relationships with relatives.
4. Increased appreciation for family and religious tradition.
5. Increased contact with neighbors.
6. More things to talk to spouse about.
7. Feeling closer to spouse.
8. Feeling of fulfillment.
9. New appreciation of their own parents.
10. Fun in playing with the baby.
11. Developing a purpose for living.
12. Enjoying baby's company.

SOURCE: Russell (1974:295).

gratifications help compensate for the stresses that parenthood brings for many parents. Studies have found that satisfaction with marriage following the transition to parenthood depends upon the ratio of rewards-to-stresses. This ratio, in turn, depends upon the following factors:

1. A satisfactory pattern of exchanging love and affection both prior to and following the pregnancy (Russell, 1974; Dyer, 1963; Hobbs and Cole, 1976; Grossman, et al., 1980).

2. The first child being planned and wanted (Russell, 1974; Dyer, 1963).

3. A baby with a pleasant temperament, one who is reasonably quiet, eats well, sleeps through the night, easily adapts to routine, and is healthy (as opposed to one who is extremely active, cries a lot, has a feeding problem, is frequently irritable, sleeps less than the average baby, or has a serious health problem) [Russell, 1974; Hobbs and Cole, 1976].

4. Having attended prenatal classes and preparing for the arrival of the child ahead of time, thereby reducing anxiety about parenthood and increasing knowledge and accuracy of expectations (Russell, 1974; Dyer, 1963; Grossman, et al., 1980).

5. A problem-free pregnancy and delivery (Russell, 1974).

6. Being married and being older (especially for men) [Russell, 1974; Dyer, 1963].

7. Looking forward to being a father or mother, and viewing the status of "parent" as important in one's system of priorities (Russell, 1974).

8. The husband assuming a greater share of the household chores, and being willing to share the child-care responsibilities (e.g., getting up with a hungry baby at night, diapering, and feeding) [Russell, 1974; Leifer, 1980].

9. Being able to cope with postpartum depression, especially if husband is understanding and willing to help (Leifer, 1980).

10. Being able to blend work outside the home, marriage, and the new roles of parenthood with a minimum degree of anxiety, feelings of isolation, boredom, and fatigue (Leifer, 1980).

THE SEXUAL RELATIONSHIP AND FAMILY PLANNING

Depending upon when during the pregnancy a couple decides to abstain from sexual intercourse, they may find an interruption in this activity for 6 to 10 weeks or more. In order to allow time for the episiotomy to heal properly (see chapter 11), most couples must wait from 3 to 6 weeks following childbirth to resume sexual activity. This delay may be difficult for some to tolerate. The need for effective husband-wife communication about sexual frustration and sexual needs is therefore acute at this time.

Once sexual activity resumes, however, the couple may find that the nature of the sexual relationship has changed somewhat, compared with the patterns that had developed prior to the pregnancy and childbirth. Infants demand time and energy on the part of both parents, especially if they are awake at odd hours during the evening and night. This can interfere with the couple's sexual activities. The wife-mother, in particular, may find herself less interested sexually as a result of fatigue caused by the demands of a new baby.

Following the transition to parenthood, there is a need for continuing the use of effective contraception once sexual intercourse resumes. Usually, it is best to delay another pregnancy until the spouses have had time to successfully negotiate this transition. Adjustments to parenthood must be made, as well as adjustments in the marriage as a result of adding parental roles to the marital career. For those who wish to have only one child, the need for immediate contraception is even more urgent. "Piggyback" pregnancies can make a stressful transition even more stressful and complicated, unnecessarily increasing the adjustment problems of parenthood.

A popular belief is that women who have recently given birth, particularly those who are nursing their babies, cannot get pregnant for a period of several months following the childbirth. Although nursing an infant delays the ovulation process for many new mothers, it does not do so for all mothers. Complicating the picture is the fact that the "safe" period varies from one woman to the next, and that ovulation can take place *before* the woman

has a menstrual period. Hence, she will not be aware of her fecundity until she has risked, and possibly experienced, another pregnancy. Consequently, the couple planning to resume sexual activity following the birth of a child must resume an effective method of birth control. It is wise to consult a physician for expert advice on the best method. For example, the birth control pill may be the best choice for some, but not for nursing mothers: the pill's hormones can dry up the supply of milk, and small amounts can work into the breast milk and be fed to the baby. Hence, a condom-foam combination is an excellent method, and may be prescribed in cases where the pill, diaphragm, IUD, or surgical sterilization are not viable choices. Also, the sympto-thermal methods (described in chapter 6) may also be a viable choice for some couples.

GENDER ROLES

Gender roles in marriage, following the transition to parenthood, have powerful influences on how satisfying and fulfilling both the experience of parenthood and the marital relationship will be. For some, parenthood pushes a marriage toward more traditional gender-role behavior (Lamb, 1978). Mothers tend to pursue the nurturant, maternal care-giving roles, and men are pressured toward greater involvement in work outside of the home. Both of these patterns reflect the cultural pressures of our society —women should care for their babies and men should financially support the family.

Research, however, consistently shows the benefits of the husband's involvement in parenting activities and helping with such household tasks as cooking, housecleaning, ironing, and washing clothes and dishes (Russell, 1974; Grossman, et al., 1980; Feldman, 1971; Leifer, 1980). *Joint conjugal-role organization,* as opposed to *segregated conjugal-role organization,* is the key here (see chapter 2). Satisfaction in marriage is related to the husband's willingness to assist in child care and household tasks after the arrival of the child. In Feldman's (1971) study, the *least* satisfied wives were in marriages where traditional segregated conjugal-role organization prevailed before the pregnancy, and where the husband failed to assume a greater share of the parental and household role responsibilities after the child's birth. Wives in joint conjugal-role organization marriages prior to the pregnancy, who found that the child's arrival interfered with the companionship and affection exchange activities enjoyed previously, also tended to express dissatisfaction. This latter group was disappointed because of the "wedge" that the child seemed to drive between them and their husbands, forcing them into a more segregated role pattern than was desirable to them. The *most* satisfied wives, on the other hand, were those who had been in segregated conjugal-role structures prior to pregnancy, but whose husbands had, after the child's arrival, moved them toward a joint conjugal-role pattern by sharing the child care and household duties. They also gave their wives emotional support. Women in joint conjugal-role organizations prior to pregnancy, whose husbands worked to maintain that pattern after the child's arrival — by sharing household tasks, activities, and affection — were also more satisfied.

Role sharing, therefore, seems to improve the chances of making a smooth transition into parenthood for many married couples. The husband's assistance and emotional support are essential for a wife and new mother: she is fatigued by the childbearing and parenting process; she may be experiencing some degree of emotional stress or depression as a result of the demands of the child on her time and energy supplies; and she may be striving to regain her figure and remain attractive to her spouse following the pregnancy (Feldman, 1971). Wives and mothers are more likely to experience parenthood and marriage in a positive way when their husbands have helped to engineer a system of *role reciprocity* in this stage.

COMMUNICATION AND CONFLICT MANAGEMENT

Open and honest communication is essential in this stage. Effective communication can help to alleviate misunderstandings caused by changes in the sexual relationship, pressures on the comfortable patterns of exchanging love and affection, and demands for flexibility and sharing placed on the gender roles in the marriage.

However, maintaining a satisfactory pattern of interpersonal communication during this stage is a difficult task. In the early years before children, spouses may have had the time and opportunity to discuss relationship problems that would arise, and to maintain a satisfying relationship by means of frequent communication with each other. During the period following the transition to parenthood, however, significant barriers arise which alter the communication habits of the couple. A new infant is a full-time, 24-hour a day responsibility which can consume most or all of the time the spouses previously had to work on building the marriage relationship. Spouses may find that increasingly they delay discussing conflicts or problems because their time and energy are concentrated on the child rather than on themselves. Priorities seem to shift, at this stage, to dealing with the problems of parenting, earning enough money to support a growing family, and changing patterns of relating to in-laws and other relatives as a result of the child's arrival. The tendency is, in many cases, to push constructive conflict management and communication processes to the "back burner" while attending to these new and more pressing issues.

It is important that couples who make the transition to parenthood reserve some time during the day (or perhaps once a week) to spend with and for each other. Whether it is to maintain some of the companionship activity enjoyed previously, or to work on problems in their own communication structure, an effort should be made to keep the relationship vital. Because many infants sleep a good portion of the day and night, new parents should plan companionship activities for times when the baby fits in — a night at the movies, dinner at a restaurant, or an afternoon visit with friends. A competent baby-sitter (perhaps a close relative, such as a sibling or in-law) can care for the child, to allow the parents an opportunity to be together and enjoy their lives *as a married pair.* Whether the new baby drives a wedge between the husband and wife, or adds a new and exciting dimension to their lives without putting an undue strain on the marriage relationship, depends on the preventive measures taken. Effective communication, particularly if it focuses on the marriage relationship and ways of keeping it strong and satisfying, lies at the very heart of this effort.

ECONOMIC FUNCTIONING

The increased expenses associated with the arrival of children begin during the wife's pregnancy, and they continue to grow following the child's birth. While she is pregnant, the expectant mother incurs costs relating to visits to the doctor, monthly at the outset and weekly toward the end of the pregnancy. Supplies need to be purchased for the newborn infant, such as a crib, diaper-changing table and storage, bedding (sheets and blankets), clothing, and toys, as well as such miscellaneous items as first-aid supplies, diapers, pins, lotions, and powders. The total cost per month for basic supplies can be as much as $75 to $100, depending on the couple's ability to budget and shop efficiently.

Then there are the costs associated with the actual childbirth. A normal hospital delivery that is free of complications can cost up to $2,000 or more. This amount includes the mother's room, nursery charges for the infant, doctor, miscellaneous supplies, labor, and delivery. This amount will increase with any delivery or postnatal complications for mother or child. Ideally, a married couple should have health insurance coverage that would cover most or all of the medical expenses related to childbirth.

Another cost, which is often not considered, is that of health and life insurance coverage (see Appendix). Health insurance premiums may rise substantially once family coverage is begun. There will be regular monthly and semimonthly medical check-ups, as well as extra visits for health problems the newborn child might develop. Life insurance coverage, too, might also be expanded at this time, so that the child will grow up in a financially secure environment in the event that one or both parents should die.

All of these costs can add up to a rather sizable amount. Nonetheless, when prorated over a monthly basis, they usually can be afforded if worked into the family budget (see Appendix). Given the fact that so many wives and mothers are employed outside of the home today, because of career interests or financial necessity, it is not surprising that 40 percent of all women return to the labor force within 12 months following the birth of their first child (McLaughlin, 1982). This will help to defray some of the costs of making the transition to parenthood.

Making the Parenthood Decision: Developmental Tasks

Because of the availability of modern, effective contraceptive devices (see chapter 6), married couples today are in a better position than ever before to choose when and where to have children, how many, how they will be spaced, and, indeed, whether they will have children at all. Unfortunately, many parents-to-be do not have access to all of the necessary information for making an informed set of decisions relating to these issues. The parenthood decision is an important one, and whether it is a good or bad decision depends on a number of factors.

PARENTHOOD: A DIFFICULT DECISION

The transition to parenthood places a number of stresses on the marriage relationship. Parenthood imposes pressures to change many of the interaction habits that have been developing during the premarital stage as well as during the early years of marriage before the arrival of children. The success of a marriage following the transition to parenthood depends, to a large degree, on the *flexibility* of each partner. In other words, each must be able to accept and accommodate to the demands for change. They must add new parental roles to their role clusters; modify their existing marital roles as companions, affection-givers, and sex partners; and they must accept new and greater pressures in roles occupied outside of the family, such as work roles and relationships with friends and relatives.

Rossi (1968) identified four "unique features" of parenthood which contribute to its difficulty for married people.

1. *Cultural Pressure to Assume the Role.* According to Rossi, men are more likely to achieve adult status and identity through their work, and women are more likely to achieve adult status and identity through maternity.

> There is considerable pressure upon the growing girl and young woman to consider maternity necessary for a woman's fulfillment as an individual and to secure her status as an adult. (148)

Although the pressure to become a mother is less today than it was years ago, the fact that such a large percentage of all married women continue to bear children (see chapters 1 and 11) indicates that some degree of cultural pressure remains.

2. *Inception of the Parental Role.* Whereas marriage is typically a conscious voluntary choice in our society, family planning failures mean that pregnancy may not be a voluntary decision—it may be the "unintended consequence of a sexual act that was recreative in intent rather than procreative." (148)

The implication of this difference is a much higher probability of unwanted pregnancies than of unwanted marriages in our family system. (148)

Given current economic conditions in our society, and women's pursuit of higher education and higher occupational status, the issue of *timing* the transition to parenthood is critical. Many young people may be entering the parenthood stage before they are fully prepared to do so — if their educations are incomplete, or if they do not have a solid job or financial base.

3. *Irrevocability.*   Parenthood is a transition which is a "point of no return" to the status of childless person. Marriage and work are less so.

> If marriages do not work out, there is widespread acceptance of divorce and remarriage as a solution. The same point applies to the work world. We are free to leave an unsatisfactory job and seek another, but once a pregnancy occurs, there is little possibility of undoing the commitment to parenthood implicit in conception except in the rare instance of placing children for adoption. *We can have ex-spouses and ex-jobs but no ex-children.* (Emphasis added.) [Rossi, 1968:150]

One response to the irrevocability of parenthood might be the *psychological withdrawal* of the parent from the child. This can lead to a child who is neglected, unloved, or possibly physically abused by one or both parents.

With the legalization of abortion, however, pregnancy is less "irrevocable" than it once was. Nonetheless, those who go through with the pregnancy and bring a new life into the world are legally bound to care and provide for their children until the child reaches the age of majority in their state of residence. Unless a child is given up for adoption, a parent cannot voluntarily relinquish this legal responsibility to care and provide for a child. Only the state has that right, if it is deemed necessary to remove the child from the custody of a parent because of parental incompetence, such as gross neglect, physical abuse, or psychological abuse. In sum, although pregnancy is no longer necessarily irrevocable, parenthood *is* irrevocable.

4. *Preparation for Parenthood.*   As a society we are inadequately trained in the skills necessary for *competent* parenthood. This lack of training complicates the transition to parenthood for many. As Rossi (1968) noted, *children are taught the skills of science, reading, art, shop,*

or math in school, but receive little or no training in the *"subjects most relevant to family life: sex, home maintenance, child care, interpersonal competence, and empathy"* (153). Parenthood is therefore undertaken by most people with no more child-care expertise than that acquired by occasional baby sitting, a college course in child psychology, or occasional care of younger brothers and sisters. Some expectant parents may do a little reading on the subject, but there is little in the way of realistic training to prepare for parenthood. Moreover, parenthood is *an abrupt transition.*

> The new mother starts out immediately on 24-hour duty, with responsibility for a fragile and mysterious infant totally dependent on her care. (153)

For women who are usually dependent on others for emotional support, such as a husband, the abruptness of the transition to parenthood can be a debilitating experience, and the new mother may be overwhelmed by the "responsibilities of maintaining a home and caring for a child" (155).

MAKING THE DECISION TO PARENT: DEVELOPMENTAL TASKS

Throughout this chapter we have referred to the transition to parenthood as a potentially stressful experience — one that challenges and possibly interferes with the key bases of the marriage relationship. A number of developmental tasks should be accomplished before a couple decides to make the transition to parenthood. By accomplishing these tasks at the critical time — that is, before the decision to become parents is made — there may be a smoother transition into parenthood. It must be noted that the accomplishment of these tasks does not guarantee a smooth transition; however, accomplishing these tasks will improve one's chances of experiencing parenthood's gratification, and will minimize its stressful aspects — its potential to be a *crisis.*

Developmental Task 1:
Have a Genuine Desire to Become a Parent
It is important that, before a pregnancy occurs, both spouses have a genuine desire to conceive a child and to become parents. This involves the tasks of accepting the pregnancy and developing an attachment to the child,

important for both the mother and the father (Valentine, 1982). A tragic aspect of human existence is the fact that children, who were initially unintended by their parents, continue to be born, and might eventually become unwanted. Parenting is a difficult and challenging enterprise requiring skill, patience, and perseverence. Given the fact that parenting skills do not come naturally to anybody, it is clear that it is difficult to establish the all-important parent-child bond when the child is an "accident," and unwanted by his or her parents.

Parents who do not develop a special bond of attachment to their children are more likely to develop psychological distance from their children (May, 1982), and to be eventual child abusers. These children usually grow up with emotional, psychological, and health problems; have less than adequate social and language skills; and perform less well in school (Matejcek, Dytrych, and Schuller, 1979; Brooks, 1981).

To be wanted, to be welcome, is basic to the beginnings of all successful human relationships . . . The life history of an unwanted child demonstrates the truth that no good can come from dislike and rejection . . . wanted children are less likely to be found on pediatric wards suffering from neglect, broken bones, or physical abuse. Wanted children rarely become wards of society, dependent upon the advocacy of society's overburdened agencies to keep them from becoming street children . . . Baby care takes a willing heart. To the simple transaction of nursing, an infant brings utter dependency and vulnerability. Everything has to be done for him . . . Gentleness breeds ease and trust, impatience breeds discomfort and distrust . . . The unwanted child senses his mother's anger, hostility, and resentment toward him. He does not know why she feels as she does and cannot avoid his own responding feelings of anxiety and tension . . . It takes an unwanting parent to produce an unwanting child . . . It is an attitude compounded of dismay, frustration, and anger; it is the attitude of the woman whose baby represents blasted hopes and ruined plans, lost chances and missed opportunities . . . [I]t permeates whole families under stress of increased family size, decreased family resources, and the endless unhappy consequences of one life too many. This "unwanting" is too well grounded to be dissolved by the charm of a new baby. (Committee on Preventive Psychiatry, 1973:45–47)

With the advent of effective methods of contraception and the legalization of abortion, the *proportion* of children who are unwanted by their parents has decreased over the past several years. Viewed in another way, however, the sheer *number* of such births is quite substantial.

As recently as 1976 in the United States, the number of live births that were reported to be "unwanted" by all ever-married mothers in the 15–44 year range was approximately 8.1 million, or 12 percent of the total 67.8 million live births (National Center for Health Statistics, 1980b). By 1982, this percentage of unwanted births had shown only slight improvement—to 11 percent of the total live births (Pratt, Mosher, Bachrach, and Horn, 1984). Unwanted children are more likely to be born to the youngest and the oldest mothers, to the less educated and lower-income mothers, and to mothers without husbands, or who have experienced marital disruption. In 1976, 26 percent of all births to Black mothers were from unwanted pregnancies, compared to only 10 percent of all births to white mothers (National Center for Health Statistics, 1980b).

Another statistical indication of unwanted births are those to unmarried women, or *illegitimate births.* After rising steadily between 1940 and 1970, in the 1970s the illegitimate birth rate began falling steadily. However, the illegitimacy rate began to rise again, increasing 6.1 percent between 1978 and 1979, and 8.1 percent between 1979 and 1980 (National Center for Health Statistics, 1981c; 1982). The illegitimacy rate among Blacks is higher than among whites, although the recent increases are because of more unmarried white women bearing children than ever before (National Center for Health Statistics, 1982). Also, teenagers are responsible for about 50 percent of all out-of-wedlock births in our society. Although a child born to an unwed mother is not necessarily unwanted by the parents, there is a good chance that this is the case.

Probably the greatest cause of unwanted or illegitimate births in our society is failure to employ effective contraceptive methods on a consistent basis. It is a tragedy that any children at all have to be conceived or be born as a result of the parents' failing to take advantage of one or more of the highly effective birth control methods widely available today (see chapter 6). In sum, whern the pregnancy is unintended or unwanted, the transition to parenthood is more troublesome; childbearing and child rearing are more difficult; and the child will experience more negative consequences in his or her own growth and development.

Developmental Task 2:
Wait Until the Marriage Relationship Is Established
Recall chapter 10. We said that it is during the years before children that marriage partners are trying to negoti-

ate the transition to marriage. Mutually satisfactory communication, conflict management, and decision-making patterns are being sought, and adjustments to each other's sexual needs, personality traits, and daily habits are being made. And, of course, this is the most divorce-prone stage of the marital career. One sure way of increasing the stress and strain of this initial stage of marriage is for the wife to get pregnant and a child to be born soon after the transition to marriage is made. This is a case of *overlapping critical-role-transition points.*

It is important that the marriage be on firm ground before the arrival of children. This includes the individual's task of accepting and resolving the relationship with one's own mother (for women) and father (for men); one must make the shift from psychological dependence as "child" to psychological independence as "parent" (Valentine, 1982). In writing about the father-to-be, Valentine (p. 247) notes:

Impending fatherhood seems to uncover memories and emotions about what it was like to be fathered. The primary experience for learning about fathering is a son's relationship with his father. As in the pregnant daughter-mother relationship at this time, to become a father means giving up being a son, to some extent, and having to face the responsibilities that had always been there to criticize.

Once the marital relationship has stabilized, a strong sense of mutual commitment between the partners has been established, and the spouses understand each other well enough to predict how each will respond in a given situation, the transition to parenthood is less stressful (May, 1982). Under these conditions, marriage partners can more readily shift their attention to the new child; they are able to meet the child's needs and to care for it in a loving and nurturing way, without being distracted by major internal conflicts and adjustment problems that have gone unresolved in the marriage.

Developmental Task 3:
Realize Educational and Income Goals

It is important to have completed one's education and to be earning enough money to support a child. There are two reasons for this. First, it is important to develop a sense of *closure* about one's life as a childless spouse (May, 1982). This includes having reached one's educational and occupational goals to a point that would allow for the intrusion of a child. Are you willing to give up the things

that usually do not include children — world travel, mountain climbing, or other kinds of companionship activities done on the spur of the moment?

Second, the costs of bearing and raising a child have grown significantly, primarily because of inflation-fueled increases in the cost of living in general. A recent United States Department of Agriculture Study (1983) has estimated the total cost of raising a child to age 18, in various categories (see Table 12.6). For example, when viewed in terms of June 1983 price levels, the cost of raising a child to age 18 in the southern region of the United States (urban areas only) was over $90,000. The combination of food and housing constitutes well over 50 percent of the total cost of raising a child in all areas of the country. Parents who desire to send a child to college for four years can expect to pay up to $100,000 or more for each child who is supported until age 18 and then sent on for a college degree. In terms of making the decision to become first-time parents, therefore, young married couples clearly must be aware of more than the short-term expenses associated with pregnancy and childbirth.

That income is a critical factor in deciding whether to have children is amply supported by statistics on infant mortality in the United States. Infants born to parents whose income falls at or below the poverty level have a 50 percent greater risk of dying, either in the weeks just after birth or within the first year of life (Gortmaker, 1979). This is true regardless of the educational level of parents, parents' age, birth order of child, birth weight, and whether or not the child was hospitalized at the time of birth.

A major aspect of this developmental task relates to the wife-mother's employment outside of the home. In chapter 8, we discussed the dilemma facing many women in our society today: they have become increasingly oriented toward work outside of the home, yet desire to bear and raise children. We noted that the percentage of women who work outside of the home has grown most rapidly for wives and mothers whose children are 6 years of age and younger (see Table 8.3). *Financial necessity* is the major reason such women work (Gordon and Kammeyer, 1980; Hiller and Philliber, 1980). The problem concerns those working mothers who would rather be at home providing the primary care for their children (Leifer, 1980). Some feel guilty about leaving the child at a day-care center or with a baby-sitter for so many hours during the week. There is less of a dilemma among job or career-

TABLE 12.6. *Cost of Raising a Child from Birth to Age 18, in Various Regions of the United States, at a Moderate Cost Level, in June, 1983*[1]

Total	Food	Food Away From Home[2]	Clothing	Housing[3]	Medical Care	Education	Transportation	Other[4]
				South				
$90,624	$17,686	$2,364	$6,244	$30,638	$5,274	$2,088	$14,568	$11,762
				West				
92,589	18,609	2,632	6,006	30,800	5,796	1,740	15,042	11,964
				Northeast				
88,016	19,870	2,256	6,176	30,150	4,752	1,740	12,646	10,416
				North Central				
83,447	17,393	2,046	5,904	28,190	4,752	1,392	13,614	10,146

[1] Child in a family of husband and wife, and no more than five children; urban areas only.
[2] Includes home-produced food and school lunches.
[3] Includes shelter, fuel, utilities, household operations, furnishings, and equipment.
[4] Includes personal care, recreation, reading, and miscellaneous expenditures.

SOURCE: Updated estimates of the cost of raising a child. *Family Economics Review*, No. 4, U.S. Department of Agriculture, 1983.

oriented women who seek personal fulfillment through work outside the home, and who believe that their children are receiving high quality substitute care during the day. A mother may, consequently, feel more comfortable if she returns to work, knowing that quality time is being spent with her child in substitute child care during this formative stage of development. One income alone is often no longer adequate to provide the standard of living desired by many families. Moreover, our occupational system does not yet provide the time or opportunities for husband-fathers to stay home and care for children while the wife resumes her career or job.

However, despite their growing rate of outside employment, the fact that married women with young, dependent children are still the least likely category of women to work outside of the home (see Table 8.3) suggests that many resolve the dilemma by staying at home to care for the child. But this decision may lead to dissatisfaction, and perhaps a feeling of inequity, in women who wish to pursue a career and attain personal fulfillment through work outside the home. It can also lead to strain in the marriage if the loss of the wife's income leads to financial difficulties for the family. Staying at home with young children is less of a dilemma for women who view as their priority providing the primary care for their children, and in marriages in which the loss of her income will not impose undue hardship on the family budget (Leifer, 1980). This development task, then, raises a number of issues that must be resolved if the transition to parenthood is to be free of economic complications. Can the husband-father's income alone cover the expenses of parenthood if the wife should decide to stay home to care for the child? If so, for how long? Perhaps a couple could afford to lose the woman's income for a period of a few months, after which she may have to begin working again to maintain the family's standard of living. If she is employed as a professional in a career, how will the birth of a child affect her ability to succeed, especially if she leaves her job temporarily to bear the child? How much money can be afforded for day care? What is the best day-care arrangement?

Developmental Task 4:
Prepare for Parenthood by Anticipatory Socialization

There is much to be learned about pregnancy, labor, childbirth, and infant care which one does not learn in the family or in school. The transition to parenthood could be less complicated if the parent-to-be prepared ahead of time by learning what to expect from the parenthood experience. The research evidence suggests that women who have prepared for childbirth by attending childbirth classes feel more in control of the pregnancy and child-delivery processes, are more excited about the arrival of the child, and feel a greater sense of satisfaction with and closeness to the newborn baby (Brooks, 1981).

Prenatal Classes.   Many hospitals, health clinics, and colleges offer six- to eight-week classes on pregnancy and childbirth. These classes increase the spouses' level of self-confidence and competence by teaching such things as proper nutritional habits for mother and child; normal infant illnesses and health problems; what supplies to have on hand prior to the child's arrival, and how to use them; how to pick up an infant without hurting it; and how to bathe the infant. Such classes also prepare the parents for the actual labor and delivery of the child by providing a tour of the hospital labor and delivery room facilities. Prenatal classes should alleviate much apprehension.

Supplementary Books.   Prenatal classes should be supplemented by books, magazine articles, or other reference materials dealing with the various aspects of pregnancy, childbirth, and infant care. There are many excellent resource books available for this purpose.

Prepared Childbirth.   A couple about to make the transition into parenthood may wish to prepare further by enrolling in a "prepared childbirth class" (also known as "husband-coached childbirth"). *Prepared childbirth* is a concept that was first developed by the British physician Grantly Dick-Read (1972) in the early 1930s, and was known at that time as "natural childbirth." Dick-Read proposed the idea that the delivery of a child did not have to be a painful experience for the mother. He stated that a "fear-tension-pain" cycle exists, such that an expectant mother can psychologically work herself into a state of pain. If she fears the hospital or doctor, or is afraid of the pain she *believes* that she will experience, she tenses up to the point of tightening her abdominal and pelvic muscles. Tightening these muscles actually works against the movement of the infant's head through the cervix and into the birth canal. Pain is there-

fore experienced because the tense pelvic-floor muscles encounter the strong muscle contractions of the uterus, contractions which are expelling the infant. This pain leads to more fear, which in turn leads to more tension, and so on, until the mother can no longer bear the pain and must take medication. Dick-Read proposed a method of breaking the fear-tension-pain cycle by removing the fear. His program included: (1) fully informing the mother-to-be about the childbirth experience; (2) providing her with relaxation exercises during her pregnancy; and (3) having the physician coach the woman during delivery.

More contemporary proponents of Dick-Read's concepts have extended his method and improved upon it. American physician Robert Bradley (1974) believed, along with other physicians, that the husband should no longer be left out of the birthing process, and emphasized the concept of *husband-coached* childbirth. Not only should men be allowed to witness the birth of their own children, but they should be able to experience the joy and excitement that childbirth can bring to *both* parents. Bradley also believed that by involving the husband in the labor and delivery process, a stronger husband-wife bond would be created and would carry over as they make the transition to the childbearing stage of the marital career. Medication of any type was also strongly discouraged by Bradley. He proposed that the husband and wife assume major responsibility for the labor and delivery, with the physician "waiting in the wings" to provide assistance only when needed ("like a lifeguard at a swimming pool").

Perhaps the most popular of the methods of prepared childbirth has been that developed by Fernand Lamaze, a French obstetrician and gynecologist (Karmel, 1959; Bing, 1977). It was Lamaze who first developed the idea of the husband coaching the wife through the delivery process. In a sense, the husband-coach and wife are trained to "roll with the punches" (temporary setbacks) during delivery of the child. Through a series of muscle relaxation, concentration, and rhythmic breathing exercises, the woman is conditioned to dissociate contractions of the uterus with pain. As a result, she is able to maintain control over her body and the birthing process. The woman is conditioned to the voice of her husband, and he is trained to keep his wife alert and relaxed during the different stages of labor. He is aware of what is happening to her body, such as the time between contractions, when to avoid pushing, when to push, and what breathing exercises to use.

The central feature of the Lamaze method is the key role of the husband-coach in helping the wife experience the childbirth process in a rewarding way. The intent here is to have the husband share in that experience so that parenthood is entered into with a sense of *solidarity* and *teamwork* betweeen spouses (Block, et al., 1981). Husband-coached childbirth can help to ease the transition into parenthood, and to create a more solid foundation in marriage as the couple enters a new stage of the marital career (Fein, 1976). Simply having the father present in the delivery room as a means of support for the wife contributes to a smooth transition to parenthood, helping to create better attachment between father and infant (Miller and Bowen, 1982; Wente and Crockenberg, 1976). Only future research, using larger and more carefully controlled samples of couples followed over a period of three or four years, will determine what effects husband-coached childbirth has on subsequent marital relationships.

Summary

The arrival of children poses a critical role-transition point in the marital career. The transition from a marriage to a family increases the demands on marriage partners — their time, energy, and economic resources. Partners expand their role clusters to include the many activities and responsibilities of parenthood, which increases the complexity of life in general at this time. Parenthood entails a certain balance of rewards and costs, which usually have a profound impact on the established patterns of exchanging affection, communication, sexuality, and work in and outside of the home. Parenthood is a "point of no return," in that married life after the arrival of children will never be the same as before.

In view of the demands and changes that parenthood imposes on marriage, the decision to become parents is extremely important. Unintended pregnancies and unwanted children too often result in tragic consequences for the family, so careful family planning decisions must be made if parenthood is to be a gratifying

experience that brings with it a minimum degree of stress and strain in the family. It is important that certain devlopmental tasks are accomplished prior to parenthood, such as (1) having a genuine desire to become a parent; (2) waiting until the marriage relationship is firmly established; (3) realizing educational and occupational goals; and (4) undertaking preparatory steps in the form of classes and books. The transition to parenthood can reap satisfaction and rewards, or disappointment and tensions, depending upon these and other conditions in the marriage relationship upon entry into this new stage of development.

Questions for Discussion and Review

1. There is growing support for the idea that the father be present in the delivery room during the birth of a child. What do you think — should he be present?

2. How do you plan to balance your work and career-related pursuits with your plans for having children? Consider timing, education, and income factors.

3. What can society do, if anything, to increase the chances of only qualified and competent people becoming parents? How can society reduce the number of unintended or unwanted children?

4. What are some of the ways children might have a positive influence on a marriage relationship? How might children exert a negative influence on marriage? In general, do children have more of a positive than a negative effect on marriage?

5. Why do you think husbands tend to participate more in role-sharing activities during the wife's pregnancy than either before or after? Given that the sharing of household tasks and parenting responsibilities in marriage is related to a positive rather than a negative parenthood experience, what can be done to encourage more role sharing between husbands and wives in this stage of the marital career?

CHAPTER 13

Marriage in a Growing Family:
The Middle Years

I n this chapter we will move forward into the stage best described as the "middle years" of the marital career. This stage covers many years, lasting anywhere from 15 to 30 years or more, depending upon the number of children a couple has and how they are spaced. Entry into the middle years is usually when the oldest child enters the 2–6 year-old range (Duvall, 1977). This stage ends when the youngest child leaves home after reaching young adulthood, usually at age 17 or 18, as the marriage returns to "just the couple" relationship. This means that couples who have only one child find themselves in the middle-years stage for approximately 15 or 16 years, whereas the couple with four or more children might be in this stage for *30 or more years!*

Development of Marriage in the Middle Years: An Overview

The effects of children on marriage continue in one shape or form into the middle years. In addition to the effects of children are the effects that *passage of time* has on marriage. The arrival of children and their normal patterns of growth and development expand the range of contacts that marriage partners have outside the boundaries of the home: teachers at school, voluntary organizations, Little League, PTA, Girl Scouts, YMCA, YWCA, and parents

of children's friends, to name a few. *Selective boundary maintenance* can be a problem in this stage, as more outside contacts are allowed to cross family boundaries. For example, teachers in the child's school and others have a key role in the child's development. (The child's entry into school is also a signal to the outside world of how good a job parents have done.) At this time, children may come into contact with the law because of delinquent acts, drug and alcohol abuse, or driving offenses. This introduces yet another intrusion, albeit an undesirable one, across family boundaries. As with earlier stages, therefore, this stage has its characteristic stresses and strains, strengths and vulnerabilities, and joys and gratification. Marriage, to be sure, continues to be influenced by other events in the family and outside of it, particularly as these relate to the arrival, growth, and development of children.

The middle years find the *role complex* of the family increasing even further if additional children are added. As can be seen in Table 13.1, as each child is added into the family, the number of two-way interpersonal relationships accelerates. This increasing complexity places growing demands on the time and energy resources of the husband-father and wife-mother.

Adding to the potential for stress and strain in this stage are the *role sequences* for marriage partners as parents (see definition of *role sequence* in chapter 2). Examples of *parental-role sequences* include changing expectations and behavior in regard to disciplining a child, or teaching

TABLE 13.1. *Plurality Patterns of Families of Various Sizes, Two Parents Present*

Number of Children	Number of Family Members (Husband-Father and Wife-Mother Present)	Number of 2-Way Interpersonal Relationships
0	2	1
1	3	3
2	4	6
3	5	10
4	6	15
5	7	21
6	8	28
7	9	36
8	10	45
9	11	55

Computational Formula

$$X = \frac{Y^2 - Y}{2}$$

Where X = Number of 2-way interpersonal relationships.
Y = Number of family members.

values and "good" behavior. The pattern may change from that of physical restraint and simple commands and statements, while the child is young, to more elaborate explanations and verbal reasoning as the child matures into adolescence. Parents who use physical means to punish a seven- or eight-year old, such as physical restraint or spanking, may find that this technique becomes less effective, and is inappropriate, as the child grows into adolescence. Another set of parents may prefer an isolation technique as a disciplinary method, and send the child to a particular room. This, too, may seem less effective, and therefore inappropriate as the child enters adolescence, at which point denying certain privileges may be more effective; for example, use of the family car, staying out past midnight, or seeing certain friends. Of course, any of these role sequences become more complicated and demanding as more children are added to the family.

An example of *marital-role sequence* might include changing the frequency of communicating with each other. The time and energy required by children, as well as the demands of work outside of the home, diminish the time available for communication. Decision-making roles

might also be changing to accommodate the expanding role-complex of the family. It may no longer be as efficient as it once was for a husband and wife to sit down for a period of time to discuss various decisions that have to be made. A growing family may mean a more *autonomic* pattern of decision making, whereby each spouse has power over his or her own realm, whether it includes children, investments, insurance, household tasks, or some other aspect of family functioning. There may be more decisions made "on the fly," as the growing demands on time and energy prevent the couple from engaging in lengthy discussions. Role sequences in other key areas may also be seen, such as in sexual roles. The frequency of sexual intercourse may decrease as, once again, children deplete a couple's energy and time resources. The opportunities for spontaneous sexual play, which were once enjoyed as a childless couple, may no longer exist because of the presence of children and the lack of privacy.

Of continuing concern is the potential for maintaining satisfaction in marriage during this stage. What are the factors contributing to each partner's satisfaction or dissatisfaction with marriage in this stage? To what extent are the basic human needs for intimacy, love, and nurturance being met by marriage at this stage? And what factors contribute to need fulfillment? There are at least two major factors relating to morale and satisfaction in marriage during the middle years. First is the *nature and flexibility of the interaction habits that have developed over the course of previous stages in the couple's relationship (premarital, early years, and transition to parenthood).* These include modes of communication; resolving conflicts; exchanging love and affection; relating sexually; making decisions and exerting influence over one another (power); and dividing household and income-earning responsibilities (gender roles). The degree of flexibility of these interaction habits will determine how well couples accommodate to the stresses and to increasing role complexity — demands on time and energy — in this stage. Also important is the degree of *role reciprocity* which each partner perceives to exist in the marriage; that is, the degree to which both partners are making contributions that meet the other's needs, and which are viewed as fair, equitable, and valuable exchanges.

The second major factor associated with marital satisfaction is *the degree to which the marriage partners have successfully accomplished development tasks in previous stages of the marital career.* Task accomplishment has a cumulative effect, from one stage to the next. For example, if a husband and wife have not adequately established a firm foundation in their marriage prior to the arrival of children (see chapter 12), then the development of effective communication and decision-making patterns, satisfying patterns of sexual interaction, and a mutually acceptable division of household chores and duties may be seriously hindered during the middle years. These *carry-over effects* assume an increasing degree of importance with each successive stage of the marital career.

Stages of Child Development: Preschool, Middle Childhood, and Adolescence

As with the previous stage of the marital career, involving the effects infants have on development in marriage, we will again examine the typical patterns of child growth and development in the family. We will divide the

childhood years following infancy into three stages: (1) preschool (ages 2 to 5); (2) middle childhood (ages 6 to 11); and (3) adolescence (ages 12 to 20).

It is important to note that children encounter a sequential pattern of developmental tasks across these three stages. A number of these are summarized in Table 13.2. Just as marriage partners who accomplish developmental tasks successfully realize easier transitions and better adjustment in subsequent stages of the marital career, so too do children facilitate their movement from one developmental stage to the next by successfully accomplishing their individual developmental tasks. Again, *timing* is important, and task accomplishment has a *cumulative* effect (see chapter 2). Failing to accomplish tasks within a certain time range can mean difficulty with other tasks in subsequent stages. Children are dependent to a large extent on their parents to assist them in accomplishing their tasks. *Effective* parenthood is that which assists children in this effort; *ineffective* parenthood hinders children or prevents them from staying on schedule with these tasks.

THE PRESCHOOL CHILD: AGES 2–5

As White (1975:153) points out, this stage of child development has its rewarding aspects, particularly at the beginning of the third year:

> The new achievements of this particular period are especially rewarding to parents. This is the time when children begin holding real conversations with family members. This activity is usually extremely enjoyable for parents and of course for grandparents. Children are now moving from babyhood into the first forms of personhood. Their personalities are becoming clearer, more reliable, and more individualistic . . . These developments . . . contribute to a general feeling that you are living with a young, very interesting person rather than a baby.

Physical Development. The child's rate of growth begins to stabilize, accelerating less, at this stage. Children will grow an average of 2 to 3 inches and 5 to 7 pounds per year until puberty (Papalia and Olds, 1978; Hall, 1975). The average height and weight of boys and girls remains about the same, although boys have a slight edge in physical strength (Garai and Scheinfeld, 1968). Girls, however, develop an edge in small-muscle coordi-

TABLE 13.2. *Developmental Tasks of Preschool, School Age, and Adolescent Children*

	Physical/Motor	Cognitive/Intellectual	Social/Emotional
Preschool Child (Ages 3–5)	1. Settling into healthy routines of rest and activity (play, sleep, rest, etc.). 2. Mastering good eating habits. 3. Mastering the basics of toilet training. 4. Developing the physical skills appropriate to this stage of development (climbing, running, throwing, catching, large-muscle and fine-motor skills).	1. Increasing ability to think symbolically and abstractly. 2. Increasing ability to use and understand language effectively and clearly. 3. Working out problems by thinking about them first, as opposed to acting first. 4. Developing an increased ability to understand cause-and-effect relationships (anticipates and understands consequences of actions). 5. Expanding dual-focusing ability (can concentrate on a task while maintaining awareness of goings-on in the immediate environment).	1. Becoming a participating and responsible member of the family (affection-giving and -receiving; appropriate household tasks; sharing with others). 2. Beginning to master impulses and conform to expectations of others (behaving in ways appropriate to a given situation; cooperating; learning obedience to authority). 3. Developing healthy emotional expressions for a variety of experiences (handling frustration and anger, learning patience). 4. Learning to communicate effectively with an increasing number of others (expanding vocabulary; talking about feelings, experiences, and impressions; getting over shyness, self-consciousness and awkwardness in relating to others comfortably). 5. Developing the ability to handle potentially dangerous situations (dangers in fire, traffic, high places, poisons, electricity; not having undue fear in situations calling for caution, such as crossing the street). 6. Learning to be an independent, autonomous person with initiative and a conscience of his/her own (taking initiative; innovating, experimenting, and being creative; developing a conscience according to expectations of family and culture). 7. Learning appropriate identifications with adult male and adult female role models.

TABLE 13.2. *(Continued)*

	Physical/Motor	Cognitive/Intellectual	Social/Emotional
Middle Childhood (6–11)	1. Mastering the physical skills appropriate to developmental stage (games and sports, coordinating large-muscle and fine-motor skills). 2. Developing abilities needed in personal and family living (bathing and dressing self; cleaning up after activities; household tasks, such as making bed and taking out garbage).	1. Learning the basic cognitive skills required of school children (logical and rational approaches to problem solving; reading, writing, calculating; reasoning and reflective thinking). 2. Expanding ability to think in symbolic or abstract terms. 3. Expanding understanding of cause-and-effect relationships.	1. Developing a practical understanding of the use of money (acceptable means of acquiring money; buying wisely; saving; coping with having fewer resources than needed to satisfy wants). 2. Becoming an active, cooperating member of the family (participating in family discussions and decision making; maturity in giving and receiving affection and gifts; assuming household responsibilities appropriate to age). 3. Extending the ability to relate effectively to others, both peers and adults (stands up for rights; adjusts to others; leader and follower abilities; basic social conventions, such as courtesies, manners, rules and customs, are followed; maintaining close friendships). 4. Continuing the learning involved in handling feelings and impulses (coping with simple frustrations; socially acceptable ways of releasing emotions effectively; gaining skill in sharing feelings with those who can help, such as parents, teachers, close friends). 5. Coming to terms with his or her own gender roles (gender-appropriate expectations for boys and girls; understanding of the nature of sex and reproduction; adjusting to a growing body). 6. Continuing to have high self-esteem (views self as a worthy person; discovering ways of gaining status and acceptance as a person in appropriate ways; growing in self-confidence and self control).

(continued)

TABLE 13.2. *(Continued)*

	Physical/Motor	*Cognitive/Intellectual*	*Social/Emotional*
Middle Childhood (6–11)			7. Developing a conscience with inner moral controls (learning and distinguishing right from wrong; accepting the necessity for rules in governing social relationships; behaving in line with morals and conscience when authority figures are absent).
Adolescence (12–20)	1. Accepting one's physique and using the body effectively (coping with changes brought about in puberty; recognizing variations between self and others as normal; understanding pubertal changes; caring for health of body; developing physical skills and overcoming awkwardness of movements brought on by puberty).	1. Confirming concepts and learning problem-solving skills (expanded ability to employ abstract mental operations; applies academic learning to everyday experiences). 2. Furthering academic skills, especially reading and writing.	1. Forming new and more mature relationships with age-mates of both sexes (getting dates and becoming comfortable with male and female friends; acquiring skills in problem solving, decision making, and conflict resolution with one's peers). 2. Achieving a masculine or feminine social role (realistic anticipation of becoming a man or woman; retaining flexibility in avoiding gender-role stereotyping). 3. Achieving emotional independence from parents and other adults (becoming autonomous and self-directed; solving own problems and making decisions; showing mature affection for parents; behaving less on impulse and more on planning and reflective thinking; accepting parental guidance while moving from childhood dependence to adulthood independence). 4. Preparing for marriage and family life (distinguishing infatuation from mature love; acquiring realistic expectations and knowledge of mate selection, marriage, homemaking, and child-rearing; planning the timing of engagement, marriage, and completion of education).

TABLE 13.2. *(Continued)*

Physical/Motor	Cognitive/Intellectual	Social/Emotional
Adolescence (12–20)		5. Selecting and preparing for an occupation and economic independence (knowing realistic possibilities for fields of work; knowing one's own interests, abilities, and opportunities; seeking helpful work experiences).
		6. Acquiring a set of ethics as a guide to behavior (implementing socially acceptable standards and ideals; developing a workable philosophy of life; resolve ambiguities in value systems observed in parents, friends, and society at large).
		7. Developing social literacy (nurturing; interpersonal skills of communication, conflict resolution, decision making and problem solving; developing civil and social responsibilities by involvement in worthwhile causes and projects; developing current knowledge of community, state, and world events).

SOURCES: Duvall (1977); Havighurst (1972); Thornburg (1982); McArthur (1962); White (1975); Tryon and Lilienthal (1950).

nation and in such skills as hopping and skipping. Again, tremendous variation exists within a normal range of growth.

The major influences on growth patterns continue to be genetically based maturational timetables, along with nutrition, disease, and socioeconomic status. Lower-social-class children are somewhat more likely than others to be undernourished, suffer from a number of different illnesses, and receive inadequate medical care (Hall, 1975). As a result of these environmental stress conditions, lower-class children exhibit lower than average height and weight norms. Good nutritional habits continue to remain a key to healthy brain and central nervous system development, as well as to normal height and weight advances.

Intellectual Development. According to Piaget's stages of cognitive development, children leave the *sensorimotor stage* of infancy (see chapter 12) and enter the *preoperational* stage during the 3- to 7-year-old period. The preoperational stage has several notable characteristics:

1. *Egocentrism* Children at this stage continue to view the world from their own perspective and have difficulty "putting themselves in another's shoes."

> He tends to think that other people see things the way he sees them and that they experience his own behavior, thoughts, and feelings about things. He even ascribes thoughts, feelings, and life itself to some inanimate objects. (Hall, 1975:211)

The preoperational child may believe that he or she is the center of the universe and that objects in the environment—including the sun, moon, mountains, and oceans—exist because he or she exists.

2. *Irreversibility* Preoperational children have difficulty reversing a cause-and-effect chain of events. For example, a preoperational child who has observed an ice cube melting into water on a warm surface will have difficulty conceptualizing the reverse process—that the water could be turned back into an ice cube by being stored in a cold environment. Another example is that of a child who is presented with a beaker of juice, which is short and wide. The child observes that the liquid is poured from the beaker into a tall narrow glass, and believes that now there is more juice. Such children have difficulty in mentally reversing the pouring process; they do not realize that the same volume of juice exists, regardless of the size and shape of the container holding it.

Other aspects of cognition and intelligence continue to develop during this stage of child development. Attention span and memory skills are improving. Language skills grow as the child's vocabulary and word pronunciation accelerate, sentence structure and grammar improve, and the ability to comprehend others increases. Children at this stage are developing the ability to engage in extended interchanges with adults.

Much of the learning which goes on during this stage is by *imitation,* or *role modeling,* of others in the child's environment, particularly parents. Much of this learning is reinforced by means of imaginative and other kinds of *play activities.* Play is an especially important aspect of a child's development at this stage, and they should be given generous opportunities to engage in play activities. Play is important for intellectual as well as social and physical development at this stage.

> Play is the work of children. Through play, children grow. They learn how to use their muscles; they coordinate what they see with what they do; and they gain mastery over their bodies. They find out what the world is like and what they are like. They acquire new skills and learn the appropriate situations for revising them. They try out different aspects of life. They cope with complex and conflicting emotions by reenacting real life. Play is so much a part of children's lives that they do not completely differentiate reality from fantasy. (Papalia and Olds, 1978:154)

Social and Emotional Development. According to Erikson's theory of psychosocial development (see Table 12.3, chapter 12), the preschool child moves through two stages: (1) *autonomy versus shame and doubt,* and (2) *initiative versus guilt.* The major tasks facing the child include becoming more independent from parents, being self-directed and self-controlled, and developing a stronger conscience than was possible at a younger age. The "psychosocial strengths" to be gained are *will power* and *purpose,* leading the child away from a paralyzing sense of shame, doubt, and guilt over taking initiative and taking charge and control of his or her life. This process depends largely on how parents and other significant others react to and nurture the child's efforts to reach out to others, trust them, and to find security in relationships with other people. If these efforts are encouraged and given supportive guidance, then successful adjustment is more likely. Conversely, if these efforts are met with rebuttals or repression, then social and emotional adjustment is likely to be difficult.

An important aspect of this stage is developing an

The preschool child strives to reach out to others, searching for trust and security in relationships with parents, siblings, and other people. *(Photo by Paula Deering.)*

identity as a boy or a girl. Children are solidifying their gender-role characteristics of masculinity and femininity, a process known as *sex typing.* What it means to be a boy or a girl is beginning to crystallize in the child's mind, and behavioral patterns associated with traditionally mascu-line- or feminine-role stereotypes begin to emerge (Kohl-berg, 1966). In addition to hormonal influences shaped by biological differences between males and females, the major sources of sex typing are parents. The child identifies with and imitates patterns of gender-role behavior ob-served in parents. Sex typing normally occurs by the child identifying with the same-sex parent during this stage. In addition, little boys and girls tend to be treated differently by parents. Achievement, aggressiveness, self-reliance, and rough and tumble games and toys are more often emphasized for boys; and obedience, nurturance, attrac-tiveness, passivity, and "being nice" for girls (Hall, 1975). Through toys and games they play, boys are also taught to aspire to occupational success, and girls, by being given dolls, playhouses, and baby carriages, are being primed for assuming domestic roles as "wife" and "mother."

Traditional gender-role stereotypes (see chapter 4) will develop to the degree that parents and other socializa-tion agents in the child's environment behave in tradi-tional ways—males dominant, assertive, aggressive, powerful, and work- or job-oriented; females submissive, shy, passive, weak, and home- or family-oriented. Chil-dren whose parents behave in less traditional ways are less likely to internalize traditional masculine and feminine gender-role expectations and behaviors, such as is the case where fathers are affectionate, nurturant, or expressive, and where mothers are career-oriented, assertive, or domi-nant in relationships with others (Balswick and Avertt, 1977).

Finally, the preschool stage is one that begins with a period known as *negativism.* Because of the striving for independence that begins during the third year of life, children typically go through a several-month period of frequent disagreement with parents. Often referred to as the "terrible two's" and "trying three's," parents' requests and directives are usually met with a resounding *"No!"* This negativism may be accompanied by temper tantrums and contests of will between the parent—who may be striving to maintain "peace and order" in the home—and the child, who is seeking to do things in his or her own way. Although this is a perfectly normal aspect of socioemo-tional development during this stage, the "friction and flying sparks" can be an especially difficult and trying period for parents (White, 1975).

THE MIDDLE CHILDHOOD YEARS: AGES 6–11

Development during these years is primarily an ex-tension of the trends initiated during the preschool years. Starting school marks the entry into this stage. The child leaves this stage during the period of pubescence, generally considered to be the beginning of adolescence.

Physical Development. The child's rate of physical growth continues to stabilize during this stage. Gains in height average about two inches per year. Boys' and girls' growth levels remain about the same. Nutrition, disease, and socioeconomic conditions continue to com-bine with hereditary timetables to direct the rate of growth. This stage normally brings on a lengthening and trimming of the body as the child's activity levels help to diminish the stores of "baby fat" acquired in earlier years.

The child's motor skills advance at a remarkable rate during the middle years of development. All aspects of physical activity improve, such as running, jumping, and throwing. Physical coordination also improves in terms of balance and eye-hand coordination. There is, for many children in this stage, a strong interest and involvement in organized sports and athletics, such as football, baseball, soccer, tennis, and basketball. Boys' and girls' abilities are approximately equal, meaning that there is probably little justification for separating them in games or in athletic competition. Any differences favoring males are most likely a result of gender-role learning in our culture.

Intellectual Development. According to Piaget's theory of cognitive development, children in the middle years are moving from the preoperational stage of the preschooler to the stage of *concrete operations.* This stage is marked by an increased ability to use abstract concepts. This ability helps the child to develop higher-level skills in reading, sentence structure, grammar, mem-orization, and mathematical computation. The child learns the concrete operations of mental *reversibility,* which we discussed before; they now know that liquid, poured from one container to one of a different size and shape, remains equal in volume. Children at this stage are becoming less *egocentric* and more able to *empathize* with others by mentally "putting themselves in the other's shoes." They have a better grasp of cause-and-effect relationships, and can solve problems more adeptly than before by applying abstract mental operations. Again, the rate at which children develop these cognitive abilities varies considerably within a normal range.

Social and Emotional Development.

According to Erikson's theory of psychosocial development, the child during the middle years goes through the stage of *industry versus inferiority,* and the major "psychosocial strength" gained is *competence.* If children are to negotiate this stage successfully, they must develop a sense of *contribution* and *participation* in the events around them. Children in this stage will view themselves as competent to the extent that they can freely exercise "dexterity and intelligence in the completion of serious tasks," and participate cooperatively in "some segment of the culture" (Erikson, 1980:25). This is a time of preparing the child for adulthood roles, laying the groundwork for a person who eventually will be a productive member of the adult society. Much of this preparation takes place in school, as well as in the family. The child's self-esteem — his or her view of the self as a valuable and worthy person — is shaped to a large degree according to how well this task of childhood is mastered.

There are two major facets to the child's social and emotional development at this stage, each of which contributes in some manner to productive involvement in the environment. First is the emerging importance of the *peer group.* Peer groups become important as the child enters school and forms friendships, and spends significant amounts of time with children of the same age and, usually at this time, the same sex. Peer groups provide several functions for the child in this stage (Thornburg, 1982):

1. They provide an important source of *identification* for the child, which assists in the *process of emancipation* from parents and family.

2. Peer groups spur healthy *competition,* which facilitates *social maturation* and prepares the child for adult life in a "society where so many attainments are necessary to success" (332).

3. Peer groups provide for the child's need *to conform,* to belong, and to subscribe to a value system, thereby

fulfilling his or her needs for acceptance, and avoiding rejection and loneliness. Popularity in the peer group is important for the development of self-esteem because of the status it provides for the child.

A second important aspect of social and emotional development at this stage is that of *moral development.* Children at this stage are developing a sense of "right" and "wrong," and a sense of "good behavior" and "bad behavior" (Kohlberg, 1963). They are discovering a number of *values* held by parents, friends, teachers, or television characters — and are trying to sort them out and behave according to the ones they think are best. It is in this stage that the roots of the child's conscience begin to grow deeper. Children learn to respond to internal controls rather than only the external controls of rewards and threats of punishment. Self-control comes about as the child develops a *sense of guilt* about misdeeds. They regulate their behavior in order to avoid the unpleasant feelings of guilt.

ADOLESCENCE: AGES 12–20

Entry into adolescence is usually marked when the child enters *pubescence,* the period of physical, emotional, and social changes that bridge the worlds of childhood and adulthood. Adolescence is often cited as a time of inevitable "storm and stress," and parent-child conflict. However, this does not have to be the case. Anthropologists Margaret Mead (1928; 1935; 1939) and Ruth Benedict (1938; 1950), for example, studied adolescents and family life in Samoa, the Arapesh of New Guinea, and a number of other cultures. They found no periods of storm and stress as have been reported in our culture. Rites-of-passage to adulthood occurred at puberty in these other cultures. Full adult rights and responsibilities had been *gradually* granted to the individual over the course of the childhood years. In essence, there was no transition period of years, or even months, between childhood and adulthood, and each person in the society knew exactly where they stood relative to the worlds of childhood and adulthood.

Adolescence, then, appears to be a cultural phenomenon unique to children in Western society. It introduces *discontinuity* in the development of the young person. Many problems associated with adolescence in our society

Peer groups and close friendships are important features of the preadolescent's life and continue to grow in importance during adolescence. *(Photo by Stephen R. Jorgensen.)*

can be traced to the fact that adults often expect adolescents to begin to act like adults in socially responsible ways—being independent thinkers, responsible for their own actions, self-controlled, and well-mannered—but at the same time denying them legitimate access to many of the rights and privileges which adults enjoy—such as alcohol consumption, sexual intercourse, gainful employment, and voting rights. So, for the adolescent, who seems to have one foot in childhood and the other foot in adulthood, and who often does not know which way to turn or which "role to play" in a given situation, this "holding pattern" can create a good deal of stress.

Physical Development. The most significant physical changes associated with adolescence are the growth spurt in both height and weight, as well as the changes in body proportions and development of primary and secondary sex characteristics (see Table 13.3). The adolescent also attains full sexual and reproductive matu-

rity, marked by the production of sperm by the male and release of ova by the female.

Pubescence actually begins with the body's release of two hormones, a process directed by the pituitary gland. The process begins earlier for girls (ages 10–11) than for boys (ages 11–13), so that girls are ahead of boys in reaching puberty by an average of one to two years. The *growth hormone* causes changes in body proportion and dimensions. For girls, it increases height, lengthens limbs, expands the pelvis region, and adds a fatty layer of tissue under the skin. For boys, this hormone increases height, lengthens limbs, widens shoulders, and adds tremendously to their muscular strength and heart and lung capacity. It is at this point that the physical strength and endurance of the average boy rises noticeably above that of the typical girl (Tanner, 1970). The average growth in height accelerates to 3 to 4 inches per year, at its peak, for boys and girls during pubescence (Hall, 1975).

The motor skills of adolescents are developing, along

TABLE 13.3. *Sequence of Development of Primary and Secondary Sexual Characteristics*

Boys	Age Span		Girls
Beginning growth of testes, scrotum, pubic hair	11.5–13	10–11	Height spurt begins
Some pigmentation, nodulation of breasts (later disappears)			Slight growth of pubic hair
Height spurt begins			Breasts, nipples elevated to form "bud" stage
Beginning growth of penis			
Development of straight, pigmented pubic hair	13–16	11–14	Straight, pigmented pubic hair
Early voice changes			Some deepening of voice
Rapid growth of penis, testes, scrotum, prostate, seminal vesicles			Rapid growth of vagina, ovaries, labia, uterus
First ejaculation of semen			
Kinky pubic hair			Kinky pubic hair
Age of maximum growth			Age of maximum growth
Beginning growth of axillary hair			Further enlargement, pigmentation, elevation of nipple, areola to form "primary breast"
			Menarche
Rapid growth of axillary hair	16–18	14–16	Growth of axillary hair
Marked voice change			Filling out of breasts to form adult conformation, secondary breast stage
Growth of beard			
Indentation of frontal hair line			

SOURCE: Rice (1981:93).

with their growth and strength spurt in this stage. However, many adolescents begin the physical growth spurt — with its lengthening of trunk and limbs — before their motor skills have had an opportunity to catch up. This may result in some degree of awkwardness or clumsiness which, although embarrassing at times, is only a temporary condition and not of major concern.

Intellectual Development. According to Piaget's theory of cognitive development, adolescents are moving from the stage of *concrete operations* to a new stage of *formal operational thought*. At about ages 11 and 12, adolescents begin to develop higher-order problem-solving abilities. They are able to think abstractly by manipulating concepts. A major function of junior high and high school programs is to assist in this process by challenging the adolescent's growing intellectual capabilities in academic areas. Adolescents are able to master increasingly sophisticated learning tasks in language, mathematics, and science as a result of these emerging cognitive abilities.

Social and Emotional Development.

According to Erikson's (1980) theory of psychosocial development (see Table 12.3), the major task facing the person at this stage is *identity* versus *identity confusion.* Identity formation involves answering the question, "Who am I?" The self-concept also entails the notion of self-esteem — "What am I worth?" "Of what value am I to others?" It is crucial that adolescents work toward developing an *integrated* identity, a view of the self that is coherent, consistent, and noncontradictory. The difficulty of this task lies in the fact that adolescents encounter a number of different, and at times conflicting, values, "teachings, creeds, and ideologies" from parents, peers, teachers, movies, and television. In addition, adolescents are striving to understand and cope with the physical and emotional changes going on within themselves, such as coming to grips with their emerging sexuality. The pressure on adolescents is typically toward *role diffusion* — the confusion and frustration resulting from all of the alternatives in deciding "who I am" and "what person I will be."

A major influence on adolescent identity formation and self-concept is the *changing balance of affiliation with peers and parents.* The peer group assumes an expanding role in the typical adolescent's life. Peer affiliation assists in the process of *emancipation* from the adolescent's parents and family. This process of seeking independence is critical as the adolescent moves toward being "launched" from the family into a job or college after high school. Peer groups continue to be an important source of *competition;* they help the child to prepare for the competitive world of adulthood in our culture. Peer groups satisfy the adolescent's *need for conformity* to a specific set of values or behavior, by which he or she will attain status and acceptance in the group. Acceptance in one's peer group is critical to the process of developing social maturity. Acceptance by peers is gauged by one's popularity in the group, which is often achieved by conforming to group values and behavior patterns. At the same time, peer groups provide the opportunity to "try on new roles and use the reactions of others to judge how well the roles fit his self-concept" (Hall, 1975:371). Peer groups also provide an avenue to *achievement,* so long as the adolescent behaves in a way that measures up to standards set by peers or the school. Being an excellent athlete or student is rewarded with popularity in the peer group, and this reward "enhances their feelings of competence and self-determination" (Thornburg, 1982:133).

However, the idea that a "generation gap" exists between parents and their adolescent children appears to be a myth (Bengtson, 1970; Thornburg, 1982). At least when gauged by the influence of parents or peers on the adolescent's values, beliefs, and occupational and educational aspirations, most studies agree that parents have the major impact throughout adolescence, and that parents and their adolescent children agree much more than they disagree over these matters (Thurner, Spence, and Lowenthal, 1974; Yankelovich, 1974; Kandel and Lesser, 1972; Munns, 1972). Nonetheless, it is common knowledge that some adolescents and their parents become involved in frequent and severe misunderstandings and conflicts, and become alienated from one another. Parents and adolescents often say to themselves, "I just don't understand her," and "she just doesn't understand me." Parents often say that their teenagers' attitudes and behavior are unacceptable, a result of their increased involvement with groups of friends who, the parents believe, have led them astray. Adolescents say that their parents are old-fashioned, "square," "not with it," or bent on interfering with their lives.

Why do such conflicts between parents and adolescent children develop? First, an important adolescent task is striving for social independence at a time when they are still emotionally and financially dependent upon parents. Parents, on the other hand, may not be psychologically or emotionally prepared to begin letting go, and therefore attempt to regulate and confine the adolescent's activities. ("Be home by midnight." "You can't date that person." "You cannot go to that party.") Parents may also believe, mistakingly so, that the adolescent's search for independence is a sign that the parents are no longer loved, wanted, or needed. This can create parental concern, and may result in more restrictions placed on the adolescent than may be appropriate or perceived as fair. Second, although parents and adolescents usually agree on major life goals and educational and career outlooks, they are much more likely to disagree and conflict over relatively trivial matters which relate to the adolescent's behavior — hair length; clothing style; music and art preferences; whether to be home by 10:30 or 11:00 P.M. Although these matters are less significant than education or career values, for example, the fact that these behavioral issues are *perceived* as significant often creates serious parent-adolescent conflict.

The second major influence on adolescent identity

and self-concept is the *changing nature of sexuality and heterosexual relationships brought on by pubescence.* The adolescent's sexual awareness, sexual drive, and ability to engage in sexual acts such as intercourse all begin to evolve with puberty and form the adolescent's *sexual self-concept* (Jorgensen, 1983a). Heterosexual attractions mean a heightened interest in and concern over physical appearance. Physical attractiveness is an important gauge of popularity with the opposite sex, and is a means of achieving status in the peer group. Positive self-images are more likely to result if adolescents view their looks as being consistent with our cultural ideals of beauty, as presented in the mass media, or by fashion models, movie stars, and athletes. Negative adolescent self-concepts are more likely to occur among those who are skinny, underdeveloped, fat and flabby, or plagued by acne. Whether or not looks contribute to a favorable self-image also depends upon how one's level of physical attractiveness compares with that of others in the peer group.

We have previously discussed the increasing rates of adolescent sexual activity and pregnancy, in addition to many of the undesirable consequences of these events in the adolescent's life (see chapter 9). However, many adolescents who progress to the point of intimate sexual activity, petting, or intercourse have not yet attained a satisfactory level of emotional development or social responsibility. A key indication of this is the poor and inconsistent contraceptive behavior of sexually active adolescents. Although they are physically capable of engaging in sexual behavior, and often do so as a result of peer-group behavior or pressure from their friends, many adolescents are not yet emotionally or socially mature enough to handle sexual responsibilities.

Another aspect of social and emotional develop-

Adolescence is at once a fascinating, exciting, and stressful experience caused by the many changes encountered in this transition from the world of childhood to that of adulthood.   *(Photo by Carl Hill.)*

ment, which influences adolescent identity and self-concept, is the *increasing risk of "problem behaviors,"* as defined by society. These include drug and alcohol abuse, running away, juvenile delinquency, and suicide. Adolescent life in our contemporary society is permeated with stress, as indicated by much of the foregoing discussion. Much of this stress is associated with the demands and challenges of a complex and ever-changing world which virtually bombards the young person with a variety of different value systems, political beliefs, and behavior patterns. Peer groups, parents, and mass media influences exert a complicated and often confusing array of "pushes" and "pulls." However, the emotional development of many adolescents does not evolve at a pace fast enough to keep up with the mounting level of stress in their lives. Adolescents may have great difficulty in coping with the anxiety, anger, hostility, guilt, shyness, or jealousy experienced at a new peak of intensity in their lives. This stress is often too much for their emotions to handle, and the resulting behavior can have tragic consequences. The most serious of these consequences may be that of damaging their health or physical well-being; but they may also fan the fire of parent-adolescent conflict over behavior which is viewed by parents as rebellious. Although a certain amount of rebelliousness is probably normal for any adolescent (Frankel and Dullaert, 1977), the problem can get out of hand for those whose temperament and internal controls are insufficiently developed to keep them from becoming deeply involved in such extreme types of behavior as "acting out" at school, lying, stealing, vandalism, alcohol and drug abuse, or running away. Many of these behaviors are peer-induced, peer-sanctioned, and peer-reinforced, meaning that they may represent to the adolescent "no more than a normal range of functioning" (Thornburg, 1982:326).

Despite the problems of adolescence, many parents and their adolescents actually enjoy each other's company, and enjoy a number of companionship and recreational activities together. Parents often take great pride in watching their children make this transition to adulthood, which is shown by the tremendous progress they make in the physical, intellectual, and socioemotional domains. Adolescents have a number of desirable personality traits which are characteristic in this stage of development (Otto and Haley, 1966). Adolescents are idealistic and concerned for the future; they have a great deal of energy and a zest for life; they are courageous and willing to take risks;

they are independent, yet can usually be relied upon to handle responsibilities well; they are open and honest, loyal to their family and friends, and generally have a positive attitude toward life; they have an active sense of humor, while developing an ability to be sensitive to the feelings of others; and many adolescents are serious and deep thinkers.

Parenthood During the Middle Years

The basic principles governing the effective parenting of infants can be extended to parenting older children —showing concern, affection, love, and guidance. The ultimate goal of effective parenthood is to assist children to reach their potential in all aspects of development—physical, intellectual, and socioemotional—appropriate to the child's age.

PARENTING THE PRESCHOOL CHILD

As White (1975) and many other experts have pointed out, preschool children need a generous amount of attention, nurturant care, and affection. They need to be held, cuddled, and hugged. It is important that both parents continue to lavish these rewards on the child, without fearing to spoil him or her. This kind of parenting behavior will help to foster a healthy and positive self-concept in the child, as well as a sense of security and belonging in the family.

A major developmental task of parents of preschoolers concerns setting realistic expectations for the child, recognizing the child's capabilities and not trying to push beyond reasonable limits (Duvall, 1977). It entails accepting the child's unique, individual qualities. Effective parenting also means parenting the "whole child." For example, there should not be an overemphasis on intellectual development to the exclusion of social skill or motor development. Some parents want their children to read and write early, to be able to add and subtract by the time they are three; they buy them expensive educational toys but fail to provide the necessary opportunities for play and large-motor activities. Children should not be pushed in any one area, if it means that other areas will be neglected.

Preschool children are known for their constant testing of parents to see how far they can go. As the child moves rapidly from a state of total dependence during infancy to increasing independence and self-direction, parents of preschoolers are presented with progressive changes in the child's capabilities, energy levels, moods, and motives. It is a period marked by extreme *unpredictability;* many parents find that their child can be a loving, cuddly, and cute person one day, and irritable, cranky, and defiant the next. Many children reach a peak of energy, and thus activity, at this stage, and this combines with their natural curiosity to lead them into mischief. Effective parenting at this stage, then, involves being firm with the child, setting and enforcing reasonable limits and expectations, while being loving and affectionate. Discipline is important, provided that misbehavior of the child is met with consistent punishment that is fair, just, and meted out at the time that the misbehavior takes place. For example, spanking a four-year-old child for accidentally spilling a glass of milk would be unfair, whereas a mild spanking for repeatedly running into the street without first looking for oncoming cars may be necessary to stop that sort of dangerous behavior. It is also important that parents explain to the preschool child the reasons why certain types of behavior are not acceptable. Verbal reasoning with the child not only increases the child's knowledge of the undesirable consequences of their behavior, but it also promotes self-respect and builds a sense of being treated fairly in the family.

PARENTING THE SCHOOL-AGE CHILD

Effective parenting of the school-age child is, in most respects, simply an extension of parenting skills exercised during the preschool years. Respecting the child as a person; showing love and affection freely; setting realistic expectations and limits and enforcing them; disciplining fairly, consistently, and with adequate explanation; and communicating openly and honestly all continue to be important aspects of effective parenting at this stage.

The most significant change in the child's life at this time is school entry. This event signals several changes in the child's life—increased importance of peer groups; pressures to achieve and do well in a competitive setting;

and relating to new adult role models (teachers), and trying to adjust to them (Klein and Ross, 1958).

There are a number of things parents can do to prepare their child for school entry and to promote the child's achievement throughout the school years. A number of research studies have concluded that patterns of communication and affection between parents and their children influence school preparedness and achievement (Milner, 1951; Hess and Shipman, 1965; Toby, 1956). Children fare better in school when their families have the following characteristics:

1. A rich verbal environment, in which parents and children talk to one another frequently, where communication has a positive tone, and where parents value reading (read books to children, and encourage their children to read);

2. A warm environment, in which affection is exchanged in a consistent and physically overt manner (hugs, kisses, cuddling);

3. A consistent environment, in which daily routines are established, where children participate in appropriate household tasks and responsibilities (e.g., make their own beds, take out the garbage, and keep their bedrooms clean and tidy), and where reasonable and fair kinds of discipline are employed.

Parents begin to experience noticeable *parental role sequences* in this stage because they must change their expectations relating to the child's physical, intellectual, and socioemotional capabilities. Parents with children in the 6- to 11-year range find that the child is seeking to communicate more as an equal. For many parents, this is the "calm before the storm" of adolescence. In order to prevent some of the conflicts, storm, and stress that adolescents can produce in a family, it would be wise for parents to try during this stage to prevent conflicts that might show up in adolescence. Following are eight developmental tasks for effective parenthood at this stage which, if accomplished, should help children better accomplish their own developmental tasks (see Table 13.2) [Thornburg, 1979; Duvall, 1977; Brooks, 1981; Baumrind, 1966].

Task 1: Encourage children to make new friends. Begin to loosen up controls on the child in order to make the emancipation process during adolescence less traumatic and difficult for child *and* parent.

Task 2: Help children develop moral concepts and values by providing the opportunities for them to (1) make free choices and decisions when possible; (2) search for alternatives when making choices and decisions; (3) weigh the consequences (positive and nega-tive) of each alternative; (4) be considerate of that which they prize and cherish; (5) confirm the things they value; and (6) act upon (do something about) the choices they make.

Task 3: Recognize and accept the range of emotions children in this stage are attempting to cope with. Love and affection, joy and happiness, fear, guilt, and anger

Effective parenting means helping children to accomplish developmental tasks in the physical/motor, cognitive/intellectual, and social/emotional realms.

are all intense emotional states of children which need to develop in a healthy way. This task can be accomplished by what Baumrind (1966) calls *authoritative parenting*. Whereas *authoritarian* parents maintain strict control over their child's behavior and deprive them of the freedom to act on their own, and *permissive* parents provide no direction and set no limits or behavioral standards for the child, *authoritative* parents combine elements of both approaches by setting firm, consistent, and fair limits and standards for the child, while allowing the child freedom and autonomy to behave within those limits.

Task 4:   Promote the healthy growth of children, who are going through a significant "growth spurt" at this time, by providing adequate nutrition; watching for illnesses or physical conditions (speech and hearing disorders, eye conditions); attempting to prevent accidents; and reducing unnecessary stress and frustration in the child's life.

Task 5:   Attempt to teach boys and girls the positive aspects of both the traditionally masculine and feminine gender roles (see chapter 4), in order to prevent them from being locked into rigid, inflexible, and potentially dissatisfying gender-role stereotypes.

Task 6:   If both parents are present in the home, they should work together as a team to provide the necessary support, guidance, and education for the child. Single parents have an especially challenging task because they often must go it alone. And spouses who rely on their partner to handle most or all of the parental responsibilities at this time are placing a heavy load on the partner's shoulders.

Task 7:   Support the child's school achievement, motivation, and activities by providing interesting learning activities in the home and limiting the amount and kinds of television which is viewed. The average child spends 8,000 hours in school and 12,000 hours in front of a television set by the time he or she graduates from high school.

Task 8:·   Try to provide the most accurate information for the child regarding the ethical problems and adverse consequences associated with alcohol and drug use, delinquent or criminal behavior, and sexual behavior. If parents lack this information, they should seek ways to

either obtain it or provide the opportunities for the child to obtain it on his or her own (books, films, classes, and so on). *Here, timing is critically important*. We discussed the problems of drug and alcohol abuse, delinquency, and sex in the foregoing section on adolescence, which is when these problems most commonly appear; they might best be *prevented* if children are educated about them *before* adolescence, in the middle-childhood years.

PARENTING THE ADOLESCENT

Effective parenting of the adolescent means promoting the adolescent's growth and development in socially desirable directions (Ford, 1982). The goal is to facilitate *social competence* in the adolescent, who can then become integrated in meaningful relationships with family and friends alike, and who can avoid becoming involved in the negative types of behavior described earlier in this chapter —delinquency, early sexual activity, alcohol abuse, and drug abuse. At the same time, it is important to nurture the adolescent's *self-concept*, fostering a sense of self-worth and a feeling of value and importance.

Each of the parenting behaviors identified in the foregoing section as being effective for preadolescents are also important in the adolescent years, although in somewhat modified forms. Parenting in this stage usually requires that parents undergo significant changes in their role expectations and role behaviors in relation to their adolescent children.

The developmental tasks of adolescents (see Table 13.2) indicate that the adolescent is growing and changing in all realms: physically, socially, and emotionally. As a result, several major issues confront adolescents and their parents: increasing separation from parents; identification with peers; establishing affectionate relationships with the opposite sex (including dating and sexual behavior); thinking about choosing a vocation; and deciding whether or not to go to college (Brooks, 1981). Duvall (1977:302) identifies five "family dilemmas" confronting parents of adolescents:

1. Maintaining firm control over the adolescent's behavior *versus* allowing freedom to behave as he or she wishes.

2. Vesting major responsibilities in parents *versus* sharing responsibilities with the adolescent.

3. Emphasizing social activities and achieving popularity *versus* academic success in school.

4. Allowing open communication, with freedom for the adolescent to openly criticize, *versus* demanding respect for peace and quiet.

5. Establishing commitments and stability in life *versus* taking an uncommitted stance toward life, or shifting from one commitment to another.

The failure to successfully resolve these dilemmas in a way that is mutually satisfying to both the parent and the adolescent is the root of many serious parent-adolescent conflicts and negative adolescent behaviors.

As with prior stages of parenting, however, there are no simple answers to the question of how to resolve these dilemmas. Adolescents are complex human beings who are in a stage of trying to be adults, trying on new behaviors "for size," and who happen to behave in unpredictable and sometimes bizarre ways. If there is ever a time for flexibility and understanding in the relationship between a parent and child, adolescence is a prime time for this.

A major aspect of the parent-adolescent relationship is *power* (Baumrind, 1968; Becker, 1964; Schaefer, 1959). The best solution appears to be a loosening of power and control, but not total abdication of control, by the parent over the adolescent. Research in this area has found seven basic types of power relationships between parents and their adolescent children (Elder, 1962):

1. *Autocratic* No allowance is provided for adolescents to express their views, nor for them to assert leadership or initiative in self-government.

2. *Authoritarian* Although adolescents contribute to the solution of problems, their parents always decide issues according to their own judgment.

3. *Democratic* Adolescents contribute freely to discussion of issues relevant to their behavior, and may even make their own decisions; however, in all instances, the final decision is either formulated by parents or meets their approval.

4. *Equalitarian* This type of structure represents minimal role differentiation. Parents and adolescents are involved to a similar degree in making decisions pertaining to the adolescents' behavior.

5. *Permissive* Adolescents assume a more active and influential position in formulating decisions that concern them than do parents.

6. *Laissez Faire* The position of adolescents in relation to that of parents in decision making is more differentiated in terms of power and authority. In this type of relationship, adolescents have the option of either subscribing to or disregarding parental wishes when making their decisions.

7. *Ignoring* This type of structure, if it can legitimately be considered such, represents no involvement of parents in directing adolescents' behavior.

Adolescents are most likely to perceive their parents as fair in their discipline, and are least likely to feel rejected, unloved, or unwanted by their parents, in the *Equalitarian, Democratic,* and *Permissive* types of relationships. These are the types of parenting behaviors that Baumrind (1968) found most effective for preadolescents, which she termed *authoritative parenting.* These kinds of parents grant the adolescent increased autonomy and freedom to make decisions and assume responsibility for themselves, but at the same time establish firm limits which are reasonable and fair (curfews, and prohibiting behavior that could harm them, such as drug or alcohol use) [Brooks, 1981]. These are the kinds of parents to whom the adolescent is likely to turn for guidance, advice, and support, and with whom the adolescent is most likely to identify (McDonald, 1980). The other four types of parent-adolescent relationships—the *Autocratic, Authoritarian, Laissez Faire,* and *Ignoring*—yield the most negative and hostile feelings among adolescents, depriving the adolescent of "involvement in self-direction and assumption of responsibility" (in the case of the *Autocratic* and *Authoritarian* modes), or weakening the bond of affection, and depriving the adolescent of the necessary guidance in moving from childhood to adulthood (in the case of the *Laissez Faire* and *Ignoring* modes) [Elder, 1962:262]. In brief, there is danger in either too much or too little control of parents over the adolescent.

In addition to loosening the reins of control over adolescents by allowing them a greater role in decisions which affect them, research has shown the need for parents to communicate with the adolescent more as peers, or friends — a step toward treating adolescents as adults who are responsible for their own behavior, rather than little girls or little boys. Adolescents want, and need, more of an equal share in decisions which affect them. Physical discipline becomes less appropriate as the adolescent responds more to reason and logic, as their values, morals, and behavior patterns are being shaped in preparation for the transition into adulthood. Adolescents also need to be reminded that parents still love them and care for them, and that they will be there to support them in times of need. Adolescent self-esteem is particularly vulnerable, and parents must strive to confirm the adolescent's intrinsic value as a person — that they are important, have much to contribute, and are appreciated. Verbal exchanges of love and affection may take precedence over physical signs (such as kisses or hugs), and parents must be ready to change behavior which was once acceptable to their little boy or girl to behavior that is viewed as appropriate for the adolescent in transition to becoming an adult.

Finally, it is important that parents *model* the behavior and values that they want their children to internalize. Adolescents are like sponges around adults. They watch and absorb what they see. For example, if parents want their adolescents to develop good manners, a cooperative and sharing attitude, and respect for the rights and property of other people, then parents must demonstrate these qualities in their own behavior toward others. Parents who smoke cigarettes and consume alcohol should not be surprised when their adolescent children take an interest in experimenting with these. What is needed is open communication, accurate information, ample use of reasoning, and modeling of appropriate behavior in order to shape the child's behavior in desirable directions.

Child Abuse and Neglect

Throughout the history of the world, children have generally been viewed as second-class citizens, and have undergone severe abuse and maltreatment as a result (Solomon, 1973). Many cultures have allowed the practice of *infanticide* — the killing of young infants who happened to be the wrong sex or who were born imperfect. As recently as the eighteenth and nineteenth centuries in Europe, children were publicly beaten or otherwise punished

for misdeeds. Parents were allowed to use whatever means they wished, no matter how cruel or inhumane, to punish their children for alleged misbehavior. Parents were granted these rights because children were defined as the property of their parents. Children were forced to work in factories during the early days of the industrial revolution, for as long as 16 hours a day. There they experienced beatings, serious illness, and unsanitary conditions, and often were shackled in chains to prevent them from running away (Helfer and Kempe, 1968). The practice of child labor was also evident in the United States in the early 1900s (Osborn and Osborn, 1978).

Later, in the twentieth century, however, the rights of children have been increasingly defined to include freedom from physical or emotional harm at the hands of parents. Laws of society today protect the welfare of children by making it a crime for parents to brutalize, neglect, or otherwise inflict physical harm on their children. Parents are legally obligated to provide for the physical safety of the child and to attend to the child's psychological and emotional needs. However, one of the most difficult aspects of this effort to protect children has been in the definition of what constitutes *child abuse;* that is, where does a parent's right to inflict physical punishment on a child *end* and the child's right to be protected *begin?* The majority of parents use some sort of physical punishment in disciplining their children, usually in the form of spanking, shoving, slapping, or grabbing the child. How much of this kind of punishment is too much? How hard should a parent be allowed to spank a child? How frequently? What about *verbal* violence toward a child, in the form of yelling, screaming, or shouting? Can this reach a point where it is defined as abusive? Just what is neglect of a child? There are no simple answers to these questions, and the definition of what is and what is not child abuse or neglect may vary from one state and legal jurisdiction to the next.

INCIDENCE AND TYPES OF CHILD ABUSE

Despite the problems of definition, it is generally agreed that abuse includes *physical assaults* on children that cause bodily injury or harm. Most common among these are hitting the child with an object, such as a coat hanger, belt, or even the hand. Brain injuries, injuries to the internal organs, and broken bones are the most common injuries that result. Some parents throw their children with great force against a wall or onto the floor, with the same results. Others burn their children in scalding hot water, or with a lit cigarette between toes, fingers, or in the mouth, in order to "get them to behave" or "stop crying." Such abuse was labeled the *battered child syndrome* more than twenty years ago (Kempe, et al., 1962). These abusive parents often permanently injure, disfigure, or kill their children.

The estimates of how many children are injured or die in the United States each year from such assaults are imprecise because a large number of child-abuse cases go undetected and unreported to authorities. Nonetheless, estimates vary between 350 and 700 child deaths per year as a result of abusive behavior of parents (Gelles, 1980). As many as 200,000 to 250,000 children are in need of protective services every year because of parents' abusive behavior, and another 30,000 to 38,000 are badly injured at the hands of their parents (Solomon, 1973). A large-scale national study, conducted by Gelles and his associates (1980) in 1975, found the frequencies which are reported in Table 13.4. These findings led to the following tragic estimates (p. 42):

There were nearly 46 million children between the ages of three and seventeen years old who lived with both parents in 1975. Of these children, between 3.1 and 4.0 million have been kicked, bitten, or punched by parents at some time in their lives, while between 1.0 and 1.9 million were kicked, bitten, or punched in 1975. Between 1.4 and 2.3 million children have been "beat up" while growing up, and between 275,000 and 750,000 three- to seventeen-year-olds were "beat up" in 1975. Lastly, our data suggest that between 900,000 and 1.8 million American children between the ages of three and seventeen have ever had their parents use a gun or a knife on them. Our figures do not allow for a reliable extrapolation of how many children faced parents using guns and knives in 1975, but our estimate would be something close to 46,000 children (based on an incidence of one in 1000 children).

Mothers are slightly more likely than fathers to admit their acts of violence toward children, and boys are slightly more likely than girls to be the victims of their parent's violent acts. And younger children are the most likely to be abused. The most dangerous period in a child's life appears to be from three months to three years of age, the infancy and preschool years.

Another kind of child abuse is *sexual* abuse. This includes cases of incest, where a parent, usually the father, fondles the child's genital area or engages in sexual intercourse with the child on a repeated basis. In cases of fathers who sexually abuse the daughter, it is often the case that she has been socialized to accept his sexual advances as a

TABLE 13.4. *Types of Parent-to-Child Violence in 1146 Families in the United States, 1975*

Incident	*Types of Parent-to-Child Violence (N = 1146)*[a]				
	Occurrence in Past Year				*Occurrence Ever*
	Once	*Twice*	*More Than Twice*	*Total*	
Threw something	1.3%	1.8%	2.3%	5.4%	9.6%
Pushed/grabbed/shoved	4.3	9.0	27.2	40.5	46.4
Slapped or spanked	5.2	9.4	43.6	58.2	71.0
Kicked/bit/hit with fist	0.7	0.8	1.7	3.2	7.7
Hit with something	1.0	2.6	9.8	13.4	20.0
Beat up	0.4	0.3	0.6	1.3	4.2
Threatened with knife/gun	0.1	0.0	0.0	0.1	2.8
Used knife or gun	0.1	0.0	0.0	0.1	2.9

[a] On some items, there were a few responses omitted, but figures for all incidents represent at least 1,140 families.

SOURCE: Gelles (1980:41), reprinted from *American Journal of Orthopsychiatry*, 1978, 48 :580–592.

normal kind of behavior for a father (Kempe, 1978). This is usually not possible without the knowledge and support of the mother, who knows about the incest and either consciously or unconsciously condones it (Nakashima and Zakus, 1977). Clearly, this sort of child abuse occurs in a family system that is pathological and in need of professional assistance.

Child abuse also includes *child neglect*. As mentioned before, parents are legally responsible for the physical care and nurturance of their children. Failure to provide for the physical needs of a child for food, clothing, and shelter — even if no physical harm is inflicted by the parent — constitutes child neglect.

The child's appearance often tells a story of neglect. If the child is inadequately dressed for the weather; is wearing clothing that is torn, tattered, or unwashed; or if the child is not clean and (is) unbathed, and has body odor — all these are signs of neglect that relate to poor household conditions and no concern for the child's welfare. (Fontana, 1973)

As in cases of physical assault, child neglect is sufficient cause for authorities to remove a child from the home, at least temporarily, in order to place it in a safer environment.

CAUSES OF CHILD ABUSE

Child abuse and neglect do not have a single major cause. There exist a great number of potential causes, many of which act in concert with one another to cause a parent to inflict harm upon a young and defenseless victim. The following "causes" are most frequently identified by social and medical scientists who have studied the problem over the past twenty years (Pelton, 1978; Helfer and Kempe, 1968; Bolton, Laner, and Kane, 1980; Martin and Walters, 1982; Vesterdal, 1980; Hunter, et al., 1978; Lamb, 1978; Garbarino, 1977; Gaines, et al., 1978):

1. Personality problems in the parents, which predispose them to violence or irrationality, or to an abnormally low level of tolerance for stress and frustration.

2. Parents' lack of information or education relating to normal patterns of child growth and development, normal problems of child-rearing, and realistic expectations about child behavior.

3. Social and emotional immaturity of the parent.

4. Economic and other life stresses — such as illness, death in the family, unemployment, divorce, and conflict in the parents' marriage — which cannot be coped with adequately. Child abuse has a clear link to economic stress among the poverty-stricken:

[T]he living conditions of poverty generate stressful experiences that may become precipitating factors of child abuse, and the poor have little means by which to escape from such stress. Under these circumstances, even minor misbehaviors and annoyances presented by powerless children may trigger abuse. Such poverty-related factors as unemployment, dilapidated and overcrowded housing, and insufficient money, food, recreation, or hope can provide the stressful context for abuse. (Pelton, 1978:93)

To the extent that middle-class parents experience economic or job-related stresses similar to those of the poverty-stricken, we would find the conditions for child abuse to be present there as well.

5. Not liking or wanting a child who is born; one born prematurely; or one with physical or mental defects (lack of parent-infant attachment).

6. Lack of a supportive network of family, relatives, or friends into which parents are integrated and through which parents develop a sense of contribution and self-esteem (social and geographic isolation).

7. Abusive parents are much more likely than other parents to have been abused themselves as children, to have been emotionally deprived and unloved, or to have been a sibling of a child who was abused.

8. A child who is unusually active, hostile, aggressive, ill-tempered, slow to learn, learning-disabled, or otherwise difficult to get along with is more likely than others to be abused. It is interesting to note that even in families with three or more children, it is usually only one child who is abused. This child may be a scapegoat for deep-rooted problems within the family system, or may be singled out for being different in some way.

9. Teenage pregnancy and parenting is associated with child abuse (and often includes many or all of the contributing factors, 1–8, identified here).

10. Alcoholism and related psychological problems in one or both parents increases the potential for child abuse.

SOLUTIONS TO THE CHILD-ABUSE PROBLEM

As a society, we are a long way from solving the child-abuse problem. Treatment programs for abusive parents seem to have limited impact. Many abused children are returned to their homes by local courts and social welfare agencies after parents have been counseled or, possibly, prosecuted. All too often the same abusive behavior recurs and the child winds up either seriously injured or dead.

Prevention seems to be the best course to follow. Family life and parenthood education programs for youngsters in school, churches, or community organizations may help to the extent that they inform these parents-to-be about the stresses and responsibilities which parenthood entails, and about realistic expectations of children's behavior and development at different stages. These programs also help the students to explore the reasons why they might someday want children of their own.

Clearly, the prevalence of child abuse in our society indicates that too many adults are not qualified to become parents—they do not possess the requisite patience to cope with the stresses of parenthood and the requisite skills to perform parental roles competently. Yet parenthood is the inalienable right of everyone. Regardless of one's ability to provide for a child's needs for food, clothing, and shelter, and regardless of one's ability to assume parental roles, anyone can have one child, three children, five children, or more. This is a basic individual freedom, one which our society does not, and perhaps should not, abridge. After all, how are we to determine, in an objective way, who can or cannot bear children? Even if such a method were developed, how would it be enforced? Would we punish such people with economic penalties? This would probably worsen the economic stress-related causes of child abuse, and lead to *more* child abuse in the long run. Moreover, this smacks of a totalitarian society, one that strives to govern the reproductive behavior of its members. And such measures could be used for political expediency, as well as for immoral and unethical purposes.

However, until we can develop preventive educational programs to reach young people *before* they become parents, and until we devise a way of persuading potentially incompetent and abusive parents to choose not to have children, the child-abuse problem will be with us for some years to come.

Development in the Marital Career: Satisfaction or Disenchantment?

We discussed in chapter 12 how the transition to parenthood can affect the marriage relationship in many ways. The process of development in marriage continues as children grow older and as additional children are added to the family. Here we will examine the five major bases of marriage and the three factors which have the greatest impact upon them during this stage of development: (1) the *passage of time;* (2) *children;* and (3) *work-related experiences inside and outside the home.*

LOVE AND AFFECTION

A host of research studies, more than can be listed here, have been conducted to determine what the *quality of marriage* is across stages of the marital career (Rollins and Cannon, 1974; Pineo, 1961; Dizard, 1968; Spanier, Lewis, and Cole, 1975; Anderson, Russell, and Schumm, 1983 to name just a few). Quality of marriage refers to a number of factors, including *how satisfied* partners are with the love and affection they receive from the partner, how *satisfied they are overall,* and how *well-adjusted* they are to each other's personal needs for love and intimacy. Does the quality of marriage improve over time? Does it deteriorate? Or does it stay about the same? Each of these studies comes to one basic conclusion:

Beginning with the transition to first parenthood, the level of satisfaction with love and affection in marriage demonstrates a gradual but consistent decline over the stages of the marital career.

The curve presented in Figure 13.1 summarizes the various studies conducted. This trend has been called the *process of disenchantment* (Pineo, 1961). Disenchantment

FIGURE 13.1.   Satisfaction and Adjustment Levels in Marriage From the Early Years (Before Children) Through the Middle Years (Children Adolescents).

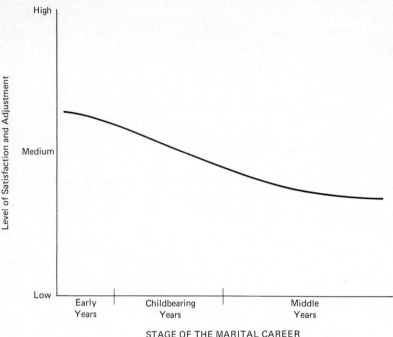

is the result of a number of factors, including the following:

1. *Growing children* in the home put a "crunch" on the time, energy, and financial resources of parents, resulting in less time and energy to devote to maintaining a satisfying marriage relationship that achieves the partner's goals for intimacy, love, and affection. However, children can be "one of the greatest and the only source of satisfaction" among spouses who otherwise view their marriage as "unsatisfying" (Luckey and Bain, 1970).

2. *Role strain,* which results from the growing demands of children and challenges of parenthood, in combination with the demands and challenges of work outside of the home. Role strain increases if one or both spouses are working outside of the home, and this strain spills over and affects the marriage.

3. A gradual *growing apart* of husband and wife as a result of different day-to-day experiences and contacts with other people and events. There is a tendency for married mates to grow less compatible over time in regard to values, role expectations, and interests, because of their different day-to-day experiences. This can happen whether one partner works outside of the home while the other cares for children and does routine homemaking activities all week, or when both partners work outside of the home.

4. *Increasing disagreement and conflict* over a number of issues relating to children, the marriage, or family-related events in general. These can include child discipline, money management, household chores and duties, and a host of other issues.

5. A decline in the number of *companionship and leisure-time activities,* such as dining out in a restaurant together, dancing, going to a sports or cultural event,

taking a walk together, or just spending an evening talking to one another.

6. A decline in the frequency of *exchanges of love and affection,* such as holding hands, touching, kissing, hugging, or other signs of intimacy. This leads to feelings of loneliness and isolation in the marriage relationship.

7. An increasing *segregation of marital roles,* such that spouses increasingly assume different responsibilities in the home — caring for and disciplining children, household tasks, and other tasks that in the early years of marriage were shared.

8. A decline in the *frequency of communication* between marriage partners — talking and listening to one another, using one another as confidants, and self-disclosure — all tend to decline in frequency from the early through the middle years of marriage.

9. A loss of the *spark of excitement, the romanticism, and the thrill of the "honeymoon effect"* in the early years of marriage. Time seems to take a toll on one important basis for marriage in our society — romantic love.

10. A growing *imbalance in the power structure* of marriage, so that one partner tends to assume increasing influence over the other in terms of making important decisions and getting what they want in the event of a disagreement.

The *process of disenchantment,* therefore, seems to affect all areas of the marriage relationship — love, communication, sexuality, affection exchange, and power. The degree of disenchantment depends, in part, on how much a spouse values those aspects of marriage that are changing — companionship, communication, love and affection, and role sharing. Recall our definition of *"successful marriage"* in chapter 1: Success depends upon the degree to which the marriage experience measures up to the partners' goals and expectations of it. Given that companionship, intimacy, and role sharing tend to decline over the years as children are added and grow up, disenchantment will be greatest for those whose goals and expectations are high at the outset.

The tendency toward disenchantment is real, and the factors contributing to it must be confronted head-on if couples are to avoid it. It is important to realize, however, that some marriages *improve and become stronger* over the stages of the marital career; but others show an even greater decline over time than is pictured in Figure 13.1. (In other words, the statistical curve in Figure 13.1 is an *average.*) For example, one study found that marital satisfaction was quite high in marriages with several children, provided that the spouses engaged in many companionship activities together (Miller, 1976). Doing things together as a couple, both with and without children present, seems to be an important buffer against disenchantment for those who place a strong value on marriage and parenthood (Rollins and Galligan, 1978).

GENDER ROLES

Partners who begin marriage with the sharing of such roles as cooking, cleaning, and household maintenance, and who begin parenthood by sharing the tasks and responsibilities of child care, socialization, and discipline, often grow more specialized and segregated in the performance of these roles over these stages of the marital career (Dizard, 1968). Wives tend to develop their own domains of functioning while husbands develop theirs. Often this increasing role segregation follows traditional gender-role lines: the husband is the primary provider, handles household repairs, financial matters, and the heavier work around the home; wives handle the cooking, laundry, housecleaning, child care and discipline, and the lighter chores around the home. This is particularly true for those couples where the husband works outside of the home and the wife is a housewife-homemaker.

However, because more and more women with dependent children at home are entering the labor force (because of either financial necessity or for personal fulfillment in a job or career [see chapter 8]), they more often share in the financial decision making, and they find that their husbands are assuming a greater interest and responsibility in child care. However, as we mentioned in chapter 8, husbands of working women today do not help much more than others with household chores and duties traditionally assigned to the wife-mother. Hence, the division of labor in marriage today still tends to follow traditional gender-role lines during the middle years of marriage, regardless of whether or not the wife-mother is employed outside of the home. In effect, many women during the middle years of marriage are working "double duty" if they are employed outside of the home.

SEXUALITY AND FAMILY PLANNING

Sexuality.   The comparative novelty of the sexual experience and freedom of sexual expression for many young couples in the early years of marriage make this a particularly rewarding aspect of marriage in that stage. As with the other aspects of marriage that change over time, however, the sexual relationship changes as well. We have seen (chapter 12) how pregnancy, childbirth, and parenting the young infant can interrupt and modify, temporarily at least, the sexual relationship in marriage. The research shows that the sexual relationship continues to change over the middle years of the marital career, following the transition to first parenthood. If we examine the classic studies of Alfred Kinsey (1948; 1953), or the more recent studies of Hunt (1974) and Tavris and Sadd (1977), we see that the average frequency of sexual intercourse and achievement of orgasm tends to drop over the middle years of marriage (see Table 13.5). Although husbands report more sexual activity during the early years of marriage, both husbands and wives report a declining frequency of sexual activity over time.

It is important to note here that "good sex does not necessarily lead to a good marriage." On the contrary, satisfaction in other areas of marriage contributes to sexual satisfaction. One study found that the sexual responsiveness of wives increased over the first several years of marriage, *if* the level of satisfaction with the marriage in general increased (Clark and Wallin, 1965). If a couple is experiencing communication problems, or if there is

TABLE 13.5. *Average Number of Times Per Week Married Couples Reported Having Sexual Intercourse, at Different Ages*

Age	Reports of Wives	Reports of Husbands
18–24	3.3	3.7
25–34	2.6	2.8
35–44	2.0	2.2
45–54	1.5	1.5
55 +	1.0	1.0

SOURCE: Hunt (1974).

chronic conflict, they are also likely to be disappointed with the quality of their sex lives in marriage. The quality of the sexual relationship during the middle years, therefore, appears to depend on whether or not, and to what degree, the "process of disenchantment" has occurred. The time and energy involved in raising children can also interfere with direct communication between husband and wife about their feelings for one another—the love and intimacy they still share (Thornburg, 1977).

An important issue, and a problem, for many couples in these middle years is *extramarital sexuality*. Traditional marriage vows state an important concept in our monogamous system of marriage—that the spouse promises "to forsake all others." However, as long as 30 to 40 years ago, Kinsey found that more than a fourth of his female respondents and nearly half of his male respondents had engaged in sexual intercourse at least once with a person other than the spouse by the time they were 40 years of age. The overall rates are about the same in more recent studies, although the covert nature of extramarital sex, and people's sensitivity to it, may lead to some underreporting of this activity (Reiss, Anderson, and Sponaugle, 1980; Johnson, 1970; Edwards and Booth, 1976; Singh, Walton, and Williams, 1976; Maykovich, 1976; Glass and Wright, 1977; Bell, Turner, and Rosen, 1975).

The following factors are associated with spouses actually becoming involved in *extramarital sexual behavior* (Reiss, Anderson, and Sponaugle, 1980; Edwards and Booth, 1976):

1. Being in an unhappy or unsatisfying marriage relationship.

2. Having the *opportunity* for becoming sexually involved outside of marriage.

3. Having a lower than average frequency of sexual intercourse within the marriage relationship.

4. Having a generally permissive attitude toward a range of sexual behaviors in general, such as premarital sex, a variety of different sexual activities within marriage (other than intercourse), and extramarital sex.

Television soap operas and "common knowledge" tell us that extramarital sexual affairs are especially exciting and gratifying. However, research evidence shows that people rate their extramarital sexual experiences as being less pleasurable (with fewer orgasms) than marital sex. According to DeLora and Warren (1977:251–52):

> Undoubtedly, for some people an extramarital relationship provides a satisfying physical and emotional experience. For others, it is a miserable and unsuccessful attempt to transcend temporarily their usual existence. Probably for most participants, the problems of guilt and fear of discovery are weighed against the delights of recaptured youth and desirability and the rediscovery of excitement and passion. Apparently in extramarital sexuality, the sexual revolution has not made the widespread changes it has in premarital and marital sexuality.

It is also commonly believed that extramarital sexual affairs necessarily have a damaging effect on the marriage relationship. However, this is not necessarily so in all cases. Entering into an extramarital sexual affair is often only a signal of strain and distress in the marriage relationship.

There are different kinds of extramarital relationships, and each has different effects on a marriage (see Figure 13.2). The major considerations here are (1) the reasons that the spouse engages in an extramarital sexual relationship, and (2) whether or not the marriage partner is aware of the activity and agrees to it. People may enter an extramarital relationship for various reasons—for sexual variety; curiosity; pressure from friends; to reaffirm one's youthful status; meeting and falling in love with another; to gain favors or resources from a person who controls them (such as having sex with one's boss in order to gain a promotion); or simply to hurt or spite a marriage partner (DeLora and Warren, 1977). These reasons can be classified as either "pleasure-focused" or "love-focused." In addition, some extramarital affairs go on with the knowledge of, and, at times, the acceptance of, the spouse. Others, of course, are kept secret in order to prevent hurting the spouse or threatening the marriage relationship. In a study of fifty wives and fifty husbands who were aware of their partner's extramarital affairs, Buunk (1982) found three basic "coping styles": (1) avoidance of the spouse; (2) reappraisal of the situation; and (3) communication. Women were most likely to avoid the issue upon discovery of their husband's extramarital affairs. Many tried to pretend that the affairs didn't exist. The most *functional response* was communicating with the

FIGURE 13.2. Types of Extramarital Sexual Relationships.

		MOTIVES FOR ENTERING EXTRAMARITAL SEXUAL RELATIONSHIP	
		Love for Another Person	Pleasure Seeking only
Spouse's Attitude	Knows About and Accepts or Agrees to the Extramarital Relationship.	1	2
	Doesn't know About or Disagrees with or Fails to Accept the Extramarital Relationship.	3	4

SOURCE: Reiss (1980); Reiss, Sponaugle, and Anderson (1980).

spouse about the affair and assessing what it meant for the future of the marriage relationship.

According to Reiss (1980), the most common is Type 4 — that which is secretive, hidden from the spouse, and based on achieving sexual gratification only. There is no particular degree of love or affection felt by the involved marriage partner for the extramarital sex partner. Adult males' use of prostitutes exemplify Type 4 extramarital relationships. Those who participate in such affairs would argue that they pose little threat to the marriage relationship because they are doing it "just for fun," and that they are not serious about the extramarital sex partner. So long as the relationships are kept secret, they believe no harm will come to the marriage partner.

Type 3 extramarital affairs rank second in frequency. They are secretive affairs involving a loving and affectionate relationship between the involved spouse and the extramarital sex partner. This is the least approved type of extramarital affair, because of the deception involved and the competitive bond of affection with the extramarital partner which, eventually, could damage the marital relationship (Reiss, 1980). Type 3 relationships are most likely to occur among spouses who are unhappily married.

Types 1 and 2 extramarital affairs are far less common, and probably account for 10 percent or less of all sexual relationships outside of marriage. Because becoming involved in these types of sexual relationships is something both partners in the marriage agree to, they are less popular.

Family Planning. Following the transition to parenthood, married couples are faced with an important decision — whether or not to have more children, and if so, how many more, and when (see chapter 6). A two-child norm has emerged in North American society in the last several years (Buckhout, 1972). That is, more young married couples view two children as the ideal number, even though a husband's and wife's preferences may not be discussed until they are confronted with having to make a decision about having more than one child. Of course, some couples may discuss these issues and formulate a plan either before marriage or in the early years before the transition to first parenthood (see chapter 9). Even those carefully formulated plans can change, however, as circumstances relating to the couple's financial status and preferences for more children change.

Couples who decide to have only one child usually do so because they believe that they will be able to devote their full and undivided attention to that child, and will thereby be most effective in their parenting. Economically speaking, they can better afford to provide for the needs and desires of one child than for two or more children. Indeed, there is some evidence to support the idea that an only child has advantages over children with siblings. In their analysis of seven national surveys drawn in the United States, Glenn and Hoppe (1984) found that, as adults, only children were more satisfied with their lives than were others who had grown up with siblings. Although the differences between only children and others were quite small on several measures of psychological well-being in adulthood (happiness, satisfaction with family life, satisfaction with friendships, and so on), they seemed to favor the only child on each measure. However, only children may also have some disadvantages (Hawke and Knox, 1977; 1978; Polit, Nuttall, and Nuttall, 1980).

Advantages of the Only Child

1. No sibling rivalry and conflict.

2. Privacy — not having to share a room.

3. Better language skills and intellectual development, grades in school, and achievement in college.

4. More self-reliant, resourceful, and self-confident.

5. Parents' marriage relationship less adversely affected than is the case with more children.

6. Feel closer to their parents than do children from larger families.

7. More participation in making decisions in the family.

8. Only children tend to achieve higher educational and income levels, and have fewer children when they grow up to be adults.

Disadvantages of the One-Child Family

1. Lack of a sibling friend and confidant.

2. Feel extra pressure to achieve and succeed.

3. Have no help in caring for aging parents.

4. Parents' fear of the child's dying and being left with no child.

5. Parents' concern about social ostracism—that they are selfish.

6. Parents' ambiguity over where to draw the line between "healthy attention" and "overindulgence" (spoiling the child).

7. The three-person group is always subject to two-against-one coalitions, such that the child or one of the parents might be "ganged-up" against.

In a study of 144 young mothers who recently had a second child, Knox and Wilson (1978) found that the total impact of the first child on the wife-mother and marriage relationship was greater than that of the second child. However, the second child meant less time for herself, more work, and more noise. It also contributed to a drop in satisfaction with the marriage, probably as a result of the added strain brought on by the "less time, more work, and more noise" they experienced. Nonetheless, the benefits outweighed the costs, because 93 percent of these mothers said their second child "was worth it," and said they never wished to return to the one-child family.

Whether or not a couple has more than one child is based on a number of possible factors. First, those who fail to employ an effective method of birth control after the first child may find a second one on the way—an unintended pregnancy. Social norms also play a major role. Those raised in large families often have large families of their own, particularly if their childhood was happy. Religious and ethnic group norms also influence the number of children a couple may have.

Because women have been entering the labor force at such a rapid pace in the last several years (see chapter 8), it has been found that their work plans and experiences play an important role in family-planning decisions. Whether she is employed for financial or personal-fulfillment reasons, the employed wife/mother actually has fewer children than do others (Cramer, 1980; Stolzenberg and Waite, 1977; Smith-Lovin and Tickamyer, 1978; Waite and Stolzenberg, 1976). However, for a majority of working women (about 55 percent), having children takes them out of the labor force for at least one year; therefore, having children usually has an adverse effect on the woman's participation in the world of work (Smith-Lovin and Tickamyer, 1978; McLaughlin, 1982).

Whatever the couple's future childbearing intentions might be, it is important to practice an effective method of birth control if they are to succeed in limiting their children to the number they can afford, in accordance with their desired standard of living, and to space them conveniently. As discussed in chapter 6, a growing number of couples in the middle years are undergoing voluntary sterilization of the husband or wife as the birth control method of choice, once they have realized their childbearing goals.

COMMUNICATION AND CONFLICT MANAGEMENT

When discussing the process of disenchantment, changes in the patterns of communication and conflict management were noted. The tendency of married partners is to change the focus of their communication from themselves and their relationship to their children and the events in a growing family. The studies of disenchantment have also found that the frequency of conflict and disagreements increases during the middle years.

In general, it appears that the manner in which conflict is resolved, and how spouses talk to one another, follow along the basic lines established in the earlier stages of the marital career. Poor communication habits and conflict-resolution strategies initiated in earlier stages, as well as the more effective ones, tend to become routine *interaction habits* that carry over into, and solidify, during the middle years.

ECONOMIC FUNCTIONING

For many families, the ratio of financial resources to financial needs grows smaller and smaller during this stage (Aldous and Hill, 1969). The costs of clothing, feeding, schooling, medical care, and a number of other incidental items children want and need grow rapidly. The costs are compounded with the addition of each child. However, the earnings of the wife-mother and husband-father usually do not reach their peak until at least some of the children have grown to adulthood and have left home. This means that the "income-per-family-member" grows smaller as children are added and as they grow during the middle years.

Even for families with only one or two children, the current state of economic conditions usually requires two incomes, if the family is to maintain the standard of living they desire. We have seen an increasing number of dual-career marriages in which the spouses must live apart from one another so that both are free to pursue their own careers. Whether it is a hundred or a thousand miles apart, couples who maintain residences in different locations undergo considerable strain (Gross, 1980). The strain of these "long-distance marriages" is greater for those married a short time, young couples, and those with children.

Recent research has shown that family income earned, and assets accumulated, during the middle years of the marital career are related to the *sequence of major adult transitions* undertaken previously by the husband-father and wife-mother. For example, couples who have their first child when they are teenagers can expect to accumulate between 20 to 25 percent fewer assets during this middle stage of the marital career (car, home, stocks, bonds, furniture, and property) than couples who wait to bear their first child for at least two or three years after marriage (Freedman and Thornton, 1979). Becoming parents during the teenage years also contributes to parents assuming low-paying, dead-end jobs, which adds further to the economic stress. Not only does early *childbearing* contribute to lower income and economic assets years later, but it appears that *marrying* before other key adult transitions are made, such as completing school or starting work on a full-time job after schooling, leads to higher rates of marital instability (divorce and separation) [Hogan, 1978] and lower income levels (Hogan, 1980) during the middle years.

Hogan (1980), for example, examined the career attainments of nearly 20,000 men between the ages of 20 and 65. He wanted to determine if the sequence of making various life transitions in adulthood affected their yearly income levels. He studied three groups of men:

1. *The Normative Group,* who underwent a normal sequence of adult transitions:

". . . When a man first completes school, next starts to work, and lastly marries."

2. *The Intermediate Group,* who deviated in one way from the normative pattern:

". . . When a man either begins a job prior to finishing school, or marries prior to beginning work but after the completion of schooling."

3. *The Non-normative Group,* who "married prior to the completion of their educations."

As expected, he found that the average annual earnings were the greatest for the *Normative Group,* less for *Intermediate Group,* and the least for the *Non-normative Group*. Among professional types of occupations, those in the Nonnormative Group earned nearly $1,500 less per year than did the Normative Group (Hogan, 1980:272). This difference was still present many years after these men first married.

The timing and sequencing of marriage and childbearing have economic effects that remain for years after they first occur. Therefore, in order to maximize one's chances for financial well-being during the middle years of marriage, a person would be wise to seriously consider the timing and sequence of completing an education, getting married, and having children. With careful planning and foresight, a married couple can shape their future financial well-being in order to carry them through the years of marriage, when a growing family places increasing pressures on the family's economic resources.

Summary

The middle years of the marital career pose a number of challenges to the married couple and the growing family. Family relationships become increasingly complex as children grow and develop through the preschool, middle childhood, and adolescence stages of development. A number of role sequences mark changes, and demands for changes, in the behavior and expectations of marriage partners relative to each other, of parents toward children, and of children toward parents. Effective parenthood involves relating to children in a manner that is caring, concerned, and respectful of their changing needs and qualities. The quality of marriage in this stage is strongly influenced by the presence of children, the eroding effects of time on the marriage relationship, and the work of both partners within and outside of the home. The morale and satisfaction of marriage partners is a direct result of how much they are able to resist the pressures toward disenchantment in marriage, which most in this stage are likely to face. This stage can provide especially rewarding and gratifying experiences, given a context of effective parenting and mutual growth and development in marriage. On the other hand, this stage can also bring conflict, disenchantment, and seemingly insurmountable crises when the stresses and challenges of children are too great for parents to handle, and when the pressures toward disenchantment become too strong for marriage partners to overcome.

Questions for Discussion and Review

1. Recall various disciplinary techniques used by your parents while you were growing up. How did they change over the years, as you grew older? How do you feel now about the ways in which you were disciplined? Which techniques, if any, do you plan to use with your own children?

2. What, in your mind, constitutes child abuse? What are your responsibilities, should you observe, or otherwise become aware of, child abuse in a particular family? What can be done to reduce the frequency of child abuse and neglect in our society?

3. Which stage of development do you think is the most difficult for a family? That is, at what ages do children pose the greatest challenge in the family? At what ages are children the least difficult?

4. In what ways do children have an impact on the marriage relationship of their parents? How do the influences of children on the family change over the years, as they grow older? In general, do children have more of a positive or more of a negative influence on marriage over the years?

5. What can marriage partners do during the middle-years stage to keep their marriage relationship vital, alive, and growth-oriented? How can they prevent the pressure toward disenchantment over the years? What, if anything, can society do to help marriage partners avoid the disappointment and growing apart, which characterizes many marriages in this stage?

6. What are your attitudes regarding extramarital sexuality? Are there any circumstances under which a sexual relationship outside of marriage would be acceptable to you? If so, what are they? Are any of the four types of extramarital sexuality identified in the text more acceptable than others? Explain your answer. Why do you think so many extramarital sexual affairs take place? Is it more acceptable for males to have an extramarital sexual affair than it is for females?

CHAPTER 14

Is There Marriage After Children?

The Postparental and Aging Years

In this chapter, we will move into the final two stages of the marital career. The postparental stage begins when the last child is launched from the home into marriage, college, or a job of his or her own, and ends when both spouses have retired from their occupations in the world of work. Retirement signals the beginning of the aging years stage, which exists until the death of one of the spouses.

The label *postparental stage* is somewhat misleading because parents continue to be parents; they maintain contacts and bonds of affection with their adult children even after they have left home to go to college, to work, or possibly to get married and begin marital careers of their own (Aldous, 1978). Nonetheless, patterns of relating to one another in this stage usually undergo dramatic changes because marriage partners are no longer directly responsible for the cares and concerns associated with having children in the home on a daily basis. As was the case in the early years of marriage, before the transition to first parenthood, spouses return to a *couple relationship* which is relatively unhindered by the demands, responsibilities, and presence of children.

This stage in the marital career is a relatively new one in our history. This is the result of trends over the past several decades in the timing of childbearing, as well as in

the lengthening human life span. Compared with people in the past 75 to 100 years, married people today have fewer children, complete their childbearing at an earlier age, are younger when their last child marries, live longer, and are older at the death of the first married partner to die (Aldous, 1978). Early in this century, the first spouse usually died about the time that the last child married. Now, on the average, there is a period of several years between the last child's marriage and the death of one spouse. For example, it is typical today to have a family with two or three children in which the last child was born before the parents reached 30 years of age (see Figure 14.1). If that child leaves the home upon turning 18 years old, the parents would enter the postparental stage at age 48. A normal retirement age of 65 would mean that *they would have 17 years of marriage in a stage which, only 75 years ago, did not even exist in the marital career.* For those who complete their childbearing later, or who retire earlier, the postparental stage would be shorter. Conversely, earlier completion of childbearing or later age at retirement would lengthen the postparental stage.

The *aging years* are entered when retirement from work takes place. Traditionally, this has been gauged by the retirement of the husband-father, who usually functioned as the primary or the only breadwinner. Today,

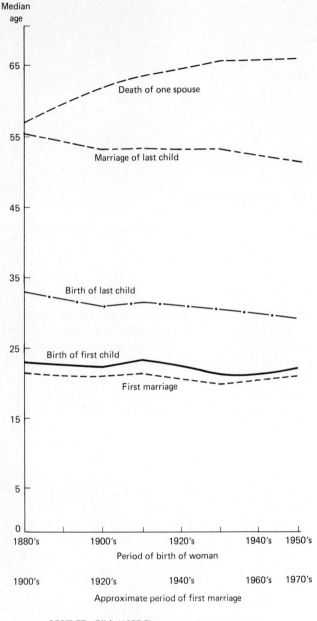

FIGURE 14.1.   Median Age of Mothers at Various Points in the Marital Career.

Median
age

65

Death of one spouse

55

Marriage of last child

45

35

Birth of last child

25

Birth of first child

First marriage

15

5

0

1880's   1900's   1920's   1940's   1950's

Period of birth of woman

1900's   1920's   1940's   1960's   1970's

Approximate period of first marriage

SOURCE: Glick (1977:7).

however, as more women are entering long-term careers and are becoming committed to a line of work for many years, we are likely to see a growing impact of the woman's retirement on the marriage relationship. For people born in the 1980s, the average life expectancy is about 70 for men and 78 for women (National Center for Health Statistics, 1984c). If retirement occurs at age 65, therefore, couples can expect to be in this stage somewhere between 5 and 10 years before the death of one spouse brings the marital career to an end. The different life expectancies for men and women means that the number of women in the aging years of life exceeds that of men to a considerable degree.

Development of the Person in the Postparental and Aging Years: An Overview

The development of a person does not stop when adulthood is reached. Just as children grow and develop over the course of the childhood and adolescent years (see chapters 12 and 13), so too do adults develop in the physical, social, emotional, and intellectual realms. Adult needs, goals, values, and expectations are in a continual state of change over the adulthood years. Sometimes the changes are gradual, and sometimes rapid. Sometimes a person changes in conformity with changes in the marriage partner, and sometimes changes occur in a totally divergent direction.

PERSONAL DEVELOPMENT OVER THE ADULT YEARS

Erikson's (1980) view of psychosocial development of the person extends throughout the life span of the individual (see chapter 12, Table 12.3). Following adolescence, the adult person is said to move through three more stages before death occurs in old age. The first is *Young Adulthood,* with the psychosocial crisis of *intimacy versus isolation.* It is at this stage of life that the person seeks to fulfill yearnings for closeness and intimacy with others. The "intimate affiliations, passionate sexual unions, or inspiring encounters" of young adulthood comprise a major part of the premarital stage and early years of the marital career (Erikson, 1980:26). Often this entails commitments to other people that demand a certain degree of self-sacrifice and compromise. The major psychosocial strength to be gained if healthy development of the individual is to proceed is *the ability to love and to be loved by others.* The danger of not developing this ability is *isolation and loneliness.* Love guides and shapes other aspects of life and gives them meaning, such as "competition and cooperation, procreation and production" (p. 27). Isolation leads to emptiness and a lack of fulfillment, possibly leading to difficulty in negotiating subsequent stages of adult development.

The second stage of adult development, according to Erikson, is *maturity.* This stage of personal development occurs at the time that many marriage partners are about to enter the postparental stage of the marital career. The psychosocial crisis of this stage, which probably occurs at about the ages of 40 to 45, is *generativity versus stagnation.* The major strength to be gained is *care.* Generativity "is primarily the concern with establishing and guiding the next generation" (p. 27). It is the "productivity and creativity" that a person is realizing during the peak years in work or career. The person develops a sense of care for others in this stage, and the "need to be needed by others" is fulfilled. The mature person, then, is one who gains fulfillment by making contributions to the family, community, or place of work that are judged by others to be meaningful and significant. The major danger in this stage is developing a feeling of *stagnation.* This occurs when one's efforts are viewed by self or others as futile, meaningless, or empty. Personal growth is denied to people who feel they are "stuck in a rut," who feel unappreciated and unneeded by family members or the boss at work, and who no longer feel a sense of contribution and creativity.

The last of Erikson's stages of development is *old age,* which parallels entry into the aging-years stage of the marital career. The major psychosocial crisis is *integrity versus despair,* and the psychosocial strength to be gained is *wisdom.* Wisdom "is a detached and yet active concern with life in the face of death" (p. 29). Wisdom includes the accumulated knowledge, understanding, and mature judgment that only those who have lived a long time, and whose lives are full of rich and meaningful experiences, can develop. Integrity comes to those who see the "meaning and paradoxes" of the "full cycle of life," and who communicate that meaning to younger generations and thereby "enhance the potentiality that others may meet ultimate questions with some clarity and strength" (p. 29). The danger in this stage is *despair*—fearing death because time is too short to accomplish those things that the person had previously set goals to accomplish. Despair involves bitterness, disgust, and cynicism toward others

because the person is unable to confront, and accept, the ultimate fate which befalls all of us: death. Despair can cause the person in old age to live in the past, to wallow in memories of how good things *were,* in order to avoid confronting the challenges of the present and events to come in the future.

MIDDLESCENCE: THE MIDLIFE AUTHENTICITY CRISIS

In her popular book describing various "passages," or critical stages through which adults in our society pass, author Gail Sheehy (1977) described the crises and passages that occur in the last half of life for some people. This "midlife passage" includes the *Deadline Decade* of ages 35 to 45 and the *Age 40 Crucible.*

The middle of the thirties is literally the midpoint of life. The halfway mark. No gong rings, of course. But twinges begin. Deep down a change begins to register in those gut-level perceptions of safety and danger, time and no time, aliveness and stagnation, self and others. It starts with a vague feeling . . . *I have reached some sort of meridian in my life. I had better take a survey, reexamine where I have been, and reevaluate how I am going to spend my resources from now on. Why am I doing all this? What do I really believe in?* (Sheehy, 1977:350)

Although not yet actually at the stage known as *middle age* (which begins around age 50), this is the midlife period, and the way it is managed will set the stage for growth and development during middle age and the aging years. Sheehy labels this the "authenticity crisis," which may have a strong negative impact on some, a strong positive effect on others, or possibly little or no effect, depending on the circumstances and events in previous stages of life. Such negative outcomes as conflict in marriage, alcoholism, divorce, clandestine extramarital sexual affairs, mental or nervous breakdown, or even suicide are some of the more extreme, and tragic, outcomes of midlife crisis of men and women. However, crises can also lead to personal growth for those who take advantage of being at a turning point in their lives; they can shift gears, and seek better and more fulfilling activities, or establish more meaningful and intimate relationships with others who are close to them, such as a spouse and children.

For women, the authenticity crisis of the midlife passage sometimes involves a genuine self-examination to determine where they have been, where they are, and where they are going in life. The midlife crisis for women who have followed the traditional gender-role pattern is clearly centered on their marriage and children. The majority of women today do not spend their entire adult lifetimes working in a career outside of the home. Many women leave the world of work to care for children and to support their husbands in their careers, or they may work in dull jobs, out of financial necessity, from time to time.

For some, the mid-life "authenticity crisis" can mean loneliness and despair if the departure of children, physical changes, and concerns about sexuality are not coped with adequately. *(Photo by Stan Levy.)*

The prospect of children leaving the home can instill fear and anxiety in the hearts of those women who see a major component of their lives coming to a close: *motherhood*. The time, energy, love, and affection they have lavished on their children for many years will be missed by mothers who feel that they are no longer going to be needed in their major adult role. They see only loneliness, boredom, and isolation in their futures. What will give their life meaning and significance — or *authenticity?* They may not have worked outside of the home for many years, and their job skills may have become rusty or even obsolete. They may question their own sexuality, and their sex appeal to their husbands, or to other men in general. Some women at this point in their lives seek extramarital affairs to reaffirm that they appeal to men, and to see for themselves if there is more to sex than they have experienced in marriage.

Women who have worked full-time in careers may also experience an authenticity crisis, which too will focus on marriage and parenthood concerns. Single career women may wonder whether or not they should have married; married career women may wonder whether or not their career had a negative impact on their children or marriage; married career women may wonder if they did the best thing by choosing not to have any, or only one or two, children; and single as well as married career women may wonder about their changing appearance and sexual attractiveness to men.

In regard to issues of midlife authenticity for men, we will turn to the work of Daniel Levinson (1978). Levinson conducted an in-depth study of 40 men, 10 each in 4 different types of occupations: executives of a large corporation, hourly workers in a factory, university biologists, and novelists. Based on his interviews with these 35- to 45-year-old men, Levinson developed a framework of stages for better understanding the major transitions and tasks critical in this period of a man's life. As depicted in Figure 14.2, these adult years can be divided into two main stages, Early Adulthood and Middle Adulthood, sandwiched between three major transition points: Early Adult, Midlife, and Late Adult Transitions.[1]

According to Levinson, a man enters the Early Adulthood stage (ages 22 to 28) by formulating his "Dream" of what he will become and what he will achieve in life. He is establishing independence from his family of origin as he makes choices in regard to occupation, love relationships, marriage and family, values, and life-styles. This stage is marked by a sense of adventure; enthusiasm

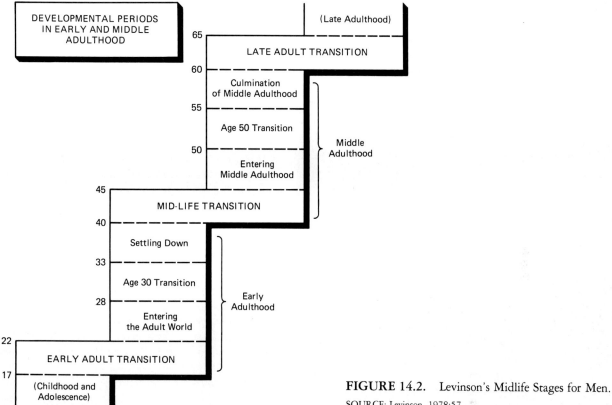

FIGURE 14.2.   Levinson's Midlife Stages for Men.
SOURCE: Levinson, 1978:57.

for future possibilities; exploration; and experimentation with different options — without making strong commitments. At the same time, the man faces the task of creating stable life patterns — developing responsibility and "making something of himself." A danger at this stage lies in the man's being unable to make a choice among the various options he has, which may lead to rootlessness — aimless wandering from one job, life-style, or love relationship to the next. Another danger is that of settling down before adequately exploring his options, which might lead to stagnation and disappointment with his job, marriage partner, or chosen life-style.

The Age 30 Transition (ages 28 to 33) is a time of reflection for the male. He must decide whether or not he is on the right career path, and he may attempt to formu-

late plans to change his path, if he can. For some, according to Levinson (p. 58), this can be a "developmental crisis" in the man's life:

. . . he finds his present life structure intolerable, yet seems unable to form a better one. In a severe crisis he experiences a threat to life itself, the danger of chaos and dissolution, the loss of hope for the future . . . At this time a man may make important new choices, or he may reaffirm old choices. If these choices are congruent with his dreams, talents, and external possibilities, they provide the basis for a relatively satisfactory life structure.

Following this transition, the man then enters the period of Settling Down (ages 33 to 40). The major tasks are "to *establish a niche* in society" by making contributions to other's lives and by being valued by his friends and family, and to _make it_ by advancing up the career or job ladder according to the usual advancement timetable (promotions, pay raises, acquiring more responsibility, and so on). He strives to "become his own man," to become a "senior member" and authority figure in his world by age 40, a world into which he entered as a "junior member" years earlier.

The Midlife Transition (ages 40 to 45) is a critical period in the man's adult development. (Sheehy [1977] described it as the _Age 40 Crucible_.) During their 40s, many men have reached the peak of their earning potential and level of advancement through the ranks of the company or organization in which they work. Many men may come to realize that they are no longer indispensible to the company and can be easily replaced by more aggressive, attractive, and less expensive younger employees. Men who had set their sights high during earlier years may realize that they are _not_ going to make it to the top, or that they can accomplish some, but not all, of their goals. Such men may experience disillusionment and despair. In a society where a man's worthiness is judged on the basis of income, achievement, and occupational success, this crisis can indeed be severe. The crisis is compounded by having to let go of the "impossible dream of youth," as he notices his "fat, the same-aged wife, his own sagging face, and graying hair" (Sheehy, 1977:403). The husband feels the loss of physical attractiveness and prowess that once were the pride of his youth, just as his wife feels the loss of her attractiveness.

Men enter the Middle Adulthood stage between the ages of 45 and 50, according to Levinson's framework. It is at this point that he must make choices and formulate a "new life structure," if he has experienced an authenticity crisis during the Midlife Transition. This stage is often marked by a significant event in the man's life, which gives it a new direction and, perhaps, a new purpose. He may change jobs, have an extramarital love affair, divorce his spouse, experience a serious illness (or the death of a loved one), or move to a new location. There are men, however, who experience little noticeable change, and "life at 45 seems to be just as it was at 39" (Levinson, 1978:61). Even in these cases, Levinson notes that subtle changes are occurring:

A man may still be married to the same woman, but the character of his familial relationships has changed appreciably for better or worse. Or the nature of his work life has altered: he is quietly marking time until retirement; his work has become oppressive and humiliating, or seemingly small changes in his mode of work have made his work life more satisfying and creative. (p. 61)

Much of a man's success in adjusting to the changes brought about during the Middle Adulthood stage hinges on his ability to be flexible, to change in the face of unsatisfying life circumstances and unresolved crises of previous years.

Despite the _potential_ for midlife authenticity crises among both men and women in our society, they are by no means inevitable. Some go through such a crisis, but others do not. In his study of midlife among men, Levinson (1978) found some for whom this period constituted "constriction and decline" in their lives. For others, though, he found quite a different pattern:

Still other men have started a middle adulthood that will have its own special satisfactions and fulfillments. For these men, middle adulthood is often the fullest and most creative season in the life cycle. They are less tyrannized by the ambitions, passions, and illusions of youth. They can be more deeply attached to others and yet more separate, more centered in the self. For them, the season passes in its best and most satisfying rhythm (Levinson, 1978:62).

There are ways to prevent the authenticity crisis from being as severe as it is for many people. For example, women who have followed the traditional gender-role patterns of full-time "housewife and mother" might branch out by joining voluntary organizations in the community, going back to college to complete a degree, or starting work in a new career. Such steps, if taken _before_ the children have all left home, will provide alternative means of self-fulfillment and self-confidence once the children are gone. Men, on approaching this stage, might prevent midlife crisis by tempering their career goals, considering a change in careers, or seeking further education or training when they realize that their dreams for the future may be "impossible dreams." Finally, for both men and women, the impact of midlife crisis will be lessened if they are able to maintain a viable marriage relationship over the years, one built on flexibility, adaptability to change, open communication, compromise, and a solid bond of mutual affection. Maintaining positive relationships with adult children and close friends also helps to prevent adjustment difficulties or crises in midlife (Levinson, 1978).

PASSAGE INTO MIDDLE AND OLD AGE

Middle age, which lasts approximately between the ages of 50 and 65, is a time of renewal and growth after the crises of midlife have been successfully resolved. It is an age of maturity. This maturity is the result of the stock-taking experience; the modifying of dreams and aspirations; and the improvements in judgment which have been developed during the midlife crises. When coupled with the departure of children, and entry into the postparental stage of the marital career, middle age can mean having more time to pursue hobbies or other interests initiated years before, such as photography, sewing, bowling, traveling, or golf, or just catching up on reading best-selling novels. Lidz (1976:493 – 495) points to a number of other satisfactions in middle age that contribute to personal well-being in this stage. Middle-aged people

1. know what will work and what will be a waste of time and energy.

2. know their abilities and have the satisfaction of feeling in control of them.

3. are wiser in approaching tasks, making decisions, and convincing others of their points of view.

4. are old and experienced hands on the job, which can yield security, special privileges, and deference from co-workers.

5. can be mentors for younger persons, to whom they can bequeath their knowledge and impart their interests to be carried forward into the next generation.

Middle age is not without its problems, however. The body is aging, sexual functions and abilities tend to decline, and the person must face up to the inevitable fact that the end of life is drawing nearer. Those who have never successfully resolved, or coped with, the midlife crises associated with children leaving the home, reaching the career plateau, or juggling work versus family problems, are likely to have trouble adjusting to the demands of middle age. Stress from the pressures and demands of the job combine with certain physical changes to increase susceptibility to hypertension, heart attacks, strokes, and other cardiovascular diseases. In addition, research has shown that midlife transitions create more stress when they are "off-schedule"—early or late, according to the per-

son's expectations (Harkins, 1978; Neugarten, 1976). For example, early or late departure of children from the home, unexpected retirement, or early death of a spouse create more problems in adjustment than the same events occuring when they are expected. Expected changes that take place "on time" can be anticipated, and psychological preparations to meet them can be made.

There are a number of factors that can give *positive* direction to middle age and help to avoid some of these problems (Levinson, 1978; Huyck and Hoyer, 1982; Lidz, 1976):

1. Adaptability to changing physical capabilities, family environment, and circumstances relating to work and career.

2. Coming to accept and approve of one's self and one's life in their own right, without concern for what others might think or what others have done, complete with successes and failures, strengths and weaknesses, wise decisions and errors in judgment.

3. Being able to meet one's personal needs for companionship, as well as privacy, in marriage by finding an acceptable balance between the two.

4. Successful resolution of any midlife crises that emerged in one's thirties and forties, especially those relating to career and family interests.

5. Maintaining an active life-style, including physical exercise, sound nutritional habits, intellectual pursuits (reading, for example), and sex. For any of these aspects of life the maxim holds true, *"Use it, or lose it!"*

6. Maintaining meaningful and satisfying relationships with the social support networks of friends and adult children, including grandchildren.

A person enters the *aging years* at about age 65, when retirement from their career or work takes place. This stage of life ushers in a distinct set of problems, as well as satisfactions. Retirement is a major turning point, and whether it has a positive or negative influence depends on whether the individual wishes to retire or was forced to retire because of advancing age; whether or not the retirement income is adequate to meet one's desired standard of living; and whether a person enters the retirement years in good health or in poor health.

Physical changes also occur in old age. Many aging people at some point enter *senescence,* that point in life when degenerative processes that lead to the breakdown of the organism gradually overtake regenerative biological processes (Huyck and Hoyer, 1982:74). Senescence is a *long-term, gradual,* and *normal* aging process that is different from *senility,* a mental disease process.[2] Senescence means that the body's immune system becomes less effective, making it more susceptible to disease, infection, viruses, and lingering injuries that take longer to heal than in earlier years. Cells break down faster than they can be replaced. The bones become more brittle and are easily broken. The veins and arteries become thickened and hardened (arteriosclerosis), the walls of the arteries continue buildup of fatty substances (atherosclerosis), and the person becomes increasingly susceptible to paralyzing strokes and heart attacks. The sensory capabilities of hearing, sight, taste, smell, and touch all decline as the person ages, and the person's ability to react quickly declines. The sex drive diminishes for many, and sexual activity becomes far less frequent and enjoyable.

Finally, the death of one spouse means that the other will be spending at least some time in widowhood. Because men die earlier than women (on the average of 7.5 years earlier), there were three times as many widows as widowers over the age of 65 in the United States in 1982 (National Center for Health Statistics, 1984c; U.S. Bureau of the Census, 1983c). This can be a time of loneliness and despair for those who have difficulty adjusting to the loss of a partner.

The aging years also have their rewarding aspects. Lidz (1976) points out that old age can bring a sense of completeness to one's life, and allows time for leisure activities that had been postponed because of work-related commitments before retirement. The aging person is free from the daily competition, demands, and struggles in the world of work. There is more free time to spend with one's grown children, and with the children's children. Factors that contribute to one's well-being in this stage are good health; sound nutritional habits; regular physical activity and exercise; adequate income and housing; satisfying relationships with friends, children, and grandchildren; and a satisfying and stable marriage relationship which provides a source of fond memories and a continuing basis for satisfying personal needs for love, affection, and intimacy.

The Postparental Stage: An Empty Nest?

The transition to the postparental stage is marked by the launching from the home of the couple's last child. For this reason, it is usually referred to as the *empty nest* stage, a phrase which has the negative connotation of "emptiness" and "loneliness" for the parents whose children no longer live with them.

The postparental years mean a return to the "couple relationship" that existed during the early years, before the transition to first parenthood took place. This entails a substantial *reduction* in the *role clusters* of each marriage partner and in the *role complex* of the family unit as a whole. Some parental roles are dropped altogether, such as caretaking and disciplinarian roles, and others are greatly modified in the form of *role sequences* (see chapter 2). As children become adults, expectations and behavior in such roles as communicator, confidant, affection-giver and receiver, and decision-maker tend to be modified, in order to conform to what is appropriate for the maturity level of the young adult. Parents and their children usually assume a *peer relationship,* which replaces the "parent superior–child subordinate" relationship that existed through the years. These changes point to a less time-consuming and energy-draining stage in the marital career than parents had known when children were present. This represents a turning point, in that the family unit is *contracting,* after several years of growth and expansion as children were added and as they grew. Without the daily responsibilities and demands of children, marriage partners now have more time and energy to devote *to each other* than they have had for many years. Whether they take up golf, tennis, traveling, or just spending the evening chatting with one another and going for long walks, new roles can be forged to add new dimensions to the marriage relationship. With the return to the couple relationship, both partners may be better able to contribute to the satisfying of each other's needs, whether they are sexual needs, needs for companionship or intimacy, or just listening to one another's troubles. Hence, the opportunity for *role reciprocity* in marriage grows in the postparental stage.

All of these changes toward a less complicated lifestyle would seem to indicate that the transition into this stage is only a mildly *critical role-transition point* for the marriage partners. It is a transition in the marital career for which partners can prepare and plan for before it arrives (Aldous, 1978). As we shall see, this is true for many couples, as satisfaction in marriage often increases with the departure of children. For others, however, the postparental stage can be a disappointment. After years of child-raising, and focusing the major portion of their time, attention, and efforts on children, marriage partners may have placed their marriage relationship on the "back-burner" for so long that they no longer know how to relate to one another in an intimate way. There may be awkwardness because they no longer have their children around to divert their attention from one another. After children leave home, a husband and wife may find they are locked into rigid and unsatisfying *interaction habits* that are resistant to the demands for change in this stage. Maintaining the *status quo* of role expectations and behavior can do more harm than good at a time when flexibility and adaptability are needed to cope with the rather significant changes pressing on both partners' personal and married lives. For example, if the wife has stayed at home raising the children, she may now be ready to seek more education or begin working in a new career. If a husband is unwilling to support his wife in these efforts, then conflict and dissatisfaction can emerge in the marriage relationship. Poor communication habits, inadequate patterns of relating intimately with each other, and the lack of a solid bond of mutual affection in earlier stages may lead to the same results in the postparental stage. Indeed, the partners' satisfaction with marriage may have dropped so low during the middle years (see chapter 13, Figure 13.1), and their patterns of relating to each other (or *not* relating) may have become so ingrained, and so brittle, that they have stayed together only for the "sake of the children." For some, the first step taken when entering the postparental stage is divorce.

At least two factors influence the quality of marriage in the postparental stage. First, the passages, turning points, and crises of personal development across the adulthood years (discussed before) can have a strong impact on the quality of marriage. The nature of the crises, how constructively they are handled, and how much marriage partners *help each other* in working through their own developmental turning points, will shape the effects they have on marriage. Second, the strength and flexibility of the *marital interaction habits* established in previous

stages of the marital career will carry over and influence the postparental stage. After several years of marriage, many couples are unable or unwilling to break out of unsatisfying patterns of communication, decision making, and exchanging affection, and fail to change as the circumstances surrounding the entry into postparenthood change. These points will be elaborated now as we look more closely at the specific domains of marriage in this stage.

LOVE AND AFFECTION

A number of studies of satisfaction with marriage during the postparental stage provide an interesting picture (see Figure 14.3). On average, it appears that satisfaction with marriage takes a significant upswing in this stage. It appears that for the average couple, the "rewards" outweigh the "costs" in the postparental stage. Whether it is "decreased role strain," "more time for each other," "heightened intimate communication and companionship with each other," "a renewed sense of love for one another," or "relief from passing through midlife crises," the quality of marriage during postparenthood appears to improve (Deutscher, 1964; Glenn, 1975a; Harkins, 1978). According to Deutscher (1964), there are a number of factors characterizing marriages in which satisfaction increases after children have left home:

1. Freedom from the financial responsibilities of children; freedom to be geographically mobile; freedom from housework and other chores; and freedom to be one's self for the first time since the children came along.

2. Better relationships with one another because one or both now get along better, are more amiable, do more "fun things" together as a couple, and can feel a "sense of accomplishment in a job well done" as a team.

3. Having a number of other involvements *before* they made the transition into postparenthood, such as hobbies, voluntary organizations, religious activities, caring for aging parents, and weekend recreational activities.

Satisfaction in marriage tends to decline when the following conditions are paramount in this stage:

1. Physical changes associated with the aging process, such as menopause, and declining physical strength and stamina.

FIGURE 14.3.   Satisfaction and Adjustment in Marriage from the Early Years Through the Aging Years.

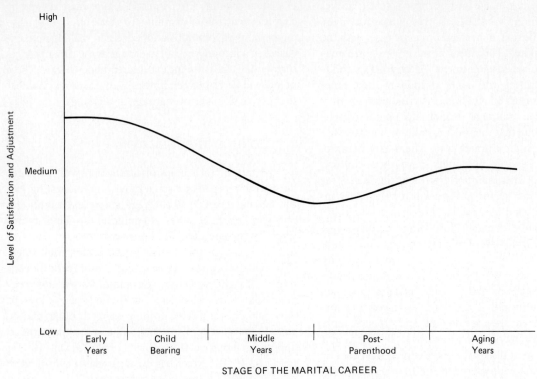

2. Looking in retrospect at one's career accomplishments and child-raising efforts, and defining those as "failures."

3. The *"family void"* — the empty place in the family resulting from the children's departure — cannot be filled because meaningful alternative roles do not exist.

Recall that in chapter 3, we said that the definition of love as a basis for maintaining intimate relationships changes over the course of a person's life. What begins as passionate and romantic love during the premarital years usually changes during the marital career to a more mature type of love, love based on mutual respect and understanding between the partners. Hence, the resurging marital satisfaction during postparenthood probably does *not,* in most cases, reflect a return of passionate love. Rather, love in this stage is based more on companionship and a mutual understanding and acceptance of each other's needs, interests, and role expectations (Feldman, 1964).

GENDER ROLES

A considerable degree of *continuity* exists in the gender-role patterns of marriage from previous stages of the marital career into the postparental stage. The typical pattern in marriage is to move from a shared, joint-role organization during the early years to a more segregated organization as children are added, grow, and place increasing demands on the time and energy resources of the husband-father and wife-mother. All of this is happening at the time when any midlife crises are at a peak. The husband may be preoccupied with the realization that he has reached the top of his career ladder, and that he has failed to reach his career goals. This situation may hasten the role-segregation process as he becomes engrossed in his problems at work. The same is true for the wife's midlife crises, as she takes stock of her marriage, parenting experiences, and decisions relating to work outside of the home.

Many women reenter the work force either just before or shortly after their children have left home, perhaps as a means of resolving a midlife crisis or because of a concern relating to her own personal development. Usually this is a seeking for personal stimulation and fulfillment, and is a means of avoiding boredom after the children have left home. Going back into the work force is likely to be an important boost to many women's self development and psychological well-being, and requires the encouragement and support of her husband. This may call for a considerable degree of adjustment on the part of the husband in a traditional type of single-earner marriage. For years, the husband may have been proud of his ability to provide for the family's financial needs so that his wife would not have to work outside of the home. He may also have grown accustomed to the wife's support of his career pursuits, and may be uncomfortable in supporting hers (Burke and Weir, 1976). If it should happen that he is undergoing his own personal midlife crisis relating to his career achievements and outlook, he may feel insecure and threatened by the fact that his wife is going back to work.

Gender-role flexibility and adaptability to change demands are clearly the keys to successful marital adjustment in this situation. Being open to change and being willing to communicate with each other about their changing personal needs and goals will contribute to the upswing in marital satisfaction in this stage. Resistance to change can create conflict, stress, and frustration in the marriage, and may hasten the process of disenchantment, which typically begins in earlier stages (see chapters 12 and 13).

SEXUALITY AND FAMILY PLANNING

The Female Climacteric and Menopause. By the time most couples enter the postparental stage, family planning is no longer an issue. Although males in this age range are still producing viable sperm and are capable of impregnating a woman, nearly all women will have undergone physiological changes that cause them to lose their fecundity, or ability to conceive children. The sum of these changes is a process called the *female climacteric*. The cessation of ovulation (production of eggs) and monthly menstrual periods, known as *menopause,* is one part of the climacteric. By age fifty, most women have undergone menopause naturally (Lake,

1979). Menopause is often a gradual process, but it varies from one woman to the next in terms of the time it takes to complete itself.

Menopause involves a decline in the body's production of the female hormones estrogen and progesterone, which causes the ovulation process to cease and the uterine wall (endometrium) to stop developing a blood-rich lining. This drop in hormone production is often linked to a number of stressful symptoms reported by menopausal women (see Table 14.1). However, many of these symptoms have not been directly linked to the climacteric and are probably associated with aspects of aging and "midlife crises" other than hormonal changes. The two that do seem to be related to change in hormone levels are *hot flashes* and changes in the vagina (Godow, 1982; Huyck and Hoyer, 1982). Hot flashes are momentary spells—marked by a sense of heat in the upper torso and face, followed by sweating and then chills. Spells can last anywhere from several seconds to a minute or two, and often occur at night and interrupt the woman's sleep. Changes in the woman's vagina include a thinning and loss of elasticity in the vaginal walls, as well as decreased lubrication

TABLE 14.1. *Symptoms Identified With the Female Climacteric*

---

* Hot flashes
* Thinning and loss of elasticity in the vaginal walls
  Dizziness
  Headache
  Muscular pain
  Depression and sadness (melancholia)
  Inflammation of the joints
  Weakness and fatigue
  Itching
  Sleeplessness (insomnia)
  Anxiety
  Weight gain
  Irritability
  Inability to concentrate
  Intolerance
  Hypersensitivity (easily upset)
  Diarrhea

---

* Only symptoms directly linked to hormonal changes.

SOURCES: Godow (1982); Huyck and Hoyer (1982); Lidz (1976).

during sexual arousal. This can result in some discomfort during the early stages of sexual intercourse, and in some women may lead to vaginal burning, aching in the lower abdominal area, and irritation of the urethra and bladder, which causes burning during urination following intercourse. Both hot flashes and vaginal changes can be treated with hormone drugs, but because of the possible medical complications from the use of such drugs, one should consult a physician and be informed about the potential risks involved in taking them.

As Godow (1982:457) points out, menopause has psychological aspects as well. It is a clear signal to many women that they are getting older, are losing their "feminine appeal," and are losing their unique biological capability for producing children:

During the climacteric women are forced to deal with the facts that they are losing their capacity to reproduce and more generally that they are aging. It is the symbolic meaning of menopause that may be most disturbing. Most women do not wish to bear children at the age of 45 or 50, but the experience of menopause may intensify the real loss they feel as their children leave home. If a woman's role as mother has been the major component of her personal identity, she may well be struggling with an identity crisis . . . In a culture that overemphasizes youth and physical beauty the 50-year-old woman may interpret menopause as a sign that she is no longer desirable as a woman and that she soon will lose her physical and sexual attractiveness.

The climacteric may also have positive outcomes and improve certain aspects of a woman's life in this stage. For example, the fear of unintentional pregnancy is no longer present, so they do not have to undergo the risks and inconveniences of birth control methods. This can increase the woman's ability to "let go" sexually and thereby enjoy sexual activity more than in previous years. The bother and discomforts of menstruation are no longer present. In any event, the number and severity of physical symptoms during the climacteric vary widely from one woman to the next.

The Male Climacteric.   Although men do not undergo a process analogous to menopause, because of obvious biological differences between the sexes, there is evidence to suggest that some men undergo a type of male climacteric. The number and viability of sperm produced tends to gradually decline after fifty years of age, and the male sex hormone testosterone is produced in slightly smaller quantities. The drop in hormone levels, in combination with the midlife stresses and strains men are going through at this point in their lives, can result in a number of climacteric symptoms: loss of sexual interest and potency; physical weakness and fatigue; mood swings involving depression and anxiety; and poor appetite and weight loss. However, these symptoms appear in less than 10 percent of all men sixty years of age and older (Henker, 1981).

Sexuality and Sexual Behavior.   A common myth is that men and women naturally tend to lose their ability to respond sexually in middle age. To the contrary, both men and women are fully capable of enjoying sexual relations in this stage (Masters and Johnson, 1966). Problems in sexual potency, or in enjoying sexual relations, are probably more a result of people thinking that these problems are going to occur. Because they *think* they will be less sexually interested and responsive, they often behave in a way that confirms their expectations — a *self-fulfilling prophecy*. They try to repress their continuing sexual urges, and may feel guilty or ashamed that they are still having them. However, the actual changes in sexuality are relatively minor, and most people in this stage are capable of maintaining a satisfying sex life. The changes in males include: (1) decreasing amount and forcefulness of ejaculation; (2) less frequent and less rigid erections; (3) longer periods of time between an orgasm and when the next erection can be developed; and (4) longer periods of stimulation in order to reach an erection and to experience orgasm (DeLora and Warren, 1977; Witters and Jones-Witters, 1980; Godow, 1982). This last change may actually add to the sexual enjoyment of the couple. The "staying power" of the male is increased, thereby allowing more time for the female to reach one or more orgasms during each sexual act.

Changes in female sexuality during middle age include: (1) changes in the vaginal walls and vaginal lubrication ability; (2) more easily fatigued during sexual intercourse; (3) decrease in engorgement of vaginal area; and (4) less frequent and less intense orgasmic contractions.

Despite this capability of most men and women to enjoy sexual relations during the middle and later years of life, the actual frequency and enjoyment of sexual activity declines rather sharply. In a large national study conducted in the 1970s, it was found that 50 percent of the women and 25 percent of the men over the age of 60 reported having no sexual intercourse in the previous six months (Wilson, 1975). Only 12 percent of the women and 27 percent of the men reported having sexual intercourse one or two times a month or more often. In another study (Pfeiffer and Davis, 1968; Pfeiffer, Verwoerdt, and Davis, 1972), 11 percent of the men and 51 percent of the women in the 61- to 65-year-old group reported no interest in sex. In terms of actual frequency of sexual intercourse, 12 percent of the men and 44 percent of the women between the ages of 46 and 71 reported that they had stopped having sexual intercourse altogether.

In view of the continuing capacity for sexual enjoyment that people have into the middle and later years, it is important to ask why the actual frequency of sexual activity drops so sharply. Apart from the fact that some people accept the myth that sexual interest and responsiveness are *supposed* to decline with age, the following reasons appear to be the most common (Godow, 1982; DeLora and Warren, 1977):

1. Illness, declining health, heart problems, and declining physical strength and energy levels.

2. Unavailability of sexual partners among the never-married, divorced, separated, and widowed.

3. Loss of interest in sexual activity by the marriage partner.

4. Monotony and boredom caused by having sexual relations with the same partner for many years.[3]

5. Taking certain drugs prescribed for older people, alcoholism, or preoccupation with career or job-related pursuits.

There are a number of ways, today, that people in the middle age years of life can help themselves reach their potential for sexual responsivity and fulfillment. First, education and reading of authoritative books will help to debunk the myths and negative social attitudes about sexuality in later life, and will teach people that the sexual drive and the ability to respond sexually are normal, natural, and acceptable throughout adulthood. Second, hormonal drug treatments can help to alleviate the problems of dryness and atrophy of the vagina, as can creams and lubricants. Third, a history of rewarding and regular sexual activity carries over into this stage and has a positive influence on sexual functioning and enjoyment (Masters and Johnson, 1966). Atrophy in the sexual organs and

inability to enjoy sex in later life are more common among people who "failed to use it" in younger years. Finally, a solid relationship with one's partner, built upon trust, understanding, and open communication about sexual needs and desires can greatly enhance the chances for realizing one's potential for sexual fulfillment.

Although changes in hormone levels and those brought on by aging may mean, for many people, a slightly lower level of sexual interest and responsivity in later life, the potential for sexual enjoyment and ability to respond sexually remains quite high for most people throughout the adult years.

COMMUNICATION AND CONFLICT MANAGEMENT

For many couples, satisfaction with marriage increases as the departure of children allows more time and opportunity for communicating with one another. However, this boost in morale is dependent upon whether or not spouses actually take advantage of the new opportunities that postparenthood provides. Recall, from the discussion of disenchantment in chapter 13, that the frequency of communication declines, and the frequency of marital conflict and disagreement increases, over time. This places the couple at a major crossroads when children leave home. Are they going to continue these trends toward less talking *to* each other *about* each other, and have more conflicts? Or will this pattern be broken — the spouses turning inward toward one another, in an effort to reestablish some of the old intimacy and affection, and to rekindle the "spark" that may have dimmed over the years?

Good communication habits are also of critical importance as individual spouses move through midlife transitions or crises. Women tend to experience such crises earlier than men. Therefore, each partner is in a position to help the other cope with the dilemmas and changes they are facing. For example, women going through menopause and other symptoms of the climacteric period need sympathy, understanding, and sensitivity from their mates. Husbands must be aware that the wife's climacteric accounts for a measure of distress and discomfort, whether in the form of hot flash spells or discomfort during sexual intercourse. (The danger here is that he might blame her or himself for her menopausal problems.) But whether it is to rekindle the spark of intimacy and love, to make joint plans for the future, or to create a satisfying sexual life in marriage, open two-way channels of communication during the postparental years are a necessary ingredient.

ECONOMICS

In chapter 13 we discussed the increasing costs of raising a family over the stages of the marital career. When children are teenagers they cost the most to feed, clothe, educate, and insure, and many parents have not yet reached their earnings peak. The ratio of economic resources to costs may therefore be gradually shrinking in many families, particularly when only one breadwinner is working outside of the home. Oppenheimer (1974) refers to this as the "life-cycle squeeze," and it is particularly devastating for low-income families in which earning levels rise only slowly and never peak at a very high level.

This trend is reversed in the postparental stage (Aldous and Hill, 1969). Many postparental couples can breathe easier once children have been launched from the home. They may now have a greater ability to save and invest money, or to go on vacation trips together, things that could only be dreamed about when children were present. Being removed from the vice-like grip of the "life-cycle squeeze" adds to the boost in satisfaction that many couples report in this stage. However, the degree of economic relief during the postparental stage depends upon the degree to which parents assume an obligation to continue financially supporting their children, either in college or in some other way.

PARENTHOOD

Significant *role sequences* in parental roles take place as children grow into adulthood and strike out on their own. Role expectations and behavior change as parents relate to their children more as peers. The role behaviors and expectations of the children change as well. Adult children are no longer as directly dependent upon their parents, either emotionally or financially, as they once were. Nor are parents any longer directly responsible for the care, safety, and well-being of their children. Their

children are now relatively free to choose their own friends and engage in the activities of their choice without parental interference. Eventually, the great majority will marry, enter work careers of their own, and have children — and the cycle will repeat itself for the younger generation. The postparental stage clearly represents a dramatic shift in the form and function of parent-child relationships. Parent-child relationships can be rewarding and gratifying, or frustrating and conflicting, in this stage.

Parents and Adult Children: Alike or Different?   Although parents and their adolescent children may undergo many conflicts, and feel that they are worlds apart on many issues in life, by the time adolescents reach adulthood they and their parents are remarkably similar to each other (Bengtson and Troll, 1978). Parents and their adult children tend to see eye to eye in terms of *political* values and orientations; *religious* attitudes, behavior, and affiliation; values placed on *work* and *achievement;* and even in *gender roles* and *attitudes toward sexual permissiveness*. Relationships between the generations are bound to be more rewarding and have fewer conflicts if parents and their adult children share similar attitudes and values in areas that are important to them.

Parents and Adult Children: Do They Keep in Touch?   In addition to shared values and attitudes, it appears that most parents and their adult children maintain contact on a fairly regular basis (Adams, 1968; Reiss, 1980). This is in contrast to the belief among some observers of the family system in contemporary society that the new nuclear family units formed by young adults who marry and bear children are isolated from their extended kin, including their parents and parents-in-law. If the parents and their adult children reside in the same community, most see each other and interact face-to-face on a daily or weekly basis. Many go out to social activities together, belong to the same organizations, or just get together to visit. For those who are separated by geographic distance, interaction takes place by means of telephone conversations, exchange of letters, and visits. However, distance does reduce the frequency of interaction to monthly or several times yearly, on the average. In any event, the typical pattern today is one of continued and fairly regular contact between adult children and their parents in this stage.

Parents and Adult Children: Do They Still Love Each Other? There is strong evidence to suggest that the bond of affection and love that kept them together during the child's years of growing up carries over into this stage. Whereas children were expected to *respect* their parents while growing up, parents now tend to reciprocate by respecting their adult children. Similarly, whereas parents felt a one-way *obligation* to care for their children while the children were growing, children tend to reciprocate as adults by assuming an obligation to care for their middle-aged parents. Hence, the entire structure of parent-adult child relationships tends to shift toward more mutuality and reciprocity than had previously been the case (Adams, 1968). Mutual feelings of love and affection between middle-aged parents and their adult children are more likely when they agree on major life values, share common interests or hobbies, and enjoy each other's company in occasional social activities.

Adult Children, Parents, and In-laws: Conflicts and Problems. A number of families experience serious conflicts and problems between the generations, many of which can pose a threat to the future quality of these relationships. First, parents and their adult children may differ in their expectations of how much influence each should have in the other's activities and decisions. Parents may attempt to influence whether or not the child will go to college; which college; the child's sexual behavior before marriage; when the child will marry; to whom the child will become married; where the young couple will live; where they will spend their holidays; when the newly married offspring will provide the parents with grandchildren; and how those grandchildren should be parented. Many adult children resent and resist this kind of interference, and serious conflict may erupt as a result. Some parents are unable to let go, and feel that they must keep a hand in their children's lives, even when they are adults. It is difficult for them to grant their children the independence they need to live their own lives, probably because they have grown accustomed to their child's dependence on them for so many years.

Adult children can also be meddlesome, and try to push uninvited advice or assistance on their parents. This is not welcomed by those middle-aged adults who are reveling in their new-found freedom from parental concerns and responsibilities, and who are enjoying their return to the couple relationship (Aldous, 1978).

If left unresolved, parent-child and in-law problems can develop into destructive long-term conflicts. When they do arise, it is important that both sides invoke effective interpersonal skills: communication, compromise, constructive conflict resolution, and above all, a high level of mutual respect and love. Those who are unable to solve their problems may find themselves and their loved ones in a position of withdrawing mutual aid, engaging in less frequent contacts, and, most tragic of all, withdrawing their love and affection from one another.

GRANDPARENTS

In addition to the couples' having a number of years together again without children in the home, the postparental stage is a time for another key transition: the transition into *grandparenthood*. Because of our increased longevity and earlier transition into the postparental stage (see page 409), more people today are grandparents than in past generations; they are becoming grandparents at younger ages; and they are able to enjoy that role, and observe the growth and development of their children's children, for a greater number of years than ever before. Grandparents today can enjoy a renewed intimacy that grandchildren can bring to their lives, enhancing the middle-aged person's sense of feeling wanted and needed. This allows them to accomplish what Erikson (1980) described as the *task of generativity* in middle-age — caring for and being concerned about younger generations and receiving care and concern in return.

Most grandparents enjoy their new roles (Neugarten and Weinstein, 1964). For many, being grandparents means having the pleasure of young children's company without the responsibilities that they knew previously as parents. Grandparenthood is found to be a significant and meaningful role in the lives of middle-aged adults, for a number of reasons:

1. *Biological renewal and/or biological continuity* with the future: "It's through my grandchildren that I feel young again." "It's through these children that we are carrying on the family line."

2. *Emotional self-fulfillment* through being better grandparents than they were parents: "I have a second chance to do the things for my grandchildren, things I could never do for my own kids."

3. *Being a teacher or resource person,* reaping satisfaction by contributing to the child's welfare through financial assistance, gifts, companionship, or sharing of the grandparents' "wisdom about life."

4. *Vicarious accomplishment and pride* via the grandchild, who represents an extension of the grandparent's self and an opportunity for ego enhancement (Neugarten and Weinstein, 1964:201–202).

However, some grandparents have difficulty in the grandparent role. For some, the idea of grandparenthood does not fit their self-image ("I'm too young to be a grandparent"), and others dislike the way the grandchildren are being raised. Still others feel a "psychological distance" from their grandchildren.

Neugarten and Weinstein (1964) found five types of grandparents in their study:

1. *The Formal* They play the "proper and prescribed role for grandparents"; although they are interested in the grandchild and provide "special treats and indulgences," they maintain clearly demarcated lines of authority between grandparent, parent, and child, and do not interfere in the parents' efforts to parent.

2. *The Fun Seeker* They maintain an "informal and playful" relationship with the grandchild, much as with a playmate, with the specific goal of having fun and providing mutual satisfaction for themselves and their grandchildren.

3. *The Surrogate Parent* This occurs when the grandparent, most often the grandmother, assumes the normal child-care responsibilities for the parents when both are working outside of the home.

4. *The Reservoir of Family Wisdom* This occurs when the grandparent, usually the grandfather, maintains a special, favored position at the top of the family hierarchy and "dispenses special skills or resources" to others ("sometimes with and sometimes without resentment").

5. *The Distant Figure* He or she maintains "fleeting and infrequent" contacts with the grandchild, usually on holidays or special family occasions. The grandparent and grandchild are not important parts of each other's lives, although the grandparent does main-

tain a "benevolent stance" by providing gifts from time to time.

Over half of all the grandparents in Neugarten and Weinstein's study were either the Fun Seeker or Distant Figure types. Both of these types were younger, on the average, than other types of grandparents. They represent new styles of grandparenthood, emerging because of the increase of relatively young grandparents in the postparental stage of the marital career.

The Aging Years: 'Til Death Do Us Part

With retirement of both spouses from the world of work outside the home comes entry into the final stage of the marital career—the aging years. The length of time a couple spends in this stage depends on two factors—their ages at retirement, and when the death of one of the partners occurs. As is true for other stages in the marital career, the transition into this stage from the postparental can be a gradual one. For most people, however, retirement occurs between the ages of 60 and 70, after the spouses have spent a number of years in the postparental stage.

GROWING OLD IN CONTEMPORARY SOCIETY

Our population grows "older" with each passing year. That is, the proportion of our population over the age of 65 increases slightly every year. In 1900, only 4 percent of the American population was 65 years of age or older, and only 72 percent born that year were expected to live to age 64 (Huyck and Hoyer, 1982:27). By 1950, the number grew to 8 percent of the population, or 12 million people over the age of 65. By 1982, nearly 12 percent of our population was 65 or older, comprising 27 million people (U.S. Bureau of the Census, 1983c). This percentage is expected to rise to 13.7 percent by the year 2000 and 21.7 percent by 2050. In 1982, there were 2.5 million people age 85 and older—the "old" old; but by the year 2050, when those people born in 1984 reach the retirement age of 65, our society will have *16 million* people age 85 and older! This aging of our society is caused by the declining birth rate of the 1960s and 1970s, combined with the longer life expectancies (longevity) of our population. A person born in 1981 has a life expectancy of just over 74 years, 70.4 for males and 77.9 for females (National Center for Health Statistics, 1984c). The relative proportion of people in the upper end of the age scale has grown as a result.

Although we might consider it to be a good thing to have people living longer, the aging of our population has caused a number of social, economic, and health-related needs, which, if unmet, threaten the personal and physical well-being of millions of people in our society. The number of years that people live after they retire has increased, whether they are married, single, or widowed. This has added to the economic problems of this age group, and has posed a heavy economic burden on society as a whole. Medical costs of the elderly have mushroomed, as their numbers grow. The Social Security System is in a perpetual state of difficulty, as the amount of money being contributed by today's workers must be regularly increased to cover the monthly benefits paid to the retired. This means that the elderly of the future may have to rely on other means of economic support, such as savings, retirement or pension funds, long-term bonds, and the yields from other investments (see Appendix).

The aging population has also added to the number of elderly dependent on their adult children or other relatives for aid and support. This places another heavy responsibility on the shoulders of the younger population. There has been a related boom in the need for services and long-term housing for the elderly, such as those provided by community agencies, nursing homes, and hospitals. The elderly often have special transportation needs, and many require special types of medical services that only a limited number of medical specialists are able to provide. For example, as of 1982, the number of *geriatricians* (medical doctors specializing in the health problems, diseases, and treatment of elderly people) was very small in the U.S. relative to many other countries. All of these problems are serious and immediate, and as a society we are still searching for the answers. If left unsolved, they will continue to have an adverse effect on the morale of this segment of our population, as well as the morale of those whose lives are touched by the problems of the elderly.

ECONOMIC FUNCTIONING AND AGING

With retirement comes a leveling off of income for some people; but many others experience a decline in income that places a severe burden on their personal well-being and ability to enjoy life in this stage. The family income of a person who voluntarily retires declines, on the average, by one-third (33 percent) [Sproat, 1983]. Many elderly people are on a fixed income, composed of their pension checks, social security payments, and perhaps some welfare assistance. With the continuing increase in prices brought on by inflation in the economy over the past several years, many elderly have become more financially troubled.

Statistics document the economic plight of many elderly in America. In 1982, 14.6 percent of all Americans 65 and older lived below the poverty line of $5,836 for elderly families and $4,626 for elderly living alone (U.S. Bureau of the Census, 1984a). This rate has remained fairly constant since 1975. The chances of an elderly person being poor are greatest among minorities, women, and those residing in small towns and rural areas. For example, in 1982 38 percent of all Blacks over 65 had incomes below the poverty line, but only 12 percent of whites did. In brief, the aging years are, for many people, a time of financial pressures that demand scrimping and careful budgeting if they are to manage.

The economic woes of the elderly are complicated even further by rising medical and health care costs in this stage of life. Older people have more frequent and serious illnesses, accidents (such as falls) and other medical problems. Therefore, their medical expenses per year average four and five times more than for a person 10 to 20 years younger. Because government insurance programs, such as Medicare and Medicaid, cover only a portion of the elderly's medical expenses, it is imperative that older people carry supplementary hospitalization and major medical insurance if unexpected catastrophic medical expenses are to be handled.

Beyond the economic problems ushered in by retirement are the social and psychological adjustments that the retiree must make. For some, retirement is a difficult transition to make, and stress is placed on retirees and their spouses as a result. For others, retirement is welcomed and gives a tremendous boost to one's morale in later life.

[R]etirement can be a period of either potential enrichment which provides freedom to pursue meaningful avocations and the search for personal wholeness and individuation, or demoralization as a result of the loss of a culturally-dominant social role. Retirement can be a pleasure or a problem. (Darnley, 1975:220)

After working for years in a particular occupation, and possibly even the same place of work, the extra time a retired person has available, the loss of companionship with workmates, and the fact that one's productive contributions are no longer being made, all mean that retirement can be a particularly difficult *critical role-transition point*. The loss of one's occupational roles can be a shock to those who feel they are no longer needed, that they are now useless to other people and to the society. This is most likely to occur to those who are forced to retire early by their companies, or who reach the retirement age of 65 or 70 and feel that they are still healthy and energetic enough to keep on working, producing, and contributing.

Other retirees, however, are able to plan for retirement both psychologically and emotionally *before* they actually retire. They begin, psychologically, to disengage from their work, and attempt to envision what life after retirement will be like (Atchley, 1977). Their adjustment is assured if they are flexible enough to meet the challenges of their role as a retired person (Darnley, 1975). Retirement means new kinds of activities, such as community volunteer work or working with youth groups; the pursuit of favorite hobbies, such as fishing, hunting, traveling; or just plain "rest and relaxation."

The degree of personal satisfaction and fulfillment in retirement depends primarily on two factors: *money and health* (Stinnett, Carter, and Montgomery, 1972; Streib and Schneider, 1971). Given the economic facts, it is clear that, at this stage, some retirees will not be able to afford the expenses of their planned activities, and they will become disappointed with the retirement role very quickly. These people must adjust their expectations and dreams downward if they are to maintain their morale in this stage of life (Atchley, 1977). Failing health or a debilitating illness at this time can also lead to adjustment problems in retirement (Quinn, 1983; Kent and Matson, 1972). Retirement per se is not a difficult or problematic transition point for most retirees. Only when serious loss of income, declining health, or both follow closely upon the heels of retirement do adjustment problems increase to a significant degree.

LOVE AND AFFECTION

As depicted in Figure 14.3, the level of satisfaction and adjustment in the aging years tends to level off following the postparenthood upswing. Many couples continue to enjoy the security and comfort reestablished in their marital relationship following the departure of their grown children. That this occurs despite the decline in economic resources is even more remarkable. One study of elderly spouses found that the majority (95 percent) rated their marriages as either "very happy" or "happy," and 53 percent reported that their marriages had become "better" over time (Stinnett, Carter, and Montgomery, 1972). A more recent study of couples married fifty years or more found that most viewed this stage of marriage to be "very satisfying," and that spouses in this stage reported understanding each other more than ever before (Sporakowski and Hughston, 1978).

A number of studies have shown that marriage and the love, nurturance, and companionship it provides in the aging years has important positive functions for the personal well-being of each partner. Very often two elderly spouses have each other, and *only* each other, to take care of and be taken care of, to love and be loved. *Role reciprocity* is therefore paramount in this stage. Elderly people who are married report being more satisfied with life, having more meaningful social relationships, and being better off psychologically than do the divorced and widowed elderly (Hutchinson, 1975; Gubrium, 1974; Longino and Lipman, 1981). An older person's sense of personal well-being is enhanced if marriage is satisfying to them (Hill and Dorfman, 1982; Lee, 1978; Stinnett, et al., 1972). The most frequently cited satisfactions with this stage are "companionship activities," "a more flexible schedule," "having time to do what you want," and "being able to express true feelings to each other." When asked what was the "most important factor in achieving marital success," most older respondents (48.6 percent) say *"being in love"* (Stinnett, et al., 1972).

Problems in marriage are most likely to be "having different philosophies of life," "being together *too* much," "declining health and financial resources," and "lack of mutual interests" (Stinnett, et al., 1972; Hill and Dorfman, 1982). For many, however, being in a satisfying marriage during the aging years provides a buffer against some of the depression and distress brought on by declining health and loss of income at retirement (Lee, 1978).

The love, nurturance, and companionship that marriage provides during the aging years has important positive consequences for the well-being of each partner; many elderly couples find this stage of marriage to be "very satisfying." *(Photo by Elizabeth Crews.)*

GENDER ROLES

Whether one or both spouses were working outside of the home, retirement means a greater amount of time spent together during the day. As Zube (1982:152) points out in writing about husband retirees married to homemaking wives:

Retirement requires both partners to assume new responsibilities and also to restructure their time. It is interesting to note that almost half the middle-aged and older men in one study reported a need to maintain a strict schedule. For such men retirement will require temporal adjustments and an understanding and tolerance on the part of their wives.

For many, the preretirement pattern of gender-role behavior will be challenged after retirement. The husband may get in the way if his wife has been responsible for the household chores. There may be confusion or uncertainty about role expectations between the spouses, resulting in awkwardness and perhaps conflict between them. Satisfaction tends to drop for women whose husbands do not have enough to do, or who spend *too much* time together with their wives. These often are husbands who feel a deep sense of personal loss when they retire, and who have difficulty coping with their new status—now located entirely outside of the "world of work."

However, research evidence reviewed by Livson (1983) suggests that gender roles often become more *androgynous* for both men and women in this stage of life. With the departure of children from the home, and retirement, men begin to behave in ways traditionally defined as related to feminine-gender roles without sacrificing their masculine qualities, whereas women tend to move toward more traditionally masculine-role behavior without losing their feminine characteristics. For example, research has shown that men in the middle years become more expressive and nurturant, and women more assertive and powerful, in their relationships with other people. As they age, and with retirement from the competitive world of work, husbands tend to become more interested in establishing closer relationships with their wives. Wives, on the other hand, become more self-confident, autonomous, and focused on developing a separate sense of identity as children are launched from the home. Livson (1983:112) describes participants in studies of couples who have followed the traditional patterns — husband employed full time in an occupation, and wife concerned with care of the home and children. Androgynous gender roles tend to emerge:

> Women become more assertive and analytic while remaining nurturant and open to feelings. Men become more giving and expressive while they continue to be ambitious and assertive. (They) developed cross-sex characteristics by age 50 *without* relinquishing same-sex characteristics. The sexes did not reverse roles; they became more androgynous.

Because of this, spouses may forge a new pattern of role sharing and equal participation in decision making, resulting in a rewarding allocation of roles that is efficient and "gets the job done." Indeed, studies of women who were housewives prior to their husband's retirement have found that the most favorable influence on satisfaction with marriage was having retired husbands who shared in household tasks (Hill and Dorfman, 1982).

Despite these changes, some couples will simply maintain the gender-role pattern established in previous stages of the marital career (Medley, 1977). Housewives may continue with their housekeeping chores and their own interests and hobbies, and their retired husbands may spend their time pursuing leisure activities. If household chores were shared before retirement, particularly if both spouses were employed outside the home, this pattern may continue after retirement. The key to satisfactory adjustment and a person's psychological well-being in this stage of marriage is the degree to which role behavior, whether traditional or androgynous, meets the changing needs and expectations of each spouse brought about by retirement and the departure of children from the home (Livson, 1983).

COMMUNICATION AND CONFLICT MANAGEMENT

Research has shown that a major part of morale and satisfaction in this stage is the presence of a spouse in whom one can confide, share problems, and just talk to (Stinnett, et al., 1972; Lowenthal and Haven, 1968). After so many years of marriage, many couples have settled into comfortable communication patterns that are effective. Brief verbal exchanges, a wink or a nod, a touch or gesture with the hand may be all that is necessary to communicate thoughts and feelings of intimacy effectively. Such forms of communicating show just how well two people can come to know and understand each other over time.

Research is lacking on conflict and conflict management in the aging years. However, it is reasonable to expect that whatever pattern of conflict resolution was established in previous stages of the marital career is likely to be firmly established in a marriage in this stage of development, and therefore extremely difficult to change if it is found to be a problem.

SEXUALITY

A popular belief in our culture is that elderly people lose their sexual drive and need for sexual intimacy. This, however, is a myth. Research has shown that for many, sexuality remains a central aspect of life well into the aging years, and that a substantial number of elderly people will participate in sexual activity and derive satisfaction from it provided that the opportunities to do so are present. According to Butler and Lewis (1976), sexuality in the aging years of marriage can serve a number of useful functions for the aging person as well as for the marital relationship of the aging couple:

1. Provides an opportunity to communicate one's continuing emotional attachment to the other, including one's affection, love, and commitment.

2. It reaffirms one's ability to be sexually assertive and physically capable, to be an effective sex partner.

3. Self-esteem grows in knowing that one continues to be sexually appealing to the partner and capable of giving sexual pleasure.

4. In an intimate relationship, one's sense of security is enhanced.

5. It provides an ongoing opportunity for the physical touching and contact so important for nurturing human growth and development across the entire life span.

Unfortunately, many aging persons believe this myth — that older adults lose their sexual capability — and unnecessarily withdraw from sexuality as a result. Compounding the problem is the disapproving social attitude held by many in our youth-oriented society, i.e., that sexual relations *should not* take place among older people; that it is "disgusting" or "degrading" for the elderly to engage in sexual intercourse or to experience an orgasm. It requires a certain degree of education to prevent this self-fulfilling prophecy from taking place.

Although the physical changes of aging may contribute to a decline in sexual interest and activity, they usually do not lead to their total demise. For the woman, menopause and changes in the uterine and vaginal environment mean that sexual intercourse can be uncomfortable if a lubricant cream or jelly is not used. The number of orgasmic contractions per orgasm is likely to be about half that of younger women, and orgasm may take longer to reach. For males, sperm production decreases with age, as do blood levels of the male hormone *testosterone*. Nonetheless, many men in their 80s and 90s are capable of producing enough sperm to be considered fully capable of impregnating a fecund woman. The major difficulty in sexual functioning for men at this age is developing and maintaining an erection long enough to complete the sexual act (impotence). The aging male also requires a long time to reach orgasm, and has a longer *refractory period* — the amount of time which lapses between ejaculation and a second erection. Each ejaculation contains less seminal fluid than was the case in younger years, and the force of the ejaculation is diminished for older men. The longer time to reach orgasm can have a positive effect on a sexual relationship, however, in that the female partner is able to enjoy a more sustained period of sexual activity, and is more likely to reach one or more orgasms as a result (Witters and Jones-Witters, 1980).

It is not surprising to find a continuing decline in the frequency of sexual activity in this last stage of the marital career. Studies of sexual interest in later adulthood (Pfeiffer and Davis, 1972; Pfeiffer, Verwoerdt, and Davis, 1972) have found that by age 71, 50 percent of the women and 10 percent of the men reported no interest in sexual activity. This compares to only 7 percent of the women and 0 percent of the men in the 46- to 50-year range. In regard to actual sexual intercourse, 95 percent of the 46- to 50-year-old men reported activity at least once a week, which dropped to 28 percent for the 66- to 71-year-old group. For women, the frequency of reported sexual activity dropped to an even lower level: from 60 percent of the 46- to 50-year-group engaging in sexual intercourse at least once a week, to only 11 percent among the 66- to 71-year-old group. Indeed, by age 66 to 71, 24 percent of the men and 73 percent of the women reported a total cessation of sexual activity.

Masters and Johnson (1966), Kinsey, et al. (1953), and Pfeiffer, et al. (1972) identify the following major reasons for the decline in sexual interest and termination of sexual activity in the aging years of marriage. Although these reasons are most commonly observed in the aging male, as reported by male and female spouses alike, they account for sexual decline in women as well.

1. *Monotony caused by repetition of the sexual act with the same person for so many years.* This problem is most likely to exist for couples whose sexual activity was a routine, predictable, and dutiful type of activity, the partners having lost interest in exploring new and creative ways of satisfying each other.

2. *Involvement in, and preoccupation with, career and economic pursuits.* The pressures and psychological stresses associated with striving to achieve success in one's career over the years can have a debilitating effect on sexuality. In a sense, the person's psychic and sexual energies are channeled in the *instrumental* direction demanded by the job and away from an *intimate-expressive* direction more appropriate for the marriage relationship.

3. *Physical and mental fatigue* can reduce sexual responsivity for several hours, or even a day or two, in the aging person.

4. *Physical and mental infirmity of the husband or wife.* Deterioration of health is a common occurrence in the aging population. A number of diseases and physical conditions — for example, arthritis, diabetes, stroke, Alzheimer's disease, heart condition, respiratory

influenza, and pneumonia—are diseases of aging that can inhibit sexual interest and ability. Also, one's interest in sex, and the sex drive, may disappear upon the death of the spouse, a problem far more common among women than men, given the life-expectancy differential between the sexes.

5. *Performance anxiety and fear of performance failure* can follow when one or two episodes of failing to achieve an erection or to reach orgasm creates tension and anxiety. When this happens, the person may wonder if sexual potency is being lost. The fear of failure and the tension it causes prevents the individual from relaxing enough to have a satisfying sexual experience, and all efforts to maintain a sexual life may cease as the person withdraws from any potential opportunities for sexual activity in the future (Godow, 1982).

Researchers and sex therapists agree that the path to a satisfying sex life in advanced years is having regular and continuing sexual activity over the previous years of life. "Use it or lose it" may be a shopworn phrase, but it is true, nonetheless.

Aging Parents and Their Children

About four in five of all people aged 65 and above have living children, and those with children have different life experiences than those with no children (Shanas, 1980). In general, the nature of parent-child relationships tends to reverse itself over the years — from dependency of young children on parents for nurturance, love, and physical support (food, clothing, and shelter) to dependency of the aging parent on the child. In a sense, many middle-aged adults in contemporary society find themselves in a position of caring for their elderly parents—caring for them physically and providing emotional support and affection during the last years of the parents' lives.

The concept of *filial maturity* describes the realization that one's aging parents are in need of substantial assistance and support, and that the adult child should not expect to receive an equal amount of support and assistance in exchange. Filial maturity implies that the child is willing to assume responsibility for taking care of an aging parent who may die at some point in the not-too-distant future (Blenkner, 1965).

Recent surveys suggest that most families achieve a satisfactory level of filial maturity. For example, Seelbach and Hansen (1980) surveyed 359 aging adults (average age of 80 years) and found that 88 percent were "perfectly satisfied" with the treatment received from their families. The "old-old" (over 75) group were more likely to give this response than were the "young-old" (under 75). More than 80 percent considered their families to be the "finest in the world," and stated that they "get as much love and affection from my family now as I ever did before" (p. 93).

After retirement, the two most important factors affecting the quality of life of the aging person are *health* and *economic status* (Streib and Beck, 1980). Aging parents are most likely to expect help from their adult children when they are very poor, ill, living alone, or very old; and adult children are most likely to assist aging parents under such circumstances (Huyck and Hoyer, 1982:291). Foremost is the aging parents' *place of residence*. In 1975, nearly 20 percent of all aging parents (over 65 years) lived in the same household with one of their children (Shanas, 1980). Thirty-four percent lived in separate households but within 10 minutes distance, and only 5 or 6 percent of all older people resided in institutions (nursing homes or hospitals). The remainder lived elsewhere in the community, in other locations, or in leisure-oriented retirement communities planned and built for the elderly.

Both aging parents and their children value independence and privacy, meaning that living together in the same household is not the preferred choice in most instances. Most aging parents want to live close to their adult children and grandchildren so that they can visit and enjoy their relationships without sacrificing their privacy and autonomy.

A major aspect of aging parent-child relationships concerns the *giving of economic aid and social and emotional support*. Adult children provide a substantial degree of financial assistance, care, and support to aging parents who have few economic reserves or who are experiencing health problems (Hess and Waring, 1978). However, the *reasons* for doing so seem to have changed in recent years. Adult children provide assistance to aging parents more on a *voluntary* basis than as a matter of *obligation*. They help because they want to help, out of trust, respect, and genuine affection for the parents, not because they feel obligated or are expected to do so. Family members still bear a significant portion of the costs of care for the aging population, despite governmental assistance programs:

> Medicaid pays something less than half of the cost of all nursing home care. Little known, apparently, is the fact that at each level of impairment sustained by the elderly, the cost borne by family and friends is greater than that borne by all government agencies combined. A recent (1977) study by the General Accounting Office . . . stated that at the "greatly impaired" level "families and friends are providing over 70 percent of the value of services received by older persons." (Montgomery, 1982:23)

Whereas adult sons are most likely to provide financial aid to aging parents, adult daughters are most likely to provide direct personal care and emotional nurturance (Huyck and Hoyer, 1982). Inviting aging parents into the home for regular visits, for Sunday dinner, or taking them on family outings (picnics, recreational events, and so on) can contribute a great deal to their morale and well-being (Watson and Kivett, 1976). These kinds of activities are particularly helpful to the elderly who live alone in widowhood, or who otherwise are unmarried.

In addition to their children, *siblings* and *close friends* can be an excellent source of emotional support and nurturance for the elderly, especially for those who are widowed or single and for those who never had children of their own (Shanas, 1980). Older adults who have never married or had children are the most likely to live with an aged brother or sister, to visit them on a regular basis, and to feel close to them. Close friends and neighbors can have an equally favorable — and, at times, greater — impact on the morale of elderly persons than do relatives (Arling, 1976; Lee and Ellithorpe, 1982). Close friends and neighbors tend to have common interests and life-styles, and associate with the elderly on a voluntary basis. Assistance is exchanged so that one person is not *dependent* upon the others for aid. This pattern often has a more favorable effect than do the relationships with adult children, if relationships with children are characterized by dissimilar life-styles and a sense of formal obligation.

The End of the Marital Career: Widowhood

By age 65, 3.5 percent of all American males and 17.3 percent of all females in 1982 were widowed by the death of a spouse, meaning that there were 5 times more widows than widowers by that age (U.S. Bureau of the Census, 1983a:44). By 75 years of age, the rates climb to 7.5 and 38.3 for males and females, respectively. For those over 75, 21.8 percent of all males and 68.5 percent of all females are widowed. This differential between males and females is exclusively the result of the fact that females outlive males by an average of 7.5 years (National Center for Health Statistics, 1984c). This means that elderly women are several times more likely than elderly men to have to confront the many problems of old age without a marriage partner, placing them at the mercy of friends, relatives, and government and private agencies for support. Three out of four American wives can expect to be widowed at some time in their lives (Balkwell, 1981).

The loss of a spouse has been classified as among the most stressful of all life experiences, and some experts consider it to be the *most* stressful (Holmes and Rahe, 1967). Widowhood inspires a great sense of loss, complicated by such ambivalent feelings as grief, despair, denial, anger at the deceased spouse for dying, and self-pity. Not only does the bereaved spouse have to adjust to the loss of the person who has been a source of personal support, understanding, trust, caring, and love, but relationships with friends and other relatives tend to change as these people modify their relationships to the one who has moved from the status of "married person" to that of "widow" or "widower." Very often role expectations become ambiguous as people fumble for the "right way" to relate to the widowed individual — "What do I say?" "How do I react?" "How can I show sympathy and sensitivity to the widowed without being offensive and making the person feel worse?" Widowhood, then, is complicated by uncertain and changing relationships with significant others in their social networks.

COPING WITH WIDOWHOOD: MAJOR INFLUENCES

Older widowed individuals evaluate everyday life more negatively and have lower morale than people who are married or who have never been married (Gubrium, 1974). The great majority of widowed persons, however, manage to work successfully through the bereavement process in time and continue to live satisfying and rewarding lives (Lopata, 1979; Pincus, 1974). Although many possible factors are involved, the following four factors appear to influence most heavily coping abilities and patterns of adjustment after widowhood: (1) *age at widowhood and length of marriage;* (2) *sex of the widowed spouse;* (3) *the nature and circumstances surrounding the spouse's death;* and (4) *the nature and extent of social-support networks, relationships with significant others, and economic resources following the loss of the spouse.*

Age at Widowhood. One of the most comprehensive studies of widowhood we have was conducted by Helena Lopata (1973; 1978; 1979) on a sample of nearly 1,200 widows in the metropolitan Chicago area. She found that relatively young widows are confronted with the decision of whether or not, and when, to return to the courtship system to find another spouse, particularly if their husbands died while they are childless and they desire to have children. They may be divided by a sense of loyalty to the deceased spouse and their own feelings of self-interest and doing what might be best for them. Especially critical is the fact that the young widowed are "off schedule" in relation to the normal course of events in our culture — people marry, have children, raise their families, launch their children, and live several years together until one spouse dies in old age. Widowhood at a young age can cause a deep feeling that life has been unfair, that they have been cheated. The young widowed person asks, "Why me?" "What did I do to deserve this fate?" This feeling can make adjustment more difficult and prolong the bereavement process.

Widowhood at an older age has its own problems, as well. The older a person is when the partner dies, the lower the chances of finding a new marriage partner (especially for women), and the greater the chances of having health and finance-related problems to complicate life (Jedlicka, 1978; Balkwell, 1981). Widowhood among older people is more likely to be followed by isolation and loneliness, because a greater proportion of one's own friends and acquaintances are already deceased, and one's social network is likely to be smaller than for the young widowed. However, the transition to widowhood is "more expected" in the later years of life, and this being "on-schedule" with a major life experience makes adjustment to widowhood somewhat easier for the older widowed (Balkwell, 1981).

Sex of the Widowed Spouse. There is no definite answer to the question, "Is widowhood worse for men or for women?" (Huyck and Hoyer, 1982). Nonetheless, research has shown that women and men tend to experience distinct types of problems with which they must cope in widowhood. For example, given the unequal earning power which favors males over females in our society (see chapter 8), widows are more likely than widowers to encounter economic difficulties after the spouse's death (Harvey and Bahr, 1974). Males, on the other hand, have been found to experience more severe *health-related effects* because of widowhood. Evidence of male vulnerability in widowhood is provided by a major study, which followed 4,032 married and widowed males and females over a 12-year-period (1963 – 1975) [Helsing, Szklo, and Comstock, 1981]. Subjects ranged in age from 18 to 75 years and older, and the researchers carefully controlled for the effects of cigarette smoking, living conditions, race, and residential history. This study focused on the death rates, or mortality, of four groups: (1) married males, (2) married females, (3) widowed males, and (4) widowed females. Table 14.2 expresses the findings in the form of *mortality rates* for each group after the entire 12 years of the study were completed. The survivorship of married and widowed females was about the same over the 12 years of the study, but widowed men had significantly higher death rates than did married men at all age levels. Also, a significant gap in survivorship was found between widowed men and widowed women — the likelihood of death among widowed men was significantly greater than among widowed women of the same age.

TABLE 14.2. *Mortality Rates Among Widowed and Married Men and Women, Per 1,000 Persons, at All Age Levels Combined*

		Marital Status		
		Widowed		*Married*
	Males	67.0	*	50.2
Sex				
	Females	25.6		21.7

* Denotes a statistically significant difference.

SOURCE: Helsing, et al., 1981:805.

Finally, it was found that a "substantial" gap in survivorship existed between widowed men who had remarried during the course of the study and widowed men who remained single. The remarried males lived longer than the single widowed males, even in the younger age categories. The researchers concluded that a social support network is of critical importance following widowhood, particularly for widowed men. At least where survival after widowhood is concerned, men appear to become lonelier, more despondent, and susceptible to death themselves, making them the "weaker sex" under these circumstances (Helsing, et al., 1981:808). Other research has shown that widowed men have higher rates of suicide (Bock and Webber, 1972; Bock, 1972), accidents, mental illness, alcoholism, and physical illness (Berardo, 1968) than do widowed women, each of which contributes to their higher mortality rates.

Nature and Circumstances of Spouse's Death.

Another factor contributing to how widowhood is experienced among different people relates to the manner in which the spouse has died. Most significant is the suddenness of the death. Lopata (1979), for example, found that wives who had cared for their husbands over the course of a lengthy terminal illness often expressed a sigh of relief that the suffering was over. Grief was much more severe among women whose husbands died suddenly and without warning, as often occurs in a serious accident or sudden heart attack. These women did not have the opportunity to go through a period of *anticipatory socialization,* during which they could psychologically prepare for his death and so begin the process of disengagement from the mate prior to his passing.

Social-Support Networks, Significant Others, and Economic Resources.

In discussing the results of her study of over 1,100 widows in the Chicago area, Lopata (1978) noted that widowhood is made considerably more difficult for those who have little in the way of a social and emotional support network upon which to rely following the spouse's death. Such sources of support were categorized by Lopata into four broad areas:

1. *Economic Supports* Gifts of money; payment of, or help in paying for, rent or mortgage, food, clothing, and medical and vacation expenses.

2. *Service Supports* Help with transportation; household repairs; housekeeping chores; shopping; yardwork; child care; automobile care and maintenance; care during illness; and legal assistance.

3. *Social Supports* Companionship in recreational activities, attending church services, and traveling out of town; visiting and entertaining in the home; cards, sports activities, or other games; and celebrating holidays.

4. *Emotional Supports* Having someone with whom one (a) is close, (b) enjoys being with, (c) can talk to and share problems, (d) can seek solace when depressed, and (e) can turn to in a crisis. Children, brothers and sisters, and close friends are the major sources of such support for the widowed.

Such community groups as neighbors, work associates, club members, and government agencies are usually not viewed by the widowed as very helpful (Lopata, 1978). Elderly widows who are left without a social network therefore live in a state of loneliness; desolation; disengagement from meaningful social ties; and helplessness in the face of changing neighborhoods, growing rates of crime, and uncertainty about their futures. Of significance here is that adult children often are unable to afford the time, money, or energy to provide the full range of supports necessary to maintain a reasonable quality of life for the elderly widowed, particularly if they live any distance from each other. Elderly widowed who have no children experience an even greater degree of social isolation than do those with children. According to Bachrach's (1980) study of nearly 2,800 persons aged 65 and older, "compared to persons who have children, the childless are more likely to live alone and, if living alone, are less likely to have had social contact in the past day or two (p. 635)." These effects of childlessness are most severe for the elderly from working-class backgrounds and among those with health problems. The more well-to-do elderly and the healthy elderly have a broader range of alternative social contacts from which to choose, despite not having children of their own to provide support.

In view of the often paltry social and economic support systems available to the widowed in our society, Lopata (1978) suggested the establishment of "neighborhood networks" that would link together those who become only "marginally engaged in societal life," by means of recreational activities and social events (p. 387). Such organizations as *Widowed-to-Widowed* now exist in sev-

Widowhood brings an end to the marital career and, for some, means loneliness and disengagement from meaningful social ties. *(Photo by James D. Anker.)*

eral communities in the United States. These help to build friendships, and to restore the person's sense of competence and self-esteem by means of telephone "hot-lines" and regular home visits by volunteers (Balkwell, 1981). Self-help, consciousness-raising, and confidante groups, led by professional counselors, have all been found to help widowed persons work through the grief process and restructure their lives in a positive direction (Barrett, 1978). Clearly, more such groups are needed to provide support for the more than 12 million widowed persons in our society, more than 11 million of whom are women (Balkwell, 1981).

STARTING OVER: REMARRIAGE AMONG THE WIDOWED

One means of overcoming loneliness for many widowed persons is *remarriage*. We have already seen that widowers who remarry suffer fewer health problems and significantly lower mortality rates than do widowers who remain single. Widowhood among men, particularly elderly men, can be more difficult than for women because of (1) their lower degree of involvement in family and friendship roles; (2) their double loss of spouse and work, as a result of retirement; and (3) their usually limited prior involvement in housekeeping and cooking (Vinick, 1978:360). Remarriage for widowers, therefore, may be a particularly effective buffer against loneliness and feelings of desolation and despair.

Unfortunately, our society does not make remarriage easy for the widowed, particularly the elderly female. Widows are less likely than widowers to remarry at all ages, and the older widowed are less likely to marry than the younger. According to national statistics reported by Pincus (1974), only 10.2 per 1,000 widows remarry, but 40.6 per 1,000 widowers remarry. The major barrier to remarriage among the widowed is the relatively small pool of eligible mates. This is particularly true for older widows, in view of our aging and mate-selection patterns. As Jedlicka (1978) notes:

> The longer lifespan coupled with current patterns of age at marriage means that it will be impossible for most women to ever remarry, enjoy companionship, sex and belonging. Only a small portion of unmarried older women could succeed in mate selection as long as it is acceptable for older men to marry younger women while at the same time it is taboo for older women to seek, date and marry younger men. (p. 137)

Hence, not only do widowed males seem to enjoy more psychological benefits from remarriage than do women, but the greater number of available partners means that widowed men are much more likely than widowed women to remarry.

Summary

Moving into the postparental and aging years of the marital career is associated with a new array of challenges, problems, and rewards. Significant changes occur in the development of adult individuals, and they often occur at different rates and to different degrees from one person to the next. For the marriage relationship, the consequences of these differences can be to promote the "growth apart" and disenchantment in marriage, which actually began years earlier in previous stages of the marital career. For women who have occupied themselves primarily in the household and domestic roles associated with motherhood, postparenthood can mean a sense of loneliness, loss of contribution, and emptiness, as departing children leave a void in their lives. For men who have immersed themselves in work and career, retirement can also prove to be a devastating blow to their identities and sense of contribution. In either case, the person may experience serious difficulties in coping with their mid- to later-life transitions.

Research shows that many marriage partners experience an increase in satisfaction as they move into postparenthood. The lessening role strain, costs and responsibilities of children, and the increased time and energy for each other often improve the level of rewards in marriage at this time. Although it is a relatively new stage of development in the marital career, and was virtually nonexistent years ago, postparenthood appears to give many couples an opportunity to arrest the process of disenchantment begun in earlier stages. Improved communication, exchanges of love and affection, and opportunities to engage in a new array of "couple-only" companionship activities exist, which were not possible when children were present. All of this is possible as they maintain contact with their adult children on more of a friendship and voluntary basis, as opposed to a superior-subordinate relationship based on obligation. For many, this stage brings back the "fun" and spark of excitement that may not have been felt for many years.

The aging years, also have their rewarding aspects. Retirement means even more time together as a married couple, pursuing leisure and recreational activities that once were only dreams. The quality of the aging years, however, hinges on the health and economic well-being of the married pair. When health is poor and income inadequate, these are bitter years, indeed.

Finally, the death of a marriage partner brings an end to the marital career. Despite our relatively high divorce rate today, most marriages continue to be broken by the death of a marriage partner. Widowhood for some means despair, grief, and uncertainty about the future. For others, widowhood represents a new beginning, especially for those who are able to meet their continuing needs for closeness, companionship, and intimacy with others. Remarriage is one option, limited of course by the size and availability of a pool of eligible marriage prospects. Involvement with friends, siblings, or other relatives can also help at this time. Social-support networks are critical for the personal well-being of the widowed.

Questions for Discussion and Review

1. What are your attitudes toward the aging person in our society? What does it really mean to be "old?" What are your feelings about growing old yourself? Are you apprehensive about it? Why or why not?

2. What is the proper level of involvement of parents in the lives of their adult children? How involved should adult children be in the lives of their parents? In what ways do your own parents continue to influence your life? How do you influence theirs?

3. What can society do to better meet the needs of the elderly? How can we better meet the needs of the widowed? Should the elderly and widowed be expected to fend more for themselves? Or are we obligated to provide more support for them than we currently do?

4. How do you plan to prepare for a possible midlife authenticity crisis (middlescence)? Is there anything you can do to improve your chances for successfully negotiating such midlife transitions as those described in the text?

5. Upon your death, what is the most important legacy or contribution you hope to leave behind for your descendents, whether they are your children, your children's children, or beyond? How do you want to be remembered in your family's history?

Notes

1. The reader should be aware that both Sheehy's and Levinson's theory's of adulthood stages and transitions have been strongly criticized (see, for example, Dannefer, 1984). The major objections of the critics have focused on two concerns. First is the claim of *universality*, which states that all adults move through this sequence of stages in the specified order. Second are the *oversimplified explanations* which both Sheehy and Levinson give to their adult transition theories. The critics of these theories are quite correct in noting that there is no solid scientific evidence to support the idea that movement through these stages occur for all, or even most, people in the order specified. The critics are also correct in noting that there are many more influences on adult development than age alone, including one's family and friend relationships, income and social class levels, and experiences in the place of work. The nature of one's movement through stages of adulthood may therefore vary substantially from one person to the next depending on the social and cultural context. At this point, then, the reader should view these ideas as interesting theories that have not yet been extensively tested scientifically.

2. *Senile dementia,* commonly referred to as senility, is a disease of the brain and nervous system that causes deterioration in memory ability, attention span, and intellectual skills, as well as changes in personality. The disease is particularly hard on family members of the afflicted person because of these symptoms. Senile dementia is most common among those over 75 years of age; more than one million older Americans have the disease. It should be emphasized, however, that the disease affects only a minority of aging persons at any one time (about 5 percent of those over 65) [(U.S. Bureau of the Census, 1983c)].

3. Couples married 30 years, who have averaged having sexual intercourse with each other one time per week over that period, have spent 520 hours of their lives (or 21.66 full 24-hour days) having intercourse with the same person (assuming an average time of 20 minutes for each sexual encounter). For those averaging two acts of sexual intercourse per week, a total of 1,040 hours (or the equivalent of 43.3 days) of their lives are spent in sexual intercourse with each other!

PART IV

Contemporary Issues in Marriage and Family Life:

Marital Dissolution and the Future of Careers in Marriage and the Family

Marriage and family careers in our society have undergone dramatic changes over the past 15 to 20 years. No more significant change has taken place than the sharp increases we have seen in the divorce rate. More than one million American marriages are terminated by divorce every year. Divorce leaves few lives untouched, whether it is experienced by members of our own family, our friends, or ourselves. In chapter 15 we will examine in some detail the major social, emotional, and legal issues relating to divorce today.

Divorce is but one of many factors that have shaped and given new direction to marriage and family careers in our society. In chapter 16 we will explore some of the emerging marriage and family life styles that are likely to be with us for some time to come. Although marriage and parenthood will remain popular choices in the foreseeable future, recent changes in social norms and preferred ways of meeting our needs for love and human intimacy now grant legitimacy to a number of viable alternatives to traditional marriage and parenting patterns. Marriage and family careers of the future will be more diverse for many, especially for those who move in and out of relatively temporary living arrangements because of cohabitation, divorce, single parenthood, remarriage, and the blending of families started in previous marriage relationships. Others will find there is a growing acceptance of legitimate life-style choices, such as permanent singlehood, childlessness, adoption, communal households, and sexually open relationships. Whatever the case, marriage and family careers of the future will involve a number of diverse possibilities, each with its own potential to satisfy basic human needs for intimacy, love, and acceptance.

Divorce:
Social, Emotional, and Legal Issues

ecall that in previous chapters we said that the basis of marriage in our culture is romantic love and mutual attraction between a man and woman. Usually this involves a high level of similarity between partners in terms of interests, values, and role expectations, as well as sexual attraction and sexual fulfillment. How is it, then, that so many marriage relationships turn sour over time and terminate in the divorce court? How do two people who were so well matched at the time of marriage become "sufficiently unmatched to unmarry?" (Foote, 1956:26). Given the recent acceleration in the divorce rate in our society, how much divorce can our family system tolerate before we get concerned that our basic institution of marriage is breaking down? What effect does divorce have on those most deeply touched by it — primarily husband, wife, and children? What, if anything, can or should be done to reverse the trend and reduce the rate of divorce in our society?

These are all important questions that deserve our most serious consideration. We will explore these and other issues in this chapter, realizing that the answers are complex and elusive. These questions have no easy answers, and the problems associated with the divorce situation have no easy solutions.

Divorce: Who Wants It?

The vast majority of people enter marriage with the sincere hope, and belief, that the marriage will survive until the death of one partner brings an end to the marital career. Few people truly believe at the outset of their marriage careers that they will be divorced (Thornton and Freedman, 1982). Otherwise, there would be little sense in their getting married in the first place! The commitment to permanence in marriage is alive and well in our society today.

However, divorce rates today are at an all-time high. At current rates, close to 5 out of 10 first marriages formed in the 1980s will terminate in divorce rather than with the death of one of the partners (Glick, 1984a). In addition, the processes often leading up to a couple's decision to seek a divorce, as well as the actual divorce itself, are a source of great emotional, and at times physical, pain and suffering. Not only are the processes leading up to divorce emotionally painful, but getting a divorce is financially costly as well.

Nevertheless, despite the many costs associated with a divorce, it is true that the decision to divorce is often the best one under the circumstances. Divorce can be the beginning of a new life for those who have been trapped in unsatisfying "empty shell" marriages, as well as for those in which the partners have had continual conflicts, negative sentiments, and hostility toward one another for a number of years. Hence, although seeking and obtaining a divorce may be a painful experience, staying together "for the sake of the children," or because of the guilt some may feel about getting divorced ("What will our friends and relatives think?"), is often far more painful.

Survival in Marriage: What Are the Chances?

We saw in chapter 1 (see Figure 1.4) that the rate and number of divorces granted in American society accelerated at a record-setting pace between the mid-1960s and the late 1970s. Between 1962 and 1981, the number of divorces nearly tripled (National Center for Health Statistics, 1983a). In 1965 there were 479,000 divorces, with an average of 2.4 divorces granted for every 1,000 people in the population. In 1981, the number of divorces granted increased, for the 19th consecutive year, to 1,213,000 (National Center for Health Statistics, 1984a). The rate per 1,000 population grew to a record 5.3 in 1979.

However, the divorce rate actually began leveling off after 1977, and in 1980 the divorce *rate* dropped for the first time since 1962 (National Center for Health Statistics, 1983b). In 1982, the total number or divorces granted in the United States also dropped for the first time since 1962. An estimated 1,180,000 couples divorced in 1982 (down 3 percent from 1981), and the divorce rate dipped to 5.1 per 1,000 population (down 4 percent) [National Center for Health Statistics, 1983a]. This may be a sign that we have reached the peak of our historic climb in the divorce rate, and that we will see only gradual "up and down fluctuations in the divorce rate for some years to come" (Glick, 1979).

There are a number of ways to calculate a rate of divorce in order to give one an idea of what a couple's chances for survival in marriage will be. Some of these are valid and provide a meaningful picture, but some are deceptive and lead to conclusions that are erroneous. A commonly used measure of the divorce rate, for example, is to calculate the number of divorces in a given year and divide by the number of marriages formed in that year. This method artificially inflates the divorce rate, however, if the marriage rate should drop on its own. What is needed is a measure of divorce that takes into account the *pool of all existing marriages,* regardless of whether they were formed in the year in question or previously. Hence, the most reliable measures, ones which provide the most useful picture of divorce in our society, are the "refined divorce rate" and the "age-specific survival rates" (Crosby, 1980).

REFINED DIVORCE RATE

An accurate reflection of the picture of divorce in our society is gained by calculating the number of divorces in a given year by the *total pool of existing marriages* in that year. The denominator in the equation is composed of *all existing marriages,* whether formed in that year or any prior year, which could have been terminated in divorce in that year. Hence, the refined divorce rate in 1970 was 15.2 per 1,000 existing marriages, meaning that 1.52 percent, or 1 in every 65 marriages, ended in divorce. In 1980, the most recent year for which this statistic was available, there were 1.2 million divorces among a pool of 51.3 million marriages. This yields a refined divorce rate of 22.6 divorces for every 1,000 existing marriages, or 2.26 percent of the total (National Center for Health Statistics, 1983b). In 1980, therefore, 1 in every 44 existing marriages was terminated by divorce.

AGE-SPECIFIC RATES AND SURVIVAL PROJECTIONS

Age-specific divorce rates provide information about the chances for divorce among people married for varying numbers of years, and who have lived through different historical, social, and economic circumstances, such as wars, depressions, and the gender-role changes we have seen in the 1970s and 1980s. The benefit of this method is that differences between generations, or cohorts, of people can be readily spotted. Glick (1984a) took this method one step further when he calculated the proportion of marriages in 1980 likely to survive without divorce, for people of various ages, *at that year's rate.* For those married couples in the 25- to 34-year age range in 1980, 51 percent were expected to survive in their first marriages without divorce. For those married couples between 45 and 54 years of age, about 70 percent were expected to survive until the marriage was dissolved by death. By 1980, only 15 percent of those marriages in which partners were in the 65-plus age range had been terminated by divorce, yielding an *85 percent survival rate!* These figures show the greater propensity of younger people to terminate an unsatisfying relationship by means of divorce, a result, perhaps, of a more liberal and accepting attitude toward divorce among the young.

ANNULMENT, DESERTION, AND SEPARATION

Annulments are binding civil or religious proclamations that a marriage never really existed in the first place. Annulment is a means of declaring a marriage *null and void,* usually on the basis of conditions existing prior to the marriage. These include teenagers who are wed without legally required parental permission; one or both spouses already in a legal marriage; failure of one spouse to consummate the marriage by engaging in sexual intercourse; and fraud or deception on the part of one or both partners. Fraud includes assuming a false identity or concealing such other pertinent information as prior conviction of a felony, drug addiction, knowledge of being infected with a venereal disease, having been previously married, and impotency (Bass and Rein, 1976).[1] Only about 3 to 4 percent of all marriages result in civil annulments that are legally binding.

According to Crosby (1980), *desertion (or abandonment)* is the second most common legal ground for divorce, (next to *irreconcilable breakdown*). Desertion is leaving the couple's residence for an extended period of time (usually weeks) without the spouse's consent, and with intent not to return (Bass and Rein, 1976). Desertion is most common among the lower-income and racial minority groups in our society. Desertion is also more common among men, although the growing number of runaway wives is closing the gap. According to the research conducted by Todres (1978), nearly 1 million American families had been victims of desertion by the wife-mother, as of 1973; and Canada reported more than 100,000 in 1971. Most desertions, however, eventually show up in divorce statistics because neither the deserting nor the nondeserting spouses can remarry until a divorce is legally declared.

Legal separations do not actually terminate the marriage (Crosby, 1980). Rather, it merely limits the legal rights and obligations of the spouses who are still legally married. Legal separation is a judgment of a court which directs the husband and wife to "live separate and apart without terminating the marriage" (Bass and Rein, 1976:53). In addition to court ordered *(de jure)* separations, a couple may live apart by mutual agreement (*de facto* separation). Legally separated couples must neither live together nor engage in sexual relations, according to the law. It is not clear, however, how enforceable such a restriction against sexual relations would be if the spouses wanted to get back together. If it is in the best interests of the marriage partners and their children, the court may allow the spouses to remain living on the same premises "provided that there is no cohabitation (sleeping together and/or engaging in sexual relations)" [Bass and Rein, 1976]. There are three major reasons why a couple may choose legal separation over divorce:

1. Religious prohibitions on divorce, which the spouses do not wish to violate.

2. To assure that inheritance, tax, Social Security, veteran's, and pension benefits will not be lost.

3. Grounds for a legal separation are often easier to prove than grounds for divorce.

In 1976, a total of 2.4 million women and 1.4 million men reported themselves as "separated" in a national population survey (Glick and Norton, 1977).

Reasons for Divorce

The underlying causes of divorce are many and complex. They vary from one society or cultural group to the next, as well as from one couple to the next. Divorce rates in American society are quite high — among the highest — in comparison with other societies around the world. There are a number of factors in our society that contribute to the high rate of divorce in the United States.

SOCIETAL INFLUENCES ON DIVORCE

The nature of social norms relating to marriage and family life, as well as the general social and economic circumstances surrounding the married couple, influence the chances for divorce in the general population.

1. *The degree to which individual freedom is granted to young people seeking a marriage partner, and the degree to which romantic love is considered a sufficient basis for marriage.* Divorce rates are usually low in cultures where marriages are arranged by parents; where parents have an important say in who children can marry, in terms of religious or social-class homogamy; and where *duty* and *obligation* are important values in a marriage relationship. In cultures like our own, where people get married on the basis of interpersonal attraction and romantic love for each other, divorce rates fall toward the high end of the continuum. If love is a sufficient basis for marrying, then falling out of love, and finding oneself in a relationship of poor quality, is a sufficient basis for "unmarrying," or divorcing (Reiss, 1980:321). When societies grant people the relative freedom to choose who they will marry, based on romantic love, those cultures also tend to give people the freedom to divorce when they feel that love is no longer present in the marriage.

2. *The degree of heterogeneity that exists within the married population.* The freedom granted to the marrying population in our society means that we will have more *heterogamy,* and less *homogamy,* than will other cultures because we are relatively free to marry across religious, social class, education, age, racial, and ethnic boundaries. Although the difference is not great, heterogamous and racially mixed marriages have somewhat higher divorce rates than homogamous couples. Heterogeneity in a culture is conducive to somewhat higher divorce rates than are found in more homogeneous cultures.

3. *The nature of divorce laws and social attitudes toward divorce.* There is no doubt that the easing of divorce laws and a movement toward greater acceptance of divorce as a legitimate means of terminating a bad marriage have paralleled the rising divorce rate. The legal grounds for divorce have been expanded in nearly every state, waiting periods have been reduced, and the concept of *no-fault divorce* has allowed for a relatively painless divorce process for many couples who agree that their "irreconcilable differences" are adequate grounds for dissolving the mar-

riage. This has reduced the adversarial nature of divorce — the accusations, blaming, fault-finding, and hostility associated with the "I'll sue you, you'll sue me" mentality of past years. The relaxing of divorce laws has also reduced the financial costs of obtaining a divorce, and those states with more permissive divorce laws have higher divorce rates than do those with more restrictive laws (Stetson and Wright, 1975).

However, there is not necessarily a cause-and-effect relationship between the institution of *no-fault divorce laws* and the *increase in the divorce rate* (Wright and Stetson, 1978). For example, people have long used evasive tactics to get around strict laws that limit the grounds for divorce. Many were put in a position of having to lie about their relationship, claiming adultery or some other legal grounds (cruelty, for example) in order to obtain a divorce. Hence, no-fault divorce and other divorce-law reforms were a legal reaction to better match what people already had been doing. And, although states with more liberal divorce laws show higher rates of divorce, those with more restrictive laws are likely to have higher rates of legal separation and desertion (Stetson and Wright, 1975). The latter are also likely to have more marriages that are intact but unsatisfying to the partners and of a generally poor quality — legally intact but emotionally broken marriages. In sum, whereas liberalized divorce laws have probably not caused the rate of marital breakdown or divorce to increase, they have made the divorce process less costly, complicated, and painful for all involved. Modern divorce laws are also a more accurate reflection of the relatively accepting social attitudes toward divorce which exist today.

4. *Change from traditional to equalitarian gender roles.* Divorce rates tend to be low in societies in which traditional gender-role prescriptions predominate. When social norms give legitimacy to male power and dominance, along with female submissiveness and deference to males, there is less cause for divorce because marital conflicts and differences are usually resolved in a manner consistent with traditional gender-role expectations. In these societies, role scripts in marriage are less ambiguous than in cultures such as ours, where more equalitarian gender-role patterns require greater skills of bargaining and negotiating between the sexes to resolve marital differences. Divorce rates increase in more equalitarian societies because people lack the necessary bargaining and con-

flict-management skills. In a study of 186 cultures around the world, Pearson and Hendrix (1979) found that divorce rates were higher in those societies where males and females were of relatively equal status. They concluded that when wives are less dependent upon husbands for care and support, as is the case in more equalitarian societies, they are more likely to leave an unsatisfying relationship by means of divorce, and the society is more likely to grant legitimacy to their request to seek a divorce.

The same processes can be seen in our own society, if one studies the divorce rate picture (see chapter 1, Figure 1.4). Beginning in the middle to late 1960s, the divorce rate began its historic climb. This is about the time when gender roles began to change because of the women's liberation movement. Women at that time began to forge a new identity as they seriously questioned their traditional roles as dutiful housewives and mothers who catered to the needs of husband and children. Women began moving into colleges and universities at a rate theretofore unknown. Many reformulated their occupational aspirations to include work-for-pay outside the home and careers in traditionally male-dominated fields (see chapter 4). Women wanted more of a say in their relationships with their male partners, as their changing self-concepts called for more power and influence in heterosexual relationships (Scanzoni, 1972). The move toward male-female equality significantly increased the strain in marriage, and, because couples lacked the necessary bargaining and conflict-resolution skills, this strain led directly to more divorces. Whenever social change occurs to the degree that it did with the woman's movement in the 1960s and 1970s, we must expect that the ripple effects will be felt throughout our society—particularly in the institution of marriage.

5. *Unrealistically high expectations for marriage.* Throughout this book, we have tried to show just how complicated the position of "marriage partner" is, and how numerous and varied the roles of a spouse and parent are. As a society, we expect people to be competent in anything they undertake, and marriage is no exception. Many people simply expect too much from their marriage partners, and are disappointed when they cannot "deliver" what is expected of them.

As we discussed in chapter 1, in relation to the concept of *successful marriage,* marriages are more apt to be defined as unsuccessful when expectations are unrealistically high. All people have certain strengths and weaknesses, and they cannot be outstanding in every way—in

the roles of provider, confidant, problem-solver, decision-maker, budget analyst, sex partner, or affection-giver.

6. *Level of socioeconomic resources in the family.* For many years in our society, people toward the higher end of the income, occupational prestige, and educational ladders have had lower divorce rates than those at lower socioeconomic levels (Glick and Norton, 1977; Goode, 1956; Cutright, 1971b). Lower-income marriages have also had significantly higher rates of desertion and separation. Lack of socioeconomic resources adds strain to marriage relationships. This is particularly true for those who fall below the poverty level, where separation and desertion rates are especially high (Brinkerhoff and White, 1978). In a society where personal and family worth, as well as the general quality of life, are gauged by income and occupational levels, *morale maintenance* is bound to suffer when the family has difficulty in providing the essentials of food, clothing, and shelter of its members.

7. *Racial background.* The divorce rate is higher for Blacks than it is for whites at all socioeconomic and educational levels. However, Blacks with a higher income and more education have lower divorce rates than do less educated and lower-income Blacks (Carter and Glick, 1976). Beyond the prejudice and discrimination against Blacks which continue to exist in our society, there is no obvious explanation of the Black-white divorce rate differences which exist at all income and education levels.

MARRIAGE QUALITY AND DIVORCE: COHESIVENESS AND COMMITMENT

Research has shown that two factors have the most weight in determining whether or not a marriage terminates in divorce: (1) *cohesiveness of the marriage relationship,* and (2) *commitment of both partners to the marriage* (Levinger, 1965; Lewis and Spanier, 1979; Reiss, 1980). *Marital cohesiveness* is the "glue" that holds partners together—the degree to which *each* partner is satisfied with the marriage and the degree to which they are satisfying each other's needs for intimacy, love, and companionship. Cohesiveness is the strength of the bond between the partners, which is solidified as each adjusts to the other over time in terms of role expectations, behavior patterns, and major life goals and values. *Marital commitment,* on the other hand, is the degree to which both partners desire to stay in the marriage relationship through thick and thin, good times and bad times, and "in sickness and in health" over the years of the marital career. Commitment is a strong desire for permanence in marriage — for continuing the marriage relationship into the future. *Commitment* is different from *cohesiveness* in that spouses may be *committed* to staying in their marriage, even though they may be having serious conflicts; are not particularly satisfied with the way they are communicating, sharing affection, or making decisions; and even though they may be doubting each other's love.

The probability that a couple will divorce is directly related to these two factors. The *lowest* chance for divorce is when *both* partners feel a mutual bond of cohesiveness, and are committed to staying together. The *greatest* chance for divorce is when partners feel a lack of cohesiveness, are not committed to making the marriage last, or lack commitment *and* cohesiveness (see Figure 15.1).

"Coming Unglued": Factors That Weaken Cohesiveness in Marriage.

A number of factors are directly related to the degree of cohesiveness in marriage, which in turn determine whether a particular married couple will divorce. Each of the following tends to *reduce* the level of cohesiveness in marriage, thereby *increasing* the chances for divorce (Dizard, 1968; Hine, 1980; Reiss, 1980; Lewis and Spanier, 1979).

1. *Many tensions and problems relative to rewards in marriage.* Inability to communicate effectively with one another; difficulty in exchanging love and affection; failing to enjoy companionship, and to have fun together; and being unable to manage and resolve conflicts effectively, result in tensions which build over time. As they do, a sense of stagnation, frustration, and disappointment pervades the marriage relationship, weakening the cohesive bond that existed in earlier years. Others simply grow tired of each other, after so many years with the same person, and look to others to meet their needs for love and intimacy, and to rekindle the spark that seems to have disappeared from the marriage relationship. When tensions build to such a level that marriage seems to have lost the potential for rewarding the partners, for meeting their needs for intimacy, love, and self-confirmation, divorce may seem to be an appealing alternative. In one study of long-term marriages, Hine (1980) found that the balance of rewards and tensions distinguished those marriages characterized as "successful" (meeting the partners' needs and expectations) from those identified as "divorce-prone" (having serious problems). See Table 15.1 for a list of these factors.

2. Related to the build-up of tensions is the *propensity for marriage partners to grow apart over time.* As we saw in chapter 14, major life changes occur in adulthood,

FIGURE 15.1. Chances for Divorce Under Varying Levels of Cohesiveness and Commitment.

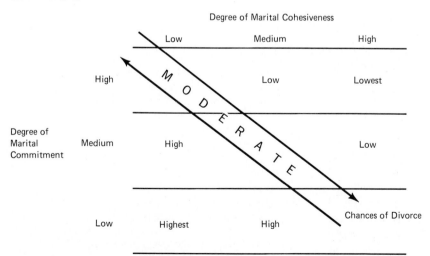

such that marriage partners may grow apart in terms of their personal needs and interests, values, and role expectations. Marriage partners who are somehow able to adjust to changes in each other, and who keep up with each other by growing and developing at the same pace, have a greater chance of maintaining cohesiveness over the years. Whether it is the husband who "outgrows" the wife, the wife who "outgrows" the husband, or whether it is simply both partners "drifting away from each other," mismatching in adulthood promotes disenchantment and leads to divorce among many.

It appears that persons who seemed matched for a time do not forever remain well-matched; pairs of persons who never grow tired of each other are few and far between . . . A marriage is not likely to stand still or continue unchanged for very long. Arrest in development of either partner makes it vulnerable to breakdown . . . To expect a marriage to last indefinitely is to expect a lot. (Foote, 1956:27–29)

3. *Being unable to cope successfully with crises and hardships that occur over the years.* In his study of marriages that had lasted several years, twenty years or more, Hine (1980) found that "being able to meet crises successfully" was the major difference between those who viewed their marriages as successful and those who were having serious problems (see Table 15.1). Whether it is such *expected* crisis situations as parenthood, seeing children grow and leave home as young adults, or retirement, or such *unexpected* crises as serious illness, death of a family member, unemployment, or legal problems, some couples are never able to recover from the stress and strain. Cohesiveness suffers as a result, and divorce may be the final outcome. However, when crises are negotiated successfully, it appears that some couples emerge as a stronger unit, with a more cohesive bond in marriage than they had before the crisis struck.

"Through Thick and Thin, for Better or Worse."

Other factors reduce the chances of divorce by promoting *commitment*. Some people are simply opposed to the idea of divorce on religious or moral grounds, and are committed to remain in a marriage even when the bonds of cohesiveness become weaker over time. A vow to remain together in marriage was made, and some are unwilling to break that commitment under any circumstances. The Roman Catholic and Mormon religions, for

TABLE 15.1. *Most Important Characteristics Differentiating Successful Marriages from Divorce-Prone Marriages After 20–50 Years of Marriage*

Successful Marriages

1. Able to meet crises successfully, with calmness and confidence.
2. Able to continue exchanging warmth and affection (*role reciprocity* in affection giving-receiving roles).
3. Loyal and faithful to each other, contributing to mutual trust and dependability.
4. Able to give reinforcement and support to each other, including compliments, praise, and positive feelings about the other.
5. Able to be honest and open in communication with each other, even if it causes some unpleasantness at the time.
6. Mental and emotional maturity of both partners, allowing for each to confront crises, solve problems, and make good decisions.
7. Generosity and unselfishness.
8. Having the "will to succeed in marriage" (maintaining a "winning" attitude and a conscious determination to make the marriage work).
9. Maintaining compatibility in major life values and goals, and adjusting to each other's role expectations as they change over time.
10. Developing and maintaining interpersonal skills of communication, negotiation, and conflict management.

Divorce-Prone Marriages

1. Not able to maintain companionship activities to a mutually acceptable degree.
2. Not able to meet crises successfully, as crisis situations throw them off course and cause great difficulty in allowing the couple to recover fully.
3. Not able to have fun together anymore.
4. Not able to exchange affection in ways that meet each other's needs for intimacy.
5. Have developed conflicts in role expectations, and which can never be resolved.
6. Can no longer find ways to give support and reinforcement to each other.
7. Are not able to remain loyal and faithful to each other because marriage has taken a "back seat" to extramarital loves, sex partners, or career pursuits.
8. Are no longer able to share in making decisions that affect the marriage and family.

SOURCE: Adapted and abridged from Hine (1980).

example, have strong rules against divorce. These faiths define marriage as a *holy sacrament,* an eternal commitment to the partner, and divorce means breaking that commitment. These religious norms function as barriers, or constraints, that keep marriages intact over the years even though they may have lost the rewards of intimacy, warmth, and fulfillment.

Another strong barrier is the presence of children. Parents may stay married for the sake of the children, if they feel that a divorce would be psychologically harmful to them. Some parents do not want their children to even suspect that they are having marital difficulties, and may do all they can to hide their distress from the children. Child custody decisions and the economic costs of supporting children in separate households may also be a consideration which delays a divorce decision.

When barriers such as restrictive attitudes toward divorce or the presence of children are not strong in a marriage, certain *alternative attractions* may contribute to a spouse's desire to leave the current marriage relationship by weakening the strength of commitment (Udry, 1981; Levinger, 1965). An extramarital love or sex partner, or feeling that one can make it alone because of a good income or other source of economic support, may cause one to leave a marriage — if sufficiently strong barriers are *not* present to keep the marriage intact. As Udry (1981) points out, believing that one would be better off without the current spouse, and that the spouse could be easily replaced with one of comparable or better quality, may be more of a factor in marital dissolution than dissatisfaction with the marriage.

The Legal Meaning of Divorce

As we discussed in chapter 10, marriage involves a complex, legally binding contract between the spouses and the state. Divorce, or the process of "unmarrying," also involves a complex interweave of the soon-to-be ex-spouses and the legal system. As with marriage laws, divorce laws vary significantly from one state to the next. Table 15.2 includes a brief summary of some of the major aspects of divorce law. Anyone contemplating divorce, therefore, would be wise to learn the legal aspects of divorce in the state where the divorce is to take place. Although legal experts have tried to formulate uniform

national divorce laws, the efforts have not been fruitful because of differences in values from one state or region of the country to the next (Monahan, 1973).

There is no doubt that the legal complexities of divorce can exacerbate an already psychologically painful

The process of "unmarrying," or divorce, involves a complex interweave between the soon-to-be ex-spouses and the legal system, involving the distribution of money, property, children, and parenting rights. *(Photo by Bruce Roberts.)*

TABLE 15.2. *Selected Laws Relating to Divorce, State by State*

State	No-Fault Divorce:	Residency Requirement	Remarriage Rules	Community Property?	Alimony Allowed?
Alabama	Yes[1]	One spouse domiciled in state. If one is a nonresident, spouse filing for divorce must have resided in state for 6 months	60 days wait after divorce	No	Yes
Alaska	Yes[2]	None	No waiting period required	No	Yes
Arizona	Yes[3]	90 days by either spouse, before filing	No waiting period required	Yes	Yes
Arkansas	Yes[4]	60 days by either spouse, before filing; 90 days before decree granted	No waiting period required	No	Yes
California	Yes[1]	6 months in state by either spouse, 3 months in county, prior to filing	No waiting period required	Yes	Yes
Colorado	Yes[3]	90 days by either spouse, prior to filing	Remarriage allowed after divorce decree granted and time for appeal has expired	No	Yes
Connecticut	Yes[1]	1 year for either spouse; either spouse domiciled in state at time of marriage	No waiting period required	No	Yes
Delaware	Yes[1]	6 months for either spouse, prior to filing	No waiting period required	No	Yes
District of Columbia	Yes[5]	6 months for either spouse, prior to filing	No waiting period required	No	Yes
Florida	Yes[1]	6 months for plaintiff, prior to filing	No waiting period required	No	Yes
Georgia	Yes[1]	6 months for either spouse, prior to filing	No waiting period required	No	Yes
Hawaii	Yes[1]	6 months for either spouse, prior to filing	No waiting period required	No	Yes
Idaho	Yes[1]	6 weeks prior to filing	No waiting period required	Yes	Yes
Illinois	No	One spouse must be domiciled in state, and domicile must be maintained for 90 days prior to final decree	No waiting period required	No	Yes
Indiana	Yes[1]	6 months for either spouse, prior to filing	No waiting period required	No	Yes
Iowa	Yes[1]	Nonfiling spouse must be a resident, or filing spouse must be resident for 1 year prior to filing	No waiting period, other than 90 days between divorce action and service of notice	No	Yes

TABLE 15.2. *(Continued)*

State	No-Fault Divorce:	Residency Requirement	Remarriage Rules	Community Property?	Alimony Allowed?
Kansas	Yes[1]	60 days for plaintiff, prior to filing	30-day waiting period after divorce is final	No	Yes
Kentucky	Yes[1]	180 days for either spouse, prior to filing	No waiting period required	No	Yes
Louisiana	Yes[1,6]	None	No waiting period. If grounds are adultery, guilty party cannot marry sex partner (accomplice)	Yes	Yes
Maine	Yes[1]	6 months for plaintiff; or defendant resident in state; or married in state, or lived in state after marriage	No waiting period required	No	Yes
Maryland	Yes[1,7]	None, if grounds for divorce arose within state; one year, if otherwise	No waiting period required	No	Yes
Massachusetts	Yes[1]	One spouse must reside in state at time of filing; one year if cause for divorce occurred outside of state	No waiting period required	No	Yes
Michigan	Yes[3]	180 days for either spouse, prior to filing; one year if grounds for divorce occurred outside of state	No waiting period required	No	Yes
Minnesota	Yes[3]	180 days for either spouse, prior to filing	No waiting period required	No	Yes
Mississippi	Yes[2]	6 months, prior to filing	No waiting period required; court may bar marriage of guilty party if adultery is grounds	No	Yes
Missouri	Yes[3]	90 days for either spouse, prior to filing	No waiting period required	No	Yes
Montana	Yes[3]	90 days for either spouse, prior to filing	No waiting period required	No	Yes
Nebraska	Yes[3]	1 year for either spouse, prior to filing	No waiting period required	No	Yes
Nevada	Yes[1]	6 weeks for either spouse, prior to filing	No waiting period required	Yes	Yes
New Hampshire	Yes[1]	Basically the same as Massachusetts	No waiting period required	No	Yes
New Jersey	Yes[1,8]	One year for either spouse, prior to filing	No waiting period required	No	Yes

(continued)

TABLE 15.2. *(Continued)*

State	No-Fault Divorce:	Residency Requirement	Remarriage Rules	Community Property?	Alimony Allowed?
New Mexico	Yes[1]	6 months and domicile in state, for either spouse	No waiting period required	Yes	Yes
New York	Yes[1,9]	Both spouses residents at filing, and reason for divorce arises in state; other conditions applicable	No waiting period required	No	Yes
North Carolina	Yes[1,5]	6 months for plaintiff, prior to filing	No waiting period required	No	Yes
North Dakota	Yes[1,9]	One year for plaintiff, prior to filing	Court determines if one or both spouses will be allowed to remarry; stated in divorce decree	No	Yes
Ohio	Yes[1,2]	6 months for both spouses for no-fault; 6 months for plaintiff if filing on other grounds	No waiting period required	No	Yes
Oklahoma	Yes[1]	6 months in state, 30 days in a county, for either spouse, prior to filing	6-month wait after divorce decree; marrying before is bigamy; cohabiting is adultery	No	Yes
Oregon	Yes[3]	Legal domicile of either spouse in state prior to filing necessary for those married in Oregon; others must be resident for 6 months	60-day waiting period after decree	No	Yes
Pennsylvania	Yes[1]	One year for either spouse, prior to filing	No waiting period required. Adulterous spouse may not marry accomplice during lifetime of ex-spouse	No	Yes
Rhode Island	Yes[1]	One year for either spouse, prior to filing	No waiting period required	No	Yes
South Carolina	Yes[1,9]	One year for one spouse, or 3 months for both spouses, prior to filing	No waiting period required	No	Yes
South Dakota	No	Plaintiff must be resident at filing, and until divorce is final	No waiting period required	No	Yes
Tennessee	Yes[1]	6 months for one spouse, prior to filing	No waiting period required	No	Yes
Texas	Yes[1]	6 months in state, 90 days in county, for either spouse, before filing	30-day waiting period after divorce	Yes	No

TABLE 15.2. *(Continued)*

State	*No-Fault Divorce:*	*Residency Requirement*	*Remarriage Rules*	*Community Property?*	*Alimony Allowed?*
Utah	Yes[1,4]	3 months for either spouse, prior to filing	No waiting period required, unless divorce action is being appealed	No	Yes
Vermont	Yes[1,5]	6 months prior to filing, and one year prior to final hearing	No waiting period required	No	Yes
Virginia	Yes[1,9]	6 months for one spouse, prior to filing	No waiting period required, unless court orders such while divorce action is being appealed	No	Yes
Washington	Yes[3]	Spouse filing for divorce must be a resident	No waiting period required	Yes	Yes
West Virginia	Yes[1,10]	Either spouse must have been resident for one year prior to filing	No waiting period required	No	Yes
Wisconsin	Yes[3]	6 months in state, 30 days in county, for either spouse, prior to filing	6-month waiting period required, regardless of state in which divorce took place	No	Yes
Wyoming	Yes[1]	60 days for plaintiff, prior to filing	No waiting period required	No	Yes

1. Irretrievable breakdown, or incompatibility of temperament, among other legal grounds.
2. Incompatibility, if both spouses agree on custody, support, property rights, and payment of debts.
3. No other grounds allowed besides "Irretrievable Breakdown."
4. After living separate and apart for three years.
5. Voluntarily living apart for six months, or living apart for one year, without sexual cohabitation (may reside under same roof).
6. No-fault allowed after living apart for two years.
7. Voluntary separation for one year, or involuntary separation for three years, without sexual cohabitation.
8. No-fault allowed after living apart for 18 months.
9. No-fault allowed if living continuously apart for at least one year; may require a decree of legal separation or written separation agreement.
10. Living apart for one year; or irreconcilable differences if one party files sworn complaint and other party files sworn answer (60-day waiting period then required).

SOURCE: Sonenblick (1981); Bass and Rein (1976). These laws were in effect in 1981. Some may have changed since that time. Current Statutes may therefore vary somewhat.

process, which was begun months or years earlier when the marriage relationship began to unravel.

Divorce is emotionally grueling, no matter how mechanical the legal process becomes; every marriage, except the most mercenary, evolves into an intimate tangle of personal hopes, visions, and commitments that cannot be cut away

with a single stroke. We do not get divorced casually; we get married carelessly, and pay handsomely in the spectacular divorce rate which follows. (Sonenblick, 1981:142)

Let us now examine some of the major ways in which our legal system regulates the process of divorce in our population.

ADVERSARIAL DIVORCE

Our legal system is based on the ancient concept of *adversarial roles* of *plaintiff* and *defendant,* the *injured* party and the party doing the *injuring,* the person *wronged* and the person in the *wrong.* Divorce laws evolved as a part of this general pattern, and one spouse was always placed in a position of having to prove the guilt of the other in violating one or more aspects of marriage laws. There had to be *legal grounds* for divorce that could be proved by the divorcing spouse in a court of law before a divorce could be granted. One partner had to be declared "at-fault" by the state, "guilty of such conduct that the state recognizes that the marriage is dead, or that continued living together would be dangerous to the physical or mental health of the injured party (spouse)" [Bass and Rein, 1976:27]. Hence, one partner had *to sue* the other for divorce, making many divorces unnecessarily bitter and hostile contests that added fuel to the fire of emotional upheaval and pain caused by the break-up of the marriage. Such law suits were also expensive, because lawyers had to be hired to protect one's interests when it came to child custody and child-support decisions, division of property, and alimony payments.

Although states have varied in terms of legal grounds for divorce, most states have included one or more of the following in its statutes (Bass and Rein, 1976):

1. *Adultery*   Voluntary sexual intercourse between a married person and anyone other than the lawful spouse, including such "deviate forms" as homosexual conduct and sodomy.

2. *Abandonment*   Intentionally deserting the lawful spouse, without his or her consent, with no intent to return.

3. *Cruelty*   Physical or mental anguish caused one spouse by the other, including (but not limited to) attacking with a weapon; hitting, slapping or kicking, or threatening to do so on repeated occasions; refusing or insisting on having sexual relations; insisting on having "unnatural" sexual relations; and insisting that a third-party sex partner live with the married couple.

4. *Drug Abuse and Habitual Intoxication*   These often are considered a form of cruelty.

5. *Imprisonment of One Spouse*   Usually for a period of years, the definition of which varies from one state to the next.

6. *Failure-to-Support*   Based upon English common law, a husband has usually been legally obligated to provide financial support for the wife. Because the wife granted title to everything she owned to the husband at marriage, it became his duty to support her and any children that were born to them. This is not considered grounds for divorce in some states, which have adopted the more modern concept that "spouses should support each other," but remains a valid grounds for divorce in others.

7. *Fraud*   A false statement willingly made by one spouse to the other who, had he or she known the truth, would not have entered into the marriage. Fraud is also present if one spouse *conceals* a "material fact" that, if known, would have influenced the other's decision to enter the marriage. The following categories of fraud are identified by Bass and Rein (1976:33–34): (a) *misrepresentation of intention,* such as refusal to have sexual intercourse; refusal to have a religious ceremony; refusal to support or set up a home; (b) *physical defects,* such as inability to have sexual intercourse (impotence, for example); (c) *concealment* of prior marriage, prior divorce, or children; of drug addiction; of venereal disease; or of homosexuality.

NO-FAULT DIVORCE

Over the years, it became evident that people were using, and divorce courts allowing, virtually any convenient legal grounds to grant a divorce in a marriage which simply had broken down following the normal process of disenchantment and growth apart of spouses over the years. Strict divorce laws only caused people to seek creative means of evading the law, such as lying by claiming adultery or cruelty existed when it in fact did not. They also increased the propensity to abandon the spouse or otherwise separate from them (Stetson and Wright, 1975).

The concept of *no-fault divorce* emerged as a response of the legal system to the reality of most divorce situations. In many instances, it was simply the case that "irretrievable breakdown" of the marriage relationship, "irreconcilable differences" between wife and husband, or simple "incompatibility" led to a divorce decision. Now all but two states — South Dakota and Illinois — have some type of no-fault divorce law available which allows "irreconcilable differences" or "irretrievable breakdown" of the marriage relationship as valid grounds for divorce (see Table 15.2). Although the nature of no-fault laws varies from one state to the next, the following conditions generally must apply in order to invoke no-fault law in a particular case.

1. Both spouses consent to seek the divorce, and neither spouse *contests* the divorce action.

2. Both spouses agree on a reasonable plan for dividing property, savings, and other assets.

3. Both spouses agree on who — wife, husband, or both — will (a) maintain legal custody of the children, and (b) provide economic support of the children.

Although the issue of guilt is generally no longer present, and one partner does not have to prove the other's guilt on the basis of some legal ground, the courts can still step in to resolve disputes over child custody or property settlements in any of the no-fault states, if that is deemed in the "best interests of the family" (Sonenblick, 1981). In addition, about 30 states still allow the question of *fault* to enter the no-fault divorce process when issues of property and children are unsettled. These are "modified no-fault" states, as compared with the 18 "true no-fault" states, which prevent any husband-wife "blaming and shaming" from entering the divorce settlement process (Sonenblick, 1981).

A major advantage of no-fault divorce laws has been to reduce the legal costs of getting a divorce, primarily in court fees and lawyers expenses. Further, the advent of no-fault divorce has had virtually no adverse impact on alimony awards, child-custody decisions, child-support awards, and equal distribution of assets between ex-spouses (Welch and Price-Bonham, 1983). [However, as we shall see, the child custody and child support situation was already in rough shape before the institution of no-fault divorce laws, at least insofar as women were concerned.] Finally, a major advantage of no-fault divorce has been that it removed a great deal of hostility and resentment from the divorce process. This has made postdivorce adjustment easier for many individuals who otherwise might have lived the rest of their lives in bitterness toward the ex-spouse. It has also made the divorce process easier on children, who are no longer torn apart emotionally by one parent battling the other in angry or hateful terms.

No-fault divorce laws have paved the way for even more facilitative divorce laws. "Do-it-yourself" divorce kits provide a means for spouses to legally dissolve a marriage without having to retain an attorney to get them through the complex legal system. In 1980, Governor Brown of California signed into law a procedure by which "default divorces" can be granted to a number of different couples at the same time, without their having to make court appearances (see Feature 15.1). There are income and property limits that must be met, and the couple must have no children, in order to use the "default divorce" process. Although there is some concern that this process makes divorce too easy, it has helped to clear the jammed calendars of the courts and further reduce the expense of getting divorced.

In the 20 percent or so of all divorces that are contested, in which one partner sues the other to prove his or her guilt according to one of the legal grounds for divorce, the costs can become astronomical. Between lawyers' and court fees, the expenses can rise to several thousands of dollars. From time to time the most notorious of these cases are publicized in the media, because they involve either large sums of money or the private lives of rich or famous people. They can also be emotionally costly because both partners drag out their "dirty linen" to prove that the other person is morally reprehensible, degenerate, or otherwise deserving of punishment by the court for malfeasance in marriage. As Sonenblick (1981:144) points out, such cases of contested divorce usually involve any one or combination of three issues: extramarital sexual affairs, large sums of money and valuable property, or children.

In divorce cases there is an eternal triangle of troublemakers which cause the bitterest battles of the "exes." Three Furies — Infidelity, Property and Offspring — with their permutations and combinations, have pursued marriages with deadly loads of acrimony since the first nuptials were recorded, and time has not sapped their trouble-making powers.

In contested divorces, where issues relating to property, children, and guilt must be decided in bloody courtroom

SAN DIEGO — Judge Raul Rosado has given new meaning to the term "quickie divorce." He summons large numbers of people into his courtroom, where they answer three questions in unison and promptly get their decrees.

Since he began the experiment last year in an effort to unclog the crowded Superior Court calendar, more than 3,000 people have gotten default divorces — an uncontested divorce in which only one partner goes to court — in a fraction of the time it used to take.

In addition, Rosado said, he favors the speedy, impersonal routine because it relieves parties to the divorces from having to sit and watch someone else's "tearful spouse on the witness stand pouring out her woes."

The American Judges Association and the Association of Trial Lawyers of America, however, both expressed concern about the practice.

"In a sense, it could make a sham of marriage by making it too easy to divorce," said Judge Allan Markert of St. Paul, Minn., president of the judges' association.

Benjamin Glosband, chairman of the Family Law Section of the lawyers' association, said marital cases "should be treated on an individual basis."

"I never heard of mass court divorces but I think each separate case should be handled individually," Glosband said in a telephone interview from Swampscott, Mass. "We owe a duty to the client to be able to establish their rights, and we can't do it in a group atmosphere."

About 35 people show up daily in Rosado's courtroom, swear before a clerk to tell the truth and stand when the judge walks in.

The judge reads their names aloud and asks three questions:

• Have you resided in San Diego County at least six months?

• Do you have irreconcilable differences with your spouse?

• Might the Conciliation Court help save the marriage?

The replies "Yes," "Yes," and "No," in unison, bring instant interlocutory decrees.

Uncontested divorces used to occupy two courts for an hour or more daily. Last year, Rosado went to his presiding judge, William A. Yale, for permission to speed them up.

Yale describes the step as "outstanding, perfectly legal in every sense."

Beginning Jan. 1, a law signed July 8 by Gov. Jerry Brown, will eliminate a court appearance from many default proceedings unless the judge sees a reason for it. Rosado's experiment has shown that will work, Yale said.

SOURCE: Dan Tedrick, *Arizona Daily Star,* August 1, 1980.

---

battles, all family members get battle scars which often remain for many years.

RESIDENCE REQUIREMENTS AND REMARRIAGE RULES

States also vary widely in terms of *residency requirements* — the length of time a spouse must legally reside in a state before a divorce is granted. In West Virginia, for example, a one-year residency requirement must be met before legal action can be taken to obtain a divorce, but in Nevada, only six weeks of residence must pass prior to filing for divorce (see Table 15.2). In general, all states respect and honor each other's divorce laws, provided that guidelines, such as residence requirements and filing procedures, have been met in the state granting the divorce.

In terms of remarriage rules, some states (e.g., Wisconsin) require a six-month waiting period following a divorce before a remarriage can take place, regardless of the state in which the individual was divorced; many other states require no waiting period, once the divorce is final.

ALIMONY

Based upon English common law, a husband has traditionally been charged with the financial support of his wife and children. Because the wife was expected to grant title of all her possessions to her husband at the time of marriage, she would generally have no independent means to support herself or her children in case of divorce. It was the husband's duty, therefore, to provide either a lump sum or periodic payment of money to his ex-wife after divorce. This payment is known as *alimony* (Bass and Rein, 1976).

Throughout our history, the majority of women in our society have stayed at home while their husbands earned the family income as the primary breadwinners. This is why some states ruled that alimony could only be an obligation of the husband and never of the wife. Most wives had little or no potential for economic independence. Therefore, alimony was viewed by the law as a fair means of helping her to maintain a reasonable standard of living. However, with the dramatic changes that have taken place during the past two decades — women moving into the labor force, seeking careers, and achieving college educations (see chapters 4 and 8), the concept of alimony is becoming obsolete. Given adequate sharing of child-support responsibilities, women today are less financially dependent on ex-husbands after divorce. The courts have recognized the income-earning potential of women, and award alimony in only 14 or 15 percent of all divorces (*Current Population Reports,* 1981). The award of alimony is more common among the very wealthy, as well as the very poor and uneducated. But, on the average, even these alimony awards are smaller today because of the expectation that women can and should support themselves, and because they are increasingly able to do so.

All states but Texas still allow alimony awards to be made (see Table 15.2). Until a recent (1980) U.S. Supreme Court decision declared the practice unconstitutional, some states (Alabama and Idaho, for example) prohibited alimony to be paid by women to support the ex-husband. Given the modern reality of women's educational and career accomplishments, however, the Supreme Court ruled that some men may be less able to support themselves after divorce than are their ex-wives. Alimony awards to males may thereby be justified in some cases. Nonetheless, the granting of such alimony awards is extremely rare.

CHILD SUPPORT AND CHILD CUSTODY

When children are born into a marriage, both husband and wife become legally responsible for their emotional and physical nurturance. This responsibility continues after divorce of the parents, and the courts must decide who will retain legal custody of the child, and how much each parent will be expected to pay for the child's continued support.

Child Custody. Custody provisions include the following: address of the child's home; who should be notified in case of accident or illness; and plans for education and religious instruction. The official criterion in awarding custody to one parent or the other is, *what is in the best interests of the child* (Bass and Rein, 1976; Sonenblick, 1981). Sometimes this involves custody hearings in the courtroom which, as in some divorce suits, can become quite hostile and messy.

The history of Western civilization has shown that *fathers* have had the absolute right to custody of their children. According to Roman Private Law, *patria potestas,* and later English Common Law, *parens patriae,* the mother could be totally excluded from even seeing or visiting with her children (Alexander, 1977). In 1839, the courts in the United States reversed this law, and mothers were uniformly awarded custody. An 1881 court ruling, which was reaffirmed in 1925, changed the emphasis from the rights of the mother to that which is in the child's best interests (Alexander, 1977).

In reality, however, the custody of children has, in this century, traditionally been granted to the mother, with the father granted *visitation* rights only. This is because of the common belief, and practice, that the mother has the role of primary caretaker of the children. The visitation agreement approved by the court would specify in as much detail as possible the time, place, duration, and any special conditions (holidays, birthdays, or vacations) related to the father's visitation. However, one problem that has recently drawn national attention is the practice of "child-snatching" — kidnapping of children by noncustodial parents who feel they should have been granted custody, or who feel that the visitation agreement is either inadequate or is not being honored by the custodial parent. In past years, the child-snatching parent could take the child across state lines and be protected from prosecution, because the states did not have reciprocal child-custody statutes. But this is not the case today; many more states are enacting uniform child-custody laws, which are honored across state lines. This is a desirable development, in view of the psychological and emotional harm that can come to a child who has divided loyalties to the two parents, and who may still be trying to adjust to the parents' divorce. Also, the child may be used as a pawn in the parents' continuing postdivorce hostility and conflict.

Traditional custody arrangements are beginning to change today, albeit gradually. The percentage of divorced and legally separated fathers receiving custody is increasing slowly, from around 10 percent during the 1950s to over 13 percent by 1972 (Orthner, Brown, and Ferguson, 1976). In some areas, as many as 29 percent of fathers are gaining custody of their children (Fischer and Cardea, 1981). The courts have come to realize the important role that fathers can play in the overall development of their children, and that fathers may actually be more effective parents than mothers. Fathers are more likely to gain custody of their male children and of older children. Older children are often granted more influence in the decision of where they will be placed, which explains why some are more likely to stay with the father (Bass and Rein, 1976).

A second trend is toward *joint custody* of children, where parents share equally in the legal custody and time spent with children (Pearson, Munson, and Thoennes, 1982). Joint custody is most likely to be awarded if the parents can agree on each one's rights and responsibilities vis à vis the child, and if they can demonstrate that they are equally competent, and deserving, as parents of the child(ren). Under these more amiable circumstances, parents are able to forge a more positive postdivorce relationship, one which has a more favorable impact on the child than is often possible in a hostile, or contested custody, situation.

A number of experts have examined the question of exactly what is in the *best interests of the child* when the courts are asked to make a child-custody decision (Alexander, 1977; Jenkins, 1977; Nichols and Troester, 1979; Robbins, 1974). There is general agreement that the decision is an extremely complicated one, which involves numerous considerations on the part of a judge. The following are of primary importance in deciding whether to award custody to mother, father, or both:

1. The parent(s) most capable of providing affection, emotional stimulation, and protection.

2. The parent(s) most able to provide a stable, consistent, and morally sound environment.

3. The parent(s) most dependable and trustworthy.

4. The parent(s) with whom the child would prefer to reside.

Programs have been developed, in family counseling centers and courts, which attempt to help the divorcing parents negotiate an agreement regarding custody and visitation privileges (Benedek, Del Campo, and Benedek, 1977; Weiss and Collada, 1977; Nichols and Troester, 1979). The results of these "divorce mediation" programs have been encouraging. Professional mediation, combined with the cooperative participation of the parents and children, helps to alleviate the tensions and hostilities that often underlie custody disputes which wind up in the courtroom. These programs also seem to de-escalate, rather than escalate, the conflicts that led to the parents' marital breakup (Nichols and Troester, 1979). The results are a better relationship between the ex-spouses after divorce; a faster and less traumatic emotional adjustment to the divorce; and children who maintain positive relationships with *both* parents, and who are not torn by divided loyalties and ex-spouse parents trying to undermine each other in the children's eyes.

Child Support. According to the law, divorce of the parents does not relieve either one from continuing to satisfy the child's basic needs for health care, food, clothing, and shelter. The courts attempt to make a fair and equitable arrangement between the ex-spouses, one which will, ideally, guarantee that the child(ren) will be taken care of to the maximum degree possible.

In determining the amount of money each ex-spouse will contribute to support of the child, the courts will take into account the current and potential income of each person—assets, debts, and other liabilities. Often the outcome is inequitable, however, particularly in divorces where the spouses agree amicably to split their property, cash holdings, and other assets equally. In such cases, the court does not become involved. The wife is sometimes unaware of her lower-income earning potential, and may lose out in the long run if she retains custody of any children. As Leslie (1979:160) points out:

No-fault generally assumes that both assets and responsibilities should be split equally. The only problem is that there are other inequalities between men and women that no-fault has not removed. One parent usually gets custody of the children and that partner is most often the woman. Even if other things are equal — which they aren't — the woman's future earning power would be handicapped. In most instances, the woman's earning power is less than the man's, even without the added burden of child care. A divorce settlement that splits assets and responsibilities equally between the couple really favors the man in the majority of instances.

What must also be taken into account, and often is not, is the full range of the child's needs, and the changing circumstances in which divorced parents and their children find themselves over time. The following considerations should be made (Leslie, 1979; Sonenblick, 1981):

1. The rate of inflation, which will erode the spending power of fixed-dollar child-support payments.

2. The possibility of the child's incurring major medical and dental expenses.

3. The possibility of the custodial parent's future loss of income because of disability or unemployment.

4. Costs of medical insurance.

5. Costs of higher education, should the child go to college, an expense incurred after the term of legally required support ends.

6. Custody and support arrangements in the event of the custodial parent's death.

7. The effect on support payments should the custodial parent remarry.

8. The tax consequences of various child-support payment plans.

9. Changes in the economic status of the noncustodial parent (unemployment, disability, or loss of income), which may affect ability to pay child support.

Clearly, if divorcing parents wish to negotiate division of their own property, child custody, and child-support settlement, both must go into the process with their eyes open. Although no-fault divorce can be a dream come true for those who wish to reduce the economic costs and emotional pain of divorce, it can be a legal nightmare for the naive person who tries, in all good faith, to negotiate child-custody, child-support, and property-settlement agreements without expert legal advice and assistance.

Given this legal background to child-support obligations, let us take a brief look at what actually happens. More than 40 percent of all divorced women who retain custody of their children are *never awarded* any child-support payments from their ex-husbands (*Current Population Reports,* 1981). Moreover, only about half (48.9 percent) of all women who were due child-support payments in 1978 received the full amount; 23 percent received only partial payment; and 28 percent received *none* of the child-support payments awarded to them by the courts. For women below the poverty line, the situation is worse. Only 41 percent, in 1978, received full payment; 18 percent received partial payments, and 41 percent received *none* of their legally granted child-support payments. The average yearly amount of child-support payments in 1978 was $1,800, constituting only about 20 percent of the average income of these women. White women are more likely to be awarded child support (71 percent) than are Blacks (29 percent) or Hispanics (44 percent), and the awards are smaller on the average for those minorities than for the white population (*Current Population Reports,* 1981).

In 1978 there were over one million women who either *never* received legally mandated child-support payments or who received *less than 25 percent* of the amount due them. This indicates the staggering number of ex-husbands who are breaking the law by reneging on their child-support obligations. Because the legal process of tracking these men is complicated, time and energy consuming, and costly, many women — particularly low-income women — are powerless to do anything about their situation. Although failure to make child-support or alimony payments can result in being arrested or imprisoned, single-parent mothers often lack the necessary resources and know-how to activate the legal system on their own behalf. The economic consequences of this situation are severe for these women and their children. As a result, many states are attempting to develop more effective means of tracking ex-husbands who are delinquent in their child support or alimony payments; are cooperating with other states; and are attempting to bring more justice to the system. These efforts are to be commended and encouraged.

PROPERTY SETTLEMENTS

In discussing marriage laws in chapter 10, we defined the concepts of *community* and *separate property*. The type of legal system influences, to a large extent, the equity and nature of property distribution after divorce. As with child-support payments and alimony awards, the ideal situation is one in which both ex-spouses are treated fairly and equitably. In reality, however, this ideal is seldom realized (House, 1975). In strict separate-property states, the spouse who has earned the most money, and who thereby provided the major means for acquisition of assets (house, car, boat, furniture, and so on), is heavily favored in property settlements. In most cases, it is the male who benefits because of his greater earning potential and more extensive work history. This is inequitable for women who had devoted their entire married lives to the care and maintenance of the home, care of the children, and to the emotional support of the husband. Such women may have even abbreviated their own educational pursuits to financially support the husband while he was pursuing advanced job-related training or a college degree.

By modern standards, this absolute rule works unconscionable hardships on the non-owning half of a broken marriage. She — it is usually she — can be utterly deprived of the family home, possessions, or savings, unless the hus-

Divorced women who have spent their married lives as homemakers and caretakers of their children often face severe economic hardships due to limited educational training and work experience; their fate may include unemployment and hours of waiting at the employment agency.   *(Photo © Gilles Peress, Magnum Photos, Inc.)*

band-breadwinner has been gracious enough to take title to these acquisitions in both names, or otherwise provide for the dependent spouse. (Sonenblick, 1981:85)

This inequity will continue so long as women participate less in the labor force; earn lower incomes than men; and experience other forms of discrimination in the family, educational, and occupational systems of society (see chapter 8). Some separate-property states, such as New York and Pennsylvania, have recognized the inequities built into their legal systems and have made serious attempts at "equitable" property settlements which take into account the needs and contributions of both spouses; length of marriage; who has custody of the children; and the present and future earning potential of the divorcing husband *and* wife (Sonenblick, 1981). Even in community-property states, however, property settlements are often inequitable (House, 1975). See Feature 15.2 for an example of how property might be distributed under different legal systems.

A national study of property settlements, made in 1979, examined the distribution of houses, real estate, cash, cars, furniture, and other personal property after divorce (*Current Population Reports,* 1981). Fewer than one half (44.5 percent) of the 12 million women who had ever been divorced as of 1979 received some form of property settlement. For those divorced between 1975 and 1979, and who received some property, the average value of their share was $4,650. Whereas 46 percent of divorced white women received property settlements, only 27 percent of divorced Black, and 29 percent of divorced Hispanics, did. These differences are a reflection of the fact that lower-income groups and ethnic minorities have less property, if any, to distribute, because of their relatively disadvantaged status in society. Nonetheless, a large number of ever-divorced women — 6,675,000 in 1979 — received nothing in the form of property settlements. As a result, the life they live is often one of economic inadequacy, frustration, welfare dependency, and poverty.

The Social and Psychological Meanings of Divorce

In addition to the legal complexities of divorce are the social and psychological problems involved in trying to cope with the fact that one's marriage has failed to provide the intimacy and permanence desired at the outset. Many people feel, and incorrectly so, that they are personal failures if their marriage has dissolved. Divorce is a signal of a *relationship* gone sour, not the personal failure of one spouse or the other. The prospect of divorce, and the

The emotional impact of divorce can be intense — with a web of such emotions as guilt, anger, hurt, loneliness, and depression often felt well before the actual legal divorce is granted. *(Photo by James D. Anker.)*

1. Mr. Jones has been the sole wage earner in a marriage of eighteen years. He has bought a private home with a market value of $75,000 and a family car, both in his name. The Joneses have, at the time they seek a divorce, two children, ages 11 and 14.

Ultra-Separate Property*

Under the property law relating to those states that apply the common-law rule, Mrs. Jones would have no interest in the house or the car. She and the children would conceivably be given the right to occupy the house, but this too is an open question if Mr. Jones decides to sell it.

Community Property

In those states that apply the community-property concept, the court would have the absolute right to divide the value of the house and car between Mr. and Mrs. Jones. Thus, the mere fact that title to these two items was taken in Mr. Jones' name is not binding — the marriage is viewed as a partnership of co-equals. (There are minor exceptions to this rule, such as in a case in which the wife is guilty of marital misconduct.)

Equitable Distribution (Most Separate-Property States)

In states that apply the equitable distribution concept, the allocation between Mr. and Mrs. Jones could conceivably be the same as in a community-property jurisdiction. Again, title is not a determining factor in the court's decision. Furthermore, it is possible that the court could award Mrs. Jones the ownership of the house if circumstances warrant.

The theoretical approach in the states that apply the equitable-distribution principle and the community-property states, is that the courts recognize the contributions made by a wife as housewife and mother, whereas in the ultra-separate-property states the wife's contribution in these vital areas is not considered in the distribution of property.

2. In 1947, when Frank and Carmela married, Carmela had a savings account containing $25,000. She advanced the entire sum to help Frank start his business and worked with him throughout the first five years of the marriage helping him to make it a viable operation. Thereafter, two children were born and Carmela continued to help in the business by entertaining business clients from time to time at their home. The business was placed in Frank's individual name and the home they lived in was purchased by them as tenants by the entirety. After twenty-five years of marriage, Frank fell in love with another woman and abandoned Carmela.

Common Law (Ultra-Separate Property)

Under the property law of a common-law state, Carmela has no absolute right to share in the value of the business. It might be possible for her to claim some equitable ownership in the business, but it is a most difficult procedure. Furthermore, it will probably be presumed that her $25,000 was a gift to Frank unless there is a written document stating that it is a debt owed to her by the business or by her husband. Furthermore, Carmela cannot claim any sums of money for the labor and service she has contributed. The house, under the law of these states, will be converted to a tenancy in common upon the occurrence of a divorce and both husband and wife will each have a one-half interest upon the eventual sale.

Community Property

Under the law of states that apply the community-property concept, Carmela is entitled to one-half of the value of her husband's business in addition to one-half of the value of the house.

Equitable Distribution (Most Separate Property States)

In states that apply the equitable distribution concept, the court has more flexibility in assessing the

FEATURE 15.2 (*Continued*)

equitable interest of husband and wife in both the business and the house. Thus, the court could award Carmela ownership of the entire house as a way of equalizing the distribution of property between the parties. If the business is valued far in excess of the house, then the court could award some from of cash

payment over a period of years to create an equitable balance between the parties.

*See Chapter 10 for the identification of community property, separate property, and ultra-separate property (common law) states.
SOURCE: Bass and Rein (1976:84–87).

---

divorce itself, can involve a tangled web of emotions ranging from guilt, anger, hurt, and hostility, to fear, despair, and depression. Divorced people are more likely to report that they are dissatisfied with life and are less optimistic about the future than are married people (Yoder and Nichols, 1980). Moreover, in examining divorce and suicide rates in all 50 states, Stack (1980) found a close correlation. Suicide rates are but one sad index of the emotional upheaval that accompanies divorce, and the degree to which people label themselves failures when a marriage relationship goes sour.

ADJUSTING TO DIVORCE: BEFORE

In many cases, the process of *psychological* and *emotional* divorce begins months, or even years, before any *legal* divorce action is taken or finalized. At some point, the relationship changes from one that is cohesive, growing, and developing to one that is stagnating, conflicting, and unraveling.

As Waller (1967) noted, once "emotional divorce" begins, once the love and rapport that had existed in the marriage are lost, once the conflicts can no longer be managed and tolerated, the wheels of marital separation are set in motion and are extremely hard to stop. Partners go through a number of stages before the divorce actually takes place. *Role reciprocity* in affection-giving-receiving, communication, and decision-making roles breaks down. The cohesiveness of the couple is further threatened when the subject of divorce is first mentioned, and the *fiction of solidarity* that the couple had maintained in the public's eye is broken. Friends and relatives know that the couple is

in trouble, and may change their previous manner of relating to the spouses by keeping their distance, avoiding them, and not involving them in activities they all used to enjoy together. Then the decision to divorce is made — sometimes carefully and with much consideration, sometimes quickly and on the spur of the moment. The couple may separate for weeks or months, living in separate residences while the legal proceedings are carried out. They may hope that somehow their differences might be resolved if they have some time on their own to think and to gain a new perspective on the situation. Lacking a reconciliation, the divorce action is finalized, and the process of coping with the divorce itself, and the emotional upheaval caused by it, begins. Each spouse is single again — each with his or her own set of problems, challenges, and new life circumstances.

It would be a mistake to think that all couples move through the disengagement and divorce process in this exact sequence, and over so long a period of time. Indeed, although half of all divorces occur before couples celebrate their seventh anniversaries, the years in which marriages are most likely to dissolve are the first two or three (see Figure 15.2) As Figure 15.2 shows, the chances of divorce drop rather sharply with each succeeding year of marriage. [National Center for Health Statistics, 1981b]. Let us examine two cases, where the conditions leading to divorce are quite different from one another.

The psychological impact of divorce is much different for young spouses married only a few months, who soon discover that they married the wrong person. They experience "reality shock" when they find that they have married a "stranger," and do not have the interpersonal skills necessary to manage their conflicts effectively, to meet each other's needs for affection and intimacy, to

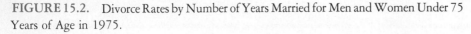

FIGURE 15.2.   Divorce Rates by Number of Years Married for Men and Women Under 75 Years of Age in 1975.

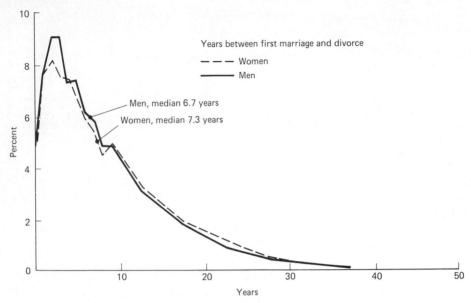

SOURCE: "Number, Timing, and Duration of Marriages and Divorces in the U.S.: June, 1975." *Current Population Reports,* Series p. 20, No. 297, U.S. Bureau of the Census, 1976.

communicate and negotiate with regard to their differences in values or role expectations, and to make decisions that are mutually agreeable. It does not take them long to decide that their marriage should end, that each would be better off with someone else. Divorce soon follows.

Contrast this sort of divorce with the one in which the partners have been married for many years, perhaps 20 or 25, and began their marriage on a firm foundation of love, mutual respect, communication, and compatibility regarding significant life values and role expectations. They had children, and raised them lovingly across the stage of child development and marital career (see chapters 11 through 14). After so many years, however, they have grown apart because they have lived in different worlds, having worked and established friendship ties in different settings. They have gone through the process of disenchantment and are no longer able to communicate about their differences. They seem to have pointless arguments that are never resolved. The feelings of intimacy and affection—the *cohesiveness of the marital bond*—are

gone. Their marriage is now an "empty shell" compared with what it used to be (Goode, 1956). They decide to divorce, perhaps because of an extramarital love affair of one partner, or some other attraction that is found to be more rewarding than their current marriage relationship. They wonder, "What happened to us?" "What did we do wrong?"

Although the outcome is the same for both couples —*divorce*—the psychological and emotional consequences and processes involved are quite different. For the younger couple married only a brief time, the divorcing spouses are hurt, and perhaps angry at themselves, that they erred so in choosing a marriage partner. They probably will go through a period of self-doubt, wondering if they as individuals are capable of surviving in a long-term relationship such as marriage. They may also feel bitterness toward the mate. However, they can take comfort in knowing that they are still young and attractive, that they can return to the "marriage market" and will have an excellent chance of finding a new mate with whom they can have a stronger, more permanent marriage. If they are lucky, the first marriage is dissolved before they have children. Otherwise, their marketability for remarriage will suffer somewhat, both for the ex-spouse who maintains custody of the child(ren) (usually the wife), and for the ex-spouse who must make child-support payments (usually the husband). Just the same, their chances of falling in love again and establishing a new bond of intimacy with another person are greater than if they had remained married for several years.

Now let us look at the second case—the longer-term marriage that ends in divorce. The marriage relationship had a much longer *history* of interaction and experiences. The emotional-divorce process evolved over a longer period of time, and the disengagement process was therefore more subtle and gradual. The decision to divorce was likely to be more agonizing and less clear-cut. There were the *barriers* that had been built up around the couple's relationship—their children, friends, the work place, and community—each with a special way of relating to and knowing the husband and wife *as a couple.* Their alternatives may not be as appealing as those of the younger couple, because their age limits the "pool of eligibles" available in the marriage market. There are also the memories both spouses have of "the way they were," of how much in love they had been, and how deeply intimate their lives once were with each other. These strong barriers, combined with the relative lack of attractive alternatives, inspire strong emotions of despair, loneliness, guilt, and perhaps fear of the unknown future. The hurt is deep, and their lives may seem shattered. According to Krantzler (1973), such spouses may move through a process of mourning following the "death of their relationship," even before the divorce is finalized. It is a crisis requiring personal strength and adaptability, and through which they must live if a sense of purpose and direction in life is to be regained.

These are but two cases of *disengagement* and *emotional divorce* which occur prior to the actual legal divorce. There are innumerable other possibilities, and other factors which can influence this process, depending upon the length of marriage, the presence and ages of children, and the particular circumstances leading up to the divorce decision. For example, consider the case of the spouse who falls in love with someone else and suddenly announces to the unsuspecting partner that he or she wants a divorce. The sense of shock and disbelief is tremendous—much as

with the sudden death of a loved one. The emotional problems in such cases can be especially severe, and adjustment to divorce much more difficult, for the "abandoned" spouse (Spanier and Casto, 1979; Price-Bonham and Balswick, 1980). The situation is also different when an unhappy spouse wants a divorce and the other wants to try to work out their differences, and does not want a divorce. The divorce is contested, and the lawsuit and legal proceedings create hostility, bitterness, and resentment in the partners.

ADJUSTING TO DIVORCE: AFTER

Once the legal divorce is finalized, there are other stages of adjustment through which the divorced person passes. However, research indicates that postdivorce adjustment is less difficult, and less of a personal crisis, than the period of time leading up to the divorce (see Table 15.3). Most people eventually adjust to divorce. In a study of 500 persons who had been divorced at least once, Albrecht (1980) found that the vast majority adjusted well to the divorce and reported that their current life situation was better than it had been prior to or immediately following the divorce. In addition, only 1 in 5 (21 percent) reported that their "most difficult period was just after the divorce, compared with 3 in 4 (77 percent) who found the most difficult time to be *before* the divorce was finalized. The period of *separation before the divorce is finalized* is often the most agonizing and stressful for the spouses (Hunt and Hunt, 1977; Pearlin and Johnson, 1977). Albrecht's (1980) study also found that wives and husbands experienced the divorce process differently, encountering different kinds of adjustment problems:

1. Wives were more likely than husbands to characterize the divorce process as stressful.

2. Wives reported greater happiness in the time period after the divorce than did husbands.

3. Wives expressed greater satisfaction than did husbands with the property settlement reached.

4. Husbands participated in social clubs and organizations after divorce, more so than wives, whereas wives maintained greater contact with relatives than did husbands.

TABLE 15.3. *Characterization of the Divorce Experience and Perception of "Best" and "Worst" Periods*

	Combined Sample	Female	Male
Characterization of Divorce Experience			
Traumatic, a nightmare	23%	27%	16%
Stressful, but bearable	40	40	40
Unsettling, but easier than expected	20	19	24
Relatively painless	17	13	20
Most Difficult Period			
Before decision to divorce	55%	58%	50%
After decision, but before final decree	22	20	25
Just after the divorce	21	19	23
Now	3	3	3
Best Time for Self and Children			
Before decision to divorce	13%	8%	22%
After decision, but before final decree	6	6	5
Just after the divorce	14	15	12
Now	67	71	62
Situation Now Compared With Predivorce Period			
Better	93%	93%	91%
Same	5	4	7
Worse	2	3	2
Situation Now Compared With Immediate Postdivorce Period			
Better	91%	92%	90%
Same	7	5	9
Worse	2	3	1

SOURCE: Albrecht (1980:61).

5. Wives had much lower income than did husbands after divorce.

When discussing postdivorce adjustment, therefore, we must take into account the different experiences of males and females.

Theories abound as to the nature of the problems and stages of postdivorce adjustment (e.g., Kressel, 1980; Krantzler, 1973; Gettleman and Markowitz, 1974; Berman and Turk, 1981; Weiss, 1975; Bohannon, 1970). Although we cannot adequately cover all of these theories here, we will summarize their common features.

First, for many couples, divorce is the most positive step they can take, given the circumstances of the marriage. Although the short-term effects may be stressful, the long-term benefits of divorce far outweigh them. The concept of *"creative divorce"* means that a person must prepare for a "new beginning" of "self-discovery" and self-examination (Krantzler, 1973). The decision to divorce should be a "serious and mature" one, which has the potential to liberate both spouses from an emotional void.

It is not at all surprising that so many people have reported to us that they began to thrive after divorce. It has been our experience that both spouses, after an initial period of confusion or depression, almost without exception look and feel better than ever before. They act warmer and more related to others emotionally, tap sources of strength they never knew they had, enjoy their careers and their children more, and begin to explore new vocations and hobbies. In one case a man who had agonized for years over getting a divorce reported that he "joined the human race" after dissolving a thirteen-year-old stagnant marriage. In dramatic contrast to the anger and desperation that consumed his energies and drove him from one casual affair to another, his postdivorce life has been filled with joy, creativity and relaxation. He earned his Ph.D. degree, became closer to his colleagues, developed a warmer and more loving relationship with his daughters, found what promises to be abiding happiness with another woman and enthusiastically started raising a new family. (Gettleman and Markowitz, 1974)

These positive views of divorce must be tempered somewhat, however, by the concern that some decisions to divorce may be made too hastily, before the spouses have given themselves a chance to work out their differences through marriage counseling or other form of professional mediation. An analogy can be made to the doctor who performed surgery that wasn't really necessary — "The operation was a success, but the patient died." Some married couples may prematurely dissolve a marriage that might otherwise have been saved, and its quality significantly improved, with professional help.

Second, the process of "picking up the pieces," of reorienting one's life and attempting to restructure one's goals and expectations in a new direction, usually begins prior to the actual divorce (Price-Bonham and Balswick, 1980). It is a process of *anticipatory socialization* during which the divorcing person psychologically prepares for the single life that is to come. Although the various stages of adjustment after divorce vary from one person to the next, the goals of the adjustment process are the same: (1) *to accept the fact of divorce* and one's fate as a single, divorced person; and (2) *to establish an autonomous, independent life-style* that is free of the constraints imposed by the previous marriage relationship. Divorced persons must decide, at some point, what it is they want from life now — a new marriage? A life alone? Making new friends? Keeping old friends? Maintaining ties with the ex-spouse? Escape into one's work? Counseling? Escape through temporary sexual involvements? (Cox, 1981:465). The sooner they begin to prepare psychologically for life after

divorce, the more rapidly divorced persons can reach these goals.

Finally, researchers have studied major postdivorce adjustment problems, coping strategies, and factors which influence them. Divorce counseling before and after the divorce can help the person move through the stages of divorce adjustment and get back on the track of personal growth (Fisher, 1973; Coogler, Weber, and McHenry, 1979; Kressel, 1980). Often, the divorce lawyer is in the best position to counsel the divorcing person, yet lawyers often lack the necessary counseling skills and knowledge of the complex psychological aspects of divorce to help the person to adjust (Shipman, 1977; Sabilis and Ayers, 1977). There is a need for the legal professional and the marriage and divorce counselor to work together in assisting the divorcing client to solve postdivorce problems, whether they are legal, emotional, or financial. As a result, a growing number of divorce courts in the United States provide professional counseling services for those who file for divorce. They do more than seek to reconcile the serious problems in these marriages; counselors in these "conciliation courts" strive to make the divorce experience less traumatic, and the legal process less burdensome, for their clients.

There are numerous other factors which favorably affect the person's ability to adjust to divorce.

1. Having support systems available in the form of friends, neighbors, relatives, community services, voluntary organizations (such as Parents Without Partners), a church, as well as one's own psychological strength to cope with the adversities, and absorb some of the shock, of divorce (Colletta, 1979; Hunt and Hunt, 1977).

2. Regaining an active level of involvement in social activities, such as recreational activities, club meetings, and dating new partners (Spanier and Casto, 1979; Berman and Turk, 1981).

3. Being able to maintain positive and rewarding relationships with one's children, regardless of whether one is the custodial or the noncustodial parent (Rose and Price-Bonham, 1973; Berman and Turk, 1981).

4. Being able to complete the process of emotional disengagement from one's former spouse, by divesting oneself of such feelings as bitterness, hostility, and anger, and rejecting the belief that one may some day

Support groups such as Parents Without Partners, as well as friends and relatives, are extremely important to the person's adjustment after divorce.   *(Photo by Josephus Daniels.)*

get back together with the ex-spouse (Bohannon, 1970; Rose and Price-Bonham, 1973). Adjustment after divorce is facilitated further if ex-spouses can forge a cooperative relationship, based on friendship and mutual respect, particularly in regard to child custody and visitation privileges, child support, and sharing of experiences they have in common—a child's birthday, graduation, or wedding—for example (Ahrons, 1980).

5. Remarriage, for those who have difficulty in adjusting to the ambiguity of role expectations and to the uncertain status of the divorced person in society, and who have problems in satisfying unmet needs for intimacy and affection (Hunt and Hunt, 1977; Rose and Price-Bonham, 1973).

6. Having adequate income to meet one's needs for food, clothing, housing, and recreation, and to maintain an adequate standard of living (Spanier and Casto, 1979; Pearlin and Johnson, 1977).

DIVORCE'S IMPACT ON CHILDREN: POSITIVE OR NEGATIVE?

As the divorce rate accelerated upward during the late 1960s and the decade of the 1970s, so too did the number of children affected by the divorce of their parents. Between 1960 and 1983, the population of children under age 18 in the United States remained about the same (64 million in 1960, 62 million in 1983). However, the number of children living with a separated parent increased by 30 percent, and the number living with a divorced parent more than tripled (Glick, 1979; 1984b). It is estimated that anywhere from 30 to 40 percent of all children born in the 1970s will experience divorce of their parents by their 18th birthdays (Welch and Price-Bonham, 1983; Glick, 1979; Payton, 1982). In 1979 alone, there were 1.17 million divorces, involving an estimated 1.2 million children (Spanier and Glick, 1981). In 1980, however, the estimated number of children involved in divorce dropped for the first time in 20 years — there were 7,000 fewer in 1980 than in 1979 (National Center for Health Statistics, 1983b). Nonetheless, as the number of divorces has climbed, "the total number of children who are 'products' of a divorce is at an all-time high" (Spanier and Glick, 1981:330) [see Figure 15.3].

What effect the parents' divorce has on the psychological health and well-being of children has for many years been a question of genuine concern and some controversy. As is the case with ex-spouses themselves, however, the answer is not simple or straightforward. The effects depend on a number of factors, including the ages, matu-

FIGURE 15.3. Trends in Number of Divorces and Number of Children Involved: 1958–1980.

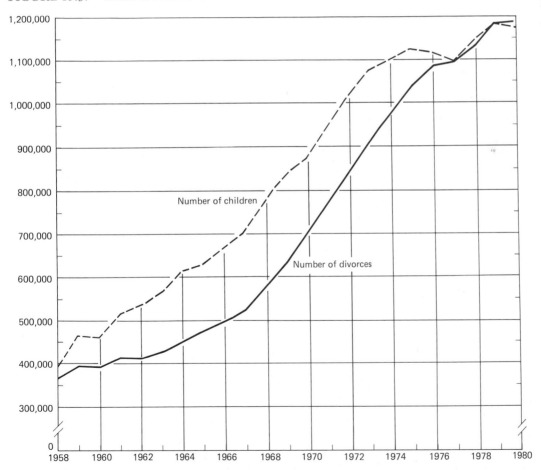

SOURCE: *Advance Report of Final Divorce Statistics, 1980.* National Center for Health Statistics, Monthly Vital Statistics Report, 32 (3), June 27, 1983, p. 2.

rity, and adaptability of the children; the quality and strength of the child's relationship with his or her parents; and the nature of the circumstances surrounding the divorce itself. Different children experience the divorce of their parents in different ways, and with varying consequences and levels of stress.

There is no doubt that most children's lives are disrupted by the fact of their parent's divorce. Divorce is "a major stressor for children" (Luepnitz, 1979). The children of divorce experience many of the complex web of emotions experienced by their parents who are divorcing: denial, fear of the unknown, anger, depression, and guilt. The children may feel guilty—wondering whether or not they caused the divorce, or at least contributed to the demise of their parents' marriage relationship. There is confusion and some ambivalence for children torn by divided loyalties to the mother and father, which can be aggravated when one parent is granted custody. They may doubt their parents' love, "If Mommy and Daddy don't love each other any more, do they still love me?" They are threatened by the loss of a major source of stability in their lives—the emotional anchor provided by their parents' bond of mutual love and affection.

Research has shown that the time just before the divorce, and the first year after the divorce, are the most disruptive and emotionally stressful for the child (Wallerstein and Kelly, 1976; Luepnitz, 1979). The level of stress experienced by the child depends in part on the level of stress and disruption experienced by the *parents* because of the divorce. That is, the children's and parents' experiences are interdependent, one influencing the other.

A study by Wallerstein and Kelly (1975; 1976; 1980) for example, followed a group of 131 children from 60 families over a 5-year period, beginning about the time the parents had separated and divorced. At the outset, these children were, typically, attempting to cope with the emotions surrounding their parents' divorce in a number of ways—by denial, courage and bravado, seeking support from others, and consciously avoiding the thought of their parents' separation. There were fears and underlying feelings of loss, anger, insecurity, rejection, helplessness, and loneliness in many of these children. A number of the school-age children experienced a "shaken sense of identity," of "who they were and who they would become in the future" (Wallerstein and Kelly, 1976:263).

One manifestation of this may be new behavior of petty stealing and lying which make their appearance around the time of family disruption. The threat the child perceives to his sense of being socialized is related, as well, to his concern of having to take care of himself.

Some children also developed such psychosomatic symptoms as headaches and stomachaches as a response to the stress caused by the parents' separation.

Despite the immediate disruption and stress caused by the break-up of their parents' marriages, however, most of the children managed over the 5 years of observation to accept the finality of their parents' divorce. About three-fourths of the children studied were coping effectively with postdivorce life, and one-third of these were judged to be extremely well adjusted. The remaining one-fourth had lingering emotional and social problems, and were still struggling to overcome the deep-rooted hurt they experienced at the time the parents divorced. Children who were able to cope effectively were more likely than the others to maintain positive relationships with *both* parents after the divorce. They also tended to be well-adjusted and emotionally stable children *before* the divorce. The unadjusted group, however, suffered from their parents' continuing negative relationship with one another, characterized by lingering conflict, resentment, and hostility.

Generally, it is not the divorce itself that causes emotional stress and disruption in childrens' lives. Rather, the *conflict and hostility in the parents' marriage prior to the divorce* seem to have the greatest impact. The parents' divorce often improves children's lives and reduces the amount of emotional disturbance and stress that they had been experiencing for the months or years prior to the actual legal divorce (Nye, 1957). Many children are relieved "in a divorce that removes them from a highly conflicted family" (Nye and Berardo, 1973:515). Childrens' feelings of self-esteem and personal well-being are far more adversely affected when parents' marriages are marked by chronic conflict and hostility (Rashke and Rashke, 1979). Although it may create temporary stress, only a minority of children experience enduring effects beyond one or two years after their parents' divorce (Luepnitz, 1979). It is the presence or absence of positive and warm relationships in a family that contribute most to the well-being of children, whether it is a one-parent or two-parent situation.

Divorces often require considerable adjustment by the individual family members . . . yet most families, and the individuals therein, seem to successfully reorganize in time. The time dimension is often overlooked. Most separations and divorce are stressful, but stress usually dissipates over time as families reorganize without the absent family member.

In summary, there is little evidence suggesting that divorce is directly related to negative developmental consequences for children. (Marotz-Baden, et al., 1979:8)

The belief that parents should remain in a poor marriage relationship for "the sake and benefit" of the children is simply not valid. In most cases, children will adjust to the divorce much better than they will ever adjust to the parents' chronic conflicts and unhappiness in marriage. Although legal divorce itself is a stressful experience for the ex-spouses (parents) and children alike, the short-term costs in the form of emotional stress and trauma are often outweighed by the long-term benefits of personal growth and development.

Disenchantment and Divorce: Can They Be Prevented?

How can divorce be prevented? Is there anything that we, as a society, can do to bring down our relatively high divorce rate? What can a particular couple do to keep their marriage healthy and cohesive so that divorce does not take place? The answers to these questions are elusive. However, we are beginning to develop a better understanding of them.

DIVORCE; GOOD OR BAD?

Divorce is often a sensible solution to an untenable and dysfunctional marriage situation. The answer to the *divorce problem* will not be found in stricter divorce laws, or otherwise forcing people to remain in unhappy marriages. The answers are to be found in the *quality of the interpersonal relationship* of the husband and wife, and the factors contributing either to its cohesiveness, growth, and development, or to its disintegration, stagnation, and disenchantment, over time in the marital career. The *divorce problem* in our society is really a problem of *emotional divorce,* of poor relationship development among a large number of couples who, for one reason or another, are unable to reach their goals for permanence, intimacy, and continuing love over the years.

MAKING MARRIAGE A TOUGHER CHOICE

A wise old sage once made the observation, "The greatest cause of divorce is marriage." This message is really less cryptic than it appears at first glance. It is no coincidence that our society has one of the highest divorce rates of all modern societies in the world. We are also one of the most *marrying* societies in existence; we have always had between 90 and 95 percent of our adult population marrying at least once during their lifetimes (Glick, 1979; 1984a). The divorce rate may be a signal that *too many* people get married in the first place.

We have seen throughout this book the heavy demands placed on marriage partners in our society. The vast number of roles and tasks marriage partners take on, each with its own set of normative expectations and guidelines to follow, make the marital career a difficult undertaking. Partners come to marriage from different family backgrounds and with different *role scripts* in their minds, which must somehow be blended together into a complementary *whole* if cohesiveness and mutual growth in the relationship are to be established. Complicating the picture are the *role sequences* that take place over time, as role scripts change with the addition of children, experiences in the work place, and with the individual stages of adult development of the marriage partners themselves. Partners can become easily mismatched over time if they do not develop *in phase* with one another in their individual marital careers (Foote, 1956). Complicating things even further is the fact that most people enter the marital career, and assume this complex array of ever-changing tasks and roles, as amateurs who lack the critical interpersonal skills so important in marriage: decision making; problem solving; communication; conflict management and resolution; and financial planning and budgeting, to name a few. A significant amount of marital breakdown and divorce can therefore be explained by the fact that too many unqualified, underprepared people enter the marriage career in the first place. They do so too soon, or do so with the wrong person. With such a large percentage of our population marrying, and with marriage the challenging and difficult task that it is, a comparatively high level of marital breakdown and divorce is inevitable.

One possible solution to this problem is *to make the marriage decision a tougher one.* One way of doing this is communicating to people that marriage is not for everyone. Just as careers in law, medicine, engineering, teaching, or business are not for everyone, because of the unique set of demands and skills each entails, so too does marriage involve skills and demands that a number of people are not prepared to assume. The idea of *permanent singlehood* (see chapter 10) should appeal to those who do not feel qualified for or interested in a marriage career. Such people should not be pressured by friends and relatives into marrying. Such pressures may be hard to resist. The decision to marry must therefore be taken more seriously. Marriage should not be entered into lightly, and with as little forethought and understanding of all that is involved in this 50- to 75-year commitment.

Some states and local jurisdictions, concerned about the rate of marital breakdown, are taking steps to make marriage more difficult to enter. In California, for example, a 1970 law (Family Law Act, Section 4101) allowed the courts to require premarital counseling of underage (under 18) couples, if it was deemed necessary, before they were allowed to marry (Elkin, 1977). This requirement could be imposed even though their parents had granted permission for their children to marry. Others have suggested raising the cost of a marriage license from the normal $10 or $20 to $100 or $200, so that with more money invested in it, couples contemplating marriage would think about their decision longer and harder. One suggestion is to have all marriage partners-to-be, *regardless of age,* enroll in a premarital education and counseling program and pass an examination (such as one does to get a driver's license) prior to the granting of a marriage license. Whether or not these or other ideas will ever be put into effect, the underlying philosophy is the same: if marriage is made more difficult to enter, perhaps more people will take the marriage decision more seriously; more potentially "bad matches" will be filtered out, and perhaps there will be fewer cases of marital breakdown and divorce.[2]

FAMILY LIFE EDUCATION

A significant number of people are naïve about the realities of marriage when they enter it. They lack accurate information about the importance of such interpersonal skills as communication, problem solving, and conflict management. They have unrealistic expectations of their own and their partner's behavior, and are unaware of the multiple role demands, role sequences, and challenges that people encounter in marriage careers. They may lack an adequate understanding of the basic principles of human sexuality and family planning, so much so that they find it difficult to communicate to their marriage partners about the pleasures and problems they might be experiencing in these important domains of the marriage relationship.

How many people would take on *any* kind of serious commitment, particularly one that is to last an adult lifetime of 50 to 75 years, with such little preparation as we give our population for marriage and family life? It is unfortunate that our primary sources of information about marriage and family life are our observations of our own parents, movie stars, television actors, and any friends or relatives we might have the opportunity to observe before we get married. Our parents usually are no more expert than we are, and often their interaction as a married couple goes on "behind closed doors," out of view, as we are growing up (Hill and Aldous, 1969). Movie stars and television performers often give us a biased and unrealistic view of marriage. We lack positive role models by which we can learn how to be skilled marriage partners or parents, and to be knowledgeable about what it takes to be successful in reaching one's goals in marriage and family life.

Numerous public school systems, colleges, and universities in our society have recognized this fact, and are beginning to provide formal instruction in *marriage and family life education.* These educational programs seek to provide accurate and up-to-date information on the nature of marriage and family roles, problems, and stresses; to educate people about the tremendous impact that marriage and family relationships have had on their lives, and will continue to have on their futures as adults; to foster an understanding of parenting skills and child development, focusing on realistic expectations for the ways in which children grow and develop; to provide an accurate picture of human sexuality and its often misunderstood and myth-laden dimensions; and to build skills in the management of time and money, particularly in establishing budgets and planning for the future (Jorgensen and Alexander, 1981).

Unfortunately, young people in the United States usually receive only a modest amount of formal preparation for marriage and parenthood before they enroll in college, marry, or have children. It is disturbing to know that people spend thousands of dollars, and four to eight years in college, preparing for such careers as law, business, or teaching, yet receive only a few hours of education (if they are lucky) in preparing for careers in marriage and parenthood—careers that often prove to be more complicated and difficult to manage. Although marriage and family life education will not prevent all marital breakdown and divorce, it is clear that ignorance of the realities of what marriage and parenthood are about will continue to foster ill-prepared marriage partners and parents who are unable to perform marriage and parental roles competently.

PREMARITAL COUNSELING

We have discussed the importance of waiting to marry until one is socially and emotionally mature enough to take on the roles, challenges, and commitment to permanence that marriage entails. We have also noted the importance of marrying the right person—the person with whom one has the potential for building a strong relationship that is viewed by each partner as "successful." But how do people *know* they are ready, that the timing is right? How do partners *know* that their relationship has the potential for success?

The answer to both of these questions is, "we never know for sure." Marriage represents a "leap of faith" in terms of what the future holds. However, there is a way to get help in making a decision—of narrowing the distance one must leap by reducing the degree to which one's future marriage is an unknown quantity. *Premarital counseling* is available to those who desire to reduce the level of uncertainty about the future. Such counseling is often available through a marriage and family counselor, minister, or other trained professional. It involves a number of sessions—perhaps six to eight sessions lasting one or two hours each—in which the counselor explores with the couple their (1) family backgrounds; (2) compatibility of values and expectations relating to marriage and parenting; (3) personality characteristics; (4) economic values and goals; (5) sexual attitudes and expectations; and (6) feelings about the degree of love and expressions of affection in the relationship (Hine, 1978). The counselor will attempt to identify potential trouble spots in the couple's relationship, and will get them on the track toward working on them before the marriage begins. The goal of premarital counseling is *not* to tell the couple whether or not they should get married. Rather, it is a useful way of diagnosing potential problem areas *before* they come up

later in the relationship. As such, premarital counseling can help the couple to accomplish premarital developmental tasks (see chapters 9 and 10). It can validate for a couple that they have made a wise decision to marry, and thereby give them confidence to meet the challenges which lie ahead. Premarital counseling may also function to filter out poor matches, or cause two individuals to delay their marriage if they learn that their marriage is destined for serious difficulties.

INTERPERSONAL SKILLS TRAINING AND MARRIAGE ENRICHMENT

Successful married couples tend to be those who have mastered the skills of communication, decision making, and problem solving. The two partners work well together as a unit when they pool their skills. However, these skills do not come naturally, as we have seen, and most of us, while we are growing up, lack good role models from whom we can learn such skills.

To fill this void, a number of skills-training programs have been developed to increase the interpersonal competence of partners in premarital, marital, and other intimate relationships (e.g., Miller, Nunnally, and Wackman, 1975; Guerney, 1977; Patterson, Hops, and Weiss, 1975). Couples who participate in such programs often improve their communication effectiveness, their ability to share feelings and otherwise self-disclose, and their ability to solve problems in their relationships (Ridley, Jorgensen, Morgan, and Avery, 1982; Guerney, 1977). These interpersonal skill improvements also lead to greater satisfaction with the relationship between the partners. However, the improvements are short-lived for those couples who do not continue to practice what they have learned, and who do not work to maintain their new skill levels over time (Wampler and Sprenkle, 1980). Such programs are currently being offered through a number of colleges, universities, and counseling centers around the country.

Another type of program that is less structured than the formal interpersonal skills programs are the *marriage enrichment workshops* provided by marriage counselors, family life educators, and some churches (Mace and Mace, 1975; Smith, Shoffner, and Scott, 1979). The Association of Couples for Marital Enrichment (ACME) provides opportunities for weekend retreats under professional supervision, so that couples can work to maintain the cohesiveness and vibrance which had already been developed in their marriages. Marriage enrichment workshops are not for couples with serious problems and conflicts for which professional therapy is needed. Rather, marriage enrichment programs provide *preventive maintenance* for couples who are relatively satisfied with relationships that are not in distress (Mace, 1979).

Regardless of whether a couple enrolls in an interpersonal skills training program, a marriage enrichment workshop, or just rely on their own internal resources, the key to divorce prevention is *hard work!* The most successful marriages are those in which the partners make a conscious effort to maintain cohesiveness and to overcome the tendency toward disenchantment. Strong marriages do not come naturally — the partners must work together at making them strong and at maintaining their strength across the years and stages of the marital career.

MARRIAGE AND FAMILY THERAPY

Family life education, premarital counseling, and interpersonal skills training are all methods of *primary prevention*. That is, they can be employed *before* a serious problem, conflict, or breakdown in the cohesiveness of the marital relationship forces the partners to seek help. *Marriage and family therapy* is a method of *secondary prevention,* which is available to those couples who are in trouble. As the word *therapy* implies, something is wrong in the couple's relationship and needs fixing, if the partners are to realize their goals and move back on the path to a successful relationship.

It is too often the case that a couple's marital problems reach such a serious level that the therapist is unable to help the couple turn things around. Often only one partner is willing to see the therapist, and the other is reluctant because of pride or embarrassment. Therapy is sometimes a last-ditch effort to save a marriage that for years has been slowly eroding and losing its cohesiveness, and seeing the professional therapist is just one more step on the path toward divorce.

Research has shown, however, that marriage therapy does help to improve distressed relationships in a number of cases (Jacobson, 1978). The greatest benefit, of course, is derived by working as a *couple* with the therapist; this is known as *conjoint marital therapy*. It is critical that *both partners* be motivated to work toward improving the rela-

tionship. It is also important to choose a qualified and well-trained therapist. A couple seeking therapy should examine the therapist's credentials. The American Association for Marriage and Family Therapy (AAMFT) has a rigorous procedure for certifying therapists, and an AAMFT certified therapist is one who probably has the requisite skills and is competent to work with distressed marriages. Finally, the therapist should not be biased toward either divorce or remaining married as a desirable outcome of a couple's counseling process. This decision is the responsibility of the couple, not of the therapist.

Family therapy is also available to those with parent-child relationship problems, which often are stressful for the marriage relationship. Family therapists examine the entire *system* of family relationships when attempting to improve life in the family group for all — parents and children alike (Gurman and Kniskern, 1981). Family relationships are *interdependent*. For better or worse, children influence the marriage relationship. Family therapy can help to improve all relationships in the family by treating problems arising in any one or more of them.

Summary

Although the vast majority of people enter marriage thinking that the relationship will last a lifetime, a growing number and percentage of marriages today end in divorce. At today's rates, nearly 5 out of 10 first marriages formed in the 1980s will be terminated by divorce. In addition, a number of marriages are dissolved by means of annulment, legal separation, and desertion. The United States has one of the highest divorce rates in the world today. This is the result of our emphasis on romantic love as the basis for marriage; the heterogeneity of our population and relative freedom to marry across social class, age, education, racial, or religious lines; increasingly relaxed social and legal attitudes toward divorce; changing gender-role expectations; and our high expectations of marriage partners. Inadequate economic resources and prejudice against ethnic minorities work against the disadvantaged members of society by increasing stress and strain in the family unit. Higher divorce, desertion, and separation rates are the result. The chances for divorce increase as the levels of cohesiveness and commitment in marriage decrease. A growing number of tensions relative to rewards; a growing apart of marriage partners over time; and an inability to negotiate crisis situations successfully all weaken the level of cohesiveness in marriage. Despite the fact that the cohesiveness in some marriages weakens over time, the partners' level of commitment to keeping the marriage intact remains strong. Often this commitment is a result of certain barriers, or constraints, such as negative attitudes toward divorce, religious values, or the presence of dependent children. When the barriers around marriage are weak or few, and when alternatives to the present marriage seem more appealing (such as an extramarital love affair or a desire to be single again), the chances for divorce increase significantly. Today our society offers a number of means by which marriage partners can help prevent the "wheels of disenchantment" from being set in motion. Family life education, premarital counseling, marriage enrichment workshops, and interpersonal skills-training programs all offer a preventive approach to the breakdown of marriage relationships. Although laws that would make marriage more difficult to enter might help to filter out poor marriage risks, their potential is limited because, in our society, we cherish and value freedom of choice. Marriage and family therapy offer hope for those couples who have serious problems and who are heading for the divorce court. However, the effectiveness of such therapeutic intervention depends upon the willingness of both partners to work toward creating a more satisfying relationship that better meets each other's needs. In any event, the marriage career is both challenging and demanding, and requires the genuine effort and work of *both partners* over the years if it is to remain cohesive, vital, and mutually fulfilling. The pressures toward disenchantment are simply too strong for those couples who, for whatever reason, are unable or unwilling to work at making marriage a successful career.

Questions for Discussion and Review

1. How permanent a relationship should marriage be? Should people enter marriage with the idea that "If it doesn't work out, we'll just get a divorce?"

2. What are your attitudes toward divorced people? Do you view them as failures? What desirable or undesirable characteristics do divorced persons have? In our society, is it better to be a divorced man or a divorced woman? Explain your answer.

3. What steps should society take, if any, to reduce the rate of divorce? Is mandatory education, including passing a marriage test, the answer? If so, how would the process be regulated? Who would set the standards for deciding who could get married? Should the fee for obtaining a marriage license be increased?

4. Why do you think that so little in the way of family life education exists in our society? What is preventing us from better preparing people for careers in marriage and parenthood?

5. Think of people you know who, as children, experienced the divorce of their parents. What effect did the divorce have on their lives? How long did it take to overcome the stress caused by the breakup of the parents' marriage?

6. Consult the list of divorce laws in effect in your current state of residence (see Table 15.2). How might the laws be changed or improved to create more equitable and humane treatment of divorcing persons?

Notes

1. Recently, the Roman Catholic Church has used annulment as a means of voiding previous marriages of divorced Catholics so that they can remarry with the blessing of the church. Because official Catholic doctrine considers marriage to be a holy sacrament, uniting the couple eternally with God, those who divorce are prohibited from remarrying under threat of excommunication (total expulsion) from the Church. In view of the growing numbers of divorced Catholics in the world, particularly in North America, the Catholic Church in 1977 expanded the grounds for annulment to include an absence of love and affection in the previous marriage. Under these conditions, a Catholic can petition a local church authority to annul the previous marriage, so that, in the eyes of the Church, it never

really existed. This "escape clause" has meant that millions of Catholics are free to remarry with the Church's blessing if they can demonstrate that their previous marriages meet the necessary conditions for annulment. However, it is important to recognize that although the Church grants annulments to allow remarriage, these annulments are *not* recognized as *legally valid* by state and local governments.

2. There are, of course, ethical issues involved in imposing stricter rules making marriage more difficult to enter. For example, it is an infringement on our highly valued individual freedom *to require* premarital counseling or education. To charge greater sums of money for a marriage license can be discriminatory to the lower-income and ethnic-minority groups in our society. When determining the proper balance between societal regulation of the marriage institution to reduce the rate of marital breakdown and divorce, versus the rights of the individual to live his or her life as desired without government interference, we must clarify our own values.

CHAPTER 16

Marriage and Family Careers of the Future:
What Choices Will We Have?

An important aspect of the marriage and family institutions in contemporary Western society is *change*. Many of these changes were described in chapter 1, as we examined the changing shape and form of marriage over the years. We no longer live in a world in which there is only one way to structure marriage and family relationships. Indeed, the pressures of our fast-paced, urbanized, *Gesellschaft* society — with its mind-boggling array of computers, high-speed communications, medical care, air and space travel, and countless other technological developments — have been accompanied by new marriage and family life-styles which provide an eye-opening array of options from which to choose.

Although many people may prefer to live as a married couple, with two or three children, two cars in the garage, a house in the suburbs, a dog or a cat, and ample money to buy whatever they need or want, a certain number choose *not* to fit into that mold. And there are those who would *prefer* that kind of life-style, but who, because of social, economic, or other circumstances in their lives, are unable to do so. Such people may find themselves in forms of intimate relationships other than marriage, or in living arrangements other than the traditional type of family household of the husband-wife pair and their children.

Only a minority of American households today are composed of a traditional nuclear family — husband and wife in their first marriage, with children present (less than 1 in 3) (Glick, 1984a). By 1983, the total percentage of American households headed by a married couple had dropped to 59 percent, compared with 79 percent in 1949 (Glick, 1984a, 1984b; Masnick and Bane, 1980). This is the result, primarily, of the increase in people who live alone in one-person households, and the number of single-parent households (see Table 16.1). A number of other trends are also clearly evident (Westoff, 1978; Glick, 1984a, 1984b; Jorgensen, 1983b).

1. The older average age at first marriage among young adults, creating a growing number of single people living alone, or with other singles who are delaying marriage or deciding to remain permanently single.

2. The growing divorce rate, which is placing more previously married people in unmarried or single-parent statuses than ever before.

3. A growing number of never-married mothers with children.

4. The increase in cohabitation (living together), which contributes to marriage delay among young

TABLE 16.1. *Changing Composition of the American Household: 1970, 1975, and 1982*

Household Composition	Year		
	1970	*1975*	*1982*
Family Households	*81.2*	*78.1*	*73.1*
Married couple only (no children under 18)	30.3	30.6	30.1
Married couple with children under 18	40.3	35.4	29.3
Single parent with children under 18	5.3	6.7	7.8
Other (such as extended families)	5.6	5.4	5.9
Nonfamily Households	*18.8*	*21.9*	*26.9*
Persons living alone	17.1	19.6	23.2
Other	1.7	2.3	3.7

SOURCES: U.S. Bureau of the Census. Household and family characteristics, March, 1978. *Current Population Reports,* Series P–20, No. 340, Washington, D.C., 1979.

U.S. Bureau of the Census. Household and family characteristics, March, 1982. *Current Population Reports,* Series P–20, No. 381, Washington, D.C., 1983b.

adults who have never been married, as well as among a growing number of older adults who have divorced or been widowed.

5. The growing number of postparental families, who have limited their number of children and completed their childbearing sooner than in previous generations (see chapter 14).

6. More families with fewer children, more voluntary childlessness, longer delays before having a first child, and earlier completion of childbearing.

Despite the fact that a declining number of households are headed by a husband-wife couple with children *at any one time,* however, it is also true that the great majority of people reside in husband-wife families with children present *at one time or another.* Many who are single parents, or who are living alone, are doing so only *temporarily;* "for a period of time {they} are living apart from a family situation" (Reiss, 1980:367). Contemporary Americans move in and out of various types of family situations more than ever before, but most will experience some or all of the stages of marriage and family careers described in this book.

The "New Wave" American Family: Expanding the Freedom to Choose

Marriage and family life in America have undergone monumental changes in the past two decades. Changing gender roles of men and women have created uncertainty in defining the roles of "what husbands and wives should be like." Wives and mothers have increased their involvement in work outside of the home, and changing attitudes toward having children, sexuality, and divorce have reshaped the very foundation upon which we structure our lives. The trademark of our contemporary family system in America is "legitimation of choice," as Reiss (1980:466) notes:

What this legitimation of choice means is that one psychological comfort once available to many Americans is fast disappearing. The comfort was the belief that one's way of life was *the* one right way of life. We are involved now in a society with a variety of life-styles that necessitates people being able to feel that their own life-style is proper for them, *even though* it may not be a proper life-style for other people. [A]lthough people feel that they can agree upon values such as integrity, honesty, concern for other human beings, happiness, and so forth, they may still disagree as to how to best achieve those values in their personal lives.

We are more tolerant today of *deviations* from the usual pattern of marriage, bearing and raising children, and moving through the stages of the marital career in an orderly manner, without divorce. It is true that the majority of young adults today *prefer and plan* to be married at some time, *prefer and plan* to have children, and *prefer and plan* not to divorce, but a growing number prefer and plan otherwise. Contemporary adults in Western society will continue to move in and out of two, three, or possibly more different types of life-style arrangements before they are finished. The range of choices available is far greater, more tolerated, and has been granted more legitimacy than ever before. In this chapter, we will explore the growing range of marriage and family life-styles that will be with us as we move toward the twenty-first century.

Future careers in marriage and the family will include a wider range of acceptable choices than ever before, as many people will move in and out of two, three, or more life-style arrangements.   *(Photo by Freda Leinwand.)*

Some of these will reflect the conscious choice and preferred pattern by those who participate in them. However, other marriage and family life-styles we shall see in the future will not be preferred by those who are in them. They will be in them from necessity, not by choice.

Permanent Singlehood and Childlessness

In previous chapters, we have examined the various advantages and disadvantages of choosing a single life-style (chapter 10) and a child-free life-style (chapter 11). Although these life-styles have grown in popularity over the past several years, this growth has been gradual, and not as rapid as many experts once thought. They will remain viable choices in the future, however, as social norms and attitudes toward those who choose them have become more relaxed and accepting.

It is unlikely that the number of adults choosing singlehood will exceed 10 or 12 percent in the foreseeable future (Glick, 1984a; Jorgensen, 1983b). Although young people are delaying their first marriages to later ages (see chapter 10), and despite the continuing popularity of cohabitation among many, the vast majority will seek the fulfillment of their needs for intimacy and companionship in at least one marriage. Marriage will continue to be a popular choice because of the permanence and security it offers in an increasingly impersonal, technological, *Gesellschaft* type of society.

The future rate of voluntary childlessness is somewhat more difficult to predict. It is difficult to know how many childless marriages today will remain so permanently, and how many are merely a reflection of delayed childbearing. Estimates of the number of married women today who will choose to be childless vary from 5 percent to 30 percent (see chapter 11). We can predict that families of tomorrow will have a smaller average number of children than in past generations, because of changing preferences, economic concerns about the costs of children, and the necessity that many wives and mothers work outside of the home. Whether the percentage of married couples who choose to remain childless exceeds 10 to 15 percent in the foreseeable future remains to be seen. Given recent increases in the birth rate, especially among older women in their 30s, such an increase is doubtful at this time.

Adoption

One choice that childless couples have is to adopt children in place of those they otherwise would have biologically produced. This alternative to the traditional careers in marriage and parenthood is not reserved just for couples who are involuntarily childless, however. A number of other couples or individuals who already have children of their own, as well as those who have chosen not to bear their own children, adopt children. Adoption is also undertaken by some who marry a previously married (widowed or divorced) person with children.

Adoption is the process by which a married couple (and more recently, a single person) achieves parenthood through legal and social procedures rather than through a biological process (Mech, 1973). The goal of adoption is to provide the child with a nurturant and protective family environment, a sense of belonging and self-worth, and the other benefits of identification and trust normally expected in natural families. The legal outcome of adoption is to terminate all rights and responsibilities between the child and the natural parents, and to transfer those rights

and obligations to the adoptive parents on a permanent basis (Mech, 1973:468). Approximately half of all adoptions are made by adoptive parents who are related to the child in some way (stepparent, grandparent, aunt, or uncle), and half are made by unrelated persons.

The proportion of American couples who adopt one or more children has always been rather low, ranging between 1 and 2 percent of married couples with wives of childbearing age (Bachrach, 1983b). However, certain people are much more likely to adopt a child than others: older couples, childless couples, those who are unable to bear children or who have difficulty in doing so, and those from higher levels of socioeconomic status.

Children become available for adoption for a number of reasons. Many, if not most, are born to unmarried women, often teenagers who will not, or cannot, raise them. Others are simply the offspring of unwanted pregnancies, unloving or abusive parents, or parents who find themselves in untenable circumstances (such as prison or drug addiction). Some are orphaned by the death of their parents. Still others are mentally retarded, physically deformed, or disabled, and their biological parents do not have the desire, motivation, or resources necessary to keep them. Some children are harder to place in adoptive homes than are others. For example, the demand for physically normal white children, especially infants, far exceeds the supply. Adoptive parents-to-be often must wait months, or possibly years, before such a child becomes available for them to adopt. Racial and ethnic minority children, those with physical or mental defects, and older children, all have more difficulty in getting placed, and often must spend most or all of their childhood in group homes, in a series of temporary foster homes, or in social welfare agencies.

One conflict that all adoptive parents face is when, if at all, they should tell the child about being adopted. Experts on the subject agree that most parents have great difficulty in sharing this information with the child, and experience anxiety as a result (Jaffee and Fanshel, 1970). However, it is also agreed that the child must be told, preferably by age two or three, and no later than age four (Mech, 1973). This will reduce the level of resentment and the sense of being deceived on the child's part, if later on he or she discovers the truth by a parent's or sibling's slip of the tongue.

Another issue concerns the adoptee's biological parents, and whether or not adoptive parents should feel threatened by the child's curiosity about them. The answer is, "No." Adopted children tend to view their adoptive parents as their "real" parents, and may ask about their biological parents solely out of curiosity. Moreover, the identity of the biological parents is, by law, kept confidential in many cases, and the adoptive parent will have little or no information to give. A few may, on their own, seek to discover the identity of their biological parents, and may try to locate them.

In past years, adoptive parents were subjected to an extremely rigorous screening procedure by the social service and adoption agencies which grant approval for adoptions. Hours of interviews, background investigations, and financial-status statements were required of the applicants, who needed to prove their worth and their ability to be "good parents." It is ironic that such stringent measures have been imposed by society on adoptive parents, yet *absolutely no such measures have ever been imposed on those who become biological parents* (see discussion on prevention of child abuse, chapter 13). The right to conceive and bear one's own children is unabridged, whereas one has had to go through a virtual test of fire to adopt a child. In recent years, however, the process has been greatly simplified, and the volume of red tape has been reduced.

Research has shown that the majority of adoptive families and their adopted children do quite well (Bachrach, 1983a). Strong bonds of love and affection develop between adoptive parent and child, and these children usually grow up to be intelligent, successful, and well-adjusted adults. One study (Bachrach, 1983a) found that adopted children and their families are better off financially than is the average child living with both biological parents or with stepparents; their mothers have higher than average levels of education, and tend to be older than mothers in other family situations. One promising trend is that more single adults and single parents are being able to adopt children. Such individuals are often child-oriented and able to give of themselves in parenting roles; and they are fully capable of being an *effective* parent (see chapters 12 and 13 on the qualities of effective parenthood). Adoption is a viable alternative to traditional patterns of parenting, and can reap untold rewards for adoptive parents, adopted children, and for a society that finds itself with too many dependent children in institutions and temporary "family" situations.

Starting Over: Divorce, Remarriage, and Blended Families

Starting in the middle 1960s, the rate of divorce in American society accelerated at an unprecedented pace (see chapters 1 and 15). However, it appears that we have reached a plateau in the divorce rate, such that only gradual up and down fluctuations around the current rate are likely to occur in the foreseeable future (Glick, 1979; Jorgensen, 1983b).

[D]ivorce will be viewed in the future as a legitimate alternative to the nuclear family model. More than today, it will be viewed as a rational means for removing one's self from an untenable marriage situation, rather than remaining in a home marked by hostility, alienation, and negative affect. (Jorgensen, 1983b:236)

Despite the increasing rate and number of divorces in our society during the 1970s and 1980s, the willingness of divorced people to enter another marriage has remained quite strong. This choice of remarriage following divorce is likely to continue into the future. Approximately three-fourths of all those who divorce are likely to remarry eventually (Glick, 1984a; Mott and Moore, 1983). Remarriage occurs at a rather young age, on the average: in 1980, the average age at remarriage was 35 for males and 32 for females (U.S. Bureau of the Census, 1983a). A growing percentage of all marriages each year are *remarriages:* they comprised only 24 percent of all marriages in 1971, but 32 percent in 1977 (Price-Bonham and Balswick, 1980). Remarriage also occurs at a fairly rapid tempo. About half occur within 3 years after the divorce, and nearly 1 in 5 occur within a year of the divorce. However, the tempo at which people remarry varies according to the following characteristics:

1. *Sex*   Men remarry faster than women, and more men than women remarry eventually.

2. *Age*   Younger people of both sexes remarry faster than do older people.

3. *Current Status*   Divorced people remarry more rapidly than do widowed people, and the divorced are four times as likely as the widowed to remarry eventually.

4. *Race*   Whites are more likely to remarry than Blacks.

5. *Education*   Those with less than a high school education are more likely to remarry than those with some college education.

6. *Working Status*   Women who are employed are less likely to remarry than those who are not employed outside the home.

7. *Income*   Men at higher-income levels are more likely to remarry than lower-income men.

8. *Children*   Those with no or fewer children remarry sooner, and more remarry eventually (Price-Bonham and Balswick, 1980; Glick, 1984a; Spanier and Glick, 1980; Mott and Moore, 1983).

It appears, then, that for most, the return to single life after divorce is not desirable. This is true whether or not children are present. Divorce is normally a temporary state that ends in remarriage for the majority. Marriage is still the preferred way for adults in our society to meet their needs for intimacy, love, and companionship. Indeed, compared to currently divorced and widowed individuals, those in remarriages report fewer health problems (especially women), are more satisfied with life, are less de-

pressed, and live longer (especially men) [Verbrugge, 1979; Pearlin and Johnson, 1977; Helsing, et al., 1981].

THE SECOND TIME AROUND: SOURCES OF HAPPINESS AND PROBLEMS IN REMARRIAGE

A number of national surveys have shown that the majority of remarriages satisfy the emotional and interpersonal needs for intimacy, love, and companionship among those who enter them (White, 1979; Glenn and Weaver, 1977; Albrecht, 1979; Glenn, 1981). Although the divorce rate among the remarried is somewhat higher than it is for first marriages, the majority of remarriages existing today will survive until terminated by the death of one of the partners. As can be seen in Table 16.2, which is based on three large national surveys, conducted annually from 1973 through 1978, the differences in marital happiness between people in their first marriages and those in subsequent marriages are small.

Many of the factors that contribute to satisfaction and adjustment in first marriages tend to contribute similarly in remarriages—such as the ability to exchange affection and caring, to communicate openly and resolve conflicts constructively, to maintain an adequate level of

TABLE 16.2. *Marital Happiness Ratings of Spouses in First Marriages (Never-Divorced) and Spouses in Remarriages (combined reports from 1973–1978 national surveys [whites only])*

	Very Happy	Pretty Happy	Not Too Happy	Marital Happiness[a]
Males				
Never Divorced (2,195)	70.7	27.7	1.6	1.69
Ever Divorced (387)	69.0	27.9	3.1	1.66
Difference	1.7	−0.2	−1.5	0.03
Females				
Never Divorced (2,507)	68.1	29.2	2.6	1.65
Ever Divorced (377)	59.4	34.2	6.4	1.53
Difference	8.7	−5.0	−3.8	0.12

(Numbers surveyed, in parentheses.)
[a] Summary Score: Very Happy = 2; Pretty Happy = 1; Not Too Happy = 0.
SOURCE: Glenn (1981:67).

economic resources, and to maintain compatability in marital-role expectations and values over time. However, a large study of 369 remarried spouses (Albrecht, 1979) found other sources of satisfaction for the remarried: having children either from the remarriage or a previous marriage, religious activity, and length of marriage were all positively related to satisfaction in remarriages. This is quite interesting, in view of the fact that children, and the number of years married, seem to have a somewhat depressing effect on the quality of *first* marriages across stages of the marital career (see chapters 13 and 14). Perhaps those who have remarried have achieved a level of maturity, knowledge, and insight as a result of their experiences in their previous marriages, and these qualities are put to use the second time around (Chilman, 1983).

There is no doubt that remarriages also present their own unique set of problems, contributing to their somewhat higher propensity to end in divorce. Many of these concern the complexities of combining children from two different families into a reconstituted, or "blended" family situation (which we shall discuss later). Remarriages are more likely than first marriages to be comprised of partners with dissimilar, or heterogamous, backgrounds (Dean and Gurak, 1978). That is, spouses in remarriages tend to have greater than average age, religious, social class, and educational differences. Many remarried persons live in close proximity to their former spouses and, if children are present, must face the complications of combining parenting styles and beliefs (Furstenberg and Spanier, 1984). New patterns of doing housework and other household chores must be established, and a new structure of relationships with each partner's kin must be forged. Spouses in remarriages may also be reeling from the emotional and legal trauma of their previous marriages. They may have developed *interaction habits* (in decision making, communication, conflict management, and affection giving-receiving) in the first marriage, which they carry into the new marital relationship. However, these patterns may not work in the remarriage relationship and, like all habits, are difficult to break. As Goetting (1982:213) points out:

Remarriage can be a complex process, and its adjustment accordingly difficult. The problems associated with remarital adjustment are often heightened by the fact that partners in remarriage may still be adjusting to their divorces . . . [A]s an individual struggles with establishing bonds of affection, commitment, and trust with a new partner, he or she may still be contending with the severance of emotional ties with the former spouse.

Perhaps this is why Albrecht (1979) found remarriages to be happier as time goes by — spouses have had a longer time to work through the disengagement process with the former spouse, and can more comfortably and freely devote their attention and love to the new spouse.

BACK IN THE MARRIAGE MARKET: MARITAL CHOICE THE SECOND TIME AROUND

Whether widowed or divorced, the previously married person must make the decision of whether or not to reenter the marriage market (see chapter 9). However, there may be awkwardness and anxiety in having to relearn the normative guides for behavior in relating to other singles who, like themselves, have probably been married in the past.

Knowing where to go to make new contacts and to establish new intimate relationships can be a problem. Singles bars are used by many, but these can turn into a series of fleeting relationships and one-night stands that yield little in the way of stability and need-fulfillment. Church organizations, social clubs, friends, and organizations such as Parents Without Partners can all provide access to new contacts with singles of the opposite sex. Dating activities can be awkward for those with children, and the single parent is often careful to balance his or her children's needs or concerns with their own. The rate of sexual intercourse between first and second marriages is quite high, higher than premarital rates before first marriage (Hunt, 1974). That birth control is a problem for some is indicated by the fact that 10 percent of all remarried women's children are *born between* marriages (Glick and Norton, 1977). Also, the rates of nonmarital cohabitation (living together) have increased for those between marriages (Glick and Spanier, 1980). In 1975, there were nearly one million individuals cohabiting after a previous marriage. Hence, just as cohabitation is another stage in the courtship process of the young before their first marriage (see chapter 9), it also appears to be so for older adults who are between marriages.

Divorced men begin dating sooner, and more extensively, following their divorces than do women (Orthner, Brown, and Ferguson, 1976). Also, given the norms of mate selection in our society (men tend to marry younger women), older women are at the greatest disadvantage in terms of "marketability." Divorced men tend to prefer younger women, and the average age gap between men who remarry and their new wives is seven years (Chilman, 1983). The pool of eligible mates for the older woman desiring remarriage is therefore quite small, and they have the lowest remarriage rates.

THE OLD AND THE NEW: STEPPARENTING AND BLENDED FAMILIES

Given the rising number of divorces, divorces involving children, and remarriages in our society over the past several years, we are seeing an increasing number of adults who become the parents of someone else's natural children, otherwise known as *stepparents*. For centuries, myth and folklore have painted a bleak picture of the "wicked and cross" stepparent, as in the story of Cinderella. There exists a stereotyped view that a stepparent takes free license to be cruel and harsh to stepchildren. Such stereotypes and other unfounded attitudes toward the stepparent have added problems to what is already for many a difficult situation in these "reconstituted families."

Some who become stepparents have no children of their own. Increasingly, however, two previously married adults, each with children of their own, enter a remarriage and *blend* the two families together. These "blended" families, which are a more complex kind of "reconstituted" family, pose formidable challenges, although they yield numerous rewards to the family members.

According to available statistics, approximately 15 percent of all American children lived with one natural parent and a stepparent in 1983 (Glick, 1984b). This totaled approximately 9.3 million children in 1983, a number that will continue to grow as we move toward the twenty-first century.

Stepparenting: A New Challenge. Because divorced mothers are awarded custody of children about 90 percent of the time, it is most often the case that the stepparent is a father. Those stepfathers who also have children from a previous marriage may experience a number of problems relating to their history. Chilman (1983:185) notes that:

> Men in remarriages often feel caught between the demands of two wives and various sets of children. Then, too, it is usually they who join an already functioning group. They often feel guilty over the plight of their previous family and the need of both families for their attention and their money. The sexuality of their stepchildren, especially the adolescent girls, may be troublesome and the issue of discipline is often difficult, especially before children form bonds of affection with their stepfathers.

The stepfather's position is in further jeopardy because his legal rights and obligations vis à vis the stepchildren are only loosely defined and ambiguous. "Under the law, the stepfather is a non-parent" (Rallings, 1976:446).

According to Duberman (1973), *stepmothers* have more difficulty in their roles as parents than do stepfathers. Stepmothers less often report being able to achieve "excellent relationships" with their children. The reasons for this are unclear, but Kompara (1980:71) speculates that the stereotype of "wicked stepparents" is more often targeted at stepmothers; that the stepmother is likely to spend more time with the children, creating more opportunity for conflict; and children are usually closer to their mothers, and it is less likely that a stepmother can follow the natural mother without encountering some resistance.

Stepparents of either sex may face a number of problems. Following is a brief description of the more common ones.

1. *Ambiguity of role expectations.* Stepparents and their marriage partners have learned their parenting attitudes, skills, and values from different family backgrounds, and because the children of stepparents have been socialized in part by the other natural parent, parental roles are often poorly defined (Kompara, 1980). Confusion and conflict can arise when children and their stepparents each bring their own established *interaction habits* and *role expectations* into the family situation. For example, the children may be used to staying up late on school nights, a behavior that the stepparent might not approve. Some stepparents who prefer to use physical means of punishment are likely to have problems with children who have never been disciplined in that way. Because role conflicts may arise in any of a number of areas in the stepparent-stepchild relationship, an important *developmental task* for step-

parents is to discuss their child-rearing philosophies and behavior preferences before they enter the remarriage.

2. *The lingering presence of former family members.* Messinger (1976) notes that ex-spouses and children from past marriages may be a haunting presence in the stepparent's new family. Their influence may be in the form of language traditions, in the stepparent's memory of their own natural children, in the stepchildren's memories of the parent who is no longer present, and in the form of actual continuing contacts with ex-spouses and their children (Kompara, 1980). The stepparent's integration into the family can also suffer a serious blow if the new partner's ex-spouse tries to turn the children against the stepparent, or if the stepchildren's grandparents conspire against the stepparent.

3. *Trying too hard.*   A common problem among stepparents is that they try too hard and move too fast to gain the children's affection and acceptance (Vischer and Vischer, 1979).

> Remarried men and women frequently try for unrealistic perfection as parents. They want to make up to their stepchildren and their biological children for the trauma that the youngsters have experienced in the past. Women, particularly, tend to take on the burden of trying to make an emotionally perfect family life. They yearn to disprove common myths about "the wicked stepmother." They attempt to deny the reality of their reconstituted family and to create the image of the traditional intact nuclear family. Stepparents, perhaps especially stepmothers, often try too hard to achieve "instant intimacy and love" from their stepchildren. Guiltily, they try to deny the anger and disapproval they may feel toward some of their stepchildren. (Chilman, 1983:158)

The three problems most often mentioned by stepparents are (1) disciplining the children, perhaps because the children do not take their commands and directions seriously; (2) adjusting to the habits and personalities of the children; and (3) gaining the children's acceptance (Kompara, 1980). The key to the resolution of any of these problems is *time,* combined with *patience.* There is no such thing as "instant love" and "instant feelings" in the families of stepparents.

4. *Financial problems* can plague stepparents who have continuing financial ties to an ex-spouse and children from a previous marriage (Price-Bonham and Balswick, 1980). Child support and alimony obligations may pinch an already tight budget. If in the previous marriage there were lingering debts, or if it was in financial difficulty, the negative effects can ripple into the new family situation.

Research has shown that children of stepparents fare no better or worse than other children, despite these potential problems (Bachrach, 1983a; Wilson, Zurcher, McAdams, and Curtis, 1975; Ganong and Coleman, 1984). Children of stepparents are like any other children in terms of delinquent behavior; grades in school; ability to maintain good interpersonal relationships; IQ; having positive family relationships; personality characteristics; self-esteem; and major life values. The stereotype of the "wicked" stepmother or stepfather is simply a myth, as parents who divorce and remarry "are often taking positive steps to improve their home situation, and hence may provide a more healthy environment for children than was possible with the original intact family" (Wilson, et al., 1975:526–527).

The Blended Family: Mix and Match. Although the stepparenting role has enough problems when stepparents enter a family situation without any children of their own, consider the added complexities and potential strain when *each* partner brings two, three, or more children together into a *blended* family. The family's *role complex* makes a dramatic leap toward greater numbers of interpersonal relationships. For example, consider the case of a remarried husband and wife who each bring three children into their blended family. Applying the formula for *plurality patterns* $\dfrac{x^2 - x}{2}$, where x is the number of people in the family, each family of 4 had 6 two-person relationships. However, the blended family now has 8 members, and the number of interpersonal relationships suddenly becomes 28! If the remarried parents decide to have their own natural children, the situation is complicated further. It is no wonder that blended families have been called "challenging," "stressful," "rewarding," and "interesting" by those who enter them.

Statistics on how many reconstituted families are

blended by combining "his" and "her" children are unavailable. However, professional counselors who have worked with blended families, and researchers who have studied them, conclude that the normal types of stepparent problems described in the previous section exist in blended families as well — but to a greater degree. Instead of one stepparent, there are *two;* instead of one set of stepchildren, there are *two*. The various cross-cutting loyalties and conflicts can be especially difficult to negotiate. Furthermore, we now have *stepsiblings* in the picture. Duberman's (1973) study of blended families, for example, found that relationships between siblings were seldom reported as "excellent," and major problems arose as a result of personality differences, rivalry, competition, and the formation of cliques. In blended families, for example, there are two firstborns, those who typically are the most achievement-oriented and leadership-oriented children. This situation can intensify the sibling rivalry in blended families (Duberman, 1973:291). Despite the potential for conflicts and difficulties among stepsiblings, however, Duberman found that 42 percent of the 45 families studied reported that "relations among the stepsiblings were improving" over time (p. 291).

Blended families start from a different developmental stage than in the traditional stages of the marital career. This situation can involve countless frustrations and difficulties: there is the remarriage relationship, stepparent-stepchild relationships, and stepsibling relationships, all rolled into one. Chilman (1983:156–158) offers some sound words of advice for those in this rather new, yet growing, alternative family life-style:

1. Work out issues relating to child discipline, either before the remarriage or soon afterwards. The disciplinary methods of both parents can be one of the thorniest problems in blended families, especially when each adult tries to be an "easygoing pal" and become popular with the other's children in order to be accepted before the remarriage takes place.

2. Maintain open lines of communication between and among *all* family members. The husband-father and wife-mother must avoid focusing too much on their own relationship if it means neglecting the children's needs and concerns. This poses a difficult balancing act for the remarried couple, who also need time to nurture and promote their own growth in marriage.

3. Parents must be sensitive to the effects that changing residences or locations can have on children, who may lose sole possession of their room and toys. This can be viewed by the child as an invasion, and loss of turf. One requisite of blended families is *that everyone must share,* which is often quite difficult for children who in the past have not had to do so.

4. An affectionately close and harmonious marriage relationship fosters harmony in other blended-family relationships — stepparent-stepchild and stepsiblings. Unresolved conflicts in the marriage can cause the children of each parent to act out their parents' problems.

5. Goal-setting is important in blended families. Regular family meetings, where all members are allowed to participate and feel that they have had a part in the *family* decision, is an excellent means of reducing jealousies and feelings of being left out or isolated.

6. Coalitions of grandparents and their own biological kin must be avoided at all costs. It is tempting to discriminate against one's stepgrandchildren in favor of one's own natural grandchildren. Again, open communication among and between all members is the best policy.

Given the continuing changes in the shape and structure of marriage and family life in our society, the number of reconstituted and blended families will continue to grow for some years to come. Hopefully, our society will be prepared with the knowledge, understanding, and resources to meet the needs, and to ameliorate the many stresses, that these alternative marriage and family life-styles will encounter.

Single Parenthood: Going It Alone

The number of children living with one parent increased sharply during the decade of the 1970s. As long as the divorce rate remains at or about its current level, this trend will continue well into the future. In 1970, 7.4 million children under the age of 18 lived with a single parent, consisting of 11 percent of all children in that age group. By 1983, the number had risen to 13.7 million, comprising 22 percent of the population of children (Glick, 1984b). This represents an 85 percent increase in just 13 years. It is predicted that 59 percent of all children born in the early 1980s will spend at least one year of their childhood in a single-parent household (Glick, 1984a). A total of 6.3 million single-parent families existed in 1981, representing 20 percent of all families with dependent children at home (Glick, 1984a).

The vast majority (90 percent) of all children of single parents live in households headed by the mother, and approximately 10 percent live in households headed by their father (Glick, 1984b; Payton, 1982). The greatest proportion of children in single-parent households are doing so because their parents have divorced (44 percent) or separated (27 percent). The remainder have a single parent who is widowed (13 percent) or who never married (16 percent) (Payton, 1982). Most striking are the changes over the years in the circumstances causing the single-parent situation. Between 1960 and 1983, the number of children living with a separated parent increased by 30 percent, those living with a divorced parent tripled, and the number living with a parent who never married increased by more than five times (Glick, 1984b).

Single-parent families are more likely to be found among the lower-income, -education, and -occupation status population. One half of all children in single-parent families have a parent with less than a high school education, whereas only one-fourth of those in two-parent families do. Moreover, there were three times the proportion of Black children living with a single parent in 1981 than there were white children: 46 percent of all Black children were in single-parent situations, compared with only 15 percent of the white children (Glick, 1984a).

Because the likelihood of remarriage among the divorced and widowed in our society continues to be quite high, most children in single-parent situations are there only temporarily. As Glick (1979:4) states, "They are in a period of transition between two successive two-parent families." Most single-parent families are therefore not a permanent alternative to the traditional nuclear family mode, but rather a temporary one. Nonetheless, it takes a number of years for most divorced or widowed parents to remarry, and some — around 20 to 25 percent — never do remarry (Mott and Moore, 1983). As a result, most single-parent families exist long enough to experience serious problems and strains.

SINGLE-PARENT MOTHERS

The problems of single-parent mothers are twofold: *economic and social,* and these impose severe hardships on many single-parent mothers.

In regard to economic conditions, single-parent mothers often find themselves in dire straits. Families headed by single-parent mothers are the most likely to fall at, or below, poverty level income. In the worst financial condition, however, are Black single-parent mothers. For example, in 1980, 40 percent of all single-parent mothers were classified as living in poverty, compared with 16 percent of families headed by single-parent fathers. In 1979, the average (median) income for single-parent families headed by women was $6,400 for Blacks and $9,200 for whites. Compare these figures with an average income of $15,300 for single-parent fathers (Payton, 1982). A large number of families headed by single-parent mothers also include at least one other relative, in addition to the mother's dependent children. In 1980, there were nearly 1.5 million such families in the United States.

Despite legally mandated child-support payments from their ex-husbands (fathers of their children), the availability of welfare and support from government agencies and, less frequently, alimony payments (see chapter 15), many single-parent families headed by women continue to experience severe economic strain. Although many are already poor when they divorce and the husband's income is removed, research has shown that many women slide down the income scale or below the poverty line following the breakup of their marriage (Weiss, 1984). The average drop in family income for divorced and separated women is 43 and 51 percent, respectively (Thompson and Gongla, 1983).

There are a number of reasons for the decline in income among women who are single-parents. First, we have seen (chapter 8) that women typically have a lower earning potential than do men because of their concentration in lower-paying occupations, many of which are considered "traditionally female" jobs. Women are also paid less than men for the same type of work — on the average of 31 percent less. Second, maintaining responsibility for the care and support of their families means that single-parent mothers cannot take time off to go back to college or receive extra training in order to enhance their job-related skills. Those women who were full-time mothers and homemakers during their marriage find that they have few marketable skills in the labor force, and must take on low-paying jobs or rely on welfare assistance just to survive. These are the growing number of "displaced homemakers" in our society who are trapped in the jaws of economic disaster. If they must pay for day-care for their children, these additional costs must be charged against the income they make. Some may be unable to locate suitable day-care arrangements they can afford—particularly if they have more than one preschool child—and must either settle for part-time work or try to find a friend or relative who can assist with child-care responsibilities while she is working.

Finally, we have seen (chapter 15) that even though divorcing women are granted child-support payments, property settlements, and sometimes alimony, this support is limited by the ex-husband's ability and willingness to pay. Many only pay a portion of the legally mandated amount of support, and others shun their responsibilities altogether. Even among those who pay the full amount, often the court's allocation is insufficient or inequitable. Such awards often do not take into account the rate of inflation, or growing costs of the single-parent mother's growing children. Children get more expensive to feed, clothe, and house as they get older. In those cases where the husband-father has *deserted* his family, of course, the woman receives nothing. Women who must go on public-assistance rolls still find a significant drop in their economic well-being (Bradbury, Danziger, Smolensky, and Smolensky, 1979). Aid to Families with Dependent Children (AFDC), welfare support, and the food stamp program fall far short of filling the economic needs of these families.

These financial problems are compounded by the strains of certain *social problems* which single-parent mothers face (Smith, 1980; Burgess, 1970). Many experience loneliness and social isolation following the loss of a spouse to divorce or death. Divorced people are more often depressed, and separated and divorced women in particular experience more than their share of health problems (Verbrugge, 1979; Pearlin and Johnson, 1977). The lack of clear, socially defined roles for divorced women, along with negative social stereotypes toward divorcées, contribute to their social isolation. According to Burgess (1970:137):

A single spouse often feels like a fifth wheel—marooned in a society that generally requires "couples" as a prerequisite to social participation. The established culture patterns regarding marriage and the family in American society do not provide institutionalized ways for single parents to resolve their special problems.

and Brandwein, et al. (1974):

Stigma is ascribed to divorced and separated women for their presumed inability to keep their men. The societal myth of the gay divorcée out to seduce other women's husbands leads to social ostracism of the divorced woman and her family. (p. 499)

As a result, many single-parent mothers often find themselves participating less in the events of the community, and enjoying less leisure-time recreation with others (Smith, 1980). Compared with divorced fathers, divorced mothers participate less in social activities and have fewer contacts with friends, and they are more likely to feel "walked on" or "trapped in a child's world" (Heatherington, Cox, and Cox 1976:422). This adds to their already heightened sense of powerlessness and alienation from society caused by their adverse economic circumstances. Moreover, having children present reduces the "pool of eligible mates" for remarriage, should she desire it. Some men do not wish to take on the responsibilities of children when they marry, particularly those children who might still have significant loyalty to, and affection for, their natural fathers. A bad marriage can cause the divorced woman to be cautious, or even fearful, of entering into another intimate relationship that could possibly result in another marriage. Divorced women also find that they have fewer contacts with and receive less support—both economic and emotional—from their relatives, particularly their former in-laws, who might at one time have been close friends and companions in recreational activities (Anspach, 1976; Spicer and Hampe, 1975).

Because social attitudes are softening toward divorced people, and toward the process of divorce itself (see chapter 15), so too is the social plight of the divorced woman. The development of support groups, such as Parents Without Partners, and the sheer growth in the number of people who are or have been divorced, means more social contacts and a quicker postdivorce adjustment period for many (Weiss, 1973: Raschke and Barringer, 1977). Despite the potential for experiencing social and economic woes, just described, a number of divorced women who are single parents will be better able to adjust in the future than was possible in years gone by. Still others

prefer the single-parent life-style, and make that their
personal choice. They may never marry, or may find that
being a single parent is far better than being married to
their ex-spouses. For most single-parent mothers, however, the stress and strain they experience present serious
adjustment difficulties.

SINGLE-PARENT FATHERS

Although only 1 in 10 of all single-parent households are headed by fathers, a proportion that has remained fairly constant for the last twenty years, a growing
number of fathers are gaining custody of their children
(Thompson and Gongla, 1983). Because they are in the
minority, most of the problems of single-parent fathers are
related to the *social* aspects of their status rather than to the
economic.

Single-parent fathers tend to experience the same
kinds of social stresses that single-parent mothers do (De-
Frain and Eirick, 1981). Social activities are curtailed until
they are able to locate other single parents and initiate new
relationships with them (Gasser and Taylor, 1976). However, dating activities start sooner for the divorced father,
and this can alleviate some of the loneliness and isolation
they might otherwise experience (Orthner, Brown, and
Ferguson, 1976). Adjustment to the single-parent situation is somewhat more difficult for the widowed father
than for the divorced, although the divorced father tends
to receive less support from neighbors, married friends,
and relatives than do the widowed (Gasser and Taylor,
1976).

A major concern often expressed by the single-parent
father has to do with the lack of *role clarity*. That is, role
expectations and behavior relating to managing a home
and caring for children are only ambiguously defined for
the single-parent father. As noted in one study:

> The single father role has not yet been institutionalized
> in American culture. The men, in this study, who undertook
> this role did so without clear prescriptions. This lack of role
> clarity contributed to the stresses many of them experienced
> as they made psycho-social adjustment to the need to coordi-
> nate employment and child-care responsibilities; manage
> their homes; respond appropriately to their children's emo-
> tional needs; and rear daughters in motherless homes.
> (Mendes, 1976:444)

Single parent fathers, while better off financially than the
average single parent mother, are likely to experience a lack of
role clarity in their child care and home management roles.
(Photo by Alice Kandell.)

Presumably, single-parent mothers have less of a problem
with role clarity because many of them have already been
balancing housekeeping, child care, and outside employment roles prior to becoming single parents. Eventually,
however, single-parent fathers learn to clarify their roles,
and most adjust to their new life-style quite well. One
study found that single-parent fathers took great "pride in

being able to cope with the challenge of parenthood,'' and felt ''quite capable and successful in their ability to be the primary parent of their children'' (Orthner, Brown, and Ferguson, 1976). These single-parent fathers grew to appreciate, and enjoy, the more nurturant relationships they were able to have with their children following entry into the single-parent status.

The economic situation of single-parent fathers is far superior to that of single-parent mothers (Espenshade, 1979), yet somewhat worse than families headed by a husband-wife couple. In 1980, single mothers functioned on about half the level of income as single-parent fathers. Single-parent fathers, however, earned only about 70 percent of what families earned with husband and wife and two children present (Thompson and Gongla, 1983). Despite the initial adjustment problems and lack of role clarity for single-parent fathers, the fact that roles do seem to clarify in time, coupled with their greater economic resources, suggests that the single-parent life-style is considerably less stressful for men than it is for women.

SINGLE PARENTS AS PARENTS: EFFECTS ON CHILDREN

Let us begin with the premise that parenting is a difficult and complex task which requires a wide range of skills, as well as a generous share of patience, understanding, flexibility, and caring. (See chapters 12 through 14 for evidence to support this premise.) Now, let us assume that complex and difficult tasks of any kind can usually be accomplished more efficiently and effectively with two people working on them rather than one. It follows, then, that the tasks of parenthood are usually more efficiently and effectively handled with two persons sharing the workload and responsibilities.

Indeed, single parenthood poses a formidable challenge to the single mother or single father. The most common problem expressed by single parents is the stress and strain caused by ''role overload'' (Thompson and Gongla, 1983; Weiss, 1979). They must handle all of the household maintenance chores as well as all of the responsibilities relating to the care, socialization, and discipline of the children. The drain on time, energy, and financial resources increases markedly. This problem is particularly evident for those who make the transition to single parenthood after having shared the responsibilities with a mar-

riage partner—the divorced and widowed. They are suddenly thrust into a situation where they must assume all of the work that was previously shared with another; and this is usually complicated by the emotional trauma of the divorce or the spouse's death. Studies of recently divorced parents, for example, have found that parents communicate less effectively with their children one year after the divorce, are more inconsistent in their discipline, and are less in control of their children's behavior (Heatherington, Cox, and Cox, 1976). By two years, however, there are signs of improvement as parents become more efficient and play the role of single parent more effectively.

After reviewing hundreds of research studies on this topic, Blechman (1982) concluded that *we simply do not know* if psychological harm or retarded social and emotional development are any more likely to occur among children in single-parent homes. The carefully designed and controlled studies necessary to answer our questions about the effects of single-parent situations on children simply have not been conducted. In single-parent situations caused by divorce, we have seen that the impact of divorce on children is greatest in the months just preceding and just following the parents' separation (see chapter 15). Nearly all children experience a significant degree of distress as a result of their parents' marital breakup. However, the majority of children appear to adjust to the dissolution of their parents' marriage within a year or two year's time. Studies of the long-term effects on children from disrupted families have found that they do not differ significantly (in terms of life-satisfaction or personal qualities) from those who lived with both parents for their entire childhood (Nock, 1982).

Single parenthood per se cannot be labeled as ''good'' or ''bad'' without understanding the circumstances of the family situation. The most important mediating factors are as follows, regardless of whether the single parent is the father or the mother:

1. *The warmth, attention and caring that exists between the parent and child.* As is the case in two-parent families, child development is fostered by *effective* parenting behaviors (see chapters 12 and 13). It is the quality of the parent-child relationship that matters in single-parent families, *not* the *number of parents* in the home at any one time (Thompson and Gongla, 1983; Marotz-Baden, et al., 1979). Single parents can compensate for their going it alone in parental roles, al-

though it may require more patience, energy, and resourcefulness than might otherwise be the case if another parent were present.

2. *In families where single parenthood is a result of divorce,* the following make a difference in whether or not children suffer maladjustment or developmental problems:

(a) *The age of the child when the divorce occurred.* Preschool children and children about to enter adolescence experience the most severe repercussions of divorce, and may therefore pose more of a problem for the single parent than children at other ages (Lamb and Lamb, 1976; Wallerstein and Kelly, 1980). Single-parent families with children in these age groups may require more support from friends, relatives, and community service networks than others.

(b) *The quality of the relationship between the ex-spouses.* Divorce is not the end of the relationship between ex-spouses. Nor does the phrase *single-parent family* necessarily mean that one parent stops being a parent. Rather, divorce signals a change in the nature of the ex-spouses' previous relationship and in the relationships between parents and children (Ahrons, 1980). Children suffer more when their divorced parents maintain resentful, hostile, or conflictual relation-

ships following the divorce (Wallerstein and Kelly, 1980). This problem is compounded if one parent tries to turn the children against the ex-spouse. Some ex-spouses, however, are able to negotiate a smooth postdivorce adjustment and maintain a relatively positive relationship with one another. They remain linked through the child(ren), and seek to cooperate and help one another in doing what is best for their offspring. Ahrons (1980) has proposed the concept of the *binuclear family system* to describe the reorganization and redefinition of nuclear family relationships, which are formed when parents divorce, remarry, and become two new nuclear-family units (see Figure 16.1). According to Ahrons, the transition to single parenthood is less stressful for the child and the parent when cooperative and mutually supportive relationships continue between the ex-spouses, particularly when they remarry and new blended family units are created. There are important events in the child's life that continue to involve both parents who wish to take part in them — birthdays, holidays, school achievements, religious rites, graduations, and weddings, for example. Children are more likely to develop an "inner peace" and maintain their satisfaction with life if their ex-spouse parents can engineer a social climate based on dignity and respect, as opposed to conflict and resentment. Parenting under these

FIGURE 16.1.   Model of the Binuclear Family With the Child at the Center.

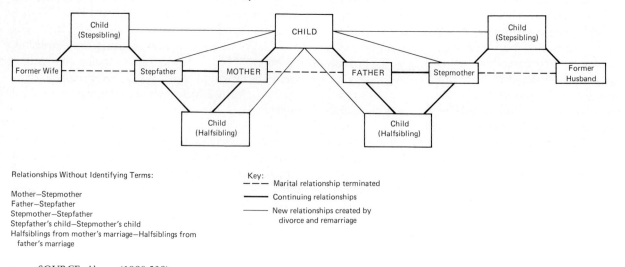

Relationships Without Identifying Terms:

Mother—Stepmother
Father—Stepfather
Stepmother—Stepfather
Stepfather's child—Stepmother's child
Halfsiblings from mother's marriage—Halfsiblings from
   father's marriage

Key:
— — — Marital relationship terminated
———— Continuing relationships
———— New relationships created by
         divorce and remarriage

SOURCE: Ahrons (1980:538).

conditions is more relaxed and fulfilling than it often is under more hostile circumstances between the ex-spouses.

(c) *Linkages to support networks in the family and in the community.* Support networks play an important role for single parents. Such groups as Parents Without Partners not only provide opportunities for social activities and meeting other members of the opposite sex. They also provide a meeting place for single parents to share information and resources, and to discuss problems relating to their roles as parents. The confidence parents gain from these contacts can make them more patient and skillful as parents, which will have a positive impact on children in the long run (Colletta, 1979).

3. *Having adequate income, substitute child care, and personal resources.* Regardless of the reason for single parenthood—divorce, separation, widowhood, or never marrying—adequate *financial* resources are critical to the well-being of children and parents alike. Inadequate income adds to the stress of the single parent's role overload, which ultimately leads to less effective parenting behaviors and tension between parents and children. We have seen (chapter 13) that the social isolation of some single parents combines with the strain of inadequate income to contribute to child-abuse behavior.

Many single parents work full-time in a job or career outside of the home. The stress induced by role overload can be reduced if they are able to find affordable substitute child-care arrangements for the child(ren). Colletta (1979) found that satisfaction with child-care arrangements is particularly important to the single parent, especially among those in low-income categories. Often a friend or relative offers assistance during the week, eliminating some of the costs associated with sending the child(ren) to private day-care facilities. Young children need supervision during the time when their parents are working, whether it is in school or with another responsible adult. Single parents are less able to provide this supervision than are two parents who can work out a schedule between them.

Finally, the *personal resources* of the single parent help to reduce the stress of role overload, and contribute to effective parenting. Such resources include having been actively involved in parenting activities prior to becoming a single parent, such as disciplining and nurturant care (Smith and Smith, 1981). Single parenting

is less stressful for those who assumed some household-management responsibilities prior to becoming single parents, such as cleaning, cooking, budgeting, and grocery shopping. This experience fosters a sense of competence and self-confidence in the single parent, who is thus able to develop a household-management system that saves time, energy, and money (Smith and Smith, 1981). In addition, having patience, empathy with their children, and flexibility in their expectations and parenting behaviors will foster a warm social climate in which their children will develop and grow in positive ways.

Experiments in Family Living: Multilateral Marriages, Sexually Open Marriages, and Communes

The 1960s and 1970s ushered in a period of rapid social change in our society. Along with these changes were experiments in alternative marriage and family structures that departed in significant ways from the traditional nuclear-family concept: a husband-wife relationship with children present. These alternatives emerged among those who were unable to fulfill their personal needs for intimacy, growth, and acceptance in the traditional marriage and family mold (Cogswell, 1975). Living in a pluralistic society, where many different kinds of people have the freedom to pursue "life, liberty, and happiness," was viewed as being fully consistent with the concept of freedom of choice in marriage and family forms. Many people involved in experimental marriage and family life styles had tried the traditional style at one time, and found it lacking.

In this section, we will take a brief look at three of the experimental forms of marriage and family living that gained acceptance during the 1960s and 1970s: multilateral, or group, marriage; sexually open marriages; and communes. None of these, however, ever developed as a popular choice among a significant number of people (Jorgensen, 1983b). Few people today are willing to participate in group marriages, sexually open marriages, mate-swapping and communal family living (Strong, 1978). Less than 5 percent of the population lives in any of these experimental forms, including premarital cohabitation, at any one time (Ramey, 1978; Glick and Spanier, 1980). Nonetheless, most people tolerate them and accept them as legitimate choices for those who desire them (Reiss, 1980). This tolerant attitude will contribute to their acceptance and continuation as choices in the future.

MULTILATERAL MARRIAGE

According to Constantine and Constantine (1973), "multilateral (or group) marriages are those involving three or more partners, each of whom considers himself/ herself to be married to more than one of the other partners" (p. 49). These "marriages" have no legal status, although they tend to be formed by currently or formerly married couples. In their in-depth study of 100 such groups over a 3-year period, the Constantines found that the average group consisted of 4 adults along with any children born into current or previous marriages. The adult members were usually in their young adult years, well educated, and held liberal social and political beliefs (Macklin, 1980). They were found to have strong personal needs for change, individual freedom, and heterosexual contact. They usually entered the multilateral marriage from a desire for more companionship, sexual variety, love, being desired by others, and to promote their personal growth (Macklin, 1980). Although sexual contacts do occur between each of the men and each of the women in most groups, *couple* relationships remain the primary focus, and internal boundaries are constructed which create a separate identity for individual couples. Often these are couples who are already legally married before entering the multilateral marriage, and who will remain together after the multilateral marriage dissolves.

The average multilateral marriage lasts less than a year, however. The most frequent problems relate to the complex role relationships of the members and the increased number of conflicts that arise. Personality clashes and communication difficulties add to the strain, as does jealousy arising from sexual interaction across couple boundaries within the group. Marriage involving only two people can be as complex and difficult, so it is no wonder that the time span of multilateral marriages is so short. The complexities and difficulties of multilateral marriage increase exponentially with greater numbers of partners (Constantine and Constantine, 1973).

SEXUALLY OPEN MARRIAGE

Sexually open marriages are those in which partners have agreed that each will be allowed to engage in extramarital sexual relations. Sexually open marriages are viewed by those in them as providing the "security and specialness of the marital commitment with the freedom and individuality required for self-actualization" (Knapp and Whitehurst, 1977:159). Sexually open marriages are intended to be pleasure-focused in most cases, as marriage partners are not supposed to become emotionally involved with any of their sex partners outside of marriage.

Macklin (1980) and Ramey (1978) note the following characteristics of sexually open marriages:

1. The husband-wife relationship in sexually open marriages focuses on equality, sharing, openness, and honesty between the partners. The relationships are usually secure and the individual spouses well-adjusted and self-assured people.

2. Wives tend to initiate the sexually open life-style, and they are usually assertive and take the initiative in forming new relationships with men.

3. Spouses in sexually open marriages tend to be upper-middle class, with above-average levels of education, income, and interest in community affairs. They occupy higher levels of occupational prestige in the academic, professional, managerial, or creative arts worlds. They tend to value individual freedom, independence, risk-taking, creativity, and nonconformity; they are usually future-oriented, and like to form their own system of values and ethics.

4. The major problems encountered by spouses in sexually open marriages are (a) the continuous work of accommodating and negotiating in the marriage; (b) jealousy, resulting from fear that one might lose the spouse to another, and lingering feelings of possessiveness; (c) loneliness; (d) conflicts over use of free time; and (e) problems in integrating the sexually open life-style into the broader social network of friends and relatives, who may not approve of it.

5. Most who are involved in such a life-style state that the rewards outweigh the costs, that their marriages are happy and cohesive, and that the quality of their mar-

riage relationships either improved or stayed about the same after beginning the sexually open life-style. They tend to report that their self-esteem has improved, as have their abilities to love, communicate, and develop awareness of the needs of others.

This last point must be tempered with a caution, however. Conclusions about the apparent success of sexually open marriages have been based on studies of couples who are still *in* them and functioning well enough to consent to being studied. We lack research on those persons who have dropped out of sexually open life-styles, who have divorced, or whose marriage relationships might have suffered as a result (Macklin, 1980). We therefore must reserve judgment about the average effect of sexual openness on marriage until further research can be conducted on those who, for one reason or another, did not continue in this life-style.

COMMUNES AND INTENTIONAL COMMUNITIES

The social changes occurring in the late 1960s and 1970s spawned the growth of an experimental life-style that promised to revolutionize the very heart of our marriage and family institutions. Because of the unpopular Vietnam war, the heightened social consciousness of those opposed to oppressive social institutions, and the many hypocrisies of a supposedly democratic society, there emerged a counterculture, wherein values were placed on peace, cooperation, sharing, and love between all people. There was a "return to nature," with survival based on only the barest necessities of life. In order to realize these values, groups of people banded together in communes to pool their social and economic resources. Communes varied in size from only a few members to one hundred or more. Communes were joined by all types of people: college students and graduates; high school drop outs; successful career persons with spouses and children; and single drifters who were looking for a place to "tune in, turn on, and drop out." Many were searching for a sort of Utopia in which they could find peace and harmony in sharing possessions and the work necessary for survival with other people in an idyllic setting. Others wished to expand the range of people available to satisfy their needs

for intimacy and companionship, possibly in a sexually open environment, as a means of personal growth through frequent physical contact with a variety of others needing the same thing. In all, communes promised to be the wave of the future, an appealing alternative life-style.

The idea of communes and their formation was not new in the 1960s and 1970s, however, nor were they even new to the twentieth century. Our own history, and that of other cultures, has shown that communes have been around for hundreds of years. For example, for centuries the Hutterites, Mennonites, Shakers, Mormons, and, more recently, the German Bruderhofs, have promoted the development of communal living centered on a unifying religious ideology (Schulterbrandt and Nichols, 1972). These groups sought isolation from the "contaminating" influences of the mainstream society and of less orthodox church members, who were perceived as a threat to the survival of the Church doctrine.

Whereas communes in the past were typically focused around a religious ideology, modern-day communes have been more politically and socially motivated, and were formed by those searching for alternatives to the traditional nuclear family unit. The practice of economic communism has prevailed, however, as the pooling and sharing of possessions and resources are viewed as an important means of achieving the goals of peace and harmony between people in the group (see Table 16.3). By 1975 there were 50,000 communes, involving 750,000 Americans (Conover, 1975).

Relationships among adults in communes range from a group-marriage type of structure, with sexual openness among all allowed, to the pairing off of couples who maintain some degree of sexual exclusivity and boundaries of privacy (Ramey, 1972). Often, legally married or previously cohabiting couples join a commune in order to experience a new life-style, or to pool economic resources with others. The vast majority of communes reject the traditional gender-role notion of male dominance-female submissiveness, and stress equality between the sexes — in household chores, decision making, conflict resolution, and any other areas in which males and females are expected to cooperate and share with one another (Conover, 1975; Kanter, Jaffe, and Weisberg, 1975).

Another important aspect of communal living concerns its *effects on children.* Communes would appear to have a number of advantages over a traditional nuclear-family situation (either one parent or two-parent) [Con-

TABLE 16.3. *Reasons for Joining or Starting a Commune*

*Reasons for Joining or Starting a Commune
(in rank order, from most (1) to least (11) important)*

1. Economic
2. Order and regularity
3. Friendship and support from caring people in a noncaring world
4. As a way to leave home
5. To break with the past
6. In search of a viable alternative to things they had tried but did not like
7. Exploratory—a way of trying out a new life-style, just for the sake of new experience
8. A way to live with a lover
9. A way to live in a single station in the company of others
10. A search for like-minded people
11. Companionship, or community

Activities Made Easier by Communal Living

1. To be single	70%
2. To find out what you want in life	70%
3. To be the kind of person you want to be	72%
4. To meet financial emergencies	72%
5. To find out who you are	74%
6. To meet new people	77%
7. To relate to people openly and spontaneously	80%
8. To solve emotional problems	81%
9. To be cared for when physically ill	82%

SOURCE: Ramey (1978:6), based on urban commune (N = 60) research of Benjamin Zablocki (1977), in Los Angeles, Houston, Minneapolis, Atlanta, Boston, and New York City.

stantine and Constantine, 1976; Kanter, et al., 1975]. These include:

1. The presence of a number of different adult role models from whom children can learn, and who can work with children to bolster their social and emotional development.

2. The presence of additional disciplinarians to help parents regulate and shape their child's behavior in the desired direction.

3. Help for parents in child-care tasks, saving their time and energy, which can then be devoted to other activities that will aid in their development as individual adults and intimate couples.

4. Support for fathers so that they can engage in more frequent interaction of an expressive nature with their children; and relief for mothers who, in traditional nuclear-family arrangements, tend to be saddled with the tasks of parenting and child-care, in addition to household maintenance activities or employment outside of the home. (see chapters 8 and 13).

5. The emphasis on sharing and cooperation, along with individual freedom and autonomy in typical communal settings, promotes the internalization of these desirable values in the children, which will facilitate their own social competence and subsequent adjustment as adolescents and adults.

By and large, children in communal settings appear to develop in quite normal and healthy ways (Berger, et al., 1972; Constantine and Constantine, 1976). Again, it is the *quality* of the parent-child bond and the personal characteristics of parents and other adults with whom the child has daily contact that determine the quality of the child's development, regardless of the particular family structure into which the child is born (Macklin, 1980; Marotz-Baden, et al., 1979).

Despite the many apparent advantages of communes, most have failed to survive for more than one or two years (Macklin, 1980). Few have survived longer than that. Nor does it seem likely that they will increase in popularity. The reasons for this concern the economic viability of the commune, the ability to divide work equitably among the commune's members, and the ability to maintain an acceptable balance of private time and time spent with others (Cornfield, 1983).

1. The complexity of the tremendous number of interpersonal relationships in communes is often too much for individual members, and the group as a whole, to handle (Ramey, 1972). The larger the group, the more complex and cumbersome it becomes. Personality conflicts, conflicts over role expectations and previously shared values, money management and economic decisions, and a host of other potential sources of conflict often play a destructive role in the commune.

2. Many commune members with children, or those who enter as couples with their own boundaries of

privacy, cannot accept the loss of control and sovereignty they experience in their own lives and that of their children. Although they may enjoy the advantages of sharing the tasks of parenting with other adults in the household,

> parents also experience diminished ability to make and enforce rules and find themselves more self-conscious about their childrearing techniques. (Macklin, 1980:915)

Having multiple rule-makers and rule-enforcers can be a problem for children, rather than a benefit, if they become confused; if the rules are ambiguous; if the discipline is uneven and rules are enforced inconsistently from one adult to the next; and if the parents disagree with the others over proper discipline, or become jealous of the influence of other adults over their children. The danger here is what Kanter, et al. (1975:451) call the "Cinderella phenomenon."

> Double jeopardy arises when the child may be reprimanded by one adult to follow one rule (such as picking up his toys in the living room) moments after another adult has reprimanded him to follow a different rule (to clean up his mess in the kitchen). This epitomizes the consequences of the "Cinderella effect"— "Cinderella, do this!" "Cinderella, do that!" "No, Cinderella, do this!"

> This phenomenon consists of arbitrary, inconsistent, and contradictory rule-enforcement where situations of "double jeopardy" (reprimands for the same offense) are likely to occur and where the child has no recourse to a higher court of appeal. Under such circumstances parents are not the dominant sources of social control for their children in the household.

3. Economic pressures on communes force many to dissipate. The most stable communes are those that have a high level of social organization and which are well-financed (Macklin, 1980; Mowery, 1978). Urban communes lack an agricultural base for sustenance through food production, so members must be employed outside the commune and must be willing to share their earnings with the group. Too many unemployed and underemployed adults in a commune places financial strains on the group, which often cannot be withstood. Some communes try to make up for income deficits by means of light cottage industries, such as making candles, clothing, toys, or other crafts which can be sold to the public. Others have relied on welfare and governmental assistance to fill the void (Berger, et al., 1972). Still others rely on such windfalls as birthday checks from parents or donations from wealthy relatives of the members. Each of these methods is far from reliable, however, and the economic survival of the commune is in a continual state of uncertainty.

4. Social attitudes and legal policies are generally not conducive to the existence of communes. Although communes and their members have encountered less resistance and social disapproval over time, there have been few changes in the structure of our social and legal institutions that would accommodate the continued growth and proliferation of communes. People living in communes have "been excluded from the benefits and legal protections normally accorded to families" (Weitzman, 1975:541). Certain income tax benefits, social security, disability, and health insurance benefits; benefits of inheritance laws relating to property and taxes; and child-custody decisions can all be adversely affected in the communal setting (Weisberg, 1975). Communal families in the 1970s often had difficulties with health care, food stamp, and housing regulations (Weitzman, 1975). Zoning regulations can deter communal groups from locating optimum housing. Legal problems can also arise in regard to children in communes. These include, but are not limited to, paternity suits in sexually open communes; adoption proceedings; custody cases; and child-support proceedings (Hauhart, 1977). Questions relating to the rights of the individual versus the rights of the group remain, for the most part, unanswered. Is the commune responsible for child support when the parent leaves the commune and abandons the child? How is paternity determined if a female engages in sexual intercourse with more than one male member of the commune? Do communes have the legal right to educate children, instead of having the children attend an approved public or private school? These are but a few of the legal issues that continue to make communal living a less viable option than it otherwise would be in a more facilitative social and legal climate.

Whether or not communal alternatives will ever increase in popularity in the future, and whether or not they will ever prove to be a viable alternative to more traditional patterns of marriage and family life, remains to be seen. One possible direction we might take is to develop communal settings for the elderly, which might ameliorate some of their serious economic, social, and psychological problems (see chapter 14) [Streib, 1978]. The Share-A-Home concept in Florida allows for "families" of nonrelated elderly persons to share the rising costs of living while enjoying more companionship and recreational activities than they would otherwise have as single persons living alone on fixed-incomes. It remains to be seen whether social norms and legal policies will change sufficiently to accommodate these and other types of communal arrangements, which are viewed by their members as viable alternatives to other types of family structures.

Homosexual Life-styles and Relationships

Although a precise estimate the number of homosexuals in our society is difficult to determine (see chapter 5), it is certain that contemporary Americans involved in homosexual relationships number in the millions. Attitudes toward homosexuality in our culture have become somewhat more tolerant since the beginning of the *homosexual liberation* movement in the late 1960s and early 1970s. As more and more homosexual individuals have come "out of the closet" to publicly express their sexual preference, homosexuality has less of a stigma than it once had. Clearly, the chosen life-style of many in the future will involve at least some degree of homosexual contact.

HOMOSEXUAL OPPRESSION AND LIBERATION

Prior to the changes effected by the homosexual liberation movement, homosexual activity could lead to a person's being arrested for criminal activity, prosecuted, and jailed, even if the activity was by mutually consenting adults; losing a job; being rejected by friends, parents, and other family members; and intense social ostracism (Godow, 1982:387). Previously married homosexuals who divorced were always determined to be "unfit" par-

ents, and were denied custody of any children as a result. Homosexual couples could be denied loans and housing because of their sexual preferences. There were countless other legal, social, and economic barriers which subjected the homosexual individual to ridicule and punishment that was unjust and inhumane. Although the sanctions against homosexuality have not been as severe as in some cultures (such as in the preliterate Rwvala of the Middle East, who sentenced male and female homosexual offenders to death), they have been quite severe for such a modern and supposedly enlightened society as our own.

Studies of attitudes toward homosexuality have shown that the general population has supported such punitive policies. For example, surveys of thousands of American adults taken in the late 1960s and throughout the 1970s showed that more than 70 percent viewed homosexuality as an illness, and as "always wrong." Another 10 percent viewed it as a criminal activity, and 9 percent considered it sinful behavior. Nearly two-thirds rejected the idea of liberalizing sex laws to protect the rights of consenting homosexual adults, and most of these people considered homosexual behavior to be "obscene" and "vulgar." Approximately one out of every two respondents stated that homosexuals should not be allowed to be teachers, members of the clergy, or judges (Godow, 1982; Weinberg and Williams, 1974; National Opinion Research Center, 1977).

This oppressive stance toward homosexuality in our society has had several adverse effects on the homosexual individual. Many have been forced to repress their sexual desires out of fear of being detected and ridiculed, or, worse yet, arrested. Others have been forced to seek clandestine homosexual relationships, forcing them into deceiving friends and family. Some homosexuals do not identify or accept their true sexual preference until after marriage and parenthood, when it is often too late to do anything about it in a way that would not offend or embarrass their loved ones. Whatever the case, the homosexual life-style of years past has often been one of frustration, alienation, loneliness, and depression. For many, there was no way out of this untenable situation, thus causing them undue suffering and emotional pain. Some actually came to accept the social stereotypes of the homosexual person, and learned to view themselves as sick, immoral, or simply undesirable people. Obviously, such self-concepts are not conducive to personal growth and development during adulthood.

It was from this repressive social context that the homosexual liberation movement sprang in the early 1970s. Groups of homosexual individuals formed political and social action groups in an effort to develop a common consciousness of self-acceptance and dignity among the homosexual population (Humphreys, 1972). Major cities across the United States saw hundreds of thousands of homosexuals marching in demonstrations in the streets. It soon became clear that homosexual people came from all walks of life and all socioeconomic levels. Out of the "closets" came clergy and cab drivers, doctors and electricians, judges and housewives, football players and musicians. Within a short time, homosexual bars, restaurants, discos, and even whole areas of large cities, became places where homosexuals could enjoy life, and meet others without fear of ridicule and social disapproval. Those who went public with their homosexuality usually expressed relief at no longer having to hide this important aspect of their lives. The American Psychiatric Association also removed homosexuality from its list of mental disturbances, and a number of changes were made in the legal system, removing some of the official discrimination against homosexuals that had always existed. For example, some courts around the country permitted divorced homosexual parents to retain custody of children, to remain in teaching positions and other professions, and to have equal access to housing and other benefits that society has to offer. Some states have either deleted sex laws banning homosexual activity or refuse to enforce existing laws.

Despite these rather significant gains, however, it must be realized that, for the most part, negative social attitudes and discriminatory laws and social policies toward homosexual people remain strong. The homosexual liberation movement has met with stiff opposition from conservative religious and political groups, who have fought hard in several states and communities to retain oppressive laws and policies against homosexuals. This means that courtroom battles and legal challenges will continue well into the future, as the homosexual population continues to fight for equal protection and equal rights under the law, which are currently enjoyed by the rest of the population. We can expect more changes to take place beyond those initiated by the homosexual liberation movement, but the current strength and determination of the opposition groups will make any further change quite gradual. In any event, the homosexual population is sufficiently large, and now sufficiently visible, to make this an increasingly popular and viable life-style option in the future.

THE HOMOSEXUAL LIFE-STYLE: AN OPTION FOR INTIMACY IN THE FUTURE

Just as marriage relationships can take on a variety of forms and functions for spouses, so too are homosexual relationships diverse in nature. Some homosexuals are committed to a monogamous relationship that is expected to last for some time; others move in and out of relatively transitory, short-term relationships, which involve fleeting sexual relationships, perhaps friendship, and little in terms of emotional involvement or commitment. At this time there is no legal basis for homosexual marriage, as the states have repeatedly denied legal status to any but heterosexual unions (Sonenblick, 1981). Although some homosexual couples go through marriage-like ceremonies to publicly announce their mutual love and commitment, these are not accorded the legal obligations, rights, and protection that heterosexual marriages receive. It is unlikely that this situation will change in the near future. Therefore homosexual relationships must continue to be developed outside of a marital context.

The homosexual bar is often viewed as the "center of the homosexual social world" (Wilson, et al. 1980:393). The homosexual bar functions in the same way that singles bars do for heterosexual men and women: a place to meet others with compatible sexual interests, and possibly to move on to more sexually and emotionally intimate levels in newly formed relationships. Physical attractiveness is an important first filter in the homosexual bar, as is the case in the heterosexual singles bar. For the covert homosexual who has not yet "come out of the closet," such bars provide a potential source of sexual partners and a friendly supportive social atmosphere, while insulating him or her from the "straight" world. This helps to reduce the risk that friends, relatives, or fellow workers will discover his or her homosexuality. In the straight (heterosexual) world, the homosexual person must act the traditional, or expected, heterosexual gender roles, but the homosexual community offers the opportunity for homosexual people to be themselves.

One of the most detailed studies of homosexual relationships was conducted in San Francisco by Bell and

Weinberg (1978). Their sample included 1,000 homosexual men and women, along with a comparison group of 500 heterosexuals of both sexes. These researchers found five basic types of relationships among the homosexual participants in the study, about equally distributed in frequency:

1. *Asexual*   Those who avoid sexual involvement with others, or who for some reason are unable to become involved.

2. *Dysfunctional*   Those who expressed little or no satisfaction with their lives.

3. *Functionals*   Those for whom establishing sexual contacts with many others was the driving force of their lives.

4. *Open-Coupleds*   Those involved in a relatively committed sexual relationship with one other person, often living together with the sex partner, but who also seek occasional to frequent sexual contacts outside the relationship.

5. *Close-Coupleds*   Those involved in sexually exclusive, and emotionally intimate, relationships with one other person.

This study, along with others (e.g., Weinberg and Williams, 1974), have found a number of other features of homosexual relationships in contemporary society. First, homosexual women (lesbians) are more likely than homosexual men (gays) to become emotionally involved and committed in longer term monogamous relationships. Although most homosexual males have engaged in a relatively committed and emotionally close gay relationship, they are more likely than females to engage in short-term sexual encounters with a variety of different partners.

Second, stereotyped images of gay men depict them as quite effeminate in their physical appearance, speech, and mannerisms, and lesbians are viewed as masculine. Although some homosexuals certainly fit these molds, most do not. Their perfectly normal, average appearance and behavior patterns allow most homosexuals to "pass" in the straight world. This helps account for the fact that some homosexuals enter into intimate heterosexual relationships, possibly eventuating in marriage and parenthood, while they are trying to conceal their true sexual preference from others. Unfortunately, these kinds of situations—where the homosexual person must act as if he or she is straight—often aggravate their sense of guilt, depression, and anxiety.

Third, the average homosexual person is just as psychologically well adjusted as the average heterosexual. Although stress certainly exists in the daily lives of homosexual people, regardless of whether or not their homosexuality is known to others, they are just as able to manage that stress as are heterosexuals. Perhaps the most stressful decision the homosexual person must make is whether or not to publicly reveal his or her homosexuality to friends, relatives, and fellow workers (Godow, 1982; Wilson, et al., 1980). A positive advantage of "coming out" is the sense of relief over no longer having to conceal one's homosexuality: no longer deceiving others on a routine basis; and no longer trying to act the role of a heterosexual. However, there is a degree of risk, because one does not know how others will respond to the revelation. Friends might be lost, relatives might become distant, and security in a job or profession might be jeopardized. There are no easy answers to this dilemma, and each decision must be made after careful consideration of the pros and cons of each situation.

The homosexual life-style and intimate homosexual relationships will continue into the future. Because of the increasingly tolerant attitudes toward homosexuality in society, and because of the vastly increased visibility of the homosexual community today, more homosexual individuals in the future will choose this life-style over traditional marriage and parenthood. It remains to be seen whether or not the homosexual life-style will ever be accorded the degree of legitimacy that more traditional marriage and family arrangements receive. We can expect that laws, public policies, and social attitudes toward homosexuality will continue to grow more tolerant in our society, but the changes will be slow in coming. In any event, the homosexual life-style and relationships will be viewed by many as a viable choice in the years to come.

Summary

Careers in marriage and the family have undergone dramatic changes over the past several years. Only a minority of American households at any one time are composed of a married couple in their first marriage with children present. People are staying single and childless longer; more are staying permanently single and childless; and divorce and remarriage rates indicate that there is a growing number of *reconstituted* families. Changes in gender roles and employment patterns of women outside of the home have challenged the traditional structure of husband and wife roles in marriage, so that bargaining, negotiation, communication, and conflict management become skills that have never been more important. With these changes in the marriage and family institutions has come an increased acceptance of such alternative marriage and family lifestyles as *multilateral marriage, sexually open marriages,* and *communal family arrangements*. Although relatively few people will ever enter into such alternative life-

styles, the important point is that our society has grown more tolerant of options such as these. They are among the growing range of choices we will have in marriage and family careers of the future, along with childlessness, singlehood, and blended families.

Despite this growing range of acceptable choices, however, all indicators point to the continuing popularity of marriage and parenthood. The vast majority of adults in our society will marry at least one time, and most who marry will either bear or adopt children. Family sizes will be kept smaller because women will continue to work outside of the home, and because current preferences for smaller families will extend well into the future. Marriage will even continue to be a

The human "touch" provided by marriage and family relationships will assure their continued popularity, in one form or another, for many years to come.   *(Photo by Nancy Durrell McKenna.)*

popular choice among the more than 2 million people who divorce each year. Most will remarry. Despite the many stresses and strains, and pushes and pulls, that marriage has undergone over the past several years, it remains the preferred means by which people seek to satisfy their needs for love, intimacy, and companionship.

More than ever before, marriage and family careers of the future will present a wide range and diversity of life-styles for the average person in our society. More people will find themselves moving in and out of temporary marriage and family situations. Although the vast majority will marry at least once, and most will experience parenthood, the individual is more likely than ever before to have extended periods of singlehood before marriage and childlessness after marriage, to move into and out of different marriage relationships by means of divorce and remarriage, and to experience life as a single parent and as a stepparent of someone else's children. Marriage and family careers will continue to be popular choices in the future, but in modified forms that will change in order to adjust to continuing changes in our society. In an increasingly high-technology and impersonal *Gesellschaft* society, the need for the human "touch" will become ever more apparent. In all likelihood, careers in marriage and the family will remain the most popular way of providing that "touch."

Questions for Discussion and Review

1. What are your attitudes toward adoption? Would you ever consider adoption as a means of parenthood? What do you see as the advantages and disadvantages facing adoptive families?

2. What do you consider to be the major problems associated with stepparenting and blended families? Do you see any advantages to them?

3. What can our society do to ease the problems associated with single parents? Why do single-parent mothers have a more difficult situation than single-parent fathers? Why do women more frequently gain custody of the children after a divorce if they have a more difficult time financially supporting them?

4. What are your attitudes toward sexually open marriage? Would you ever consider such a life-style? What problems might be anticipated? What might be some of the advantages? Would you ever consider a multilateral marriage situation? Why or why not?

5. Would you ever consider a communal type of arrangement? Explain your answer. Compare the advantages of a communal life-style with the disadvantages. Why do you think so few communes survive more than a year or two? What are the constraints in society operating against their survival?

6. What will the "average American family" be like in the year 2000? What about in the year 2050? How will the family of the future be different from the family of today? Structure your response according to the major bases of marriage discussed in this book: love and affection; gender roles; family planning and childbearing; communication; and economic functioning. Will marriage and family be necessary in the future? Why or why not?

7. Do you think that homosexual relationships will ever be accorded a degree of legitimacy comparable to heterosexual relationships? Will homosexual marriages ever be given legal status? What effect will the homosexual life-style and relationships have on more traditional careers in marriage and the family of the future?

Appendix
Managing Income:
Budgeting, Credit, and Investments

The quality of marriage and family life today is influenced not only by the total number of dollars earned, but also by the ability to *manage the dollars earned*. In fact, the budgeting, spending, and investing of income earned is often more critical to economic functioning than is the absolute income level. We will now explore the key areas of family financial planning and management that contribute to the ability of marriage partners to turn a limited amount of economic resources into a safe, secure, and growing economic base for the family.

Inflation: The Great Dollar Disease

The dominant trend of the American economy in recent years has been *inflation*. Simply stated, *inflation is a continuing rise in prices* for goods and services. Inflation erodes the purchasing power of a given monetary unit, such as the dollar, so that it buys less this year then it did last year. Inflation has many causes, including (1) increasing supplies of money circulating in the economy; (2) increasing cost to produce goods or services; (3) increasing demand for goods being made by a growing population who wish to share in the reward structure of modern society; (4) shortages of major consumer goods; and (5) any decline in the value of the dollar relative to other nations' currencies, causing higher prices to be charged for imported goods.

The rate of inflation is greater than the growth of income for many families. These families are slipping behind, as they see their dollars purchase less and less with each passing year. For those on fixed-incomes, or with declining incomes caused by unemployment or some other economic misfortune, the effects of inflation are particularly devastating. The need to budget income effectively is therefore becoming increasingly pronounced for the American family that seeks to enjoy a style of living that is commensurate with its expectations, hopes, and dreams.

The inflation rate in the American economy has varied between 3 and 11 percent over the past several years. At a 10 percent rate of inflation, a dollar earned in one year would purchase only 90 cents worth of goods and services in the next. Viewed over the longer term, a worker who earned $25,000 a year in 1960 had to earn at least $58,500 in 1978 just to maintain an equivalent standard of living (Cohen, 1979:40). As shown in Table A.1, the 1967 purchasing power of a dollar had declined to only 34 cents by 1983. For example, a bag of groceries which cost $10.00 in 1967 would, in 1983, cost the shopper nearly *three times* that amount — *$29.30!* Inflation appears to

*"I've called the family together to announce that, because of inflation,
I'm going to have to let two of you go."*

be a fact of life that must be confronted by American families, at least for the next several years. (See Table A.1.)

Effective Budgeting

In view of the continuing rise of prices in our inflation-fueled economy, and the economic uncertainty that many families must face as a result, the need for sound budgeting practices becomes critical. Budgeting is a means of assuring that income earned is sufficient to cover all expenses incurred, as well as meeting long-range economic goals by means of saving. A budget is typically formulated on the basis of *monthly* income and expenses. However,

inflation means that household budgets must be occasionally revised, because a given level of income will purchase less as time goes by. Although we typically measure inflation rates on a year-by-year basis, the key point to remember is that inflation represents a *continuing* rise in prices, meaning that prices are rising monthly, weekly, and even daily. Periodic budget reviews for a family are therefore essential if they are to keep on top of the erosion in purchasing power caused by inflation.

There are two major objectives in budgeting: (1) *to implement a system of disciplined spending,* and (2) *to reduce the amount of money wasted through needless expenditures* in each expense category (Bailard, Biehl, and Kaiser, 1980:59). The first objective means that a carefully developed plan of spending must be followed so that you do not

TABLE A.1. *Purchasing Power of the Dollar, 1960–1983 (1967 = $1.00)*

Year	Value of One Dollar Relative to 1967	Annual Inflation Rate (Approximate)
1960	$1.13	1.6
1961	1.12	1.0
1962	1.10	1.1
1963	1.09	1.2
1964	1.08	1.3
1965	1.06	1.7
1966	1.03	2.9
1967	1.00	2.9
1968	.96	4.2
1969	.91	5.4
1970	.86	5.9
1971	.82	4.3
1972	.80	3.3
1973	.75	6.2
1974	.68	11.0
1975	.62	9.1
1976	.59	5.8
1977	.55	6.5
1978	.51	7.7
1979	.46	11.3
1980	.41	13.5
1981	.37	10.4
1982	.35	6.1
1983	.34	3.5

SOURCE: U.S. Bureau of the Census, *Statistical Abstract of the United States, 1984,* 104th Ed., Washington, D.C., 1983, pp. 796–797.

run out of money before all of the monthly expenses have been covered. The plan must be an accurate reflection of your actual monthly take-home income and expenditures. This can be developed by first keeping track of how money is spent — how much and for what — over a one- to two-month period. You must become *aware* of your spending patterns if a useful budget is to be developed. The second objective means that family members must develop some degree of consensus over what types of expenditures are either necessary, important but not essential, or unnecessary. A certain amount of discretionary funds, sometimes referred to as "mad money," could be set aside each month in order to keep the budget from being too restrictive. This would allow occasional impulse purchases of something desired without having to feel guilty about violating the previously agreed upon budget.

There are certain budgeting rules which, if followed, will make a budget a tool working *for* you rather than *against* you. We have already mentioned developing an awareness of expenditure patterns by keeping a detailed and accurate record of monthly income and expenditures. This can be accomplished with the use of a form such as that in Figure A.1. After a number of months of record-keeping, this form can be transformed into a more permanent monthly guide, which is periodically revised to take into account inflation, changing family priorities, and changes in income.

It is important to group similar types of expenses, according to meaningful categories, for the final budget. These categories should not be so large that certain regular expenses get "lost," making it difficult to pinpoint the cause of overspending at any time. Nor should the categories be so small that they make recordkeeping cumbersome and difficult to monitor. It is not necessary to account for every penny and dime spent.

As can be seen in Table A.2 and Figure A.2, the combined monthly expenditure for food and housing alone constitutes roughly 50 percent of the average four-person family's budget. Moreover, in comparing "lower," "intermediate," and "higher" levels of living, it is interesting to note the larger percentages of income required for food and medical expenses among the "lower" life-style categories, and for taxes and housing among the "higher." The remaining categories are roughly equivalent for all three groups. These include transportation, clothing, personal care, and a number of miscellaneous expenses that most families will incur.

In view of the large percentage of family income devoted to food and housing, a third rule of budgeting assumes importance: *setting priorities.* Many people who cannot afford it want to have everything — a car, house, furniture, vacations, and three nights a week out at their favorite restaurant — and they want these things *now*. They begin buying and spending money they don't have, often with the use of a modern invention known as the "credit card," only to find themselves wallowing in a quagmire of debt. Effective budgeting means identifying and establishing priorities among these desired commodities and then purchasing them one at a time, without overspending in any of the monthly budget categories. This plan would require setting a top priority on the most

FIGURE A.1. Example of a Monthly Budget Form.

Our Plan for Spending 19

Item	Jan.	Feb.	Dec.	Total
Total money income				
Major fixed expenses: Taxes: Federal				
State				
Property				
Auto				
Rent or mortgage payment				
Insurance: Medical (including prepaid care)				
Life				
Property				
Auto				
Debt payments: Auto				
Other				
Savings for: Emergency fund				
Flexible expenses: Food and beverages				
Utilities and maintenance (household supplies and services)				
Furnishings and equipment				
Clothing				
Personal care				
Auto upkeep, gas, oil				
Fares, tolls, other				
Medical care (not prepaid or reimbursed)				
Recreation and education				
Gifts and contributions				
Total				

SOURCE: U.S. Department of Agriculture, "A Guide to Budgeting for the Young Couple." *Home and Garden Bulletin,* Number 98, July, 1977, p. 7.

TABLE A.2. *Average Monthly Expenditures for a Family of Four at Three Levels of Living, United States, 1981*

	Lower	Intermediate	Higher
Total Budget	$15,323	$25,407	$38,060
Food	30%	23%	19%
Housing	18	22	22
Transportation	9	9	8
Clothing	6	5	5
Personal Care	2	2	2
Medical Care	9	6	4
Other Family Consumption[1]	4	5	5
Other Items[2]	4	4	5
Taxes and Deductions (incl. Social Security and Personal Income Taxes)	17	24	30

[1] Includes average costs for reading materials, recreation, tobacco and alcohol products, education, and miscellaneous expenditures.

[2] Includes allowances for gifts, contributions, life insurance, and occupation-related expenses.

SOURCE: U.S. Department of Labor, Bureau of Labor Statistics, *News,* Washington, D.C., April, 1982, p. 2.

basic physical needs: food, clothing, and shelter. These come first in determining the quality of life and standard of living of a marriage or family. Part of this plan would also involve setting a priority on *saving* a certain amount every month. Saving provides a cushion in the event of emergencies such as sudden unemployment, illness or hospitalization, or a major household repair. Ideally, there should be some sort of consensus generated in a family as to what the budget priorities will be. However, this requires a cooperative mood, effective communication, and problem-solving skills (see chapter 7) if consensus is to be reached. Remember, money management is the most frequent source of conflict in marriage.

A fourth rule of effective budgeting is to *remain flexible.* Remember that priorities change as the goals of family members change. Neither are the monthly average income and expenditures of a family set at a constant rate.

Periodic budget review, along with a *realistic* assessment of the income/expenditure ratio, will help here. Also realize that certain expenses are inflexible, or "fixed," every month, but some are flexible (see Figure A.1). The flexible categories allow some leeway in trimming monthly expenses if spending is approaching or exceeding income.

Credit

"Drive now, pay later." "Small down payment required, 48 months to pay." "Eat at our restaurant, and charge it." "Low monthly payments." "Six months deferred payments." These are only a few of the many slogans in our "credit-crazy" society. More than one-half of all retail sales in the United States are handled on a credit card basis, and virtually all "big-ticket" purchases made by American families—houses, cars, boats, furniture, major household appliances, and even vacations—are made possible by the ease of borrowing money. Credit use allows a person to make purchases without having the cash on hand. Borrowing money from financial institutions by means of installment loans provides the consumer with the opportunity to enjoy goods and services before enough money has been saved to pay for them. The borrower then pays back a certain amount each month, for a predetermined amount of time, until the debt has been repaid. However, credit-card use and borrowing money are not free. The borrower must also pay a "service" charge, called *interest*, which covers the cost of "using" the lender's money for that period of time.

In order to obtain credit cards and borrow money, a person must have an acceptable *credit rating.* A good credit rating is established by reliably paying back previous loans and proper use of credit cards by making payments on time. Stability also counts heavily—being in a particular location, or at a certain job, for a number of years. People who spend cash for everything do not have an established credit rating and may not be viewed as good credit risks in certain circumstances. The more you borrow, and the more you pay back on time, the better your credit rating and the easier it will be to obtain sizable loans in the future.

A person's credit rating is kept on file at the local or regional credit bureau. When you apply for a loan, the lender can check at the credit bureau on your past record of

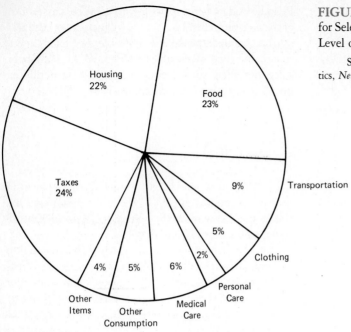

FIGURE A.2.   Percentage of Monthly Income Required for Selected Expenditures, Family of Four at an Intermediate Level of Living, 1981.

SOURCE: U.S. Department of Labor, Bureau of Labor Statistics, *News,* Washington, D.C., April, 1982, p. 2.

borrowing money and paying back the loans to determine if you are a good credit risk. There is a national network of credit bureaus, so that the credit rating established in one locale can be determined if you should move to a new city or town.

A number of federal laws have been enacted to protect the rights of those who seek and use credit. The Truth-in-Lending and Fair Credit Billing laws help to protect the borrower from being deceived by the lender. The consumer must be informed in writing of all conditions of the credit agreement, including the rate of interest, prior to entering it. The consumer also has the right to question the accuracy of the billing statements provided by the lender, and must be notified by the lender of appropriate channels for doing so. No interest charge or penalty can be levied against the consumer for any amount of money that is being disputed with the lender. The Fair Credit Reporting Act of 1971 has closed your file at the credit bureau to anyone but yourself and those who have a legitimate need to evaluate your credit rating at certain times — insurance agents, government agencies, banks, potential employers, or creditors. You have the right to know what is contained in your file, including comments that you might consider unfair or underserved, and the

source of those comments. If you can verify that these comments are inaccurate or misleading, the credit bureau must purge them from your file, and notice of the change must be sent to any creditors who have inspected your file over the previous six months. You also have the right to insert a 100-word refutation into your file when you and the credit bureau dispute the validity of any of the information you are contesting. There are stiff penalties for those who seek information about someone from a credit bureau under false pretenses, or who violate any conditions of this law.

Another important federal law pertaining to credit use is the Equal Credit Opportunity Act. This law states that discrimination on the basis of race, sex, age, religion, national origin, or marital status against anyone seeking credit is prohibited. No longer can divorce be considered as a "black mark" against the person being considered for credit. The lender must also regard child support and alimony payments as part of a person's income, although a person is not *required* to list these sources of income on a loan application. A woman's application for credit must be given equal weight relative to that of a man in comparable circumstances, and both a husband and wife can now establish separate credit ratings on the basis of loans obtained during the marriage. Previous to this law, the husband's credit rating would usually be the only one affected by borrowing and repaying money. Following divorce, many women found themselves without any credit rating at all, making it extremely difficult to take advantage of the credit system, even if they might have been excellent credit risks by all other standards. The Equal Opportunity Credit Act thereby seeks to prohibit the denial of credit to anyone solely on the basis of race, sex, or marital status.

The major advantage of credit use is that a family does not have to wait several years and save thousands of dollars before owning those material things that are valued by them. They can live in a home, furnish it, enjoy the use of a car, add a room to accommodate a growing family, or even build a swimming pool in their backyard by borrowing the thousands upon thousands of dollars these items cost. In a sense, borrowing is a form of forced saving — the money is spent before it is earned, then paid back on a monthly basis until the debt no longer exists. One major disadvantage of credit use, however, is that the borrower must pay for use of the money through interest payments, which can be quite costly. The actual cost of the item is therefore much greater than the amount on its price tag, when money is borrowed to pay for it. When you pay for an expensive item with cash, you avoid paying any interest and pay only what the item costs at that time. In addition, when you save money, the bank is paying interest to *you,* instead of you paying it to someone else. Hence, a general rule of thumb is that *whenever possible, major purchases should be made with cash rather than credit.*

A second disadvantage of using credit is that many people get into financial trouble by borrowing too heavily, relying too much on their assortment of credit cards. Monthly payments, which at first seem small, add up quickly when credit is used extensively. Therefore, many experts advise that if you must use credit, *limit the number of times you borrow, but maximize the amounts borrowed at the lowest possible interest rates,* provided your budget can handle the monthly payments (Bailard, et al., 1980). Borrow only for those expensive items that either have investment potential (home, car, education, property), or that are essential in order to live comfortably (furniture, washing machine, refrigerator). Items with investment potential will either maintain a reasonable value or appreciate (increase their value) over time. Never borrow to pay for items that are a regular part of your budget, such as food, clothing, utility bills, and entertainment. In deter-

mining how much you should borrow and still manage to stay within your budget, a rough guide is to limit the total amount of your debt payments (excluding home mortgage) *to no more than 15 to 20 percent of your disposable* (take-home) *income.* For every debt incurred by borrowing money or other type of credit use, a separate line should be added to your budget to cover the monthly payments of principal-plus-interest that must be made to the lender. Failing to do this can lead to excessive debt, inability to repay loans, repossession of the valuable item(s) that have been purchased, and possibly even bankruptcy. There are approximately 250,000 cases of personal bankruptcy declared in the United States every year, the vast majority resulting from families overextending their credit use. Bankruptcy devastates a person's credit rating, making it difficult to use credit again for some time to come, and results in lost assets for both the borrower and the lender.

Although there are many types of credit and loan outlets, we will be concerned here only with the two primary means by which American families use credit purchases: *credit cards* and *installment loans.*

CREDIT CARDS

Over one half of all American families have at least one credit card. Many families have five or more credit cards. Credit cards far exceed the use of cash at hotels and restaurants, filling stations, and large retail stores. Using the credit card is a convenient service for the consumer who does not have the cash-on-hand to pay for particular goods or service. Credit cards also allow the consumer to borrow money from the company handling the credit account. The item is paid for with the consumer's credit card, the cost is then covered by the company, and the consumer is expected to pay off the loan either in regular monthly installments or all at one time.

Experience has shown two major dangers in the use of credit cards. First, the interest rates on the money "borrowed" are quite steep. At this writing, the typical interest rate for almost all types of credit cards is 21 percent annually on the unpaid balance of the loan. It is therefore wise to pay off as much of the balance as possible, preferably all, on the first payment of a credit card bill, when the interest charges have not yet begun to accrue.

The second danger of credit card use is related to the first. Credit cards for some people are *too* convenient. They can easily be viewed as "plastic" money that at the time of a purchase is not "real." The temptation, then, is to make extensive use of credit cards without considering any monthly budget constraints that might exist. It becomes extremely difficult to manage an effective budget when bills from four, five, or six different credit cards pour in every month, some with previous loan balances and accumulated interest charges. It is easy to lose control of credit-card use because people tend to forget in a few weeks' time the loan amounts they had been accumulating through various purchases. When the monthly bills arrive, some people are confronted with the shocking realization that they do not have enough money left over, after other expenses, to cover the bills.

In sum, credit cards should be used with great caution. They become unnecessarily expensive conveniences as soon as people begin to carry too many balances from one month to the next because they are unable to pay them in full. The interest expense that results adds significantly to the costs of the goods and services purchased with the credit card.

INSTALLMENT LOANS

The second major form of credit use is the *installment loan contract*. Installment loans are made to the consumer through banks, credit unions, or other types of financial agencies. Whereas credit cards usually have quite a low debt ceiling, usually around $1,000–$2,000, installment loans are made for more expensive durables, such as new and used cars, houses, appliances, boats, swimming pools, and home improvements. The borrower agrees to pay back the loan in predetermined monthly installments (principal-plus-interest) for a specified period of time (3 or 4 years for most new-car loans, 30 years for home-purchase loans). The interest rates charged for installment loans vary considerably from one lending institution to the next and depend on the item being financed. At this writing, interest rates have been gradually climbing for several years, and currently vary between 15 percent for loans from a credit union, to 18 percent for loans from a bank, to 25 percent or more for loans from a private commercial finance company. When borrowing money by means of installment loans, three rules apply:

1. *Shop around* at various lending institutions to obtain the best possible rate of interest on your loan.

2. Be sure that the *monthly payments can be scheduled* so that you are able to handle them *within your budget*. Remember, though, that the longer the time period over which you spread your payments, the more money you pay in interest charges on the loan. You should be able to arrange a pay-back schedule which allows you to pay as much as your budget will allow per month, allowing the loan to be paid off in as short a time as possible.

3. *Read the loan agreement carefully.* Never borrow money without knowing what each of the terms and clauses in the loan contract means. Ask questions of the loan officer, if necessary, if you do not understand something about the conditions of the loan, interest and principal payments, or relationship between borrower and lender.

Rule Number Three is geared to protect you, the consumer, in the loan market. There are six common "oppressive clauses" which can be inserted by a lender in a loan agreement (Bailard, et al., 1980:279; Cohen, 1979:341–343). If the borrower fails to read and understand the terms and conditions of the installment-loan contract, those oppressive clauses will have legal force if one or more are included by the lender in a signed contract.

1. *Wage assignment, or garnishment.* If you should fall behind or default on your loan payments, the lender would have the legal right to take a percentage of your regular wages or salary to pay on the outstanding principal and interest of the loan.

2. *Confession of judgment* This clause states that you willfully waive your right to legal counsel or due process in the courts, should you fall behind or default on your loan payments; it constitutes an "admission of debt" with legal authorities.

3. *Repossession.* The creditor has the right to take possession of whatever it is you have purchased with the loan money, should you fail to make payments.

4. *Add-on Clause.* This clause states that the lender has the right to repossess items you have purchased over several years with loan money from the lender, and *already paid for,* if you should fail to make a payment on any items purchased with future loans.

5. *Acceleration Clause.* If you should miss a single payment on your loan, the lender has the right to make

the entire outstanding balance of the loan immediately due. Of course, if you have to miss one payment, you are not going to be able to pay the entire loan balance at one time. The lender can then repossess whatever it was that was purchased with the loan money.

6. *Balloon Clause.* The borrower pays relatively low, and constant, monthly amounts on the loan until the last payment, which is substantially larger than the rest. The lender makes out well in this situation because the borrower is often forced to refinance the loan, two or possibly three times, pushing the total interest charges paid on the initial loan amount higher and higher.

In sum, using credit, whether in the form of credit cards or installment loans, can be a useful tool in the hands of a cautious person. Simply knowing how easy it is to become overextended through the misuse of credit should cause one *to save and pay with cash whenever possible*. If credit is to be used, be sure to enter it as part of your total monthly budgeting process.

Investment

Investment is a way of using money to make more money. Wise investing is an excellent hedge against the shrinking value of the dollar, if you are able to generate money at a rate faster than the rate of inflation. Even investments that return less than the rate of inflation are useful in that they *slow down* the eroding impact that inflation has on your financial welfare.

There are many types of investments. Indeed, there are so many, and they are so technically complicated, that we can cover only the most common ones in this section, noting their basic characteristics, advantages, and disadvantages. In a time of significant dollar inflation, which we are likely to experience for some time to come, anyone would be wise to investigate investment possibilities in greater detail.

In examining the characteristics of various investment alternatives, it is important to consider seven things (Bailard, et al., 1980).

1. *Risk* (chance of losing money from the investment in the future);

2. *Approximate percentage return* for every dollar invested;

3. *Liquidity* (time it takes to convert the current value of your investment back into cash);

4. *Personal effort* required to manage the investment;

5. *Maturity* (minimum time it takes to realize the rate of return expected when the investment was made);

6. Its *power to protect* against inflation;

7. *How much and in what ways your investment is taxable* by the local, state and federal governments.

Before investing a penny of your earnings, however, you must be certain that you are able to *afford* the money that must be tied up if the investment is to realize its maximum potential benefit. It is useful to plan your investments according to the pyramid concept (see Figure A.3). The base of the pyramid constitutes the basis of your financial planning. You must first take adequate care of your family's basic needs for food, clothing, and shelter, according to your life-style expectations. It is also important to have enough cash on hand in savings to cover an unexpected financial problem, such as that caused by an accident or by the sudden illness of a family member. You must also have adequate insurance to protect against major financial calamities caused by fire, natural disaster, catastrophic illness, or the unexpected death of a breadwinner. After the base of the pyramid is set, and you have discretionary income left over in your monthly budget, then consider moving up the "ladder of risk" in the investment pyramid. You might begin in the stock market, and then diversify your investments as your budget allows. In this way, the standard of living you have attained will not be threatened by having dollars tied up in the higher-risk and potentially higher-yield investment alternatives. Nor will your family suffer if you should experience losses as the result of various speculative investments that might turn sour.

In this section, we will briefly discuss various investment alternatives that you eventually might wish to consider. We will begin with the lowest-risk investments and work our way up.

SAVINGS ACCOUNT AND CERTIFICATE OF DEPOSIT (CD'S)

Most people are familiar with the operation of a savings account. These are low-risk, low-return accounts

FIGURE A.3.   The Investment Pyramid.

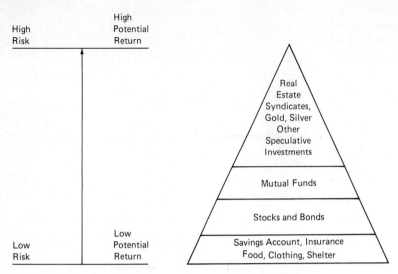

The author gratefully acknowledges Earl Mendenhall of William Ipema and Associates, Tucson, Arizona, for sharing this idea with his marriage education classes.

at a savings and loan association, bank, or credit union. The money deposited usually earns from between 5 and 7 percent interest, lower than the rate of inflation has been in recent years. Interest earned on savings accounts is also taxed by federal and state governments. Although savings accounts may not yield a return that is greater than the current rate of inflation, meaning that a dollar saved is slowly losing value over time, savings accounts do have certain important advantages. They provide security in the event of emergencies that require quick access to cash. That is, they are a *liquid* asset. Also, purchasing such major items as a car or appliance with money deposited over time in a savings account reduces your reliance on credit. Rather than going into debt and paying interest on a loan, you can pay only what the item costs with your cash-on-hand that has been accumulating with interest someone else has paid *to you*.

Certificates of deposit (CD's) are similar to a savings account. They are safe, low-risk investments that have grown tremendously in popularity. However, they usually require that the individual deposit money in $1,000 to $10,000 increments, whereas for savings accounts any amount can be deposited at any time. In addition to requiring a higher initial investment, CD's yield higher

interest to the depositor (varies from between 10 and 15 percent). Because of their higher interest yields, CD's must be left on deposit for longer time intervals than savings accounts, usually for at least 6 months to 1 year or more, meaning that their liquidity is less. The depositor must pay a substantial interest penalty for premature withdrawal on CD's.

HOME AND PROPERTY OWNING

One of the safer low-risk investments young married couples have been able to make is the purchase of a home or property. The value of a home or property has generally grown faster than the rate of inflation, making home and property owning a reasonably low-risk hedge against inflation. In comparison with renting a home or apartment, where the renter gets none of the rental dollars back, owning a home allows the homeowner to get back all of the money put into it, plus the increased value. This is known as *equity*. For example, the average home in 1968 could be purchased for $24,700, and could be sold in 1978 for $55,600 (Bailard, et al., 1980). This is a 125 percent increase in value, whereas the rate of inflation was considerably lower during that time period (see Table A.1).

Most young couples have been able to own a home after saving a certain amount of money for a down payment, and then borrowing the remainder from a bank or home loan corporation. Such home loans are known as *mortgages,* which allow the lender to repossess the home in case the borrower fails to make regular monthly payments on the loan. Mortgages are similar to installment loans in that a level principal-plus-interest payment schedule is established, usually for from 25 to 30 years, to allow for the gradual pay-back of the loan. As with installment loans, the more cash you are able to put down on a home at the outset, and the shorter the repayment schedule you are able to arrange in the context of your budget, the less interest money you will have to pay in addition to the amount borrowed over the loan period.

The down payment required for a typical, conventional mortgage loan is 25 to 50 percent of the market value of the home. Because most young couples do not have that kind of money available, the federal government has created a loan-guarantee program (the Federal Housing Administration, or FHA) which requires only a 3 percent down payment on the first $25,000, and 5 percent on the balance. Although the government does not actually lend the money, it *insures* the loan so that the lender feels safer in giving the money to the home buyer. The down payment required is therefore less on FHA loans in comparison with conventional mortgages. Qualified veterans of the armed services are also entitled to low-down-payment mortgages that are insured by the federal government's *Veterans Administration.* Known as *VA loans,* they have made it easier for many young couples to get started in building the financial equity that comes with home-owning.

STOCKS AND BONDS

The stock market offers a somewhat higher-risk investment alternative to people who have money available above and beyond that required by their monthly budgets. Common stocks provide an ownership interest in a particular company, so that profits earned by the company are shared with the stockholders. Stocks may also accrue in value over time (which is known as *capital gain* of the stock), providing a reasonably good hedge against infla-

tion. In order to reap the maximum benefits from stock ownership, however, the investor must expect to leave money in the stock market for a considerable amount of time. Owning stock, therefore, is a less liquid investment than the lower-risk alternatives already discussed. Also, the dividends and capital gains acquired through stock ownership are taxable.

Depending on the company, and the condition of the stock market as a whole, the investor can enjoy significant gains or suffer significant losses. This is the risk feature of stock ownership, and this is why investors should be sure that their family's needs for food, clothing, shelter, savings, and insurance are taken care of *before* investing in the stock market.

Stocks are issued by companies to raise investment capital in order to provide for expansion and growth. *Bonds,* too, are issued by companies, or by federal, state, and local governments to raise money for growth and expansion purposes. Bonds are long-term investments, usually in increments of $1,000, and range anywhere from 5 to 30 years for their maturity to be realized. State and municipal bonds, and U.S. government securities (Treasury bills, for example) not only pay a fixed amount of interest, but are also a more secure investment alternative than the stock market. After the period of maturity, the investor is guaranteed to receive the initial amount invested. Interest earned from state and municipal bonds is also exempt from federal and state taxes, which increases their desirability for many investors.

MUTUAL FUNDS

Mutual funds involve a pooling of investment dollars by a number of individuals in an investment company. The company manages the dollars, in turn investing them in a wide range of stocks, bonds, and other securities for the benefit of the group of investors. Each investor must pay about 1 percent of the amount invested each year as a service charge to the investment company. It is a convenient way to enter the investment market because someone else is handling all the work for you, worrying about what companies to invest in, when to buy and sell stocks, and how to manage all the assets involved. Mutual funds can be risky, however, if they are poorly managed by the investment company. The investor must therefore take great care in selecting a mutual fund with investment objectives and an investment record that are viewed as satisfactory. The rate of return on mutual funds parallels that of the stock market in general, ranging from substantial gains to substantial losses, depending upon their management. Some mutual funds are highly speculative, meaning that particularly strong gains or losses may occur. Money invested in mutual funds is *low on liquidity;* that is, it must be left in the fund for a long term if benefits are to be realized. Dividends and capital gains distributed to investors from the investment management company are taxable by federal and state governments.

There is far more to effective investment practices than can be included here. Owning real estate and participating in real estate syndicates, for example, is a potentially high-yield, yet high-risk, investment alternative which some may wish to consider. Owning rental property can yield significant annual gains if the property appreciates in value at a reasonable rate, costs relatively little time and money to maintain, and if renters can be found who are willing to pay enough to make the investment worthwhile. Owning rental property also provides certain tax advantages to the property owner. No matter what investment alternative, or set of alternatives, you choose, careful investigation and planning is essential *before* the investment is made. Also, remember that investment is reserved for those who have money left over after their basic needs have been taken care of: food, clothing, shelter, savings, and insurance.

References

Bailard, T.E., Biehl, D.L., & Kaiser, R.W. *Personal money management,* 3rd ed. Chicago: SRA, 1980.

Cohen, J.B. *Personal finance,* 6th ed. Homewood, Ill.: Irvin, 1979.

Glossary

Achieved Roles. Roles attained by a person on the basis of his or her own efforts, rather than one the basis of some ascribed characteristic (such as age, race, or sex).

Affinal Relatives. Persons related to us by virtue of marriage (father-in-law, brother-in-law, and so on), and who are *not* related to us "by blood" (i.e., biologically).

Agape. The Greek concept of love that includes its respectful, caring, and emotional aspects.

Alimony. Periodic payment from one ex-spouse (usually the husband) to the other ex-spouse (usually the wife), who has little or no means of support following a divorce. Alimony awards are declining in frequency and amount today as more women are entering the work force and completing higher levels of education.

Androgyny. The quality of having characteristics of both traditionally masculine and feminine roles, promoting more flexibility in meeting new situations and fewer restrictions in expressing one's thoughts and feelings. Androgynous people are independent, yet gentle; leaders, yet compassionate; and assertive, yet cheerful.

Annulment. Civil or religious proclamation that a marriage never existed between two individuals. Only civil annulments are legally binding.

Ascribed Roles. Roles assigned on the basis of some characteristic over which the person has little or no control, such as sex, age, or race.

Breech Birth. A childbirth characterized by the child's buttocks or feet moving through the birth canal first, as opposed to the normal head-first (cephalic) delivery.

Cesarean Section. A surgical childbirth procedure accomplished by removing the child from the mother's uterus through a horizontal or vertical incision in the abdominal wall.

Climacteric. Among women, the climacteric includes the physical changes associated with the loss of fecundity. Symptoms include menopause for most by age 50, and "hot flashes" and vaginal changes for many, because of declines in the production of the hormones estrogen and progesterone. Among men, climacteric-like symptoms are less common or severe. They include gradual decreases in sperm production, testosterone levels, loss of sexual interest and potency, physical fatigue, mood swings, and loss of appetite and weight.

Cohabitation. The practice of living together with a person of the opposite sex without being legally married. Cohabitation usually includes sexual intercourse, and is practiced by young people before their first marriage (most commonly); by older adults following divorce and before remarriage; and by the elderly.

Common-Law Marriage. A type of legal marriage relationship granted when a male and female live together for a period of years (no set number), present themselves in the community as a married couple would, and agree to be married. They can be married without ever going through a state-authorized ceremony.

Communication. Effective communication is the exchange of information between two or more people, such that the message sent by one is accurately interpreted and understood by the other.

Community Property. Property and debts acquired during a marriage by either or both spouses and which belongs equally to both. Eight states have community-property laws that pertain to property settlements between spouses following divorce.

Conjugal-Role Organization. The structure of household roles in marriage, such as cooking, cleaning, repairs, child care, and child discipline. *Joint* conjugal role organization exists when marriage partners share most or all of the household duties. *Segregated* role organization exists when tasks are divided between husband and wife, with relatively little overlap.

Consanguineal Relatives. Persons related to us biologically, or "by blood," such as parents, brothers, sisters, and cousins.

Critical Role-Transition Point. Periods of time in the marital career signaling normal discontinuities in role expectations, role clusters, and interaction structures of power, affection, and communication. Old patterns of relating are inadequate to meet the demands of the new situation, and new patterns must be developed if the transition is to be successfully negotiated. Getting married, first parenthood, school entry of a child, departure of the last child from home, retirement, and death of a spouse are all critical role-transition points in marriage and family life.

Demographic Transition. Rapid population growth in societies experiencing continuing high birth rates, coupled with declining mortality (death) rates. Most likely in developing societies moving from traditional agricultural economies to modern postindustrial and high-technology economies, where medical technology and eradication of disease are expanding.

Desertion. Leaving the residence of the married couple with no intent to return, and without the spouse's consent.

Developmental Task. A task that must be faced at or about a certain point in a person's life, or in a social relationship such as marriage, successful accomplishment of which will enhance the chances of success with other tasks later on, and failure may lead to difficulty with subsequent tasks. The *timing* of task-performance is important, as being off schedule (early or late) in attempting to accomplish tasks is often more difficult than being on schedule. Developmental task-accomplishment also has a *cumulative* effect, as successful accomplishment of earlier tasks will help in accomplishing later ones.

Divorce. A legally binding declaration of the state that terminates the existence of a marriage relationship.

Dizygotic Twins. Twins conceived by sperm cells fertilizing two separate eggs. Dizygotic twins are not physically identical, and can be of opposite sexes.

Ectopic Pregnancy. A fertilized egg that implants in the Fallopian tube rather than in the uterus. As it grows, the egg expands and places pressure upon the tube, causing severe pain and possible rupture. This is a serious medical condition which merits immediate attention by a physician.

Embryo. The stage of prenatal development beginning around the third week after conception, in which the development of skeletal, muscular, nervous, circulatory, and excretory systems begins. This stage ends in the sixth to eighth week after conception.

Endogamy. A cultural norm prescribing that one should marry within a certain group, such as a racial or religious group. Failure to do so can result in serious sanctions, such as social ostracism or being expelled from the group.

Engagement. The period of time in an intimate relationship, beginning when each partner intends and fully plans to marry the other and makes these intentions known, and ending either when the marriage takes place or when at least one partner decides that they do not intend to marry the other.

Eros. The Greek concept of love that includes its physical, sensual, sexual, and erotic aspects.

Estrogen. The female hormone that builds in the woman's system during each menstrual cycle, and which helps to release the mature egg during ovulation. Synthetic forms of estrogen are used in the manufacture of birth control pills to prevent ovulation from occurring. By maintaining estrogen at a constant level in the woman's system, the birth control pill inhibits the release of hormones necessary to produce a mature egg following the menstrual period.

Ethnocentrism. The belief that the practices, values, and attitudes of one's own culture are naturally superior to, or better than, those of another culture.

Fecundity. The biological capability of a male-female couple to conceive and bear children.

Fertility. The number of children actually born to a woman, or group of women, in their lifetimes.

Filial Maturity. The realization that one's aging parents are in need of substantial assistance and support, and a willingness to assume responsibility for the care of aging parents who are becoming less able to care for themselves over time.

Gemeinschaft. Social relationships based on the belief that the bond between people is sacred, personal, and friendly. Ferdinand Töennies (1855–1936) believed that such relationships were more prevalent in rural agricultural societies of years gone by, where people related to each other as "whole persons," rather than on the basis of one specific role or function.

Gender. Behavioral and psychological aspects of being male or female that are shaped by one's interaction with the physical and social environment.

Gender Roles. Concepts of masculinity and femininity based upon what are considered to be appropriate rights, obligations, and behaviors of males and females.

Genes. The material that determines our physical traits and characteristics following conception. Genes are carried on cell structures known as chromosomes.

Gesellschaft. Social relationships based on the belief that the bond between people is distant, cold, and based on purely rational considerations. Ferdinand Töennies (1855–1936) believed that such relationships are more prevalent in contemporary industrialized societies than in traditional societies of the past. Rather than relating to others as "whole persons," people in modern societies are more likely to relate impersonally, on the basis of one or two specific roles or functions.

Heterogamy. Marriage of two persons from notably different social backgrounds in terms of age, education, social class, or type of residence (urban vs. rural), or between two individuals who share dissimilar interests, values, and role expectations for marriage and family life.

Homogamy. Marrying someone with similar social characteristics, such as age, education, or social-class background (social homogamy), or one who shares similar values, interests, and role expectations (cultural homogamy). Usually, marriage partners who are socially homogamous tend to be culturally homogamous as well.

Homologies. Anatomical counterparts of males and females in the sexual and reproductive systems (for example, the female clitoris is the counterpart of the male penis, in terms of location and function).

Human Chorionic Gonadotropin. A hormone released by the placenta, following a woman's pregnancy, which appears in the urine, and which is tested in order to determine if the woman is indeed pregnant.

Illegitimate Birth. Birth of a child to an unmarried woman.

Immature Love. Known also as infatuation, immature love is based on such superficial qualities as eye appeal, surface enchantment, fantasy projection, and the need for self-aggrandizement in the eyes of others. Immature love is not a firm basis for long-term relationships, such as marriage.

Impotence. The inability of the male to achieve and maintain an erection, because of either physical or psychological problems, or a combination of the two.

Interaction Structures. The characteristic patterns of role relationships in marriage and the family, focusing on power, communication, and affection. Interaction structures emerge as people develop comfortable "habits" of relating to each other over time.

In Vitro Fertilization. Also known as "test-tube pregnancy," a fertilization that occurs when medical scientists combine sperm and egg cells in the laboratory in specially designed equipment, and them implant the fertilized egg into the woman's uterus for normal growth and delivery of a child.

Looking-Glass Self. The means by which we develop identity — a sense of who we are and what we are worth — on the basis of how others close to us react to us, and appear to be evaluating us.

Marital Career. The existence of a married couple, from their initial dating and courtship activities to their dissolution either by divorce or by death of one of the partners, as demarcated by a sequence of stages of development.

Marriage. A social, emotional, and legal commitment between a man and woman to live together and share a sexual relationship. Children born in marriage relationships are recognized as legitimate in the society, providing them certain rights relative to the mother and father (inheritance, support, and so on).

Mature Love. Love that enhances the growth potential of both partners in an intimate relationship. Mature love provides a firm basis for long-term relationships, such as marriage, because of the genuine caring, concern, responsibility, respect, and knowledge of each partner relative to the other that mature love entails.

Menopause. A part of the female climacteric, menopause involves the cessation of ovulation (production of eggs) and menstrual periods.

Menstrual Cycle. The process by which the woman develops a blood-rich lining in the uterus that can support and nourish a fertilized egg. If fertilization does not occur during the menstrual cycle, then the blood lining is sloughed off during the menstrual period. Menstruation is guided by the female hormones estrogen and progesterone, and varies in duration from one woman to the next, as well as from one cycle to the next for many women (irregular menstrual cycles).

Metacommunication. Communication about the nature of an interpersonal relationship, including how the partners communicate with each other.

Monozygotic Twins. Twins conceived by a single sperm cell and single egg, which divides into two parts after conception. Chromosomes in each twin thereby carry the same genetic material and appear to be identical in physical characteristics.

Multilateral Marriage. Also known as "group marriage," these are relationships between three or more persons who consider themselves to be married. Although they are neither legally accepted or binding, multilateral marriages involve sexual relationships among the members and boundaries that identify them as a unit distinct from other marriage and family units (i.e., separate identity, residence, rituals, and rules for relating to each other).

No-Fault Divorce. Legal grounds that allow divorce between spouses who agree that "irreconcilable differences" in the relationship have led to an "irretrievable breakdown." Removes the adversarial "plaintiff-defendent" aspect of divorce, provided that a reasonable degree of consensus is reached over property distribution, child custody, and child support.

Norms. Culturally defined "shoulds" and "ought to's" that provide guides for acceptable behavior. Norms *prescribe* behavior (should) as well as *proscribe* behavior (should not), and play an important role in the conduct of marriage and family relationships.

Orgasm. The peak of sexual intensity and pleasure. Orgasm involves a series of physical reactions in both men and women which, for most, are the ultimate goal of sexual intercourse or other types of sexual play.

Orgasmic Dysfunction. The inability of the female to experience orgasm, usually the result of fears or anxieties relating to sexual behavior.

Ovulation. The release of mature eggs by the female's ovaries, for potential fertilization by the male sperm.

Parturition. The entire child-delivery and child birth process.

Philos. The Greek concept of love, which includes one's feelings toward other people and toward humanity.

Polyandry. A type of polygamous marriage involving one woman with two or more husbands. Few cultures have preferred, or extensively practiced, this pattern of marriage.

Polygyny. A type of polygamous marriage involving one man with two or more wives. Many cultures in the world have preferred this pattern of marriage, and have practiced it before the Western value on monogamy and economic considerations made it impractical.

Position. The cluster of roles assumed by a person in the family at any one time. Husband, father, wife, mother, son, daughter, brother, and sister are the major positions in the family unit of our society.

Primary Groups. The groups composed of the significant others in a person's life, and that are characterized by intimacy, cooperation, and love. The major sources of personal-need fulfillment, recognition, and affection.

Progesterone. The female hormone produced in the ovaries, which functions to maintain the development of the blood-rich lining of the uterus during the menstrual cycle and, if conception should take place, during pregnancy.

Residential Propinquity. The limitations on one's pool of eligible marriage partners imposed by geographic proximity of residences. We tend to meet, fall in love with, and marry another person who lives in our neighborhood, college campus, or local community.

Role. An organized set of specific norms which define a given activity for an individual. In marriage, husbands and wives play a number of roles, such as provider, sex partner, affection giver and receiver, confidant, money manager, and decision maker. Parents and children also play roles in such areas as discipline, teaching and learning of values and norms, and exchange of love and affection.

Role Cluster. The full complement of norms and roles a person has at any one time in the family. The size of the role cluster expands as children are added, and contracts as children are launched from the home.

Role Complex. The full complement of norms and roles in a marriage or family unit at any one time. The role complex is the sum total of all role clusters of all family members.

Role Reciprocity. The degree to which two individuals in a social relationship, such as marriage, are rewarding each other by meeting their obligations and role expectations in the relationship. Strong, stable relationships tend to be those where role reciprocity is present.

Role Sequence. The changes in role expectations and behavior that occur over time as a result of age changes among family members and changing stages of marriage and family development.

Selective Boundary Maintenance. The practice of establishing and maintaining marriage and family relationships as separate entities, allowing influences of outsiders to penetrate on a more or less selective basis. Boundaries can be physical or social, and help to establish the identity of the marriage or family unit by setting them apart from others. Separate residence, pet names, and special rituals are some of the ways people establish boundaries.

Self-Actualization. The process by which a person moves toward reaching his or her potential as a human being, which requires prior fulfillment of such essential human needs as intimacy, closeness, security, love, food, clothing, and shelter.

Self-Disclosure. A communication skill that involves the ability to communicate one's thoughts, feelings, beliefs, and fears about oneself, about other people, and about the surrounding world.

Senile Dementia. A disease of the brain and nervous system that attacks at older ages. Its symptoms include loss of memory, attention span, sensory capabilities, and reaction time, as well as personality changes.

Separate Property. Property acquired before of during a marriage, which belongs to only one of the spouses, and which, in most cases, cannot be divided with an ex-spouse in the event of a divorce.

Separation. Legal *(de jure)* separation is a judgment by a court of law, directing a husband and wife to live apart from each other without terminating the marriage. Separation by mutual agreement of the spouses *(de facto)* is also practiced.

Sex. The biological and physiological aspects of being male or female, based on one's genetic make-up (genotype).

Sexually Transmitted Disease (STD). Any disease that can be transmitted from one person to another by means of sexual contact. STD's include traditionally defined venereal diseases, such as syphilis and gonorrhea, as well as such others as Herpes Simplex II, urethritis, and trichomoniasis.

Social Stratification. The system by which individuals and families are ranked according to income, assets, and social prestige.

Successful Marriage. A marriage that fulfills the needs, and achieves the goals, expectations, and values of both marriage partners over time.

Surrogate Mother. A woman who agrees to be impregnated in order to carry another couple's baby to term and to deliver it. She is impregnated with the sperm of the husband in the couple, and is then paid a fee for carrying and delivering the child.

Testosterone. The male hormone that stimulates the growth and development of the external male genitalia (penis and scrotum) prior to birth, and directs such physical changes as deepening of the voice, body and facial hair growth, and growth in physical strength and body dimensions of the male at puberty.

Toxemia. A set of interrelated health problems that can occur during pregnancy. Symptoms include fluid retention and swelling (edema), high blood pressure, and excess protein in the blood (proteinuria). If not treated or stopped, toxemia can develop into a life-threatening situation for the woman.

Tubal Ligation. Contraceptive sterilization of the female achieved by severing the Fallopian tubes, thereby preventing the male's sperm from reaching the mature egg released by the woman during ovulation.

Vasectomy. Contraceptive sterilization of the male, achieved by severing the *vas deferans,* the tubes connecting the male's testes and seminal vesicles, so that no sperm cells are allowed to reach the ejaculatory duct.

Zygote. A fertilized egg.

References

Adams, B. N. *Kinship in an urban setting.* Chicago: Markham, 1968.

Adams, J. K. The hidden taboo on love. Pp. 27–41, in Otto, H. A. (Ed.) *Love today.* New York: Association, 1972.

Addegio, F., Belzer, E. G., Jr., Comolli, J., Moger, W., Perry, J. D., & Whipple, B. Female ejaculation: A case study. *Journal of Sex Research,* 1981, *17:*13–21.

Ahrons, C. R. Divorce: A crisis of family transition and change. *Family Relations,* 1980, *29:*533–540.

Ainsworth, M. D. Patterns of attachment behavior shown by the infant in interaction with his mother. *Merrill-Palmer Quarterly of Behavior and Development,* 1964, *10:*51–58.

Albee, E. *Who's Afraid of Virginia Woolf?* New York: Atheneum, 1962.

Albrecht, S. L. Correlates of marital happiness among the remarried. *Journal of Marriage and the Family,* 1979, *41:*857–867.

——— Reactions and adjustments to divorce: Differences in the experiences of males and females. *Family Coordinator,* 1980, *29:*59–68.

——— Bahr, H. M., & Chadwick, B. A. Changing family and sex roles: An assessment of age differences. *Journal of Marriage and the Family,* 1979, *41:*41–50.

Aldous, J. *Family careers: Developmental change in families.* New York: Wiley, 1978.

——— & Hill, R. Breaking the poverty cycle: Strategic points for intervention. *Social Work,* 1969, *14:*3–12.

——— Osmond, M. W., & Hicks, M. W. Men's work and men's families. Pp. 227–256, in Burr, W., et al. (Eds.) *Contemporary theories about the family: Vol. 1.* New York: Free Press, 1979.

Alexander, S. J. Protecting the child's rights in custody cases. *Family Coordinator,* 1977, *26:*377–382.

Anderson, J. E. Planning status of births, 1975–1976. *Family Planning Perspectives,* 1981, *13:*62–70.

Anderson, S. A., Russell, C. S., & Schumm, W. R. Perceived marital quality and family life-cycle categories: A further analysis. *Journal of Marriage and the Family,* 1983, *45:*127–139.

Anspach, D. F. Kinship and divorce. *Journal of Marriage and the Family,* 1976, *38:*323–330.

Arafat, I., & Yorburg, B. On living together without marriage. *Journal of Sex Research,* 1973, *9:*97–106.

Arizona Daily Star, Two-thirds of mothers to hold jobs by 1990, experts say. Sept. 25, 1979.

——— 11% favor 4 children or more; lowest percentage in 44 years. Jan. 1, 1981.

Arizona Family Planning Council Newsletter. Out-of-wedlock births increased 50% in past decade, Vol. 30, No. 12, Dec., 1981.

——— Silicone tubal plug sterilization technique. Vol. 31, No. 1, Jan., 1982a.

——— Voluntary sterilizations top one million mark, Vol. 31, No. 8, Aug., 1982b.

——— Phoenix conference on population issues, Vol. 33, No. 1, Jan., 1983a.

——— Population bomb still ticking. Vol. 32, No. 9, Sept., 1983b.

Arling, G. The elderly widow and her family, neighbors and friends. *Journal of Marriage and the Family,* 1976, *38:*757–768.

Atchley, R. C. *Social forces in later life* (2nd. ed.) Belmont, Calif: Wadsworth, 1977.

Atkinson, L. S., Shearer, B., Harkavey, O., & Lincoln, R. Prospects for improved contraception. *Family Planning Perspectives,* 1980, *12:*173–192.

Bach, G. R., & Wyden, P. *The intimate enemy: How to fight fair in love and marriage.* New York: Morrow, 1969.

Bachrach, C. A. Childlessness and social isolation among the elderly. *Journal of Marriage and the Family,* 1980, *42:*627–637.

——— Children in families: Characteristics of biological, step-, and adopted children. *Journal of Marriage and the Family,* 1983a, *45:*171–179.

——— Adoption as a means of family formation: Data from

the national survey of family growth. *Journal of Marriage and the Family,* 1983b, *45*:859–875.

Bahr, S. J. Effects on power and division of labor in the family. Pp. 167–185, in Hoffman, L. W., & Nye, F. I. *Working mothers.* San Francisco: Jossey-Bass, 1974.

———Chadwick, B. A., & Stauss, J. H. The effect of relative economic status on fertility. *Journal of Marriage and the Family,* 1975, *37*:335–343.

Baldwin, W. Adolescent pregnancy and childbearing—rates, trends, and research findings. Unpublished report. *Center for Population Research, National Institute of Child Health and Human Development,* Nov. 1982.

Balkwell, C. Transition to widowhood: A review of the literature. *Family Relations,* 1981, *30*:117–127.

Balswick, J. O. The inexpressive male: Functional-conflict and role theory as contrasting explanations. *The Family Coordinator,* 1979, *28*:331–336.

———Explaining inexpressive males: A reply to L'Abate. *Family Relations,* 1980, *29*:231–233.

———& Avertt, C. Differences in expressiveness: Gender, interpersonal orientation, and perceived parental expressiveness as contributing factors. *Journal of Marriage and the Family,* 1977, *39*:121–127.

———& Peek, C. W. The inexpressive male: A tragedy of American society. *The Family Coordinator,* 1971, *20*:363–368.

Barrett, C. J. Effectiveness of widows' groups in facilitating change. *Journal of Consulting and Clinical Psychology,* 1978, *46*:20–31.

Barry, H., Bacon, M. K., & Child, I. L. A cross-cultural survey of some sex differences in socialization. *Journal of Abnormal and Social Psychology,* 1957, *55*:327–332.

Bass, H. L., & Rein, M. L. *Divorce law: The complete practical guide.* Englewood Cliffs, N.J.: Prentice-Hall, 1976.

Baumrind, D. Effects of authoritative parental control on child behavior. *Child Development,* 1966, *37*:887–907.

Bayer, A. E. Sexist students in American colleges: A descriptive note. *Journal of Marriage and the Family,* 1975, *37*:391–397.

Beach, F. A. (Ed.) *Human sexuality in four perspectives.* Baltimore: Johns Hopkins, 1977.

Becker, W. C. Consequences of different kinds of parental discipline. Pp. 189–208, in Hoffman, M., & Hoffman, L. W. (Eds.) *Review of Child Development Research,* New York: Russell Sage, 1964.

Bell, A. P., & Weinberg, M. S. *Homosexualities: A study of diversities among men and women.* New York: Simon & Schuster, 1978.

Bell, R. R. *Marriage and family interaction,* 5th ed. Homewood, Ill.: Dorsey, 1979.

———& Coughey, K. Premarital sexual experience among college females, 1958, 1968, and 1978. *Family Relations,* 1980, *29*:353–357.

———Turner, S., & Rosen, L. A multivariate analysis of female extramarital coitus. *Journal of Marriage and the Family,* 1975, *37*:375–385.

Bem, S. L. The measurement of psychological androgyny. *Journal of Consulting and Clinical Psychology,* 1974, *42*:155–162.

———Probing the promise of androgyny. Pp. 48–60, in Kaplan, A., & Bean, J. (Eds.) *Beyond sex-role stereotypes: Readings toward a psychology of androgyny.* Boston: Little, Brown, 1976.

———Androgyny vs. the tight little lives of fluffy women and chesty men. Pp. 165–172, in Morrison, E. S., & Borosage, V. (Eds.) *Human Sexuality: Contemporary Perspectives.* Palo Alto, Calif.: Mayfield, 1977.

Benedek, R. S., Del Campo, R. L., & Benedek, E. P. Michigan's friends of the court: Creative programs for children of divorce. *Family Coordinator,* 1977, *26*:447–450.

Benedict, R. Continuities and discontinuities in cultural conditioning. *Psychiatry,* 1938, *1*:161–167.

———*Patterns of culture.* New York: New American Library, 1950.

Bengtson, V. L. The generation gap: A review and typology of social-psychological perspectives. *Youth and Society,* 1970, *2*:7–32.

———& Troll, L. Youth and their parents: Feedback and intergenerational influence in socialization. Pp. 215–240, in Lerner, R. M., & Spanier, G. B. (Eds.) *Child influences on marital and family interaction: A life-span perspective.* New York: Academic, 1978.

Berardo, F. M. Widowhood status in the U.S.: A perspective on a neglected aspect of the family life cycle. *Family Coordinator,* 1968, *17*:191–203.

Berelson, B. *The population council annual report.* New York: Population Council, 1972.

Berger, B., Hackett, B., & Miller, R. M. The communal family. *Family Coordinator,* 1972, *21*:419–427.

Berman, W. H., & Turk, D. C. Adaptation to divorce: Problems and coping strategies. *Journal of Marriage and the Family,* 1981, *43*:179–189.

Bernard, J. The adjustments of married mates, Pp. 675–739, in H. T. Christensen (Ed.) *Handbook of marriage and the family.* Chicago: Rand McNally, 1964.

———*The future of marriage.* New York: Bantam, 1972.

————Comments on Glenn's paper. *Journal of Marriage and the Family,* 1975, *37*:600–601.

Berscheid, E., & Walster, E. H. *Interpersonal attraction.* Reading, Mass.: Addison-Wesley, 1969.

————Walster, E., & Bohrnstedt, G. Body image. *Psychology Today,* July 1972, *6*:57–66.

Bianchi, S. M., & Farley, R. Racial differences in family living arrangements and economic well-being: An analysis of recent trends. *Journal of Marriage and the Family,* 1979, *41*:537–551.

Bieber, I. *Homosexuality: A psychoanalytic study.* New York: Basic, 1962.

Bing, E. *Six practical lessons for an easier childbirth,* Rev. ed. New York: Bantam, 1977.

Blake, J. Is zero preferred? American attitudes toward childlessness in the 1970's. *Journal of Marriage and the Family,* 1979, *41*:245–257.

Blau, P., & Duncan, O. D. *The American occupational structure.* New York: Wiley, 1967.

Blechman, E. A. Are children with one parent at psychological risk? A methodological review. *Journal of Marriage and the Family,* 1982, *44*:179–195.

Blenkner, M. Social work and family relationships in later life with some thoughts on filial maturity. Pp. 46–59, in Shanas, E., & Streib, G. R. (Eds.) *Social structure and the family: Generational relations.* Englewood Cliffs, N.J.: Prentice-Hall, 1965.

Block, C., Norr, K. L., Meyering, S., Norr, J. L., & Charles, A. G. Husband gatekeeping in childbirth. *Family Relations,* 1981, *30*:197–208.

Blood, R. O. Resolving family conflicts. *Journal of Conflict Resolution,* 1960, *4*:209–219.

————& Blood, M. *Marriage,* 3rd ed. New York: Free Press, 1978.

————& Wolfe, D. M. *Husbands and wives: The dynamics of married living.* New York: Free Press, 1960.

Bloom, D. E. What's happening to the age at first birth in the United States? A study of recent white and nonwhite cohorts. Paper presented at the annual meeting of the Population Association of America, Washington D.C., March 26–28, 1981.

Blumenthal, M. D. Mental health among the divorced: A field study of divorced and never divorced persons. *Archives of General Psychiatry,* 1967, *16*:603–608.

Bock, E. W. Aging and suicide: The significance of marital, kinship, and alternative relations. *Family Coordinator,* 1972, *21*:71–79.

————& Webber, I. L. Suicide among the elderly: Isolating widowhood and mitigating alternatives. *Journal of Marriage and the Family,* 1972, *34*:24–31.

Bohannon, P. (Ed.) *Divorce and after.* New York: Doubleday, 1970.

Bolig, R., Stein, P., & McKenry, P. The self-advertisement approach to dating: Male-female differences. *Family Relations,* 1984, *33*:587–592.

Bolton, F. G., Jr. *The pregnant adolescent.* Beverly Hills, Calif.: Sage, 1980.

————Laner, R. H., & Kane, S. P. Child maltreatment risk among adolescent mothers. *American Journal of Orthopsychiatry,* 1980, *50*:489–504.

Booth, A. Wife's employment and husbands's stress: A replication and refutation. *Journal of Marriage and the Family,* 1977, *39*:645–650.

————Does wives' employment cause stress for husbands? *Family Coordinator,* 1979, *28*:445–449.

Borland, D. M. An alternative model of the wheel theory. *Family Coordinator,* 1975, *24*:289–292.

Bormann, E. G., & Bormann, N. C. *Speech communication: An interpersonal approach.* New York: Harper, 1972.

Bott, E. *Family and social network: Roles, norms, and external relationships in ordinary urban families.* London: Tavistock, 1957.

Bower, D. W., & Christopherson, V. A. University student cohabitation: A regional comparison of selected attitudes and behaviors. *Journal of Marriage and the Family,* 1977, *39*:447–453.

Bowlby, J. The nature of the child's tie to his mother. *International Journal of Psychoanalysis,* 1958, *39*:350–374.

————Separation anxiety. *International Journal of Psychoanalysis,* 1960, *41*:89–113.

————*Attachment and loss, Vol. 1: Attachment.* New York: Basic, 1969.

————*Attachment and loss, Vol. 2: Separation.* New York: Basic, 1973.

Bradburn, N. *The structure of psychological well-being.* Chicago: Aldine, 1969.

Bradbury, K., Danziger, S., Smolensky, E., & Smolensky, P. Public assistance, female headship, and economic well-being. *Journal of Marriage and the Family,* 1979, *41*:519–535.

Bradley, R. A. *Husband-coached childbirth,* Rev. ed. New York: Harper, 1974.

Brandwein, R. A., Brown, C. A., & Fox, E. M. Women and children last: The social situation of divorced mothers and their families. *Journal of Marriage and the Family,* 1974, *36*:498–514.

Brazelton, T. B., Koslowski, B., & Main, M. The origins of reciprocity: The early mother-infant interaction. In Lewis, M., & Rosenblum, L. (Eds.) *The effect of the infant on its caregiver.* New York: Wiley, 1973.

Brim, O. G., & Wheeler, S. *Socialization after childhood: Two essays.* New York: Wiley, 1966.

Brinkerhoff, D. B., & White, L. K. Marital satisfaction in an economically marginal population. *Journal of Marriage and the Family,* 1978, *40*:259–267.

Broderick, C. Going steady: The beginning of the end. In Farber, S. M., & Wilson, H. L. (Eds.) *Teen-Age marriage and divorce.* Ann Arbor, Mich.: Diablo Press, 1967.

Bromwich, R. M. Stimulation in the first year of life? A perspective on infant development. *Young Children,* 1977, *32*:71–81.

Brooks, J. B. *The process of parenting.* Palo Alto, Calif.: Mayfield, 1981.

Brown, D. G. *Annual Report of the Conciliation Court of Pima County, Arizona, 1979.*

Brown, H. *The challenge of man's future.* New York: Viking, 1954.

Buckhout, R. Toward a two-child norm: Changing family planning attitudes. *American Psychologist,* 1972, *27*:16–26.

Bumpass, L. L., & Sweet, J. A. Differentials in marital instability: 1970. *American Sociological Review,* 1972, *37*:754–766.

Bureau of Labor Statistics. Children of working mothers. Special Labor Force Report, Bulletin 2158, U.S. Department of Labor, Washington D.C., March 1983.

Bureau of Labor Statistics News. U.S. Department of Labor. Washington, D.C., Dec. 2, 1983.

Burgess, E. W., & Cottrell, L. S., Jr. *Predicting success or failure in marriage.* Englewood Cliffs, N.J.: Prentice-Hall, 1939.

Burgess, J. K. The single-parent family: A social and sociological problem. *Family Coordinator,* 1970, *19*:137–144.

Burke, R. J., & Weir, T. Relationship of wives' employment status to husband, wife and pair satisfaction and performance. *Journal of Marriage and the Family,* 1976, *38*:279–287.

Burr, W. R. *Successful marriage: A principles approach.* Homewood, Ill.: Dorsey, 1976.

Butler, R. N., & Lewis, M. I. *Sex after sixty: A guide for men and women in their later years.* New York: Harper, 1976.

Buunk, B. Strategies of jealousy: Styles of coping with extramarital involvement of the spouse. *Family Relations,* 1982, *31*:13–18.

Calderone, M. S. Eroticism as a norm. *Family Coordinator,* 1974, *23*:337–341.

Calhoun, L. G., & Selby, J. W. Voluntary childlessness, involuntary childlessness, and having children: A study of social perceptions. *Family Coordinator,* 1980, *29*:181–183.

Cameron, C., Oskamp, S., & Sparks, W. Courtship American style: Newspaper ads. *Family Coordinator,* 1977, *26*:27–30.

Capellanus, A. *The art of courtly love.* New York: Ungar, 1957.

Carr, D. H. Chromosomal abnormalities in human fetuses. *Research in Reproduction,* 1972, *4*:3–4.

Carter, H., & Glick, P. C. *Marriage and divorce: A social and economic study,* Rev. ed. Cambridge, Mass.: Harvard U. P., 1976.

Casler, L. This thing called love is pathological. *Psychology Today,* 1969, *3*:18–76.

Cates, W., Schulz, K. F., Grimes, D. A., & Tyler C. W., Jr. The effect of delay and method choice on the risk of abortion morbidity. *Family Planning Perspectives,* 1977, *9*:266–273.

Chafetz, J. S. *Masculine/feminine or human?* Itasca, Ill.: Peacock, 1974.

Chelune, G. J. (Ed.) *Self-disclosure: Origins, patterns, and implications of openness in interpersonal relationships.* San Francisco: Jossey-Bass, 1979.

Cherlin, A., & Walters, P. B. Trends in United States men's and women's sex role attitudes: 1972–1978. *American Sociological Review,* 1981, *46*:453–460.

Chester, R. Is there a relationship between childlessness and marriage breakdown? *Journal of Biosocial Science,* 1972, *4*:443–454.

Chiappa, J. A., & Forish, J. J. *The VD book.* New York: Holt, 1976.

Chilman, C. S. Families in poverty in the early 1970's: Rates, associated factors, some implications. *Journal of Marriage and the Family,* 1975, *37*:49–60.

——— Social and psychological research concerning adolescent childbearing: 1970–1980. *Journal of Marriage and the Family,* 1980, *42*:793–805.

——— Remarriage and stepfamilies: Research results and implications. Pp. 147–163, in Macklin, E. D., & Rubin, R. H. (Eds.) *Contemporary families and alternative lifestyles.* Beverly Hills, Calif.: Sage, 1983.

Clark, A. L., & Wallin, P. Women's sexual responsiveness and the duration and quality of their marriages. *American Journal of Sociology,* 1965, *21*:187–196.

Clarke-Stewart, K. A. Interaction between mothers and their young children: Characteristics and consequences. *Monograph of the Society for Research in Child Development,* 1973, *38*.

Clayton, R. R., & Bokemeier, J. L. Premarital sex in the seventies. *Journal of Marriage and the Family,* 1980, *42:*759–775.

——— & Voss, H. L. Shacking Up: Cohabitation in the 1970s. *Journal of Marriage and the Family,* 1977, *39:*273–283.

Cogswell, B. E. Variant family forms and life styles: Rejection of the traditional nuclear family. *Family Coordinator,* 1975, *24:*391–406.

Cohen, J. B. *Personal Finance,* 6th ed. Homewood, Ill.: Irvin, 1979.

Cole, C. L., Cole, A. L., & Dean, D. G. Emotional maturity and marital adjustment: A decade replication. *Journal of Marriage and the Family,* 1980, *42:*533–539.

Colletta, N. D. Support systems after divorce: Incidence and impact. *Journal of Marriage and the Family,* 1979, *41:*837–846.

Colston, L. G. Love and creativity. Pp. 172–184, in Otto, H. A. (Ed.) *Love today.* New York: Association, 1972.

Comfort, A. *The Joy of Sex.* New York: Crown, 1972.

Committee on Preventive Psychiatry. *Humane Reproduction.* New York: Scribner, 1973.

Conover, P. W. An analysis of communes and intentional communities with particular attention to sexual and genderal issues. *Family Coordinator,* 1975, *24:*453–464.

Constantine, L. L., & Constantine, J. M. *Group marriage: A study of contemporary multilateral marriage.* New York: Macmillan, 1973.

———. *Treasures of the island: Children in alternative families.* Beverly Hills, Calif.: Sage, 1976.

Constantinople, A. Masculinity-femininity: An exception to a famous dictum. *Psychological Bulletin,* 1973, *80:*389–407.

Consumer Reports. Is breast-feeding best for babies? March 1977.

Contraceptive Technology Update. Sponge survives first year; emerges top seller. 1984, *5:*81–88.

Coogler, O. J., Weber, R. E., & McKenry, P. C. Divorce mediation: A means of facilitating divorce and adjustment. *Family Coordinator,*1979, *28:*255–259.

Cooley, C. H. *Social organization.* New York: Schocken, 1962.

Coombs, K. N. Can midwives mean happier birth days? *TWA Ambassador,* Oct. 1980.

Coombs, R. H. Value consensus and partner satisfaction among dating couples. *Journal of Marriage and the Family,* 1966, *28:*166–173.

Cooper, D. *The death of the family.* New York: Random, 1970.

Coser, L. A. *Masters of sociological thought.* New York: Harcourt, 1971.

Coutts, L. M., & Schneider, F. W. Visual behavior in an unfocused interaction as a function of sex and distance. *Journal of Experimental Social Psychology,* 1975, *11:*64–77.

Cox, F. D. *Human intimacy: Marriage, the family and its meaning.* St. Paul, Minn.: West, 1978.

Cramer, J. C. Fertility and female employment: Problems of causal direction. *American Sociological Review,* 1980, *45:*167–190.

Cromwell, R., & Olson, D. H. (Eds.) *Power in families.* Beverly Hills, Calif.: Sage, 1975.

Cronkite, R. L. The determinants of spouses' normative preferences for family roles. *Journal of Marriage and the Family,* 1977, *39:*575–585.

Crosby, J. F. A critique of divorce statistics and their interpretation. *Family Coordinator,* 1980, *29:*51–58.

Cuber, J. F., & Harroff, P. B. *Sex and the significant Americans.* New York: Penguin, 1965.

Current Population Reports. A statistical portrait of women in the United States: 1978. Special Studies, Series P-23, No. 100, Feb., 1980.

———Child support and alimony: 1978. Series P-23, No. 112, Washington, D.C., 1981.

Cutler, B., & Dyer, W. Initial adjustment processes in young married couples. *Social Forces,* 1965, *44:*195–201.

Cutright, P. Income and family events: Getting married. *Journal of Marriage and the Family,* 1970, *32:*628–637.

———Income and family events: Family income, family size, and consumption. *Journal of Marriage and the Family,* 1971a, *33:*161–173.

———Income and family events: Marital stability. *Journal of Marriage and the Family,* 1971b, *33:*291–306.

Dannefer, D. Adult development and social theory: A paradigmatic reappraisal. *American Sociological Review,* 1984, *49:*100–116.

Darnley, F. Adjustment to retirement: Integrity or despair. *Family Coordinator,* 1975, *24:*217–226.

Dean, D. Emotional maturity and marital adjustment. *Journal of Marriage and the Family,* 1966, *28:*454–457.

Defrain, J., & Eirick, R. Coping as divorced single parents: A comparative study of fathers and mothers. *Family Relations,* 1981, *30:*265–273.

Defronzo, J. Cross-sectional areal analyses of factors affecting marital fertility: Actual versus relative income. *Journal of Marriage and the Family,* 1976, *38:*669–676.

DeLamater, J. D., & MacCorquodale, P. *Premarital sexual-*

ity: Attitudes, relationships, behavior. Madison, Wis.: U. of Wis. P., 1979.

DeLora, J. S., & Warren, C. A. B. *Understanding sexual interaction.* Boston: Houghton, 1977.

DeMartino, M. F. How women want men to make love. *Sexology,* Oct., 1970: 4–7.

Derlega, V. J., & Chaikin, A. L. *Sharing intimacy: What we reveal to others and why.* Englewood Cliffs, N.J.: Prentice-Hall, 1975.

Deutscher, I. The quality of postparental life: Definitions of the situation. *Journal of Marriage and the Family,* 1964, *26*:52–59.

Diamond, M. Human sexual development: Biological foundations for social development. In Beach, F. A. (Ed.), *Human sexuality in four perspectives.* Baltimore: Johns Hopkins, 1976.

———Sexual identity and sex roles. In V. Bullough (Ed.), *The frontiers of sex research.* New York: Prometheus, 1979.

Dick-Read, G. *Childbirth without fear,* 4th ed., New York: Harper, 1972.

Diepold, J., Jr., & Young, R. D. Empirical studies of adolescent sexual behavior: A critical review. *Adolescence,* 1979, *14*:45–64.

Dizard, J. *Social change and the family.* Chicago: Community and Family Study Center. U. of Chicago, 1968.

Duberman, L. Step-kin relationships. *Journal of Marriage and the Family,* 1973, *35*:283–292.

———*Gender and sex in society.* New York: Praeger, 1975.

Duvall, E. *Family development,* 5th ed., Philadelphia: Lippincott, 1977.

Dyer, E. D. Parenthood as crisis: A re-study. *Marriage and Family Living,* 1963, *25*:196–201.

Eckland, B. K., & Bailey, J. P., *National longitudinal study of the high school class of 1972: Second follow-up.* Research Triangle Park, N.C.: Research Triangle Institute, 1976.

Edmonds, V. H. Marital conventionalization: Definition and measurement, *Journal of Marriage and the Family,* 1967, *29*:681–688.

Edwards, J. N., & Booth, A. Sexual behavior in and out of marriage: An assessment of correlates. *Journal of Marriage and the Family,* 1976, *38*:73–83.

Elder, G. H., Jr. Structural variations in the child rearing relationship. *Sociometry,* 1962, *25*:241–262.

Elkin, M. Premarital counseling for minors: The Los Angeles experience. *Family Coordinator,* 1977, *26*:429–443.

Ellis, A. A study of human love relationships. *Journal of Genetic Psychology,* 1949, *75*:61–71.

———Frigidity. Pp. 450–456, in Ellis A., & Abarbanel, A. (Eds.) *The encyclopedia of sexual behavior, Vol. 1.* New York: Hawthorne, 1961.

Elstein, M. Effect of infertility on psychosexual function. *British Medical Journal,* 1975, *3*:296–299.

Erikson, E. H. Life cycle. Pp. 19–30, in Bloom, M. (Ed.) *Life span development: Bases for preventive and intervention helping.* New York: Macmillan, 1980.

Ewer, P. A., Crimmins, E., & Oliver, R. An analysis of the relationship between husbands' income, family size and wife's employment in the early stages of marriage. *Journal of Marriage and the Family,* 1979, *41*:727–738.

———& Gardner, E. C. Income in the income and fertility relationship. *Journal of Marriage and the Family,* 1978, *40*:291–299.

Family Planning Perspectives, Cigarettes plus pill: Deadly for women 30 and over. 1977, *9*:36.

———World population: Wide regional variations in fertility, mortality rates, 1984a, *16*:145.

———Sterilizations off sharply in 1982. 1984b, *16*:40–41.

———Study of some 20,000 men finds no evidence vasectomy has any adverse health consequences. 1984c, *16*:35–36.

Fein, R. A. Men's entrance into parenthood. *Family Coordinator,* 1976, *25*:341–348.

Feldman, H. *Development of the husband-wife relationship.* Ithaca, N.Y.: Cornell U. P., 1964.

———The effects of children on the family. Pp. 104–125, in Michel, A. (Ed.) *Family issues of employed women in Europe and America.* Leiden, Belgium: E. J. Brill, 1971.

Fendrich, M. Wives' employment and husbands' distress: A meta-analysis and a replication. *Journal of Marriage and the Family,* 1984, *46*:871–879.

Ferreira, A. J. The pregnant woman's emotional attitude and its reflection on the newborn. *American Journal of Orthopsychiatry,* 1960, *30*:553–561.

Fischer, J. L., & Cardea, J. M. Mothers living apart from their children: A study in stress and coping. *Alternative Lifestyles,* 1971, *4*:218–227.

Fisher, E. I. A guide to divorce counseling. *Family Coordinator,* 1973, *22*:55–61.

Fontana, V. J. The diagnosis of the maltreatment syndrome in children. *Pediatrics,* 1973, *51*:780–782.

Foote, N. Matching of husband and wife in phases of development. *Transactions of the Third World Congress of Sociology,* London: International Sociological Society, 1956.

Ford, C. S., & Beach, F. A. *Patterns of sexual behavior.* New York: Harper, 1953.

Forrest, J. D., & Henshaw, S. K. What U.S. women think and do about contraception. *Family Planning Perspectives,* 1983, *15:*157–166.

Frank, L. K. Tactile communication. *Genetic Psychology Monographs,* 1957, *56:*209–255.

Frankel, J., & Dullaert, J. Is adolescent rebellion universal? *Adolescence,* 1977, *12:*227–236.

Frankel, V. E. *The doctor and the soul,* 2nd. ed. New York: Bantam, 1965.

Freedman, D. S., & Thornton, A. The long-term impact of pregnancy at marriage on the family's economic circumstances. *Family Planning Perspectives,* 1979, *11:*6–21.

Friedan, B. *The feminine mystique.* New York: Norton, 1963.

Friedrich, W. N., & Boriskin, J. A. The role of the child in abuse. *American Journal of Orthopsychiatry,* 1976, *46:*580–590.

Fromm, E. *The art of loving.* New York: Bantam, 1956.

Furstenberg, F. F. Industrialization and the American family: A look backward. *American Sociological Review,* 1966, *31:*326–337.

——— & Spanier, G. B. The risk of dissolution in remarriage: An examination of Cherlin's hypothesis of incomplete institutionalization. *Family Relations,* 1984, *33:*433–441.

Gaines, R., Sandgrund, A., Green, A. H., & Power, E. Etiological factors in child maltreatment: A multivariate study of abusing, neglecting, and normal mothers. *Journal of Abnormal Psychology,* 1978, *87:*531–540.

Ganong, L. H., & Coleman, M. The effects of remarriage on children: A review of the empirical literature. *Family Relations,* 1984, *33:*389–406.

Garai, J. E., & Scheinfeld, A. Sex differences in mental and behavioral traits. *Genetic Psychology Monographs,* 1968, *77:*169–299.

Garbarino, J. The human ecology of child maltreatment: A conceptual model for research. *Journal of Marriage and the Family,* 1977, *39:*721–735.

Gasser, R., & Taylor, C. M. Role adjustment of single parent fathers with dependent children. *Family Coordinator,* 1976, *25:*397–401.

Gauger, W. H., & Walker, K. E. *The dollar value of housework.* Information Bulletin 60, Cooperative Extension Service, Ithaca, N.Y.: Cornell University, 1980.

Gebhard, P. Factors in marital orgasm. *Journal of Social Issues,* 1966, *22:*88–95.

Gelles, R. J. Violence toward children in the United States.

Pp. 35–48, in Cook, J. V., & Bowles, R. T. (Eds.) *Child abuse: Commission and omission.* Toronto: Butterworth, 1980.

Gettleman, S., & Markowitz, J. *The courage to divorce.* New York: Simon & Schuster, 1974.

Gilbert, S. J. Self-disclosure, intimacy and communication in families. *Family Coordinator,* 1976, *25:*221–231.

Glass, S. P., & Wright, T. L. The relationship of extramarital sex, length of marriage, and sex differences on marital satisfaction and romanticism. *Journal of Marriage and the Family,* 1977, *39:*691–703.

Glenn, N. E. Psychological well-being in the post-parental stage: Some evidence from national surveys. *Journal of Marriage and the Family,* 1975a, *37:*105–110.

———The contribution of marriage to the psychological well-being of males and females. *Journal of Marriage and the Family,* 1975b, *37:*594–600.

———The well-being of persons remarried after divorce. *Journal of Family Issues,* 1981, *2:*61–75.

———Interreligious marriage in the United States: Patterns and recent trends. *Journal of Marriage and the Family,* 1982, *44:*555–566.

——— & Hoppe, S. K. Only children as adults: Psychological well-being. *Journal of Family Issues,* 1984, *5:*363–382.

———Hoppe, S. K., & Weiner, D. Social class heterogamy and marital success: A study of the empirical adequacy of a textbook generalization. *Social Problems,* 1974, *22:*539–550.

——— & Weaver, C. N. The marital happiness of remarried divorced persons. *Journal of Marriage and the Family,* 1977, *39:*331–337.

Glick, P. C. A demographer looks at American families. *Journal of Marriage and the Family,* 1975, *37:*15–26.

———Updating the life cycle of the family. *Journal of Marriage and the Family,* 1977, *39:*5–13.

———Future American families. *The Washington COFO Memo,* 1979, *2:*2–5.

———Marriage, divorce, and living arrangements: Prospective changes. *Journal of Family Issues,* 1984a, *5:*7–26.

———American household structure in transition. *Family Planning Perspectives,* 1984b, *16:*205–211.

——— & Norton, A. J. Marrying, divorcing, and living together in the U.S. today. *Population Bulletin,* 1977, *32:*1–39.

——— & Spanier, G. B. Married and unmarried cohabitation in the United States. *Journal of Marriage and the Family,* 1980, *42:*19–30.

Godow, A. G. *Human sexuality.* St. Louis: Mosby, 1982.

Goetting, A. The six stations of remarriage: Developmental tasks of remarriage after divorce. *Family Relations,* 1982, *31:*213–222.

Gold, R. B. Depo Provera: The jury is still out. *Family Planning Perspectives,* 1983, *15:*78–81.

Gonzalez-Mena, J., & Eyer, D. W. *Infancy and caregiving.* Palo Alto, Calif.: Mayfield, 1980.

Goode, W. J. *After divorce.* New York: Free Press, 1956.

Gordon, H. A., & Kammeyer, K. C. W. The gainful employment of women with small children. *Journal of Marriage and the Family,* 1980, *42:*327–336.

Gordon, M. (Ed.) *The nuclear family in crisis: The search for an alternative.* New York: Harper, 1972.

———Was Waller ever right? The rating and dating complex reconsidered. *Journal of Marriage and the Family,* 1981, *43:*67–76.

Gordon, T. *P.E.T. Parent effectiveness training.* New York: New American Lib., 1970.

Gortmaker, S. L. Poverty and infant mortality in the United States. *American Sociological Review,* 1979, *44:*280–297.

Gouldner, A. W. The norm of reciprocity: A preliminary statement. *American Sociological Review,* 1960, *25:*161–178.

Gove, W. R. The relationship between sex roles, marital status, and mental illness. *Social Forces,* 1972, *51:*34–44.

———Sex, marital status, and mortality. *American Journal of Sociology,* 1973, *79:*45–67.

Gross, H. E. Dual-career couples who live apart. *Journal of Marriage and the Family,* 1980, *42:*567–576.

Grossman, F. K., Eichler, L. S., & Winickoff, S. A. *Pregnancy, birth, and parenthood.* San Francisco: Jossey-Bass, 1980.

Gubrium, J. F. Marital desolation and the evaluation of everyday life in old age. *Journal of Marriage and the Family,* 1974, *36:*107–113.

Guerney, B. G. *Relationship enhancement.* San Francisco: Jossey-Bass, 1977.

Gurin, G., Veroff, J., & Feld, S. *Americans view their mental health.* New York: Basic, 1960.

Gurman, A. S., & Kniskern, D. P. (Eds.) *Handbook of family therapy.* New York: Brunner/Mazel, 1981.

Hall, E. (Ed.) *Developmental psychology today,* 2nd ed. New York: Random, 1975.

Hallenbeck, P. N. An analysis of power dynamics in marriage. *Journal of Marriage and the Family,* 1966, *28:*200–203.

Harkins, E. B. Effects of empty nest transition on self-report of psychological and physical well-being. *Journal of Marriage and the Family,* 1978, *40:*549–556.

Harlow, H. F., & Harlow, M. K. Effects of various mother-infant relationships on rhesus monkey behaviors. Pp. 15–36, in Foss, B. M. (Ed.) *Determinants of infant behavior, Vol. 4.* London: Methuen, 1969.

———The young monkeys. Pp. 154–159, in *Readings in developmental psychology today,* 2nd ed. New York: Random, 1977.

Harrell, J. E., & Ridley, C. A. Substitute child care, maternal employment, and the quality of mother-child interaction. *Journal of Marriage and the Family,* 1975, *37:*557–564.

Harrington, M. *The other America: Poverty in the United States.* New York: Penguin, 1962.

Harvey, C. D., & Bahr, H. M. Widowhood, morale, and affiliation. *Journal of Marriage and the Family,* 1974, *36:*97–106.

Hatcher, R. A., Stewart, G. K., Stewart, F., Guest, F., Stratton, P., & Wright, A. H. *Contraceptive technology, 1978–1979.* New York: Irvington, 1978.

———Guest, F., Stewart, F., Stewart, G. K., Trussell, J., & Frank, E. *Contraceptive technology, 1984–85.* New York: Irvington, 1984.

Hauhart, R. C. Children in communes: Some legal implications of a modern lifestyle. *Family Coordinator,* 1977, *26:*367–371.

Havens, E. M. Women, work, and wedlock: A note on female marital patterns in the United States. *American Journal of Sociology,* 1973, *78:*975–981.

Havighurst, R. J. *Human development and education.* New York: Longmans, 1953.

———*Developmental tasks and education,* 3rd ed. New York: McKay, 1972.

Hawke, S., & Knox, D. *One child by choice.* Englewood Cliffs, N.J.: Prentice-Hall, 1977.

Heatherington, E. M., & Frankie, G. Effects of parental dominance, warmth, and conflict on imitation in children. *Journal of Personality and Social Psychology,* 1967, *6:*119–125.

Heer, D. M. Economic development and the fertility transition. *Daedalus,* 1968, *97:*447–462.

———The prevalence of black-white marriage in the United States, 1960 and 1970. *Journal of Marriage and the Family,* 1974, *36:*246–258.

Helfer, R. E., & Kempe, C. H. *The battered child.* Chicago: U. of Chicago, 1968.

Helsing, K., Szklo, M., & Comstock, G. W. Factors associated with mortality after widowhood. *American Journal of Public Health,* 1981, *71:*802–809.

Henker, F. Male climacteric. In Howells, J. G. (Ed.) *Modern perspectives in the psychiatry of middle age.* New York: Brunner/Mazel, 1981.

Hess, B. B., & Waring, J. M. Changing patterns of aging and

family bonds in later life. *Family Coordinator,* 1978, 27:303–314.

Hess, R. D., & Shipman, V. C. Early experience and the socialization of cognitive modes in children. *Child Development,* 1965, 36:870–886.

Hetherington, E. M., Cox, M., & Cox, R. Divorced fathers. *Family Coordinator,* 1976, 25:417–428.

———— & Frankie, G. Effects of parental dominance, warmth, and conflict on imitation in children. *Journal of Personality and Social Psychology,* 1967, 6:119–125.

Hicks, M. W. An empirical evaluation of textbook assumptions about engagement. *Family Coordinator,* 1970, 19:57–63.

Hill, E. A., & Dorfman, L. T. Reaction of housewives to the retirement of their husbands. *Family Relations,* 1982, 31:195–200.

Hill, R., & Aldous, J. Socialization for marriage and parenthood. Pp. 885–950, in Goslin, D. (Ed.) *Handbook of socialization theory and research.* Chicago: Rand McNally, 1969.

———— & Hansen, D. A. The identification of conceptual frameworks utilized in family study. *Marriage and Family Living,* 1960, 22:299–311.

Hiller, D. V., & Philliber, W. W. The derivation of status benefits from occupational attainments of working wives. *Journal of Marriage and the Family,* 1978, 40:63–69.

———— Necessity, compatibility, and status attainment as factors in the labor-force participation of married women. *Journal of Marriage and the Family,* 1980, 42:347–354.

Hine, J. R. *Will you make a wise marriage choice?* Danville, Ill.: The Interstate Printers and Publ., 1978.

———— *What comes after you say "I love you?"* Palo Alto, Calif.: Pacific, 1980.

Hirsch, G. T. Non-sexist childrearing: De-mythifying normative data. *Family Coordinator,* 1974, 23:165–170.

Hite, S. *The Hite report: A nationwide study on female sexuality.* New York: Macmillan, 1976.

Hobbs, D. F., & Cole, S. P. Transition to parenthood: A decade replication. *Journal of Marriage and the Family,* 1976, 38:723–731.

Hobson, C. F., Skeen, P., & Robinson, B. E. Review of theories and research concerning sex-role development and androgyny with suggestions for teachers. *Family Coordinator,* 1980, 29:155–162.

Hodge, M. B. *Your fear of love.* New York: Doubleday, 1967.

Hofferth, S. Day care in the next decade: 1980–1990. *Journal of Marriage and the Family,* 1979, 41:649–658.

Hoffman, L. W. Effects on child. Pp. 126–166, in Hoffman, L. W., & Nye, F. I. (Eds.) *Working mothers.* San Francisco: Jossey-Bass, 1974.

Hogan, D. P. The variable order of events in the life course. *American Sociological Review,* 1978, 43:573–586.

———— The transition to adulthood as a career contingency. *American Sociological Review,* 1980, 45:261–276.

Hoge, D. R. Changes in college students' value patterns in the 1950's, 1960's and 1970's. *Sociology of Education,* 1976, 49:155–163.

Holmes, T. H., & Rahe, R. H. The social readjustment rating scale. *Journal of Psychosomatic Research,* 1967, 11:213–218.

Hood, J., & Golden, S. Beating time/making time: The impact of work scheduling on men's family roles. *Family Coordinator,* 1979, 28:575–582.

Hornung, C. A., & McCullough, B. C. Status relationships in dual-employment marriages: Consequences for psychological well-being. *Journal of Marriage and the Family,* 1981, 43:125–141.

Hotchner, T. *Pregnancy and childbirth: The complete guide for a new life.* New York: Avon, 1979.

House, B. G. *Analysis of economic status of women in divorce.* Unpublished Masters thesis. Texas Tech U., 1975.

Houseknecht, S. K. Childlessness and marital adjustment. *Journal of Marriage and the Family,* 1979, 41:259–265.

Hubbard, C. W. *Family planning education,* 2nd ed. St. Louis: Mosby, 1977.

Humphreys, L. *Out of the closets: The sociology of homosexual liberation.* Englewood Cliffs, N.J.: Prentice-Hall, 1972.

Hunt, M. M. *Sexual behavior in the 1970s.* Chicago: PEI Books, 1974.

———— & Hunt, B. *The divorce experience.* New York: McGraw-Hill, 1977.

Hunt, R. A., & Rydman, E. J. *Creative marriage,* 2nd ed. Winchester, Mass.: Allyn and Bacon, 1979.

Hunter, R. S., Kilstrom, N., Kraybill, E. W., & Loda, F. Antecedents of child abuse and neglect in premature infants. *Pediatrics,* 1978, 61:629–635.

Hutchinson, I. W. The significance of marital status for morale and life satisfaction among lower-income elderly. *Journal of Marriage and the Family,* 1975, 37:287–293.

Huyck, M. H., & Hoyer, W. J. *Adult development and aging.* Belmont, Calif.: Wadsworth, 1982.

International Planned Parenthood Federation (IPF) Bulletin, 1976, 10:4.

Istvan, J., & Griffitt, W. Effects of sexual experience on dating desirability and marriage desirability: An experimental study. *Journal of Marriage and the Family,* 1980, *42*:377–386.

Jacobson, N. S. A review of research on the effectiveness of marital therapy. In Paolino, T. J., & McCrady, B. S. (Eds.) *Marriage and marital therapy: Psycho-analytic, behavior, and systems perspectives.* New York: Brunner/Mazel, 1978.

Jacques, J. M., & Chason, K. J. Cohabitation: Its impact on marital success. *Family Coordinator,* 1979, *28*:35–39.

Jaffee, B., & Fanshel, D. *How they fared in adoption: A follow-up study.* New York: Columbia U. P., 1970.

Jedlicka, D. Sex inequality, aging, and innovation in preferential mate selection. *Family Coordinator,* 1978, *27*:137–140.

——— Formal mate selection networks in the United States. *Family Relations,* 1980, *29*:199–209.

Jenkins, R. L. Maxims in child custody cases. *Family Coordinator,* 1977, *26*:385–389.

Johnson, M. P., & Leslie, L. Couple involvement and network structure: A test of the dyadic withdrawal hypothesis. *Social Psychology Quarterly,* 1982, *45*:34–43.

Johnson, R. E. Extramarital sexual intercourse: A methodological note. *Journal of Marriage and the Family,* 1970, *32*:279–283.

Jorgensen, S. R. *Antecedents of marital conflict: Sociocultural heterogamy and socioeconomic rewards in marriage.* Unpublished doctoral dissertation, U. of Minnesota, 1976.

——— Beyond teenage pregnancy: Research frontiers for early adolescent sexuality. *Journal of Early Adolescence,* 1983a, *3*:141–155.

——— The American family of the future: What choices will we have? Pp. 227–245, in Gutknecht, D. B., Butler, E. W., Criswell, L., & Meints, J. (Eds.) *Family, self, and society.* New York: U. P. of America, 1983b.

——— & Alexander, S. Reducing the risk of adolescent pregnancy: Toward certification of family life educators. *High School Journal,* 1981, *64*:257–268.

——— & Gaudy, J. C. Self-disclosure and satisfaction in marriage: The relation examined. *Family Relations,* 1980, *29*:281–287.

——— & Johnson, A. C. Correlates of divorce liberality. *Journal of Marriage and the Family,* 1980, *42*:617–626.

——— & Klein, D. M. Sociocultural heterogamy, dissensus, and conflict in marriage. *Pacific Sociological Review,* 1979, *22*:51–75.

——— *Conflict in marriage.* New York: Guilford (Forthcoming).

Jost, A. Embryonic sexual differentiation. Pp. 15–45, in Jones, H. W., & Scott, W. W. (Eds.) *Hermaphroditism, genital anomalies and related endocrine disorders.* Baltimore: Williams and Wilkins, 1958.

——— A new look at the mechanisms controlling sex differentiation in mammals. *Johns Hopkins Medical Journal,* 1972, *130*:38–53.

Jourard, S. M. Healthy personality and self-disclosure. *Mental Hygiene,* 1959, *43*:499–507.

——— *The transparent self.* New York: Van Nostrand, 1971.

——— Some dimensions of the loving experience. Pp. 42–48, in Otto, H. A. (Ed.) *Love today.* New York: Association, 1972.

——— & Richman, P. Disclosure output and input in college students. *Merrill-Palmer Quarterly of Behavior and Development.* 1963, *9*:141–148.

Juhasz, A. M. A chain of sexual decision-making. *Family Coordinator,* 1975, *24*:43–49.

Kagan, J. Acquisition and significance of sex typing and sex role identity. Pp. 137–167, in Hoffman, M. L., & Hoffman, L. W. (Eds.) *Review of child development research,* Vol. 1. New York: Sage, 1964.

Kahl, J. *The American class structure.* New York: Holt, 1957.

Kammerman, S. B. Child-care services: A national picture. *Monthly Labor Review,* 1983, *106*:35–39.

Kandel, D. B., & Lesser, G. S. *Youth in two worlds.* San Francisco: Jossey-Bass, 1972.

Kanter, R. M., Jaffee, D., & Weisberg, D. K. Coupling, parenting, and the presence of others: Intimate relationships in communal households. *Family Coordinator,* 1975, *24*:433–452.

Kantor, D., & Lehr, W. *Inside the family: Toward a theory of family process.* New York: Harper, 1975.

Karmel, M. *Thank you, Dr. Lamaze.* Philadelphia: Lippincott, 1959.

Katz, A. M., & Hill, R. Residential propinquity and marital selection: A review of theory, method and fact. *Marriage and Family Living,* 1958, *20*:27–35.

Keith, P. M., & Schafer, R. B. Role strain and depression in two-job families. *Family Relations,* 1980, *29*:483–488.

Kelly, R. K. *Courtship, marriage, and the family,* 3rd ed. New York: Harcourt, 1979.

Kempe, C. H. Sexual abuse: Another hidden pediatric problem. *Pediatrics,* 1978, *62*:382–389.

——— Silverman, F. N., Steele, B. F., Droegemueller, W., & Silver, H. K. The battered child syndrome. *Journal of the American Medical Association,* 1962, *181*:17–24.

Kenniston, K. The sources of student dissent. *Journal of Social Issues,* 1967, *23*:108–137.

Kent, D. P., & Matson, M. B. The impact of health on the aged family. *Family Coordinator,* 1972, *21*:29–36.

Kieren, D., Henton, J., & Marotz, R. *His & hers: A problem solving approach to marriage.* New York: Holt, 1975.

——— & Tallman, I. Adaptability: A measure of spousal problem solving. *Minnesota Family Study Center,* Tech. Report No. 1, U. of Minnesota, 1971.

King, K., Balswick, J.O., & Robinson, I. E. The continuing premarital sexual revolution among college females. *Journal of Marriage and the Family,* 1977, *39*:455–459.

Kinsey, A. C., Pomeroy, W. B., & Martin, C. E. *Sexual behavior in the human male.* Philadelphia: Saunders, 1948.

——— & Gebhard, P. H. *Sexual behavior in the human female.* Philadephia: Saunders, 1953. (Pocket Ed.)

Klaus, H., & Kennel, J. *Maternal-infant bonding.* St. Louis: Mosby, 1976.

Klein, D. C., & Ross, A. Kindergarten entry: A study of role transition. Pp. 60–69, in Krugman, M. (Ed.) *Orthopsychiatry and the school.* New York: American Orthopsychiatric Association, 1958.

Knapp, J. J., & Whitehurst, R. N. Sexually open marriage and relationships: Issues and prospects. Pp. 147–160, in Libby, R. W., & Whitehurst, R. N. (Eds.) *Marriage and alternatives: Exploring intimate relationships.* Glenview, Ill.: Scott, Foresman, 1977.

Knapp, M. L. *Nonverbal communication in human interaction.* New York: Holt, 1972.

Knox, D. *Marriage happiness: A behavioral approach to counseling.* Champaign, Ill.: Research Press, 1971.

———*Exploring marriage and the family.* Glenview, Ill.: Scott, Foresman, 1979.

——— & Wilson, K. The differences between having one and two children. *Family Coordinator,* 1978, *27*:23–25.

——— & Wilson, K. Dating behaviors of university students. *Family Relations,* 1981, *30*:255–258.

Knox, S. *VD quiz: Getting the right answers* (Student text). Palo Alto, Calif.: American Social Health Association, 1977.

Kobrin, F. E., & Hendershot, G. E. Do family ties reduce mortality? Evidence from the United States, 1966–1968. *Journal of Marriage and the Family,* 1977, *39*:737–745.

——— & Waite, L. J. Effects of childhood family structure on the transition to marriage. *Journal of Marriage and the Family,* 1984, *46*:807–816.

Kohlberg, L. Moral development and identification. Pp. 277–332, in Stevenson, H. W. (Ed.) *Child psychology.* Chicago: U. of Chicago, 1963.

———A cognitive-developmental analysis of children's sex-role concepts and attitudes. Pp. 82–172 in Maccoby, E. (Ed.) *The development of sex differences.* Stanford, Calif.: Stanford U. P., 1966.

———Stage and sequence: The cognitive-developmental approach to socialization. Pp. 347–480, in Goslin, D. A. (Ed.) *Handbook of socialization theory and research.* Chicago: Rand McNally, 1969.

Kohn, M. *Class and conformity.* Homewood, Ill.: Dorsey Press, 1969.

Kolbe, R., & LaVoie, J. C. Sex-role stereotyping in preschool children's picture books. *Social Psychology Quarterly,* 1981, *44*:369–374.

Komarovsky, M. *Blue-collar marriage.* New York: Random, 1962.

Kompara, D. R. Difficulties in the socialization process of stepparenting. *Family Relations,* 1980, *29*:69–73.

Krain, M., Cannon, D., & Bagford, J. Rating-dating or simply prestige homogamy? Data on dating in the Greek system on a midwestern campus. *Journal of Marriage and the Family,* 1977, *39*:663–674.

Krantzler, M. *Creative divorce.* New York: Evans, 1973.

Kressel, K. Patterns of coping in divorce and some implications for clinical practice. *Family Coordinator,* 1980, *29*:234–240.

Lake, A. *Our own years: What women over 35 should know about themselves.* New York: Random, 1979.

Lamb, M. E. Influence of the child on marital quality and family interaction during the prenatal, perinatal and infancy periods. Pp. 137–163, in Lerner, R. M., & Spanier, G. B. (Eds.) *Child influences on marital and family interaction.* New York: Academic, 1978.

——— & Lamb, J. E. The nature and importance of the father-infant relationship. *Family Coordinator,* 1976, *25*:379–385.

Landis, J. T. Marriages of mixed and non-mixed religious faith. *American Sociological Review,* 1949, *14*:401–407.

——— & Landis, M. G. *Building a successful marriage,* 7th ed. Englewood Cliffs, N.J.: Prentice-Hall, 1977.

Larson, J.H. The effect of husband's unemployment on marital and family relations in blue-collar families. *Family Relations,* 1984, *33*:503–511.

Leboyer, F. *Birth without violence.* New York: Knopf, 1975.

Lederer, W. J., & Jackson, D. D. *The mirages of marriage.* New York: Norton, 1968.

Lee, G. R. Marriage and morale in later life. *Journal of Marriage and the Family,* 1978, *40*:131–139.

———— & Ellithorpe, E. Intergenerational exchange and subjective well-being among the elderly. *Journal of Marriage and the Family,* 1982, 44:217–224.

Leifer, M. *Psychological effects of motherhood: A study of first pregnancy.* New York: Praeger, 1980.

Lein, L. Male participation in home life: Impact of social supports and breadwinner responsibility on the allocation of tasks. *Family Coordinator,* 1979, *28*:489–495.

LeMasters, E. E. Parenthood as crisis. *Marriage and Family Living,* 1957, 19:352–355.

Lenski, G. *Power and privilege: A theory of social stratification.* New York: McGraw-Hill, 1966.

Lerner, R. M. *Concepts and theories of human development.* Reading, Mass.: Addison-Wesley, 1976.

———— & Spanier, G. B. (Eds.) *Child influences on marital and family interaction.* New York: Academic, 1978.

Leslie, G. R. Personal values, professional ideologies, and family specialists: A new look. *Family Coordinator,* 1979, *28*:157–162.

Levine, S. One man's experience. Pp. 156–159, in Pleck, J. H., & Sawyer, J. (Eds.) *Men and masculinity.* Englewood Cliffs, N.J.: Prentice-Hall, 1974.

Levinger, G. Marital cohesiveness and dissolution: An integrative review. *Journal of Marriage and the Family,* 1965, *27*:19–28.

———— Husbands' and wives' estimates of coital frequency. *Medical Aspects of Human Sexuality,* 1970, *4*:42–57.

———— Senn, D. J., & Jorgensen, B. W. Progress toward permanence in courtship: A test of the Kerchoff-Davis hypothesis. *Sociometry,* 1970, *33*:427–443.

Levinson, D. J. *The seasons of a man's life.* New York: Knopf, 1978.

Leupnitz, D. A. Which aspects of divorce affect children? *Family Coordinator,* 1979, *28*:79–85.

Lewis, R. A. Social reaction and the formation of dyads: An interactionist approach to mate selection. *Sociometry,* 1973, *36*:409–418.

———— & Spanier, G. B. Theorizing about the quality and stability of marriage. Pp. 268–294, in Burr, W. R., Hill, R., Nye, F. I., & Reiss, I. L. (Eds.) *Contemporary theories about the family (Vol.1).* New York: Free Press, 1979.

Libby, R. W. Creative singlehood as a sexual lifestyle: Beyond marriage as a rite of passage. Pp. 37–60, in Libby, R., & Whitehurst, R. (Eds.) *Marriage and alternatives: Exploring intimate relationships.* Glenview, Ill.: Scott, Foresman, 1977.

Lidz, T. *The person: His and her development through the life cycle.* New York: Basic, 1976.

Livson, F. B. Gender identity: A life-span view of sex-role development. Pp. 105–127, in Weg, R. (Ed.) *Sexuality in the later years: Roles and behavior.* New York: Academic, 1983.

Locke, F. W. Introduction. Pp. iii–vii, in Andreas Capellanus, *The art of courtly love.* New York: Ungar, 1957.

Locksley, A. On the effects of wives' employment on marital adjustment and companionship. *Journal of Marriage and the Family,* 1980, *42*:337–346.

Longino, C. F., & Lipman, A. Married and spouseless men and women in planned retirement communities: Support network differentials. *Journal of Marriage and the Family,* 1981, *43*:169–177.

Longstreth, L. E. *Psychological development of the child,* 2nd ed. New York: Ronald, 1974.

Lopata, H. Z. *Widowhood in an American city.* Cambridge, Mass.: Schenkman, 1973.

———— Contributions of extended families to the support systems of metropolitan area widows: Limitations of the modified kin network. *Journal of Marriage and the Family,* 1978, *40*:355–364.

———— *Women as widows: Support systems.* New York: Elsevier North-Holland, 1979.

Lowen, A. The spiral of growth: Love, sex and pleasure. Pp. 17–26, in Otto, H. A. (Ed.) *Love today.* New York: Association, 1972.

Lowenthal, M. F., & Haven, C. Interaction and adaptation: Intimacy as a critical variable. *American Sociological Review,* 1968, *33*:20–30.

———— Thurner, M., & Chiriboga, D. *Four stages of life.* San Francisco: Jossey-Bass, 1977.

Luckey, E. B., & Bain, J. K. Children: A factor in marital satisfaction. *Journal of Marriage and the Family,* 1970, *32*:43–44.

Luft, J. *Group processes: An introduction to group dynamics.* Palo Alto, Calif.: Mayfield, 1984.

Lugo, J. O., & Hershey, G. L. *Human development.* New York: Macmillan, 1974.

Lyness, J. L., Lipitz, M. E., & Davis, K. E. Living together: An alternative to marriage. *Journal of Marriage and the Family,* 1972, *34*:305–311.

Maccoby, E. E. Sex differences in intellectual functioning. Pp. 25–55, in Maccoby, E. E. (Ed.) *The development of sex differences.* Stanford, Calif.: Stanford U. P., 1966.

Mace, D. Marriage and family enrichment: A new field? *Family Coordinator,* 1979, *28*:409–419.

———— & Mace, V. C. Marriage enrichment: Wave of the future? *Family Coordinator,* 1975, *24*:131–135.

Macklin, E. D. Heterosexual cohabitation among unmarried

college students. *Family Coordinator,* 1972, *21*:463–472.

———Students who live together: Trial marriage or going very steady? *Psychology Today,* Nov. 1974, 8: 53–59.

———Nontraditional family forms: A decade of research. *Journal of Marriage and the Family,* 1980, *42*:905–922.

Maine, D. Depo: The debate continues. *Family Planning Perspectives,* 1978, *10*:342–345.

Makepeace, J. M. Courtship violence among college students. *Family Relations,* 1981, *30*:97–102.

Malinowski, B. *The sexual life of savages in North-Western Melanesia.* New York: Harvest Books, 1929.

Marotz-Baden, R., Adams, G. R., Bueche, N., Munro, B., & Monro, G. Family form or family process? Reconsidering the deficit family model approach. *Family Coordinator,* 1979, *28*:5–14.

Marriage and Divorce Today, The full extent of family violence. New York: Atcom, Inc., 1978.

Marriage and Divorce Today, Marriage losing popularity in Canada. 1980, *5*:4.

Marshall, J. Cervical mucous and basal body temperature method of regulation of births. *Lancet,* 1976, *II*:282.

Martin, M. J., & Walters, J. Familial correlates of selected types of child abuse and neglect. *Journal of Marriage and the Family,* 1982, *44*:267–276.

Martindale, D. *The nature and types of sociological theory.* Boston: Houghton, 1960.

Maslow, A. H. *Motivation and personality.* New York: Harper, 1954.

———*Toward a psychology of being,* 2nd ed. New York: Van Nostrand, 1968.

Masnick, G., & Bane, M. J. *The nation's families.* Cambridge, Mass.: Joint Center for Urban Studies of MIT and Harvard University, 1980.

Masters, W. H., & Johnson, V. E. *Human sexual response.* Boston: Little, Brown, 1966.

———*Human sexual inadequacy.* Boston: Little, Brown, 1970.

Matejcek, Z., Dytrych, Z., & Schuller, V. The Prague study of children born from unwanted pregnancies. *International Journal of Mental Health,* 1979, *7*:63–74.

May, K. A. Factors contributing to first-time fathers' readiness for fatherhood: An exploratory study. *Family Relations,* 1982, *31*:353–361.

May, R. *Love and will.* New York: Norton, 1969.

Maykovich, M. K. Attitudes versus behavior in extramarital sexual relations. *Journal of Marriage and the Family,* 1976, *39*:693–701.

McArthur, A. Developmental tasks and parent-adolescent conflict. *Marriage and Family Living,* 1962, *24*:189–191.

McCary, J. L. *Sexual myths and fallacies.* New York: Van Nostrand, 1971.

———*Human sexuality: Physiological, psychological and sociological factors,* 2nd ed. New York: Van Nostrand, 1973.

McDonald, G. W. Parental power and adolescents' parental identification: A reexamination. *Journal of Marriage and the Family,* 1980, *42*:289–304.

McLaughlin, S. D. Differential patterns of female labor-force participation surrounding the first birth. *Journal of Marriage and the Family,* 1982, *44*:407–420.

Mead, M. *Coming of age in Samoa.* New York: Mentor, 1928.

———*Growing up in New Guinea.* New York: New American Library, 1935.

———*From the South Seas: Studies of adolescence and sex in primitive societies.* New York: Morrow, 1939.

Meadows, D. H., Meadows, D. L., Randers, J., & Behrens, W. W. *The limits to growth.* New York: New American Library, 1972.

Mech, E. V. Adoption: A policy perspective. Pp. 467–508, in Caldwell, B. M., & Ricciuti, H. N. (Eds.) *Review of child development research,* 1973, Chicago: U. of Chicago P.

Medley, M. L. Marital adjustment in the post-retirement years. *Family Coordinator,* 1977, *26*:5–11.

Mehrabian, A. *Silent messages.* Belmont, Calif.: Wadsworth, 1971.

Melville, K. *Marriage and Family Today,* 2nd ed. New York: Random, 1980.

Mendes, H. A. Single fathers. *Family Coordinator,* 1976, *25*:439–444.

Messinger, L. Remarriage between divorced people with children from previous marriages: A proposal for preparation for remarriage. *Journal of Marriage and Family Counseling,* 1976, *2*:193–200.

Meyerowitz, J. H., & Feldman, H. Transition to parenthood. Pp. 78–84, in Cohen, I. M. (Ed.) *Family structure, dynamics and therapy.* New York: American Psychiatric Association, 1967.

Miller, B. C. A Multivariate developmental model of marital satisfaction. *Journal of Marriage and the Family,* 1976, *38*:643–657.

———& Bowen, S. L. Father-to-newborn attachment behavior in relation to prenatal classes and presence at delivery. *Family Relations,* 1982, *31*:71–83.

Miller, H. L., & Siegel, P. S. *Loving: A psychological approach.* New York: Wiley, 1972.

Miller, S., Corrales, R., & Wackman, D. B. Recent progress

in understanding and facilitating marital communication. *The Family Coordinator,* 1975, *24*:143–152.

——— Nunnally, E. W., & Wackman, D. B. *Alive and aware: Improving communication in relationships.* Minneapolis: Interpersonal Communications Program, Inc., 1975.

Milner, E. A study of the relationship between reading readiness in grade one school children patterns of parent-child interaction. *Child Development,* 1951, *22*:95–112.

Minuchin, S. *Families and family therapy.* Cambridge, Mass.: Harvard U. P., 1974.

Monahan, T. P. National divorce legislation: The problem and some suggestions. *Family Coordinator,* 1973, *22*:353–357.

Money, J. Sexually dimorphic behavior, normal and abnormal. Pp. 201–212, in Kretchmer, N., & Walcher, D. N. (Eds.) *Environmental influences on genetic expression: Biological and behavioral aspects of sexual differentiation.* Washington, D.C., U.S. Government Printing Office, 1971.

——— & Ehrhardt, A. A. *Man & woman, boy & girl.* Baltimore: Johns Hopkins, 1972.

Montagu, A. *Touching: The human significance of the skin.* New York: Columbia U. P., 1971.

Montgomery, B. M. The form and function of quality communication in marriage. *Family Relations,* 1981, *30*:21–30.

Montgomery, J. E. The economics of supportive services for families with disabled and aging members. *Family Relations,* 1982, *31*:19–27.

Morbidity and mortality reports, annual summaries, 1970–1979. Vols. 19–28. Atlanta: Center for Disease Control.

Morgan, M. *The total woman.* Old Tappan, N.J.: Revell, 1973.

Mosher, W. D., & Bachrach, C. A. Childlessness in the United States: Estimates from the national survey of family growth. *Journal of Family Issues,* 1982, *3*:517–543.

Mosher, W. D., & Pratt, W. F. Fecundity and infertility in the United States, 1965–1982. National Center for Health Statistics, *Advance Data,* No. 104, Feb. 11, 1985.

Mott, F. L., & Moore, S. F. The tempo of remarriage among young American women. *Journal of Marriage and the Family,* 1983, *45*:427–435.

Mouly, G. J. *Psychology for effective teaching,* 2nd ed. New York: Holt, 1968.

Movius, M. Voluntary childlessness — The Ultimate Liberation. *Family Coordinator,* 1976, *25*:57–63.

Mowery, J. Systemic requisites of communal groups. *Alternate lifestyles,* 1978, *1*:235–261.

Mueller, C. W., & Campbell, B. G. Female occupational achievement and marital status: A research note. *Journal of Marriage and the Family,* 1977, *39*:587–593.

Munns, M., Jr. The values of adolescents compared with parents and peers. *Adolescence,* 1972, *7*:519–524.

Murstein, B. I. Stimulus-value-role: A theory of marital choice. *Journal of Marriage and the Family,* 1970, *32*:465–481.

——— Mate selection in the 1970s. *Journal of Marriage and the Family,* 1980, *42*:777–792.

Mussen, P. H. Some antecedents and consequents of masculine sex-typing in adolescent boys. *Psychological Monographs,* 1961, *75* (2, Whole No. 506).

——— Long-term consequents of masculinity of interests in adolescence. *Journal of Consulting Psychology,* 1962, *26*:435–440.

Naffziger, C. C., & Naffziger, K. Development of sex role stereotypes. *Family Coordinator,* 1974, *23*:251–259.

Nakashima, I. I., & Zakus, G. E. Incest: review and clinical experience. *Pediatrics,* 1977, *60*:696–701.

National Center for Education Statistics. Fall enrollment of 12.3 million sets record high for colleges. Reported in the *Arizona Daily Star,* Dec. 11, 1981.

National Center for Health Statistics. Reproductive impairments among currently married couples: United States, 1976. *Advance Data,* No. 55, Jan. 24, 1980a.

——— Wanted and unwanted births reported by mothers 15–44 years of age: United States, 1976. *Advance Data,* No. 56, Jan. 24, 1980b.

——— Trends in breast feeding. *Advance Data,* No. 59, March 28, 1980c.

——— Socioeconomic differentials and trends in the timing of births. *Vital and Health Statistics,* Series 23, No. 6, Feb. 1981a.

——— Duration of marriage before divorce: United States. *Vital and Health Statistics,* Series 21, No. 38, July 1981b.

——— Advance Report of final natality statistics, 1979. *Monthly Vital Statistics Report,* Vol. 30, No. 6, Sept. 29, 1981c.

——— Advance report of final natality statistics, 1980. *Monthly Vital Statistics Report,* Vol. 31, No. 8, Nov. 30, 1982.

——— Births, marriages, divorces, and deaths for 1982. *Monthly Vital Statistics Report,* Vol. 31, No. 12, March 14, 1983a.

————Advance report of final divorce statistics, 1980. *Monthly Vital Statistics Report,* Vol. 32, No. 3, June 27, 1983b.

————Annual summary of births, deaths, marriages, and divorces: United States, 1982. Vol. 31, No. 13, Oct. 5, 1983c.

————Advance report of final natality statistics, 1981. *Monthly Vital Statistics Report,* Vol. 32, No. 9, Dec. 29, 1983d.

————Advance report of final divorce statistics, 1981. *Monthly Vital Statistics Report,* Vol. 32, No. 9, Jan. 17, 1984a.

————Births, marriages, divorces, and deaths for 1983. *Monthly Vital Statistics Report,* Vol. 32, No. 12, March 26, 1984b.

————Advance report of final mortality statistics, 1981. *Monthly Vital Statistics Report,* Vol. 33, No. 3, June 22, 1984c.

National Opinion Research Center. Cumulative codebook for the 1972–1977 general social surveys. Chicago: U. of Chicago, 1977.

Neugarten, B. L. Middle age and aging. In Hess, B. B. (Ed.) *Growing old in America.* New Brunswick, N. J.: Transaction, 1976.

————& Weinstein, K. K. The changing American grandparent. *Journal of Marriage and the Family,* 1964, 26:199–204.

Newcomb, P. R. Cohabitation in America: An assessment of consequences. *Journal of Marriage and the Family,* 1979, 41:597–603.

Nichols, R. C., & Troester, J. D. Custody evaluations: An alternative? *Family Coordinator,* 1979, 28:399–407.

Nilson, L. B. The social standing of a housewife. *Journal of Marriage and the Family,* 1978, 40:541–548.

Nock, S. L. Enduring effects of marital disruption and subsequent living arrangements. *Journal of Family Issues,* 1982, 3:25–40.

Nye, F. I. Child adjustment in broken and in unhappy unbroken homes. *Marriage and Family Living,* 1957, 19:356–361.

————Husband-wife relationship. Pp. 186–206, in Hoffman, L. W., & Nye, F. I. (Eds.) *Working mothers.* San Francisco: Jossey-Bass, 1974.

————Is choice and exchange theory the key? *Journal of Marriage and the Family,* 1978, 40:219–233.

————& Berardo, F. M. *The family: Its structure and interaction.* New York: Macmillan, 1973.

————& Lamberts, M. B. *School-age parenthood: Consequences for babies, mothers, fathers, grandparents and others.* Extension Bulletin 667, Cooperative Extension Service, Washington State. U., Pullman, Wash., 1980.

Olson, D. H. Marriage of the future: Revolutionary or evolutionary change?, *Family Coordinator,* 1972, 21:383–393.

O'Neill, N., & O'Neill, G. *Open marriage: A new life style for couples.* New York: Avon, 1972.

Oppenheimer, V. K. The life-cycle squeeze: The interaction of men's occupational and family life cycles. *Demography,* 1974, 11:227–245.

Orlinsky, D. E. Love relationships in the life cycle: A developmental interpersonal perspective. Pp. 135–150, in Otto, H. A. (Ed.) *Love today.* New York: Association, 1972.

Orthner, D. K., Brown, T., & Ferguson, D. Single-parent fatherhood: An emerging family lifestyle. *Family Coordinator,* 1976, 25:429–437.

Ory, H. W. The noncontraceptive health benefits from oral contraceptive use. *Family Planning Perspectives,* 1982, 14:182–184.

Osborn, D. K., & Osborn, J. D. Childhood at the turn of the century. *Family Coordinator,* 1978, 27:27–32.

Osmond, M. W., & Martin, P. Y. Sex and sexism: A comparison of male and female sex-role attitudes. *Journal of Marriage and the Family,* 1975, 37:744–758.

Osofsky, J. D., & Osofsky, H. J. Androgyny as a life style. *Family Coordinator,* 1972, 21:411–418.

Otto, H. A. The prospects of love: An introduction. Pp. 9–16, in Otto, H. A. (Ed.) *Love today.* New York: Association, 1972a.

————Communication in love. Pp. 66–72, in Otto, H. A. (Ed.) *Love today.* New York: Association, 1972b.

Otto, H., & Haley, S. Adolescents' self perception of personality strengths. *Journal of Human Relations,* 1966, 14:483–490.

Ovid. *The art of love, and other poems.* Mozley, J. H. (Tr.) London: Heinemann, 1929.

Packard, V. *The sexual wilderness.* New York: McKay, 1968.

Palmer, S. *The violent society.* New Haven: College & Univ. P., 1972.

Papalia, D. E., & Olds, S. W. *Human development.* New York: McGraw-Hill, 1978.

Parade Magazine, Mating game. May 18, 1980a, p. 8.

————Women's ideal lifestyle. Dec. 28, 1980b.

Parelius, A. P. Emerging sex-role attitudes, expectations, and strains among college women. *Journal of Marriage and the Family,* 1975, 37:146–153.

Parke, R. D., & Sawin, D. B. The father's role in infancy: A re-evaluation. *Family Coordinator,* 1976, 25:365–371.

Parsons, T., & Bales, R. F. (Eds.) *Family, socialization, and interaction process.* New York: Free Press, 1955.

Patterson, G. R. *Families: Applications of social learning to family life.* Champaign, Ill.: Research Press, 1975.

Patterson, G. R., Hops, H., & Weiss, R. L. Interpersonal skills training for couples in early stages of conflict. *Journal of Marriage and the Family,* 1975, 37:295–303.

Payton, I. S. Single-parent households: An alternative approach. *Family Economics Review,* Winter, 1982.

Pearlin, L. I., & Johnson, J. S. Marital status, life strains and depression. *American Sociological Review,* 1977, 42:704–715.

Pearson, J., Munson, P., & Thoennes, N. Legal change and child custody awards. *Journal of Family Issues,* 1982, 3:5–24.

Pearson, W., & Hendrix, L. Divorce and the status of women. *Journal of Marriage and the Family,* 1979, 41:375–385.

Peele, S., with Brodsky, A. *Love and addiction.* New York: Taplinger, 1975.

Pelton, L. H. Child abuse and neglect: The myth of classlessness. *American Journal of Orthopsychiatry,* 1978, 48:608–617.

Peterman, D. J., Ridley, C. A., & Anderson, S. M. A comparison of cohabiting and non-cohabiting college students. *Journal of Marriage and the Family,* 1974, 36:344–354.

Peterson, W. *Population,* 2nd ed. New York: Macmillan, 1969.

Petrakis, N. L., Gruenke, L. D., Beelen, T. C., Castagnoli, N., & Craig, J. Nicotine in breast fluid of nonlactating women. *Science,* 1978, 199:303–305.

Pfeiffer, E., & Davis, G. C. Sexual behavior in aged men and women. *Archives of General Psychiatry,* 1968, 19:753–759.

————Verwoerdt, A., & Davis, G. C. Sexual behavior in middle life. *American Journal of Psychiatry,* 1972, 128:1262–1267.

Piaget, J. *The origins of intelligence in children.* New York: International U. P., 1952.

Pincus, L. *Death and the family: The importance of mourning.* New York: Random, 1974.

Pineo, P. C. Disenchantment in the later years of marriage. *Marriage and Family Living,* 1961, 23:3–11.

Piotrkowski, C. S. *Work and the family system.* New York: Free Press, 1979.

Plato, *The symposium of Plato.* Groden, S. Q. (Tr.) Amherst, Mass.: U. of Mass. P., 1970.

Pleck, J. My male sex role—and ours. Pp. 253–264, in David, D. S., & Brannon, R. (Eds.) *The forty-nine percent majority: The male sex role.* Reading, Mass.: Addison-Wesley, 1976.

————Men's family work: Three perspectives and some new data. *Family Coordinator,* 1979, 28:481–488.

Polit, D. F. Stereotypes relating to family-size status. *Journal of Marriage and the Family,* 1978, 40:105–114.

————Nuttall, R. L., & Nuttall, E. V. The only child grows up: A look at some characteristics of adult only children. *Family Relations,* 1980, 29:99–106.

Polonko, K. A., Scanzoni, J., & Teachman, J. D. Childlessness and marital satisfaction: A further assessment. *Journal of Family Issues,* 1982, 3:545–573.

Porter, J. *The vertical mosaic: An analysis of social class and power in Canada.* Toronto: U. of Toronto Press, 1965.

Pratt, W. F., Mosher, W. D., Bachrach, C. A., & Horn, M. C. Understanding U.S. fertility: Findings from the National Survey of Family Growth, Cycle III. *Population Bulletin,* 1984, 39(No. 5).

Price-Bonham, S., & Balswick, J. O. The non-institutions: Divorce, desertion, and remarriage. *Journal of Marriage and the Family,* 1980, 42:959–972.

Queen, S. A., & Habenstein, R. W. *The family in various cultures,* 4th ed. Philadelphia: Lippincott, 1974.

Querec, L. J. Apgar score in the United States, 1978. *Monthly Vital Statistics Report,* Vol. 30, No. 1. Washington, D.C.: National Center for Health Statistics, May 6, 1981.

Quinn, W. H. Personal and family adjustment in later life. *Journal of Marriage and the Family,* 1983, 45:57–73.

————& Dennis, M. B. An examination of marital behavior, process, and quality during the early years. Unpublished manuscript. Texas Tech U., College of Home Economics, 1982.

Radloff, L. Sex differences in depression: The effects of occupation and marital status. *Sex Roles,* 1975, 1:249–265.

Rainwater, L. *And the poor get children.* Chicago: Quadrangle, 1960.

————*Family Design.* Hawthorne, N.Y.: Aldine, 1965.

Rallings, E. M. The special role of stepfather. *Family Coordinator,* 1976, 25:445–449.

————& Nye, F. I. Wife-mother employment, family, and society. Pp. 203–226, in Burr, W., et al. (Eds.) *Contemporary theories about the family: Vol. 1.* New York: Free Press, 1979.

Ramey, J. W. Emerging patterns of innovative behavior in marriage. *Family Coordinator,* 1972, 21:435–456.

———Experimental family forms—The family of the future. *Marriage and Family Review,* 1978, *1*:1–9.

Rao, S. L. N. A comparative study of childlessness and never-pregnant status. *Journal of Marriage and the Family,* 1974, *36*:149–157.

Rapoport, R. Normal crises, family structure and mental health. *Family Process,* 1962, *2*:68–79.

———& Rapoport, R. *Dual-career families.* New York: Penguin, 1971.

Raschke, H. J., & Barringer, K. D. Postdivorce adjustment among persons participating in parents-without-partners organizations. *Family Perspective,* 1977, *11*:23–34.

———& Raschke, V. J. Family conflict and children's self-concepts: A comparison of intact and single-parent families. *Journal of Marriage and the Family,* 1979, *41*:367–374.

Raush, H. L., Barry, W. A., Hertel, R. K., & Swain, M. A. *Communication, conflict, and marriage.* San Francisco: Jossey-Bass, 1974.

———Goodrich, W., & Campbell, J. D. Adaptation to the first years of marriage. *Psychiatry,* 1963, *26*:368–380.

Razani, J. Ejaculatory incompetence treated by deconditioning anxiety. In LoPiccolo, J., & LoPiccolo, L. (Eds.). *Handbook of sex therapy.* New York: Plenum, 1978.

Reiss, I. L. Toward a sociology of the heterosexual love relationship. *Marriage and Family Living,* 1960, *22*:139–145.

———*The social context of premarital sexual permissiveness.* New York: Holt, 1967.

———*Family systems in America,* 3rd ed. New York: Holt, 1980.

———Anderson, R. E., & Sponaugle, G. C. A multivariate model of the determinants of extramarital sexual permissiveness. *Journal of Marriage and the Family,* 1980, *42*:395–411.

———& Miller, B. C. Heterosexual permissiveness: A theoretical analysis. Pp. 57–100, in Burr, W., Hill, R., Nye, F. I., & Reiss, I. L. (Eds.) *Contemporary theories about the family, Vol. 1.* New York: Free Press, 1979.

Rendina, I., & Dickerscheid, J. D. Father involvement with first-born infants. *Family Coordinator,* 1976, *25*:373–378.

Renne, K. S. Health and marital experience in an urban population. *Journal of Marriage and the Family,* 1971, *33*:338–350.

Rheingold, H. L. The modification of social responsiveness in institutionalized babies. *Monographs of the Society for Research in Child Development,* 1956, *21*:5–48.

Rice, F. P. *The adolescent: Development, relationships, and culture,* 3rd ed. Newton, Mass.: Allyn and Bacon, 1981.

Richardson, J. G. Wife occupational superiority and marital troubles: An examination of the hypothesis. *Journal of Marriage and the Family,* 1979, *41*:63–72.

Ridley, C. A., Jorgensen, S. R., Morgan, A. G., & Avery, A. W. Relationship enhancement with premarital couples: An assessment of effects on relationship quality. *American Journal of Family Therapy,* 1982, *10*:41–48.

———Peterman, D. J., & Avery, A. W. Cohabitation: Does it make for a better marriage? *Family Coordinator,* 1978, *27*:129–136.

Risman, B. J., Hill, C. T., Rubin, Z., & Peplau, L. A. Living together in college: Implications for courtship. *Journal of Marriage and the Family,* 1981, *43*:77–83.

Robbins, N. N. Legal standards for determining best interests of child. *Family Coordinator,* 1974, *23*:87–90.

Rollins, B. C., & Cannon, K. F. Marital satisfaction over the family life cycle: A reevaluation. *Journal of Marriage and the Family,* 1974, *36*:271–282.

———& Galligan, R. The developing child and marital satisfaction of parents. Pp. 71–105, in Lerner, R. M., & Spanier, G. B. (Eds.) *Child influences on marital and family interactions.* New York: Academic, 1978.

Roper, B. S., & Labeff, E. Sex roles and feminism revisited: An intergenerational attitude comparison. *Journal of Marriage and the Family,* 1977, *39*:113–119.

Rose, V. L., & Price-Bonham, S. Divorce adjustment: A woman's problem? *Family Coordinator,* 1973, *22*:291–297.

Rosen, B., Jerdee, T. H., & Prestwich, T. L. Dual-career marital adjustment: Potential effects of discriminatory managerial attitudes. *Journal of Marriage and the Family,* 1975, *37*:565–572.

Rosenberg, B. G., & Sutton-Smith, B. *Sex and identity.* New York: Holt, 1972.

Ross, C. E., Mirowsky, J., & Huber, J. Dividing work, sharing work, and in between: Marriage patterns and depression. *American Sociological Review,* 1983, *48*:809–823.

Rossi, A. S. Transition to parenthood. *Journal of Marriage and the Family,* 1968, *30*:26–39.

Roy, R., & Roy, D. Essay, pp. 60–77, in Hart, H., et al. (Eds.) *Marriage: For and against.* New York: Hart, 1971.

Rubin, L. B. *Worlds of pain: Life in the working class family.* New York: Basic, 1976.

Rubin, Z. *Liking and loving: An invitation to social psychology.* New York: Holt, 1973.

Russell, C. S. Transition to parenthood: problems and gratifications. *Journal of Marriage and the Family*, 1974, 36:294–302.

Rutter, M. Parent-child separation: Psychological effects on the children. *Journal of Child Psychology and Psychiatry*, 1971, 12:233–260.

Ryder, N. Contraceptive failure in the United States. *Family Planning Perspectives*, 1973, 5:133–142.

Sabalis, R. F., & Ayers, G. W. Emotional aspects of divorce and their effects on the legal process. *Family Coordinator*, 1977, 26:391–394.

Sampson, W. A., & Rossi, P. H. Race and family social status. *American Sociological Review*, 1975, 40:201–214.

Satir, V. Marriage as a statutory five-year renewable contract. Paper presented at the annual meeting of the American Psychological Association, Washington, D.C., 1967.

Saxton, L. *The individual, marriage, and the family*. Belmont, Calif.: Wadsworth, 1977.

——— *The individual, marriage and the family*, 4th ed. Belmont, Calif.: Wadsworth, 1980.

Scanzoni, J. H. *Opportunity and the family*. New York: Free Press, 1970.

——— *Sexual bargaining: Power politics of the American marriage*. Englewood Cliffs, N.J.: Prentice-Hall, 1972.

——— Strategies for changing male family roles: Research and practice implications. *The Family Coordinator*, 1979, 28:435–442.

——— & Polonko, K. A conceptual approach to explicit marital negotiation. *Journal of Marriage and the Family*, 1980, 42:31–44.

Schaefer, E. S. A circumplex model for maternal behavior. *Journal of Abnormal and Social Psychology*, 1959, 59:226–235.

Schafer, R. B., & Keith, P. M. A causal analysis of the relationship between the self-concept and marital quality. *Journal of Marriage and the Family*, 1984, 46:909–921.

Schaffer, H. R., & Emerson, P. The development of social attachments in infancy. *Monographs of the Society for Research in Child Development*, 1964, 29 (3).

Schlesinger, Y. Sex roles and social change in the kibbutz. *Journal of Marriage and the Family*, 1977, 39:771–779.

Schulman, M. L. Idealization in engaged couples. *Journal of Marriage and the Family*, 1974, 36:139–147.

Schulterbrandt, J. G., & Nichols, E. Ethical and ideological problems for communal living: A caveat. *Family Coordinator*, 1972, 21:429–434.

Seelbach, W. C., & Hansen, C. J. Satisfaction with family relations among the elderly. *Family Coordinator*, 1980, 29:91–96.

Seligman, M. E. Depression and learned helplessness. Pp. 83–113, in Friedman, R. G., Katz, M. M. (Eds.) *The psychology of depression: Contemporary theory and research*. Washington, D.C.: V. H. Winston, 1974.

Sexually transmissable diseases. National Institute of Allergy and Infectious Diseases. U.S. Government Printing Office, 1976.

Shanas, E. Older people and their families: The new pioneers. *Journal of Marriage and the Family*, 1980, 42:9–15.

Sheehy, G. *Passages: Predictable crises of adult life*. New York: E. P. Dutton, 1976.

Shipman, G. The role of counseling in the reform of marriage and divorce procedures. *Family Coordinator*, 1977, 26:395–407.

Shostrom, E. L. Love, the human encounter. Pp. 185–196, in Otto, H. A. (Ed.) *Love today*. New York: Association, 1972.

Simirenko, A. From vertical to horizontal inequality: The case of the Soviet Union. *Social Problems*, 1972, 20:150–161.

Singh, B. K. Trends in attitudes toward premarital sexual relations. *Journal of Marriage and the Family*, 1980, 42:387–393.

——— Walton, B. L., & Williams, J. S. Extramarital sexual permissiveness: Conditions and contingencies. *Journal of Marriage and the Family*, 1976, 38:701–712.

Skinner, D. Dual-career family stress and coping: A literature review. *Family Relations*, 1980, 29:473–481.

Smith, M. J. The social consequences of single parenthood: A longitudinal perspective. *Family Coordinator*, 1980, 29:75–81.

Smith, R. E. (Ed.) *The subtle revolution: Women at work*. Washington, D.C., The Urban Institute, 1979.

Smith, R. M., Shoffner, S. M., & Scott, J. P. Marriage and family enrichment: A new professional area. *Family Coordinator*, 1979, 28:87–93.

Smith, R. M., & Smith, C. W. Child rearing and single-parent fathers. *Family Relations*, 1981, 30:411–417.

Smith-Lovin, L., & Tickamyer, A. R. Non-recursive models of labor force participation, fertility behavior, and sex role attitudes. *American Sociological Review*, 1978, 43:541–557.

Solomon, M. A developmental conceptual premise for family therapy. *Family Process*, 1973, 12:179–196.

Solomon, T. History and demography of child abuse. *Pediatrics*, 1973, 51:773–776.

Sonenblick, J. *The legality of love*. New York: Jove, 1981.

Sorensen, R. C. *Adolescent sexuality in contemporary America*. New York: World, 1973.

Spanier, G. B., & Casto, R. Adjustment to separation and divorce: An analysis of 50 case studies. *Journal of Divorce,* 1979, 2:241–253.

——— & Glick, P. C. Paths to remarriage. *Journal of Divorce,* 1980, 3:283–298.

——— Marital instability in the United States: Some correlates and recent changes. *Family Relations,* 1981, 39:329–338.

——— & Lewis, R. A. Marital quality: A review of the seventies. *Journal of Marriage and the Family,* 1980, 42:825–839.

——— & Cole, C. L. Marital adjustment over the family life cycle: The issue of curvilinearity. *Journal of Marriage and the Family,* 1975, 37:263–276.

Spence, J. T., Helmreich, R., & Stapp, J. Ratings of self and peers on sex role attributes and their relation to self-esteem and conceptions of masculinity and femininity. *Journal of Personality and Social Psychology,* 1975, 32:29–39.

Spicer, J. W., & Hampe, G. D. Kinship interaction after divorce. *Journal of Marriage and the Family,* 1975, 37:113–119.

Spiegel, J. P. The resolution of role conflict within the family. *Psychiatry,* 1957, 20:1–16.

Spiro, M. *Kibbutz: venture in Utopia.* Cambridge, Mass.: Harvard U. P., 1956.

——— *Gender and culture: Kibbutz women revisited.* Durham, N.C.: Duke U. P., 1979.

Spitz, R. A. Hospitalism: An inquiry into the genesis of psychiatric conditioning in early childhood. Pp. 53–74, in Fenschel, D., et al. (Eds.) *Psychoanalytic studies of the child, Vol. 1.* New York: International U. Press, 1945.

Spitze, G. D., & Waite, L. J. Wives' employment: The role of husbands' perceived attitudes. *Journal of Marriage and the Family,* 1981, 43:117–124.

Sporakowski, M. J., & Hughston, G. A. Prescriptions for happy marriage: Adjustments and satisfactions of couples married for 50 or more years. *Family Coordinator,* 1978, 27:321–327.

Spreitzer, E., & Riley, L. E. Factors associated with singlehood. *Journal of Marriage and the Family,* 1974, 36:533–542.

Sproat, K. How do families fare when the breadwinner retires? *Monthly Labor Review,* 1983, 106:40–44.

Stack, S. The effects of marital dissolution on suicide. *Journal of Marriage and the Family,* 1980, 42:83–91.

Stafford, R., Backman, E., & Dibona, P. The division of labor among cohabiting and married couples. *Journal of Marriage and the Family,* 1977, 39:43–57.

Stayton, D. J., Hogan, R., & Ainsworth, M. D. Infant obedience and maternal behavior: The origins of socialization reconsidered. *Child Development,* 1971, 42: 1057–1069.

Stein, P. J. Singlehood: An alternative to marriage. *Family Coordinator,* 1975, 24:489–503.

——— *Single.* Englewood Cliffs, N.J.: Prentice-Hall, 1976.

Steinmetz, S. K., & Straus, M. A. (Eds.) *Violence in the family.* New York: Harper, 1974.

Stetson, D. M., & Wright, G. C. The effects of laws on divorce in American states. *Journal of Marriage and the Family,* 1975, 37:537–547.

Stinnett, N., Carter, L. M., & Montgomery, J. E. Older persons' perceptions of their marriages. *Journal of Marriage and the Family,* 1972, 34:665–672.

Stokes, B. Men and family planning. *Worldwatch Paper No. 41.* Washington, D.C.: Worldwatch Institute, 1980.

Stolzenberg, R. M., & Waite, L. J. Age, fertility expectations and plans for employment. *American Sociological Review,* 1977, 42:769–783.

Streib, G. F. An alternative family form for older persons: Need and social context. *Family Coordinator,* 1978, 27:413–420.

——— & Schneider, C. J. *Retirement in American society.* Ithaca, N.Y.: Cornell U. P., 1971.

Straus, M. Leveling, civility, and violence in the family. *Journal of Marriage and the Family,* 1974, 36: 13–29.

——— Gelles, R. J., & Steinmetz, S. K. *Behind closed doors: Violence in the American family.* New York: Anchor/Doubleday, 1980.

——— & Hotaling, G. T. (Eds.) *The social causes of husband-wife violence.* Minneapolis: U. of Minn. Press, 1980.

Swenson, C. H. Love: A self-report analysis with college students. *Journal of Individual Psychology,* 1961, 17:167–171.

——— The behavior of love. Pp. 86–101, in Otto, H. A. (Ed.) *Love today,* New York: Association, 1972.

Talmon-Garber, Y. *Sex-role differentiation in an equalitarian society.* Jerusalem: Hebrew-U. P., 1959.

Tanner, J. M. Physical growth. Pp. 77–155, in Mussen, P. H. (Ed.) *Carmichael's manual of child psychology, Vol. 1,* 3rd ed. New York: Wiley, 1970.

Tavris, C., & Sadd, S. *The Redbook report on female sexuality.* New York: Delacorte, 1977.

Theodorson, G. A. Cross-national variations in eagerness to marry. Pp. 119–134, in Geiger, H. K. (Ed.) *Comparative perspectives on marriage and the family.* Boston: Little, Brown, 1968.

Thomas, A., Chess, S., & Birch, H. G. *Temperament and*

behavior disorders in children. New York: New York U. P., 1968.

Thomas, E. J. *Marital communication and decision making: Analysis, assessment, and change.* New York: Free Press, 1977.

Thompson, E. H., & Gongla, P. A. Single-parent families: In the mainstream of American society. Pp. 97–124, in Macklin, E. D., & Rubin, R. H. (Eds.) *Contemporary families and alternative lifestyles.* Beverly Hills, Calif.: Sage, 1983.

Thompson, L., & Spanier, G. B. Influence of parents, peers, and partners on the contraceptive use of college men and women. *Journal of Marriage and the Family,* 1978, *40*:481–492.

Thomson, E. The value of employment to mothers of young children. *Journal of Marriage and the Family,* 1980, *42*:551–566.

Thornburg, H. D. Effect of children on parents' sexual relationships. *Family Therapy,* 1977, 4:67–76.
———— *The bubblegum years: Sticking with kids from 9–13.* Tucson, Ariz.: H.E.L.P. Books, 1979.
———— *Development in adolescence.* Monterey, Calif.: Brooks/Cole, 1975.
———— *Development in adolescence,* 2nd ed. Monterey, Calif.: Brooks/Cole, 1982.

Thornton, A., & Freedman, D. Changing attitudes toward marriage and single life. *Family Planning Perspectives,* 1982, *14*:297–303.

Thurner, M., Spence, D., & Lowenthal, M. G. Value confluence and behavioral conflict in intergenerational relations. *Journal of Marriage and the Family,* 1974, *36*:308–319.

Time Magazine. Superkids? A sperm bank for Nobelists, March 10, 1980.

Toby, J. Orientation to education as a factor in the social maladjustment of lower-class children. *Social Forces,* 1956, *35*:259–266.

Todres, R. Runaway wives: An increasing North-American phenomenon. *Family Coordinator,* 1978, *27*:17–21.

Töennies, F. *Gemeinschaft and Gesellschaft (community and society).* East Lansing: Mich. State U. P., 1957.

Tryon, C., & Lilienthal, J. W. Guideposts in child growth and development. *NEA Journal,* 1950, *39*:188–189.

Turner, R. H. *Family interaction.* New York: Wiley, 1970.

Tyrer, L. B. Poverty, family planning, and health. *Planned Parenthood Review,* 1984, *3*:11–12.

Udry, J. R. Marital alternatives and marital disruption. *Journal of Marriage and the Family,* 1981, *43*:889–897.

U.S. Bureau of the Census. Number, timing and duration of marriages and divorces in the U.S. *Current Population Reports.* Series P-20, No. 297, Oct., 1976.
———— Household and family characteristics, March, 1978. *Current Population Reports,* Series P–20, No. 340, Washington, D.C., 1979.
———— A statistical portrait of women in the United States: 1978. *Current Population Reports, Special Studies.* Series P-23, No. 100, 1980.
———— *Statistical Abstract of the United States, 1984,* 104th Ed. Washington, D.C., 1983a.
———— Household and family characteristics, March, 1982. *Current Population Reports,* Series P–20, No. 381, Washington, D.C., 1983b.
———— America in transition: An aging society. *Current Population Reports,* Series P–23, No. 128, 1983c.
———— Characteristics of the population below the poverty level. *Current Population Reports,* Series P–60, No. 144, Washington, D.C., 1984a.
———— Money income of households, families, and persons in the United States: 1982. *Current Population Reports,* Series P–60, No. 142, Washington, D.C., 1984b.
———— Marital status and living arrangements: March, 1983. *Current Population Reports,* Series P–20, No. 389, Washington, D.C., 1984c.

United States Department of Agriculture. Updated estimates of the costs of raising a child. *Family Economics Review,* No. 4, 1983.

U.S. Department of Health and Human Services. *Income of the population 55 and over, 1982.* Social Security Administration, No. 13–1187, Washington, D.C., March, 1984.

Valentine, D. P. The experience of pregnancy: A developmental process. *Family Relations,* 1982, *31*:243–248.

Vaughan, B., Trussell, J., Menken, J., & Jones, E. F. Contraceptive failure among married women in the United States, 1970–1973. *Family Planning Perspectives,* 1977, *9*:251–258.

Veevers, J. E. Voluntary childlessness: A review of issues and evidence. *Marriage and Family Review,* 1979, *2*.
———— *Childless by choice.* Toronto: Butterworth, 1980.

Ventura, S. J. Trends in births to older mothers, 1970–1979. *Monthly Vital Statistics Report,* Vol. 31, No. 2. Washington, D.C.: National Center for Health Statistics, May 27, 1982.

Verbrugge, L. Marital status and health. *Journal of Marriage and the Family,* 1979, *41*:267–285.

Vesterdal, J. Psychological mechanisms in child abusing parents. Pp. 165–169, in Cook, J. V., & Bowles, R. T.

(Eds.) *Child abuse: Commission and omission.* Toronto: Butterworth, 1980.

Vinick, B. H. Remarriage in old age. *Family Coordinator,* 1978, *27*:359–363.

Visher, E. B., & Visher, J. S. *Stepfamilies: A guide to working with stepparents and stepchildren.* New York: Bruner/Mazel, 1979.

Waite, L. J., & Stolzenberg, R. M. Intended childbearing and labor force participation of young women: Insights from nonrecursive models. *American Sociological Review,* 1976, *41*:235–252.

Waldron, H., & Routh, D. K. The effect of the first child on the marital relationship. *Journal of Marriage and the Family,* 1981, *43*:785–788.

Walker, K., & Woods, M. *Time use: A measure of household production of family goods and services.* Washington, D.C., American Home Economics Association, 1976.

Wallace, K. M. An experiment in scientific matchmaking. *Marriage and Family Living,* 1959, *21*:342–348.

Waller, W. The rating and dating complex. *American Sociological Review,* 1937, *2*:727–734.

———*The old love and the new: Divorce and readjustment.* Carbondale, Ill.: Southern Ill. U. P., 1967.

———& Hill, R. *The family: A dynamic interpretation,* Rev. ed. New York: Holt, 1951.

Wallerstein, J., & Kelly, J. The effects of parental divorce: Experiences of the preschool child. *Journal of the American Academy of Child Psychiatry,* 1975, *14*:600–616.

———The effects of parental divorce: Experiences of the child in later latency. *American Journal of Orthopsychiatry,* 1976, *46*:256–269.

———*Surviving the break-up: How children actually cope with divorce.* New York: Basic, 1980.

Walster, E. Passionate Love. Pp. 85–99, in Murstein, B. I. (Ed.) *Theories of attraction and love.* New York: Springer, 1971.

———Aronson, V., Abrahams, D., & Rottman, L. The importance of physical attractiveness in dating behavior. *Journal of Personality and Social Psychology,* 1966, *4*:508–516.

———& Walster, W. *A new look at love.* Reading, Mass.: Addison-Wesley, 1978.

Walum, L. R. *The dynamics of sex and gender: A sociological perspective.* Chicago: Rand McNally, 1977.

Wampler, K. S., & Sprenkle, D. H. The Minnesota couple communication program: A follow-up study. *Journal of Marriage and the Family,* 1980, *42*:577–584.

Watson, J. A., & Kivett, V. R. Influences on the life satisfaction of older fathers. *Family Coordinator,* 1976, *25*:482–488.

Watzlawick, P., Beavin, J. H., & Jackson, D. D. *Pragmatics of human communication: A study of interactional patterns, pathologies, and paradoxes.* New York: Norton, 1967.

Weber, M. *The Protestant ethic and the spirit of capitalism.* Parsons, T. (Tr.) New York: Scribner, 1958.

Weeks, J. R. *Population.* Belmont, Calif.: Wadsworth, 1978.

Weinberg, M. S., & Williams, C. J. *Male homosexuals: Their problems and adaptations.* New York: Oxford U. P., 1974.

Weisberg, D. K. Alternative family structure and the law. *Family Coordinator,* 1975, *24*:549–559.

Weiss, R. S. The contributions of an organization of single parents to the well-being of its members. *Family Coordinator,* 1973, *22*:321–326.

———*Marital separation.* New York: Basic, 1975.

———*Going it alone: The family life and social situation of the single-parent.* New York: Basic, 1979.

———The impact of marital dissolution on income and consumption in single-parent households. *Journal of Marriage and the Family,* 1984, *46*:115–127.

Weiss, W. W., & Collada, H. B. Conciliation counseling: The court's effective mechanism for resolving visitation and custody disputes. *Family Coordinator,* 1977, *26*:444–446.

Weitzman, L. J. To love, honor and obey? Traditional legal marriage and alternative family forms. *Family Coordinator,* 1975, *24*:531–548.

———*Sex role socialization.* Palo Alto, Calif.: Mayfield, 1979.

Welch, C. E., & Price-Bonham, S. A decade of no-fault divorce revisited: California, Georgia, and Washington. *Journal of Marriage and the Family,* 1983, *45*:411–418.

Wente, A. S., & Crockenberg, S. Transition to fatherhood: Lamaze preparation, adjustment difficulty and the husband-wife relationship. *Family Coordinator,* 1976, *25*:351–357.

Westoff, C. F. Some speculations on the future of marriage and fertility. *Family Planning Perspectives,* 1978, *10*:79–83.

———The decline in unwanted fertility, 1971–1976. *Family Planning Perspectives,* 1981, *13*:70–72.

White, B. *Human infants experience and psychological development.* Englewood Cliffs, N.J.: Prentice-Hall, 1971.

———*The first three years of life.* Englewood Cliffs, N.J.: Prentice-Hall, 1975.

White, L. K. Sex differentials in the effect of remarriage on global happiness. *Journal of Marriage and the Family,* 1979, *41:*869–876.

Whitehurst, R. N. Youth views marriage: Awareness of present and future potentials in relationships. Pp. 294–301, in Libby, R. W., & Whitehurst, R. N. (Eds.) *Marriage and alternatives: Exploring intimate relationships.* Glenview, Ill.: Scott, Foresman, 1977.

Whitley, M. P., & Paulsen, S. B. Assertiveness and sexual satisfaction in employed professional women. *Journal of Marriage and the Family,* 1975, *37:*573–581.

Williams, F., LaRose, R., & Frost, F. *Children, television, and sex-role stereotyping.* New York: Praeger, 1981.

Williams, R. *American Society,* 3rd ed. New York: Knopf, 1970.

Wilson, K. L., Zurcher, L. A., McAdams, D. C., & Curtis, R. L. Stepfathers and stepchildren: An exploratory analysis from two national surveys. *Journal of Marriage and the Family,* 1975, *37:*526–536.

Wilson, S., Strong, B., Robbins, M., & Johns, T. *Human sexuality,* 2nd ed. St. Paul: West, 1980.

Wilson, W. C. The distribution of selected sexual attitudes and behaviors among the adult population of the United States. *Journal of Sex Research,* 1975, *11:*46–64.

Winch, R. F. The theory of complementary needs in mate-selection: A test of one kind of complementariness. *American Sociological Review,* 1955a, *20:*52–56.

———The theory of complementary needs in mate-selection: Final results on the test of the general hypothesis. *American Sociological Review,* 1955b, *20:*552–555.

———*Mate-selection: A study of complementary needs.* New York: Harper, 1958.

———The functions of dating in middle-class America. Pp. 506–510, in Winch, R., McGinnis, R., & Barringer, H. (Eds.) *Selected studies in marriage and the family,* Rev. ed. New York: Holt, 1962.

———Ktsanes, T., & Ktsanes, V. The theory of complementary needs in mate-selection: An analytic and descriptive study. *American Sociological Review,* 1954, *19:*241–249.

———Empirical elaboration of the theory of complementary needs in mate-selection. *Journal of Abnormal and Social Psychology,* 1955, *51:*508–513.

Witters, W. L., & Jones-Witters, P. *Human sexuality: A biological perspective.* New York: Van Nostrand, 1980.

Wood, B. (Ed.) *A pediatric vade-mecum,* 8th ed. London: Lloyd-Luke, 1974.

Wright, G. C., & Stetson, D. M. The impact of no-fault divorce law reform on divorce in American states. *Journal of Marriage and the Family,* 1978, *40:*575–580.

Wright, J. D. Are working women *really* more satisfied? Evidence from several national surveys. *Journal of Marriage and the Family,* 1978, *40:*301–313.

Yankelovich, D. *The new morality: A profile of American youth in the 1970s.* New York: McGraw-Hill, 1974.

Yarber, W. L. Waging war on V.D. *The Science Teacher,* 1978, *45:*38–42.

Yarrow, L. J. Separation from parents during early childhood. Pp. 89–136, in Hoffman, M. L., & Hoffman, L. W. (Eds.) *Review of child development research,* Vol. 1. New York: Sage, 1964.

Yoder, J. D., & Nichols, R. C. A life perspective comparison of married and divorced persons. *Journal of Marriage and the Family,* 1980, *42:*413–419.

Zablocki, B. *Alienation and investment in the urban commune.* New York: Center for Policy Research, 1977.

Zarate, L. *VD quiz: Getting the right answers* (Teacher's manual). Palo Alto, Calif.: American Social Health Association, 1977.

Zehv, W. How men and women differ in sex. *Sexology,* May 1968: 666–668.

Zelditch, M., Jr. Role differentiation in the nuclear family: A comparative study. Pp. 307–352, in Parsons, T., & Bales, R. F. (Eds.) *Family, socialization, and interaction process.* New York: Free Press, 1955.

Zelnik, M., & Kantner, J. F. Sexual and contraceptive experience of young unmarried women in the United States, 1976 and 1971. *Family Planning Perspectives,* 1977, *9:*55–71.

———Sexual activity, contraceptive use and pregnancy among metropolitan area teenagers: 1971–1979. *Family Planning Perspectives,* 1980, *12:*230–237.

Zimmerman, S. L. Alternatives in human reproduction for involuntary childless couples. *Family Relations,* 1982, *31:*233–241.

Zube, M. Changing behavior and outlook of aging men and women: Implications for marriage in the middle and later years. *Family Relations,* 1982, *31:*147–156.

Name Index

Subject Index